The
Decisive
Duel

Spitfire
vs
109

DAVID ISBY

ABACUS

First published in Great Britain in 2012 by Little, Brown
This paperback edition published in 2013 by Abacus

A CIP catalogue record for this book
is available from the British Library.

ISBN 978-0-349-12365-3

Typeset in Bembo by M Rules
Printed and bound in Great Britain by
Clays Ltd, St Ives plc

Papers used by Abacus are from well-managed forests
and other responsible sources.

MIX
Paper from
responsible sources
FSC® C104740

Abacus
An imprint of
Little, Brown Book Group
100 Victoria Embankment
London EC4Y 0DY

An Hachette UK Company
www.hachette.co.uk

www.littlebrown.co.uk

For all who knew the aircraft and lived the events I have written about, but especially my father, Joseph Isby, who flew with the Eighth Air Force; my mother, Peggy Carpenter Isby, who worked at Vickers; my grandfather, George 'Jack' Carpenter, who trained the RAF; my grandmother, Rachel 'Ray' Carpenter, who did voluntary work, waited to buy rationed food, and sewed clothing during the Blitz; my aunt and uncle, Lily and Charles Lane, who were aircraft construction foremen at Vickers; and, finally, my cousin, Flying Officer Richard Whitby, Royal Canadian Air Force, who did not have the chance to grow old.

David Carpenter Isby

Contents

Acknowledgements

I first met Ian Drury playing wargames many years ago and he was still willing to be my editor and now my agent. He made this book happen. At Little, Brown, I had the skilful reading and editing of Iain Hunt and Tim Whiting.

I was fortunate to benefit from advice, in-depth reading, editing and inputs by some of the finest current practitioners of creative non-fiction writing: Tom French, Diana Hume George, Leslie Rubinkowski and Laura Wexler.

Many people helped me write this book. Nothing would have been possible without those whose lives were touched by these aircraft and who flew, built or maintained them, most now sadly gone; this is their book. My friends who volunteered to read the manuscript and shared their expertise have my deep gratitude: Gray Boak, Lee Brimmicombe-Wood, Boris Ciglic, Stephen Glick, Chris Goss, E.R. 'Ted' Hooton, Karl Mueller, Alex Smart, Andrew Smith, Charles Vasey and Ian Wedge. Many sources provided insights in person, by mail or online. They include Andrew Arthy, Nick Beale, John Beaman, Christer Bergström, Donald Caldwell, Carl-Frederick Geust, Thierry Kleinprintz, Hans Naufta, Murray Rubinstein and Andy Saunders.

I appreciate the help received from people at: Alexandria, VA Library interlibrary loan; Archives Canada, Ottawa; Bundesarchiv Militärarchiv, Freiburg; Deutsches Museum, München and Oberschleissheim; Fairchild Library, Maxwell AFB, AL; The Imperial War Museum, Duxford and Lambeth; The Library of Congress, Washington (which, alas, loses books like the Luftwaffe lost fighters); The National Air and Space Museum, Washington and Dulles; The National Archives (US), College Park, MD; The National Archives (UK), Kew; The RAF Museum, Hendon; The USAF Historical Research Agency, Maxwell AFB, AL; and US Navy Operational Archives, Washington.

Finally, as ever, thanks for all her help and support to Anne Shackleton, whose father flew with the Eighth Air Force.

1

Introduction

Over London, 15 September 1940

She could no longer hear the noise of the anti-aircraft guns, the deep, repeated booming. At her office building, working on a Sunday afternoon, 15 September 1940, Peggy Carpenter had heard the air-raid sirens sound for the first attack that morning. She had heard nearby anti-aircraft guns in action against the German bombers attacking London at noontime, when she had sheltered in the office building's basement. Now, the guns fell silent. Though she had not heard the 'All Clear' sirens, she thought that the raid had passed. She went downstairs from her office and stepped outside to see what had happened.

She was thrust into a climactic moment in history, walking out of a familiar office with its teacups, typewriters and filing cabinets and into a day, like that of the battles of Marathon or Tours, when the future of western civilisation was shaped. The familiar cloudy late summer afternoon sky over London was that day a historic battleground. Looking up from the pavement, she saw, through a gap in the clouds, a mass formation of big, twin-engine German Heinkel He 111 bombers flying 12,000 feet overhead, their silhouettes unmistakable.

One aeroplane of the mass formation was pursued by a smaller plane. A single Royal Air Force (RAF) fighter. A lone Spitfire.

She watched as the one tiny Spitfire noiselessly – too high for her to hear the engines – flew closer, coming up on the formation of Heinkels from behind. Closer.

One Heinkel belched smoke and flame and started going down.

The Spitfire's pilot pulled up from his attack and threw his craft into a spontaneous victory roll, spinning 360 degrees around its line of flight for about two seconds. A noiseless shout of triumph, a gesture for the benefit of the embattled men fighting for their lives in the remaining bombers: you are next, you *will* be going down too.

Peggy's eyes were still fixed on the drama above, on the victorious rolling Spitfire and the burning Heinkel that would not be bombing its target in central London that day or any other day, when, from out of her field of vision, another spectator to history yelled loudly,

'Take cover, miss!'

She did not look for the source of the warning. She retreated inside the doorway to her office building a second before all the bullets fired by the attacking Spitfire and the Heinkel formation's gunners that had missed their targets splashed down on the street outside, a terrible rain, instantaneous and lethal. She decided to stay inside her office building, under cover, until the 'All Clear' sirens sounded.

The 16-year-old typist, who would have been at school had her school not been evacuated from London, had had a brush with history. But even for her, the battle over London represented the culmination of events of which she had already been a part.

She had seen a Spitfire for the first time not that afternoon but back in 1936, when war had seemed far away. The prototype, streamlined in powder-blue paint, had appeared at the annual Hendon air display. It stood out from the biplanes whose flying thrilled the crowds that day. It represented the future, not yet filled with foreboding. She had attended with her parents and sister, all dressed up for the day out.

Then, last year, in the summer of 1939, on what everyone knew would be the last school break and the last family holiday before the out-break of another, more terrible war, she had sipped her lemonade, sitting next to her father on a bench in the garden of a pub outside the gate of RAF Eastchurch, on the Isle of Sheppey in Kent. George 'Jack' Carpenter, a Royal Artillery and Royal Flying Corps veteran of the Great War, was back as an RAF armament instructor thanks to his

Edwardian sense of duty, his comprehensive knowledge of machine guns, and a Masonic handshake in the right office in the Air Ministry. But what had impressed her most were all the handsome 20-year-olds in their RAF service blue uniforms and issue neckties, crowding around, who obviously thought the world of her poor old dad.[1]

'Let me buy you a beer, Chiefy.'[2]

His trainees learned how to service the guns of Spitfires. One of them may well have loaded the raining bullets that she had just dodged on a London street. But her father, his trainees and their neckties had also been part of the story that put the Spitfire into the air and had sent the Heinkel, burning, down rather than home in triumph that afternoon. It was a story about aircraft and technology, but also about people, not only brilliant aircraft designers, far-sighted air marshals and brave fighter pilots, but teenage typists and their middle-aged fathers.

All wars must have at least two sides. That afternoon, the parallel story was not apparent from that London street. Peggy Carpenter had seen on other days, briefly, German Messerschmitt Bf 109 fighters over London. She knew their silhouette – she had memorised aircraft recognition books – appearing like a shark's fin off a bathing beach, alien and deadly, before vanishing. The Bf 109s had appeared over London as the culmination of another, parallel story, with a separate but in many ways similar set of characters.

The Bf 109 had enabled Germany to come close – closer than anyone outside a few in government then knew – to defeating Britain in the summer of 1940. The Spitfire had prevented it. Spitfires had defeated the German attempt to destroy the British Army as it evacuated from Dunkirk and, later, the attempt to conquer Britain by air attack, potentially enabling a cross-Channel invasion.[3] The Spitfire, making its victory roll in the skies over London as the Heinkel burned, was a symbol, but it was also a capstone, the highest and most apparent element of a complex set of relationships of people, organisations and ideas that stretched around the world and back through the decades.

2

The Race to Design the Modern Fighter

To October 1936

Before the Spitfire and Bf 109 were legends, before they were aeroplanes, and before those aeroplanes could develop their own personalities and become as much characters in their own story as any machine can become, they were the visions of single individuals that were eventually pushed and pulled, from designs on drawing boards, into reality. The transition from personal idea to aeroplane was made by relatively small teams of people, operating at what was then the limit of technology. The pull came from organisations that needed planes because of other changes. Germany became a Nazi dictatorship. Europe went from a post-war to a pre-war era. Aeroplanes were not the only thing that started as a vision, dream or, more often, nightmare that became a reality.

Willy Messerschmitt
They rode on the wind, soaring above the trees, fields and green hills of the German countryside. Gliders were his first love; delicate white birds of wood and linen, with long wings. A skilful pilot could seek out moving air, then fly high, above any eagle, and alight on the wooden skid under the glider's belly on a patch of level grass. Then do it all again.

In the summer of 1914, Wilhelm Emil 'Willy' Messerschmitt was obsessed with gliders. A 16-year-old student who had been building model gliders since he was ten, he was spending the summer as an assistant to Friedrich Harth, Germany's foremost glider designer and pilot. Willy helped maintain the gliders and get them into position on a grassy hilltop for each flight. He would fly them or, with Harth at the controls, he would attach a tow line to the glider and run downhill with it as fast as he could, dragging Harth's craft into the air.

Once airborne, the glider's flight was smooth and gentle. Going forward just fast enough to keep the air moving over the wings to create lift, avoiding a stall, it turned to seek rising air currents as an eagle would look for a pigeon. Catching a breath of warm air, the long thin wings climbed over the green valley.

At the end of each flight, Willy, bicycling furiously, would be first on the scene wherever Harth had landed, discussing how the flight had gone and what would be needed to make the next one better, longer or higher. Willy would disassemble the glider. The first step was unfastening the wings, always a struggle. When he designed his own gliders, they would have easily detachable wings. Finally, he would help load the glider into a horse-drawn wagon and haul it away for the next flight from the top of the Ludwager Kulm, a hill near Willy's home town of Bamberg, Bavaria, or back to its shed to await tomorrow's flying.

Until everything went to hell that summer. A crisis in the Balkans became a European war. The gliding stopped. Harth joined Imperial Germany's small band of military aviators. He gave Willy the plans for his next glider design for safekeeping. The war would surely be over before Christmas.

It was not. The European war metastasised into the Great War. Harth, finally back to Germany on leave, stopped in to visit Willy. He had not only kept the plans safe, he had gone ahead and built the glider. Willy used French prisoners of war, supposedly working for his family's wine business, to help him. Examining the glider, Harth saw that the teenager had indeed improved his design.

Gliders had no value in the war that had swept away the summer afternoon flights. Harth worked to develop German Army aeroplanes. He made sure that when Willy reached eighteen and was called up, he was transferred from trench mortars to the Air Service. Willy was trained to fly planes at Schleissheim in Bavaria, then, with Germany running out of aviation fuel, before he could be awarded his pilot's badge, he was sent to use his talents working on new designs.

In the four years of the Great War, aircraft technology advanced further than it would have done in a generation of peacetime development. German aviation technology was threatened when the Treaty of Versailles in 1919 banned Germany from developing or operating military aircraft. The German aircraft industry – what was left of it after demobilisation and the post-war economic collapse – took the wartime advances and applied them to civil aviation. The General Staff kept Germany's military aviation capability alive clandestinely. Research and development was shifted to German-controlled firms in other countries. Pilot training and aircraft testing were carried out in cooperation with the Soviet Union, where a secret training school was set up at Lipetsk. The rosters of post-war German cavalry regiments included pilots and technicians who never sat on a horse. Others found jobs in civil aviation. In the 1920s, German aviation managed to stay alive (the aircraft engine industry was closed down by the Treaty of Versailles) but could build only a few aircraft, so each one had to represent an aeronautical advance.

Possessed of brilliant intelligence and a formidable work ethic, Willy Messerschmitt was part of all of this. Leaving the army in 1919, he completed an engineering degree in Munich. He persuaded the university to accept the plans of his latest glider design, the S 14, in place of a thesis. 'You can't design a good plane unless you know how to build a glider,' Messerschmitt recalled, years later.[1]

Messerschmitt set up a partnership with Harth to design and build aircraft. Messerschmitt's glider designs minimised drag and weight and stressed cheapness and ease of construction. On 13 September 1921, Harth set a world duration record with a flight of 21 minutes 30 seconds in the S 8 glider he and Messerschmitt had designed. However, the two split over differences in aircraft design; Harth thought Messerschmitt's structures were too light.

In 1925, Messerschmitt established his own company, Messerschmitt AG. This merged, in 1927, into Bayerische Flugzeugwerke (Bfw), with Messerschmitt as chief designer.[2] The merger was an obvious one; Bfw had been building Messerschmitt's light aircraft and glider designs under licence. Bfw received a subsidy from the regional government to bring employment to its factory near Augsburg in Bavaria. Messerschmitt would merge his company into Bfw, keep the subsidy but retain control, which required him to borrow money from wealthy relatives of his girlfriend, Baroness Lilly von Michel-Raulino Stromeyer, a divorcée eight years his senior (her family's business imported tobacco). She kept the shares in her own name and played a hands-on role in management at Bfw, recruiting her ex-husband for a term on the board of directors. Messerschmitt bought out Bfw using funds secretly provided by the General Staff, intended to keep the German aircraft industry going. The German Defence Ministry in Berlin then purchased 62.5 per cent of the stock in the 'new' Bfw. While he had succeeded in getting funds from both the German military and the Bavarian government, Messerschmitt was unimpressed with their officials: men of the previous century who did not understand when he told them what he could do if only he had the resources and no Versailles treaty restrictions.

Messerschmitt's negotiation of the merger agreement brought him into contact with Ernst Udet, Germany's highest-scoring surviving fighter ace from the Great War. Udet had set up his own aircraft manufacturing company after the war, soon merged into Bfw. Udet was a romantic *bon vivant*, happy to travel the world barnstorming in his Bfw-built Flamingo biplane. He liked Messerschmitt's designs. The two soon became friends.

Messerschmitt designed and built light aircraft, but it was airliners that paid the bills, starting with the M 18 of 1925. Messerschmitt and his design team could make each airliner design a little bigger, carrying more mail (their primary function) and passengers faster and farther. He patented a single-spar (the main structural member that supports the wing) design. He started using metal in place of wood and fabric in his designs. Germany's Luft Hansa airline wanted all-metal airliners such as the Junkers W 33, built by Messerschmitt's old friend Dr Hugo Junkers at his factory in Dessau.

Luft Hansa ordered a dozen of Messerschmitt's single-engine high-wing monoplane M 20 and M 20B airliners – a huge purchase by the European standards of the time. The M 20 applied Messerschmitt's philosophy of lightweight, technology-stretching design to airliners. It featured a cantilever wing, without the external struts for support that most aircraft then used, and a powerful 500 horsepower (hp) engine.

In 1928, the first M 20 crashed. A Bfw-built prototype biplane twin-engine night fighter, the M 22, crashed while on a test flight over Augsburg in 1930. Improved M 20B airliners crashed in 1930 and 1931. An inquiry blamed Luft Hansa for having imposed an unworkable and unsafe specification on Messerschmitt. This enraged Erhard Milch, head of Luft Hansa. He had lost a close friend, test pilot Hans Hackmack, in the first crash. Now his airline was being blamed. Though neither an engineer nor a pilot – he had flown as an observer during the war – Milch was convinced that it was not his specification at fault, but rather that Messerschmitt had made the structure too light.

This led to a confrontation in Milch's office in the terminal building of Berlin's Tempelhof Airport with Messerschmitt and Kurt Tank, his chief designer. Tank, a wartime infantry officer and, more recently, a designer of all-metal flying boats, explained to Milch that the design had indeed met all required structural standards imposed by the German civil aviation authority.[3] Milch was unimpressed. However lacking the specification and the standards might have been, Messerschmitt had sold him aeroplanes that failed.

Milch resolved to ruin Messerschmitt, making a start by cancelling Luft Hansa's order for ten remaining M 20Bs and suing for a refund of payments. Milch had political connections that could allow him to carry out his threat: he was a secret member of the Nazi party. He made Luft Hansa airliners available for the rising Nazi leader, Adolf Hitler, whom he personally admired. The Nazi party was never billed. Milch's actions had helped enable Hitler's rise as a national figure, campaigning by airliner even when he was not yet well funded. Milch paid 'consultancy' fees to senior Nazi party members, including Hermann Göring, a Reichstag deputy and former Great War fighter pilot who had become Hitler's right-hand man. Göring took his money, voted for continued subsidies to Luft Hansa, but resented that Milch thought that he could be bought.[4]

The German Defence Ministry dumped its Bfw stock. Although the Baroness arranged further investments from her family, without Luft

Hansa's money Messerschmitt was bankrupt within a year. He sold his car in an effort to stay in business and keep his employees working. Kurt Tank was one of many employees who left. Dr Ernst Heinkel, the aircraft manufacturer, started negotiating with the Augsburg local government to take over the Bfw factory.[5]

Fortunately for Messerschmitt, his lawyer Konrad Merkel won a settlement. Luft Hansa agreed to take delivery of modified M 20B airliners. The M 20B was re-certified by German civil aviation authorities, showing that the modified design was acceptable. But once Luft Hansa had cancelled its initial order, no one else wanted Messerschmitt's airliners. Messerschmitt needed to design and build new types of planes to keep Milch from gloating as the receiver's padlock went on the factory gates.

R.J. Mitchell

The seaplane's engine produced a long ear-shattering roar as they ran it up on shore. The pilot eased the throttle forward. The seaplane strained at the restraints that held it down. Watching were other pilots in flight suits, technicians and ground crew in overalls, and one man in a three-piece suit, a pipe stem clenched between his teeth, sometimes making notes on a clipboard he was holding, watching and listening to the massive roar. It was not all just noise to him.

The run-up finished and the engine turned off; the seaplane was released from its bonds. It was eased forward onto a metal cradle with four automobile wheels and, with ground crew and technicians pushing, gently rolled down a concrete ramp that led into the Solent.

The waters of the Solent were busy with international commerce. Everyone handling the seaplane could look up and see a great ocean liner cruising to or from Southampton. Nearby, several motorboats were already purposefully cruising up and down, searching for any floating debris. Another motorboat came in, close to the cradle, and picked up a tow line as the seaplane entered the water, towing it onto the Solent and into the wind.

The mighty engine started up again. The propeller blew a plume of spray, the wind catching it as it accelerated; the spray almost concealed the plane itself, soon hurtling forward through the water. The pilot pulled his head well down, trying to shield his goggles from the spray.

The nose swung slightly from side to side as it picked up speed and the pilot tried to get a view straight ahead, where the sheer size of the engine blocked his vision.

The little blue seaplane's wings started to lift it into the air. The motorboats raced behind, at a respectful distance, soon outpaced as the seaplane picked up speed, 'on the step', its two streamlined floats skimming the surface of the water, until it broke free and lurched into the blue summer sky. The spray disappeared. On the edge of a stall, it seemed to hang on its propeller for an instant, a few feet above the water. The pilot eased the stick forward. A brief plume of water rolled off its floats as the seaplane climbed away. A dissipating wake on the surface of the water showed where it had taken off. The elegant royal blue low-wing monoplane racer seaplane, taking off from the waters of the Solent on a practice flight that summer day, was wearing the RAF's red–white–blue rudder stripes.

Speed and power: what the Supermarine S.6B seaplane racer embodied in the summer of 1931, powered by a Rolls-Royce R in-line engine producing an astounding 2700 hp at a time when the RAF's principal fighter, the biplane Bristol Bulldog, used a 450 hp engine. The S.6B had been designed to win the Schneider Cup – the premier international air racing prize for seaplanes since before the Great War – permanently for Britain. Any country winning three times in a row would keep the Cup and conclude the series of competitions, held first annually and then biennially. The British, with strong aviation and marine industries, thought the Cup rightfully belonged to them.

The RAF's specialist High Speed Flight trained through the summer of 1931 at the seaplane base at Calshot Castle, on the Solent near Southampton. Watching them fly and maintain the S.6Bs was Supermarine's chief designer, Reginald James Mitchell. Mitchell – 'RJ' to his friends, 'Mitch' only to the pilots of the High Speed Flight – was born in 1895, three years before Willy Messerschmitt. His wife, Florence, eleven years his senior, was a former primary school headmistress. They had a teenage son at school. The quiet, shy, intense, pipe-smoking engineer knew speed and power.

Mitchell had started building model aeroplanes as a child and had learned engineering through apprenticeship at a locomotive works rather than at university. In 1920, at the age of twenty-four, he had become chief designer for Supermarine, a small Southampton-based aircraft manufacturer that specialised in seaplanes. His best-known designs were large biplane flying boats with a forest of struts and bracing wires that might make a stately progress of up to 100 miles per hour (mph) with a tailwind.

Mitchell immersed himself in the details of airframe and engine design and construction. He observed the work of his design team, asking for explanations as they transformed his ideas into the complex structure of an aircraft. On the shop floor, he watched as wood and metal came together, covered with fabric, to become an aeroplane. He learned to smell the varnish of the dope on the fabric that covered the wooden framework of control surfaces; if it did not smell right, it would not work in the air. He felt stitching in the fabric, placed so it would not be pulled apart by a slipstream at hundreds of miles per hour. At the test stands, he listened to the engines being powered up, until he could tell from the sound how fast they were turning over and whether something was amiss. The chief designer relied on others to turn his vision into an actual design, but it was his decisions that determined an aeroplane's success or failure.

In the 1920s, other countries had beaten the British in the Schneider competition. Italy did so with Macchi seaplanes. But a Supermarine design, the Sea Lion, prevented the Italians from winning the Cup outright in 1922. The US won in 1925 with the Curtiss R3C Racer seaplane, flown by James 'Jimmy' Doolittle, an Army Reserve lieutenant and test pilot who held a doctorate from the Massachusetts Institute of Technology.

'Speed in the air must always be a measure of aerodynamic efficiency, which in turn must always be the most important consideration of all in aircraft design', Mitchell had written.[6] Mitchell was able to put this into practice in his racing seaplane designs thanks to new engines made first by Napier and then by Rolls-Royce. The earliest version was the wooden-winged S.4B, which had failed to beat the Italians in 1926. Mitchell-designed racers won two Schneider competitions in a row. The all-metal S.5 won in 1927, and the S.6 won again in 1929. Mitchell refined his basic racer design.

Racing accelerated aircraft development. Mitchell said that his work on the racers showed 'it is essential to break new ground and to invent and involve new methods and new ideas'; the S.6's engine 'would have taken at least three times as long to produce under normal processes of development'.[7] Mitchell's ultimate refinement of the design, the S.6B, was prepared for the decisive 1931 competition that could mean a third-time, permanent win. Then the Treasury pulled the plug. The great depression precluded funding to build and race the S.6B. Mitchell knew that winning the Schneider Cup permanently would give the struggling British aircraft industry – increasingly overshadowed by foreign competition – a massive boost. But this did not sway bureaucrats in Whitehall. The opportunity to win the Cup for a third and last time was about to slip away.

Mitchell and his plane were saved by Lady Lucy Houston, a well-known philanthropist and former actress, wealthy through marriage, whose humble origins, right-wing politics and eccentric lifestyle made her a media favourite. Anxious to help Britain achieve an international aviation success (and embarrass the Labour government she detested), she provided £100,000 of her own money to build two S.6Bs. These new Mitchell-designed racers allowed the RAF High Speed Flight to compete in 1931.

Once the money was provided, the S.6Bs still had to be made ready to fly. The High Speed Flight brought together RAF members of the teams that had won the two previous Schneider Cup competitions and representatives of Supermarine and Rolls-Royce. In the summer of 1931, S.6Bs were flying from the RAF seaplane ramps at Calshot Castle. Mitchell was on the scene to deal with technical problems. During a practice run, an S.6B experienced dramatic rudder flutter that nearly caused a fatal crash. High-level meetings were convened at Calshot and at the Air Ministry in London. Mitchell instead examined the damaged racer. He spoke to all the pilots and technicians involved with the S.6B, not just the senior men. One of the pilots, Flying Officer Richard 'Batchy' Atcherley,[8] recalled: 'He was always keen to listen to pilots' opinions and never pressed his views against theirs. He set his sights deliberately high, for he had little use for "second bests". Yet he was the most unpompous man I ever met.'[9] Mitchell came up with a solution –

external rudder mass balance weights, tested and installed in time to participate in the 1931 Schneider Cup competition.

Faced with the difficulties of fielding racing seaplanes, the potential competitors – Italy, France and the US – folded. Britain was unopposed in the 1931 competition and won the Cup. Soon after, the S.6B set the world absolute air speed record, 407.5 mph. This success made Supermarine world famous. Vickers, the armaments manufacturing conglomerate, bought the company, in no small measure to gain access to Mitchell and his design team.

Mitchell designs a fighter
On 1 October 1931, eighteen days after the Schneider Cup was won outright for Britain, the Air Ministry had issued Specification F7/30, for a new fighter plane to replace the Bristol Bulldog. Its top requirement was a speed over 250 mph. Designs using the steam-cooled Rolls-Royce Goshawk engine (a development of the Kestrel) would be preferred. Mitchell and his design team, at Supermarine's Woolston factory near Southampton, were among several working to design an aeroplane to meet this specification. Sydney Camm and his team at Hawker, in Kingston-on-Thames, had designed the RAF's newest fighter, the Hawker Fury. Other British airframe designers also submitted designs.

Mitchell lacked Camm's experience with biplane fighter design. Supermarine's smaller, less well-funded design team had experience with racers but this was not directly applicable, although they had learned much about streamlining and powerful engines. While Camm worked on two designs, a biplane and a monoplane, Mitchell's team concentrated their efforts on a single design, a monoplane. Their plans arrived at the Air Ministry on 20 February 1932, 106 hectic days after receiving the specification.

A monoplane fighter was revolutionary. Every fighter in the RAF was a biplane. Months of ominous silence followed. The Air Ministry studied the plans, checked their budgets, then studied the plans some more. They also looked over their shoulders at what might be coming. In 1931, Britain had agreed to a League of Nations 'armaments truce', effectively halting aircraft procurement, and hoped that the League would eventually negotiate an 'air pact' that would ban bombing, removing any need for a fighter. But the League's authority was fading. Japan had invaded Manchuria in 1931. The League failed to act. In 1932, the British Cabinet abandoned the ten-year rule, that no major conflict was to be anticipated for that length of time. Finally, Mitchell heard back from the Air Ministry: build one prototype. A contract followed on 2 August 1932.

The fighter Mitchell designed to Specification F7/30, the Supermarine Type 224 prototype, took form in Supermarine's factory. This all-metal monoplane had a thick low inverted gull wing, its fixed undercarriage shrouded in streamlined 'trousers', an armament of four machine guns, and an open cockpit. To Mitchell, the least satisfactory element of the design was the engine. The 600 hp Rolls-Royce Goshawk provided insufficient power. Its steam cooling system proved unreliable and ineffective.

Even as the prototype was taking shape, Mitchell worked hard with his team, looking for ways it could be improved. Soon, he began to feel unwell. He ignored it. It was only overwork. His team found him more demanding than ever. The work came home with him. Florence Mitchell recalled:

> He'd be talking to you one moment, and the next minute, he'd be miles away and you knew he'd thought up something new. He loved snooker, but even in the middle of a game he'd suddenly put down his cue and out would come an old envelope or a scrap of paper and, as he began to draw, he would give a rapid explanation of the diagrams he was making ... In those days we lived aeroplanes. There were always people from Supermarine or pilots at our Southampton house, talking about their aircraft or the speeds at which they could fly and they often sat up into the early hours of the morning.[10]

As a result, recalled Supermarine's chief draughtsman Joseph 'Joe' Smith, 'I can remember many occasions when he arrived at the office with the complete solution of a particularly knotty problem, which had baffled us all the night before.'[11]

Mitchell grew sicker. He was soon in the hands of the doctors, then the surgeons. The diagnosis was bowel cancer. This led to major surgery and the fitting of a colostomy bag in August 1933. Following his operation, as the Type 224 approached flight, Mitchell was under strict orders to rest. His prognosis was clouded. If the cancer did not recur within four years, it would mean he had beaten it. The odds were not good. Nor was the Type 224 progressing as he wished. Without an adequate engine, it appeared that it would meet neither Mitchell's expectations nor the Air Ministry's specifications.

The future of flight arrives

The future of flight reached England on the morning of 16 October 1934. Flying Officer Jeffrey Quill of the RAF did not see it arrive. He, like Britain's other fighter pilots, was flying an elegant biplane such as the Armstrong Whitworth Siskin, or his favourite, the Bristol Bulldog.[12]

In the air, Quill was separated from the wind rushing past, at almost 200 mph, by a small windscreen, his leather flying helmet and his RAF-issue goggles. The biplane he was flying, like every fighter plane built since the Great War, was covered with doped fabric and armed with the same armament of two synchronised rifle-calibre .303 Vickers machine guns.

What had changed in fighter design since 1918 was not evident to those watching the Bulldog from a distance. Its framework, aluminium rather than wood, along with struts and wire rigging, provided structural strength. Its engine had a supercharger for improved performance at higher altitudes, allowing flights as high as 16,000 feet. The pilot could even communicate through a radio telephone rather than hand signals.

Quill loved it. He loved the wind, the sound it made as it whistled through the knife-edged bracing wires that held the biplane's two wings in alignment, and he adored the Bulldog's manoeuvrability. With two pairs of wings providing lift and external struts and bracing wires providing support for them against the stress of intense manoeuvring, the Bulldog could change its direction, pitch, yaw or roll, in instant response to a move of the control stick and rudder pedals. The 440 hp Jupiter radial engine made the aircraft some 60 mph faster than the fighters of 1918, years after Mitchell's S.6B had set the speed record at 407.5 mph.

The future of flight was a Douglas DC-2 airliner of KLM, the Netherlands' airline. It was on its first flight to RAF Mildenhall, the starting point of the Mac Robertson England to Australia air race that was to begin on 20 October 1934. The race had become a focus not just of the aviation world, but of worldwide attention. Mitchell had even proposed that the Type 224 prototype be allowed to compete, an idea disapproved by the Air Ministry.

The DC-2 was everything that Quill's Bulldog fighter was not. The airliner, built in Long Beach, California, and the first of its kind to arrive in Europe, moved fast and could have outrun him in a race. A twin-engine, low-wing monoplane, with streamlined lines and swept-back wing leading edges that minimised resistance and the amount of area presented to the airflow, the DC-2 was all-metal, built of light but rugged aluminium alloys. Unlike the Bulldog, its structural strength came not from an internal skeleton but its polished silver 'stressed' skin, 0.8 mm thick, which carried the aerodynamic stresses. The DC-2's metal skin was more durable than the Bulldog's doped fabric. While the Bulldog, like all its contemporaries, had a fixed undercarriage, the DC-2's main undercarriage retracted, pulled inside the wing in flight to reduce drag, increasing speed and range.

The DC-2's two Wright Cyclone radial engines each provided 875 hp, almost twice that of the biplane fighter. Each engine was housed in a streamlined metal cowling, whereas the cylinders of the Bulldog's engine were exposed to the wind, like Quill himself in his open cockpit. The cowlings, like the retractable undercarriage, smoothed the flow of the air passing the engines and decreased drag. The Bulldog, with its struts, fixed undercarriage and rigging wires, could never be described as streamlined.

Like the Bulldog's engine, each of the DC-2's engines had a super-charger, forcing air into the intake manifolds at altitudes where the air was markedly thinner and its pressure less than at sea level. An engine without a supercharger loses some 45 per cent of its power at 15,000 feet, the highest altitude where flight without oxygen equipment is feasible. To get greater power from a piston engine, the supercharger squeezed more oxygen into its cylinders.

While the Bulldog's two-blade propeller was of beautifully laminated wood, the DC-2's engines used constant-speed propellers that could vary their pitch – the angle at which the blades cut through the air – automatically between take-off, climb, cruise and landing to ensure the optimal use of the engines' thrust. Where the Bulldog's radio telephone had to be supplemented by wing-waggling, hand signals or signal flares, the DC-2 had two reliable radio systems, both a voice radio and a Morse key radio set with its own operator.

Although Quill was an all-weather flying specialist, most of the RAF's biplanes could not fly unless the sky was clear. The DC-2 had blind flying avionics, including an artificial horizon and a radio compass to allow it to home in on radio beacons and so keep a schedule even in Europe's overcast skies. The DC-2 could fly year round; it was equipped with a heated cabin, de-icer boots on each wing's leading edge, which prevented the formation of ice that could otherwise decrease lift and increase drag and weight until an aircraft could no longer fly, and carburettor heating, so ice would not choke off the engine's air.

Coming in to land at Mildenhall, the low-drag, high-speed DC-2 could not glide in gracefully to land like Quill's biplane, back to a grass strip, sideslipping to bleed off excess airspeed. Rather, the DC-2 had flaps that could be lowered from the trailing edge of the wings to provide more lift (and drag) at low speed, as required while landing. Some monoplanes (though not the DC-2) also had slats that extended from the leading edge of the wing at low speed to smooth the airflow. The DC-2 was designed to fly from concrete runways, not grass.

The DC-2 flying into Mildenhall that morning was a virtual catalogue of technological innovations that the resource-constrained RAF's biplane fighters lacked. It had been made in the US, where larger distances meant money could be made with airliners, and where its advanced technology had already been applied to build the Boeing YB-9 and Martin B-10 bombers. The RAF had little money to invest in developing or procuring these technologies in 1934. The careful, punctual Dutchmen flying the DC-2 for KLM were earning money. The DC-2 had a schedule to keep, picking up paying passengers and a full load of mail while flying the race. It came in second place overall and first in the handicap division.

Air power and the future

Winning war without the trenches, without the bloody months-long battles and without the conscript armies of infantrymen whose losses had led to social revolution in Germany and Russia: this was his vision. Marshal of the Royal Air Force Sir Hugh 'Boom' Trenchard cast a long, gaunt shadow over British air power in 1934. His nickname referred to his loud parade-ground voice, bestowed in an era when dropping bombs from flying machines constituted science fiction rather than national strategy. He had commanded the Royal Flying Corps in France in the Great War. His maxim had been 'use scouts offensively' and he had sent his pilots over German lines relentlessly, the airborne counterparts of the 'big push' offensives on the ground. In 1918, he directed the Independent Bomber Force: British bombers based in France to target Germany in retaliation for the bombing of London by German Zeppelins and bombers.

The bomber force emerged as the RAF's primary rationale for its continued existence as an independent service, equal with the Royal Navy and the British Army. Post-war, as the RAF's first chief of staff (to 1929), Trenchard had been the foremost advocate of strategic bombing. Starting in the 1920s, with budgets strictly limited by the 'ten-year rule' but building on their limited 1918 experience of bomber attacks on German industry, the RAF had planned for strategic bombing, the launching of direct attacks on an enemy's industry (destroying its ability to wage war) and population (crushing the morale of its people). In this way, future wars would not have to be fought like the Great War, with massive land battles. Trenchard was seen as a prophet, even at the Treasury; if bombers were capable of winning future wars, they would not have to invest in tanks and warships.[13]

The airmen of many nations had spent the 1920s and early 1930s planning for strategic bombing. Italy's General Giulio Douhet was the leading theorist, writing influential books and articles. He argued that bombers, rather than armies or navies, would win future wars. Trenchard's counterpart in America, Brigadier General William 'Billy' Mitchell, advocated bombers. He wanted a US Air Force, independent like the RAF, but the US Army Air Corps remained part of the US Army.

Trenchard's vision of emphasising strategic deterrence through bombers had been set out in an Air Staff memorandum in 1924. 'Bombing squadrons should be as numerous as possible and the fighters as few as popular opinion and the necessity for defending vital objects will permit.'[14] Bombers meant peace, fighters an ineffective defence. But the British, with the bitter but instructive experience of German air raids during the Great War fresh in their memories, never abandoned a commitment to air defence. The Air Defence of Great Britain (ADGB) headquarters, organised in 1925, included both bombers and fighters. But there was little money for either.

In Britain, as in other countries, professional airmen such as Trenchard believed that 'the bomber must always get through' to its target. This had been accepted wisdom for years before Stanley Baldwin, the prime minister, used the phrase in a speech before the House of Commons on 10 November 1932. At that time, biplane bombers were almost as fast as biplane fighters. Without a reliable way (other than inaccurate sound detectors) to detect incoming bombers until they could be seen overhead, defenders were unlikely to intercept before the bombers had dropped their bombs. Without reliable long-range radios, fighters could not be directed to intercept them. In the wake of the Great War, it was assumed that poison gas would be used against civilian populations. The winner in the next war would be the side with more and better bombers, able to render factories and cities unusable before the enemy could do the same. Air power was a balance of terror.

The RAF held its largest peacetime exercises in the summer of 1933. The lessons reinforced established wisdom. Bombers would get through, by night or day. It was an easy stretch to incorporate the emerging technologies used by the DC-2 into a new generation of all-metal twin-engine bombers. Indeed, artists' impressions of such designs on drawing boards worldwide appeared in the aviation press. Larger, four-engine bombers were likely to follow. This was the goal of the US Army Air Corps' Tactical School at Maxwell Field, Alabama, an incubator of pro-bomber thinking. The RAF's leaders thought the same way. In both air arms, dissenting fighter pilots believed they could intercept the bombers. But they were not the ones allocating scarce resources within the services.

Yet fighters could also use at least some of the new technologies the DC-2 represented. No one was sure what a high-technology fighter plane would look like. Indeed, many professionals thought fighter aircraft impractical without the biplane's superb manoeuvrability and the all-round visibility of the open cockpit. This was what had led to the F7/30 specification. The Air Ministry aimed to find from the British aircraft industry's designers if a modern fighter was practical.

Willy Messerschmitt builds a plane
While Willy Messerschmitt drew up new designs and tried to earn money as a professor of aerodynamics in Munich, most of his work went into light aircraft (which won a number of prestigious competitions) and gliders. Early 1930s Germany was obsessed with gliders. All the world's gliding records were set by Germans or Austrians.

In 1932, no German wanted to fly more than did Adolf 'Keffer' Galland, a 20-year-old who lived for gliding even more than hunting and girls, the only things that came close. Rather than going to college, he won glider championships for speed, endurance and distance covered. He was selected for a highly competitive (4000 applicants for 18 slots) place to train for an 'airline' flying job.

But Galland's 'airline' training was intended to turn him from a glider pilot into a fighter pilot. In 1932, Germany was still banned from having an air force under the Treaty of Versailles. The Weimar Republic's clandestine development of military aviation had been apparent for years to anyone who cared to see it (one of the few in England who did was Winston Churchill, then a backbench Member of Parliament and writer). They had been paying Messerschmitt, Junkers and all Germany's aircraft designers for warplane designs.

The 'airliners' being prepared for Galland were products of the German aviation industry. Messerschmitt's long-time rival, Dr Ernst Heinkel, had as his chief designers the twin Günter brothers, Siegfried and Walther, Great War *Frontschweine* who had been captured together on the Somme. The brothers' need for speed was such that they would drive fast cars and fly fast aeroplanes, even in formal attire (top hats included). The talented brothers had, along with Heinrich Hertel, Heinkel's technical director and chief of development, designed some of the world's fastest planes, as well as the Heinkel He 70, a high-speed single-engine low-wing 'airliner' with elegant elliptical wings.

Messerschmitt's 1932 M 29 was intended to repeat the successes of his previous designs in the Circuit of Europe air race. It was a low-wing two-seater, with a cantilever wing, though its horizontal stabiliser was externally braced by struts. Four M 29s were built for the August 1932 race. They never got to compete. Two crashed fatally days before the competition began. The survivors, withdrawn from competition, had their structure strengthened.

Messerschmitt built an aerobatic competition monoplane, the M 35, to demonstrate that his lightweight designs would stay together in the air regardless of the manoeuvres a pilot put it through. Finally, he started a new aircraft, to be ready in time for the 1934 Circuit of Europe. The M 37 was a low-wing all-metal design, a two-seater with a single engine and a retractable undercarriage. Messerschmitt hired Rakan Kokothaki, an engineer, as a manager and assistant, and relied on him to manage new projects. But Bfw was still in the hands of the receivers.

The 30 January 1933 appointment of Adolf Hitler as Chancellor changed everything. In March, he established the *Reichsluftfahrt-ministerium* (RLM), the Reich Air Ministry, in readiness for a formal renunciation of the Versailles Treaty and the creation of an overt air force. The new RLM, which would buy Germany's military planes, was under Göring's jurisdiction, but the real power was Erhard Milch, appointed as the secretary of state for air. He soon demonstrated that, despite his arrogant personality, he had a thorough knowledge of aircraft and management alike. He remained convinced that Messerschmitt's designs were unsound.

Milch renewed his campaign against Messerschmitt in June 1933, obstructing government contracts to build Messerschmitt-designed aircraft. He even sought to deny Bfw contracts to build other aircraft under licence. Milch demanded that Bfw post a two-million-mark surety bond against the structural failure of any of the aircraft they produced.

Faced with ruin, Messerschmitt was able, through the Baroness's family connections, to deliver the banker and financier Friedrich Seiler to Milch's office in Berlin to sign the unprecedented surety bond. Milch, outraged, lashed out at Seiler: 'You are bailing out a would-be industrialist who will never make the grade.'[15]

However, the new regime's first target in the German aircraft industry was Dr Junkers, a strong nationalist and opponent of Versailles but a long-time social democrat.[16] In June 1933, threatened with imprisonment, Junkers signed away all 170 of his patents, and transferred 51 per cent of the stock of his firm to the Reich. Messerschmitt, given his history with Milch, feared he would be next. He said nothing in public about the Nazi treatment of Junkers. No one in the German aircraft industry did.

But Messerschmitt had friends too. He had known Rudolf Hess, Hitler's deputy, in the 1920s. Hess took time out from Nazi politics for flying and gliding. Messerschmitt had given Hess a good deal on an M 23 aerobatic monoplane that he had used to win a number of competitions. Through Hess, Messerschmitt met Hitler for the first time. It would be the first of many meetings. Hitler was impressed by Messerschmitt and considered him a genius, the possessor of a particularly and uniquely Germanic creativity and insight that he could count on to realise his vision of turning the bankrupt and defeated country into a dominant power.[17] Messerschmitt, in return, appreciated Hitler's interest in aircraft and his willingness to talk about the details of technology, recognising him as a twentieth-century man of genius who realised the importance of ensuring that it was Germany that led in advanced aeronautics and that the dead hand of Versailles was preventing this.

Theo Croneiss, a wartime fighter pilot who was now a leader of the paramilitary Nazi SA (Brownshirt) organisation, Hitler's street fighters, was another of Messerschmitt's old friends. He had run an airline in the 1920s that flew Messerschmitt designs and had volunteered to act as test pilot for the M 20B airliner. Milch had tried to run him out of business for competing with Luft Hansa. Croneiss became chairman of Bfw's board of directors in October 1933.

In 1933, Willy Messerschmitt filled out his application form to join the Nazi party and became member 342354. He often wore a swastika lapel pin on his business suits. A combination of gratitude for support against Milch and a vital need to ingratiate himself meshed with his nationalist politics and a desire to provide employment for loyal workers who had stuck with him in the lean years. He indeed was a national socialist (in lower-case letters) but no insular fanatic. He was used to interacting freely with people in aviation worldwide. His stepfather was an American citizen. His older brother, who ran the Messerschmitt family wine and restaurant business in Bamberg, had spent much of his career in California. Messerschmitt's friend Ernst Udet was one of the many other Germans applying to join the party in 1933.

For the M 37 programme, Messerschmitt hired a new chief designer: Robert Lusser, a record-setting pilot as well as a graduate engineer. He had previously designed all-metal aircraft for Junkers and then for Heinkel, where the Günter brothers had blocked him from the chief designer's position he coveted. The design bureau chief, Richard Bauer, brought in from Arado, another aircraft manufacturer, used his all-metal design expertise to turn Lusser's project sketches into the detailed design and construction drawings that would be needed to build the new aeroplane. Hubert Bauer, head of production, would often be found on the shop floor, welding aluminium, showing craftsmen and engineers alike what he wanted on the emerging M 37 design.

The fast M 37 may have been intended for a 1934 prestige air race, but in 1933 it required no prescience to see that it could also be an advanced trainer, capable of developing Germany's thousands of glider pilots into fighter and bomber pilots. But the RLM ignored the M 37. Instead, Messerschmitt's Augsburg factory built Heinkel He 45 biplanes under licence as well as Dornier Do 11s, an under-powered monoplane twin-engine bomber-trainer, thinly disguised as a mail plane. The German air industry was stretched to over-capacity by the first round of RLM orders. In 1933 the German aircraft industry had employed 3500 personnel, mainly highly skilled craftsmen, and was building an average of thirty-one planes a month. This level was about to expand by orders of magnitude. With the money from the licensed production orders, in May 1933 Messerschmitt was able to get Bfw out of the hands of the receivers, relaunch it, and prepare for the first flight of the M 37 the following year. But he had yet to sell any Messerschmitt designs to the RLM.

The RLM and the War Ministry in Berlin were at work on answering a fundamental question: what kinds of combat aircraft would the new German air force need when it finally shed its clandestine nature? This was the primary focus of General Walther Wever, chief of staff of the Luftwaffe in all but name. A staff officer who had learned to fly late in his career and embraced it with a convert's zeal, he was respected by the professional military, the aircraft industry and the new regime alike. In 1933, Germany feared primarily a pre-emptive strike by France, Poland and perhaps other neighbours.[18] German military staff officers produced studies and played wargames to identify Germany's combat aircraft needs. These were reflected by the RLM's 1933 *Technisches Amt* (Technical Department, better known as *C-Amt*) programme. The *C-Amt* planned that once trainers were built, Germany would need combat aircraft in four broad categories, designated *Rüstungsflugzeug* (aircraft armaments) I–IV: respectively, a multi-seat medium bomber, a smaller tactical bomber, a single-seat interceptor fighter and a two-seat heavy fighter. *C-Amt* started to work on detailed specifications for each of these requirements. They would then invite tenders from German aircraft manufacturers.

RLM Specification LA 1432/33 reflected the Luftwaffe's vision of what a single-seat fighter plane would have to do in a future war, replacing biplane Heinkel He 51s and Arado Ar 68s.[19] It specified an interceptor, intended to defeat high-technology twin-engine bombers sent to bomb Germany by day. The specification's primary evaluation criterion for the new fighter was speed. To enable it to catch incoming bombers, it had to sustain a speed of no less than 400 km/h (250 mph) for twenty minutes at an altitude of 6000 metres (19,690 feet). This showed the RLM's understanding of how the fast bomber had changed air combat: speed was needed to intercept them. Second, rate of climb would be considered, reflecting the need for the new fighter to quickly reach the high altitudes – made possible by their supercharged engines and oxygen equipment – at which the new bombers would be operating. The new fighter had to be able to climb to 6000 metres in seventeen minutes. It would have an operational ceiling of 10,000 metres; the engine would require a supercharger and the pilot oxygen. Total endurance was to be ninety minutes in the air, reflecting a need to patrol rather than a specific requirement for range or to carry an external fuel tank under the fuselage, like the He 51 biplane. An interceptor would operate close to its home base.

Manoeuvrability, considered the *sine qua non* of biplane fighters, was only the third-placed criterion, displaced by the bomber threat. It was thought that at the high speeds of modern aircraft, there would be few fighter versus fighter dogfights on the Great War model. The new design would have to have a wing loading of less than 100 kg per square metre; the lower the wing loading (the amount of lift each area of the wing must develop to keep an aeroplane flying) and the greater the engine power, the higher the manoeuvrability. The specification required the 670 hp Junkers Jumo 210 engine. The armament specified was the usual two rifle-calibre synchronised machine guns that current German biplane fighters carried. However, the RLM also asked for the new fighter to have provision for an engine-mounted 20mm cannon. The Luftwaffe realised that heavier firepower might be required to bring down all-metal multi-engine bombers.

Willy Messerschmitt knew about the upcoming competitions. He most wanted to win those for the two *Rüstungsflugzeug* fighter designs. But he had never produced a combat aircraft. Lusser's new design, the M 37, would not fly until 1934. Even if the M 37 were adopted by the RLM as a trainer and liaison aircraft, its importance to Messerschmitt was dwarfed by the numbers of potential aircraft that would be produced to meet the two fighter requirements. But Milch could prevent Messerschmitt submitting a design or receiving government funding to build a prototype.

In designing the M 37, Messerschmitt's team overcame many of the same problems that would be encountered in a modern fighter. The team had little experience designing aircraft with a retractable undercarriage, but produced an effective lightweight design. An enclosed cockpit, leading-edge slats and slotted flaps, previously used on larger all-metal airliners, were adapted to a small airframe. The M 37 design, though it had yet to fly, looked so promising that even the RLM had to pay attention. In September 1933, the RLM awarded Bfw a development contract, including six prototypes, for the former M 37, now redesignated the Bf 108A. With construction under way, Messerschmitt hired as chief engineer Walter Rethel, formerly Arado's chief designer, a man with extensive experience in building all-metal aircraft.

In October 1933, Germany had walked out of the League of Nations' Disarmament Conference. In Britain, Winston Churchill was one of the few public figures to call attention to German rearmament. Britain had wanted the 'air pact' that would effectively end bombing through international agreement. For this, Britain even offered Germany in exchange the remilitarisation of the Rhineland, which had been demilitarised under Versailles and occupied by Allied troops until 1931. Hitler was not receptive. Soon after, Germany withdrew from the League of Nations. The Luftwaffe's need for modern fighter aircraft became urgent.

R.J. Mitchell builds a better fighter

In the summer of 1933, Mitchell was recuperating from his bowel cancer surgery in a sanatorium in Bournemouth. Away from the office, Mitchell pondered political developments in Germany as well as his Type 224 design. Neither looked encouraging. Mitchell ignored his doctors and went back to Woolston.

Mitchell's son Gordon recalled, 'He never let himself be discouraged by failure. If a design failed, he went straight back to the drawing board and started again.'[20] Even before the Type 224 had flown, Mitchell decided that rather than devoting his time and that of his design team to improving the original design with the hope of winning the competition under Specification F7/30, they would prepare an entirely new design.

Mitchell had no assurance the RAF would buy the new fighter he was designing in the absence of an official specification. But RAF intelligence and some of its high-level leadership had already realised the implications of the 1933 German air expansion programme. In 1934, the RAF started planning for a war with Germany.

The Type 224 prototype first flew on 19 February 1934. But Mitchell was already at work on the new design. Always demanding with his team, Mitchell now became driven. Drawings that were not what he wanted would be flicked aside or even ripped to pieces. His team, even Joe Smith, leader in his absence, learned not to disturb Mitchell's concentration when he was focusing on a problem. His son Gordon recalled, 'He had no time at all for anyone he considered a fool and could be very rude.'[21] Mitchell faced his medical problems with a stiff upper lip and, told his cancer could soon return, was soon working harder than ever, even flying planes himself. He brought his son to the office when he worked through weekends. Alan Clifton, Smith's assistant, who had been at Supermarine since 1923, had no idea Mitchell had had a colostomy.

Mitchell's gamble, to devote his and his team's efforts to his idea – not that of the RAF – for a new fighter design rather than work on improving the Type 224, was backed up by his management. Sir Robert McLean, chairman of Supermarine's owner, Vickers, had previously supported Mitchell's work on the Type 224 prototype and had been frustrated by what he perceived as a technically backward Air Ministry. He had suggested its unofficial name, Spitfire. He funded Mitchell's new design, designated the Type 300. McLean recalled:

> I felt that they [Mitchell and his team] would do much better by devoting their qualities not to the official experimental fighter [the Type 224] but to a real killer fighter. After unfruitful discussions with the Air Ministry, my opposite number in Rolls-Royce, the late A.F. Sidgreaves, and I decided that the two companies together should finance the building of such an aircraft. The Air Ministry was informed of this decision and we were told that in no circumstances would any technical member of the Air Ministry be consulted or allowed to interfere with the designer.

Mitchell was on his own for the design. McLean felt 'the only thing to do was to build one ourselves. We had a large development fund and I used my own discretion, and we were on our own.'[22]

But if McLean was taking a risk in using company funds to back the gamble, it was an informed one. They had paid for Mitchell's team to work on the new design since February 1934. The Air Ministry had asked Supermarine for costing information for the new project, a first step to issuing a contract. Two days after the Vickers board meeting that authorised the use of company funding on 6 November 1934, McLean spoke to Air Marshal Sir Hugh Dowding at the Air Ministry, who assured him that he would expedite the issuing of a contract and that there was no intention to impose an engine choice on Mitchell's design. Dowding helped shape Air Ministry support for McLean's desire for Mitchell to create his own vision of a 'killer fighter'.[23] The Spitfire was only briefly a private venture, and the Air Ministry, looking for solutions to its requirements, soon supported Mitchell's independence and demonstrated this by its rapid response in creating a contract.

Mitchell sketched out the new fighter, which took shape on Smith's and Clifton's drawing boards. Smith recalled that Mitchell 'was an inveterate drawer on drawings, particularly general arrangements. He would modify the lines on an aircraft with the softest pencil he could find, then re-modify over the top with progressively thicker lines, until one would be faced with a new outline about three sixteenths of an inch thick. But the results were always worthwhile and the centre of the line was usually accepted when the thing was redrawn.'[24] The copying of design drawings was the responsibility of the team's junior members, the 'tracers', male and female. With Smith, Mitchell would 'spend almost all of the time in the drawing office, on the various boards. Here he would argue out the details with the draughtsmen concerned and show a complete grasp of the whole aircraft.'

The design team's chief aerodynamicist, Beverly Shenstone, a former Royal Canadian Air Force (RCAF) pilot with a degree in aeronautical engineering, had worked in Germany with Dr Junkers.[25] Arthur Black, the chief metallurgist, provided expertise vital to a team that had started out building wooden aeroplanes. Mitchell's technical assistant, Squadron Leader H.J. 'Agony' Payn, a Great War fighter pilot, provided the new design with operational insights. Other members handled radio, armament and other complex sub-systems. Ken Scales was the foreman in charge of assembling the prototype on the shop floor. Vera Cross, hired as Mitchell's secretary, took over the team's administrative duties as well.[26] Mitchell, Smith recalled, 'won the complete respect and the confidence of his staff, in whom he created a continuous sense of achievement ... But in spite of being the unquestioned leader, he was always ready to listen to and consider another point of view, or modify his ideas to meet any technical criticism he thought justified.'[27]

The Type 300 design would have all the elements of a modern fighter that were missing from the Type 224: an enclosed cockpit, a radio, a retractable undercarriage, all-metal stressed skin construction rather than a heavy rigid internal framework, and multiple machine guns in the wings. The control surfaces mounted on the trailing edges – the rudder on the fin, the elevators on the horizontal stabilisers and the ailerons on the wing – had a metal structure but were covered in fabric. These were vital because they were what a pilot would use to direct the flight of an aircraft. All were hinged and moved by wires and pulleys in response to manual pressure (the reason why a light, fabric-covered structure was specified) on the controls in the cockpit: the control stick (for ailerons and elevators) and the rudder pedals. Moving the ailerons, deflected against the airflow in flight, one going up while the other goes down, alters the lift of a wing and so produces roll, changing the heading on which the aircraft is flying. The elevators control the pitch, making the nose go up or down, while the rudder controls yaw, the side-to-side motion. The Type 300 would have trim tabs on its elevators and rudder, adjustable by the pilot in flight by a wheel-like control, used to stabilise or 'trim' the aircraft in flight.

Mitchell emphasised performance rather than ease of production, though he had designed the new fighter's tail fin to be built as an integral part of the fuselage, simpler to assemble than as a separate component. Beverly Shenstone thought, 'Had we had mass production in mind for the Spitfire from the beginning, we should almost certainly have arranged the internal structure rather differently.'[28]

The Type 224 was doomed by the lack of a powerful and reliable engine. For Mitchell, who had seen the S.6B set records, the Type 224's maximum speed of 238 mph was inadequate. He turned again to Rolls-Royce in-line engines, at that time the best in the world. The company had continued to work on the V12 engine designs that powered Mitchell's S.6B Schneider Cup racers. These engines had the cylinders in-line in two banks and were water cooled rather than having the cylinders arranged around the crankshaft and air cooled, as in a radial engine. Rolls-Royce were working on a new engine in this series, designated the PV 12 (to be renamed the Merlin), and designed to provide 760 hp, with the potential for additional increases in power. Their Derby factory became the hub of advanced piston engine development, led by Ernest 'Hs' Hives.[29]

Mitchell designed his Type 300 fighter around the new engine – rather than the alternative, the Napier Dagger – assuming that it would do everything that Rolls-Royce said it would do. If the engine failed to deliver or proved unreliable, or if its development were too protracted, Mitchell's design would be useless. The PV 12 engine determined the form of Mitchell's design, basically the smallest aircraft that could be designed around the engine and carry a multi-gun armament. Mitchell asked McLean and Sidgreaves to approach the RAF on his choice of engine. The Air Ministry decided in November 1934 not to push the Dagger on Mitchell and affirmed there was no objection to the use of the PV 12.[30] The Air Ministry's Royal Aircraft Establishment (RAE) at Farnborough developed an improved liquid cooling system that proved applicable to the new Rolls-Royce design.

At Hawker, Sydney Camm was also building a fighter, backed by his company's resources, after his 'Fury Monoplane' design to the F7/30 specification had been turned down by the Air Ministry. Camm also intended to use Rolls-Royce's PV 12 engine. But his design philosophy was different from that of Mitchell. Camm wanted to make his monoplane fighter as similar to his successful biplane fighters as possible, allowing an easier transition to the new technology for the manufacturer, ground crew and pilots alike. Camm, working independently from Mitchell, decided that, instead of using all available advances to maximise performance, he would instead aim to design the Hawker Hurricane, a fighter that it would be possible to develop, produce and put into service before the next crisis in Europe.

The Type 300 design progressed through the summer of 1934. Mitchell submitted a proposal for the new design to the Air Ministry on 16 July. It proved timely. In July 1934, rearmament began.[31] The government announced Scheme A, a programme to expand the RAF to 1304 aircraft in five years, with seventy-five home-based bomber and fighter squadrons. The RAF had been training some sixty pilots a year. Over the next two years, thirteen civilian flying schools would be formed to dramatically increase this number.

The press brought more news of advanced fighters being designed and built abroad, in the United States and the Soviet Union. Mitchell's vision, that all-metal construction need not be limited to planes like the DC-2 with multiple engines and a strong structure, was shared by other aircraft designers throughout the world, even while others, such as Sydney Camm at Hawker, were designing monoplane fighters that would retain at least some of the old technology, the fabric-covered fuselages.

But no one had yet seen what was considered inevitable: a German all-metal monoplane fighter design. When it did come, Mitchell and his team were well aware it was likely to make use of the expertise in all-metal design and construction available in Germany. In November 1934 Mitchell sent Beverly Shenstone to the Paris Air Show, where he closely examined the He 70; he admired the Günter brothers' streamlined wooden cantilever elliptical wing design, ran his hand over the fuselage's fine low-drag flush riveting and felt the cool touch of its lightweight high-magnesium-content alloy skin. The He 70 mutely asked the uncomfortable question: what do you get if you make a smaller version and arm it? Likely, something that would be able to sweep the skies of the RAF's biplane fighters. Ralph Sorley, then a squadron leader serving in the Air Ministry, recalled, 'The point came when Mitchell saw, I think more plainly than anybody else at that time – and mark you it was 1934 – that German aircraft design effort was something that we were going to feel and suffer from.'[32]

In November 1934, Mitchell made the decision to use the Rolls-Royce engine in his design. By the end of the year, Mitchell's team had prepared detailed drawings of the Type 300. On 1 December, Supermarine received a £10,000 contract for the Type 300 from the Air Ministry. The project had been funded. Any doubts that the RAF had about Mitchell's design were put aside on 5 December, when Mitchell came up from Southampton to the Air Ministry in Kingsway, London, for a meeting, accompanied by Alan Clifton carrying the design drawings. For all Robert McLean's perception of having to force an outside design on a bureaucracy entrenched in the biplane era, Mitchell now sat across the table from RAF officers and civil servants committed to building monoplane multi-gun fighters. No objections were raised to Mitchell's choice of the PV 12 (Merlin) engine for his design. A few weeks later, the RAF issued a specification, F.37/34, written explicitly for the Type 300 and intended to meet the Air Ministry's Operational Requirement OR.17 for an interceptor. In January 1935, construction began on the first prototype.

Mitchell now had another chance at building a fighter. His health and the European political situation both appeared clouded. He needed to finish the Type 300 before, one way or the other, time ran out.

Willy Messerschmitt designs a fighter

In January 1934, Willy Messerschmitt was unhappy. Money was coming in to Bfw. It had made a modest profit of 166,000 Reichsmarks in 1933. But the aeroplanes being produced were not Messerschmitt designs. Milch's bureaucratic empire at the RLM in Berlin could succeed in keeping Bfw limited to building other manufacturers' designs under licence. Messerschmitt might not be invited to bid on any of the new *Rüstungsflugzeug* military aircraft contracts from the RLM.

Messerschmitt had received no interest from the RLM beyond the order for six prototypes of the Bf 108. He sought to license his designs to Romania. Messerschmitt felt loyalty to the few dozen Bfw employees who had hand-crafted his planes during the worst years. Now, over the course of 1933, he hired a larger workforce – about 600 – without their expertise or the links of personal loyalty to build other men's designs. So when an offer of a prestigious appointment as a professor in Danzig arrived, Messerschmitt gave it strong consideration.

Milch turned his attention to stripping assets – including ownership and management of his aircraft business – from Dr Junkers, arrested for treason on 17 October 1933. It seemed Messerschmitt would be next. Milch used Messerschmitt's proposed deal with Romania – in the absence of a German production order – as grounds for an investigation of violation of export laws. The chief of *C-Amt*, Oberstleutnant Wilhelm Wimmer, considered to be the most technologically proficient officer in the RLM and a protégé of Wever, led the attack.

Messerschmitt called his Nazi friends. He had loaned Rudolf Hess an M 35 aerobatic monoplane, which Hess had used to win a major competition. Hess was powerful enough to save Messerschmitt's friend Theo Croneiss from being murdered along with many of his old

Bavarian Brownshirt comrades in the Night of the Long Knives, 30 June 1934, as Hitler consolidated power.[33] Croneiss switched sides at the last minute.

Milch found he had more pressing concerns than Messerschmitt. At the same time as Messerschmitt was discovering that he had friends in high places, Milch instead found out that his many personal enemies – his management style tended to create them – had spread the word that Milch's father was Jewish. Theo Croneiss, remembering Milch's attempts to run his airline out of business, compiled a genealogical dossier, complete with photographs of the headstones of Milch's relatives buried in Jewish cemeteries. He shared the fruits of his research with Göring as well as his fellow directors of Bfw.[34] As momentum gathered for the purging of anyone with Jewish blood, this intervention appeared timely; in 1934, the German military purged itself on its own account, with few protests, and none from the incipient air force, over the seventy officers and NCOs dismissed.

Milch was faced with ruin. Explaining to Göring, Milch told him that his real father was not his mother's (deceased, Jewish) husband but rather her (suitably Aryan) long-time lover. While Göring saw Milch as a rival, he had a degree of sympathy. Göring had been aware of his own mother's Jewish lover during the many years when Göring's father, a diplomat and colonial administrator, was overseas. With his famous comment '*I* decide who is a Jew', he signalled that Milch would remain in the inner circle and halted enquiries into Milch's mother's Jewish background.

Göring knew he needed Milch to use his links with the semi-clandestine Weimar aviation industry to build the new National Socialist air power. Göring lacked Milch's managerial experience. Successful and self-assured, Milch had run a large business. He could read a balance sheet and make things happen on schedule. Milch now aimed not to take over the German aircraft industry, but to prune his own family tree. Göring ensured that, now racially pure, Milch stayed. Milch's power, increasing in 1933, was now overshadowed by that of his boss, to whom he owed his job and, indeed, his life and that of his daughter (who had Down's Syndrome and so was at risk from Nazi euthanasia programmes). This removed a check on Göring's leadership style, which reflected active intelligence combined with loyalty to Hitler, undercut by often spectacular self-indulgence coupled with his near-total aversion to technology and ignorance of any advances in aircraft since 1918.

Göring's pre-industrial and post-rational worldview and need to please Hitler at all costs set the tone for many of the decisions made with regard to German air power. He was a politician, and only a military leader because Hitler promoted him over the heads of the entire officer corps. Yet military men were still responsible for making key decisions on resource allocation, intelligence, and technology development. The German military remained dominated by the army and its thinking by the General Staff, whose exclusive ranks included few airmen.

With Milch preoccupied, Messerschmitt's friends in the leadership arranged a production order for Bf 108 trainers, soon after the first one flew in June 1934. Messerschmitt would build them at his Augsburg plant. He used one of the first, civil registered as D-IMTT, as his personal aircraft ('MTT' was how Messerschmitt initialled documents). It was a success for the man who had sold his car to help keep a padlock off his factory door three years before. He declined the professorship.

The Bf 108 proved to be a record-setting, technology-pushing design. Early Bf 108 examples, though, suffered from structural weakness. Rudolf Hess had heard about the new design. No one was willing to tell the deputy leader of the Third Reich that the aircraft should not be flown. At Staaken, near Berlin, Hess put on a spontaneous aerobatic display and landed with the Bf 108 crippled by structural failure but still just in one piece. The Bf 108 design was swiftly modified as the Bf 108B and became a classic; some thirty-five years after its first flight, Squadron Leader John R. Hawke, a former RAF aerobatic instructor, called it 'the finest flying machine of its type I have ever flown'.[35]

But before the drama with Milch had played out and the first Bf 108 had flown, the competition for the new German fighter had opened with C-Amt's issue to Messerschmitt, among other companies, of specification LA 1432/33. Messerschmitt was aware of the detailed designs for a monoplane fighter Ernst Heinkel had already passed to C-Amt for review. Yet for all the promise inherent in the Bf 108 design, Messerschmitt had never designed a single-engine fighter. Messerschmitt at first limited his investment in the new programme to a preliminary design, designated Project P 1034, concerned that the RLM would not fund him to build prototypes. But his links to the Nazi leadership and the excellent potential of the Bf 108 could not be ignored by the RLM.

When Messerschmitt visited Berlin, flying in to the grass strip at Tempelhof Airport in D-IMTT, he did not need Milch or Wimmer to tell him that the RLM thought it knew better. Their offices said it for them. The RLM's first act upon its formation in 1933 had been to build a massive 4500-office building, the largest in Europe, on the Wilhelmstrasse. Milch had sent 5000 men to clear the site overnight, plans to preserve the previous buildings be damned.[36] Quarries throughout Germany had been mined for the marble façade and floors. The seventeen staircases, grand and red-carpeted, had gleaming banisters, polished daily, under glowing chandeliers and elaborately patterned ceilings. A great hall allowed indoor ceremonies on the model of the Nuremberg rallies. Even the minor offices in this edifice were occupied by self-imagined Men of Destiny, for whom failure or mistakes were inconceivable. When it came to measuring themselves against outsiders, no matter how distinguished, those who sat at massive desks in the RLM's office building did not think they had much to learn. The massive carved swastika and eagle was inside, in the great hall. When the building opened in October 1935, it was the modernist public expression of a regime whose inner nature, timeless as torture and hunger, was revealed by the opening for business of Dachau in 1933.

Milch did not think he had to worry about Messerschmitt winning the competition. He had already taken a good look at the He 112 design, which Wimmer favoured. Milch thought that having Messerschmitt in the competition would motivate others to improve their performance and lower their prices; he had no desire to see Ernst Heinkel, whom he considered a prima donna, sweep the competition.[37] Milch told Gerhard Geike, head of the RLM's technical centre at Rechlin, where the competing designs would be evaluated, he 'was not keen on going along with Messerschmitt, but in the end he gave in'. General Wever, impressed by the Bf 108B's performance, wanted to see what Messerschmitt could do with a fighter design. Göring wanted to develop the aircraft industry in Bavaria, to include 'a very fast courier aircraft that need only be a single seater', a necessary euphemism for a fighter, still banned under the Versailles Treaty.[38] But Göring made it clear that while he wanted fighters built in Bavaria, they did not have to be designed there; the building of Heinkel designs under licence was acceptable. Milch went along, adding: 'Nothing much will come of it, but, as a pike in a carp pond, Messerschmitt may be quite useful.'[39]

A head-to-head competitive evaluation and fly-off would decide the winner between the prototypes. In February 1934, Messerschmitt, Heinkel and Arado each received contracts from the RLM for three prototypes, to be powered by Junkers Jumo or BMW 116 in-line engines, both then still in development. Messerschmitt attributed his inclusion to the military's desire to access the best aircraft technology: 'Wever, a very intelligent man, saw to it that I got the contract without any preconditions attached and that I was able to build an airplane as I imagined a fighter to be.'[40] A fourth manufacturer, Focke Wulf, received a development contract months later. With the RLM contract came an official designation for Messerschmitt's new fighter: the Bf 109. From then on, it would be known to the Germans simply as the 'one-hundred-nine'.

Everything was at stake for Messerschmitt. Considering Milch's dislike and Heinkel's strong position, his design would be an underdog. The winner would take home production contracts for an unprecedented number of aircraft. The losers would potentially be marginalised, reduced to building other firms' designs, or, at worst, treated as Dr Junkers had been, with the RLM taking everything, including their name.

Messerschmitt distrusted *C-Amt*'s wisdom about Germany's modern fighter design: 'I studied the requirements in detail and went back to Berlin, where I told the gentlemen that the specifications were not to my liking. Such a fighter would never be able to bring down a bomber embodying the latest technological advances.'[41] Messerschmitt and his team, led by Lusser, Rethel and Bauer, with Kokothaki handling management, had no access to the RLM and their wisdom. They therefore designed their fighter as they thought fit. Messerschmitt took a hands-on role in the design. The Messerschmitt fighter design was small, light yet aerodynamically highly efficient. Intended to use the Jumo, Messerschmitt ensured that the design would be adaptable to a better engine when one became available. Messerschmitt stressed lightness and ease of construction, 'a true application of light construction principles: minimal dimensions, minimal surface area, lightest materials, equal distribution of stress loads, and above all using a single component for multiple functions ... It also led to simplification of construction. In spite of its extremely light weight, we were able to keep construction time down ... requiring fewer man-hours per kilogram of weight to build than any contemporary design.'[42]

In May 1934 a basic mock-up of the new fighter was completed. A low-wing monoplane, its state-of-the-art elements included an outwardly retracting undercarriage, an enclosed cockpit and a radio. For lightness and ease of production, old-technology approaches were also used. The horizontal stabilisers were externally braced with struts. The tailwheel was non-retracting.

The new fuselage design was built in two halves, joined along the centre line, and used monocoque stressed-skin construction (as had Mitchell's design). Structural loads were carried by the 0.6mm-thick aluminium skin. The fuselage had no load-carrying structure other than the firewall, which was where the two legs of the cantilever undercarriage (an innovation on the Bf 108), the engine and the main spar pick-up points were all attached. A fuel tank, below and behind the cockpit, and a radio behind it could both fit inside the fuselage.

Messerschmitt knew that, with a given source of engine power, speed can be increased by reducing wing area, hence less drag. But a smaller wing area created a higher wing loading, hence less manoeuvrability, and higher landing speed (with a smaller wing, an aeroplane has to fly faster to generate the minimum amount of lift to keep it in the air). Messerschmitt had been one of the first designers to introduce the single-spar metal wing; the new fighter's main spar was a single aluminium I-beam, positioned near the leading edge of the wing.

Messerschmitt decided to use thin, tapering wings. He kept weight down by thinning the covering, from 1.4mm thick at the root down to 0.7mm at the tip. The *C-Amt* specification's armament of two machine guns and an engine-mounted cannon (firing through the propeller hub) could all be concentrated in the nose rather than accommodated inside the wing. With no provision for guns, the wings could be kept light and

easily removable because they did not have to support the retractable
undercarriage, attached to the fuselage structure at the firewall. To keep
the wing design light and low-drag, Messerschmitt accepted a higher
wing loading.

To compensate for higher wing loading and get the maximum in
manoeuvrability from the thin, simple light wing, the landing speed
could be reduced by slotted flaps, lowered from the trailing edge of the
underside of the wing on approach to landing, effectively creating more
lift and drag. The leading-edge slats smoothed the airflow going over the
wing as it approached a stall (caused when air is not moving fast enough
over the wing to generate lift). This generated more lift, reducing landing speed, and allowed the pilot better control in a tight
high-performance turn than would have been possible without slats.
Automatic (self-deploying) leading-edge slats had been originated in
Britain by Handley Page. Messerschmitt himself had met Sir Frederick
Handley Page and the German designer of the slats, Gustav Lachmann,
back in the 1920s. Since then he had been convinced of the potential
value of leading-edge slats. Mutual licensing had been agreed over 'a liter
of good German beer in a beer garden in Frankfurt', Messerschmitt
recalled.[43]

The specification showed that the RLM was concerned about spin
performance, and with good reason. With the potential higher performance of all-metal aircraft, pilots were likely to black out during
intense manoeuvring and lose consciousness. This was exacerbated at
high altitude, where the 1920s-technology oxygen masks then used in
Germany often slipped off and did not provide a reliable flow under the
pressure of several times the force of gravity. It was important to the
RLM that if a fighter went into a spin, through the pilot having blacked
out or stalled during too tight a turn, he could easily recover even if he
was blacked out for several turns. Though any fighter plane could expect
to stall during air combat manoeuvres, it was important to be able to
recover; fighter planes needed to be flown to their design limits.

While no single element of the Bf 109 design was original, the way
Messerschmitt and his team pulled it all together and reduced drag and
weight while simplifying construction amounted to a considerable
advance. Early 1930s all-metal aircraft had over-designed structures; the

DC-2 and DC-3 will never wear out. Such structures were acceptable on transports or even bombers, which had to carry heavy loads but not fly at high speed or dogfight. Fighters had remained biplanes into the 1930s because monoplane wings that would not fail under the stresses of air combat manoeuvring had to be so big that an early 1930s engine could not make them fly fast enough to achieve a fighter's required level of performance. Messerschmitt, undeterred by the history of structural failures of his all-metal aircraft designs, created what was effectively a 'light fighter'. This, along with the promise – for that was all it was – of more powerful engines from German industry, allowed Messerschmitt to turn the basic Bf 108 design into the Bf 109 fighter.

Messerschmitt's team had an advanced mock-up ready in January 1935. Greater haste was apparent throughout the German aircraft industry. Its overall rate of production increased to 265 aircraft a month by 1935, almost nine times what it had been just two years before.[44] In January 1935, Milch announced a further plan to increase production to 526 a month by 1936.

On 1 March 1935, the Luftwaffe officially abandoned its clandestine status. The new service started co-equal with Germany's army and navy. Its 20,000 personnel, most of them highly trained aircrew and technicians, would be reinforced by the reintroduction of conscription. The 'airline' training school where Galland had learned to be a fighter pilot became a military training base with just a change of signage and uniforms.

While Milch had guided the RLM in 1933–4, Göring, new commander-in-chief of the Luftwaffe, saw himself as the central figure in all of German aviation. His considerable intelligence and wartime experience as a fighter pilot, however, was tempered by his limited understanding of both the technology and the operations of modern military aviation. Göring was interested in reporting to Hitler only the number of combat aircraft. He did not care much about sustainability, strategy, tactics or investing in the future. The Luftwaffe did have the benefit of a small cadre of highly professional staff officers transferred from the army, including General Walther Wever, but this led to enduring tensions in the Luftwaffe. The high-level staff officers were not aircrew and the aircrew were not staff officers.

The first prototype of Messerschmitt's fighter, the Bf 109V1 (*Versuchs*, experimental), was completed in May 1935. But the Junkers Jumo 210 engine was not ready. Messerschmitt had never been happy with the Jumo. It did not provide enough power for its weight and size to be other than an interim powerplant for Messerschmitt's fighter. Dr Junkers' heirs – Messerschmitt's old friend had died, under house arrest, in March – were 'persuaded' to transfer their remaining interest in the aviation business to the RLM for a fraction of its worth. The new RLM-owned Junkers would be responsible for future development of the engine.

Messerschmitt had, from the inception of the Bf 109 design, planned on its ultimate powerplant being the advanced design Daimler-Benz had been working on for years, a twelve-cylinder inverted-V in-line engine. In 1933, they had received RLM funding and an order for six prototypes, but it had yet to be tested. Taking a risk on this unproven technology, Messerschmitt pressed the RLM to accept the Daimler-Benz DB 600 series engine as an alternative power source for his original Bf 109 design. But the specification remained for the Junkers Jumo, with the BMW 116 – rather than the Daimler-Benz that Messerschmitt wanted – the only approved alternative engine.[45] Until Daimler-Benz could prove its design, Bf 109s had to be built with Jumo 210 engines.

No Jumos, BMWs or DB 600s were available for the impending competition for Germany's new fighter. For a short-term solution, the RLM turned to Britain and acquired four of Rolls-Royce's latest 695 hp Kestrel VI V12 in-line engines by trading a He 70. This gave Milch another opportunity to thwart Messerschmitt, concerned that his engine would be allocated elsewhere or received too late.

In the end, two of the engines went to Messerschmitt, the others to competitors. The Augsburg factory modified the Bf 109V1 to accept the Kestrel VI. The British engine, lacking a suitable constant-speed propeller, used an old-style two-bladed wooden fixed-pitch propeller. The Bf 109's design called for an inverted engine, but the Kestrel fitted better upright.

While these changes were going on, Ernst Udet visited Messerschmitt at Augsburg. He sat in the Bf 109V1 prototype. If this was the future of

German fighter aircraft, Udet was not buying it. He disliked the enclosed cockpit. The retractable landing gear design was unreliable. Udet (like many contemporaries) saw no value in monoplanes except as airliners or bombers.[46] Pulling himself out of the cockpit, he slapped Messerschmitt on the back. 'Messerschmitt, this will never make a fighter ... A fighter pilot must feel the speed and the one wing you've got there needs another above it with struts and wires between ... then it will be a fighter.'[47] This, from Germany's greatest living fighter pilot!

The Bf 109V1 first flew on 28 May 1935 from the Bfw factory at Augsburg, with Messerschmitt's senior test pilot, Flugkapitan[48] Hans 'Bubi' Knotzech, at the controls: five months before the Hawker Hurricane's initial flight and ten months before the Spitfire took to the air. But Messerschmitt was more concerned with his German competitors than potential foreign rivals.

Udet rejoined the Luftwaffe in June 1935. In February 1936, he became Inspector of Fighters and Dive Bombers. In June, Göring appointed him the head of the RLM's Technical Office, with authority over the *C-Amt*, using him to remove Milch's control over the production and technical decisions of Luftwaffe expansion. Having an old friend in the RLM was obviously beneficial for Messerschmitt.

After the Bf 109V1's flight tests were completed at Augsburg in September 1935, it was sent to the RLM's *Erprobungstelle* (proving centre) at Rechlin. In the autumn of 1935 Rechlin was a vision of the new and the modern, where every day the old world – of the Versailles Treaty and biplanes and German humiliation and exclusion from both European power and dominance in military aviation – was being washed away. Hitler's new Germany and Germany's new air force had arrived together to shake the world.

On its flight from Augsburg to Rechlin, the Bf 109V1 landed to refuel at a Luftwaffe fighter field at Doberitz. Adolf Galland, now a Luftwaffe *Leutnant* flying biplane He 51s, saw it. He knew immediately that this was the plane for him. As a champion glider pilot, he appreciated the thin tapering wings and the low-drag design. Galland sat in the cockpit, viewing the enclosed canopy with suspicion. Knotzech told him, 'we would not need any more visibility rearwards, because no one could attack us from the rear on account of our superior speed'.[49]

Galland persuaded Knotzech to fly the Bf 109V1 in a mock dogfight against Galland in his He 51. Galland's training emphasised dogfighting. His commanding officers, Great War veterans, insisted on having dozens of fighters simulating close combat, turning to get behind each other. Knotzech, he said, 'though a brilliant test pilot, was without any air combat training or experience. Consequently he did not make the right use of his superiority in acceleration, speed, and climb.'[50] Galland resolved that, if he ever flew the Bf 109 in combat, he would not make the same mistakes.

At Rechlin, RLM, Luftwaffe and company test pilots turned out to watch the new Bf 109V1 arrive. The favourite in the competition, the He 112V1, had already been test flown. Knotzech made a flawless approach and gently landed the new light grey fighter. The main wheels gently touched the runway together. And then: disaster. Its left main undercarriage leg broke. As Heinrich Beauvais, a Rechlin test pilot, saw, 'The aircraft stood straight up on its nose, hesitated, and then decided to fall back onto its belly rather than completely nose over.'[51] Knotzech was able to keep the Bf 109V1 from suffering substantial damage. Repairs were soon made, but it was a terrible way to begin the competition.

In the weeks that followed, Knotzech demonstrated the Bf 109V1's speed; capable of 467 km/h (290 mph), it was 27 km/h (17 mph) faster than the He 112V1. But this was a fighter evaluation, not an air race. When Knotzech flew the Bf 109V1 back to Augsburg, the He 112V1 was still the favourite. Messerschmitt, furious at the crash, fired Knotzech and supervised the hurried completion of another prototype. Unless Messerschmitt could turn the competition around, the 'pike in the carp pond' would only give the RLM better bidding leverage with Heinkel.

The Spitfire emerges

At a meeting between the pair in March 1935, Hitler told the British foreign secretary, Anthony Eden, that the Luftwaffe already equalled the RAF in striking power. Within two months, the British government announced a new expansion plan, Scheme C, with a goal of 112 squadrons by 1937.

At the same time, the Italians started to reinforce their army on the border of Ethiopia in preparation for their eventual invasion of that country, making them another potential enemy. The British Mediterranean Fleet's main base at Malta suddenly looked vulnerable in the face of Mussolini's much-publicised air power. The RAF, with no interceptors available to defend Malta, considered it the Royal Navy's problem. Without effective air defences, its ships withdrew to Gibraltar and Egypt. How Malta would be defended from air attack went unresolved.

Mitchell's work on the new Type 300 fighter went on as the Type 224's flight test programme continued. Evaluated by the RAF at Martlesham Heath, the Type 224 failed to offer the improved performance the RAF wanted, just as Mitchell had thought it would. In July 1935 the RAF ordered the Gloster Gladiator biplane fighter, which could at least be built immediately. This was an improved version of the Gloster Gauntlet fighter with flaps, an enclosed cockpit, a radio and four machine guns. Some thought even the Gladiator used too much new technology. The commander-in-chief of the ADGB, Air Marshal Robert Brooke-Popham, opposed the Gladiator's enclosed cockpit.

It was accepted that the Gladiator was a stopgap until the sort of fighter envisioned the year before in Specification F.37/34 could become a reality. The Type 300 and a corresponding specification written around Sydney Camm's Hurricane design were to be fighters with a top speed of greater than 300 mph and a maximum ceiling of more than 30,000 feet. This required a streamlined design with a retractable undercarriage. Their structures had to be strong enough to manoeuvre at high speeds, with an airframe capable of holding up under stresses several times the force of gravity.[52] Enclosed cockpits and oxygen were required for high-altitude flight. A radio would be required to communicate. But the new fighters needed to be flyable by service pilots and to operate off RAF stations' short (4000 feet or less) runways, usually of grass. Good low-speed performance and low landing speed required flaps to be included in the design.

There were now two modern fighters being designed for the RAF, both powered by the Merlin engine. But the Hurricane differed from the Spitfire in that it also used partial wood-and-fabric construction stiffened by metal tubes. It could be built by the current workforce, used to old-technology aircraft, without as lengthy a learning curve. The Hurricane's designers were not trying to push the outer limits of mid-1930s airframe technology. Camm had a larger design team than Mitchell. The Hurricane would be ready for production first.

The two new RAF fighters would also share the same armament. The RAF had come to the conclusion that a fighter needed to fire a thousand .303 bullets in two seconds to bring down the modern bombers that would be its primary target. Dogfights with other fighters, as in the Great War, were seen as less likely, considering the high speed of modern aircraft. It was strategic bombing that threatened Britain, and the fighter's mission was to protect against it.

Squadron Leader Ralph Sorley, in the Air Ministry's Operational Requirements Branch, became the most vocal advocate for any new fighter to have an armament of eight .303-calibre machine guns in the wings, so they did not have to be synchronised through the propeller. This would increase the rate of fire, but decrease its concentration and make aiming more problematic (the guns were no longer in front of the pilot's gunsight).[53] He encountered high-level opposition – Brooke-Popham had said in July 1934 that an eight-gun armament was 'going too far' – but more of those in charge eventually supported the enhanced armament. While the Hurricane's thick wing easily accommodated eight guns and enough ammunition for fifteen seconds' firing, it was difficult to incorporate them into the thinner, tapering wings that Mitchell had been planning for the Type 300. Sorley proposed firing trials of an eight-gun armament in December 1934. While he later recalled encountering high-level opposition, the concept was quickly approved in the Air Ministry and was being tested within months.

In spring 1935 the RAF made it clear it wanted to arm the Type 300 with eight machine guns. A new specification, F.10/35, issued for comment only, suggested that this was to be an interim step and that future fighters would be armed with multiple cannon. At the final mock-up conference in May 1935, the Air Ministry's Operational Branch made its case for an armament of eight machine guns and this was accepted. Mitchell abandoned the tapering wing for an elliptical wing to accommodate the increased armament along with the retractable undercarriage. The wing's chord – its width from leading to trailing edge – was longest at the wing root, where it was attached to the fuselage, contributing to greater structural strength. This reduced wing loading, increasing speed and manoeuvrability; a 10 per cent increase in wing area, for a fighter, could mean the difference between excellent and adequate manoeuvrability. It also provided space inside the wing, where Mitchell intended to put the multi-gun armament.

Mitchell and Shenstone had decided they wanted to keep the wing thin. This would reduce drag and improve airflow at high speeds, providing better high-speed performance. An elliptical design seemed the best way to reconcile a thin wing with the need to accommodate not only a retractable undercarriage but also internal space for heavy armament, plus additional wing area for high manoeuvrability. Elliptical wing designs were not revolutionary on fighters; they had been used by the Günter brothers in Germany and Alexander Kartveli in the US. Mitchell told Shenstone, who had pushed for an elliptical wing design, 'I don't give a bugger whether it's elliptical or not, as long as it covers the guns.'[54] The Spitfire wing (13 per cent of chord at the thickest point) was thinner than that of the Bf 109 (14 per cent) and much thinner than the Hurricane (19 per cent). Deciding on a thin wing would minimise drag at high speeds.

For the wing design, Mitchell and his team were reaching beyond the evidence provided by wind tunnel tests. 'We made hardly any use of wind tunnel testing in evolving the shape of the new fighter,' Beverly Shenstone wrote.[55] Mitchell was relying on the experience of the high-drag Type 224 and his own judgement. He was turning away from his S.6B Schneider Cup design, straight lines faired into other straight lines with a simple box spar, and instead used compound curves for the elliptical wing and its fairing to the fuselage, relying on a complex 'leaf spring' spar to provide strength. Working under pressure of the deteriorating international situation as well as his deteriorating health, Mitchell did not explain his design decisions to the team, nor to the Air Ministry. It was their specification, but his design.

The design of the fairing where the wing joined the fuselage was important to the handling of low-wing monoplanes. Mitchell's design for the wing and its fairing would allow control in high-speed stall conditions (as might be considered in future air combat manoeuvres), Mitchell effectively anticipated that the problem of high-speed stalls would be encountered by a high-performance modern fighter. With the Spitfire's wings joining the fuselage at an angle – another one of the compound curves that literally shaped the aircraft – a pilot would better feel the initial severe juddering as it started to stall, giving greater control, as a juddering Spitfire was still in full control and able to turn tightly on the brink of a stall.[56]

It also appeared to Mitchell that the design would offer advantages in maintaining control if it encountered the recognised but little-understood transonic phenomena that made an aircraft uncontrollable as it approached the speed of sound. This seemed to impose an absolute limit on the speed an aircraft could achieve, even in a dive, hence the term 'sound barrier'. But the wind tunnels Mitchell had access to were unable to achieve such speeds. This advantage could only be demonstrated on paper.

'"Joe" Smith, in charge of structural design, deserves all credit for producing a wing that was both strong enough and stiff enough within the severe volumetric constraints,' Shenstone recalled.[57] The 'leaf spring' design of the main spar, the wing's structural support, consisted of five overlapping boxes of high-grade aluminium at the wing root, gradually thinning down to a single box at the wing tip. This gave structural strength at the wing root and flexibility at the tip. It was a brilliant design, but few industrial machines in Britain could produce such aluminium structures, and, like the wing-fuselage joint, it added to the difficulty of construction.

Forward of the main spar, Mitchell's team designed what was essentially a rectangular aluminium box for strength. This was faired over with light-grade aluminium to form the wing's leading edge and outer skin. In addition to carrying the new fighter's armament, its wings would also carry the engine's radiator and oil cooler on the underside. Split flaps were built in under the trailing edge.

To accommodate the weight of the eight guns without reducing performance, other elements of the design were lightened. This included reducing the maximum fuel capacity from ninety-five to eighty-five gallons, all in the fuselage, and dispensing with any plumbing for external fuel tanks.

Mitchell's design for the Spitfire gave it an advantage over the Bf 109. It was physically larger, with a wingspan 10 per cent longer, had a greater wing area and a deeper fuselage. Yet Mitchell was able to reduce the Spitfire's drag until it was almost equal to that of the smaller Bf 109.[58] The Spitfire was all compound curves where the Bf 109 was linear and angular. The Spitfire design minimised drag, but its complex structure – especially the elegant, precisely curved, elliptical wings – meant it would be more difficult to build.

The prototype Hurricane first flew on 6 November 1935. After the November 1935 election, which left the National government under the Conservative Stanley Baldwin in power but with a reduced majority, the RAF approved its new expansion Scheme, 'Plan F', in February 1936. Its goal of 107 squadrons would now be sustained by planning for spare parts and reserve aircraft. Perhaps most importantly, it recognised the vital importance of expanding the British aircraft and engine industries. Lord Swinton, the new secretary of state for air, created the 'shadow' factory scheme, where each existing factory would help create a second factory as its shadow, located away from the threat of enemy air attack.[59] These factories would be built at government expense. Some would be managed by car manufacturers; they had greater experience of mass production than the aircraft industry, which relied on hand-crafting. Rolls-Royce started shadow engine factories at Crewe, Manchester and, later, Glasgow, the latter set up by Ford to build engines on an assembly line rather than maintaining the traditional reliance on craftsmen. While work started on the construction of factory buildings and scarce machine tools were ordered, the aircraft manufacturers' network of sub-contractors and experience in building to Air Ministry specifications proved harder to duplicate. Industrial weakness limited expansion.

Despite the failure of the League of Nations, the 1935 Anglo-German naval agreement had revived hope that negotiations would succeed. Trade as well as talk continued between the two countries. The Spitfire might not be part of the RAF's rearmament programme; it might not even be funded.

The prototype Type 300 took shape at Supermarine's Woolston plant. In February 1936, it started ground tests. The Air Ministry named it 'Spitfire', the name which McLean had previously tried to give to the

Type 224. 'Just the sort of bloody silly name they would choose' was Mitchell's reaction. The prototype Spitfire was dismantled and taken by lorry to nearby Eastleigh Airport. Its first flight was on 5 March 1936, with Supermarine's veteran test pilot Joseph 'Mutt' Summers at the controls; the plane was fitted with a two-blade fixed-pitch wooden propeller and its undercarriage was fixed down (they had not yet checked out the retracting mechanism). Mitchell and most of the team watched the hour-long flight. Those who were there recalled Mitchell's tension as his design started its engine, taxied out and took off. Joe Smith recalled, 'Although he witnessed the first flights of so many aircraft he never grew accustomed to it.' Mitchell did not relax until Summers had safely landed, the engine had been switched off and the wheels chocked. Summers' first words were 'Don't change a thing.'

In the weeks that followed, the Spitfire was flown by Summers and his colleague Jeffrey Quill, who had flown with the RAF. Supermarine's test pilots, like their counterparts worldwide, were an indispensable part of the design team.[60] Their position had evolved from daredevil pilots before the Great War to the design teams' eyes in the cockpit. Technology to monitor and record performance of aircraft instruments in flight was rudimentary – some instrument readings were recorded on paper rolls – so the design team relied on the judgement of the test pilots. They quickly demonstrated the Spitfire's potential. One test flight achieved a speed of 430 mph in a dive.

Mitchell valued the test pilots' reports and insisted on having them verbatim, not 'edited' by his team. Sorley recalled, 'He could talk pilots' language, could understand the pilots' feelings and expressions and generally speaking you could get on with him. He could understand what you thought about it and he would tell you what it all meant.'[61] Mitchell told Quill, 'Look, I'll give you a bit of advice, Jeffrey. If anybody tells you anything about aeroplanes which is so bloody complicated you can't understand it, take it from me, it's all balls.' Quill went on to become one of Britain's most successful test pilots.

Mitchell continued to plan ahead about what would need to change when the Spitfire was developed. On 29 March, less than a month after the first flight, he issued an internal specification to start designing a version of the Spitfire armed with 20mm cannon in response to Air

Ministry Specification F.37/35, issued on 15 February 1936, to meet Air Ministry Operational Requirement OR.31 for a day and night fighter for home defence or overseas operations.[62] Many manufacturers submitted designs to this specification. It appeared possible that whatever aircraft was selected could expect more extensive production than the current Spitfire. By submitting a cannon-armed Spitfire, Mitchell was already envisioning such fighters as the eventual replacement for the current eight-machine-gun Spitfire.

The prototype Spitfire finished its initial testing at Eastleigh. On 26 May 1936, it was delivered for evaluation by the RAF at the Aircraft and Armament Experimental Establishment at Martlesham Heath. Flight Lieutenant Humphrey 'EJ' Edwards Jones, an RAF test pilot at Martlesham Heath, was put on alert to start flight testing within minutes of the Spitfire's delivery and to call the Air Ministry directly after the first Spitfire flight by an RAF pilot:

> At about 4:30 pm, 'Mutt' Summers, the firm's chief test pilot, brought K5054 in and at about 5:30 pm, I took off after a thorough briefing from 'Mutt' ... I flew the aircraft for about 20 minutes and found it delightful to handle and no problems in normal flight ... It was not until I was on what is now known as 'finals' [final approach to landing] that I remembered something was missing and that I had not lowered the undercarriage! I decided at first to open up [the throttle] and go around again, but before doing so put the undercarriage lever into 'down' and as the wheels came down with a satisfactory clonk, decided to carry on with the landing which was easy and normal.

Edwards Jones had come perilously close to bringing the Spitfire programme to a halt by inadvertently belly-landing the only flying prototype. On landing, he called the Air Ministry. He was switched through to the chief of RAF research and development, Air Marshal Sir Wilfrid Freeman. Air marshals did not normally spend spring evenings waiting in their offices for pilots' phone calls. Sir Wilfrid asked, 'I know you can't tell me what the aircraft does after one short flight. All I want to know is, do you consider that the novice pilots that we are going to get into the RAF under the expansion scheme would be able to cope with such an advanced aircraft?' Edwards Jones, the highly experienced pilot who had minutes before come close to wrecking the Spitfire, replied, 'Yes, provided they are given adequate instruction in the use of flaps and retracting undercarriages.'[63]

Despite his worsening health, Mitchell came up to Martlesham Heath for the official trials on 8–9 June 1936. The RAF's report was that 'The aeroplane is simple and easy to fly with no vices. All controls are entirely satisfactory ... can be flown without risk by the average full trained fighter pilot.'[64] On 3 July 1936 the Air Ministry issued Supermarine a £2 million contract for 310 Spitfire Is, part of Expansion Scheme F. Specification F.16/36 was issued for these production aircraft. This followed the first production order for 600 Hurricanes; all were to be ready by March 1939.

Now came the hard part: the size and scope of the order, while gratifying in that it marked the success of the Spitfire, was also overwhelming. Supermarine's factories had fewer than 500 employees and still hand-crafted aircraft, mainly biplane amphibians and flying boats that were nothing like the Spitfire. Initially, Supermarine was supremely confident that they could handle even a huge order of new-technology Spitfires by themselves. But they were unable to present the Air Ministry with a coherent statement of how they were actually going to carry this out. Instead, the Air Ministry directed Supermarine to make maximum use of subcontractors in Spitfire production, with Supermarine concentrating on final assembly. But subcontracting would be problematic. Much of the British aircraft industry was already committed to contracts from earlier RAF expansion schemes. While orders had massively increased, the numbers of machine tools and skilled workers had not. Engine production was another bottleneck. Many different designs would be effectively competing for every Merlin that Rolls-Royce could produce at their Derby factory.

Getting the Spitfire into production and into the hands of the RAF would require close cooperation between the design team and the factory, making changes so that components could be subcontracted out and then reassembled. Night after night, when Mitchell had not come home for dinner and was not answering his phone, his wife Florence

called Vera Cross at her desk. She would search him out, in the drawing offices or on the factory floor, and tell him it was time to go home.

Even at this stage, the Spitfire was not Mitchell's only project. He was
also working on a bomber design. Like Willy Messerschmitt, a man he
had never met, Mitchell had always prided himself on his ability to
design many types of aircraft. Despite his doctor's orders, Mitchell
worked longer and longer hours.

The Bf 109 competes

As the first Bf 109V1 prototype was being evaluated at Rechlin, Messerschmitt was at work on the second prototype, the Bf 109V2, powered
by a prototype Jumo 210A 610 hp engine and first flown in October
1935. The Bf 109V3 followed. It was the first prototype to mount armament – two synchronised 7.92mm machine guns – in the cowling. Still,
no engine was available for it until another Jumo 210A was hand-made
in May 1936.

The Bf 109V2 went through the acceptance trials at Rechlin, and in
March 1936 flew to Travemünde on the Baltic, where its main competitor was already in residence for the first-stage competitive fly-off.
The Heinkel He 112 was still the favourite. The all-metal He 112 used
a version of the He 70's elliptical wing. This gave it lower wing loading
than the Bf 109, providing better manoeuvrability and lower landing
speed. Its thicker wing could accommodate a robust, outward-retracting
undercarriage. The He 112V2 prototype retained an open cockpit. Ernst
Udet had flown it and liked it. A number of countries were already
interested in export sales. But Germany was starting to run short of
money for aeroplane-building.

The two other competitors arrived at Travemünde in early March.
The Arado Ar 80 was the German equivalent of Mitchell's Type 224,
underpowered, with a gull wing and a fixed undercarriage. Attracting
more interest was the Focke Wulf Fw 159, designed by their chief
designer, Kurt Tank. He had eschewed the low wing of all the other
designs for a high parasol wing, intended to preserve the advantages of
a biplane fighter and provide good visibility. At the last minute, Focke
Wulf's design team – Tank had relinquished the project after setting out
the original concept – had added a retractable undercarriage attached to

the fuselage. When the undercarriage collapsed, it put the Fw 159 out of the competition.

As the flying evaluation started, the Bf 109V2 proved surprisingly capable in comparison with the He 112V2. Messerschmitt's lightweight design approach had paid off. Although both fighters were powered by the same engine, the lighter Bf 109 demonstrated a higher rate of climb, top speed (17 mph faster), speed in a dive, and a greater rate of roll. The Bf 109 design offered greater ease of construction, especially in comparison with the He 112V2's elliptical wing. The Bf 109 required significantly fewer rivets and less building cradle and jig work to complete. Messerschmitt's light fighter approach had created a design that could be mass produced; the He 112's elliptical wing required extensive use of skilled workers. Heinkel might not be able to handle the production of the new Luftwaffe's standard fighter as well as its twin-engine bombers. The skilled pilots flying the Bf 109 at Travemünde did not find the light, narrow-track undercarriage a drawback. What they found most compelling was the Bf 109's excellent low-speed performance, with gentle stalls due to the leading-edge slats and an ability to easily recover from a spin.

After the company test pilots and the Travemünde test pilots had flown the competitors, the heavyweights had their turn. They included Udet, fighter ace Oberst Robert Ritter von Griem (who opposed monoplane fighters), and two senior Rechlin test pilots, Karl Francke and Leo Conrad. The RLM relied on their reports. Udet's and von Griem's previous concerns about the Bf 109 design were overcome after they had flown it. The previous flying trials had assuaged many of Udet's concerns about the reliability of the leading-edge slats (if only one wing's slats extended, the other wing could stall and the aircraft would spin), the enclosed canopy, the narrow-track undercarriage, and poor ground visibility from the cockpit. They recognised that the basic design was faster, cheaper to build and easier to maintain than that of the He 112.

Spinning and dive pull-out performance remained a major concern. It increased when the He 112V2 was lost; the test pilot had bailed out when it went into a flat spin. Messerschmitt followed this by having their chief test pilot, Dr Hermann Wurster, demonstrate the Bf 109's ability to spin and dive safely.

On 2 March, Wurster took up the Bf 109V2 for a demonstration flight.[65] He climbed to 7000 metres, gently spiralling up over the airfield and the Baltic coastline beyond. He was using a cumbersome and inefficient old-technology oxygen mask that he had to adjust with care. As he reached his altitude, Wurster tightened his shoulder straps and seat belt. He checked that everything was secure in the cockpit. He flew in a gentle circle, looking for air traffic. All was right, it was time to go into a dive.

He started by performing a half roll, turning the aircraft on its back, reducing the power to idle, and pulled it into a sixty- to seventy-degree dive.[66] Wurster moved the control stick, with careful movements of the elevator to establish control against the force of the air rushing past at high speed. The Bf 109 lacked a rudder trim tab, so he pressed hard on the left rudder pedal to counteract torque. As the Bf 109V2 dived steeply, accelerating from gravity, a glance at the airspeed indicator showed Wurster that the indicated airspeed was fast approaching 650 km/h (404 mph). The ground loomed up, coming closer second by second. 'Finally, using both hands, I pulled back on the stick and recovered the dive … and had to deal with stick forces that no one could expect a pilot in aerial combat or the regular line of duty to handle.'[67]

Now Wurster encountered the Bf 109's problems with control response at high speed. He would have had to pull hard on the stick before any perceptible change in flight attitude was evident. Then the change became uncomfortably violent. He was pressed into the seat.[68] The Bf 109's cramped cockpit – designed to minimise weight and drag – made it hard for the pilot to apply leverage. Increased g force demanded greater force to pull back the control stick and get the Bf 109V2 out of its dive. The Bf 109's control surfaces tended to be stiff and hard in order to bite the air. Rechlin test pilot Heinrich Beauvais had also encountered the same difficulty: 'There was very little initial response to the control input and then a sudden and violent over-response. I was able gradually to reduce the oscillations and, most importantly, to reduce the speed and pull out of the vertical dive.'[69]

When Wurster pulled the Bf 109V2 out of its dive, he imposed 7.8 g on its structure. With the maximum force a Bf 109 pilot could exert on the controls estimated to be some 40 lb of leverage, he exerted the equivalent of 312 lb of leverage to pull up, demonstrating that the real limit of the Bf 109 was the physical strength of the pilot. While the Bf 109's low, reclined seat reduced the pilot's leverage, it did make it easier to sustain g forces without losing consciousness. In addition to its structural strength, the Bf 109 design had the pilot sitting low in the cockpit with his legs thrust out in front rather than in a more conventional chair; this delayed the onset of blacking out in a 5 g turn by up to one or two seconds. Because it was difficult for the pilot to apply enough leverage to move the controls in a high-speed dive and subsequent pull-out, the Bf 109's never-exceed limits were set at 750 km/h (466 mph) and 7 g forces.

Having demonstrated the Bf 109V2's diving and pull-up performance, Wurster climbed back to altitude to demonstrate its spin capabilities. Again, tighten straps, check the cockpit for anything that could become a lethal missile, do the checklist, oxygen to full 'on', a clearing turn, and it was time to go again. This time in a spin.

Wurster slowed down, pushing back the throttle to idle. As the Bf 109V2 slowed, the automatic leading-edge slats deployed and the warning horn sounded in the cockpit. The controls gently shuddered. The plane was now on the edge of a stall. With both the rudder and ailerons ineffective, the control stick going forward towards the instrument panel, he pushed the nose about ten degrees below the horizon. The left wing dropped and the aeroplane went into a spin. As the Bf 109 started sinking towards the ground, whirling around and around like the blades of a helicopter rotor, the 360 degrees of the horizon would pass in front of his eyes, revolving slowly at first, but then with ever-increasing speed.[70]

Wurster went around and around, the first turn steep, with the nose pointing down at the Travemünde airfield below. Next, he gently pulled back on the stick. The Bf 109V2 revolved in a flat spin, Wurster watching the horizon whip around through the windscreen.

He alternated the types of spin until he had put the Bf 109V2 through twenty-one rotations to the right. He pulled back on the stick, applied opposite rudder (i.e. opposite to the direction of the spin). Then, with the hand that had been on the throttle throughout, he added power — slowly. The aircraft pulled out of the spin.

Wurster climbed back up to altitude for the third time that flight. He spun the Bf 109V2 again, this time with seventeen rotations to the left.

None of the Rechlin test pilots had been among the audience for Wurster's performance, but they soon learned what he had done. Word even penetrated the marble corridors of the RLM. The Bf 109V2 had demonstrated it could do everything the specification demanded of it.

The competition between the Bf 109 and the He 112 now took on greater significance. During the evaluation, the Luftwaffe learned that the RAF had flown an all-metal monoplane fighter, the Spitfire, on 5 March. With the Hurricane having flown the previous November, the British had two monoplane single-engine fighter designs heading towards production. Germany had none.

News of Germany's reoccupation of the Rhineland on 7 March electrified those evaluating the new fighters at Travemünde. They knew that if the French decided to fight, the Luftwaffe lacked the numbers and quality to defeat them, regardless of what Germany's leaders may have claimed. On 12 March 1936, the RLM awarded a pre-production contract for ten aircraft each to Bfw and Heinkel.

Now the Bf 109 was no longer the underdog, but the favourite to receive a production contract. Heinkel tried to take back its favoured position with a new prototype. The improved He 112V4 used a more powerful Jumo 210DA engine, a redesigned wing that could accommodate weapons, and an enclosed cockpit. Udet flew the new version. He advised his friend Ernst Heinkel to stick to building bombers. Heinkel's plant was at capacity and having trouble fabricating the He 112's labour-intensive elliptical wings. Udet believed that Germany required a single standard fighter and could not afford to bring a less advanced design to production, as the British appeared to be doing with the Hurricane. The He 112V4, not ready for preliminary evaluation at Rechlin, could not take part in the Travemünde trials.

The final outcome of those trials was that, while Heinkel still had funding to continue to develop the He 112 design, the Bf 109 alone was selected for production. The end of the competition was marked by a display at Rechlin where, with Göring in attendance, Udet flew the Bf 109V3 prototype in a simulated dogfight in which he 'shot down' four He 51 biplane fighters and several bombers they were 'escorting'.

This turned out to be one of the most decisive dogfights in history, showing even Göring, ignorant of modern technology, the potential power of the modern fighter. After that, no one in Germany argued for fabric-covered fighters.

Messerschmitt's team modified the design of what was now designated the Bf 109B with a Jumo 210 engine. Its armament was increased to three 7.92mm machine guns. One, mounted between the cylinder banks on the engine, fired through the propeller hub. But the Bf 109B would not be ready until February 1937. It was uncertain how quickly the British would have Hurricanes and Spitfires in production. Messerschmitt started building a new factory at Regensburg, after the municipal authorities at Augsburg denied him permission to expand the existing plant. The new plant, intended for production lines rather than hand-crafting aeroplanes, was designed to reflect the ideal of a National Socialist 'beauty and labour' workplace, with modernistic architecture, but still depended on a relatively few skilled technicians; it had 530 workers when it opened in 1937.[71]

The race to create the modern fighter had ended with the decision to go into large-scale production. A new race now began, to deploy the modern fighter as an effective element of air power. In this, both Britain and Germany were starting even, with a few prototype aircraft. This new race would involve a new set of people. The origins of the fighter had involved first the designers, their design teams, and the RLM and the Air Ministry who had the power to fund or quash their ideas. Now, there would be aircrew and ground crew in operational units, concerned not with developing technology but using it effectively. The aeroplanes themselves would have to be produced in large numbers; this would require many more workers than the few skilled craftsmen who had created the prototypes. The new race would be contested by a much wider field, with more opportunities to stumble and fall. Both the Spitfire and the Bf 109 designs had been pushed by the new technology, but in this new race they would increasingly also be pulled by outside events, by changes in the European political situation, by the needs of the air arms that would use them, and by changes in doctrine and tactics. The first to deploy large numbers of modern fighters would be able to control the skies over Europe in any future conflict.

3

The Race to Deploy the Modern Fighter

June 1936–September 1938

Flying into the future. In a high-speed, low-altitude pass, its Jumo engine throttled up, the Bf 109V1 overflew the opening ceremonies at the 1936 Olympic Games in Berlin on 1 August.

It was all about the future. The Bf 109V1's low pass showed the world what the Luftwaffe would be flying in that future. The swastika on its tail, echoing those on the massive banners displayed on the ground, stated unequivocally that the future would be dominated by National Socialism. Those who watched the Bf 109V1 fly in Berlin that day, and the millions more who saw its pass in Leni Riefenstahl's documentary *Olympia*, in newsreels or on television – the broadcast of that day's ceremony was the first-ever Olympics coverage – saw that, in the air as in politics, Germany and the Bf 109 had arrived, together, and would be shaping *their* future.

With their initial designs completed, prototypes flying and production orders placed, the Spitfire and the Bf 109 were now no longer ideas, but actual things, with their own characteristics. They were now creating their own history rather than being created by others. Other players were now more important as the race became not to design but to deploy the Spitfire and Bf 109. Not just the design teams and the factories but the air forces and national industries were involved to an ever greater degree.

Throughout this time, the European security situation continued to deteriorate. Many saw another war approaching. To some, war was something to be avoided at almost any cost. A war, made more devastating by the emergence of the bomber threat since 1918, would likely complete the destruction of the old world initiated by the Great War. To others, a new war would be welcomed to wipe away a dying order and decades of disgrace, stretching back beyond Versailles.

A troubled transition

The prototype Spitfire was introduced to the public on 27 June 1936 at the RAF Hendon air display. In its light blue paint, the clean compound curves of the Spitfire design demonstrated modern technology rather than an ideology of domination. Despite the swastika flags now flying over the Rhineland, Britain's leaders still saw no need for warlike camouflage paint on its aeroplanes. Each RAF squadron advertised itself with colourful markings on each silver biplane – and in 1936, military aircraft in Britain were almost all biplanes – with no thought for operational security. Only the night bombers, in a businesslike drab green, suggested that they possessed a purpose beyond the sheer joy of flying in a clear blue English early summer sky.

The first production order for 310 represented more aircraft than Supermarine had ever built at one time. It presented the company with immense difficulties in making the transition from creating a single prototype to large-scale, simultaneous production. Supermarine had too little of everything, especially skilled workers. The factory at Woolston was at capacity with flying boats and amphibians. Preparing the plans for the first production Spitfire I took a year and occupied the skilled draughtsmen, too few in number, also needed to document changes in the design from the flight test programme. Other programmes also clamoured for resources. The ailing R.J. Mitchell and Supermarine's management were both overwhelmed by the size and scope of the problem.

Supermarine and Vickers were reluctant to subcontract out many of the components. This reflected concerns not only over workshare but also quality control and standardisation. Other industry leaders subcontracted only under protest. But Supermarine could not produce the initial order for 310 Spitfires by themselves. From early on in the Spitfire programme, it had been agreed with the Air Ministry that Supermarine must accept a degree of subcontracting greater than had previously been the practice in the British aircraft industry. For example, it was originally planned that Supermarine would carry out final assembly, but build only the fuselage. The entire Spitfire wing assembly was subcontracted to Pobjoy, one of many 'fringe' aircraft manufacturers that did not sell their own designs to the Air Ministry and so were now available to build others' aircraft.[1] But the complex elliptical wing, its leaf-spring spar, and the compound curves where the wing joined the fuselage proved difficult to fabricate even for the firm that had designed it, with the design team on site to answer questions and make changes. Drawings and plans were often not ready in time for the subcontractors to train their workers and start work to meet the required deadlines. The high-technology Spitfire design required finer tolerances than British industry had previously worked to. With the subcontractors floundering, the overburdened Supermarine factories carried out many of the more challenging construction tasks as well, including wing fabrication.

Development flying of the Spitfire continued. Mitchell's team was kept busy identifying and incorporating changes in the production Spitfire I design. The prototype received its armament of eight machine guns in December 1936. Flight testing had shown that the guns did not interfere with the Spitfire's speed and manoeuvrability or throw off the centre of gravity. In March 1937, the guns were fired for the first time. All worked perfectly.

A few days later, the prototype climbed up to 32,000 feet and its guns were fired. After a few rounds, they froze solid from the cold. Mitchell's team needed to find a way to keep the guns from freezing at high altitude or the Spitfire would be militarily useless. Sydney Camm's larger team at Hawker had encountered the same problem with the Hurricane and had so far not come up with an answer. Other changes were carried out to make mass production easier or incorporate changes directed by the Air Ministry. Mitchell, despite his colostomy bag and health problems, worked hours that would have exhausted a fit man.

Mitchell was again in the hands of the surgeons. An operation in March 1937 revealed that his cancer had returned and was far advanced.

Soon, Mitchell was so ill he could no longer come into the office. Instead, he would be driven in his car to the airport at Eastleigh from his home in Southampton. He would watch the prototype Spitfire in its test programme, taking off and landing. He would listen to the note of the Merlin engine, using it to understand at what power settings the test pilots were landing. After each flight, he called over the test pilot, 'Mutt' Summers or Jeffrey Quill, to talk with him where he sat in the back seat. He listened to their reports and wrote down notes for his team. Joe Smith took over as chief designer.

Smith, like Mitchell, had been an apprentice (in the motor car industry) before coming in 1921 to Supermarine, where he had been chief draughtsman since 1926. He had always been in Mitchell's shadow. This had not bothered him. Shunning publicity, he proved an effective manager of the team as well as a designer and carried on Mitchell's practice of working closely with those building the aircraft at Supermarine. Cyril Russell, a metal worker, recalled him as 'a dedicated, clever, and polite man with a sense of humour'.[2] But his overall approach was different from that of Mitchell, just as Mitchell's style, supporting his leaps of design with solid engineering, differed from the wide-ranging innovation of Willy Messerschmitt. 'Although he had been a great admirer of Mitchell, Smith had never tried to imitate his visionary boldness, for his own talent lay in developing things which were already known to be good.'[3]

The problem was that, while Supermarine and the RAF both knew the Spitfire to be good, they had been frustrated in bringing it into service. Smith incorporated Mitchell's inputs while dealing with the RAF's urgent demands for Spitfire production. The subcontractors needed plans, jigs and explanations. The Spitfire had made the transition into production in March 1937. Months later, none had been completed. The design team was fully occupied with making the changes required to enable production, while on the shop floor Supermarine was failing the RAF. The Spitfire remained only an unfulfilled promise.

A plane crash in Germany
General Walther Wever, chief of staff of the Luftwaffe, was killed when his He 70 light bomber crashed on 6 June 1936. His death removed a

leader with a clear vision of how to expand the Luftwaffe and the German aircraft industry. Inherent in his plans had been the military's assumption that, while Germany needed a near-term capability, a major war was not likely until 1942 or after. The Bf 109 had been envisioned, as part of Wever's strategy, to be the shield that made possible the use of the sword, defending Germany's bomber bases (from which air war would be waged), cities, industries and, if required, troops.

With Wever gone and Milch's power diminished, the Luftwaffe lost the vision that had created the Bf 109 specification in 1933. Göring saw this as an opportunity to reassert control. Udet replaced Wimmer in the *C-Amt* with Oberst Franz Löb, friendlier to Messerschmitt. The highest priority in the new Luftwaffe, as before, went to the bombers. The Luftwaffe's bombers would be supported by twin-engine heavy fighters, the Messerschmitt Bf 110 *Zerstörer* ('destroyer'), with longer range and a radio operator, able to communicate reliably with the bombers. Willy Messerschmitt had been able to win the competition for that design on the momentum of his Bf 109 success, and now was increasingly preoccupied with management responsibilities.

While Wever had taken a realistic view of what a war would entail, without him it was thought that the next war would be a short, victorious conflict against Germany's neighbours. The Bf 109's role was increasingly seen as top cover for what would become the *Blitzkrieg*, to protect the advance of the German Army, enabling it to defeat the enemy decisively and win the war. The Bf 109's role as an offensive fighter was seen as secondary to that of the Bf 110. Even before it fired a shot in anger, the Bf 109 evolved. It carried out new missions without relinquishing those it was designed to perform.

Inventing the shield

Still hindered by limited funding, the RAF was struggling to reconcile its bombers-first vision of future air war with the realities of rearmament. British government policy was to avoid appearing aggressive. Britain stressed diplomacy in order to avoid another European conflict that would be more devastating than that of twenty years before. If it was true that 'the bomber will always get through', and fighters appeared inadequate to deal with the threat of new-technology bombers, the British had to look to an alternative approach. Previously, this had been seen primarily in terms of achieving a limitation on the use of aircraft in war through the League of Nations or, failing that, through bilateral agreement. But with Hitler's rise to power and Germany's exit from the League this appeared less feasible. New technology provided another possible answer.

In 1934, Henry Tizard and Harold Wimperis, members of a new scientific committee formed by the Air Ministry to review potential air defences, asked Robert Watt,[4] a radio expert at the National Physical Laboratories, whether it would be possible to create a 'death ray' for air defence, beaming radio energy at incoming bombers so intense it would disable their crews or scramble their ignition systems.[5] Watt was able to use elementary physics to show the committee that, even with all the electrical power in Britain at its disposal, such a weapon would have a range of tens of feet rather than miles. But, he added, if the committee were interested in using transmitted radio energy to solve Britain's air defence problems, he would be happy to discuss a 'method of [aircraft] detection by reflected radio waves'.

At the committee's first meeting in January 1935, Watt explained how this method of detection might be developed. Funding depended on the man then in charge of the RAF's research and development: Air Marshal Sir Hugh Dowding. A pilot in the Great War, 'Stuffy' Dowding did not believe the bomber would always get through. He had commanded the defending side in the 1930 summer manoeuvres and improvised a ground-based early warning network for his fighters by deploying observers in wireless-equipped vehicles.

At their first meeting at Dowding's office in the Air Ministry, Watt had written the range equation on a blackboard, showing how it was physically practical to detect an otherwise unseen aircraft by reflected radio waves. Dowding responded, 'You scientific blokes can prove anything by equations. I want a demonstration.'[6]

What would become known as radar (though that term is now universal, it was known as radio direction finding until 1942) was first tested on 26 February 1935, using radio waves from an existing transmitter to detect a biplane bomber at a range of eight miles. Watt watched the radio waves bounced off the bomber move along a cathode ray tube. He recognised its potentially revolutionary significance for air warfare.

But radar was still far from an effective system. Following the successful demonstration, Dowding arranged funding – difficult to do in 1935 – for Tizard and Watt to build on this work and start bringing in RAF personnel. Within six months, the range of detection in follow-on experiments had been increased to forty miles. Contracts were placed for the first six radar stations on the English coast. Training schools were set up.[7]

Radar set the precedent for how the British military could reach out to the civilian scientific and technical base to identify and help implement solutions. The air marshals in their beribboned tunics and the scientists in their tweed jackets soon found that together they could create and refine new operational capabilities. Their German counterparts, however brilliant, proved unable to work together in the same way.

Dowding had been instrumental in the outcome of the 1935 RAF fighter evaluation. Rather than procure a too-slow all-metal monoplane fighter such as the Type 224, instead he had invested in the development of what would become the Hurricane and the Spitfire, and a host of new technologies had subsequently been developed: improved engines and radios, all-metal structures, retractable undercarriages, variable-pitch propellers, high-octane fuel. The Spitfire would offer the first opportunity to pull all these together in a fighter plane design, while the Hurricane, sharing its Merlin engine but with its partially old-technology structure of wood and fabric, served as an alternative.

Sydney Camm realised that not only the Hurricane's structure but more significantly its greater drag, compared with the Spitfire, would put it at a disadvantage in air combat. His answer was to start preliminary design work on two new fighter designs: the Hawker Tornado, which would use the new Rolls-Royce Vulture engine, and the Hawker Typhoon, using the Napier Sabre, an improved version of the smaller Dagger engine that offered twice the power of the Merlin.[8] Together, they were intended to replace both the Hurricane and the Spitfire. The Air Ministry, impressed, ordered thousands 'off the drawing board', before any prototypes could be built.

Dowding was one of the senior officers who had pushed for eight-gun fighter armament. By 1936 he had come to believe that cannon would be required to bring down modern bombers. He insisted that the new Spitfires and Hurricanes should have bulletproof glass for their windscreens, even though other RAF senior officers laughed at his idea. Dowding retorted, 'If Chicago gangsters can have bullet-proof windows for their cars, why can't my pilots have bullet-proof windscreens?'[9] He funded the development of new tactics, in which fighters would be directed against incoming bombers through radio messages from a ground controller – a new type of air warrior. Dowding helped establish the Air Fighting Developmental Establishment (AFDE) to develop tactics using the new technologies, which would entail different fighting methods from those of their biplane predecessors.

Not all of Dowding's technical investment decisions, in hindsight, were the right ones. He emphasised trying to create a crash-proof fuel tank while neglecting the potentially easier development of self-sealing tanks that would make aircraft less prone to fire or catastrophic structural failure if hit by enemy weapons. The AFDE developed tactics that looked good in flying displays and in the RAF *Manual of Air Tactics*.[10] Only after several years had passed and many fighter pilots had died in combat would it become apparent that these tactics had been imposed by Fighter Command through stamping an *imprimatur* on untried and undeveloped notional methods. Training concentrated on set-piece tactics involving only a few fighters at a time.

Dowding had hoped to be appointed as the RAF's chief of staff in 1937. Instead, as RAF expansion led ADGB to be divided in July 1936 into two organisations, Bomber Command and Fighter Command, Dowding became commander-in-chief of Fighter Command, moving into his newly acquired headquarters at Bentley Priory, west of London. He turned over the research and development responsibilities to Air Marshal Wilfrid Freeman, his 1914 flying-school classmate, who was in that position when the key decisions on the Spitfire prototype were made.

Dowding was disappointed not to be chief of staff. But his selection for the new command was a brilliant and inspired choice by the Air Ministry. Dowding helped provide the pull for the Spitfire while

Mitchell led the technology-pushed development. Dowding knew technology, even if he was not a 'scientific bloke'. He had been instrumental in both the development and deployment of radar and the integrated air defence system. Having authorised the development of what became radar, he had a personal understanding of, and a stake in, the outcome. Interwar Britain in general and the RAF in particular suffered from a lack of understanding of changed conditions (technological and strategic), a lack of leadership and a lack of imagination. Dowding had all three.

The governmental pull for turning the Spitfire from Mitchell's idea into Britain's defender was increased when Sir Thomas Inskip was appointed minister for the coordination of defence in 1936 (outraging Winston Churchill, who had wanted the position). Inskip recognised the importance of air defence.[11] He also realised that political reality pointed to more investment in fighters. Cheaper and quicker to produce, fighters would increase RAF numbers faster than buying bombers. The electorate was also more likely to support rearmament if they could see that it was to defend them from bombing.

The RAF started to provide the pilots that would be required by the Hurricanes and Spitfires on order. The RAF Volunteer Reserve (RAFVR) was formed in 1936, training 800 aircrew a year. The Auxiliary Air Force, consisting of squadrons of part-time aircrew, was expanded. Without conscription, and with service pay still at a low level, getting the personnel for an expanded RAF was a problem. Volunteers for pilot and officer training were never lacking, the greater need was for competent technicians and NCOs.

The RAF aimed to recruit worldwide, throughout the Commonwealth and Empire, but the governments involved were reluctant to lose personnel that they might eventually need. The RAF turned to recruit from the British lower middle class and skilled working class, traditionally not the source of enlisted personnel in peacetime. To symbolise this, in 1936, the RAF changed its uniforms so that all its personnel, not only officers and NCOs, wore shirts and ties with their uniform tunics.[12] All those over twenty-one would have the right to live 'off', outside RAF stations, and claim a housing allowance, encouraging older men with families to enlist. This followed the RAF's decision to abolish the post of sergeant major. Although these individuals served on as before, as warrant officers, the image of brass-voiced disciplinarians was not one the RAF wanted to project. While pilots in the Great War had mostly been officers, the RAF now reserved many of its cockpits for NCOs.[13] You could still aspire to fly with the RAF even if you did not qualify for a commission, academically or financially (the academy at Cranwell charged tuition fees). The message was clear in the class-conscious Britain of the 1930s. Being in the RAF was different from being in the army or navy. Issuing neckties helped Spitfires fly.

The Spitfire enters production

The Spitfire's design team, now led by Joe Smith as chief designer and Alan Clifton as his assistant, was still trying to cope with fixing problems identified in testing and with the transition to production. Supermarine was struggling to set up production in factories that proved too small and had too few workers who knew how to build modern aeroplanes. The subcontractors, further behind, beseeched Supermarine for plans and tooling. The scope and timeframe of their tasks was far beyond anything anyone in the British aircraft industry could have imagined just a few years previously.

Too sick now to work even from his car, Mitchell flew to Vienna for treatment. The design team came out to Eastleigh Airport to wish him farewell. But the cancer was too advanced. Mitchell returned to his home in Southampton where he died on 11 June 1937, aged forty-two.

Florence Mitchell called Vera Cross one last time and told her. Vera left her desk and told Joe Smith. Then she went to each of the team members, first in the drawing offices then out to the shop floor, and told those who had built the first Spitfire.

Though the design work of the Spitfire was unaffected – management had been in Smith's and Clifton's hands for months (Beverly Shenstone had gone to the Air Ministry) – the overall feeling of the Spitfire team when they went, in a group, to Mitchell's funeral was indeed sombre. With its creator dead and the RAF increasingly enraged at the absence of deliveries, the future of the Spitfire was clouded. Neville Chamberlain became prime minister in May 1937, replacing Baldwin, and the following month directed the services to postpone plans for further expansion. Back in February 1936, Sir Robert McLean had guaranteed that Supermarine would start to deliver a Spitfire a week fifteen months after the production order was received. When that deadline arrived, in November 1937, no production Spitfires had been delivered. At that point, it appeared that it would be months, if ever, before any could be delivered. The RAF, looking at their now-constrained future plans, which had been evolving with bewildering rapidity as politics and technology pulled them in multiple directions, started to reconsider whether the Spitfire should be part of those plans.

Limiting the troubled Spitfire programme to the 310 already on order, or cancelling it outright, started to seem a good idea to some in the Air Ministry. The unresolved problem with freezing guns led the chief of Air Staff, Marshal of the Royal Air Force Sir Cyril Newall, to say, 'If the guns will not fire at heights at which the Spitfires are likely to encounter enemy bombers, the Spitfire will be useless as a fighting aircraft.'[14] The Spitfire seemed to many likely to be only an interim type, soon superseded.

The Bf 109 goes to war

While the Spitfire programme was falling behind, the Bf 109 went straight to air combat. The Spanish Civil War had broken out in August 1936. The Luftwaffe provided the major element of German military intervention in Spain, the Condor Legion. It had been organised by Milch, who had resumed his RLM empire-building. But the Condor Legion's fighter element flew He 51 biplane fighters, inadequate in the face of an answering Soviet intervention.

The Soviets brought to Spain more advanced fighter designs than the Germans had in operation. The monoplane Polikarpov I-16 *Rata* (rat)[15] fighters outperformed the He 51. The Luftwaffe, despite past years of cooperation with the Soviets, were surprised by the capability of their combat aircraft. By November 1936, the Condor Legion was at a disadvantage in air combat over Spain. *Ratas* helped end bomber attacks on Madrid.

In an emergency move, the fourth Bf 109 prototype, the Bf 109V4, with its three-machine-gun armament, which was designed to reflect the first production Bf 109Bs, was pulled out of its flight test programme and rushed to the Condor Legion in December, followed by the Bf 109V5 and V6 in January. These two planes received improved Jumo 210B engines intended for the Bf 109B. The three fighters carried out a seven-week combat evaluation in Spain, the Bf 109's first combat missions.

While it was difficult to maintain three hand-crafted prototypes at the end of a lengthy supply line from Germany, the three Bf 109s proved to be the only German fighters in Spain capable of dealing with the highest-performing Soviet-designed aircraft. When the prototypes returned to Germany in February 1937 to continue the disrupted flight testing programme, the Condor Legion demanded that production Bf 109Bs be provided as soon as possible.

Messerschmitt now needed to translate the Bf 109 design to production. If the transition proved prolonged or difficult, as that of the Spitfire was proving, the Condor Legion would find its biplane fighters shot out of the skies of Spain when the spring weather of 1937 brought a renewal of air combat.

Bf 109 – production and prestige

Messerschmitt was able to rush through the start of Bf 109 production to meet the urgent needs of the Condor Legion, get them built and deliver them to the Luftwaffe to train pilots, before their deployment to Spain in time for the spring offensive. Thanks to the use of workers trained to build the Bf 108 and the adaptation of its tooling and jigs, the Bf 109B, the first production version, made its initial flight in February 1937, powered by a 650 hp Jumo 210DA. After testing, it entered service with the Luftwaffe's JG (*Jagdgeschwader*) 132 'Richthofen' fighter wing.

Having started level with Britain, Germany now had its first operational modern fighters before its rival. This claim was more than simple pride or bragging rights. The perception of the Luftwaffe's power was vital to Hitler's diplomatic leverage. In addition to deterring Germany's potential enemies, the German aircraft industry aimed to win (paying) export contracts from countries throughout Europe. With aircraft would go advisors and instructors, enabling German internal penetration, using the prestige of German air power to win over neutral countries such as Hungary, Sweden, Yugoslavia, Turkey and Romania. The export of combat aircraft became an important aspect of competition between the great powers in Europe.

The Bf 109B had been hurried into production without many of the design elements that the 1936 tests had identified as important. These included a radio, a reflector gunsight and a two-bladed variable pitch propeller, a US-designed Standard having been hurriedly licensed until German versions could be incorporated when the building of later Bf 109B models started at Augsburg. At the same time, the RLM directed extensive licensed production of the Bf 109 to begin. Major German aircraft companies, including Fieseler and Erla, set up Bf 109 production lines, using plans and tooling provided by Bfw. Other companies would join them by 1938, including Focke Wulf and Arado. Willy Messerschmitt himself was increasingly involved in other programmes (including the Bf 110), management (including getting the Regensburg factory, which eventually split into two major facilities, operating), and dealing with the leadership in Berlin.

Germany looked for ways to demonstrate the Bf 109 and the implied power it gave the Luftwaffe. Three prototype Bf 109Bs took part in the July 1937 Zurich *Flugmeeting*, one of them flown by Udet. They were painted in unit markings misleadingly to suggest operational rather than developmental aircraft. The competitions at Zurich became a stand-in for air conflict to demonstrate to the world which country had the superior air designs. The Bf 109s were able to make a clean sweep of many of the speed competitions as well as scoring in the shadowy game of deception played out in pre-war air intelligence.

The only flying Hurricanes and Spitfires were the prototypes, but they still had an impact on the Bf 109. In 1937, the RLM learned that the RAF's new fighters would have an armament of eight machine guns. The Bf 109B could carry a maximum of three and most carried only two. Messerschmitt received direction from Berlin: the Bf 109 needed more firepower, immediately.

The Bf 109C's wing was redesigned to accommodate improved wing slats (reducing but never solving the concerns about failure to deploy in a tight turn) and two 7.92mm machine guns, replacing the Bf 109B's propeller-hub machine gun. Putting guns in the wing of the Bf 109 proved to be difficult. The wing design, critical to Messerschmitt's lightweight concept, proved too thin to accommodate boxes of ammunition. These had to be put in the fuselage and fed out to the guns in the wings. Such an arrangement worked on the firing range, but not under the strains of air combat.

Ernst Heinkel was not about to accept defeat at the hands of Willy Messerschmitt. The Günter brothers' new fighter design, unveiled on 25 May 1937, was the DB 601-powered, cannon-armed He 113 (soon renumbered He 100 in recognition of the triskaidekaphobia of some in the Nazi leadership), which used a sophisticated steam evaporative surface cooling system to achieve high-speed performance. Heinkel's second attempt at building Germany's single-engine fighters suffered a setback in September 1937 when Walther Günter was killed in a plane crash. Siegfried carried on the project.

Heinkel lobbied Milch and the leadership in Berlin throughout 1937 for He 100 development funding and a production order for the He 112. Milch arranged for three pre-production He 112s to go to Spain for combat evaluation by the Condor Legion. But while it did not order the He 112 into production, the RLM did decide, in autumn 1937, to ask German industry for a new fighter design that would be available to fight alongside the Bf 109. This would be a turn away from the idea of a single 'standard fighter'. Among the designers responding to the 1937 RLM requirement was Messerschmitt's former employee Kurt Tank, chief designer at Focke Wulf. The He 100, while offering the potential for better performance than the Bf 109, would not be as advanced as this new design.

Return to Spain
Guernica was burning. Modern war had arrived in Spain.

Spanish Republican sources (and the journalists they briefed) reported that the first Bf 109Bs were among the fighters that escorted German and Italian bombers attacking the Basque city of Guernica on 25 April 1937. High estimates of civilian casualties, released by the defending Republican forces to gain international sympathy, were used by the Germans as evidence of the power of the bombers that were the Luftwaffe's primary weapon.

The Germans had to put modern fighters in combat or risk their Spanish Nationalist allies losing control of the skies of Spain. Soviet 'volunteers' flew the Tupolev SB, a twin-engine bomber, one of the most advanced designs of the early 1930s. He 51s could not catch them.

Milch put together a force of Bf 109s for the Condor Legion. In April 1937, the first batch of sixteen production Bf 109Bs, their volunteer Luftwaffe pilots hastily trained by the Richthofen *Geschwader*, were rushed to Spain. Most of the Bf 109Bs lacked radios and had only two synchronised machine guns in the nose for armament. Throughout the spring and summer of 1937, the Bf 109Bs, their numbers increased to two *Staffeln* (the size of RAF squadrons, about twelve fighters), outperformed the Soviet I-15s and I-16s, even if they could not match their counterparts' manoeuvrability.

In Spain, the Condor Legion recognised that their fighter tactics needed to change. The Luftwaffe's biplane fighters had flown in rigid three-plane *Kette*, usually in V formation. Adolf Galland later recalled of them, 'Only the leader could see, all the other pilots are occupied holding their positions.'[16] With too few Messerschmitts to make up enough *Ketten*, they flew in a two-aircraft *Rotte*. Using these tactics, the Germans found out that even a small number of Bf 109s could ensure air superiority against a numerically superior enemy.

By mid-July, the Bf 109Bs had achieved air superiority over the battlefront. At altitudes above 10,000 feet, the Bf 109Bs' advantage in speed and rate of climb became more pronounced. Only if a Bf 109B pilot ended up dogfighting at low speed and altitude – turning tightly in the attempt to get behind a fighter – would he be at a disadvantage. Rather than manoeuvring to get behind their opponent in a classic tight-turning dogfight, as the Luftwaffe's He 51s had done, the Bf 109Bs' pilots learned to make slashing, diving attacks, using their rate of climb and ceiling to gain the altitude advantage and their speed to close quickly with the enemy while minimising the effects of the heavy control forces that made tight turning a physical struggle. If a *Rata* spotted an attacking Bf 109 and swiftly turned to meet the attack – the more manoeuvrable *Rata* could turn faster – the German would break off, climb, and look for another target.

The Bf 109B's two rifle-calibre machine guns lacked the power needed to destroy all-metal aircraft. The Condor Legion wanted explosive shells fired from cannon to bring down SBs. Messerschmitt quickly modified the Bf 109V3 with an experimental 20mm cannon mounted between the engine cylinders, firing through the propeller hub. But the vibration made this unworkable. Upgrading the Bf 109's armament with cannon was not going to be the subject of a quick fix.

The Germans learned in Spain that effective use of air power in support of ground forces could be operationally decisive, basing their fighters near the battlefield and ensuring they had skilled ground crews to keep the aircraft flying and a supply of fuel and spare parts. This enabled Bf 109Bs to fly up to seven sorties a day in September 1937. The Bf 109's narrow-track undercarriage did not prevent it from operating from improvised grass strips.

These improvisations were intended to solve the Condor Legion's immediate tactical problems and take advantage of the Bf 109's performance superiority. Together, they became the basis of modern fighter tactics. Relatively few Bf 109Bs were thus enabled to change the course of the air war over Spain. The more numerous He 51 biplanes could concentrate on fighter-bomber missions.

While the Luftwaffe started applying the combat lessons from Spain, its main focus remained increasing Germany's leverage in the European balance of power. This would require improving technology. The surprise of finding out that the Soviets were flying aircraft, such as the SB, that were in many ways superior to those used by the Luftwaffe helped motivate investment in Germany's aircraft and engine technologies.

Building capabilities
While the Luftwaffe was learning about modern air war in Spain, the Spitfire still had not made the transition from brilliant prototype to mass-produced weapon. The larger system into which the Spitfire was to fit was still primitive and the operational aspects of how modern fighters would be used to defend Britain had yet to be worked out. But the advocates of defending Britain by air – most notably Inskip in the Cabinet and Dowding at Fighter Command – were able to achieve progress. The radar network started to take shape. More airfields were built.

It would take a while, however, before these actions yielded significant results. In the first Fighter Command exercises in 1937, the RAF's biplane fighters demonstrated little ability to intercept new monoplane twin-engine Bristol Blenheim bombers.[17] In these exercises, the bomber did get through.[18] But only one radar station was working in 1937. The exercise also demonstrated the techniques of ground-controlled interception. These had first been tried in experiments earlier that year at RAF Biggin Hill, an airfield which now became a 'sector station', controlling fighters in a designated sector of airspace between London and the coast.

To coordinate the different sector stations, an intermediate level of command between them and Fighter Command was required. The 1937 exercises were the first test of the reformed 11 Group, responsible for the air defence of London, formed from the old ADGB's Fighting Area air defence headquarters that had defended against German air raids in 1917–18.

From the 1937 exercises, the RAF rediscovered the Great War lessons of the importance of having operations rooms, where those directing the defence could rely on a 'plot': a display of the current operational situation, showing friendly and enemy aircraft, ground defences and objectives to be defended. The information displayed on the 'plot' was generated at an adjacent 'filter' room, where controllers would 'filter' out spurious or multiple reports by comparing them on a map out of sight of the controllers and confirming by telephone or radio as required, before they 'fused' these inputs into the situation reflected on the 'plot'.

The impetus to order more fighters as part of the air defence system came not from the Air Ministry but rather from the Cabinet. The first production Hurricane, which flew in October 1937, encountered many problems during manufacture and in service. Only four, beset with a host of technical difficulties, had been delivered to the RAF when the Cabinet accepted Inskip's recommendations on the priority of air defence on 22 December 1937. Even though fighter production was lagging, bombers would no longer be the RAF's unchallenged priority; in any case, production of these aircraft was also suffering from technical problems. RAF Expansion Scheme L, which had been approved by the Cabinet on 27 April 1938, increased the ratio of fighter to bomber squadrons in the objective UK-based force structure, which would now include forty fighter and fifty-seven bomber squadrons. An additional 200 Spitfires were ordered. Despite the problems still inherent with the RAF monoplane fighters, the Cabinet imposed a mandate to increase their numbers dramatically. This encountered widespread opposition in the RAF, press and Parliament. The politicians had effectively overruled the air marshals on the question of what kind of military aircraft Britain should build. The RAF leadership, their view of air power focused on strategic bombing, was strongly opposed. 'Boom' Trenchard, in the House of Lords, said the decision 'might well lose us the war'.

Challenge to the Bf 109

The lessons learned from using the Bf 109 in action in Spain reached the Bfw plant at Augsburg as the first DB 600 series engines started to arrive. Both Messerschmitt and the Luftwaffe saw that, while the initial production DB 600 had problems, the engine produced more power for its weight than the Jumo ever could and, perhaps more important, gave the promise of further development.

The Luftwaffe continued to emphasise bombers in its procurement programmes. Messerschmitt wanted funding to develop a DB 600-powered, cannon-armed Bf 109. Ernst Heinkel thought the answer was his new He 100 design, taking advantage of improvements in technology since the basic Bf 109 design of 1934. Using the DB 600 engine, the He 100 had a higher top speed than the Bf 109 prototypes. Instead of the Bf 109's narrow-track undercarriage, the He 100 had a broader, inwards-retracting design. The He 100 featured less complex construction than had the He 112. However, its cooling system, an engineering achievement, was also a plumber's nightmare of tubing that Heinkel eventually replaced with a conventional radiator. Heinkel pressed Udet and the RLM for a production order.

The He 100 first flew in January 1938, designed from the outset with two wing-mounted 20mm cannon. Messerschmitt's team was having problems adapting cannon armament to the Bf 109. The Bf 109 had of course originally been designed with provision for a 20mm cannon mounted between the engine's cylinder banks, firing through the propeller hub, where the Bf 109B design instead had a machine gun. The mount did not work well. The engine-mounted 20mm cannon had vibration problems. Changing the Bf 109 to accommodate a 20mm FF cannon in each wing required a redesign. The new wing design had two streamlined fairings, bumps in the skin under the wings outboard of the undercarriage, each accommodating a sixty-round ammunition drum. The Luftwaffe's 20mm FF cannon was based on the Swiss-designed Oerlikon, with relatively low muzzle velocity, achieved by using shells with less propellant. The breech mechanism could be made lighter and the wings reinforced for less recoil force, although the weapon also had shortened range.

Adapting the DB 600 series engine to the Bf 109, unlike the wing cannon, was something the basic design had provided for from its inception. The potential of the new engine was demonstrated by the Bf 109V13 prototype. On 11 November 1937, Hermann Wurster flew the Bf 109V13, powered by a prototype DB 601 engine boosted to 1650 hp for brief periods, to a speed of 611 km/h (380 mph), winning the world absolute speed record. It was the first time this record had been held by a German. It also demonstrated the potential of the Daimler-Benz engine that Messerschmitt had wanted for his fighter since the original design.

With the wing cannon installation not yet ready, the Bf 109D was fitted with a single 20mm cannon firing through the propeller hub, mounted as in the original design between the two cylinder banks of the engine, but this arrangement led to unresolved vibration problems. The Bf 109D went into service with four 7.92mm machine guns, two in the nose and two in the wings. Its Revi C/12D reflector gunsight offered a skilled pilot greater accuracy, especially in deflection shooting, 'leading' a target when the fighter was not directly behind it. Graduated crosshairs and a glowing white circle were projected on to the sight's glass screen, giving a way to estimate the range; a fighter would fill the circle at 100 metres range, a bomber at twice that.

Messerschmitt had hoped to power the Bf 109D with the 1000 hp DB 600A, which offered about 400 hp more than the Bf 109C's Jumo for an additional 400 lb of weight. But only a few Bf 109D prototypes flew with these engines. All production Bf 109Ds were powered with a 661 hp Jumo 210D with a new two-speed supercharger to increase take-off power and altitude performance.

The DB 600 was not available to power production Bf 109Ds. Bombers were top priority in the Luftwaffe's build-up programme and they had first claim on these engines. The engine shortage undercut Heinkel's push to put the He 100 into production. Göring was concerned with numbers above all else. The Bf 109 was already in production. Heinkel, on the other hand, was fully committed to building bombers.

Heinkel could not make a case to reverse the decision made in 1933 that Germany should standardise on one single-engine fighter. But Udet did. Previously the great proponent of having a standard single-engine fighter, Udet decided, in summer 1938, to award Kurt Tank at Focke Wulf a development contract for a new fighter design to meet the previous year's requirement, powered not by scarce DB 600s but rather by an air-cooled radial engine. The He 100 was sandwiched between the need to keep up Bf 109 and Heinkel bomber production while providing resources for Tank's fighter design. It lacked effective armament and there were problems with its cooling system. The He 100 lost its chance for production orders as the RLM pressed manufacturers to concentrate on producing fewer standard types.

Despite his haphazard managerial style, Udet assumed the post of the RLM's *GeneralLuftzeugmeister* (Director General of Equipment, GL) in 1938, replacing Milch.[19] Furious, Milch told Göring he was resigning. Göring refused. He told Milch resignations were not accepted, only suicides.[20]

Anschluss *and Spain: the Luftwaffe in action*

The sky over Vienna was filled by aeroplanes flying low. The crowds saw the swastikas painted on their tails, the noise of the engines clearly audible.

But this was not about the power of aircraft engines, but of Germany and of the Nazi idea. On 13 March 1938, Milch stood next to Hitler on the reviewing stand in Vienna, watching the Luftwaffe put all the aircraft of the former Austrian military into the air alongside the Luftwaffe.

It was a show of National Socialist brotherhood that sent a message: the Germans could have levelled the city had they been resisted.

Austrian military and civil pilots were incorporated into the Luftwaffe. Luftwaffe units moved into Austrian bases. Austria had ordered redesigned He 112Bs. These aircraft became Luftwaffe fighter trainers, their pilots wishing it rather than the Bf 109 were the standard fighter.[21] Messerschmitt opened a new factory at Wiener Neustadt, with workers from the Austrian aircraft industry, building sixteen Bf 109s a month by September 1939. In Britain, after the *Anschluss* (German annexation of Austria), even the Treasury realised the end of business as usual had arrived.

The Bf 109B continued to dominate the skies over Spain. On 7 February 1938, during the Battle of Teruel, Oberleutnant Wilhelm Balthasar led an attack on fast-moving bombers. The son of an artillery officer killed in the Great War, he had become one of the Condor Legion's most proficient fighter leaders, though what his comrades valued most was his organising of excellent parties on the ground. He was now going to do what air marshals and pundits alike knew was impossible, defeat a formation of Tupolev SB monoplane twin-engine bombers, so capable that the Germans called them 'Glenn Martins', after the US designer, assuming no one in the Soviet Union could design a world-class bomber.

'The machines in front of me grow larger by the second. I can see the broad red stripes [wing markings of the Spanish Republic] clearly. I dive through the column at high speed and approach the second vic [three-aircraft V formation] from the front from below. They have seen me and a shower of fire reaches out for me. The crosshairs are aligned on its right engine. My fingers are on the triggers. The range is 20 meters when my three guns begin to rattle. There, flames. I pull up sharply and the bomber explodes before me and falls to earth a mass of flames. I am quite calm.'[22]

Balthasar's Bf 109s claimed ten (and actually destroyed four) of a formation of twenty-two SBs and two escorting I-16s, with a single Bf 109 lost to defensive gunfire from a bomber. He personally claimed three SBs (which post-war records suggest he actually shot down) and one I-16, the highest single-mission score of the Spanish Civil War. Even with escort, it had again been proven that the bomber would not always get through. By the end of the Tereul campaign in 1938, Bf 109s had defeated the Spanish Republic's fighter force in air combat.

Bf 109Cs arrived in the Condor Legion in April 1938, followed by Bf 109Ds in August. In 1938, the Bf 109 tactics that had been developed were written down and systematised by a senior pilot, Hauptmann Werner 'Vati' Mölders, who shot down fourteen Spanish Republican aircraft.[23] A keen hunter, personally studious and a pious Catholic, as a youth he had consumed every memoir and article by the German Great War fighter pilots who were his role models. He was able to infuse the lessons of the current war with the tactical lessons – largely overlooked by the staff officers writing manuals, who had not been trained as fighter pilots – of the earlier one.

In addition to systematising the tactics devised by Bf 109 pilots in Spain, Mölders made innovations of his own. On those occasions – more frequent than in 1937 – when the Germans had enough Bf 109s, a four-fighter *Schwarm* enabled each two-fighter *Rotte* to fight together for mutual support. Mölders knew German fighters had fought this way in 1917–18. The formation of four became the building block of effective modern fighter tactics.

The lessons included the need for fighter units to be able to rapidly rebase themselves. This supported ongoing Luftwaffe efforts to form mobile servicing units that could advance and set up forward airstrips, following the army. Luftwaffe Ju 52 transports provided a vital support and resupply capability and made possible a new ground combat force that the Luftwaffe was developing: paratroopers. The importance of close cooperation with the army emerged in Spain, which also demonstrated the value of being able to operate at night and in bad weather. As result, the Luftwaffe formed *Staffeln* trained for night operations in each Bf 109 *Jagdgeschwader* in Germany, exercising with searchlights.

Galland was one of those cooperating with the army. Now an *Oberleutnant*, he had volunteered for combat in Spain in the hopes of hunting *Ratas* at the controls of a Bf 109. Instead, he led a *Staffel* of He 51 biplanes, carrying out ground attack missions. He still longed for air combat, but Galland's 280 combat missions in Spain resulted in none of the air-to-air victories he sought.

The Spitfire enters service

Messerschmitt had built, put into service, and used in combat hundreds of Bf 109B/C/D models before the first production Spitfire was turned over to the RAF. But even after it was delivered to 19 Squadron at RAF Duxford, an airfield south of Cambridge, on 4 August 1938, the Spitfire was still far from operational. The problems with guns freezing at high altitude remained unresolved. The Spitfire's future remained at risk. When Air Marshal Sir Wilfrid Freeman visited the Supermarine factory, he found seventy-eight fuselages – many without engines or equipment – but only three sets of wings ready to be assembled.[24] Aligning wings and fuselage proved more difficult than anticipated and required both be assembled to precise tolerances. The RAF was not sure whether the Spitfire was going to be a vital part of its build-up or merely an interim measure until better designs came along.

Faced with a Luftwaffe bomber threat and the reality that Britain remained out of range of fighters such as the Bf 109 based in Germany, the solution appeared to be to build not Mitchell's interceptor but instead specialised bomber-destroyers. In 1936, Wing Commander John 'Jack' Slessor, a future marshal of the RAF then considered to be one of the brightest advocates of strategic bombing, urged investment in two-seat fighters, with longer range and reliable Morse radios, as better for air defence (and, potentially, offensive operations as well) than single-seaters.

Potential bomber-destroyer designs included the Westland Whirlwind, powered by two unproven Rolls-Royce Peregrines, designed around a battery of four 20mm cannon in the nose. Sydney Camm's Tornado and Typhoon fighters, with thick wings suitable for cannon armament (and promising but untested high-technology engines), seemed future replacements for the troubled Spitfire as well as the Hurricane. The cannon-armed twin-engine Bristol Beaufighter, developed from the Blenheim bomber, offered the advantage of longer range (able to patrol) and a radio operator for reliable communications. It so impressed the Air Ministry that it considered ordering Supermarine to build Beaufighters under licence instead of Spitfires.

The British bomber-destroyer closest to production was the Boulton

Paul Defiant, a Merlin-powered two-seater. It had no forward firing guns, but was instead fitted with a powered turret armed with four machine guns and a gunsight. The RAF was counting on the powered turret for bomber defence in daylight. They would now be used to attack bombers.[25] While the accuracy attainable by the Defiant's turret was impressive – the maker's expert could stick a pencil in a gun muzzle and sign his name – Dowding considered the Defiant design flawed. He limited the numbers being procured for Fighter Command; Spitfires and Hurricanes would retain priority for Merlin engine deliveries.

Despite the political push for fighters, the RAF continued to emphasise bombers. The Castle Bromwich shadow factory in the West Midlands, where Spitfires were to be produced when it was finally set up, was reallocated to build four-engine bombers. Then, following the Cabinet's approval of Inskip's increased emphasis on air defence, it was decided that Castle Bromwich would instead be used to produce the Whirlwind. Finally, in April 1938, the automotive industry's Nuffield Organisation, given management responsibilities at Castle Bromwich, received an order for 1000 Spitfires, ensuring that the factory would be a second source for Spitfires. This order, for improved Spitfire II versions designed by Joe Smith and his team, was expected to start production in 1939 and be complete by 1940. By then, the Air Staff modernisation plans assumed, a more modern fighter would succeed the Spitfire in production.

The commitment of Castle Bromwich, set up from the outset for assembly-line mass production unlike the Supermarine factories at Woolston (and now at Eastleigh) in Southampton, with their roots in hand-crafting, was a great step forward for the Spitfire. So was the design of the Spitfire II, the first, incremental, upgrade of the original production Spitfire I. In the eyes of many, the Spitfire would in any case eventually be supplanted by cannon-armed fighters and multi-engine bombers. The future was with such aircraft, not with Spitfires.

Munich
As the focus of the security crises in Europe shifted from Austria to Czechoslovakia, in July 1938, Bfw was renamed Messerschmitt AG

(*Aktiengesellschaft*, joint stock company). Reflecting the increased power and influence of Udet on Göring (then eclipsing Milch, who was focusing on operational concerns), the RLM allowed Messerschmitt to lead a group of stockholders (including the Baroness) to acquire the company, which reverted to its original pre-1928 name. From then on, all the company's designs would receive the RLM designation prefix 'Me' instead of 'Bf'. Those already designed, such as the Bf 109, would retain their original designations, but the British, Messerschmitt, the RLM and the Luftwaffe alike would often refer to the 'Me 109' – or simply 'the one-hundred-nine' – in place of 'Bf 109'. Willy Messerschmitt's personal star continued to ascend. In October, he was awarded the German National Prize, the Nazi alternative to the Nobel Prize.

In 1938, with the introduction of the Bf 109D, production shifted to Regensburg; Augsburg would now be used for research and development, production of other types of aircraft, and administration. By October 1938, Messerschmitt AG had 9267 workers (compared with eighty-two in May 1933); its expansion was built on the success of the Bf 109 and subsequent Bf 110 designs.

As Germany demanded the annexation of Czechoslovakia's Sudetenland in the summer of 1938, it was apparent that the Bf 109 had won the race that had started in March 1936. Germany had an effective force of modern monoplane fighters. The RAF did not.

Yet to a large extent, German air power was a creature of bluff and propaganda. Even Göring was reluctant to go to war. The Luftwaffe's professional leaders realised, following a series of exercises and wargames, that, for all its success in Spain, it was still operationally incapable against Britain.[26] Wargames suggested that, rather than defeating the RAF, the Luftwaffe would be most successful at minelaying, helping a U-boat blockade. On 1 August 1938, the Luftwaffe had 2929 aircraft; 650 of these were fighters, fewer than 300 of them Bf 109s. Operational were 582 bombers, 159 divebombers and 453 fighters, with less than half of those Bf 109s. Even though the bulk of the Luftwaffe fighter force still flew He 51 and Ar 68 biplanes, the Bf 109 was capable of ensuring air superiority even before a rush effort by the factories increased the number in Luftwaffe service to 583 by 19 September. But many of these were operational only on paper, lacking trained fighter pilots or spare parts.[27]

The Luftwaffe's potential opponents were all too aware of the limitations of their own air arms. Impressed by the numbers of German aircraft being produced and newspaper accounts of cities devastated in Spain, they were unwilling to risk a war with Germany. British rearmament lagged. When the crisis over the Sudetenland began, only one of the RAF's five squadrons of Hurricanes was operational. The teething troubles of those aircraft were extensive. Pilot Officer D.H. 'Nobby' Clarke recalled that 'there were snags, snags, and snags and serviceability was about nil'.[28] Machine guns froze solid above 15,000 feet. Only a single one of 19 Squadron's handful of Spitfires was operational at the start of the crisis, along with five radar stations. The August 1938 air defence exercises had shown both the potential of radar and the deep limitations that remained in Britain's air defences, especially in the operations rooms set up after the failures in the 1937 exercises.[29] For all its limitations, the Luftwaffe was closer to being ready for war than was the RAF.

The French had modern fighters on order but had invested few resources in developing an integrated air defence system or adapting their radar and radio technology to such a system. The British had shared little with them. Development of French combat aircraft had lagged. As a result, France had placed extensive orders in the US, but the first of these aircraft had not yet been delivered. The French felt exposed and vulnerable to the German air threat to an even greater extent than did the British.

At the height of the crisis, the RAF did all it could to ready itself for war. Its silver fighters were camouflaged, the blue-white-red roundels on their upper wings repainted a less conspicuous blue-red. The RAF's remaining biplane bombers were among the aircraft loaded with the few available bombs and their crews briefed to hit the RLM's grand edifice in Berlin, even though they were unlikely to navigate anywhere near the city, let alone to a specific street address.

But neither gunless Hurricanes nor biplane bombers were called on to go to war in 1938. The Munich agreement did many things. It aimed to appease. It bought time.[30] It also eventually allowed the Reich to incorporate Czechoslovakia's economic strength, including a sophisticated aircraft industry: a Luftwaffe victory, achieved without fighting.

4

The Race to Decisive Combat

October 1938–May 1940

Longer than an ocean liner, but lighter than air, the massive airship LZ-130 *Graf Zeppelin II* churned through the night-time clouds off the east coast of England on the night of 30/31 May 1939. The successor to the ill-fated *Hindenburg* that had exploded in 1937, the huge silver Zeppelin, its tail marked with massive swastika flags, was on an intelligence-gathering mission, listening for transmissions of the British Chain Home radar network.[1]

The huge airship crossed the North Sea in vain. Its electronic intelligence receivers picked up nothing the Germans recognised as radar transmissions. This was not because the British had turned off their radar once its massive bulk was detected, though this would have been a wise precaution. Rather, the Germans were listening to the wrong part of the electromagnetic spectrum. Large steel radar antennas had been built along the English coast. The Germans, more advanced in radar technology, doubted that such primitive transmitters were actually part of an integrated air defence system. Because they were only trying to intercept the sort of electronic emissions to be expected from a more advanced radar, the Germans were to learn little about the British radar network. They did not invest in developing countermeasures, such as jamming.

Intelligence collected on both sides had tended to focus on the number of aeroplanes produced. In Britain, the intelligence services, the Foreign Office and the Air Ministry all had competing sources of information and provided differing analyses.[2] The intelligence-gathering flight of the *Graf Zeppelin II* was evidence of how little the Luftwaffe understood about the air defences of Great Britain. Milch ordered books from London booksellers that told him more than official intelligence reports.

The Luftwaffe and the Bf 109E

Hitler disregarded the Munich agreement and made a personal threat that he would use the Luftwaffe to level Prague. In March 1939 he annexed the remainder of Czechoslovakia, incorporating its aviation industry and airfields, after the government had capitulated without resistance. The German occupation of Prague was accompanied by a massive fly-past to demonstrate the power of the Luftwaffe.

On 1 February 1939 the Luftwaffe had received a new chief of the general staff, a position held by interim appointees since the death of Wever. General der Flieger Hans Jeschonnek was a 40-year-old pilot who had seen combat in the Great War. While active and energetic, he lacked the bureaucratic and political power to affect the German Army's control of preparation and plans for the coming war. Like his ally Udet, he was a strong advocate of the dive bomber. Though he greatly admired Hitler, he was soon at odds with Göring and Milch, who aimed to keep control over Luftwaffe operational matters.

The Germans' monthly aircraft production had dipped to 436 in 1938, reflecting the transition to more complex bomber designs. It increased to an average of 691 in 1939. Fighters still constituted only a small fraction of the overall numbers. The Luftwaffe was also hindered by underproduction of spare parts, which amounted to 10 to 25 per cent of total production rather than the standard 50 per cent. Reserves of ordnance and aviation fuel were low. The Bf 109 remained the one German single-engine fighter in production. While Germany pursued parallel aircraft developments in a highly politicised process, it was apparent even to Ernst Heinkel by late 1938 that the RLM would not order the He 100 into production.

To those Luftwaffe pilots who had flown earlier versions of the

Bf 109, the new Bf 109E's differences were discernible at first glance: the cowling indicated a new, more powerful engine and gun muzzles protruded aggressively from each wing leading edge. The Bf 109E-1 entered production in late 1938, powered by the 1100 hp DB 601A engine. The Bf 109 now had the engine Messerschmitt had wanted from the start. Daimler-Benz had used the one-year production delay to improve the DB 600 engine to create the DB 601, giving the Bf 109E increased speed and rate of climb.

The DB 601 was the first German aircraft engine to go into large-scale production that offered performance equal to its foreign counterparts.[3] The DB 601 had a capacity of 33.93 litres (larger than the 26 litres of the Merlin, which required higher manifold pressure to generate similar horsepower) and produced its highest power output at lower revolutions per minute (rpm) of the crankshaft than the Merlin. This increased reliability and decreased fuel consumption, although it later proved a limitation on modifying the design. The DB 601's crankshaft was a massive piece of steel compared to that of a Merlin, reflecting German lack of access to speciality metals. Fabricating crankshafts was to prove a critical bottleneck when the Germans tried to increase engine production.[4] German aircraft engines typically had higher compression ratios (creating increased power at all altitudes) but less boosted manifold pressure (creating the potential for increased power up to the critical altitude – the altitude at which the engine's supercharger developed maximum power) than their British counterparts.

While most of the Jumo series and all British engines used a carburettor, the DB 601 had a fuel injector. This made possible rapid dives without cutting off power, providing better mixture control and distribution. But it required a high standard of workmanship (a Daimler-Benz speciality). The DB 601 introduced an automatic variable-speed drive for the supercharger. This meant that, at lower altitudes, an air pressure sensor would automatically slow the speed of the supercharger, preventing too great an air pressure in the intake manifold.

Drooping ailerons, a high-technology Messerschmitt innovation, were added to the BF 109E-1. When the flaps were lowered, the ailerons automatically dropped twenty degrees and the horizontal stabiliser's angle of incidence increased, all allowing better low-speed performance.

This was important because, with the heavier engine, the Bf 109E's wing loading went up, leading to less manoeuvrability and a higher (by 10 mph) landing speed – the latter putting additional strains on the under-carriage, always a problem even in lighter Bf 109 versions. Many experienced pilots ended their first flight in the Bf 109E by collapsing the undercarriage. In 1939 alone, Bf 109s experienced 255 landing accidents resulting in damage.[5]

The first Bf 109E-1s were delivered with the same four-machine gun armament as the Bf 109D. Messerschmitt again tried an engine-mounted 20mm cannon, but vibration problems made it useless. The Bf 109E-3 model was the first to show the results of a redesign of its wing. Enlarged teardrop-shaped blisters were added to the underside of Messerschmitt's thin wing to accommodate the breech mechanism and ammunition drums for 20mm Oerlikon FF cannon. While the Bf 109E-3 retained provision for the engine-mounted cannon, it was seldom fitted.

Leutnant Ulrich Steinhilper, though experienced in the Bf 109D, was unsure about the fast new fighter. 'Somewhat nervously, I stepped into the cockpit and dropped down into the close fitting interior. The air-craft smelled new with a rich mixture of odours; parts still being "burned off" as the engine began to gain hours and the new parts still being covered in preservative or fresh paint. The mechanic helped strap me in and I began my pre-flight checks. All was in order.'

Except for Steinhilper himself. He had not been properly checked out in the Bf 109E. He had invited himself on an unauthorised hop at the controls of the new fighter.

'I give the signal to [stand] clear [of the] prop and start and the "black man" [ground crew, wearing black overalls] who was standing on the starboard wing root began to wind the heavy eclipse [inertial] starter. At that moment, I pulled the lever and the starter turned the great DB 601 engine over, roaring into life on the first turn. The whole airframe shook with the power as I made my running checks prior to takeoff. Again all was in order and so I gave the signal to clear chocks [the wooden blocks that keep the main wheels from rolling on the ground] and I released the brakes.'

Steinhilper was now in the Bf 109E's most dangerous element, on the ground, where the combination of a heavier airframe and a more powerful engine with the same narrow-track undercarriage made taxiing difficult.

'Taxiing around to line up I opened the throttle and the aircraft leapt forward, the long engine cowling clearing my view as the tail came up smartly. I was soon in the air.'[6] Unfortunately for Steinhilper, he could not stay in the air. On landing, he collapsed his Bf 109E's undercarriage.

By 1939, Bf 109 production was at a level where Germany could afford to permit exports. Bf 109Ds and Es went to Switzerland in a cash sale and Bf 109Es to Yugoslavia in exchange for vital raw materials. Bf 109E-1s arrived in Spain in the final months of the civil war, after the Luftwaffe had pulled many fighter pilots out during the Sudetenland crisis. The Condor Legion stayed in action. Their remaining Bf 109s were turned over to the Spanish Nationalists at the end of the war. By the end of the conflict, some 405 Luftwaffe fighter pilots had gained combat experience.[7] Many would become leaders of the fighter force.

Speed record

While the stars of the German aircraft industry, like Messerschmitt, had higher status and more access to national political figures than their British counterparts, Germany lacked the close integration of science, industry and air force that Britain achieved. The German military were jealous of the industry's autonomy and hostile to outsiders and their ideas. Germany's scientists and engineers were world class, but their projects required patronage from an increasingly dysfunctional leadership which had politicised the development and production of aircraft.

So it was a political event when the Messerschmitt team that had brought the Bf 109 from specification to production in two and a half years fell apart over the troubled design and development of the Me 210 twin-engine fighter. Intended to be one of the RLM's 'standard types', allowing economies of scale in production, to replace the Bf 110, the Ju 87 dive bomber and the Do 215 reconnaissance aircraft, it was able to do none of this. Messerschmitt personally 'improved' the original design, shortening the fuselage and making it unstable. Lusser, the chief designer, left in March 1939 to work for Heinkel. Walter Rethel took over his position. Waldemar Voight, original designer of the Me 210, took over the project team and would be responsible for future designs. Dr Ludwig Bölkow was brought in to work on Bf 109 development.

While Hitler continued to think him a genius, Willy Messerschmitt's credibility with Berlin never recovered. It became apparent to everyone except Messerschmitt himself that, regardless of his brilliance as an aircraft designer, he was unable to manage a large industrial organisation. 'A man like Messerschmitt is an artist. One should never put an artist at the head of such a large firm,' was the post-war judgement of Dr Albert Speer, who was, in 1939, still Hitler's favourite architect.[8]

In practice, Udet did not prevent industry, especially his friends Messerschmitt and Heinkel, from competing for limited development resources by having their teams produce many different designs, rather than concentrating on the few 'standard types' he had advocated. While Messerschmitt AG was supposed to be concentrating on fighter designs, Willy Messerschmitt devoted much effort to competing for Udet's funding, expanding his design capabilities to other types. Reversible-pitch propellers (a Messerschmitt innovation), jet fighters, giant front-loading (another first) gliders and long-range bombers appeared on the Augsburg drawing boards. This fed Messerschmitt's talent for innovation and new technology, but failed to provide the Luftwaffe with aircraft that could be mass produced. Willy Messerschmitt focused on creating innovations in aviation technology, rather than supervising production, testing, management, or issues such as aircraft structural reliability.[9] The engineering staff, some 250 in 1938, did not expand as fast as new programmes appeared.

Udet, as Director General of Equipment, was far beyond his level of competence, as his direction of the Me 210 programme demonstrated. He aimed to conceal his personal failings by relying on a high-level inner staff even less capable than himself. Udet avoided coming into his RLM office in Berlin, going either flying or drinking.

Udet funded (in two separate secret programmes) high-speed aircraft from Messerschmitt (and Heinkel) to make an attempt on the world speed record for Germany. On 26 April 1939, Messerschmitt test pilot Fritz Wendel set a new world record of 469 mph with the specially designed Me 209, which did not so much fly as hurtle. German

propaganda reported that the record-setter was a 'Bf 109R', a modified
fighter, but the Me 209 owed little to the Bf 109. Wendel was happy to
have survived. 'The 209 was a brute. Its flying characteristics still make
me shudder ... In retrospect, I am inclined to think that its fuel was a
highly volatile mixture of sweat from my brow and goose pimples from
the back of my neck.'[10] The Me 209V1's record stood for piston-engine
aircraft until 1969.[11]

Messerschmitt devoted a major effort by the design team at Augsburg
to an Me 209 fighter design that used little of the original except the
designation. Heinrich Beauvais tested the Me 209V4 fighter version at
Augsburg on 4 June 1939. 'The *Fischschwanz* (fishtail), as we called it,
required less rudder on take-off than the 109 and I remember no difficulties during the flight. I recall that we definitely tried to stall but had
no reason to explore spin characteristics. Landing, however, was quite
exciting – for one thing, visibility from the cockpit was worse than the
Me 109 and judging one's height above the ground was not easy.'[12]
Messerschmitt put the design aside, though testing continued through
summer 1940. It was followed by a new fighter design designated the
Me 209 II, but this had nothing in common with the 1939 record-setter
or the Me 209V4 fighter version except the charisma imparted by the
shared designation. The Messerschmitt design team was to invest many
man-hours on this project in 1940–1.

His experience with high-speed piston-engine flight made Messerschmitt realise that the future of the fighter was the jet engine: 'the use
of air-propellers would be limited with increasing flying speeds, i.e., their
efficiency would become less and their top speed probably would not
exceed 700 km/h (420 mph)'.[13] Messerschmitt's interest in jet propulsion had dated back to March 1935, when he had been called in to
observe work on pulse jets and had met Dr Wernher von Braun, a scientist working on rockets for the army. They and their colleagues agreed
that pulse jet technology had promise. Meetings with von Braun had
sparked Messerschmitt's interest in rocket power for aircraft. An interceptor that could rocket up to high altitude and then glide back to a
landing appealed to Messerschmitt. He started to combine von Braun's
rocket engine with the tailless aircraft designs developed by Alexander
Lippisch.

The RLM had awarded Messerschmitt a jet fighter development contract in 1939. Robert Lusser had worked on an initial design before his split with Messerschmitt. Willy Messerschmitt had personally drafted *Provisional Technical Terms of Reference for Fast Fighter Aircraft with Jet Engines* on 4 January 1939. But with war seemingly getting closer, Germany was reluctant to invest scarce resources in jet technology.

RAF rearmament

Rearmament was finally being pursued in earnest. Conscription was introduced in Britain, limited at first but eventually expanded to include civilian labour, male and female, as well. As production increased – Britain produced almost as many aircraft as Germany in 1939 – RAF Fighter Command re-equipped from biplanes to Spitfires and Hurricanes.[14] The RAF had time for one last set of air exercises, in August 1939. Fighter Command demonstrated that operations rooms and the radar system were working better together. Radio communication with fighters had improved.

Spitfires arrived at more RAF stations. Each squadron was commanded by a squadron leader and had some sixteen (later eighteen) Spitfires; a squadron was divided into two flights, each under a flight lieutenant. At full strength, a squadron would generally have about twenty pilots at various levels of proficiency and over 100 ground crew and support personnel and would be expected to put twelve Spitfires into the air, usually flying in four sections of three.

In April 1939, when the initial order for Spitfires was supposed to have been completed, only 130 had been delivered. Often, the established procedures of having pilots go for transition training, being introduced to innovations such as flaps and retractable undercarriage on trainer aircraft, were put aside. Instead, squadrons had to convert themselves.

The Spitfire was like no fighter anyone had flown before. Pilots figured out how to fly them from manuals and shared ignorance. Ground crew handled the culture shock of having to service a new-technology aeroplane. They ran their hands over the aluminium skin, feeling the rivets, all so different from the fabric-covered biplanes. The ailerons, still covered in fabric to minimise weight, were pushed up and down, the flaps lowered and retracted again. They opened the panels of the Spitfire's all-metal skin, were introduced to the wonderful song of the Merlin engine as it was revved up, and viewed with suspicion the retractable undercarriage.

One of the pre-war fighter pilots having to make a hasty conversion was Flying Officer Allan 'Al' Deere, a native of New Zealand, flying Gladiators in 54 Squadron. 'On 6 March 1939, I flew my first Spitfire ... The transition from slow biplanes to the faster monoplanes was effected without fuss, and in a matter of weeks we were nearly as competent on Spitfires as we had been on Gladiators.'[15]

When his unit converted to Spitfires in August 1939, Pilot Officer David Crook of 609 Squadron's experience was in a larger sense applicable to Fighter Command as a whole. 'Having mastered the cockpit drill, I got in and taxied out on the aerodrome, stayed there for one moment to make sure that everything was OK, and opened up to full throttle. The effect took my breath away. The engine opened up with a great smooth roar, the Spitfire leapt forward like a bullet and tore madly across the aerodrome, and before I had realised quite what had happened I was in the air.' The pilots proved adaptable but many elements – tactics and technology alike – lagged behind.

The pilot of a Spitfire coming in to land would throttle back to fly a curved approach, enabling him to keep the airfield in sight at all times. On a grass field, he would be landing directly into the wind, determined by reference to a windsock flying from a pole. He would then lock the cockpit hood open in the full aft position and leave the side half-door ajar, so a hard landing would not end up trapping him in the cockpit. As the Spitfire's speed came down, the pilot checked the brake pressure and extended the undercarriage (once his speed dropped below 160 mph). Two green indicator lights came on in the cockpit when the undercarriage was down and locked. Rich engine mixture was selected (more fuel in the fuel–air mixture the engine burned), the propeller pitch was selected to fully fine, and, as the speed dropped under 140 mph, the flaps were lowered. Unlike the Bf 109, the Spitfire could only fully extend its flaps; it had no intermediate positions. The Spitfire would come 'over the hedge' above the airfield boundary at 85 mph, then, descending, the pilot would ease back on the control stick, keeping the plane off the grass until, at 64 mph, it would flare and touch down gently.

Dowding pressed for resources for Fighter Command: radar and Spitfires. He worked hard to improve Fighter Command, its aircraft, radar, airfields and command and control network, from the perceived weakness – one squadron of operational Hurricanes – that had so under-cut British diplomacy at Munich. His ally in the Cabinet, Sir Thomas Inskip, had left his position. Sir Kingsley Wood, who had succeeded Lord Swinton as secretary of state for air, announced after Munich that priority would go to fighters. The Air Ministry's response was to extend by an additional year the two-year production contracts for Spitfires and Hurricanes then in force. While this was claimed as a 50 per cent increase, it simply resulted in orders already planned being placed ear-lier. This was made possible by the first Rolls-Royce shadow factory, at Crewe, starting production as the second source for Merlin engines.

The eighth and last RAF rearmament plan, the post-Munich Scheme M, was intended to make the RAF ready for war by 1942. Yet the num-bers of aircraft ordered under the plan were only enough to maintain the current production rate. Despite the politically driven emphasis on air defence, the Air Staff still wanted more bombers. Scheme M allocated £175 million for bombers (including, for the first time, 1360 new heavy bombers) but only £45 million for fighters. As a result, Supermarine received an order for 450 Spitfires in August 1939. Castle Bromwich, finally approved to start building Spitfires, was floundering and had not yet delivered any.

The RAF build-up went beyond aeroplanes. The Women's Auxiliary Air Force (WAAF; later WRAF, Women's Royal Air Force), formed in June 1939, worked in the vital operations rooms, or driving vehicles, or packing parachutes. More RAF bases were built, continuing an effort that had started in 1937. These had permanent runways as well as the grass fields Spitfires used, with dispersal sites so that parked aircraft could be dispersed around the perimeter, less vulnerable to attack. Revetments (blast pens with an open side and roof) and walls were built to protect aircraft, fuel and explosives storage.

After extensive negotiations, the Empire (later British Common-wealth) Air Training Scheme (EATS/BCATS) was finally started in

December 1939. It allowed integration of aircrew and technician training throughout the Commonwealth in Canada, Australia, New Zealand, South Africa and Southern Rhodesia.

The Luftwaffe attacks

The August 1939 crisis resulting from Hitler's territorial demands on Poland brought most of Germany's Bf 109 fighter units out of their permanent bases to grass fields near the Polish frontier. The Luftwaffe had 1056 (946 operational) Bf 109s on 1 September 1939. Training flights were cut back, minimising the opportunity for an unplanned clash with the Poles, as well as conserving scarce fuel and spare parts.

When Hitler attacked, on 1 September, the first objective was the defeat of Poland's air force. Its PZL-11 and PZL-7 fighters, early 1930s designs with a high monoplane wing that had worried the RLM in 1933, were no match for the Bf 109.

The Polish Air Force had dispersed from its peacetime permanent airfields to grass airstrips. Few aircraft were destroyed on the ground, but at the dispersal strips the Poles could not coordinate air defence or repair damaged aircraft. Luftwaffe fighters effectively defeated the Polish Air Force in air combat in the first few days. Following pre-war Luftwaffe operational thinking, Bf 109E units were largely held back, defending German cities, airfields and forces in case of Polish bomber attacks. Offensive operations, including bomber escort missions, were largely the responsibility of the *Zerstörer* units, flying Bf 110s and, as an interim measure, older and less capable Bf 109Ds. This was reflected in the air-to-air victories against the Poles: ninety-three for Bf 110s, only thirteen for Bf 109s.[16]

The Germans' air superiority enabled them to use dive bombers in close support of advancing Panzers and to launch bombers against besieged Warsaw. Once Polish aircraft were shot down or out of action, Bf 109s strafed ground targets. The Luftwaffe's mobile ground technical support units, able to follow advancing troops – tactics they had exercised before the war – allowed Bf 109s to move into forward airfields, resupplied by Ju 52/3m transport aircraft. German losses included thirty-five Bf 109s, only nine in air combat.

While the Luftwaffe's role in Poland demonstrated its power, its resources were stretched, expending some 60 per cent of its ammunition. In the months following the defeat of Poland, despite access to Soviet resources granted through the Hitler–Stalin pact – the payment for which included three Bf 109Es for testing – Germany was cut off both from the international economy and from the resources it needed. Aircraft production was hard pressed to keep pace with that of the year before. Germany prepared for a decisive blow that would upend the strategic situation: an offensive in the west.

The war in the west

The day Britain declared war, 3 September 1939, the RAF had nine operational Spitfire squadrons, with 171 Spitfires (150 of which were serviceable). A further seventy Spitfires were in reserve or being made ready for squadron service. Held back for home defence against an anticipated bomber offensive, possibly with chemical weapons, none of the Spitfires deployed to France, where RAF Hurricane fighters and Fairey Battle and Bristol Blenheim bombers operated alongside the ground troops of the British Expeditionary Force (BEF). Just about all of the British Army's re-equipped units, slowly and painfully built up through rearmament, were transported to France, but the feared massive battle there did not materialise. Both sides instead settled down to months of a static situation without ground combat.

Spitfires awaited the German bomber offensive that had, since the 1920s, been assumed to follow immediately after any declaration of war. It did not materialise. The Spitfire's first combat was on 6 September, east of London. In the 'Battle of Barking Creek', two Hurricanes were shot down by Spitfires from 74 Squadron. All had been directed by ground controllers against the same false alarm.

With both sides avoiding any attacks on the civilian population, the Luftwaffe and the Royal Navy clashed in the North Sea. German bomber attacks on British naval bases were intercepted and two German Ju 88 bombers were shot down on 16 October 1939 by Spitfires based in Scotland. The Royal Navy, now that their aircraft carriers were equipped with radar, realised that a fast-climbing interceptor could take off in time to protect the fleet and asked the Air Ministry about the feasibility of operating Spitfires from aircraft carriers. In January 1940, Joe

Smith's team at Woolston offered the Royal Navy a Griffon-powered Spitfire only to have it rejected by Winston Churchill, First Lord of the Admiralty, in favour of additional existing two-seat naval fighters. Smith then submitted a plan to modify the Spitfire I, with an arrester hook for deck landing and folding wings for carrier storage. Months later, when Supermarine were ready to start production of a batch of fifty, Sir Wilfrid Freeman, in need of every Spitfire to meet the coming storm, rebuffed the Royal Navy. No Spitfires would go to sea in 1940.

In the few combats between Bf 109s and French fighters and British Hurricanes – Spitfires were still being held back to defend Britain – over the western front, the Germans shot down two Allied fighters for every one they lost. The RAF, prevented by government policy from launching the bomber offensive that their pre-war strategy had emphasised, instead probed German airspace with bombers. The Battle and Blenheim bombers based in France went into action first. They suffered heavy losses from Bf 109s with minimal results. A series of RAF daylight bomber missions against German naval vessels culminated on 18 December 1939. The RAF put up a daylight 'armed reconnaissance' mission with twenty-four Wellington bombers, believing any German fighters would be shot down by the concentrated gunfire of their defensive armament.

Unlike RAF Fighter Command, the Luftwaffe had not created an integrated air defence system, nor was this seen as a priority. Although German radar technology was ahead of that in Britain, their air defence radar coverage was limited, as was training of ground controllers to direct fighters. Many senior officers agreed with Adolf Galland, who had said in a pre-war exercise, 'It would be best to throw out all these damned radios! We don't need them. We didn't need them in Spain and without them we could fly higher and faster.'[17]

But radio direction from the ground proved to be critical when German radar warned of the approaching Wellingtons. Bf 109s and Bf 110s, alerted in time to climb to altitude, shot down twelve Wellingtons, many bursting into flames. British bombers, unlike their German counterparts, were not then fitted with self-sealing fuel tanks. Three more, riddled with 20mm cannon fire, crashed after making it back to Britain. Two Bf 109s were lost to bomber defensive fire.[18]

This climactic air battle over the Heligoland Bight demonstrated that, in daylight, bombers such as the Wellington would not get through to Germany. However, designing an escort fighter with range enough to fly from England to Germany and then dogfight on equal terms with a Bf 109 was considered unrealistic. The RAF recognised that bombers attacking Germany would have to do so primarily at night or, in daylight, at low level, stressing the element of surprise. But despite night bombing having been a part of RAF strategic theory since the Great War, they had made few investments in all-important navigation systems.

That Spitfires would be needed for the daylight reconnaissance mission was apparent even before it was seen that aircraft such as the Wellington and Blenheim were too vulnerable. Two Spitfire Is, their guns removed, had already been fitted with large American-made Fairchild F.24 cameras and deployed to France. The first Spitfire photo reconnaissance mission over Germany was flown on 11 November 1939. While bad weather and technical problems with the camera led to these two aircraft being withdrawn to England, they demonstrated the feasibility of using the Spitfire in a new role.

Other Spitfires took over reconnaissance. On 22 March 1940, a Bf 109 of I/JG 20, flown by Oberleutnant Harald Jung, intercepted and shot down a reconnaissance Spitfire over Kleve, the first Spitfire to be lost to a Bf 109. Pilot Officer Clive Wheatley was killed when his parachute failed to open. He received a full military funeral from the Luftwaffe. Jung received the Iron Cross First Class. Subsequent clashes were to receive less recognition.

But the reconnaissance Spitfire had proven its capability where most of Britain's improvised reconnaissance aircraft had proved wanting. A few dozen Spitfire Mk I were modified as PR Types A–C and rushed into service (over Dowding's objections; he wanted all the Spitfires for fighter squadrons). With additional fuel tanks in the wing and fuselage, they could reach Berlin from English bases. The Supermarine design team started modifying two prototypes, ready in late October 1940, with additional 66-gallon tanks inside each wing, giving a total range of 1750 miles. Subsequent reconnaissance Spitfire PR IDs were modified from Spitfire Vs (redesignated Spitfire PR IV, though different from the prototype Spitfire IV) and proved capable of ranging inside Germany as far as Stettin. RAF intelligence started reviving the science of photographic interpretation to extract vital data from examination of the photographs. The Spitfire, in addition to being an interceptor, could be the eyes of the British war effort.

Bf 109 development

Hitler was confident of a short, victorious war. On 7–9 February 1940, a high-level conference presided over by Göring and attended by Milch discussed the acceleration of Germany's armament programme. RLM investment in upgrading the Bf 109 would be secondary to that made in new fighters such as the Me 210.[19] Developments (such as turbojet engines) not likely to be ready within months would receive few resources. The short-term focus of German policy led Messerschmitt to feel subjected to 'planlessness'.

One of the Bf 109 developments was its adaptation to operate from an aircraft carrier. In 1939, the German Navy was in the process of building its first aircraft carrier, the *Graf Zeppelin*. The design team at Augsburg provided an initial modification of the Bf 109E-1 as it came off production lines. Final design modification and production were delegated to Fieseler, producing Bf 109s under licence. The ten Bf 109T-0s (T for *Träger*, carrier) were produced with an arrester hook, catapult points and longer folding wings with additional spoilers on the upper wing surfaces to allow slower landings. When, in 1940, work was halted on the *Graf Zeppelin*, the Bf 109T-0s were sent to reinforce fighter units in Norway; their wing design provided enhanced short field operations. Several dozen Bf 109T-2s – modified Bf 109E-4s which lacked the arrester hook and folding but retained the modified wing – were built. These too never went to sea and were mainly deployed to Norway.

1940: Invasion in the west

The Luftwaffe trained intensively, absorbing the combat lessons of the Polish campaign. Some 1100 Bf 109 pilots were ready for combat, flying about 1370 Bf 109s.[20] One of the Bf 109 pilots was Adolf Galland. He had spent the Polish campaign, as he had his combat time in Spain, leading a *Staffel* of ground attack biplanes. Transferred to the staff of a Bf 109

Jagdgeschwader, Galland's natural skill as a pilot, evident since his glider-flying youth, found its full expression in the Bf 109.[21] 'Vati' Mölders even gave him a short tutorial on using the improved Revi 3c A265 gunsight – which incorporated an adjustable sliding screen of neutral-density glass to filter out glare – on the Bf 109E-3 for deflection shooting. Now, he was ready to go hunting for enemy fighters. Galland respected Mölders: 'He was a far more analytic creature than I was. He was a very detail-oriented person, but this is not to say he was not a deadly pilot. He was one of the best.'

Galland not only wanted the thrill of the hunt he knew from the field, but was keen to achieve a score to rival the flying aces of the Great War that he, like his friend Mölders and many of the pilots on both sides of the current conflict, had idolised as a youth. The fighters who were going to be in the gunsights of Galland and his comrades were pre-dominantly from the French Air Force. The French flew a mix of fighter designs, ranging from excellent (such as the Dewoitine D.520) to inad-equate (the Potez 63). The D.520, the only other fighter in Europe in 1940 to be competitive with the Spitfire and the Bf 109, was only just entering service. The French also flew US-built Curtiss Hawk 75s, which offered superior performance to the indigenous Marcel Bloch MB 151/152 and Morane-Saulnier MS 406 that equipped most fighter units. France had split its resources over some half-dozen single-engine fighter types, showing that Udet's original insistence that Germany should decide on and concentrate on a standard fighter design did indeed provide a competitive advantage. Late in rearming, France had lacked time to produce necessary spare parts. Many French units had only some 40 per cent of their fighters flyable. The French military, rely-ing on conscription, had failed to recruit the technicians like those who kept the Luftwaffe and RAF flying; they had less than a quarter of the numbers required.[22] Most importantly, France had neither radar nor an effective way of massing fighters over a critical sector or directing them against enemy aircraft. The Luftwaffe would have the edge over them.

Fall Gelb (Case Yellow), the German offensive in the west, opened in the early morning of 10 May 1940. German bombers attacked airfields throughout the Netherlands, Belgium and northern France. The most important contribution of the Bf 109 in the opening days of the campaign was preventing Allied air reconnaissance from understanding the size, scope and direction of the German mechanised thrust through the rugged Ardennes region of Luxembourg and Belgium into northern France. By 12 May reconnaissance sorties, including those by photo reconnaissance Spitfires based at Heston in London's western suburbs, had alerted the Allies of the German penetration. It was too late for their armies to shift troops; they lacked mobile reserves. However, the French Air Force allocated air power to the Sedan sector as a priority.[23]

Panzer spearheads had penetrated the Ardennes and were in a position to break through French defences along the River Meuse and advance into the Allied armies' undefended rear areas on 13 May 1940. Bf 109s enabled German Panzer divisions, supported by attacks by Ju 87 Stuka dive bombers, to break through.[24] The Stukas were vulnerable to any Allied fighters. On 12 May, a *Staffel* of twelve had been caught by French fighters and wiped out. But on 13 May, the Stukas were able to make repeated sorties, rearming and attacking again, thanks to the protection of the Bf 109s and the failure of the Allies to mass their fighters to stop them. The Germans crossed the River Meuse near Sedan, Dinant and Mezières.

While even the accurate Stukas did limited damage – the French lost only two tanks to bombers that day – the overall impact was decisive.[25] French troops, untrained to deal with air attack, were unable to defeat the simultaneous German ground attacks. To add to the noise of the aircraft engines, the gunfire and the explosions, many Stukas carried wind-driven sirens on their fixed undercarriage to intensify the psychological effect of the bombing.[26] These devices emitted a terrifying shriek audible even above the explosions. No one who has ever taken cover from enemy aircraft needs to be told air attacks have an effect beyond the kinetic power of their weapons. The French Army found this out on 13 May.

RAF and French bombers that could potentially have bombed the advancing Germans to a standstill until French reserves could block the way were absent from the skies over the Meuse on 13 May. The RAF was unaware of the impending crisis; their bombers had suffered heavy losses the day before and had spent the day recovering. Winston Churchill (British prime minister since 10 May), rejected a proposal on

13 May to send more RAF fighters to France; he was concerned about weakening Fighter Command. The French did not call for air support, unaware that the German advance was potentially decisive.[27]

When the escorted Allied bombers did come into the fight on 14 May, they found German bridges over the Meuse defended by flak (anti-aircraft guns), and the sky full of Bf 109s. The French Air Force started the desperate attacks on the Meuse crossings by throwing in every bomber they could muster. After the French attacks failed, it was the turn of the RAF's Battle and Blenheim bombers, escorted by any Hurricane fighters airworthy after four days of intensive fighting. Of seventy-six RAF bombers, some forty fell to the Bf 109s and flak. Like the French bombers, they inflicted little damage. Throughout the day, 170 Allied aircraft were shot down. Watching from the battefield, a German officer saw 'Again and again an enemy aircraft crashes out of the sky, dragging a long black plume of smoke behind it . . . Occasionally from the falling machines one or two white parachutes release themselves and float slowly to earth.' In return, eleven Bf 109s were shot down, seven by RAF Hurricanes.[28] French Prime Minister Paul Reynard called Churchill and asked for ten more squadrons of fighters; the British War Cabinet and Chiefs of Staff Committee, meeting that evening, agreed Fighter Command should not be further weakened.

The Bf 109s defended the German bridgeheads over the Meuse without radar to warn of incoming bombers. Only a small fraction of the German fighter strength was in the air over the bridges at any given time. But Allied attacks were uncoordinated. The Germans flew 814 fighter sorties over the bridgeheads on 14 May. Many Bf 109 pilots flew three or four patrols. In contrast, French fighters, without the Luftwaffe's well-developed ground support staff, could not even achieve one sortie per fighter a day.

'We have been defeated.' These were the first words of Reynard, calling Churchill early on 15 May. That day's Allied bomber attacks, much weaker, could only delay rather than prevent the German breakthrough across northern France. The RAF restricted their surviving bombers to night operations. On the night of 15 May, the RAF opened the long-awaited night bomber offensive against transportation targets in the Ruhr. This, along with Churchill's appointment as prime minister, was a sign that the 'phony war' mentality that had predominated since the outbreak of the war was coming to an end. But it could not end quickly enough to save the collapsing battlefield situation in France.

On 13–14 May, over the River Meuse in northern France, the Bf 109 effectively won the Battle of France – and what appeared to be the war – for Germany. Neither the RAF nor the Luftwaffe recognised this at the time. The Bf 109 did not win the battle by itself or by shooting down planes. It did so by enabling other forces – the Panzer divisions. To the RAF, focused on strategic bombing, this was so antithetical that they failed to notice. The Luftwaffe's focus was on the Stukas and bombers that had made the attacks on 13 May, not on the Bf 109s that kept them from falling prey to Allied fighters. The Bf 109 pilots, however, understood the importance of what they had done and referred to 14 May 1940, when they protected the vital bridgeheads, as 'the day of the fighters'.[29]

The first Spitfire–Bf 109 clash

When the invasion of France began, Dowding withheld the Spitfire squadrons from combat, anticipating German bomber attacks on Britain. He thought that committing Spitfires to combat without radar or ground controllers would make them vulnerable. In response to an urgent demand for reinforcements, he authorised the sending of additional Hurricanes to reinforce the hard-pressed fighter squadrons in France. On 12 May, Spitfires based in England started flying over the Continent.[30]

On 13 May, six Spitfires of 66 Squadron, along with six Defiants of 264 Squadron, crossed the Dutch coast to look for German aircraft supporting the invasion of the Netherlands. The thwarted spring sky over the invaded countries was full of sullen rainclouds.

Flying through heavy Dutch and Belgian anti-aircraft fire, the Defiants found the Luftwaffe first, a *Staffel* of Ju 87 Stukas, dive-bombing a target near Rotterdam. The Defiants attacked.

Each of the Spitfire pilots of 66 Squadron, going into combat for the first time, performed the same quick actions. The knurled knob on the top of the control stick was twisted from 'safe' to 'fire', arming the eight Browning machine guns in the wings. They turned on their reflector sights, making the range-finding circles, deflection crosshairs and central aiming dot glow brightly on the angled glass plate under the bulletproof windscreen. While German sights had one fixed circle, the Spitfire pilots had to quickly adjust theirs to frame a Stuka-size wingspan in lethal range. They switched the fuel mixture to full rich and opened the radiator to prevent overheating.

'Tally ho!' The traditional fox-hunter's call announcing the adversary sighted and the chase beginning came over the voice radio.

The Spitfires followed the Defiants into the attack. Four Stukas were quickly shot down. At higher altitude, a *Staffel* of Bf 109s – the fifth *Staffel* of II/JG 26[31] – saw the attack and dived to the aid of the Stukas.

Pilot Officer Charles Cooke of 66 Squadron had been attacking the Stukas when the Bf 109s showed up. Neither he nor any other Spitfire pilot had seen a Bf 109 in combat before. 'After using all ammunition I joined formation with two Messerschmitt 109s by mistake. On realizing this I immediately climbed into cloud and returned to base.'[32]

Most of the Bf 109s attacked the Defiants – which they identified as Spitfires – and shot five down. The Defiants, two-seaters with all their armament in the gun turret that weighed them down, lacked the performance to escape as Cooke had done, despite their Merlin engines. The 66 Squadron Spitfires claimed one Bf 109 shot down. Either they or the Defiants did shoot down Oberleutnant Karl Borris' Bf 109. He bailed out and was captured.

Flying Officer George Brown of 66 Squadron followed down one Stuka he had attacked. He watched it crash. 'I rejoined my flight, which was then reforming over the southern end of Rotterdam.'

Then the battle changed. 'Nine Me 109s appeared at about 6,000 feet which immediately went into line astern and came down to attack us. One got on my tail and I observed tracer ammunition [machine-gun bullets that trace their trajectory in flight by chemical action] going past me. I used my emergency boost cut-out and I opened my throttle fully at the same time, doing a violent right-hand climbing turn into a cloud.'

But the Merlin engine and its supercharger would take seconds to respond. The additional drag imposed by the high-speed climbing turn was immediate. Inside the cloud, without ability to see the horizon, Brown felt first the Spitfire's characteristic shudder, the aircraft on the edge of a stall: 'severe shudder and clattering noise throughout the air-craft, which tends to flick over laterally and unless the control column is put forward instantly, a rapid roll and spin will result'.[33]

Normally, as the Spitfire announced a stall by the shuddering of the control stick, the pilot could take preventative action by relaxing the back pressure on the stick. But Brown was already pulling several g forces and, instead of stalling gradually, the entire right elliptical wing effectively stopped lifting at one instant. Brown stalled his Spitfire; a high-speed stall.

The wing dropped of its own accord. The Spitfire pitched violently and the tail spun. Brown was thrown around the cockpit, smashing into the aluminium structure, no longer flying the stricken Spitfire. He could feel the g forces tighten as the Spitfire whipped around in a spin. It seemed as if it might flip on its back at any instant. Nose and tail rapidly changed places in a spiral that, unless he recovered, would only end with a lethal impact. But, at the same time, he had another worry – the Bf 109s that had chased him into the clouds were waiting for him as he spun out of them.

'I came out of the cloud in a spin which apparently gave the Me 109s the impression that I was about to crash.'

With the Bf 109s convinced that the spinning Spitfire was finished, Brown now had the chance, outside the clouds, to recover from the spin. Fortunately for him, it was something the Spitfire did well. The recovery manoeuvre had been drilled into every RAF fighter pilot: throttle closed, full rudder opposite to the direction of spin. The Spitfire was now no longer spiralling but diving. But it could flick back into a spin in either direction. Then, centralise the controls, a firm but gentle pressure back on the control stick, open the throttle, and as the airspeed indicator crept back past 150 mph again, Brown brought the Spitfire back to level flight. 'When I pulled out I observed the enemy aircraft making off in another direction.'

The Bf 109s apparently gone, Brown had a chance to survey the damage. 'I noticed then that my main planes [wings] had sustained damage from enemy fire and that almost the whole of my port exhaust manifold had been shot away and that when I opened the throttle, sheets of flame appeared. I then decided to proceed leisurely to Knokke [a Belgian airfield that had been the prebriefed emergency field for the flight] and was proceeding southwest, just east of Tholen.'

But he had devoted too much attention to keeping the damaged Spitfire in the air and not enough to looking around him. 'I heard steadily, above the engine noise, the impact of fire on my fuselage and at the same time observed tracer bullets from behind. I again opened the throttle fully and when the fire had ceased looked round and, looking round, I found an Me 109 pulling out of range.'

For the second time that day, a 109 pilot had assumed Brown was going down and did not stay around to watch him crash or follow him down. Anyway, their job was to escort the surviving Stukas, their vulnerability to modern fighters, even ones as ill-conceived as the Defiant, painfully demonstrated. 'After this I maintained as much throttle as my broken exhaust would allow and kept a look out behind.'

By now on this grey spring day, the cloud was down to 1500 feet and it was raining, with Dutch and Belgian anti-aircraft guns impartially firing at the crippled Spitfire. Despite these hazards, Brown made a landing at Aalst airfield in Belgium. His Spitfire turned over on landing. The damage to the wings had flattened one of the tyres.

One of the surviving Defiants, low on fuel, followed him to the airfield. With only two seats, it left Brown behind when it headed back to England. Abandoning his crashed Spitfire, Brown headed back cross-country towards British forces in France along with the Belgian military, joining a retreat that seemingly involved a whole country.

Flying towards Dunkirk

The RAF reinforced the six Hurricane squadrons that had been fighting in France since 10 May. By 15 May, the equivalent of six more squadrons had been sent to France. A further four were operating over France during the day and returning, if possible, to bases in England. Winston Churchill, desperate to keep France in the war, agreed to send more fighters, despite his earlier resolve and having informed the War Cabinet on 13 May that Fighter Command could not be weakened to reinforce France. Dowding, as commander-in-chief of Fighter Command, realised that the defence of Britain was his primary responsibility.

Dowding asked Air Marshal Sir Cyril Newall, the Chief of Air Staff, to go to the Cabinet on his behalf. Dowding attended the 15 May meeting of the War Cabinet. They were sympathetic to his plea to retain fighters for defence of Britain. The meetings' conclusions were that 'no further Fighter squadrons were to be sent to France for the present'.[34] Despite this, on 16 May, four Hurricane squadrons deployed to France; another six squadrons were being made ready. Churchill thought the move 'a very great risk, but seemed essential to bolster the French'.[35]

In response, Dowding sent a formal message to the under-secretary of state for air. The RAF had estimated fifty-two squadrons were required to defend Britain. Fighter Command had already been effectively reduced to the equivalent of thirty-six squadrons. Dowding was anxious to conserve his nineteen Spitfire squadrons, which he saw as the key to Fighter Command's ability to defend Britain. He said, 'If the Home Defence force is drained away in desperate attempts to remedy the situation in France, defeat in France will involve the final, complete and inevitable defeat of this country.'[36] Dowding prevailed, although not until 19 May did Churchill finally agree that no more fighter squadrons should be sent to France and that those able to withdraw should fly back to England. But Fighter Command now faced a new challenge.

The German Panzer spearheads reached the Channel on 20 May, cutting off the BEF and the French armies in the north from the rest of France. The few photo-reconnaissance Spitfires were able to report on their progress. The Netherlands had already surrendered on 14 May, the same day that Luftwaffe bombers devastated much of the city of Rotterdam. Belgium was largely overrun and on the brink of surrender. Evacuation by sea to England through the French port of Dunkirk appeared the only way the British troops could be saved.

5

The Battle Opens

May–August 1940

The opening rounds of the air battle over Dunkirk took place on 23 May, as the Germans moved against British forces defending the nearby ports of Calais and Boulogne. Fighter Command's 11 Group, responsible for the air defence of London and its approaches from the south and east, now also had to defend the evacuation at Dunkirk from the intensive German air attacks.

It took days before the British realised how bad the situation really was. The BEF, forced to retreat by the German advance from the Meuse bridgeheads, was in danger of being cut off and forced to surrender. It was bad enough that all its heavy equipment would have to be abandoned. Without an evacuation, Britain would have few trained soldiers to defend against an increasing threat of invasion. Initially, the evacuation was carried out by warships and Channel steamers. But it soon became evident that this would not be enough. The result was the famous appeal to the British public for privately owned pleasure craft and their owners to go to Dunkirk and ferry soldiers from the beaches. As a result, boats from throughout England were soon converging on Dover. The Royal Navy started planning a massive evacuation in the teeth of the enemy, drawing together all these ships and boats.

The German spearheads, which had seemed unstoppable, had halted, at the end of their supply lines. Besides, Göring, on 25 May, promised

Hitler that *his* Luftwaffe would personally defeat the evacuation while the army prepared to finish the job in France. The army's generals, who had been forced to halt their advance, eagerly agreed.

Operation Dynamo, the evacuation from Dunkirk, started on 26 May. RAF Fighter Command's 11 Group, commanded by Air Vice Marshal Keith Park, based in south-east England, would provide air cover. Since 10 May, 11 Group's sixteen fighter squadrons had seen intense combat while flying from their fields in England, losing eighty-two fighters, including fifty Hurricanes and twenty Spitfires. When the losses of Hurricanes based in France were added in, the first twelve days of air combat had cost the RAF a quarter of its first-line fighters. Dowding authorised the large-scale commitment of Spitfires to defend the evacuation. In its opening days, the orders were for 11 Group to keep a continuous presence over Dunkirk.

Park was in a difficult position. British radar did not have the range to provide warning of German bombers leaving their bases to attack Dunkirk. Fighters could not be scrambled from British bases in time to defend Dunkirk, but the alternative of keeping permanent standing patrols of squadron or smaller strength over Dunkirk would mean that the Germans could overwhelm them at any time with a mass attack. Massing multiple squadrons could improve the odds in air combat, but 11 Group lacked enough fighters to keep strong forces over Dunkirk continuously. Spitfires, even if operating from forward airfields near the Channel, such as RAF Manston and Hawkinge in Kent, could spend a maximum of forty minutes over Dunkirk.

Yet, for all the RAF's problems, the Luftwaffe was in a weak position to fulfil Göring's promise. At Dunkirk, Göring intended to demonstrate the power of the Luftwaffe. But he did not consider the difficulties the Luftwaffe, especially the Bf 109 units it relied on, was facing.

The Luftwaffe had been in constant action since 10 May. Despite its overall success, losses had been relatively high. Aircrew were exhausted. Stocks of ordnance and spare parts, slowly built up since the Polish campaign, were depleted. Only the use of captured fuel sustained operations, despite Germany receiving petroleum from the Soviet Union. Bf 109s had flown four sorties a day – sometimes as many as six – since 10 May.[1] The Bf 109 units were also finding out that their pilots lacked sufficient instrument flying skills. An emphasis on 'blue sky' flying proved costly when blue skies were few and far between. Many Bf 109 units had moved into forward bases in France and Belgium. The French airfield at Charleville near the Meuse had become a base within hours of being overrun. But some bomber units were still based in Germany. The French Air Force was still in action despite its defeats in mid-May, with increasing numbers of D.520 fighters.

Air battles over Dunkirk

The initial Luftwaffe attacks on Dunkirk, aimed at port facilities and troops on the beaches, did not lead to the decisive results Göring wanted. Over Dunkirk, Bf 109s and Spitfires clashed in large numbers. In the words of Major Werner Kreipe, then flying Do 17 bombers with III/KG 2 (*Kampfgeschwader*, bomber wing), 'the days of easy victory were over. We had met the Royal Air Force head on.'[2]

The Luftwaffe concentrated its fighters and bombers of all different types against Dunkirk, though the French Air Force, still fighting desperately, absorbed much of their effort. Kreipe's III/KG 2 was introduced to Spitfires on 27 May, after taking off on a mission to Dunkirk:

> With its full complement of 27 aircraft and was soon flying north at 11,000 feet, which was just below the cloud base. From this height the crews had a veritable bird's eye view of Dunkirk and the beaches already crowded with soldiers, horses, vehicles and equipment of every sort. But before the Dorniers could unload their bombs on this ideal target, the wireless sets began to crackle: 'Enemy fighters coming in from astern.' Within a matter of seconds a squadron of Spitfires – the first these German airmen had met – had hurled itself upon the bomber group. Despite the heavy defensive fire of the German air gunners, the British fighters attacked again and again and succeeded in driving the Dorniers away from their target.[3]

KG 2 lost seven Do 17s shot down.

The Luftwaffe was stunned by its initial encounters with large numbers of Spitfires over Dunkirk. The Bf 109 did not have a clear-cut advantage over the Spitfire. The German pilots had been used to superiority over their opponents, even the RAF Hurricanes that had been the most capable fighters they had encountered in the preceding weeks. The II *Fliegerkorps*, on 27 May, lost more aircraft over Dunkirk than they had in all the preceding fighting since 10 May.[4] Faced with the fresh British squadrons, the Luftwaffe switched to launching larger, more concentrated attacks on Dunkirk, aiming at ships. British casualties increased.

For most of the Spitfire squadrons, Dunkirk was their first sustained combat experience. All but three Fighter Command squadrons saw combat over Dunkirk, fighting without ground control. The Spitfire squadrons had trained to intercept unescorted German bombers over Britain. Now Spitfires were facing large numbers of German fighters.

The RAF squadrons operating over Dunkirk had little knowledge of the situation unfolding below them and no way of coordinating with the other services, firing at every plane that came within range regardless of type. Pilot Officer Allan Wright was flying Spitfires with 92 Squadron. 'We were, however, given the limits of our patrol area, not to patrol below 10,000 feet and told to attack any German aircraft seen. We were also warned to conserve fuel and to leave the battle area with sufficient fuel to get back. Not easy to assess in the heat of battle.'[5]

When gaps opened in the dense billowing black clouds that covered much of the evacuation site up to an altitude of 30,000 feet, Spitfire pilots patrolling Dunkirk could see the whole extent of the drama, even if its meaning was not apparent in the view from their cockpits. Flashes of gunfire marked the front line on the ground, where French troops held the line against German attacks on the perimeter. The German Army, ordered to halt, first by their Army Group commander and then by Hitler, could be seen resupplying itself after its advance across Belgium and northern France. Convoys of supply trucks, now moving in daylight without fear of air attack, stretched back to the German border, off in the hazy distance to the east, where tree-lined roads and the towns and villages of northern France provided them with cover. As William Shirer, an American journalist accompanying the Germans, found, 'One of the sights that overwhelms you at the front is the vast scale on which the Germans bring up men, guns and supplies unhindered.'[6]

What RAF pilots remembered most about Dunkirk were those huge clouds of black smoke. They blocked visibility, concealed escaping enemy (and friendly) aircraft, and even permeated the cockpits of Spitfires that had flown through them, with the pilots going on oxygen until they flew clear. The burned petroleum smell remained.

When the clouds opened, high-flying Spitfire pilots had brief views of the harbour, breakwater and beaches at the centre of the cauldron. Flames and large billowing dark clouds rose from the targets of earlier German bombing attacks. Oil tanks, port facilities and ships were all burning, creating their own clouds that covered much of the area. Evacuating British troops burned their equipment. All the tanks, artillery and motor transport – the BEF was the first army ever to depend wholly on trucks rather than horses – that had been the product of Britain's late and painful rearming were being destroyed to keep them out of German hands.

On the beaches – where improvised piers were created from lorries pushed into the water at low tide – and around the port, massive, orderly lines of troops waited to embark. In the first days of the German air attacks, troops were the targets for bombing Stukas or strafing Bf 109s. It was days before the Germans realised that the troops were more vulnerable when closely packed in a returning ship rather than able to take cover among the dunes. Ships were everywhere: sunk and sinking ships, sleek grey destroyers, stubby minesweepers, Channel steamers still in peacetime livery. Some were alongside a breakwater, loading troops. Shuttling between the beaches and the ships were the little boats, 700 mainly privately owned British pleasure craft, sailed by their civilian owners, which had crossed the Channel from their anchorages and boatyards in England after the radioed appeal for volunteers. Fading into the smoke and haze to the west were the ships returning to England with evacuated troops and, passing them, those returning to pick up more, their white bow waves and wakes catching the pilots' eyes.

RAF fighters were originally ordered to fly over Dunkirk at an altitude above 10,000 feet. This was intended to reduce vulnerability to friendly anti-aircraft fire, which was still directed at any aircraft its operators spotted. But these orders prevented the RAF from diving down against low-altitude attackers and ensured that the only aircraft seen by the men on shore or on the ships would be German. The RAF soon realised that they had to operate at all altitudes, accepting losses from friendly anti-aircraft fire.

The RAF's apparent absence led to much bitterness and hostility directed at shot-down aircrew looking to rejoin their squadrons and get back into action. The view from the ground was different from that from the cockpit. Having been shot down himself, fighter pilot Pilot Officer Roy Morant of 222 Squadron was trying to get on board a ship. 'I could see the difficulties the fighters are up against. At times we could see Hun bombers bombing from the cloud when our own fighters were about half a mile away obviously unable to see them. The troops could not understand that one could see an aircraft in thin cloud above one, but from the air one could not.'[7] Pilot Officer Peter Cazenove of 92 Squadron had been forced to belly-land his Spitfire on a beach at Calais on 24 May, when it was still held by the British. He made his way to the port, where the evacuation was in progress. British destroyers alongside the breakwater were loading troops. Cazenove was, in turn, 'told to f— off' by the navy at the gangways of no less than four destroyers. As the destroyers sailed away with evacuated troops, Cazenove picked up an abandoned rifle and joined the last British soldiers holding the ruins of Calais, left behind to be captured by the Germans two days later.[8] Later, at Dunkirk, Al Deere and Pilot Officer Ken Manger of 17 Squadron were both barred from destroyers by army officers until they forced their way on board. Feelings of abandonment and resentment were as commonplace as heroism.

The RAF response

In the face of Luftwaffe attacks that were increasing in tempo, the RAF improvised tactics. Park had opposed the initial orders (from the Chief of Air Staff) requiring him to keep fighters continuously over Dunkirk.[9] This made them vulnerable to being overwhelmed by German mass attacks. During the height of the air fighting over Dunkirk, Park would leave 11 Group headquarters and fly, in his personal Hurricane, to the airfields from where his pilots flew multiple sorties every day. He would listen to their reports of combat over Dunkirk, then fly back and modify the plans of the next day's operations. The result had been the shift to sending multiple squadrons together over Dunkirk.

Starting on 28 May, Park paired Hurricane and Spitfire squadrons to operate together, so that the Hurricanes would go after the bombers while the Spitfires held off the fighters.[10] But the larger formations were unwieldy. The high-frequency RAF radios in the Spitfires and Hurricanes proved ineffective in coordinating multiple squadron forces in the air. Sometimes no Spitfires or Hurricanes at all patrolled over Dunkirk.

Air warfare requires quick and effective adaptation, of aircraft, technology and tactics. The Germans were, in turn, quick to respond to the new British mass formations. On the evening of 29 May, the Luftwaffe started sending more mass attacks over Dunkirk. Three of the five mass raids in the afternoon met with wing-size RAF fighter forces. The other two, attacking between patrols, caused heavy damage. On 30 May, despite bad weather, the Luftwaffe, now targeting the evacuation ships, was able to take advantage of the gaps between 11 Group's wing-size formations patrolling above Dunkirk and sank ten large ships and dozens of smaller ones.

On the afternoon of 1 June, Flight Lieutenant Douglas Bader's Spitfire was flying over Dunkirk, part of a wing of 222 and 19 Squadrons. He recalled, 'You could identify Dunkirk from [over] the Thames Estuary by the huge pall of smoke rising straight up in a windless sky.'[11] Bader, a pre-war regular, was then the RAF's only fighter pilot with two artificial legs, the result of a crash in a Bristol Bulldog. Told at first he would never walk again, he not only walked, but also, after Munich, went back into the RAF to fly fighters, which is what he insisted he was going to do from the start. Douglas Bader did not have a lot of time for obstacles in his way, whether they be handicaps, senior officers or, as now, Bf 109s.

Bader and the wing flew towards Dunkirk, over the ships. 'It was solid with shipping. One felt one could walk across without getting one's feet wet.' That afternoon, Bader reported, '19 and 222 Squadrons in Sections line astern [were] flying just beneath a cloud layer at approximately 4,000 feet.' This was an unwieldy formation; section line astern meant that only the leader could devote his attention to seeing the enemy; the other two pilots had to try to stay in line.

But the wing managed to spot what Bader described as '12 Me 110s flying on a southerly course near Dunkirk. The Me 110s were just breaking through the cloud base. 19 Squadron followed by 222 went in to attack in aeroplanes line astern, the 110s also circling in line astern.' Bf 110s, big twin-engine fighters with a rear gunner, often formed defensive circles when under attack by more manoeuvrable Spitfires and Hurricanes, each rear gunner covering the plane behind.

Bader advanced his Spitfire's throttle to full, flicking on his reflector sight and twisting the knob on his control column that armed his guns. He could see the Spitfires stringing out in one ragged line as they went in for an attack on the Bf 110s.[12]

Rather than focusing on the Bf 110s, Bader had kept up his search. He saw Bf 109s, diving down from his left, coming to the aid of the Bf 110s.[13] 'As 19 Squadron started their attack, 12 Me 109s dived through the clouds in an east to west direction, right into the Spitfires which were by that time in an approximate circle turning left handed.'

Over the radio, he warned the squadron,

'Break left!'

This was an urgent warning and a command: turn and face their attackers.[14] Or be shot down.

Bader now broke off his attack on the Bf 110s. Applying one of the basic rules of air combat tactics – turn into your attacker to present him with a more difficult shot – he rammed his stick and rudder over and pulled his Spitfire into a tight right turn, bringing the Spitfire's nose around as quickly as he could, the two wingmen in his section who had been following him now struggling to keep up with him in the tight turn and not to stall.

'I saw a Messerschmitt 109 diving towards and to the side of me, firing twin [machine guns] on top of the engine cowling, so I turned into its path.' Bader was standing the speeding Spitfire on its wing tip, in a steep turn in the same direction as the 109 was heading, so that the Spitfire's nose – and guns – were pointed directly ahead of it at the point where he judged the target would be when the bullets hit.[15]

Bader jabbed the firing button on the circular top of the Spitfire's control stick with his thumb.[16] 'Gave it a short full deflection burst.' Bader had set up a full-deflection shot, the hardest a fighter pilot can make, firing at an enemy aircraft that is basically broadside. He did not hit it. He kept the Spitfire in a tight turn, manoeuvring for a position straight behind the Bf 109.

'Turning onto its tail as it went past,' Bader was now at the Bf 109's six o'clock position, 150 yards directly behind it. He aimed through the reflector gunsight, where the Bf 109's wings were almost touching the inner red circle projected onto the glass panel in front of his windshield.

'I saw my tracers hitting the 109 and as I turned behind it, it burst into flames.' Bader saw a spurt of orange flame appear and spread behind the cockpit as the Bf 109 rolled over on its back and started going down, a long black smoke trail behind it.[17]

Bader had successfully demonstrated the characteristics that would make him a legend in Fighter Command: aggressiveness, determination, accurate close-range shooting (a two-second burst at 150 yards, closing to 100, firing 285 rounds from each of his Spitfire's eight machine guns) and disdain for all who opposed him, regardless of uniform. He concluded his report: 'All the German pilots appeared to me to be below average.'[18]

From the ground, however, all of these battles, including Bader's tight turn and well-aimed deflection shooting, even the burning Bf 109, adding its own contribution to the smoke and flame that covered Dunkirk, appeared indistinct or were totally obscured. When they could see the aeroplanes, British troops either took cover or opened fire.

The end at Dunkirk

On 1 June, another twelve large ships were sunk. German artillery started to pound the troops remaining on the ground. Faced with heavy loss of life, the evacuation was scaled back, limited to the hours of darkness.

The Luftwaffe daylight attacks continued, hitting the beaches and troops. On the morning of 2 June, over Dunkirk, Adolf Galland first encountered Spitfires.[19] He had gained nine victories since 10 May, but he had never seen combat of this intensity. The RAF sent five squadrons over Dunkirk that morning and engaged three massed raids of escorted bombers. RAF losses were heavy. 611 Squadron, on their first patrol, had two Spitfires shot down and six more damaged; the squadron was immediately withdrawn from combat. However pleased Galland may have been to have destroyed a Spitfire (one of seven shot down that morning, for the loss of a single Bf 109), the attacking German bombers did not get through on this occasion. No attacks on shipping were reported that morning. Fighters shot down do not equate to tactical success.

Some 198,000 British and 140,000 French troops had been successfully evacuated when, after the surrender of the two French divisions defending the evacuation from the German Army, the evacuation ended on 4 June. Park flew the last combat mission over Dunkirk in his personal Hurricane.[20]

Dunkirk was more than a successful evacuation. It was Germany's first strategic rebuff, the first time Hitler had failed to achieve his goals. The Spitfire had enabled the rest of the RAF to carry out their missions over Dunkirk. Generalfeldmarschall Albert Kesselring, commanding *Luftflotte* Two during the campaign, said after the war that 'Only the Spitfires really bothered us. The Me 109 still had the edge.'[21] But, over Dunkirk, the Bf 109 had no longer been able to assure the sort of air superiority that had proven so decisive above the Meuse crossings. The Luftwaffe had been fought to a standstill.

Fighter Command had shot down some 130 German aircraft over Dunkirk but at a cost of 90 fighters and 80 pilots. Forty-two Spitfires had been shot down. Of 261 Hurricanes sent to France, only 66 returned to Britain. More important, the 435 RAF fighter pilots lost were irreplaceable in the months to come. In May and June, the Luftwaffe had lost 257 Bf 109s, 169 in action, 66 on operations not due to enemy action, and a further 22 not on operations.[22] Some 169 Bf 109 pilots became casualties, about a fifth of the force that had started the campaign. Many of the Bf 109 pilots taken prisoner were soon back in the cockpit, including Karl Borris, shot down over Rotterdam, and 'Vati' Mölders who, despite being one of the top-scoring Luftwaffe aces, had lost a fight with a French Hawk 75. The rest would be sorely missed in the coming climactic battle with the RAF.

Preparations – Spitfire transitions
On 14 June, the German Army entered Paris; France stopped fighting on 25 June. Britain's only alternative to a negotiated peace on Hitler's

terms was to defeat the impending German air offensive that would pre-
cede any attempt at invasion. As Britain organised its defences, industry
worked overtime to replace the weapons left behind at Dunkirk and the
aircraft shot down over France. The changes that turned the initial
Spitfire design into the combat-ready Spitfires of summer 1940 demonstrated the close relations between RAF, science and the aircraft industry
that allowed needs to be rapidly identified, solutions developed and the
results put quickly into service. Civilian scientists at operational RAF
headquarters, including Fighter Command and 11 Group, developed
working relationships with Dowding, Park and other RAF leaders. The
British command relationships recognised that the war in the air would
be shaped by technology.

In these weeks, the British were able to put in place a series of
changes to the Spitfire that turned Mitchell's original design into an
effective fighting machine and, more importantly, integrated it with the
overall defence of Britain. Some of these had been incrementally carried
out, but many of the most important were only reflected in Spitfires in
Fighter Command at the last moment, in the weeks following Dunkirk,
and were made without slowing production. Many of the changes made
in the years between the aircraft's initial design and the summer of 1940
would not yield results in the form of advanced marks of Spitfire in the
hands of operational squadrons until 1941 or later. But critical upgrades
were delivered, many just in time, to make a difference in the upcoming decisive struggle.

The most important single innovation would not be ready in time for
the coming battle. In 1939, despite being committed to developing
many advanced engines, Rolls-Royce started work on a new engine
design. Ernest Hives, head of the Rolls-Royce design office, called his
new engine the 'second power string for the Spitfire'. It was to be longer
and heavier than the Merlin, with a 37-litre capacity (10 litres more than
the Merlin). Based on the experimental 'R' racing engine from
Schneider Cup days, it had been designed to squeeze tremendous power
into a small, low-drag package. Despite also having multiple short-term
commitments, Joe Smith and 'Hs' Hives and their teams both went to
work integrating the new engine, soon named the Griffon, with the
basic Spitfire design on their own initiative. Smith, with his unmatched

knowledge of the Spitfire design, knew that, even though Mitchell had designed the airframe around the smaller Merlin, it could accommodate the larger Griffon, while Hives relied on Rolls-Royce's unmatched supercharger design and fabrication capability. In December 1939, the Griffon prototype was running on a test stand.

The design of the Griffon-engine Spitfire started, like the original 1934 programme, with Supermarine and Rolls-Royce working together on a private venture. As before, the Air Ministry soon saw its potential. The Spitfire still had not proven itself in combat, so once again Sir Wilfrid Freeman demonstrated he was able to recognise the potential of a design and help pull it into service. In October 1939, Freeman gave authority to develop the Griffon-engine Spitfire.

But Freeman still did not abandon the idea, which he had seriously considered in March 1939, that the Spitfire was merely an interim design to be replaced in production by twin-engine Beaufighters (or advanced fighters with engines still in development). Until the shock of combat put an end to the idea in 1940, meetings considered how Supermarine was going to wind up Spitfire production and make the transition to Beaufighters.[23] But, for all its promise, in June 1940 the first Griffon-powered Spitfire (soon designated Spitfire IV) was literally still on the drawing board. For short-term gain, Hives' team started the process of modifying the Merlin design to make it easier and quicker to produce.[24]

While near-term improvements were incorporated on the production line and retrofitted to existing Spitfires, at Woolston Joe Smith and Alan Clifton were leading the design team on a thorough redesign of the Merlin-engine Spitfire that would incorporate all the upgrades and reflect the improved technology available since Mitchell's initial design. The improvements in the Merlin and the potential for upgrades in the Spitfire design made it apparent to the Air Ministry that continued investment was needed. But Smith believed that with such investment, the basic Spitfire design could be developed to yield greatly increased performance. The Air Ministry realised that, in a long war, they needed to have an alternative to the as yet unproven designs that, in peacetime, had appeared the obvious successors to the Spitfire.

The Spitfire III prototype first flew on 15 March 1940, powered by

Hives' 1390 hp Merlin XX engine, with a two-speed single-stage super-charger, a retractable tailwheel (by itself increasing top speed by 5 mph), clipped-back wing tips, improved canopy, provision for cannon arma-ment, and other upgrades. But the need to come up with immediate improvements and integrate them in the existing production aircraft lim-ited the resources Supermarine had available to develop the Spitfire III throughout 1940. Merlin XXs were needed for other aircraft. The Spitfire III, which would require extensive modifications to the airframe to accommodate the more powerful engine, would not be ready to go into production in time to meet the crisis.

On 15 May 1940, Lord Beaverbrook, the Canadian-born newspaper magnate, former appeaser and now Churchill's political ally, was appointed to the Cabinet as the first-ever minister of aircraft production. Most of the improvements in British aircraft production had already been put in place months before Beaverbrook took office, but he provided a badly needed leadership figure with Churchill's confidence at a time of crisis. Disregarding layers of bureaucracy, he called Dowding every evening, asking him how many fighters he needed delivered the next day and where they should be sent. On Beaverbrook's first day in office, the Spitfire was identified by Sir Wilfrid Freeman as one of five designs to receive priority in resources. In September 1940, Britain produced 470 single-engine fighters, Germany 178.[25] Supermarine delivered a monthly average of 121 Spitfires from its Southampton factories alone in the third quarter of 1940; Castle Bromwich added a further 39. Spare parts pro-duction was temporarily cut back to 6 per cent of total output; more aircraft were what was desperately needed. The Bf 109 was losing the critical battle of numbers.[26]

Spitfire deliveries were handled by the Air Transport Auxiliary (ATA), an organisation of civilians, private pilots, Great War veterans and women who would fly the planes from factories to the maintenance units (MUs), where they would be made ready to be turned over to operational squadrons. Jeffrey Quill, test pilot at Supermarine, recalled that 'Before long, every Spitfire which left our works was collected by a woman. In their dark blue uniforms they looked neat and smart and they did the job quietly and efficiently and with a minimum of fuss.'[27]

Diana Barnato was one of these women. Initially limited to flying trainers and light aircraft, the Spitfire became her favourite. 'They all flew beautifully, with the Spit characteristic of it feeling it was part of you. The Mark I was really light on the controls.'[28]

Beaverbrook took over the RAF's Civilian Repair Organisation (CRO), which the Air Ministry had established in 1938. Under the Ministry of Aircraft Production, the CRO was better able to work with industry. Badly damaged RAF aircraft were repaired by the aircraft industry while the RAF concentrated on repairing those aircraft that could be quickly returned to combat. In coming months, some 40 per cent of the Spitfires and Hurricanes reaching the RAF did so through the CRO.[29]

With no time to develop a new mark of Spitfire, existing Spitfire Is received an important performance upgrade in the weeks after Dunkirk. Mitchell had pointed out back in 1929 that variable pitch propellers would become more important as aircraft speed increased. Without such a propeller (and flaps), landing speed would be too high for contemporary airfields. Yet the first Spitfires and Hurricanes had been delivered to the RAF with fixed pitch two-blade propellers, the same as those used by biplane fighters. Spitfires and Hurricanes had gone to war with two-speed variable pitch propellers, which required the pilot to change the pitch control. These had been introduced on the Spitfire production line after seventy-seven had been built.

Despite its potential performance advantage, it was not until after Dunkirk, in response to demands by operational squadrons, that a constant-speed propeller, which changed pitch automatically through the use of a governor mechanism rather than requiring the pilot to adjust it, was hurriedly fitted to Spitfires. The original plan had been for the Spitfire to receive a Rotol-design constant-speed propeller, but production had lagged and delivery priority went to Hurricanes (in greater need). A few Spitfires had used these propellers over Dunkirk. The RAF then looked at an alternative De Havilland design, spurred on when, days after Dunkirk, an RAF engineering officer contacted De Havilland, the designer of the propeller, to see if 'without red tape or bother' his squadron could test their constant-speed propeller. A combination of low-level push, high-level pull, successful testing and desperation accelerated the programme. De Havilland was personally authorised by Lord

Beaverbrook to retrofit all existing Spitfires and Hurricanes within two weeks of the initial test. Constant-speed propellers would be fitted to all new construction fighters. Teams of De Havilland engineers went from squadron to squadron fitting in the new propellers, often arriving without notice and working until all the fighters were modified, then returning to their factory to load their vans with new propellers just off the production line and going out again, working around the clock. In less than two months after Dunkirk, over 1000 propellers were delivered. Spitfires using the new propeller had a shorter take-off run, faster climb, and an increase in maximum altitude.

Another innovation to improve Spitfire and Hurricane performance was the introduction of 100-octane aviation fuel, supplanting the original 87-octane type.[30] This more powerful fuel had been used by the RAF as far back as the 1931 Schneider Cup race. Processes to enable its mass production were developed in the US in the 1930s, with 'Jimmy' Doolittle, who had competed for the Schneider Cup in the 1920s, among those playing a major role. It had taken years to get a production stream established and the refining technology distributed, but enough was imported from the US or refined in the UK for Fighter Command. Soon RAF fighter airfields had separate 100-octane storage tanks and fuel trucks.

The use of 100 octane made it possible for Spitfires to receive an additional 'emergency boost' capability. (This is what Brown had used to escape over Rotterdam.) Emergency boost increased the pressure in the intake manifold of the Spitfire's Merlin III for five minutes. This provided increased speed – an additional 34 mph at 10,000 feet – and climb performance. To prevent unintentional use, the Spitfire's throttle was modified with an aluminium wire barrier. Breaking the wire allowed the engine to reach war emergency power. The new fuel provided RAF fighters with a performance advantage: Bf 109s, like the rest of the Luftwaffe, continued to use 87 octane.

The Spitfire, like the Hurricane, had been designed without armour. After initial clashes in 1939, RAF fighter pilots realised their vulnerability, even if the Air Ministry did not. Hurricane units in France started fitting their fighters with improvised armour before the German offensive. A Supermarine-designed Spitfire armour package, pushed through by Dowding, had been designed in 1939. Now, the pro-gramme to retrofit it to all existing Spitfires accelerated after Dunkirk. The 73 lb weight of the armour was counteracted by the increased power made available by the constant-speed propeller and the 100-octane fuel.

Self-sealing fuel tanks were installed, preventing fuel leaks if the tanks were penetrated by bullets, and helping prevent the structure of a fighter that had been hit in the fuel tank being damaged by hydraulic ram effect (where the energy of the incoming bullets was transferred, through the fuel, to damage the target aeroplane's structure). Dowding's pre-war keenness to develop fuel tank protection against post-crash fires meant that Spitfires first received an upgrade to cover their fuselage fuel tanks with aluminium armour and a fire retardant coating in April 1940. Combat lessons then accelerated the effort for Spitfires to receive improved self-sealing tanks, starting in July. But the fuel tanks in the fuselage forward of the Spitfire's cockpit still provided a hazard to the pilot in the event of in-flight fire. There was not room for the upper of the two fuel tanks to receive the protective Linatex coating. The Spitfire I would go into battle with only the 37-gallon lower tank self-sealing, while the less protected 48-gallon upper tank would be emptied first in the course of a sortie. Dowding was unsatisfied with this modification, telling the Air Ministry, 'I would very much welcome the provision of a self-sealing tank.'[31] The Bf 109's L-shaped fuel tank, below and behind the cockpit, was less vulnerable.

The months between the start of the war and the summer of 1940 had been used for improvements to the 'situational awareness' of both the Spitfire pilot and the Fighter Command system that directed him. Spitfires were retrofitted with a 'bubble' bulge dome sliding cockpit canopy and enlarged rear-view mirrors. This provided Spitfire pilots with a better view to the rear than Bf 109 pilots, sitting low in the fuselage under a canopy with heavy-framed flat top and sides and a smaller mirror. Reflecting the vital importance of radar to Fighter Command and the lessons of the 1938 exercises, even before the 'Battle of Barking Creek' and the heavy friendly fire Fighter Command had endured over Dunkirk, the British developed Identification Friend or Foe (IFF) transponders, so that friendly aircraft could be distinguished from the enemy on radar. The first 500 IFF transponders had been ready in September 1939, but by February 1940 only one Spitfire had been retrofitted. In the months after Dunkirk, transponders were retrofitted to all of Fighter Command's aircraft. The improved IFF Mark II was introduced in July 1940, and had re-equipped Fighter Command by October.

Not all the upgrades intended for RAF fighters were ready in time. Pre-war exercises had brought home to the RAF the limitations of the TR 9 high frequency (HF) radio. 'Nobby' Clarke called it 'the most unreliable set in the world'.[32] It would pick up BBC programmes at crucial moments. Combat lessons over France and Dunkirk had brought its failures home. The RAF had planned for years to equip all its fighters with the TR Type 1133, using new US-developed very high frequency (VHF) radio technology. But problems with this new technology delayed deliveries. During the fighting above Dunkirk, Dowding decided to withhold fighters with VHF radios from combat to ensure a common standard among all the aircraft. When it became apparent, after Dunkirk, that insufficient VHF radios would be available to re-equip all of Fighter Command before the German attack, the order was given to convert the whole force back to the HF radio.[33]

Two-step rudder pedals, with an upper step for high-g manoeuvres, allowing the pilot to better handle the stresses of air combat, were added to new production models and retrofitted to Spitfires starting in summer 1940.

Upgrades of the Spitfire's armament had been in progress since the problem of frozen guns had made the first production Spitfires militarily worthless back in 1938. Spitfire Is were modified on the production line so that heat was ducted from the engine exhaust to keep the guns from freezing at high altitude, especially after encountering condensation when climbing through cloud. Later, this was replaced by electric gun heating. A short-term solution, using adhesive patches on the wing's leading edge to cover the muzzles, was universally practised by 1940, and helped prevent gun icing (as well as dirt and insects) from disarming Spitfires.

Initial production Spitfires had been delivered with the same simple ring-and-bead gunsight that had been used on biplane fighters. This was soon replaced by a Barr and Stroud GM 2 reflector gunsight, similar to the Revi gunsight used by Bf 109s. In 1939, the RAF modified fighters' Browning .303 machine guns to be able to fire bursts of up to 300 rounds. The modification required a redesign of the muzzle attachment and the improved guns were not installed on all RAF fighters until May 1940. The Browning could fire the new, more lethal Mk 6 Incendiary Round, the Belgian-designed De Wilde, in service by mid-1940.

Improving the Spitfire gunnery was a change in how its eight machine guns were harmonised. Before the war, all eight guns were supposed to be aligned so their fire would strike an area the size of a bomber's cockpit at 400 yards range. Even before the German offensive, the France-based Hurricane squadrons harmonised the guns to produce concentrated fire at 250 yards range, more realistic under combat conditions. After Dunkirk, the rest of Fighter Command followed suit. But the Hurricane, with all its guns mounted close together in the wing, could always achieve better concentration of fire than the Spitfire, whose two outermost guns were easily put out of alignment by the flexing of the wing during air combat manoeuvres.

The biggest failure in the many upgrades the Spitfire received was the initial attempt to arm it with 20mm cannon.[34] For years, the cannon-armed bomber-destroyer had been seen as the successor to the Spitfire. Now, with these designs still far from operational, the Spitfire would have to become its own successor. Integrating the Hispano 20mm cannon with the Spitfire's thin wing proved difficult. The 20mm-armed Spitfire IB, which entered production in 1939, never overcame the cannon's technical problems. These aircraft were ultimately withdrawn and replaced by standard Spitfire IAs.

By early June, the Spitfire Mark II – similar to the Mark I but with a more powerful Merlin XII and more armour – was finally in production at the shadow factory at Castle Bromwich. After the years of problems with starting Spitfire production, the factory's management had been taken over by Vickers, which also owned Supermarine, as part of a reorganisation that included the sacking of Sir Robert McLean, who had encouraged the initial Spitfire design. The new management addressed the chronic labour-management issues that had hindered production.[35] A third Rolls-Royce Merlin factory, near Glasgow, was approaching completion, but would not deliver its first engines until October, while an even larger factory on the banks of the Manchester Ship Canal, to be run by Ford, would not be ready until 1941. Rolls-Royce had opened negotiations for licensed production of the Merlin in the still-neutral US, but were finding that adapting the engine to US mass production standards would require substantial redesign. After Henry Ford refused to build engines for Britain, the licence went to Packard Motors in September 1940, but it would be years before any Merlins were made in the US.

Shortage of fighters was no longer the key weakness in Fighter Command. In 1940, Britain would produce 15,049 aircraft (and received many from the US) while Germany produced 10,247.[36] The Luftwaffe's numerical advantage was fading.

What was critical to the RAF was the shortage of trained fighter pilots. Everything depended on 3080 men, the aircrew of RAF Fighter Command, about the strength of a single infantry brigade. Losses over France and Dunkirk had been painful. In addition to those shot down, the RAF found out that a number of its fighter pilots, especially senior men, were too old or too fixed in the ways of peacetime flying in the biplane era. Many experienced pilots lacked air combat and gunnery skills or the aggressive instincts of a successful fighter pilot; the pre-war RAF had not inculcated these. They were eventually moved on to non-combat assignments, replaced by younger men.

The RAF cut back training to rush pilots to the squadrons. The time fighter pilots spent in the operational training units (OTUs), where they went after flight training to learn to fly Spitfires, was reduced to some twenty hours, including minimal training in gunnery and none in air combat tactics. The Fighter Command OTUs had been established in spring 1939. Flying Officer J.E. 'Johnnie' Johnson, an engineer before the war, went through Spitfire OTU: 'Although the instructors were good fellows, they were few and we were many and they seemed content to teach us to fly the Spitfire and not to fight it. We searched desperately for someone to tell us what to do and what not to do because this, we fully realized, would shortly mean the difference between life and death.'[37]

Tactical improvisation made some squadrons more effective than when they had fought over Dunkirk. They abandoned the pre-war tactics and started flying in pairs rather than threes.[38] 'Weavers', aircraft flying behind and above each squadron, weaving back and forth along its course looking for the enemy, were often added. Park provided guidance to 11 Group squadrons, but the judgement of each squadron's commanding officer decided the tactics. The skipper's influence and character was vital to the morale and effectiveness of their largely inexperienced pilots.

While the vast majority of Fighter Command's aircrew in 1940 were from the United Kingdom, RAF squadrons had recruited an increasing percentage of volunteers from the Commonwealth countries since the late 1930s. The RAF also started integrating pilots from occupied Europe. Poles, Czechoslovaks, Frenchmen and Belgians who could speak English, already the international language of aviation before the war, were quickly added to RAF squadrons. Soon, these air forces would have their own squadrons as part of the RAF. The first few US volunteers were already flying with Fighter Command. This was the start of a great transition: RAF Fighter Command was becoming a multinational fighting force.

Neither the Spitfire, Fighter Command, nor Britain itself had been ready for combat at the opening of war. Together, they all changed in the months that intervened before the opening of the decisive battles in August 1940, especially in the weeks after Dunkirk. They had seen what defeat would look like and what was required, if not to win the war, then to survive it.

Bf 109s versus the Luftwaffe

During the air fighting over Dunkirk, some Bf 109s found themselves in air combat *against* the Luftwaffe. Switzerland's Bf 109s were the first to see such action.[39] During the German invasion of France, Luftwaffe aircraft frequently penetrated Swiss airspace. Swiss Bf 109s intercepted them and, when they would not land, opened fire.

In the first battle, on 10 May, Swiss Bf 109s brought down a Do 17 bomber. These battles escalated until, on 1 June, a Swiss Bf 109E-1 shot down a He 111, killing the crew. This was followed by a pitched air battle, as a formation of thirty-six unescorted He 111 bombers penetrated Swiss airspace to bomb targets in France. The Swiss responded by scrambling twelve Bf 109E-1s. As a result of these initial clashes six He 111s were shot down or forced to land in Switzerland. One Bf 109E-1 had been shot down by the He 111s' gunners.

Tensions between Germany and Switzerland mounted. The German ambassador sent a memorandum to Berlin describing Switzerland as a 'huge armaments factory . . . working almost exclusively for France and England'. The Swiss prepared for invasion. But Göring, who saw the downed planes as a personal affront to *his* Luftwaffe, wanted, as over Dunkirk, to demonstrate its power for independent action. He ordered Bf 110C-equipped II/ZG 1 to teach the Swiss a lesson. On 4 June, a large formation of Bf 110s entered Swiss airspace. They attacked a Swiss biplane on border patrol. This provoked the reaction by Swiss Bf 109s Göring had wanted. In the battle, two He 111s, one Bf 110 and one Swiss Bf 109D were shot down.

On 8 June, after an angry exchange of diplomatic notes between the two countries, II/ZG 1 repeated their attack. This time, they caught and shot down a patrolling Swiss C-35 observation biplane. Fifteen Swiss Bf 109E-1s – Bf 109D models were withheld from combat after the loss on 4 June – intercepted twenty-eight Bf 110Cs, escorting He 111s. The Bf 110Cs formed defensive circles. The Swiss had no radar. Many of their Bf 109Es had been delivered without radio. Despite this, the Swiss were able to defeat the Luftwaffe forces, shooting down five Bf 110Cs in return for one Swiss Bf 109E damaged and forced to land.

Smarting from this defeat, the Germans turned to other ways to put the Swiss Bf 109s out of action. On 16 June, the Swiss arrested a group of saboteurs, armed with explosives, outside an airfield. Since 1 June, the Swiss had shot down eleven German aircraft against two of their own.

Hitler was furious at the use of Bf 109s to shoot down German planes. He had a message sent to the Swiss government that threatened invasion. Within a few days the Swiss had suspended border patrol flights. While they would still intercept overflights, they announced their aircraft would open fire only in self-defence. On 8 August, Switzerland agreed to curtail Allied access to its industrial production. Germany had succeeded in its object lesson, but for the Bf 109 and the Swiss Air Force, it remained a victory.

The Luftwaffe gets ready

Following their success against France, the Germans were confident of ultimate victory. Hitler and the German leadership were still committed to mobilising their economy, including the aircraft industry. Pre-war, they had purchased as many machine tools from the USA as their foreign exchange holdings, largely looted from Austria and Czechoslovakia, would allow. But the mobilisation of the aircraft industry was being totally mismanaged in 1940.[40]

Instead, they gave out rewards. Willy Messerschmitt was summoned to Berlin to receive Hitler's personal thanks. Göring was made the only *Reichsmarschall*. Milch, who had added to those he already held the post of Inspector General of Luftwaffe the previous year, was promoted to *Generalfeldmarschall*. Jeschonnek, the chief of staff, was promoted to *Generaloberst*, as was Udet, who also received the Knight's Cross. Galland, having demonstrated his skill as a fighter pilot by becoming one of the top-scoring aces of the French campaign, received promotion and caught the eye of the Luftwaffe command. He was given command of a *Gruppe* of JG 26, consisting of three *Staffeln*. The ground crews that had kept the Bf 109s in the air received Iron Crosses. But few Luftwaffe fighter pilots shared in the bounty of promotions. This had an importance beyond hurt egos. The German military traditionally exalted hierarchy. Few fighter pilots achieved positions working for the General Staff or had the rank and authority to enable them to stand up and contradict army and party leaders profoundly ignorant of aviation in general and fighters in particular.

Despite his new command responsibility, Galland still took the opportunity to fly, looking for combat, whenever he could. On one mission, Galland, who had had the sky-blue fuselage sides of his Bf 109E-3 camouflaged to be less conspicuous, heard a voice over his radio he recognised as Hauptmann Wilhelm Balthasar, with whom he had flown in Spain and during the French campaign. Galland heard Balthasar talking to his *Staffel*:

'Below us is a Hurricane. I will destroy it. Watch closely. I dive and approach from below.'

Galland listened intently to the running radio commentary Balthasar gave as he dived on the target that had appeared some 3000 feet below him. He admired his colleague's coolness in the attack and his effort to show his less expert wingmen how to do it, diving down in the Messerschmitt's signature slashing attack until it was in the blind spot behind and beneath the target's tail, then using the momentum from the dive to pull up into a climb, quickly closing to lethal range.

'My range is 500 metres, 300, 200. The fool is asleep. I close to 50 metres.'

Streams of tracer bullets shot past Galland's cockpit. He realised exactly who Balthasar's target was. Galland, already on the right radio frequency, shouted a warning. He racked his Bf 109E-3 around in immediate evasive action. The wing slats extended with their familiar loud clacking noise. In a tight turn, Galland showed his attackers the unmistakable Messerschmitt wing and its black cross markings.

Waggling his Bf 109E-3's wings as a recognition signal, Galland joined up with Balthasar, flying on his wing and grinning broadly at his old comrade. On landing, Balthasar had several bottles of champagne sent over to Galland. But few of the many friendly fire incidents on either side worked out so well. Luck and flying skill had saved Galland even in the gunsights of an ace pilot.[41]

The Bf 109, which had received the benefits of incremental improvements since 1936, had less need than the Spitfire for last-minute upgrades. The most important was retrofitting the Bf 109Es in France with the improved protection armour to the cockpit and fuel tank that was also fitted to new Bf 109E-4s coming off German production lines.

Bf 109 units were flying out of improvised airfields in northern France. In terms of serviceability – the percentage of aircraft that could be made ready to fly combat missions – this put them at a disadvantage compared to RAF Fighter Command, flying from their home bases. Serviceability ranged from about 65–80 per cent for the Germans to 80–90 per cent for the British. Oberst Fritz Löb, implementing one of Udet's rare practical ideas, commandeered a factory near Antwerp, Belgium, as the Erla VII aircraft overhaul facility, starting work before the end of June.[42]

The Battle of Britain, July–August 1940

With the surrender of France on 25 June, the Luftwaffe began preparing the air offensive against Britain. After success as part of Germany's effective capability for joint war-fighting in Europe, the Luftwaffe was going to have to defeat the RAF above Britain on its own.

With his earlier assumption that Britain would accept German terms fading, Hitler saw this battle as crucial to bringing about the negotiated peace he saw as taking Britain out of a war he had already effectively won. But, if Britain did not see reason, he set out his goal in his Führer War Directive 16, issued on 16 July 1940. 'As England, despite her hopeless situation, still shows no sign of willingness to come to terms, I have decided to prepare, and, if necessary, to carry out, a landing operation against her. The aim of this operation is to eliminate the English motherland as a base from which war against Germany can be continued and, if necessary, to occupy completely.' Three days later, he made a final appeal for peace to the British government.

Göring had savoured the triumph over France so long that he was shocked to find that his generals had not come up with a coherent plan to win the air war over Britain in the time permitted between the opening of the air offensive and when autumn weather would render an invasion impossible. He was also shocked to find that his combat units were still understrength and short of munitions and spares; he asked, 'Is *this* my Luftwaffe?'

The opening phase started on 10 July 1940 with German air attacks on British coastal convoys in the Channel. Dowding was urged by Churchill to commit his fighters to defend the convoys. Once again, limiting the number of fighters sent up to protect the convoys, Dowding held back his forces in order to safeguard his fighters against premature battle in a situation where German numbers and superior fighter tactics would give them an advantage. This was despite pressure from the Air Ministry, who told him to send up larger forces, and Churchill, who thought the convoys were useful 'bait' for the Luftwaffe.

But even if both sides held back from launching maximum efforts, the air battles over the Channel and southern England were intensive. More and more Bf 109 pilots received a demonstration of the Spitfire's superb manoeuvrability and the RAF's determination. They also found out how quickly their red 'fuel low' warning lights came on in the cockpit when in combat over the Channel. Many of their comrades were lost when trying to disengage from combat due to lack of fuel.

Others came down over England or the Channel from mechanical failure.

The RAF, for their part, learned how lethal were the Bf 109E's diving attacks, especially if they were able to attack the Spitfires while still climbing to altitude. The Luftwaffe, in turn, learned they had the advantage if they could catch the Spitfires lower down. The Bf 109E-3's DB 601A engine reached its critical altitude (the height where its supercharger is operating at full capacity and above which power will fall off rapidly, also known as full throttle height) at 14,765 feet, lower than the 18,500 feet of the Spitfire IA's Merlin III engine. The German engine's automatically variable speed supercharger (its gears changed performance with the air pressure) gave it an advantage equivalent to some 200 hp at low altitude.[43] Despite the Spitfire's excellent manoeuvrability, which allowed it initially to turn more sharply and tightly than the Bf 109, at low altitude the Bf 109 could sustain climbing turns that a Spitfire could not match.

Over Dunkirk, the RAF had been able to plan their own missions so that their planes could climb to operational altitude before going into battle. Now, with Luftwaffe fighters taking the offensive, they often did not have that option.

These opening attacks allowed Fighter Command to better understand German air operations and tactics. Radar and the ground control system, which had not had the fighter pilots' experience over Dunkirk, soon became combat veterans. Fighter Command was, for all its limitations, able to get ready to defeat an air offensive spearheaded by Bf 109s.

The battle opens

With Hitler's 'last appeal to reason' refused by the British, the tempo of German air operations increased. On 6 August, Göring told senior Luftwaffe leaders that the invasion would take place in the first two weeks of September. It was up to them to make it possible through a series of massive air attacks.

RAF Fighter Command was fortunate in that it was going into decisive battle flying both the Spitfire and the Hurricane. Not enough aircraft of any single design could have been produced to prevent the

Luftwaffe triumphing through sheer weight of numbers. The Hurricane, designed a year earlier than the Spitfire and using old-technology structural elements, had enabled the aircraft industry and the RAF alike to make the transition away from the biplane era during the Spitfire's delayed entry into production. In January 1940, it took 15,200 man-hours to build a Spitfire, 10,300 to build a Hurricane (compared to about 9000 for a Bf 109E).[44] The Spitfire prevented the Hurricane from being dominated by the Bf 109.

The RAF – except for Fighter Command – was still far from an effective fighting force. It had been less successful than the Luftwaffe in developing aircraft and tactics and late in starting substantial aircraft production. But the RAF, and particularly Fighter Command, had been better in building up the organisations and infrastructure needed to help the Spitfire win a protracted war in the air. Britain's integrated air defence system, the most effective air fighting force on either side, had been made possible by successful British investments including radar, intelligence (including the vital Ultra signal interception and decryption as well as photo-reconnaissance Spitfires), the sector stations and their plot rooms, the shadow factories (British aircraft output exceeded Germany's from 1940 onwards)[45] and training.

But it was in the human dimension that the British advantage was perhaps most profound. At the highest levels, the dysfunctional elements of the Nazi regime had been obscured by brilliant military success. Now, when they were forced to make strategic and operational decisions, Hitler's failures as a strategist and Göring's as a service chief would become all too apparent. Jeschonnek, the Luftwaffe's chief of staff, believed Hitler would once again produce an easy victory and declined to press for more resources and aircraft. Other senior officers implemented flawed plans without protest.

The British system, for all the years of hesitation and half-measures, now gave Churchill a capability for effective war-fighting greater than that of his opponent, for all Hitler's dictatorial powers. Having been First Lord of the Admiralty since the outbreak of the war and having been in the Cabinet in the Great War, Churchill brought personal experience of wartime leadership as well as an understanding of the aircraft and technology involved. A devoted supporter of ingenuity and invention,

Churchill's closest advisor was Dr Frederick 'Prof' Lindemann, a scientist who had been a RFC test pilot in the Great War.

This difference also applied to industry. There was no German equivalent, in 1940, to Lord Beaverbrook and the Ministry of Aircraft Production. That Spitfires had received more last-minute upgrades than Bf 109s in 1940 showed both how belated rearmament had been and how British science and industry were proving more responsive than their German counterparts.

The senior leaders at the RLM, such as Milch and Udet, and in German industry, like Willy Messerschmitt, would not be direct participants in the coming battle. Messerschmitt personally led an accelerated design effort for a massive front-loading glider, intended to carry heavy weapons for an airborne invasion of Britain, but this would not be ready until the following year. The vision of the RLM and industry alike was on upcoming aircraft and how they would be produced. With Germany poised for victory, immediate improvements to current designs were not a priority.

Of the men in uniform who would be making plans and giving orders for the attacks on Britain, no one at the top of the German command structure had approached Wever's sorely missed realism and drive. The Luftwaffe had competent senior commanders. While they had performed effectively in Poland and France, however, few understood the technological nature of modern war in the air and none of them had ever been faced with the task they now confronted: defeating a major power by air power alone, with little cooperation from the other German services. No German had the experience and authority of men like Dowding and Park, who had been instrumental in creating the fighters and forces they would now lead into battle, and had spent the last years of peace thinking and exercising about the task they now faced: defending Britain from air attack. While, before the war, both the Luftwaffe and the RAF had emphasised the bomber, the RAF fighters had benefited greatly from their high-level advocacy while, as Galland recalled years after the war, 'Hitler built first the air offensive but neglected the fighters.'[46]

The Luftwaffe did have an advantage in fighter leaders. While many of the senior commands were still held by undistinguished Great War veterans, those with recent combat experience were now refining tactics and leading missions. The RAF's Spitfire squadrons' combat experience had been largely limited to Dunkirk. But Galland, who had encountered them there, later recalled that he considered, 'at this time, the English fighter pilots were equal to our own', though German tactics were superior. All these men now looked ahead with little to guide them. Would the Luftwaffe be able to overcome the RAF as quickly and decisively as it had their Polish and French opponents?

6

The Battle of Britain

15 August 1940, 'Black Thursday'

The German bombers were coming. Air Vice Marshal Keith Park, who commanded RAF Fighter Command's 11 Group, responsible for the air defence of south-east England, saw all the signs.

At 11 a.m. on 15 August 1940,[1] he was not in the air but rather underground, in 11 Group's headquarters operations room at RAF Uxbridge. In one glance, he could assess the 'plot' table, a large map of England and northern France, gridded like a chessboard. At the same time that he received reports of enemy actions, the plot was updated to show Park and his staff the locations of all aircraft in the air in the vital sector that the group defended. One of the WAAF 'plotters' placed a coloured wooden block with identifying numbers over the Pas de Calais. This was the first indication of a German air attack coming across the English Channel. Seeing the numbers on the block, Park knew that the British radar network estimated the incoming formation as more than one hundred enemy aircraft, probably fighters escorting bombers.[2]

The plot (and the 11 Group operations room) was more than just a game board. It was a powerful weapon in its own right. Looking at the plot, the commander – Park – could make command decisions and, forwarded by controllers via telephone on the ground and wireless in the air, have them obeyed by men in aircraft within minutes. Looking at the plot, Park could see more than any squadron leader could see from the cockpit. He could watch the whole of the air battle over 11 Group. Making this advantage in situational awareness more important was that the Germans had no counterpart. Once their plans were made and their aircraft sent off on missions, the Luftwaffe's radar did not cover England, nor was there any way for those on the ground to know more than the men in the cockpits. While Luftwaffe intelligence monitored British transmissions (and knew they were directed from the ground), they were slow at producing useful electronic intelligence (ELINT).[3] The Luftwaffe could not change plans, order formations to alter course or avoid RAF interception, once their planes were in the air. Whatever the advantages or disadvantages of the Spitfire as compared to the Bf 109, Spitfires benefited greatly on 15 August from the situational awareness provided by the plot and its usefulness in enabling Park to give his orders.

Park, a cool, highly professional and much-decorated airman originally from New Zealand, had expected an attack since dawn, when the weather had started to clear into a fine, if cloudy, English summer day. Having himself been a fighter pilot since the Great War, Park knew the skies above England thoroughly. 'I never saw or heard him laugh. He was always so taut. I do not think he knew how to. But he knew all about fighters and fighter tactics,' recalled Group Captain Cecil 'Boy' Bouchier, who had flown with Park in the previous war and now commanded the vital sector station at RAF Hornchurch.[4]

While he did most of his fighting underground, wearing his RAF blue service dress tunic and necktie, Park took every opportunity to get into his white flying overalls, strap a steel helmet on top of his leather flying helmet and fly his personal Hurricane to the RAF fighter stations that were now the first line of Britain's defences. He liked to talk with the young fighter pilots on whom so much depended; he was a popular leader and his personal touch was widely appreciated.

The Luftwaffe offensive that Churchill had dubbed the 'Battle of Britain' had now entered a new and more intense phase. The Germans launched heavy attacks on British airfields, aircraft factories and the all-important radar stations.

The German build-up for the invasion of England accelerated. Their soldiers in France and Belgium were issued life jackets for the Channel crossing to England. The Channel ports were crammed with invasion barges and forward airfields filled up with transport aircraft for para-troops. The German General Staff was planning Operation Sea Lion, their code-name for the invasion, with the same Prussian efficiency that had won such stunning victories over Poland and France. Even though some of the Nazi and military leadership felt Hitler was still looking towards achieving a political settlement, he was serious enough to give the preparations for invasion high priority.

The British monitored all this with Ultra, their top-secret commu-nications interception and decrypting operation. If Hitler was only bluffing about invading England, nobody told his generals. Today's attack could clear the way for the invasion. Both sides understood that the Germans had to win air superiority over the beaches in Kent and Sussex before launching their invasion.

Two days before, on 13 August, Park's command had intercepted a series of mass air attacks on southern England. The Germans had lost forty-six aircraft for only thirteen RAF fighters shot down in return. Of the forty-seven British aircraft destroyed on the ground, only one was a fighter. Fighter Command had proven resilient, but now it faced the full power of the Luftwaffe.

The RAF was much stronger than it had been only a few months earlier. Nevertheless, the British were still outnumbered in fighters and – crucially – in experienced fighter pilots. On the morning of 15 August, most of 11 Group's squadrons were at airfields built before the war. They had been incorporated into Britain's integrated air defence system in the wake of the 1938 Munich crisis. The most important were 11 Group's seven sector stations, major airfields that also contained the all-important sector operations rooms and their landlines to Group and Fighter Command headquarters. At these stations, Park's orders were turned into the radio messages that directed fighters in the air to the enemy.

The big German raid Park was watching take shape over the Pas de Calais was the first attack 11 Group would face, but it was the second major German raid of the day. The onslaught had begun with a series of intense attacks launched across the North Sea from bases in Denmark and Norway. This was far beyond the range of single-engine fighters.

Two raids with a total of seventy-two Heinkel He 111 and sixty Junkers Ju 88 bombers escorted by Messerschmitt Bf 110 twin-engine fighter aircraft crossed the North Sea that day.

The Luftwaffe had some 335 Bf 110s operational on the morning of 15 August. Much was expected from the Bf 110, especially in the bomber escort mission, even though, to an even greater extent than the Bf 109, it needed to fight at high speed for its greatest tactical advantage or use the element of surprise to bring its powerful nose-mounted armament to bear.

Flying Officer Hugh 'Cocky' Dundas – nicknamed from his imagined resemblance to a bantam rooster – flying Spitfires with 616 Squadron, was one of the RAF fighter pilots who intercepted the North Sea raids that day. Dundas had been a pilot before the war, having joined the Auxiliary Air Force straight from school in emulation of his older brother Johnnie. His brother was already running up a score of German aircraft shot down. Cocky had himself seen combat over Dunkirk and had acquired enough Spitfire time to appreciate its performance, while he had the flying experience and skill – both in short supply in Fighter Command in the summer of 1940 – to fly to the limits of its performance.

Before the war, RAF regulars disparaged the Auxiliary Air Force as the 'millionaires' mob', where most of the pilots paid for their own training. To reassure them, regulations required the Auxiliaries to wear two brass letter 'A's on their tunics, showing that regulars need not pay them too much attention. Cocky fitted the stereotype. Coming from a wealthy family, he kept a retriever, which specialised in slobbering on senior officers, and took every opportunity to live well, and expensively, in austere wartime Britain.

When 616 Squadron was scrambled that day, Cocky jumped at the chance finally to get at the enemy.

I set a course and rammed the throttle 'through the gate' [breaking the aluminium wire], to get the maximum power output, permissible for only a very limited time. Some of the others were ahead of me, some behind. We did not bother to wait for each other or try to form up into flights and sections. We raced individually across the coast and out to sea. About fifteen miles east of Bridlington I saw them, to the left front, and slightly below – the thin, pencil shapes of German twin engine bombers, flying in loose, straggling, scattered formation toward the coast.[5]

Park was cheered to learn that the German attacks across the North Sea were intercepted by the RAF's 13 Group, defending the north of England, and had been repulsed with the loss of fifteen bombers and seven Bf 110s, while no RAF fighters were lost. The German bombers' defensive armament, mainly of manually operated single-mount 7.92mm machine guns, was no match for the eight-gun battery of attacking Spitfires and Hurricanes. Adolf Galland realised, after several other defeats of Bf 110s such as this one, 'they often needed our 109s to escort them, as they were easy targets'. The Germans had only managed to bomb one target, an RAF bomber airfield. Even then, they had been unable to inflict decisive damage.

With the events further north earlier that morning in mind, Park had no doubt he was seeing the opening move of another mass air assault on southern England. He responded with an action of his own. Park ordered the Hurricanes of 501 Squadron, on alert at Hawkinge airfield in Kent, and the Spitfires of 54 Squadron at Hornchurch, east of London, to intercept. These units were able to take off within five minutes.

The two squadrons had been waiting at the alert status the RAF defined as 'at readiness'. The pilots were awaiting the order to scramble – make an immediate take-off – at the dispersal sites, a short sprint from where their fighters were parked.

Dispersal sites were often around the borders of the airfield, reducing vulnerability to air attack, yet near enough to the end of the runway that pilots could quickly taxi into position for take-off. It was a far cry from the peacetime practice of having all a unit's fighters lined up neatly on an airfield.

The highest level of alert was two-minute readiness, or 'stand-by'. This was cockpit alert, meaning the pilots were to wait strapped in. This situation could not be sustained for too long before fatigue and foreboding took the edge off the airmen's alertness. Other of Park's squadrons were at 'available' status, requiring fifteen minutes to get airborne, or 'released', meaning that they would not be called upon for a specified period.

Park could tell the status of each of his squadrons from the large 'tote' status display positioned over the plotting table at Uxbridge. On the tote, under each sector station and airfield, 11 Group's fighter squadrons were listed by number, type of fighter and home base, next to a column of lights which changed colour to show the units' status. Fighter Command had some 570 Spitfires and Hawker Hurricanes (plus a further 235 available as replacements), a few dozen twin-engine Bristol Blenheims, gun turret-armed Boulton Paul Defiants and even a few biplane Gloster Gladiators operational that day.[6] While most were under Park's command, the rest were split between 10 (covering southern England west of London), 12 (covering from the north of London to the Midlands) and 13 (covering northern England and Scotland) Groups.

As Park made his response to the Germans' opening move, he watched as the lights on the tote board under 501 and 54 Squadrons noiselessly changed from the green representing 'at readiness' to the amber of 'detailed to raid', which meant their aircraft were making their take-off rolls and climbing to altitude, following the ground controller's instructions to intercept the enemy. Within minutes, blocks representing those squadrons were placed on the plot table, their progress tracked by radio triangulation. By then, the squadrons had started to climb to altitude over their bases to intercept the incoming raid. The radar only looked over the coast – it did not cover inland – and could not tell the difference between incoming bombers and fighter sweeps. For that the Observer Corps on the ground and a few individual spotter Spitfires provided voice reports. The British systematically monitored German radio transmissions, not just for intelligence but also to provide Fighter Command with information about the Germans' intentions and attacks in progress.[7]

The Luftwaffe improvises

While the British spent the morning of 15 August waiting, and then responding to the attacks, the Germans were frantically improvising. The Luftwaffe had expected bad weather on 15 August. Its units based in

France had called off any offensive operations against England. Many senior commanders were summoned to fly to a conference with Göring at his estate at Karinhall near Berlin. He demanded reasons for their failure to defeat the RAF two days before. To make a confusing situation even more so, the pre-planned air attacks across the North Sea against the north of England went ahead, uncoordinated with simultaneous strikes from the south, as had been originally intended.

About 0700 hours, the fog and low cloud over France started to clear. The Luftwaffe's *Obersts* and *Majors*, left in charge while their commanding generals were busy being insulted by Göring, decided to launch a major air attack on their own initiative. At Luftwaffe headquarters throughout northern France, Belgium and the Netherlands, urgent telephone conversations and clattering teletypes issued orders as to how many planes each unit was to put into the air, where they would rendezvous, and where they would fly to. But the hasty planning that morning, as throughout the Battle of Britain, was undercut by the Luftwaffe's lack of actionable intelligence. They did not know what the radar system was or how it operated, nor yet where Spitfires were based, and thought the RAF was so weak in fighter numbers that a few weeks' hard fighting would lead to collapse.

On the airfields, ground crews in black overalls fuelled and armed aircraft as quickly as possible. Most German fighter units' workshops and equipment were in improvised field conditions, in farm buildings or under canvas, making the hasty start of another mission after a week of maximum-effort attacks even more difficult. At their quarters, pilots who had hoped for a chance to sleep late were awakened and pulled on their flying clothes.

That morning, of the some 800 Bf 109s available to the Luftwaffe, over two-thirds were operational on the German side of the Channel and the North Sea. The largest concentrations were at improvised grass fields in France's Pas de Calais and Normandy regions, although a lucky few operated from pre-war civil airports such as Abbeville and Le Touquet. Despite the alert and the frantic activity at each airfield, putting Bf 109s into the air on the morning of 15 August was a challenging prospect. Many aircraft had been damaged or required maintenance after the previous week of intense air attacks against England. The Luftwaffe had only had a few weeks to recover from its costly victories in the French campaign. The pilots were tired. At the end of a supply line stretching back to Germany, spare parts and consumable items had not yet been replaced by a German economy that, though mobilised, was proving inefficient.

The Luftwaffe fighter pilots' pre-mission briefings were given at about 0800. Customarily, the briefings were given outside by the *Gruppenkommandeur* (commanding officer of a *Gruppe* of three or more *Staffeln*).[8] He would announce information the pilots needed to fly the mission, the area, time and kinds of missions and formations to be flown, and time of take-off. If flying an escort mission, the briefing would stress measures for coordination with bombers; what altitude and speed they would fly. The bombers' HF radios could not communicate with the VHF radios in the Bf 109s. They relied on wing-waggling signals. A rapid weaving from side to side by the fighters was something the bomber crews did not want to see: it signified that they were short on fuel and turning back to base, leaving the bombers to defend themselves against the RAF alone. These steps were compressed or abbreviated due to the improvised nature of 15 August's mission.

One of the *Gruppenkommandeure* giving hurried briefings to his pilots that morning was Adolf Galland. His first encounters over Dunkirk had left him with great respect for the Spitfire, which he saw as a superb defensive fighter because of its excellent low-speed manoeuvrability. When, after the height of the Battle of Britain, Göring asked Galland what fighters he would like, he famously asked for Spitfires – not because he preferred them to his beloved Bf 109, but to drive home the idea that by being tied to escorting bombers, the Germans were failing to use the Bf 109's best qualities for cut-and-slash offensive tactics. 'The 109, with its high wing loading, needs to keep its speed up, the Spitfire, with lower wing loading, can slow down more,' Galland later explained.

Neither Göring, with his ignorance of technology, nor the senior Luftwaffe leaders, focused on the bombers that were their main offensive weapon, realised that by determining that the Bf 109s would have to stay within 100 to 200 metres of the bombers and so fight at the German bomber's cruising altitude of about 15,000 feet, he was committing them to decisive combat at an altitude that was above the critical altitude of their own engines but, at the same time, below the higher critical altitude of the British Merlin engines. The Bf 109s would fight at a disadvantage at that altitude.

The Bf 109 needed to keep its speed up for manoeuvrability. Its structure was stressed so that it could make its tightest possible instantaneous turn,[9] imposing a load of 8 g. However, if a Bf 109E-3 tried such a steep and violent turn at any speed less than 312 mph, it would stall (for a Spitfire and Hurricane, the comparable figures were 284 and 290 mph, respectively).[10] A Bf 109 trying to stay with bombers or conserve fuel would fly at about 225–233 mph.

The Bf 109's best manoeuvring speed – the speed at which it could change direction most quickly and have the most compact turn radius – was considerably higher than its economical cruising speed, where it burned the least fuel. If surprised by a Spitfire, Bf 109s at cruise speed were at a disadvantage until they could accelerate, by throttling up their engines – which would take precious seconds – or, more swiftly, by diving away. This would leave the bombers vulnerable to attackers. Reflecting this, Unteroffizer Willi Ghesla of I/JG 53 spoke for most Bf 109 pilots. 'We much preferred the *freie Jagd* (fighter sweep),' he said. 'Close escort was unpleasant and we were always in an unfavourable position when attacked by the RAF.'[11]

The bomber crews wanted to see Bf 109s flying close escort. These airmen, considered more important to the Luftwaffe than the fighter pilots, now realised that their pre-war assumptions about being able to operate without an escort, or rely on sweeps ahead of the formations by the twin-engine Bf 110 fighters, were wrong. But by 15 August, it was not only the bombers that were wary of the RAF. 'Over the coast we were usually attacked by Spitfires coming by above and out of the sun – they were already waiting for us,' wrote Leutnant Erich Bodendiek, a Bf 109 pilot in II/JG 53.[12] 'We didn't know at the beginning that they were guided by radar.'

To Galland, defensive close-escort tactics were anathema to what he saw as the primary mission of the fighter pilot: 'to attack, to track, to hunt and destroy the enemy, only in this way can the eager and skilful fighter pilot display his ability. Tie him to a narrow and confined task, rob him of his initiative, and you take away from him the best and most valuable qualities he possesses: aggressive spirit, joy of action and the passion of the hunter.'[13] Galland was no ordinary fighter pilot. His desire to increase his personal score of enemy aircraft shot down was only the most visible manifestation of his total commitment to seek out and engage the enemy, and the Bf 109 made all this possible. Galland was one with his chosen fighter in the summer of 1940.

Galland had taken command of the III *Jagd Gruppe* (JGr) of *Jagdgeschwader* 26 (III/JG 26) as the Germans completed their victory in France. With nineteen air-to-air victories, he was Germany's second-highest-scoring air ace, trailing only his friend and rival Major 'Vati' Mölders, from whom Galland acknowledged he learned a lot, and whose tactical skills he greatly respected.[14] Galland brought a potent mix of personal charisma, charm, self-regard and cunning to his new command, backed up by the first-rate flying skills that had served him so well at the controls of Bf 109s in the French campaign. Now, he had enough rank and authority to start doing things his way, not like his non-flying Luftwaffe superiors. One of his first acts in his new command was to order his 'personal' Bf 109 to be modified with the addition not only of his personal insignia of an armed Mickey Mouse but also of an in-cockpit cigar lighter and ashtray, regulations against smoking while flying be damned.

The pilots of III/JG 26 were soon won over by the keen-eyed hunter with the big moustache, slicked-back hair and omnipresent (twenty a day) big cigars.[15] They respected his tactical instincts, honed in previous campaigns. They appreciated his policy of giving them one day off after eight of operations. 'The Casanovas arrived the following day with weak knees, the day after the leave only easy missions were flown,' Galland recalled.[16]

At the briefing, Galland told his pilots that they would be leading the Luftwaffe's assault on southern England that day and that he in turn would be leading them. Galland may have shaken his head at the higher headquarters' lack of organisation, but he was always ready to fly or head out for a hunt. His optimism and aggressiveness spread to the rest of III/JG 26.

The fighting over Dunkirk and battles with the RAF since then had revealed that the British were a different type of opponent than they had encountered before. The German fliers knew better than their own high command, with its inaccurate intelligence reports, that the Spitfire was the first enemy fighter over which the Bf 109 did not have a clear-cut performance advantage. While Germany's military depended on conscription, as did those of all Europe's major combatants, fighter pilots had volunteered for their jobs and had competed to be accepted for long and difficult training. The men in the Bf 109s' cockpits wanted to fly and fight. They believed in the inevitability of ultimate victory for Germany. Officers were losing little sleep over the personal oaths they had sworn to Adolf Hitler. But, since Dunkirk, it was evident the RAF would not be defeated the way the Polish and French air arms had been. The confidence remained alongside increasing acceptance of a hard fight ahead.

After listening to the *Gruppenkommandeur*, with the pilots gathered around him at the dispersal site, the commander of each twelve-fighter *Staffel* assigned the pilots to their aircraft – pilots would fly their 'own' Messerschmitt as much as possible – and designated who would lead each four-aircraft *Schwarm*. The *Schwarm* formation was the classic 'finger four' (with the fighters' positions resembling the parallel four fingers of a hand). Two pairs of fighters would search and fight together, providing mutual support. The two-aircraft *Rotte* had been the indivisible unit of German single-engine fighter tactics since the Spanish Civil War, with a leader, who would shoot down the enemy, and a wingman, who would protect the leader. A lone fighter was a liability.

Heinz 'Pritzl' Bär – the nickname was from a brand of chocolate bars he favoured[17] – was a *Feldwebel* (sergeant) leading a four-fighter *Schwarm* of I/JG 51, one of the units that would be part of the Luftwaffe's air offensive.[18] He would be flying escort to the Do 17 bombers of KG 3. While any bomber escort mission would tie down his four Bf 109s, the Do 17s at least cruised faster than the He 111s or, worst of all, the painfully slow Ju 87 Stuka dive bombers. At twenty-seven, Bär was older and had more flying experience than most of the men flying Bf 109s that day. A natural, instinctive fighter pilot with an impulsive and flamboyant character, he was a farmer's son who spoke with a strong Saxon accent that evoked an old rural Germany. His leadership skills were not those of a Prussian officer but of the toughest and best fighter, and no one would have dreamed of disappointing him. His fellow pilots even listened to the stories he told of how he and his brothers had once painted a farmer's goat to look like the devil. But what impressed them most was his deflection shooting skill. He was able to hit near-impossible targets with short bursts of fire. A short, compact man with an intense gaze who lacked Galland's charm, Bär shared his exceptional flying skills. He had been credited with three aerial victories over France.

Take-off

The Bf 109s' ground crews worked on their aircraft while the fighter pilots received their briefing. Time permitting, after the crew had finished, each Bf 109 pilot and its crew chief would carry out a full walk-around inspection. They pushed control surfaces to ensure nothing impeded them; they unscrewed fuel tank covers and checked the fuel, both for contamination and, important in light of their impending flight over water, to ensure that the tanks were full. German aircraft had a unique smell, a mixture of the aluminium alloy, oils and lubricants. D.H. 'Nobby' Clarke, who test flew captured German planes, called it 'the smell of death'.

After the briefings and inspections, with their take-off time looming closer, Galland and his comrades squeezed into the tiny cockpits of their Bf 109s, which sat noses pointing skywards at a steep angle because of their short tailwheels. The cockpits had to be entered standing on the left wing root; the hinge was on the right. Grasping the windscreen handgrip, each pilot had to duck under the open canopy and its attached slab of armour plate before easing down on the deep seat, legs almost horizontal as he attached the stirrups of the aluminium rudder pedals, the control joystick upright between his legs. The cockpits were so cramped that freedom of movement was minimal. RAF trials on captured Bf 109s found that this limited the amount of force the pilot could apply by up to 50 per cent. Once strapped in their narrow, semi-reclining, low-slung seats, German pilots found it hard to move, even to look over their shoulders. The small bulletproof windscreen and heavy canopy frame provided an uncurved, undistorted view but also restricted forward vision, like thick-rimmed spectacles.

Over his flight suit and parachute each pilot wore or attached a life vest, a one-man life raft (inflated by a compressed air bottle), a flare pistol and ammunition, sea dye markers, a knife and a survival kit with 'a packet of Schoka-Kola, Pervitine tablets, and many other things including one small bottle of good French cognac' according to Unteroffizer Rudolf 'Rudi' Rothenfelder of III/JG 2.[19] While bulky, this equipment was often envied by RAF fighter pilots, who had only their own inflatable 'Mae West' yellow life vests (named from a fancied resemblance to the buxom actress), worn over their flight clothes, for survival if shot down over the Channel.

Cockpit checks were straightforward. As with all German aircraft, the instruments were in metric units. The instruments were simple: absent were an artificial horizon (providing a reference to the pilot in clouds) and a radio compass; the Bf 109E was a blue-sky plane. It lacked even a manifold pressure gauge; the supercharger operation was automatic. The fuel–air mixture control and the throttle were positioned to come easily to a pilot's left hand. The throttle, unlike those of British aircraft, was pulled back to accelerate. A clock-like instrument showed the pitch of the constant-speed propeller; the pilot had to set the pitch himself, unlike those of their British counterparts, where pitch changed automatically.

The briefings specified the exact minute to start engines, an effort to conserve fuel. Each pilot signalled for a ground crewman to close and latch the canopy. Then, with a final check of the instruments – switch and magnetos on, propeller pitch set, fuel–air mixture full rich – each pilot pushed the primer button on the instrument panel, cracked the throttle open and signalled the ground crew to stand clear, then pushed the starter button on the instrument panel as the engine started to turn over. The DB 601 should burst into life, with a short burst of flame and black exhaust. If it did not, the ground crew would have to use a crank to hand-start the engine's inertia starter. Throttled up to check the oil pressure and coolant temperature and then throttled back to taxiing speed, the big Daimler engine emitted a loud continuous growl, a steel predator.

After waiting a minute for their engines to run up, the Bf 109s taxied slowly and ungracefully from their dispersal sites. Never mind the impending mission, German pilots had enough to worry about just trying to take off safely. Not all did. Hauptmann Douglas Pitcairn, the

Luftwaffe fighter leader with Scottish ancestors who had led a Bf 109 *Staffel* in the Spanish Civil War, had his flying career ended by injuries from a collision on take-off from a crowded French airstrip.

The Bf 109 was not built for the ground; some two thousand were written off in landing or ground accidents during the war. Its landing gear was tall (in order to permit use of a large propeller for maximum thrust) and narrow. On the ground, the engine cowling blocked forward vision, and pilots could see nothing in front of them but a huge engine and propeller. The hinged cockpit canopy, which Ernst Udet had found too confining before the first Bf 109 had ever flown, had to be shut before taxiing, further reducing visibility. On the ground, Bf 109Es moved in a snaking S–curve, or relied on a ground crewman as a guide.

The stiff undercarriage meant that the pilot felt every bump in the grass taxiway. Turns had to be made gradually; the Bf 109E was prone to ground-looping, skidding while moving that would often damage the undercarriage or wing tips. Worse still, the Bf 109Es' brakes tended to 'grab', causing numerous accidents. Summer rains softened the ground on many improvised airfields, and many a pilot came to grief, tipping up his Bf 109E in a 'headstand' as the fighter nosed over on its propeller. The damage was rarely serious, but it put the aircraft out of action until it could be repaired.

In position for take-off, the pilot would check the two magnetos to make sure the ignition system was working. Then the flaps and elevator trim controls, vertical wheels on the left side of the cockpit, would be adjusted for take-off. Bf 109Es would use positive elevator trim and twenty degrees of flap for take-off. Even with the radiator flaps open for maximum cooling, the engine would overheat unless throttled back or in the air. It was time to go, one way or the other.

Usually a *Schwarm* of four Bf 109Es would take off together at the leader's hand signal. Each pilot moved the lever back to full throttle, left leg extended on the rudder pedal to counteract torque as the fighter rolled and, as speed built up and the Bf 109E quickly accelerated, bumped over the ground, the tail rising so that the pilot could see straight ahead. This made the Bf 109E's small rudder vital for keeping the plane pointed in the right direction, once it was moving fast enough to 'bite'.

The stiff undercarriage imposed a slight lateral rocking as the Bf 109E built up speed over the grass runway. The control stick was pushed hard forward at first to get the tail up. The pilot felt the pressure in the fingers of the hand on the control stick – the other on the throttle – as the ailerons started to lift and then, with a glance at the airspeed indicator, gently eased back on the stick so the fighter would climb. Then the main wheels came off the grass and were retracted, along with the flaps, by the pilot's left hand on the controls. The Bf 109E was now in its element. A pilot flying a trimmed-out Bf 109E always had to use the rudder gently to compensate for torque forces in flight due to the powerful engine, the small size of the rudder itself, and the lack of a rudder trim tab. In the air, the electric undercarriage retraction brought the wheels up into the wells with a loud double-clunk noise. Quick movement with the left hand raised the flaps and brought the trim down. Then, adjusting the throttle and propeller pitch and partially closing the radiator flaps, he was ready to climb to altitude.

Taking off next to him on the morning of 15 August, Galland's wingman was Oberleutnant Joachim Müncheberg, adjutant of III/JG 26. He had flown with Galland since the ace had taken over his new command and together they made a formidable team, demonstrated by the number of RAF aircraft Galland had destroyed. Tall, quiet and highly professional, Müncheberg's personality contrasted with that of Galland. Having served in the Luftwaffe since it was a covert force, Müncheberg had the rank and experience to lead a Bf 109 formation himself, which would give him the chance to improve his own victory score. Instead, he preferred to fly as Galland's wingman.

Galland and his pilots set up a quick scan on the Bf 109's cockpit instruments as they climbed. Survival required that each should keep looking outside the cockpit for most of the mission. Anything that brought the pilot's attention inside the cockpit, such as changing propeller pitch, had to be done quickly. Flying in formation allowed bombers' defensive gunners to cover each other in mutual defence, creating overlapping fields of fire to concentrate against an attack by fighters from any angle. For fighters, formation was about attack as well as defence; the key to being a successful fighter pilot included retaining constant all-round visibility, to see the enemy before they saw you – or, at least, before they could launch a lethal attack of their own.

III/JG 26's Bf 109s climbed to their operational altitude of 18,000 feet as top cover. They formed up with the planes they were to escort, Ju 87 Stuka dive bombers heavily laden with bombs slung under their fuselages and wings, lumbering to altitude over French airfields; this took almost half an hour before they could head for England.[20]

The Germans' inability to supplement the Bf 109's limited internal fuel capacity with an external fuel drop tank that could be jettisoned before combat was a severe operational limitation. Bf 109s could fight over Kent and Sussex, but could not take the battle to the airspace over the RAF sector stations. For a Bf 109, a one-hour mission was long. A mission lasting an hour and a half was an in-flight emergency; many Bf 109s landed with the red 'fuel low' light in the cockpit burning bright. Willy Messerschmitt's gliding background gave the Bf 109E design an exceptional 13:1 glide ratio, travelling thirteen feet forward for every foot of altitude it lost. Gliding home saved many Bf 109 pilots.[21]

Others found themselves in more difficulty. 'Pritzl' Bär, having ended another mission shot down by a Spitfire, was one of many pilots who ditched an out-of-fuel Bf 109. He was twice picked up by a He 59 seaplane of the Luftwaffe's efficient air–sea rescue service. Many German fighter pilots were less lucky still. Even on a warm day, the English Channel will kill a floating fighter pilot in about four hours.

The attack on Hawkinge

That morning, Galland and the Bf 109s of III/JG 26 were flying top cover as a detached escort for forty Ju 87 Stuka dive bombers, heading to attack two RAF forward airfields, just across the Channel, at Hawkinge and Lympne in Kent. Bf 109 units at lower altitude were throttled back as close escort to the slow-flying Stukas. It was a large formation, with the top cover up to a mile above the bombers in what the RAF called a 'Balbo' after the 1930s Italian flier famous for leading masses of aircraft. The Luftwaffe, in a Wagnerian reference, called such formations a 'Valhalla'.

The Bf 109 pilots' need to stay close to the bombers put them at a disadvantage. Their most fuel-efficient cruising speed was higher than that of the bombers, heavily loaded with fuel and ordnance, so to keep pace the fighters weaved back and forth over the bombers, burning precious fuel. Some Bf 109s cruised with their flaps partially extended in order to reduce speed, a technique that was still harder on fuel consumption. In the very best conditions, a Bf 109 would have just ten minutes over London for a combat mission that would last for an hour to an hour and a half, and close escort could erode this further. And even on short-range missions over Kent, such as this one, Bf 109 pilots knew that throttling back made them vulnerable to fighter attack.

Surprise, pilot skill and effective tactics were usually the decisive elements in air combat, but once in close combat, what a fighter pilot needed most from his plane was speed and manoeuvrability. Speed gave the initiative in combat: the ability to pursue and engage an enemy or, conversely, escape when conditions were unfavourable. Manoeuvrability – how rapidly it was possible to change the direction the fighter's nose was pointing, either horizontally or vertically – enabled either attack or escape. A fighter's fixed forward-firing armament could only hit targets it was pointing at. Pointing your guns at the enemy while preventing his from pointing at you was the basic objective of this deadly competition.

The Bf 109's automatic leading-edge slats popped out of the wing when the Bf 109 was flown at slow speed – making a clanging noise so loud that pilots could hear it above the roar of the engine. The slats increased lift and drag but were not for the faint of heart. Oberleutnant Erwin Leykauf said, 'For us, the more experienced pilots, real manoeuvring only started when the slats were out.'[22] Less experienced pilots could put a Bf 109 into a stall and spin when the slats deployed on one wing and not the other in a tight turn. When slats deployed unevenly in tight turns, they would disrupt the airflow, causing the ailerons to 'snatch' enough to shake a Bf 109, spoiling the pilot's aim. Similarly, an experienced pilot could take advantage of the Bf 109E's manual propeller pitch control to maximise performance in combat better than any automatic governor; inexperienced pilots tended to set the pitch before fighting and forget about it.

Even with their advantage of an integrated air defence system in which the pilots were directed by command centres based on information from radar and ground observers, only a third of British fighter sorties managed to contact the enemy. The Bf 109s, once they left the ground, had only their pilots' eyes and their on-board radios. The odds of the Germans catching RAF fighters were even smaller. It bears repeating that their success – and survival – depended on seeing the enemy first. What made the situation survivable was the advantage of numbers. On the offensive, Bf 109s were able to climb to altitude before crossing the British coast. But this had not availed 'Rudi' Rothenfelder four days previously, on 11 August. 'Our *Rotte* had been jumped by six Spitfires who had pounced on us out of the sun. I shouted a warning over the radio but my wingman failed to react,' he said. 'A Spitfire bore in on my tail, preparing to attack. I threw the throttle wide open, pulling up the nose of my machine. My adversary shot past me while I flung my machine down into a steep dive, pulling out at 6,000 meters.'[23]

'When we took off, we were immediately detected by English radar,' Galland later recalled. That morning Galland's III/JG 26 and the heavily escorted Stukas approached the target, Hawkinge airfield, at about 11.40. Ten Hurricanes of 501 Squadron and twelve Spitfires of 54 Squadron, led by the quiet and determined Squadron Leader James 'Prof' Leathart – nicknamed for his engineering degree – were ready. The RAF fighters had climbed to altitude and were in position to attack. As the Stukas started dive-bombing the airfield, the RAF fighters dived down to attack them and their Bf 109 close escort. This gave Galland and his top cover the advantage of height. Instinctively, Galland looked around, a sweep of the head to check the location of both his fighters and any additional enemy, while with a finger he flicked his gun's safety switch to 'fire' and gave III/JG 26 the order to attack.[24]

'*Horrido!*' This was the Luftwaffe's fighter pilots' call, which originated on the hunting field. Someone had seen the enemy. Whoever gave it quickly had to add the callsign of the formation of aircraft he was talking to – otherwise Luftwaffe planes all over southern England might be looking for a non-existent threat – and the number of enemy planes, type and altitude, with location being given in terms of either a ground reference point or in relation to the spotting aircraft. But the pilot making the radio call was pumping pure adrenaline and excitement often trumped accuracy.

The call over the radio brought the eyes of each pilot to the location reported, but even then it took precious seconds to spot the enemy themselves. Galland had to act immediately; the rest of the top cover Bf 109s would follow. When Galland saw the Spitfires attacking the Stukas, his countermove was to launch the Bf 109 pilots' preferred response: a diving attack. Bf 109s accelerated quickly in a dive.

'The first rule of all air combat is to see the opponent first,' Galland said. If they could seize the initiative, Bf 109 pilots would throw the fight into the vertical, climbing and diving rather than trying to turn horizontally with Spitfires. The Bf 109 had a faster rate of climb. In a dive, the Bf 109's pilot could push the nose down and the DB 601 engine's fuel injector would keep delivering fuel to the engine. The Spitfire's Merlin engine had a conventional float carburettor, so when its pilots shoved the control stick forward, they effectively cut off the flow of fuel to the engine. A Spitfire would have to roll inverted before diving, which gave the Bf 109 a head start when attempting to dive away. However, even with this advantage, many Bf 109 pilots would roll inverted anyway. An inverted aeroplane does not have to 'push' against the lift from its wings. Lift was not keeping the inverted aeroplane up but pushing it down, the way the pilot wanted to go. An inverted pilot would also have a better view of the airspace. Superior diving acceleration gave the Bf 109 an 'escape corridor' in its air battles with the Spitfire.

Galland had hoped to surprise the British fighters. But 'Prof' Leathart had anticipated an attack by the Germans' top cover. Leathart and half of 54 Squadron had followed 501 Squadron's Hurricanes against the Stukas and their Bf 109 close escort. He left two three-Spitfire sections up high to guard against a German diving attack. Galland and Müncheberg led the top cover of III/JG 26 as they dived on these Spitfires, which turned to face the attack. From above, the high-altitude layer of this battle appeared as a microcosm of the Battle of Britain as a whole: six Spitfires turning at bay against several times their number of Bf 109s. At lower altitude, Leathart and five other Spitfires attacked the close escort of Bf 109s, which turned to meet them, interposing themselves between the British fighters and the Stukas.

Head-on attacks were often lethal against the slower German bombers, which had demonstrated an ability to absorb up to 200 .303 bullets and still fly home. The eight .303 machine guns of a Spitfire could shatter the nose of a Heinkel, which had nothing but thin aircraft aluminium and Plexiglas between the crew and the bullets and often only a single 7.92mm machine gun shooting back.

In head-on attacks between fighters, both would be moving so fast that they were in range and then overshoot each other so quickly that few pilots were able to land a killing blow. Although Spitfires and Bf 109s differed in armament, they were alike in that their weapons were fixed and forward firing. To hit, the entire fighter was pointed at the enemy.

Galland and Müncheberg did not hit any of the Spitfires in their initial attack. To shoot down a fighter whose pilot has seen its attacker is very difficult, a feat most fighter pilots never achieve. Experienced Bf 109 pilots would not even try to manoeuvre with a Spitfire that had seen them. It was wiser to climb or, more often, dive away, disengage, and come back either to re-engage the Spitfire from a blind spot or find a British pilot who had lost mutual support and was alone, or was concentrating so hard on attacking another German aircraft he wouldn't see the proverbial 'Hun in the Sun'.

But Galland was not an average pilot. Keeping his eyes glued to the six Spitfires, the ace realised as he shot past that he had two advantages over his opponents. He understood that he and his wingman had the momentum from their diving attack to carry them up into a zoom climb, keeping the fight in the vertical. He also saw that the two sections of three Spitfires had, in meeting his diving attack, now become split into six separate fighters.

Two elements of three Spitfires was something Galland would have been wary of; six separate Spitfires was an opportunity for victory. What made Galland exceptional was his ability not just to fly, but to size up a tactical situation instantly and keep it in his head as he concentrated on shooting down the enemy: what a later generation of fighter pilots would call 'situational awareness'. Galland may have been unaware of the term, but his accounts of the air battles he fought show that he instinctively used the concept. In the Second World War, 'situational awareness' was provided by visual acuity, experience and messages from others; in any event it was vital for survival, let alone success.[25] Most Spitfire squadrons in the Battle of Britain took off and fought in 'vics' of three aircraft. Vics would often fracture into three lone Spitfires in combat, as these two sections of 54 Squadron had just done.

Galland's next move was to turn around and renew his attack on the Spitfires he and Müncheberg had just overshot, before they could join up and renew the attack on the two Bf 109s. The two German fighters turned vertically in an outside loop, and were now back pointing at the scattered Spitfires with the advantage of height regained. Galland had used the Bf 109's performance and his own skill to keep the initiative. Focusing on a Spitfire diving away in a right turn, he launched another diving attack, aiming to get on the tail of this Spitfire.

Galland followed the Spitfire down, keeping the target in his sights. This particular target was likely the Spitfire flown by Sergeant Wojciech Klozinski, a former bomber pilot and flight instructor in the Polish Air Force. He had joined 54 Squadron two weeks before and had claimed a victory over a Bf 109 since then.

The manoeuvring became more intense. From the ground, it would have been hard to pick out the Spitfire in a diving spiral and the two Bf 109s behind it as being locked in a life and death pursuit. Other fighters from the high battle over Hawkinge were diving down as well, trading altitude for airspeed, trying to escape attacks and position themselves for a renewed assault. They may have crossed paths with Galland's and Müncheberg's pursuit of Klozinski. Galland could keep his eyes focused on Klozinski. Müncheberg would come to his defence or would warn him to break off the pursuit if another Spitfire came to Klozinski's aid. But at that moment, with Sergeant Klozinski fighting for his life against Galland and Müncheberg, his commanding officer 'Prof' Leathart was in no position to come to his aid. Leathart, along with the other six Spitfires of 54 Squadron, had his hands full with the Stukas and their Bf 109 close escort in a separate, low-altitude battle over Hawkinge airfield. He was in the thick of the fighting but scored no kills.

As their Bf 109s turned tightly to pursue the Spitfire, Galland and Müncheberg felt – and heard – their automatic slats bang open on the leading edge of each wing. The control sticks shook, but the two Bf 109s, diving, traded altitude for airspeed and avoided stalling. They could also lower their flaps to ten degrees, to give their turning aircraft more lift at the expense of more drag, something the Spitfire, whose flaps only opened to the full forty-degree position, could not do. Because of the Bf 109's heavy controls and the high g-force turns, Galland and Müncheberg were using all their strength to manoeuvre, their bodies pressed against the sides of the tiny cockpits for leverage. Experienced pilots, they could feel the control stick and rudder pedals responding the way they wanted, as they twisted closer and closer to the Spitfire.

The diving, spiralling pursuit of Klozinski by Galland and Müncheberg put severe stress on the structure of the aircraft and the pilots alike. A successful fighter pilot is usually able to think in all three dimensions, making the best decisions and implementing them near-instantaneously. But success demands great physical strength too. Even a superbly responsive fighter like the Spitfire had heavy control forces at high speeds. Jeffrey Quill, the Supermarine test pilot, flying a Spitfire, had to 'struggle with both hands on the stick at well over 400 miles per hour and sweating and swearing profusely'.[26] Fighter pilots fought and died sitting down, but they were no chairborne warriors.

Tight turns and combat manoeuvres imposed forces of up to eight times normal gravity (8 g) on the aircraft – and their pilots. Each g force multiplied the effective weight of the pilot's own limbs, so that moving the controls quickly became even more tiring. Many pilots were unable to parachute from spinning aircraft; the g forces pinned them to their seats. 'Pulling' g forces in a tight turn led to pilots blacking out, losing peripheral and then direct vision before becoming unconscious, as the blood drained away from the head. They would be unable to see the enemy or sustain the tightest turn. Douglas Bader, with his two artificial legs, was said to turn tighter than any other pilot because his blood had less distance to flow. Galland now in effect imitated him, raising his legs and leaning forward to counteract the g forces that were bringing him to the edge of losing consciousness.

Turning inside its path was one way that an attacker could shoot down an enemy fighter whose pilot was aware he was under attack. Making a turn with a smaller radius than an opposing aircraft eventually allowed the attacking pilot to 'pull deflection' – to point the nose of the aircraft ahead of where the enemy fighter was turning, to where it would be a few seconds later when the bullets arrived at the aim point.

A fighter being manoeuvred at its performance limits was always on the verge of stalling and going into a spin, making it first a target and then liable to crash. George Brown had done this over Rotterdam on 13 May. 'Prof' Leathart, making a tight turn with a Spitfire on the verge of a stall, felt 'that lovely feeling of the gluey controls and the target being slowly hauled into the sights'. Leathart was able not only to control his Spitfire, but to use it as an effective gun platform against a manoeuvring target. It required rare skill to keep a fighter shuddering on the brink of a stall while aiming through a reflector gunsight, allowing for the deflection needed to hit a manoeuvring target. As Leathart said, 'Then thumb down on the trigger again and the smooth shuddering of the machine as the eight-gun blast let go.'[27] All the while he had to remain aware of other aircraft nearby to ensure no one was about to make him an easy kill.

Galland was as concerned with scoring more kills as the average fighter pilot was about doing his job and staying alive. He stayed with Klozinski in pursuit of the Spitfire as it spiralled down towards the green fields of Kent, looming larger every second, the two Bf 109s twisting their way towards firing position.

Galland claimed that he never had a Spitfire turn inside him in a Bf 109, despite the Spitfire having the smaller turning circle.[28] His skill as a pilot allowed him to wring every bit of possible performance from his Bf 109, turning just on the brink of a stall. Galland, who had been flying Bf 109s for years, was able to out-turn Klozinski, who had only been flying Spitfires for a few weeks. He managed to turn inside the Spitfire and was now in firing position, with Müncheberg hanging on, turning alongside him, his head spinning around to search for any Spitfires that might be coming to join the fight to even the odds against Galland.

Galland saw the Spitfire's wings inside the illuminated outer circle of his gunsight. Galland's Revi optical reflector gunsight projected a red dot on a flat transparent panel behind the windscreen, above the instrument panel, inside the illuminated circles that provided range indication when the target's wingspan filled the circle at firing range. A Spitfire's wingspan filled the circle of the Revi gunsight at 100 metres range, lethal against a manoeuvring fighter. Yet any pilot who spent too much time peering through the gunsight was likely to make himself vulnerable. A fighter pilot needed to acquire the target, focus and shoot quickly without losing overall situational awareness.

Galland was running out of altitude. He had to pull up, but he could not do so suddenly. The Bf 109's ailerons had less effect at high speeds. Galland had to make his first burst count or the Spitfire would be able to run for home at treetop height. The Spitfire was turning tightly. Galland would have none of the advantages of attacking an unsuspecting target from directly to its rear. He had to calculate his aiming point ahead of the Spitfire by eye and judgement. Galland knew how to judge deflection, to lead the target, to focus on it, aware that his wingman would warn him of any threat. The Bf 109, under his controls, was transformed from a flying machine into a firing platform.

Galland had two triggers, one for synchronised machine guns and one for cannon, on the top of his control stick. Until the guns were armed in flight on each mission, the triggers remained collapsed against the control column. Now, they were ready for his gentle squeeze. This was his first shot of the day, one that had to count. Galland, the expert hunter of birds and aeroplanes, knew skilful aiming required less firing.

Following the red pyrotechnic paths of his tracer ammunition, Galland saw his bullets hit the Spitfire's fuselage, moving forward as the Bf 109 slightly overhauled its target, first hitting near the roundels and then moving forward to the engine exhausts. The Spitfire went down. Galland saw no need for a second firing pass. Klozinski was wounded. He managed to belly-land his Spitfire and ended the day in hospital. He was not to return to duty, as a ground instructor, for over two years.

Galland's battle with Klozinski had been less than two minutes of pure adrenaline-charged action. Now, he and Müncheberg pulled up at about 3000 feet, amid the Stukas that had finished their dive-bombing attacks on Hawkinge. Galland had so fully concentrated on Klozinski during the spiralling pursuit that it was hard for him to have a sense of the direction of the other battles above, below and around him. But observers on Hawkinge airfield – those who were not taking cover from the Stukas – would have seen a blue sky full of many individual battles, with groups of one, two or three fighters manoeuvring.

To any such observers, the 'high' battle, which pitted only a few

RAF fighters against the much larger force of the bulk of III/JG 26 and the rest of the top cover, would have appeared as a large number of specks, with the identity of Spitfire, Hurricane and Bf 109 indistinct as they rolled, twisted and turned. Unless someone had kept their eyes focused on one fighter throughout, they would not have made sense of the manoeuvres. Witnesses remembered the intricate patterns left by the white contrails – the streaks of frozen water crystals from engine exhaust, depending on air temperature and winds aloft – that marked the track of each fighter, turning and weaving like strands in a tapestry.

To those same observers, the low battle would have been impossible to ignore. The Stukas attacked the airfield in near-vertical dives, pulling up at low altitude, barely missing the explosions of their own bombs on the target.

By the time Galland was able to take in the situation, the Stukas were heading for home. Gaps in their formation showed three had been shot down by RAF fighters. Nonetheless the Stuka attack on Hawkinge was a victory for Galland and the other escorting Bf 109s, for without their action, the slow, ungainly Stukas would likely have been massacred. And, even more importantly, smoke clouds rising from Hawkinge showed Galland that their bombing had been accurate.

Galland called his fighters on the radio to break off action and rejoin the formation to cover the withdrawal of the Stukas. Once the Stukas were on their way home, he led III/JG 26 back up to 18,000 feet and started looking for RAF fighters. He saw a Spitfire heading home and made a diving attack. This may have been Sergeant Nigel Lawrence of 54 Squadron, who had attacked the Stukas at low altitude over Hawkinge. He parachuted from his Spitfire. Pulling up from this attack, Galland saw another Spitfire, turning to get behind one of his unit's Bf 109s. He was able to turn in behind it and open fire. The Spitfire broke away, apparently damaged but still flying. Galland was too low on fuel to pursue. He led his fighters back across the Channel to their base.

For all its intensity, the air battle over Hawkinge did not lead to mass casualties. Of the dozens of individual battles that made up the larger action, the vast majority ended with no one being shot down, confirming the larger truth of fighter-to-fighter combat: only when the target was unaware, or, as with Galland, the pursuer had the time and the skill to manoeuvre into a position where it did not matter that the target was aware, was it highly lethal. In this hectic fight, the RAF had lost two Spitfires and two Hurricanes; the Germans, in addition to the three Stukas, had lost two Bf 109s. While the Stukas had inflicted considerable destruction on Hawkinge airfield, it was not one of the sector stations at the heart of Fighter Command. The damage did not reduce the RAF's ability to intercept the next wave of raiders that were now crossing the Channel. In fact, the most serious damage the Stukas had inflicted was inadvertent: they had severed the power cables to three British radar stations that ran by the airfield. Yet, as happened throughout the Battle of Britain, the Germans' intelligence left them blind. The Luftwaffe had had no idea about the cables. Unaware that the radar stations had been put out of action, they were unable to take advantage of their success. Galland recalled, 'We learned very soon that English radar was just perfect, but we neglected to attack the system.'[29]

The cutting edge of the fighters

The Spitfire and the Bf 109, during the Battle of Britain, differed in their armament. The Spitfire's eight .303 Browning machine guns were less powerful than the Bf 109's two 20mm FF cannon and two 7.92mm machine guns. Before the war, the RAF had considered the Browning capable of hitting aircraft at ranges as long as 600 yards. Now, in the summer of 1940, even the range of 200 or 250 yards at which most RAF squadrons' guns were harmonised after their combat experience in France and over Dunkirk proved to be too long.

Widespread retrofitting of additional armour protection and self-sealing fuel tanks to fighters and bombers alike reduced the effectiveness of the Brownings (as well as the Bf 109's 7.92mm guns). Many German aircraft made it home during the battle perforated by .303 bullets that had failed to hit a vital spot. It required the explosive power of the 20mm shells to give a pilot high confidence of bringing down a target. Nevertheless, to those hit by them, the destructive force of the Spitfire's machine guns was real enough. Leutnant Albert Striberny, of I/LG 2 (*Lehr* – demonstration – *Geschwader* 2), once said, 'I heard the sound as if one throws

peas against a metal sheet and my cockpit filled with dark smoke.'[30] But
the fact that Striberny survived was evidence of how important it had been
to add effective armour protection for the Bf 109 pilot's back in the weeks
before the Battle of Britain opened.

The Luftwaffe strikes – afternoon of 15 August

As the day continued, more German attacks targeted RAF bases. Many
of these missions were against targets in the south-east corner of
England, covered by the extensive fighter sweeps that the Bf 109 pilots
did so well. Ominously, the RAF was unable to do much about them.
Their fighters were kept at arm's length by the powerful Bf 109 formations. By mid-afternoon, it appeared that the RAF had lost control
of the sky over much of Kent and Sussex, where the Germans were
expected to try to invade in the coming weeks. The poor weather always
to be expected at some point in an English summer was Fighter
Command's most powerful ally in 1940, often providing a respite when
the German air offensive had gathered momentum. Yet many days, like
this one, had a clear sky made for contrails at the altitudes where the
Luftwaffe flew, the light blue arcing upwards until it started to darken at
the highest altitude. Park and 11 Group were being stretched to their
limits.

As Galland and III/JG 26 rearmed for another mission, the Luftwaffe's
improvised planning was making ready two series of coordinated raids,
one against targets in Kent and the other against targets to the west of
London, in Hampshire and Devon. They would hit their targets in early
evening, taking advantage of the long-lasting August daylight. Before
then, at about 3 p.m, a high-speed low-altitude raid with Bf 109s escorting bomb-carrying Bf 110s sped across the Thames Estuary. They
attacked Martlesham Heath airfield in Suffolk, inadvertently taking
advantage of the gaps in British radar coverage created by the Hawkinge
attack in the morning.

The first of the large evening raids, formed up over Normandy, hit
its targets in the west of England between 5.30 and 5.50. Bombers
with Bf 110 escort fought their way through to attack airfields at
Middle Wallop and Worthy Down while Stukas hit the Portland naval
base.

The other evening raid was gathering over France. Galland and III/JG 26 were back in the air, again providing top cover; 190 Bf 109s would escort 88 Dornier Do 17 bombers to targets in Kent. The other two *Gruppen* of JG 26 flew a fighter sweep in advance of the main force.

The huge formation built up like a thundercloud over northern France. At 6 p.m., it moved across the Channel. While it did so, the Germans mounted another series of smaller attacks on airfields south of London, using small groups of Bf 110s and Do 17s, coming in low and fast.

By the time the block representing this raid was being pushed across the English Channel on the plot table at Uxbridge, Park had precious few aircraft with which to stop it. Few of the lights on the tote board showed squadrons at 'available'. Most were rearming and refuelling after the battles earlier in the day, and he knew their pilots were exhausted. Nevertheless, Park ordered four fighter squadrons to take off and engage this massive raid. The sector station at Biggin Hill diverted four squadrons already in the air away from what now appeared diversionary raids. But as each squadron, independently, attacked the mass formation, it was swatted away by the Bf 109 escort. Galland, ordered to stay with the bombers, was unable to add to his morning's score. But the Dorniers made it through to their targets with only two bombers lost to the RAF, more a successful juggernaut than a hard-fought battle. The formation split up. Some Dorniers hit an aircraft factory in Rochester, disrupting production of the RAF's four-engine bomber, the Short Stirling, for four months. Other bombers struck RAF Eastchurch on the Isle of Sheppey in the Thames Estuary, a Training Command airfield where a dozen Spitfires had been temporarily based that morning. Only one was caught on the ground as German bombs devastated the airfield. 'Jack' Carpenter, Peggy Carpenter's father, helped fight the fires. Later, when asked about the Battle of Britain, what he remembered best was how tired everyone was, all the time.

As the mass attack withdrew, the low–flying Bf 110 fighter-bombers and Do 17s struck, but against the wrong airfields and not the crucial sector stations: Croydon instead of Kenley and West Malling instead of Biggin Hill. The attackers fought their way home as Park sent fresh squadrons, rearmed after the earlier attack, against them. The Germans again suffered severe losses. The Bf 110 fighter-bomber specialists lost seven. The vital sector stations had escaped damage.

German formations returned home with little cause for triumph. They had inflicted painful blows on several airfields and an aircraft factory, but the cost was prohibitive. The Germans had lost fifty-five aircraft in the air, and many of the returning bombers came back with damage. The defeat of the raids across the North Sea early in the day forced the Norway- and Denmark-based units of the Luftwaffe effectively out of the daylight battle.

The day's events also showed the Luftwaffe leaders – if not Göring – that the Luftwaffe could not use all its bombers over England. It could only use as many as could be effectively escorted by Bf 109s. Three Bf 109s were required to escort a single Stuka dive bomber effectively. This led to the Stukas' withdrawal from combat over England.

Despite the Luftwaffe's claims, they had been able to shoot down only thirty-four RAF fighters. The Luftwaffe was soon calling 15 August *Schwarze Donnerstag*, 'Black Thursday'.

Just after 7 p.m., Galland, who had returned to base after the successful top cover of the Do 17s' strike on Rochester and Eastchurch, quickly rearmed. He and Müncheberg took off on their third mission of the day. They did not have far to go to find combat; it came to them in the fading daylight at around 7.30, directly over Calais–Merck airfield.

One of the Bf 109s escorting the low-level airfield attacks had been chased across the Channel by a particularly determined Spitfire. The pursuer was Flight Lieutenant Al Deere of 54 Squadron, who had fought the Stukas over Hawkinge that morning. Deere had opened fire at long range and the Bf 109 had dived down to escape from 5000 feet. Deere had won the Distinguished Flying Cross (DFC) for heroism over Dunkirk. Like Galland, he had an aggressive desire to shoot down enemy aircraft that, in these days, meant he lived for air combat. That was what brought him, alone, low on fuel, into the midst of hundreds of Bf 109s.

Deere had barely enough fuel to make it back to England when Galland and Müncheberg came to the rescue of the fleeing Bf 109. Confronted by two fresh Bf 109s with full fuel tanks, Deere had no option but to break off and run for home, with Galland and Müncheberg in hot pursuit.

This time, Galland and Müncheberg split up, one on each side of Deere, and accelerated after him. 'Down came the first one to the attack, around went my Spitfire in a vicious turn in his direction causing him to break without firing,' Deere later recalled. 'In came number two, around the other way I went and he too broke without firing. And so it went on.'[31]

Galland put the aiming point of his Revi reflector sight in front of Deere's fleeing Spitfire. The skilled hunter raked it with his 7.92mm machine guns, shattering the instrument panel, riddling the Merlin engine's oil tank so that the windscreen was coated black. Other bullets thudded against the armour plate behind the back of Deere's seat. Deere could no longer see in front of him or break into each attack, but he used his rudder to skid, trying to evade the Germans' fire.

The result was a high-stakes air race with Deere in the lead. Leading the two Bf 109s in a low-altitude chase across the English Channel, Deere, in the gathering darkness, crossed the English coast over the white cliffs of Dover at about 7.45, his crippled Spitfire trailing black and white smoke.

Deere's engine quit. Using his remaining forward momentum, he pulled the crippled Spitfire up to 1500 feet, jettisoned the shattered cockpit canopy, opened the side half-door, unstrapped himself and rolled inverted. Rather than falling free, as he had expected, he was hung up. His seat parachute pack had caught on part of the mangled cockpit.

Deere's Spitfire was now in a vertical dive. With a final effort, he separated himself at the last instant. He pulled the parachute's ripcord. Just above the ground, it successfully opened with a gentle tug. He landed in a field near where his burning Spitfire had embedded itself, Merlin first, deep into the chalk soil. It was one of the five times he escaped from a destroyed aircraft during the Battle of Britain. Along with his flying skill and aggressive hunting, Deere shared, with Galland and 'Pritzl' Bär, extraordinary luck.

Having hit their target, Galland and Müncheberg turned back for France in the gathering darkness, landing at the end of a day already part of history. Not for the Luftwaffe but for Galland, with three air-to-air victories claimed, it had been a good day.

7

'Battle of Britain Day'

15 September 1940

Shortly after dawn on 8 September, Keith Park slowly flew his Hurricane down the River Thames through spirals of smoke. Below him, London burned. Smoke and flames rose hundreds of feet into the air from warehouses, docks and residential neighbourhoods. Exhausted firemen fought fires for a second successive day while crowds of refugees fled burned-out areas. And yet, looking down from the cockpit at the devastation, Park was thankful: 'It was burning all down the River [Thames]. But I looked down and said "thank God for that", because I realized that the methodical Germans had at last changed their attack from my vital aerodromes to the cities.'[1]

From 8 August until 7 September, the Luftwaffe had hammered the RAF's airfields. Their campaign was scarcely checked by the setbacks of 'Black Thursday' on 15 August. In the last ten days of August alone, RAF Fighter Command lost some 126 fighter pilots, 14 per cent of those available, 60 per cent of them experienced and thus irreplaceable.[2] New RAF fighter pilots were no longer being produced quickly enough to replace losses; those arriving at squadrons were often rushed through training and so at a disadvantage against their experienced Luftwaffe enemies. Squadrons sent to 11 Group were decimated and exhausted before the squadrons they had replaced were rested and reinforced on airfields out of range of Bf 109s. By

6 September, no fresh RAF squadrons were available to commit to 11 Group.

Some of the secondary airfields that the Luftwaffe's bombers attacked, like Manston and Eastchurch, were so badly damaged that 11 Group stopped forward-deploying fighters to them. Most that had been attacked, like the vital sector station at Biggin Hill on the direct air route to London, continued to be operational despite intensive bombing. Bomb craters in the runways were quickly filled in and Biggin Hill's all-important operations room, which directed fighters in the air, left its bombed-out building and set up in a butcher's shop in a nearby village that still had two working telephone lines. But the damage still told. On 5 September, Park had reported to Dowding, 'The absence of many telephone lines, the use of scratch equipment in emergency operations rooms, and the general dislocation of ground organization was seriously felt in the handling of squadrons.'[3]

But the weakness of Luftwaffe intelligence had undercut their offensive operations. The Germans were unable to distinguish airfields vital to the British defence from those that could be easily replaced. The factories the Germans attacked were not the ones producing fighters or Merlin engines. Nor were the vital radar stations bombed. The Germans did not realise that their efforts were misdirected; their poor intelligence reported that RAF Fighter Command had been effectively defeated.

Meanwhile, the German pre-invasion build-up continued. At a conference held on 14 September at his headquarters, Hitler announced that naval preparations for invasion were complete and a successful invasion would be the quickest way for Germany to win the war. Hitler saw the Luftwaffe offensive against Britain was succeeding, but air superiority had not yet been achieved. He would personally review the situation on 17 September, with 27 September or 8 October as likely invasion dates.[4]

Hitler's orders reflected the German high command's confidence in their inevitable success, as yet untempered by the reality their pilots were experiencing on a daily basis, that the RAF remained unbeaten and was inflicting painful losses on the attackers. Yet RAF Fighter Command, weakened by the attrition in aircraft and especially in experienced pilots, looked with unease at the opening weeks of September, when the weather in England is often at its best. That, they predicted, would be when the Germans would launch their invasion of England.

But the course of the battle changed. Massed raids on the civilian population, expected before the war, had not yet materialised. Army Generaloberst Alfred Jodl, the chief of the operations staff of the OKW (Wehrmacht Supreme Command) had in June 1940 prepared a memorandum for Hitler that terror attacks would be required to break the morale of the British population. But Hitler had not agreed; so far German day bombing attacks, like the British night attacks on German targets, had tried to hit at least nominally military targets. As a result, Hitler was enraged by a British bombing attack on Berlin on the night of 28/29 August, retaliation for the unintentional bombing of central London by a number of lost German bombers on the night of 24/25 August.

Hitler decided that the only way to win the war against Britain was to shift the German daylight air attacks on to London. He had previously given orders to accelerate invasion preparations, with more barges towed to the Channel ports. The objective was to force Britain to ask for a negotiated peace. He gave notice of his new objective in a screaming speech in the Berlin Sportspalast on 4 September; he announced the Luftwaffe would bomb British cities off the map, although the bombers would still be targeted on nominally 'military' targets, such as railway stations.

On 7 September, the Germans started the daylight bombing of London. Göring even came to visit the Luftwaffe's forward airfields to see the attack launched. The first day's attack surprised the British, who expected a renewed attack on their airfields. Park held back the fighters from intercepting the raids targeting London on 7 September, thinking it a diversion. Most squadrons scrambled too late, after the Germans had bombed the capital. The first wave of bombers had hit around 1700 hours, flying up the Thames with strong fighter escort, targeting Woolwich Arsenal, power stations and docks but hitting many residential areas with high explosive and incendiary bombs. A second wave of about 150 bombers hit the same targets at twilight, about 8.10 p.m., and added to the fires. More bombers attacked through the night.

The Germans repeatedly attacked London in the days following 7 September, but weather limited the size and scope of these attacks on 8–10 September, then grounded the attackers completely from 11 to 14 September. The Luftwaffe planned to follow up these raids with their most massive attack in over a month on 15 September, targeting strategic objectives such as transport lines and docks. In practice, the lack of accuracy even in daylight bombing meant that the Luftwaffe was going to try to do to London what it had already done to Warsaw and Rotterdam: level large urban areas.

Park knew the attacks were coming. Ultra had decrypted Göring's order not long after the Germans received it themselves. Fighter Command had made use of the days since 7 September to prepare. Fresh squadrons had been brought into 11 Group from the north. Fighter Command allowed the transfer of experienced pilots from squadrons in the north to those in the front line in the south. Fighter Command had nineteen Spitfire squadrons operational on 15 September, seven of them part of 11 Group. Park issued new tactical instructions. The German high-altitude escorts would be engaged by only some of the Spitfire squadrons. The remaining Spitfires and all the Hurricane squadrons would concentrate on defeating the bombers. Squadrons would operate in pairs, usually one of Spitfires and one of Hurricanes.

With no signs of a mass raid as dawn broke at 6.34 on 15 September, Park had time for breakfast with his wife in their house in RAF Uxbridge's married quarters, a short walk from the operations room. She reminded him he had forgotten her birthday. Park, surprised, apologised until she told him she could ask for no better gift than a large bag of German attackers.[5] He arrived in the operations room in time to order one squadron at each of 11 Group's seven sector stations to 'readiness' alert status from 0700 hours. Standing patrols of RAF fighters took off. But throughout the early morning, only single German reconnaissance aircraft penetrated British airspace, the lone petrels giving indication of the coming storm.

Fighter Command – 15 September
Most RAF fighter pilots had been awakened before dawn. Officers were greeted by an airman with a cup of tea or coffee; non-commissioned

officers by a form they were to sign, showing that if they rolled over and went back to sleep it was their own fault. Washed, shaved (stubble interfered with the oxygen masks) and dressed, they went to their dispersal sites, near their aircraft or a quick lorry ride away.

They kept their flying clothes on or near at hand: leather fleece-lined Irvine jackets, the pullovers – either RAF-issue 'frock, white' or knitted for them – that they relied on to keep them warm at high altitude, padded leather flight helmets (with built-in oxygen mask and radio microphone and earphones), yellow 1932 temperate model 'Mae West' inflatable life jackets, and seat-type parachutes. Goggles were supposed to be worn at all times in flight, but many pilots reserved them for landing, otherwise preferring to risk their eyes rather than impair their vision. Pilots who could get them wore white naval socks under their fleece-lined flying boots. Some pilots, finding the jackets and pullovers confined strenuous action, flew in shirtsleeves or overalls regardless of the cold sky that awaited them, colder by 2° C for every thousand feet above sea level. The cold, along with the passive solar heating, made pilots simultaneously sweat and freeze.

But, to begin, they simply waited. Many dispersal sites had chairs outside, where the pilots would await the telephone call that would launch them into battle. The morning of 15 September was warm enough that some tried to read outside or throw a ball around. Smoking and cards offered diversions. Others quietly enjoyed the late summer day. The casual outdoor furniture and the attempts at relaxation contrasted with the anticipation.

Some RAF pilots, like Douglas Bader and Al Deere, shared Galland's love of the chase and desire to improve his score of enemy kills; that was what they lived for, all else was but waiting. For such men, their score was no game-playing, it was evidence of their skill in destroying the enemy and keeping themselves alive. Increasing the score became a near-obsession with some. As long as they were still scoring, they were still alive. Others, such as many of the increasing number of Polish, Czechoslovak and other foreign fighter pilots in RAF squadrons, felt a grimmer desire: retribution for the loss of their homes and families. Most of the pilots were quietly aware that, soon, that day, they would likely be both the hunters and the hunted. They resolved not to let their comrades down.

Squadron Leader Brian 'Sandy' Lane of 19 Squadron waited at a dispersal site at RAF Fowlmere, near Duxford. He was twenty-three years old, and had left a job as an industrial supervisor to join the RAF. Now he had been commanding the squadron for ten days, following extensive combat since Dunkirk. 'Calm and reassuring' in the words of one 19 Squadron pilot, he had been awarded the DFC and was an ace, with five confirmed victories. The squadron, having turned in its unreliable cannon-armed Spitfires, was now on the fringes of the battle as part of 12 Group.

Newly commissioned Pilot Officer George 'Ben' Bennions, of 41 Squadron, was among those waiting near his Spitfire at RAF Hornchurch, still operational despite German attacks. He had started his RAF career as an apprentice at the technical training school at Halton and then served as an engine fitter before pilot training. One of Fighter Command's most successful Spitfire pilots, he had shot down a Bf 110 and one of the German bombers that had tried to attack the north of England on 15 August, while the remainder of his eleven victories were all Bf 109s or Bf 110s.

At 10.50 British radar started picking up German formations climbing to altitude over France. Fighter Command began bringing squadrons to higher levels of alert. At 10.55, Park brought all his squadrons to 'readiness' and warned 12 Group to the north of London and 10 Group to the west that a large-scale attack was coming.

At 11.03 Park made his first move. He ordered Spitfires of 72 Squadron to scramble from Biggin Hill to intercept the anticipated raid over the coast of Kent, between Canterbury and Dungeness. By 11.08, within five minutes of receiving the order to scramble, the Spitfires were climbing. Other squadrons followed them into the air. At Uxbridge, the lights of squadron after squadron changed on the tote board.

At 11.25 Park called Fighter Command headquarters at Bentley Priory and spoke to Air Marshal Sir Hugh Dowding. Park requested that 12 Group cover some of 11 Group's airfields. He also requested that 12 Group mass a 'big wing' of five squadrons together over London, something that the forceful and outspoken Douglas Bader, then commanding 242 Squadron at RAF Duxford in 12 Group, and 12 Group's Air Officer Commanding, Air Vice Marshal Trafford Leigh-Mallory, had advocated for weeks. But they had never managed to bring a 'big wing' into battle successfully. It had taken too long – twenty-five minutes – to form up five fighting squadrons, circling as they climbed, over RAF Hornchurch at 20,000 feet. By the time they could be sent into action as a fighting force the Germans had often dropped their bombs and were on the way home. 11 Group usually received ten to fifteen minutes' warning of incoming raids before they crossed the coast; obviously not enough time to form up such a wing.

For each squadron, the summons came in the form of a telephone call to a dispersal site or, if already at cockpit readiness, a radio message.

'Scramble!'

At the order for immediate take-off, waiting pilots tossed aside books, grabbed parachutes and flying clothes, bolted from their deck-chairs and ran to their fighters. The uncertainties of anticipation were pushed aside by the action of take-off. 'When you were running to your machine, the adrenaline took over,' Sergeant Frank Usmar of 504 Squadron recalled.[6]

Those who had not been wearing seat-type parachutes would hastily step into the straps, inserting their metal ends into the circular quick-release buckle with a metallic click.

Getting into a Spitfire required the orchestrated cooperation of pilot and ground crew. The hinged half-panel door in the left-hand side of the fuselage under the cockpit made it easier to manage the ballet of a scramble. The pilot stood on the left wing root and started by putting his right foot on a step set into the left side of the fuselage, then brought up his left leg on to the wing root, enabling him to straddle the cock-pit with his other leg and lower his parachute into the metal bucket seat, where it functioned as a cushion. Usually a ground crewman standing on the wing root helped with the strapping in, pulling the Sutton harness straps tight, securing him firmly in the seat, then closing the hinged panel. Pilot and plane were now one, attached. They would likely, man and machine, return or perish together.

The petrol flow was started by the pilot flicking a switch on the instrument panel. Releasing the manual primer, he gave it a few quick pumps, spraying fuel into the Merlin engine's waiting cylinders. Then, the ignition switch was flicked on.

The next step was to ensure the Spitfire's brakes were locked and, with a thumbs-up signal to the ground crew to stay clear of the turning propeller, to start the engine, pushing the starter button on the instrument panel with a gloved finger.

In a scramble, the Merlin engines of Spitfire IIs could be started with a Coffman cartridge. An explosive about the size of a shotgun shell, it would detonate when the pilot turned on the electrical power. A flight of Spitfires starting their engines at the same time provided a display of gunshot explosions. The gas produced would turn over the engine, creating a bright flash out of the exhaust pipes when it fired, then leaving a black plume of smoke over each Spitfire. More black smoke belched from the triple-tier exhaust as the Merlin coughed and started. For Spitfire Is' less dramatic take-offs, an accumulator trolley, a cart full of batteries and a fire extinguisher were wheeled from Spitfire to Spitfire, starting each in turn. The Merlin's power vibrated through the control stick, rudder pedals and the metal seat.

Communication was by radio, or by hand-and-arms signals, because of the noise from the Merlin. In the heat of battle, the engine would drown out any sound, even the fighters' own guns. It was said that if a pilot could actually hear the noise of an exploding anti-aircraft shell, he was going down.

The pilot checked the oxygen flow to the soft kid mask attached to the flying helmet to ensure it was working, and made sure the helmet's microphone and earpieces were connected to the Spitfire's radio. If the oxygen system failed, malfunctioning or suffering battle damage at 15,000 feet or higher, a fighter pilot could easily succumb to lethal hypoxia (oxygen starvation) and become disoriented and then unconscious, spinning out of control.

Checking the instruments – no time to go through the complete cockpit checklist – and the brake pressure was the bare minimum required to make sure the Spitfire could be taxied. Then, check the voice radio. No fighter would take off without a functioning radio. The pilot throttled back and, ready to taxi, gave the signal for 'chocks away'. The ground crew used attached ropes to pull from in front of the wheels the wooden wedges that kept the Spitfire from lurching forward. The pilot released the brake lever on the control stick – it gave a hissing noise as the pressure was released – and then, gently, advanced the throttle to get the Spitfire rolling on the ground.

Spitfires taxied with an S-curve fishtailing motion. While not as bad as the Bf 109, the Spitfire had poor forward vision on the ground, even with the canopy open and the pilot's seat raised to the uppermost position. On the ground, the Spitfire was steered with its brakes on the rudder pedals, but this required depressing the brake lever on the control stick. Taxied into position at the end of the runway, the pilot would stop, pull the brake lever hard, run up the engine and cut off each magneto in turn to check the ignition system. Then he would perform a quick cockpit checklist, making sure that the trim controls were set for take-off, flaps set to full up, checking the gauges: petrol, temperature, electrical systems.

A scramble permitted only time gently to swing the nose from side to side for a forward glance to make sure no one was in the way as the Spitfire turned into the wind. Then a check to see that oil pressure and engine coolant temperature were normal, the propeller pitch was fine and fuel mixture was full rich, both correct for take-off. Elevator and rudder trim was quickly set with the trim wheels. The pilot smoothly advanced the Merlin engine, and then, waiting for a signal from the leader of the three-fighter section, released the brake lever on the control column.

As with any aircraft with a supercharger, the pilot thought in terms of boost and manifold pressure. The fighters bounced as they picked up speed. The tail lifted, and then the pilot gently pushed the throttle all the way forward. Take-off was achieved with full power on the Merlin and left rudder applied to keep the torque forces of the engine from pulling the Spitfire off to the side.

After a take-off run of about 1200 feet, back pressure on the control column eased the Spitfire into the air. Once trimmed out, with trim wheel control in the cockpit moved to ensure that the trim tabs on the control surfaces were adjusted, a Spitfire – highly responsive and with a powerful engine – was flown with the fingertips. With a rudder trim tab, the Spitfire, unlike the Bf 109, did not require constant rudder pressure in flight.

Spitfires needed to get into the air quickly not only to engage the enemy, but to minimise their own vulnerability. Only rarely did RAF pilots have to take off when already under attack. This had happened to Flight Lieutenant Colin Gray and 54 Squadron when at cockpit readiness at Hornchurch two weeks earlier, on 31 August. 'I hear the controller panicking: "54 Squadron take off, take off, for f—'s sake take off". So for f—'s sake I took off, hotly pursued by George [Gribble] and his section who had not heard the message but figured there must be something very wrong for me to act like that,' Gray recalled. 'As I reached the far boundary I looked back and saw the whole airfield covered in the smoke and dust of exploding bombs . . . Three of our aircraft didn't make it.'[7] The surviving pilot of one of those three Spitfires was Al Deere, whom Adolf Galland had shot down on 15 August. His Spitfire, blown on its back by a bomb, slid 100 yards along the runway upside down. Once again, Deere walked away, his longevity determined by luck as well as skill.

In the air, a Spitfire pilot squeezed the brake lever once more, then selected 'undercarriage up' and looked for the red light on his instrument panel that confirmed the wheels had successfully retracted. He reached one arm above him and slid the cockpit canopy's hood shut; it had been kept open for take-off in case of a ground accident requiring a quick exit. Engine mixture, trim and throttle were adjusted for the climb to altitude. The radiator, which had been fully open for take-off, was partially closed, reducing drag. Climbing past 10,000 feet, the pilot switched on the oxygen flow to his mask, already soaked in sweat from the bright sun despite the cold temperatures at altitude. Pilots belched frequently into the masks, with less air pressure to keep the gas in their stomachs.

In the air, the squadrons were directed by radio messages from their sector station controller, responding to telephoned orders from 11 Group headquarters. The Chain Home radar stations were all on the coast, looking outwards for early warning. Fighter Command kept track of its fighters with 'Pip-Squeak', a radio signal that automatically broadcast at intervals, allowing ground stations to triangulate their locations. Once the Germans crossed the English coast, they too disappeared from radar. Fighter Command relied on visual reports from the Observer Corps or sighting reports from aircraft. When over the coast, the Spitfires would be identified as friendly to British radar by their IFF transponders.

Now the Spitfire pilots were searching, a matter of life and death; 'left, right, above, below, behind, and into the sun, always searching, never relaxing', recalled 'Nobby' Clarke.[8] Climbing, RAF pilots flew 'spinning their head like a top', in the words of the contemporary cliché. Fighter pilots kept up a scan, a regular movement of the head from side to side, up and down, with occasional glances at the flight instruments. Both RAF and Luftwaffe fighter pilots wore silk scarves, so they would not rub their necks raw on their flying clothing from their heads' constant swivelling.

The design of the Spitfire and the Bf 109 both left blind spots astern and below the cockpit, which became especially vulnerable when these blind spots pointed towards the sun. Fighters needed to change course frequently to prevent enemy diving on them in their blind spots and to keep up the mutual all-around search for potential attackers.

One of the *Rules for Air Combat* developed by Squadron Leader Adolph 'Sailor' Malan, the keen South African-born RAF tactician commanding 74 Squadron, and his pilots was 'never fly straight and level in the combat area for more than 30 seconds'. Awareness and min-imising vulnerability made survival possible. The Spitfire's curved Plexiglas cockpit canopy also tended to distort the pilot's vision. Some Spitfire pilots would fly with the canopy slid open; others removed it completely to prevent anything from getting in the way of their searching.

From many angles – especially ahead and behind – the Bf 109 and Spitfire could easily be mistaken for one another. 'Nobby' Clarke once turned his Spitfire into firing position behind a Ju 87 Stuka dive bomber, whose rear crewman waved at what he thought was a Bf 109. Clarke hes-itated for an instant, then pushed the firing button on the top of the Spitfire's control column.[9]

Looking kept a fighter pilot alive *and* enabled him to do his job: destroying enemy aircraft. The best pilots often had acute vision. They trained themselves – the air forces as organisations had not yet learned – *how* to look but also *where* to look. They knew through hard experience or instinct where, in a given tactical situation, the enemy was likely to be. The old RAF training posters that said 'Beware of the Hun in the Sun' demonstrated awareness that a competent enemy would use the advantage of being able to determine the time and place a battle would start to climb higher and gain the advantageous 'up-sun' position.

Spitfires were vulnerable to any German fighters on a 'free hunt'. Bf 109s could drop down on them from 'out of the sun', where glare would make them practically invisible until too late. Fighter pilots unable to keep their place in formations became vulnerable, including wingmen who spent too much time trying to keep up and not enough looking. Less experienced pilots diverted their attention from looking for the enemy to keeping formation – especially when flying in the then-standard RAF three-fighter 'vic' tactical formation – or devoted their attention to flying the plane, looking inside the cockpit at the flight instruments.

'Sailor' Malan had his unit fly in three-Spitfire line-astern formations with two 'weavers' zigzagging behind the squadron to keep an eye on their blind spots. Many other RAF squadrons tried to minimise their vulnerability by having one or two such 'weavers' behind their formations as they climbed. But, lacking mutual support, too many 'weaver' Spitfires themselves fell to the first burst of fire from a Bf 109 that then disengaged, climbing or diving away before the rest of the Spitfires could do anything.

As the RAF fighters climbed, strong winds from the west sped them towards the enemy, who fought headwinds all the way to their targets. This morning, the Germans were concentrating fighters to escort their air armada. Some sixty Bf 109s were making 'free hunts' in advance of 240 bombers and their escorts heading for London, with no major feints or diversionary attacks.

Viewed from above, the Spitfire's brown-and-green camouflage matched the summer fields of the English countryside, brown and green alternating. Even with ground controllers using voice radio to direct the Spitfires towards the enemy, the absence of radar coverage inland and the lack of ability to provide exact positions made each squadron's commander responsible for finding the enemy, then manoeuvring their aircraft into position for an attack. Finding the enemy – especially without being spotted first – depended on what the

RAF called the 'Mark I Eyeball', the skills of the pilots and the capabilities of their aircraft.

The morning attack

At 11.36 the first attackers crossed the English coast at Dungeness. The Spitfire pilots of 72 Squadron, and the other squadrons joining them, saw more than 100 Do 17s and an even larger number of Bf 109s. Their leaders radioed their tally-ho reports back to 11 Group, giving the numbers, height and position of the enemy.

The Germans, spread back towards the Channel, flew in nine-bomber 'V of V' formations, each following by a few hundred metres, close enough for mutual support. The close escort of Bf 109s and, higher up, their top cover searched for interceptors. Bf 109 fighter-bombers were part of the attack, modified aircraft from LG 2, each carrying a 250 kg bomb under the fuselage. The Luftwaffe high command had ordered Bf 109Es modified to carry bombs after the Polish campaign. Though unable to manoeuvre while carrying this load, they could still fly higher and faster than the Dorniers.

On 15 September, 72 Squadron put up twelve Spitfires, led by Flight Lieutenant John 'Pancho' Villa, and 92 Squadron put up eight. Villa received orders from the ground controllers to attack the fighter escort, stripping them away from the bombers.[10] He swiftly assessed the situation and the enemy, before giving his own orders over the voice radio: 'Tennis Squadron, tally ho!' To Villa, the German formation, with the multiple formations of escorting Bf 109s stacked up above, looked like a swarm of midges in the distance.[11]

Having gained the advantage of altitude, Villa formed the twenty Spitfires of 72 and 92 squadrons into a long line-astern formation.

Villa peeled off – rolling his Spitfire inverted and, upside down, going into a diving turn to starboard, followed within seconds by each of the other Spitfires in turn. It was an impressive sight. 'I ordered the squadron into echelon starboard, thus attacking as many enemy fighters (Me 109) as possible,' Villa reported.

72 Squadron's diving attack hit the Bf 109s of I/JG 53. Their leader, Oberfeldwebel Alfred Müller, saw the Spitfires in time to give the Luftwaffe's warning over the radio: '*Achtung Indianers!*'

Villa and the Spitfires of both squadrons shot down four or five Bf 109s without loss. 'Villa attacked an Me 109 . . . and saw it on fire and explode in mid air. He then attacked another Me 109 which was on his tail. This machine also burst into flame,' the combat report stated.[12]

But more Bf 109s joined the fight. Villa saw the Dorniers slide below him as he fought off a numerically superior force of Bf 109s. A dozen Spitfires from 603 Squadron dived down and joined the mêlée, but the Bf 109 escorts were able to keep the Spitfires from breaking through to their bombers. The Spitfires did, however, pull the escorts away from the Do 17s. Ahead, two squadrons of Hurricanes climbed for their attacks, one of them 303 (Polish) Squadron, its pilots anxious to try out the head-on attacks that had been part of pre-war Polish fighter tactics. Alfred Müller was flying one of the Bf 109s that went down.

Starting at about 11.40, as the German formation flew across Kent to London, 303 Squadron led the attack as more RAF squadrons joined the battle.[13] Most of the squadrons had time to climb to gain the advantage of altitude over the attackers, then were directed by the ground controllers until behind them, able to curve in with a diving attack. In opposition were the same Do 17 crews that had landed hard blows on RAF Eastchurch and Rochester a month before, on 15 August.

Bf 109s roamed back and forward along the flanks of the Dornier formation, burning precious fuel, trying to meet the repeated RAF attacks on the bombers. The Bf 109 escort reached the limits of their radius of action as they approached London.

By the time the formation reached London, six Do 17s had gone down from British attacks. Another four had been damaged. They jettisoned their bombs and turned out of the formation, trying to make it back to France. Many of the other Dorniers were hit repeatedly by .303-calibre machine-gun bullets. Crewmen were wounded. Some of the Dorniers' machine guns fell silent, ammunition expended. Their formation became more dispersed. Rather than the precision of the nine-bomber formations, each following another, that they had been flying when they crossed the English coast, the beleaguered Dorniers now clumped together as best they could for mutual protection.

'Ben' Bennions won a battle with one of the escorts, as he said in his combat report immediately after landing that day. 'Leading Blue Section I was attacked by [an] Me 109,' he reported. 'After a steep right hand climbing turn the Me 109 with a yellow nose fell out of the turn and I turned on to his tail.'

The Bf 109, trying to turn with the Spitfire, had apparently stalled, giving Bennions the chance to turn inside him enough to get behind him, where the German was most vulnerable and Bennions' shots were more likely to hit. To regain airspeed and escape, the German's next move was to dive.

'He rolled over and went vertically downwards and pulled out heading south east.' Bennions followed and, with the ground looming, the Bf 109 pulled up into Bennions' gunsights. 'As soon as he straightened up, I gave him three short bursts. He burst into flames and after knocking off his roof [jettisoning the cockpit canopy] bailed out.' It was Bennions' tenth victory.

By 11.55, as the escorted formation had fought its way to the eastern edge of London, Park made his move: a coordinated mass attack. Four Hurricane squadrons launched a head-on attack on the leading edge of the formation. At the same time, the Duxford 'big wing' of two Spitfire and three Hurricane squadrons, led by Douglas Bader, hit its northern flank. The coordinated attack disrupted the German formation as it approached its target. Their bombs, instead of being concentrated on central London, were spread out to the south and east. The Germans turned away and fought their way back to the coast.

The Bf 109s' lack of endurance often required them to disengage from fighter combat before their RAF opponents did, putting them at a tactical disadvantage. Even if they managed to disengage, they were vulnerable to RAF fighters, especially at low altitude, throttled back to conserve fuel. Bf 109 pilots considered RAF fighters who attacked them when they were short of fuel and low on altitude and airspeed unsporting, and called those who did so *Leichenfledderer* (grave robbers).

Some RAF squadrons pursued the retiring raid, but most were recalled to their airfields by the controllers at the sector stations. Park knew the Germans were not finished. He wanted as many fighters as possible quickly rearmed, refuelled and brought back to readiness against the next attack.

At each airfield, the RAF ground staff would be looking for the returning fighters, whether still in formation – which showed no contact with the enemy – or in ones, twos and threes – which showed they had been in a fight. RAF Fighter Command's airfields were a main source of its resiliency. Sector stations included an operations room where telephonic or teletype orders were received and relayed to the fighter squadrons by voice radio. Before the war each of Fighter Command's major airfields included workshops, spare parts and trained ground crew, all in close proximity. Fighters with minor battle damage could be repaired at the airfield by unit personnel, rather than disassembled and transported by road to a depot for more extensive work. A Hurricane's fabric-covered metal frame fuselage was easier to repair than the Spitfire's all-metal structure.

Following a quick debriefing with intelligence officers and the unit commander, claims for victories were recorded and passed up to higher headquarters, along with reports of how many fighters and pilots had been lost or damaged.

Many pilots were exhausted, especially if they had been in combat. The physical effort of flying and the passive solar heating at altitude left them soaked in sweat. At the debriefing they were often emotionally and psychologically drained, or were so high on the adrenaline still flowing that, when it ran out, they tended to run down, regardless of where they were. Despite their exhaustion, the pilots were ready to fly again within minutes, waiting to scramble as soon as their fighters were made ready. The mess would often send over tea and sandwiches, but many went uneaten.

At the dispersal sites, ground personnel worked to get as many fighters as possible ready for the next scramble. Ground crew whose fighters had not returned had to shake off their shock and sorrow and join in preparing those that had come back. Lorries – bowsers in RAF parlance – rushed from Spitfire to Spitfire with 100-octane fuel. A Spitfire, after landing, was refuelled, rearmed and ready to take off again in less than twenty minutes. The ground crews checked that the oil tank was full and that the fuel tanks held 85 gallons of 100-octane aviation petrol.

The canopy access rails were lubricated so they would not freeze in place from moisture if the pilot had to bail out at high altitude. The radio fitter popped open the fuselage access panel and checked the crystals in the radio set, high technology by 1940 standards.

Kneeling under the wing, armourers removed the panels that gave access to the Spitfire's eight Browning .303 machine guns. In ten minutes, a team of four armourers could clean the bores and breeches and change the 300-round ammunition boxes for each gun. They fed the new ammunition belts holding the dull, glittery brass cartridges through the breech mechanisms of each machine gun. Red adhesive fabric patches applied to the leading edge of the Spitfire's wing covered each machine gun's muzzle, to protect it from condensation and reduce drag until firing. Then the armourers cocked each gun in turn, drawing back its bolt. The Spitfire was ready for combat as soon as the pilot turned the round knob on the control column from 'safe' to 'fire'.

The afternoon attack

Soon after 1 p.m., the next attack formed up over northern France. Larger than the previous assault, it included more than 150 bombers in three waves and 40 Bf 100s and 450 Bf 109s in escort, including Galland and III/JG 26. Only a few dozen Bf 109s were flying close escort. The remainder were flying 'free hunts' or top cover, the better to engage the RAF's fighters in a final decisive battle for London.

This time, Park waited as long as he could, giving extra time to refuel and rearm the fighters and to allow the pilots to get a second wind. Between 1.50 and 2.08, squadron after squadron scrambled. Park aimed to position as many squadrons as possible to meet the incoming raid close to London.

Park ordered up his spotters, a few Spitfires deployed at forward air-fields. They were soon climbing to altitude. The spotters' task was not to attack, but to count the number of German aircraft and their direction. The spotters radioed this back to the sector stations, who forwarded it to Uxbridge. Using this information, Park held some squadrons back, over their airfields or near London, so that the Bf 109s would be low on fuel when they engaged.

The massive formation, almost ten miles wide, crossed the English coast, heading for London. At 2.15, twenty-seven Spitfires of 41 and 92 squadrons attacked the incoming raid over Dungeness. This time, however, they were not heading for the bombers, but aimed to strip away the Bf 109s by forcing them to burn their fuel in dogfighting, for the benefit of the squadrons climbing near London. Diving out of the sun, the two squadrons claimed fourteen German fighters while losing only a single Spitfire.

Through the clouded light blue of 15,000 feet now came the formations of German twin-engine bombers. The big formations looked terrifying, but the RAF had learned that individual bombers carried modest payloads and weak defensive armament.

The battle at 11 Group

At Uxbridge, as RAF squadron after squadron took off and hundreds of German aircraft started to fill the skies over England, 11 Group's plot table filled up with blocks, pushed across the map by croupier-like rakes deftly applied by the WAAF plotters. On the tote, the lights of squadron after squadron changed colour as they were ordered to intercept the incoming raids.

Winston Churchill, with the instincts of both a politician and a historian, had picked that particular day, 15 September, to make another of his occasional visits to the operations room at Uxbridge, accompanied by his wife, Clementine. Sitting in a gallery that gave him a full view of the action, the prime minister sucked on an immense unlit Havana cigar and watched the story told by the changing situation on the plot table and the tote board as the Germans fought their way from the Channel to London.

The fury of the running battles appeared distant as the WAAF plotters pushed the blocks representing the German attackers closer and closer to London; those representing the RAF squadrons in contact with them were pushed along as well, until they signalled they were breaking off to refuel and rearm. Churchill watched, the tote board lights from each squadron going from 'available' to 'airborne' or 'detailed to raid' until no more 'available' lights were lit. As he described it in his memoirs:

Presently the red bulbs showed that the majority of our squadrons were engaged ... The Air Marshal [Park] walked up and down behind, watching with a vigilant eye every move in the game, supervising his junior executive hand,[14] and only occasionally intervening with some decisive order, usually to reinforce a threatened area. In a little while all our squadrons were fighting and some had already begun to return for fuel. All were in the air. The lower line of bulbs was out. There was not one squadron left in reserve.[15]

Churchill then spoke to Park, who appeared to him to be nervous in a way he had never been before. He asked him what reserves 11 Group had.

Park's reply: 'There are none.' He was all-in, gambling no larger raid was behind this one. He had committed every fighter available of the 315 that had been operational with 11 Group that morning. If the Germans launched more raids, perhaps aimed at the sector stations, everything was at risk. When he told him the news, Park thought that Churchill looked grave.

Park was making a gamble, but it was an informed one. He was counting on squadrons from 10 Group and 12 Group to reinforce his fighters. He could see that, despite German jamming, the Chain Home radars were still working. If a large-scale attack on 11 Group's airfields or the radar stations were planned, he would already be seeing indications. Clouds covered many of his airfields from bombers. He was relying on the power of his squadrons making a massed attack against the afternoon raid on London for his gamble to pay off.

The squadrons Park had committed were now in position to launch a coordinated attack against the German formation as it approached London: nineteen squadrons with 185 RAF fighters. 12 Group's Duxford Wing, rearmed and refuelled, attacked the north flank of the German formation. Six 11 Group squadrons, reinforced by another two from 10 Group to the west, hit the Germans head-on as they came over London. Too few Bf 109s with too little fuel defended the front of the formation against the RAF attack. One formation of Do 17s saw the Bf 109s, short on fuel, turn for home. Their targets covered in cloud, these bombers also turned around before they had reached their

109 origins: the Harth and Messerschmitt designed S 10 glider (in a 1922 competition) was an improved version of the S 5 of 1914–15. (National Archives RG-18-WP)

Spitfire origins: the Schneider Cup–winning Supermarine S.6B racer. (National Archives RG-18-WP)

Spitfire creator: R.J. Mitchell (right) in his element, conferring next to the floats of his Supermarine S.6B racer in 1931. (Getty Images)

Mutual admiration: Willy Messerschmitt and Hitler before a performance of *Lohrengrin* in Augsburg, 1939. (National Archives RG-242)

Mutual antipathy: Willy Messerschmitt makes a point with Erhard Milch, 1937. (National Archives RG-242)

109 predecessor: a Bf 108 in a pre-war propaganda photo. (National Archives RG-242-GLP)

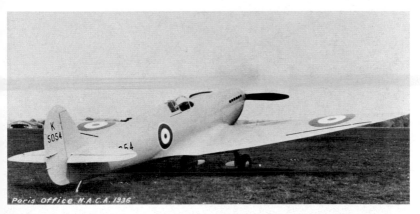

Spitfire predecessor: the prototype Spitfire K5054. (National Archives RG-18-WP)

109 enters production: a Bf 109B. (National Archives RG-18-WP)

Spitfire enters production: Spitfire Is with early variable–pitch three-bladed propellers equip 19 Squadron RAF, 1939. (National Archives RG-208-AA)

Behind the 109: groundcrew help start a Bf 109E-1 removing the chocks, 1939.
(National Archives RG 242-GLP)

Behind the Spitfire: RAF armourers (with issue shirts and neckties under their overalls) rearm a Spitfire. (National Archives RG 242-GLP)

109s in combat: a *Schwarm* of Bf 109E-4s from I/JG 3, late in the Battle of Britain, in a still from a German newsreel. (National Archives RG 242-GLP)

Spitfires ready for combat: 19 Squadron RAF puts up twelve Spitfires for the camera, RAF Digby, 20 May 1939, showing the three-plane vee formations, impressive for photographs, less good in combat. (National Archives RG 208)

109 men: Willy
Messerschmitt congratulates
test pilot Fritz Wendel after
his Me 209 set the world
landplane piston speed
record, 26 April 1939.
(National Archives RG-18-WP)

109 men: Udet, Galland and Moelders, all of whom flew Bf 109s in some of their
most important battles (and survived them). (National Archives RG-242-GLP)

Spitfire master: the greatest air battle in history was won by a pilot nicknamed 'Stuffy' – Air Marshal Sir Hugh Dowding. (Getty Images)

Spitfire man: Douglas Bader, shown as a group captain in 1945, swings his artificial legs into the cockpit of his personal (marked with his initials) Spitfire IX (which retains its wartime rearview mirror). (Gamma-Keystone via Getty Images)

target of the Surrey Commercial Docks. They scattered their bombs widely over London's docklands and headed for their bases in northern France.

At about 2.50, the oncoming planes appeared distant to 'Sandy' Lane. He was leading 19 Squadron over the Thames, east of London, as part of Bader's 'big wing', attacking the German formations.[16] They started to move, growing bigger, then catching the slanting rays of the mid-afternoon sun; more aeroplanes than he had ever seen before. They were all German, thirty Do 17s with Bf 109 and Bf 110 escorts, stacked up to 30,000 feet, and all flying away from him and the other Spitfires of 19 Squadron.

The Spitfire squadrons were to attack the escort while Bader and the Hurricane squadrons attacked the bombers. Once Lane had seen the German formation, he made sure his two wingmen were with him, one on each wing in the RAF's 'vic' fighting formation. One of them, Flight Sergeant George 'Grumpy' Unwin,[17] was 19 Squadron's leading ace, with eight victories. Lane slowly pushed the throttle forward – the Merlin engine's 1175 hp kicked in as the Spitfire accelerated – and quickly armed the eight machine guns with a twist of his gloved trigger finger. He checked the reflector sight behind the windscreen. It was set at the bright 'daylight' position for illumination of the circular range-finding rings that would bracket a Bf 109's wingspan at 250 yards, where all eight machine guns were harmonised to strike together in an area the size of a Bf 109's cockpit. All three Spitfires went into a climbing turn, aiming to get behind and below the Bf 109s for an attack.

A flash of tracer bullets – three Bf 109s dived on the Spitfires from above. They fired from straight ahead of the Spitfires; rather than pulling deflection, a head-on shot. The combined closing speed of the fighters brought them together at some 700 mph. The Bf 109s had almost instantly grown from specks to full-size planes, their light blue bellies a few feet above the Spitfire's canopy.

Two of the Bf 109s broke away to starboard, followed by Lane's wingmen. A swirling dogfight then followed. 'Grumpy' Unwin said, 'The next thing I knew, literally thousands of yellow-nosed Messerschmitts were whistling by me less than 100 yards away, so I pulled the bloody stick back, went into a steep turn and held it there.'

Lane went for a formation of Bf 110s before seeing a single Bf 109, probably one of the three that had attacked him moments before, just above him. Without a wingman, the vulnerable Bf 109 would be his target. 'Pulling around half stalled, I tore after him.'

The Spitfire was in a near-vertical bank. It turned to get behind the Bf 109s that had just overshot his section. Lane kept his eyes focused ahead as his peripheral vision faded towards a blackout. Increasing g forces compressed him into his seat. Still he turned, on the verge of a stall.

Now he was behind and below the Bf 109, whose pilot had probably lost sight of him. Lane's Spitfire was in his blind spot. 'I got in a short burst as I closed on him before he was out of my sights again.' Alerted, the Bf 109's pilot went into a tight turn, aiming to get on Lane's tail.

'That German pilot certainly knew how to handle a 109 – I have never seen one thrown about as that one was.' But Lane was able to turn inside the Bf 109. He swivelled his head around. He checked his rear-view mirrors, 'clearing his tail'. Lane had added a second mirror to his Spitfire, so important did he consider them to keeping an effective look-out. He strained against the shoulder straps that held him in the seat in his cockpit as he turned from side to side. Shifting his vision to the illuminated rings on the reflector sight, he pushed the trigger button on the Spitfire's control column, holding it down for about two seconds.

'Get in close. Get in close. When you think you're too close, get in closer.' Douglas Bader's advice to his pilots reflected his direct and blunt personal approach to defeating all obstacles. 'Sailor' Malan's first rule of air fighting was 'Wait till you see the whites of his eyes.' In other words, a fighter pilot often fired so close to his enemy that, on several occasions in the battle, RAF fighters were hit by pieces they had shot off enemy aircraft and were forced down themselves.

'Twice I managed to get in a short burst but I don't think I hit him.'

The Bf 109's pilot hauled it around in a tight turn, its leading-edge slats springing out to keep it flying on the verge of a stall, doubtless craning his neck hard around to keep in sight the Spitfire hunting him down.

'He was obviously turning as tightly as his kite could and I could see his slats were open, showing that he was nearly stalled. His ailerons were obviously snatching too, as first one wing and then the other would dip violently.' This suggests that the slats might have been jamming, with some not extending properly. The effect would be to create an asymmetric flight condition or, worse, stall one wing of the Bf 109.

Still in a tight turn, Lane saw the Bf 109 getting closer and closer to being in his gunsight. With the Spitfire about to open fire, the Bf 109's pilot decided to play his plane's strong card, superior acceleration in a dive. It half-rolled and dived away, heading for a cloud deck beneath the fight, with Lane following. 'He flew on inverted for several seconds, giving me the chance to get in a good burst from that quarter.' This time, Lane's gloved finger held down the button for a full five seconds of concentrated fire from the Spitfire's eight Browning machine guns.

The Bf 109's superior dive acceleration allowed him to open the range. 'Half righting himself for a moment, he slowly dived down and disappeared into the clouds, still upside down.' While Lane claimed it as a 'probable', German records show no Bf 109 likely to have been lost at the time and place of this combat.

'Grumpy' Unwin had finished his dogfight in much the same way. 'I gave the odd machine a quick burst as it flew past me and succeeded in forcing one to half roll and dive into cloud below. I followed him down, but my windscreen froze at 6,000 feet and he escaped.'

The exertion demanded in even a short manoeuvring dogfight was tremendous. Lane recalled, 'The sweat was pouring down my face and my oxygen mask was wet and sticky about my nose and mouth. I felt quite exhausted after the effort and my right arm ached from throwing the stick around the cockpit.'

At the end of a fight with a particular enemy aircraft, a fighter pilot often found himself in an empty sky. Having concentrated on the enemy – whether as the hunter or the hunted – he was unaware of the changing overall situation. His individual fight had gone one way and the rest of the war had gone another. This happened to both Lane and Unwin, separately, a few minutes later.

Lane was able to reorient himself and, alone, returned to the battle. He attacked two formations of Do 17s, one head-on and one from astern. The Do 17 crews 'did not appear to like head-on attacks as they jumped about a bit as I flashed through. I observed no results from these attacks.' Attacking from astern, Lane opened fire at about 1000 yards, too long a range to have an effect. His ammunition expended, he headed back to his airfield.

His wingmen had also survived the German attack. Unable to follow his tight turn, they had let him conduct his dogfight by himself. Like Lane, they returned from the afternoon battle, with 'Grumpy' Unwin scoring two confirmed Bf 109s shot down. Filling out his combat report, in the blank thoughtfully labelled 'number of enemy aircraft', Lane entered: 'Whole Luftwaffe'.

Throughout the day, air battles raged over London and its southern and eastern suburbs. The heavy RAF attacks had scattered the German formations and prevented concentrated bombing of London. The German aircrew, told at their morning briefings by Luftwaffe intelligence that the RAF was down to its last fifty Spitfires, were shocked to see repeated attacks from hundreds of fighters intercepting them. The Luftwaffe again suffered from massive intelligence failure. They had derived their estimate from an unrealistically modest guess at Spitfire production, unaware that Castle Bromwich was finally producing improved Spitfire IIs, and had then simply subtracted the number of Spitfires claimed destroyed by the Luftwaffe, discounting the fact that in the heat of combat, substantial overclaiming was inevitable. Despite the weeks of attacks on RAF airfields, as the damaged German aircraft struggled to get back across the Channel, losing altitude, it became obvious they had not defeated Fighter Command.

By 3–3.15, the Germans were turning for home. RAF squadrons returned to base to refuel and rearm.

Park turned to Churchill again. 'I am very glad, sir, that you have seen this.' At an earlier visit to the 11 Group operations room on 16 August, where he had watched the course of the defence of England on the plot and tote, Churchill had left saying, 'Don't speak to me. I have never been so powerfully moved.' After a few minutes of silence, he had added, 'Never in the field of human conflict has so much been owed by so many to so few.'[18] This comment, incorporated in his speech to the House of Commons on 20 August, ensured that the aircrew of RAF Fighter Command in the summer of 1940 would forever be known as 'The Few'. Of 15 September, Churchill wrote in his memoirs: 'It was one of the decisive battles of the war.'

Churchill was concerned about history. Park was concerned that German bombers had penetrated to bomb London, but encouraged by reports that large numbers of German aircraft had been shot down. Bombers going down over London had been seen by many people. One Do 17, before crashing into the bus station in front of Victoria Station,[19] jettisoned its bombs, damaging Buckingham Palace. Park saw that this day had brought Fighter Command its greatest success to date, even if not a complete one.

As the bombers returned to base, the Bf 109s that had escorted the earlier mission, now rearmed and refuelled, took off in a series of large-scale fighter sweeps to cover their withdrawal and help prevent a significant RAF pursuit. Galland even attacked Bader's 'big wing' as it returned to base. He claimed a Hurricane, his thirty-third victory putting his total score four behind that of his friend 'Vati' Mölders.

German fighters continued to range over southern England until after 3.30. In the afternoon and early evening, the Germans launched a number of escorted bomber raids at targets to the west of London. While these resulted in several hard-fought battles as the RAF intercepted, they were anti-climactic.

The bombers did not return to London that day until after sunset. Some 180 bombers then hit the capital, with smaller raids on other cities. Aiming at the same 'strategic' targets – mainly transport hubs – in central London that they had been unable to hit during the day, the night bombing did more damage than the two defeated mass raids. By bombing at night, the Germans could achieve better results.

In September 1940, RAF night-fighting capability was still in its infancy. The few radar-equipped Blenheim night fighters could not catch many German bombers once they had dropped their bombs. Spitfires had occasionally flown night training missions since 1938 but had proved unsuitable due to the narrow-track undercarriage and limited cockpit vision. The two-seat Defiant was eventually modified to mount a radar set; the Spitfire was too small.

The Luftwaffe had so far failed to land a telling blow on London. The daylight air offensive had not been able to defeat the RAF in time for a successful invasion of England before autumn closed in. Nor were they going to be able to trigger a political collapse and a negotiated peace.

They would now shift their effort to night bombing. For the Germans, 15 September had not been seen as a decisive defeat but only as requiring another change in tactics.

More large-scale attacks followed in the weeks ahead, with more intense fighting. At the end of September, some 28 per cent of the RAF fighter pilots who started the month had been lost (compared with 23 per cent for the Luftwaffe). In the 15 September air battles, the British at the time claimed 185 German aircraft destroyed. The actual number was fifty-six, compared to twenty-nine RAF fighters and thirteen RAF pilots lost. Although the British had destroyed far fewer aircraft than they first estimated, the effects of 15 September were truly decisive, even in the light of hindsight. The Germans learned they were not going to be able to defeat Britain by air attack in 1940. Daylight attacks would continue, but never again such a massed air assault on London. The British victory also had an impact on the US and the Soviet Union, the two neutral great powers. It demonstrated that Britain would remain in the war with the hope of ultimate victory. Hitler no longer appeared Europe's inevitable master, as he had in May.

The British, from the outset, had planned for a long and bitter conflict. Hitler's Germany had envisioned a short, victorious war. The Battle of Britain denied it that result. The Luftwaffe, which had succeeded from the start of the war until the Battle of Britain, was unable to defeat the integrated air defence system the British had raced to deploy in the months before July 1940.

Its bombers having failed to bomb England to defeat by daylight, the Luftwaffe now looked to the Bf 109 to carry the offensive air battle to the British. At the same time, Messerschmitt was starting production of a new version, the Bf 109F. The first examples were already in action over England; Mölders had claimed one of the first to be delivered as his personal fighter.

A new battle between the Bf 109 and the Spitfire, less decisive but still costly, was being set up for the autumn and winter months. The Luftwaffe's pilots, for all their exhaustion, were still confident in their own skills, in Hitler and in Germany's ultimate victory; they were ready to play the game again. Even Oberfeldwebel Gottfried Leske, an He 111 pilot, who wrote, 'We know the English are our enemies and that we must beat them and that we will beat them, but we can't keep hating every damned pilot of every damned Hurricane.'[20]

On 17 September, Ultra picked up the first messages from the German high command giving orders that the invasion was to be 'temporarily postponed'. Hitler had been considering such a move even before the air battle of 15 September. The shift to bombing London the week before had been a tacit admission that creating a political impact by hitting Britain's capital was more likely to push the government towards the negotiated settlement Hitler really wanted than attacks on airfields and aircraft factories were to yield the air superiority the Germans believed they needed before an invasion could take place. Despite the defeat of the Luftwaffe's daylight bomber offensive over London, the Germans would continue to rely on air power to keep the pressure on Britain while Hitler turned his attention to new objectives.

For the Luftwaffe, 15 September was not seen as a decisive defeat. It was a setback in the ongoing air offensive that would require a change of tactics, just as the week before they had shifted to attacks on London. Now, improvising its air war against England, the Luftwaffe would try to adapt again, seeking to maintain the offensive while recognising that its twin-engine bombers could seldom operate in daylight over England. Instead, these bombers would now carry out their missions by night, while day bombing would be carried out by Bf 109s.

To Göring, the change was so much the better. He would now have another opportunity to win an independent strategic victory over Britain, succeeding in what he had failed to do over Dunkirk. Defeating Britain without an invasion had the potential to raise his political position in the Reich. Meanwhile, the General Staff turned their attention to planning the invasion of Germany's current ally, the Soviet Union, Hitler's new goal. The staff officers locked back up in their safes their tide tables and aerial photographs of the Channel ports (the bombing of which Göring had thoughtfully prohibited to allow for their use in the invasion) and in their place brought out maps of the long road to Moscow.

8

The Continuing Battle

18 September 1940–end of 1941

The Germans had not finished their attacks on Britain when the threat of invasion receded, at least until the following spring. The Luftwaffe turned to tactics that the British defence system had not been designed to counter.

The Luftwaffe's autumn offensive
In the autumn of 1940, Bf 109 *JaBos* (*Jagdbomber*, fighter-bomber) took on a greater role in the daylight offensive over England. Twin-engine bombers were now largely used for night attacks; only rarely would they again come within range of British-based Spitfires in daylight. The main object of the autumn's *JaBo* offensive was the bombing of Britain's urban areas. In fighter units, 20 to 35 per cent of Bf 109Es were modified to carry a single 250 kg bomb, although this was never enough for mass raids. The remainder of the Bf 109s provided large-scale fighter escort for the bomb-laden planes on the way to the target.

The Bf 109 pilots and their aircraft were tired. As of 28 September, 712 Bf 109s were serviceable, but only 676 pilots were ready for operations (out of a total of 917), putting an increasing strain on fewer men. Oberleutnant Ulrich Steinhilper, who had recovered from wiping out the undercarriage of a Bf 109E on his first flight in the type to become a five-victory ace, was one of the pilots experiencing *Kanalkrankheit* (Channel sickness), described as:

> A combination of chronic stress and acute fatigue. At first there were isolated cases but, as the battle dragged on, there were to be more and more cases of the evil disease. The symptoms were many and various but usually surfaced as stomach cramps and vomiting, loss of appetite and consequently weight and acute irritability. Typically the patient's consumption of alcohol and cigarettes would increase and he would show more and more signs of exhaustion. There was little leave and, unlike the RAF pilots, we were not to be circulated to quiet zones for short periods of rest and refitting. There was nothing our doctors could do either. The principle of battle fatigue had not yet been established and it was felt that as soon as anyone was taken out of the line because he was showing signs of stress, there would be a flood.[1]

There was increasing resentment of higher command that failed to provide reinforcements. Some pilots in III/JG 53, angry with actions they saw as disrespectful of their commanders and unit, painted over the swastikas on the tails of their Bf 109Es. Their commanding officer, Hauptmann Wolf-Dietrich 'Fürst' (Prince) Wilcke, who made no secret of his lack of Nazi politics, did not order the aircraft restored to regulation condition. Eventually, grievances addressed, the swastikas reappeared.[2]

Serviceability for Bf 109s, which had been at 95 per cent on 15 July and 85 per cent on 17 August,[3] was now hard to sustain at 68 per cent. The pilots were not trained for fighter-bomber missions. The Bf 109 had no bombsights. The Revi gunsight was useful only if the Bf 109 dived on its target at a 45-degree angle; at a 65-degree dive angle or greater, the bomb was likely to strike the propeller. Some pilots drew grease-pencil lines on their windscreens to allow them to attack at the appropriate angle.

The fighter-bomber offensive was also intended to continue to weaken Fighter Command, in part by attacks on airfields and factories but primarily by forcing the RAF into combat with superior numbers at high altitude. But the Spitfire, with its higher critical altitude, larger wing and lower wing loading, had an advantage in manoeuvring at high altitude over the Bf 109E-3. Since July, the Luftwaffe fighter units had received an increasing number of Bf 109E-4s, many converted from earlier Bf 109E models. The new design differed in having rearranged armour plate and wing cannon with the capability to fire more powerful 20mm shells.[4]

Major Adolf Galland, now a *Geschwaderkommodore* in command of all three *Gruppen* of JG 26, gave orders that Bf 109s escorting fighter-bombers would fly at 9750 metres (32,000 feet).[5] But often this was not high enough. Steinhilper was flying with his wingman at 32,000 feet when Spitfires at even higher altitude dived down on them from out of the sun and shot them both down. Both survived as prisoners of war.[6]

New versions of the Bf 109E started arriving at Luftwaffe units in France soon after the climactic battles. The Bf 109E-5 was a reconnaissance version, with the wing cannon removed to compensate for the weight of a large camera in the fuselage. Unlike the RAF's reconnaissance Spitfires, it did not have a long-range capability. Reconnaissance versions of subsequent Bf 109 models were also used, but the Luftwaffe's lack of a suitable camera for low-altitude oblique photography limited them to high-altitude (16,000–26,000 feet, later higher) vertical photography.[7] The Bf 109E-7 had underbelly hardpoints with plumbing for external 300-litre droppable fuel tanks (drop tanks), but these were mainly used to carry bombs. With the drop tank, Galland, used to having thirty minutes of flying time when he crossed the English coast, now found he had a further thirty.

The Bf 109E-4/N was powered by the more powerful DB 601N engine that required C3 fuel, the German counterpart of the RAF's 100-octane fuel, rather than the Luftwaffe's standard 87-octane B4 fuel. The engine had a service life of about forty hours (compared to 100 hours for a standard DB 601). Poor reliability, a high catastrophic failure rate (due to increased stresses on the engine) and the need for extra engines limited the number deployed.[8]

Mölders had asked Göring for these planes for his unit.[9] Despite that, the first Bf 109E-4Ns had instead been delivered to II/JG 26, which was largely equipped with them by 19 July.[10] Galland claimed one of the first

Bf 109E-4/Ns for his personal use; he used it to score twenty-eight victories.[11] The Bf 109E-6 was this aircraft modified for short-range photo reconnaissance (the earlier Bf 109E-5 had been a version of the Bf 109E-3). Armament was reduced to the two nose machine guns to allow for an in-fuselage camera.

The Bf 109E-8's DB 601N engine used the GM-1 nitrous oxide injection system to increase power. This was laughing gas, giving the system its Luftwaffe nickname of 'Ha Ha' or '*Göring Mischeng*' (Göring's blend). From now on the Luftwaffe increasingly used boosts and additives to improve engine performance as they pushed their designs to the limit. Injected into the supercharger inlet, the gas provided additional oxygen for combustion at high altitude and acted as an anti-detonant, cooling the fuel–air mixture.[12] It enabled a supercharged engine to deliver higher power above its critical altitude. Any engine with a single-stage supercharger starts running out of power above 20,000 feet, and even before the Battle of Britain, it had become apparent that air combat was taking place at altitudes above those where the DB 601 series engine had been designed to deliver its best performance. The GM-1 produced an increase of around 25 per cent, boosting maximum speed by 65–105 km/h (40–65 mph) at high altitudes. Other Bf 109E sub-types were fitted with upgrades in power, engines and equipment. From now on the Bf 109 would be deployed in a bewildering variety of sub-types that defeated attempts at standardisation.

The new Bf 109E versions and the fighter-bombers posed a challenge to Fighter Command. Park found that the interception tactics by which 11 Group had gained success against escorted twin-engine bombers were less effective against the fighter-bombers. Climbing to high altitude over the Channel and moving faster than the bombers, Bf 109 fighter-bombers could penetrate to targets before 11 Group's squadrons could be ordered to scramble and make the long climb up to the fighter-bombers' operational altitude. Park kept Spitfires on standing patrol, some at high altitude, to engage incoming raids until reinforcements could be vectored by ground controllers at the sector stations. The 11 Group spotters, brought up to squadron strength and re-equipped with stripped-down Spitfire IIs, were kept in the air at high altitude to pass information to controllers so that they could direct squadrons during their long and vulnerable climbs. Hurricanes, still constituting a majority of the RAF's fighter strength, with their slower rate of climb and lower ceiling, were less effective against the new tactics.

To Spitfire pilots, even veterans of the fierce battles of previous months, the high-altitude offensive presented them with an inhospitable battlefield of icing and bitter cold. Merlin engines, despite their superchargers, gasped in the thin air, where the dark blue of infinity arched above the familiar sky of an English autumn. Despite the Spitfire's superior high-altitude performance, the Bf 109s were not the only enemy. The De Havilland constant-speed propeller's governor mechanism would freeze in the intense cold of high altitude, often leading to engine failure.[13] RAF oxygen systems, designed for lower altitudes, often proved inadequate at 30,000 feet or above. The strain of repeated high-altitude flights told on pilots who had come through months of intense fighting. Losses from hypoxia increased. Spitfires nosed out of formation and went into a spin without a word. Cockpit canopies frequently fogged over, blocking any sight of the enemy until it was often too late. Heating proved inadequate. Even small air leaks could focus paralysing cold air on a pilot. RAF pilots flew wearing thick, heavy clothing, but this hampered their ability to respond if they encountered the enemy.

The Air Ministry turned to Supermarine to modify the Spitfire to make it better able to fight at high altitude. They feared that, the next year or later, the Germans would resume the daylight offensive against Britain with improved bombers capable of flying above British fighters. Dowding warned of 'a new series of four-engine bombers which will have a ceiling in the neighbourhood of 35,000 feet'.[14] The Air Ministry directed Joe Smith's design team to start work on the Spitfire VI, a high-altitude fighter development of the Spitfire I with a more powerful 1415 hp Merlin 47 engine, a four-bladed Rotol constant-speed propeller, a pressurised cockpit (giving the pilot the effects of flying at an altitude of 28,000 feet when he was at 40,000 feet) and extended wing tips. But it would be many months before this version could fly.

The RAF took the opportunity offered by the reduced tempo of German attacks to expand the use of 100-octane fuel (used until now only by Fighter Command) and to carry out their long-planned transition from HF to VHF aircraft radios (the latter having been ordered on

19 August).[15] The use of VHF radio enabled more effective wing-size operations, such as those of 11 Group over Dunkirk and 12 Group over London on 15 September. More aircraft could communicate, while the radios had better performance over longer range with more frequencies available. This meant that Spitfires were better able to fight as a multi-squadron wing rather than in individual squadrons. Radar was supplemented by the intercepts of the 'Y' service, which monitored German radio communications. These could be filtered and 'fused' together with the other sources of situational awareness, radar information and that from the Observer Corps at the group level quickly enough for the controllers at the sector stations to use it to vector interceptors.

The German day offensive, while not capable of doing damage such as that inflicted on London on 7 September, could still strike painful blows. The Supermarine factory at Woolston in Southampton was hit by two devastating attacks on 24 and 26 September 1940. Spitfire production by Supermarine came to a halt.

Whatever Supermarine production facilities could be salvaged were dispersed. Soon, parts of Spitfires were being produced in business premises throughout southern England. Wings were assembled in a converted bus garage in Salisbury. Despite the dispersal to a total of sixty-six sites, all the parts had to be built to fine tolerances to enable them to be brought together for final assembly at Supermarine's surviving Eastleigh Southampton-area plant. The production rate slowly recovered, but it would be over a year before it was back at pre-dispersal levels.

Joe Smith and his design team set up shop at Hursley Park, a country estate near Winchester, where they were to remain – with the owners still in residence – among the oak-panelled rooms and staircases, the administrative staff being housed in temporary buildings on the stately lawns. The team was to have the twin advantages of being able to concentrate primarily on improving the Spitfire design and its derivatives and work closely with 'Hs' Hives' team at Rolls-Royce. This meant that, in practice, the future development of the Spitfire would be as an integrated system, airframe and engine together. Alan Clifton, Smith's deputy and head of the technical office, recalled that 'frequent meetings were held between the firms at a managerial and technical level and the team spirit characteristic of the war period was nowhere more evident'.[16] Both teams' close relationship with the Air Ministry and the RAF allowed operational needs and requirements to be quickly assessed and met.

With Supermarine's production rate effectively halved until March 1941,[17] other production lines were set up. By September, the Castle Bromwich factory had finally, after a long and troubled start, built up its production capacity under Vickers' management.[18] The plant had been designed from the outset for mass production, and Cyril Russell, one of the skilled craftsmen on whom Supermarine relied, marvelled at its 'tooling – rubber presses, brake presses and the like – which the Woolston Supermarine factory had never known'.[19] The Westland factory at Yeovil, previously a subcontractor, received its first order for 300 Spitfires in August (and went on to produce 685 in total).[20] Approaches to other manufacturers to take on licensed production went less smoothly. Sir Richard Fairey insisted that his namesake firm would continue to build its own naval aircraft designs rather than Spitfires.

The question of what should come after the Spitfire became important to the RAF. The improved versions that Joe Smith and the Supermarine design team had been developing in 1939–40, the Merlin-engine Spitfire III and the Griffon II-engine Spitfire IV, were not ready to go into production. An interim model, the Spitfire V, would be built until the more advanced Spitfires could be produced. This decision preceded the bombing attacks on Supermarine's Woolston factory, which made it apparent that the Spitfire V was the only way to keep the Spitfire production lines going. Better versions would have to wait.

Though Fighter Command had lost 28 per cent of its pilots in September and 26 per cent in August, its pilot strength had increased from 1396 on 10 August to 1492 on 14 September and 1752 on 12 October.[21] The Germans were not winning the battle of attrition. They had lost 11 per cent of their Bf 109 pilots in July and a further 15 per cent in August. Bf 109 units had started September 1940 with 735 pilots for 740 operational Bf 109s. By the end of the month, some 229 of these pilots had been lost, almost a third.

On 30 September, German twin-engine bombers were sent against

London in daylight. Forty-seven German aircraft were lost as opposed to twenty by the RAF. On 12 October, Hitler reaffirmed that Operation Sea Lion was postponed indefinitely. The General Staff had never been enthusiastic about an invasion plan that, in the final analysis, would likely not work at all, and certainly not unless the Luftwaffe's fighter pilots achieved air superiority. The German Army turned in the life jackets they had been issued over the summer. The dispersal of invasion barges from the Channel ports began. The photo-reconnaissance Spitfires that had reported on the build-up of the barges were now able to watch them leave.

By the end of the daylight battle in October, the Luftwaffe had lost 610 Bf 109s – at least 122 to Spitfires – as well as 235 Bf 110s. The RAF had lost 403 Spitfires and 631 Hurricanes, with between 160 and 219 Spitfires, and 272 Hurricanes, lost to Bf 109s. Total losses, from July to October, are estimated at 550 Spitfires, 750 Hurricanes, 780 Bf 109s and 340 Bf 110s, with 329 victories by Spitfires, 603 by Hurricanes, 534 by Bf 109s and 196 by Bf 110s.[22] The precise numbers can never be known. But it is apparent that throughout the battle, the Bf 109 had an advantage in fighter-to-fighter combat over the Spitfire. This reflected a broad range of influences: the Luftwaffe's numbers, superior German fighter tactics and an overall higher level of training and experience among veteran German fighter pilots, while 11 Group squadrons were trying to disrupt bomber attacks rather than run up scores against fighters.

The RAF was now replacing fighters faster than the Luftwaffe. Fighter Command ended the Battle of Britain with more aircraft and aircrew than it had when it began. But it lacked fully trained fighter pilots, scarcer still fighter leaders who could improvise and improve tactics – a necessity in the absence of strong top-down direction – while training new pilots who had learned little of tactics or gunnery at the OTU. Both sides had lost large numbers of fighter pilots. From May to December, a total of 720 Bf 109 pilots were lost, 65 per cent of the 1110 on duty the day Germany invaded France.[23] The RAF, fighting over their own territory, did not effectively lose a pilot with every plane shot down. The victor was Fighter Command – although, at a Defence Committee meeting in the Cabinet War Room on 31 October, 'Sir

Hugh Dowding said that although we had been successful in defeating the German air attacks by day, we had only done so by a narrow margin.'[24] That margin lay in Britain's intelligence, research and development, industry, training, and, above all, the integrated air defence system that pulled everything together.

The war changes

Daylight air battles with Luftwaffe fighters and fighter-bombers continued through autumn 1940. The losses included many on both sides who had distinguished themselves in the earlier fighting. Johnnie Dundas, Cocky Dundas' ace brother, was shot down and killed in a dogfight moments after he had himself shot down and killed Major Helmuth Wick, then the Luftwaffe's top-scoring ace with fifty-six victories. But the main battle was not the daylight fighting between Spitfires and Bf 109s but rather the Luftwaffe's twin-engine bombers' night bombing campaign, waged against British cities with the aid of radio-navigation systems and specially trained target-marking crews, developed before the war.

Spitfires were of limited use against this German night offensive, dubbed 'the Blitz' by the British press. At night, the Spitfire was less safe than the Hurricane because of its narrower undercarriage that made night landings more hazardous. Most Spitfire pilots were not trained for night flying, limiting combat to moonlit 'fighter nights', when they flew over London through a gap in the searchlight defences, patrolling at predetermined heights to reduce the risks of mid-air collision and friendly anti-aircraft fire. The pilots' only means of detecting the enemy was the 'Mark I Eyeball', supported by directions from ground controllers. Radar coverage, which months before had only been available along the coast, was still limited. The answer was radar-equipped night fighters – inadequate Blenheims and a few new-production Beaufighters.

On 17 October, Dowding and Park had gone through an acrimonious high-level meeting on tactics. Trafford Leigh-Mallory had brought in Douglas Bader (as the only operational pilot to appear, uninvited) as his support when he confronted Park across the conference table in a heated argument. As a result, the 'big wing' rather than 11 Group's tactics would be emphasised. Beaverbrook, shocked by the destruction of the Supermarine factory, had by October lost confidence that Dowding could defend 'his' aircraft factories. Beaverbrook had a 'streak of vindictiveness and even cruelty', according to future prime minister Harold Macmillan, then a junior minister, and wanted Dowding replaced.[25]

Churchill had trusted Dowding throughout the Battle of Britain. He had not interfered with him, nor with Park, who was Dowding's hand-picked man. Churchill had supported Dowding in July when the Air Ministry had considered removing him, saying, 'He is one of the very best men you have got.' But he also could not forget that Dowding had demonstrated iron resolve over the question of reinforcing France in May and he had wavered.[26] Now, German night bombing demonstrated that Fighter Command had built little capability to defeat night attacks under Dowding in the years before the war, even though Dowding had been among the first to urge the development of radar-equipped night fighters.

The controversy over tactics and frustration over Fighter Command's inability to counter the Blitz were among the reasons Dowding, well past his pre-war retirement date, was sacked on 25 November. Given a series of peripheral high-level assignments, he was then retired from the RAF. Air Marshal William Sholto Douglas, who had been Assistant Chief of Air Staff, took over Fighter Command. Douglas had been a strong supporter of the development of radar but instead of backing the Spitfire had wanted Defiants and 'bomber destroyers'. He believed in the RAF's tradition of emphasising the offensive. Douglas would have to expand and rebuild Fighter Command to get it ready to meet the potential threat of a renewed German daylight air offensive in the spring.

As had Dowding, Douglas wanted his hand-picked man commanding 11 Group. Park, exhausted by the Battle of Britain, was replaced by Leigh-Mallory, 'an extremely ambitious man', according to his new staff officer, Group Captain 'Boy' Bouchier.[27] Leigh-Mallory had wanted the job. He listened to Bader, attracted by his charisma, and was able to use Bader's combat experience and his own insistence on 'big wings' to lever Park from command of 11 Group. Park's 'junior executive hand', Lord Willoughby de Broke, was also replaced and sent to RAF public relations.

Bader had made a politically valuable ally. His adjutant at 242 Squadron at Duxford, Flight Lieutenant Peter 'Boozy Mac' Macdonald, was, in civilian life, a Member of Parliament. He ensured that Bader's views received a hearing at the highest levels of government.

Bader wanted to lead large formations of fighters and to be in command, not following the directions of a ground controller. Soon after the 15 September battle the RAF took a serious look at the failings of many of their ground controllers and instituted intensive training. Controllers were increasingly selected from fighter pilots who understood the importance of an altitude advantage, the direction of the sun and that the directions they gave were literally a matter of life and death.[28]

The RAF relied increasingly on Spitfires, even as the first up-engined Hurricane IIs were delivered. Other fighters that, in the pre-war years, had been seen as replacements for the Spitfire all proved unsatisfactory. The Beaufighter, while an effective night fighter, could not defeat Bf 109s by day. The Hawker Tornado had been cancelled when its Vulture engine proved a failure. The Napier Sabre-powered Hawker Typhoon's development was marked by engine problems and structural failures. The twin-engine Westland Whirlwind was produced only in limited numbers.[29] US-built fighters began arriving in ever greater numbers, first purchased by the British or taken over from French contracts, later supplied under Lend – Lease. But the RAF, testing each design in turn, came to the conclusion that none was suited to high-altitude combat against the type of opposition the RAF had encountered over England.

Although the RAF now had access to US aircraft production, this would not help it get the fighters it needed. Future US production would go primarily to the US Army Air Forces (USAAF), the renamed Army Air Corps. USAAF fighter designs reflected its own pre-war thinking rather than British combat lessons. In response to a British specification, North American Aviation's president, James 'Dutch' Kindelberger, managed a programme that, in 117 days, went from blank paper to first flight. Kindelberger's chief designer, Edgar Shmued, was a German-trained engineer, now an American citizen. Among the innovations in the design was a laminar flow wing, thicker than that on the Spitfire and the Bf 109 alike.

The British liked the design, which they named the Mustang, but were concerned that its US-designed Allison engine would be uncompetitive in high-altitude air combat. The RAF ordered the Mustang from North American for low-level tactical reconnaissance, setting up a production line in California.

Spitfire upgrades

In spring 1941, Spitfires and Hurricanes received a partial solution to one of their tactical disadvantages. The carburettor float in the Merlin engine would shut off the flow of fuel under negative gravity, giving Bf 109s a head start in a dive. A quick interim solution was devised by Beatrice 'Tilly' Shilling, one of the few female engineers working at the Royal Aircraft Establishment at Farnborough. A specialist in engines (and a champion motorcycle racer before the war), she designed a simple cut-off allowing fuel to flow through to the carburettor without flooding the engine.[30] Quickly designed, tested and approved, it was rushed into production. In early 1941, Shilling and an RAE team went from base to base modifying every fighter engine. The RAF remained open to ideas that came from outside, from 'scientific blokes' (even when they were not blokes). The British system recognised the importance of the individual innovator.

Officially known as the 'RAE Restrictor', pilots called it 'Miss Shilling's Orifice'. The performance advantage it enabled was greatly appreciated. Rolls-Royce subsequently modified new production Merlins with a carburettor designed to function under negative-g conditions, such as occur when a plane accelerates downwards faster than the natural acceleration due to gravity. Without a modified carburettor (or a fuel injector), this effect would effectively cut off the supply of fuel to the engine. The first deliveries were made in October 1941.

The device made more effective the negative-g bunt evasive manoeuvre that the RAF had improvised during the Battle of Britain. A pilot would slam the control stick towards the forward left corner of the cockpit while his left foot kicked the rudder pedal hard forward and he opened up to full throttle, going 'through the gate' – breaking the wire barrier to cut in emergency boost – if he had not already done so. As the nose of the Spitfire lurched down and it skidded to the left, helped in that direction by engine torque, the pilot would be thrown up against his shoulder straps, his eyes first experiencing white flashes and then 'redding out' as the blood rushed to his head. At this point, without the orifice, his engine would pack up from lack of fuel. In either case, the next step would be to roll and pull into a positive-g turn, pulling hard enough to induce a blackout as the blood now rushed to his feet. This was a manoeuvre better done with power.

But this was an emergency, temporary fix. And in any case, neither approach always worked properly. Pilots learned in combat in the subsequent months that they could not always rely on either technique. Douglas reported, 'Our engines are still liable to temporary failure in flight under negative "g" conditions.'[31]

In 1941, 20mm cannon-armed Spitfire IIBs were coming off the production line at Castle Bromwich. Teardrop fairings added above the wing provided room for the breech mechanism. The shift to a belt-fed cannon design had made possible a weapon that could operate even under the multiple g forces of air combat. The Rotol-design constant-speed propeller was also reintroduced in the IIB, eventually supplanting the De Havilland model that had proven crucial during the Battle of Britain.

The Spitfire V followed the Spitfire II in production, starting in early 1941. Being an interim version, intended to cause minimum disruption to production lines with Supermarine lacking time to develop the Spitfire III or IV, the Spitfire V differed from its predecessors primarily in using the more powerful 1315 hp Merlin 45 engine. But this lacked the two-speed supercharger of the Hurricane II's Merlin XX, a disadvantage at low and medium altitude. Diana Barnato, the ATA ferry pilot, thought that the Spitfire V 'gave a fluttering feeling in flight'.[32]

Compared to the Spitfire II, the Spitfire V was faster (369 mph at 19,500 feet) and had a better rate of climb. Some of the initial production Spitfire VAs were armed with the same eight .303 machine guns as previous Spitfires. Most were Spitfire VBs, with two 20mm cannon and four machine guns. Later, the Spitfire VC had the 'universal wing' that could be armed either with four cannon or two cannon with four .303 machine guns. Spitfire Vs started to equip RAF fighter squadrons in mid-1941, replacing the Spitfire IIs that had, in turn, finished replacing Spitfire Is in April. Not all pilots saw it as an improvement. John

Freeborn, an ace and a veteran of the Battle of Britain, thought, 'It wasn't a patch on the Spitfire II which was replaced by them. The airframe was standard, but the engine was, in my opinion, makeshift, underpowered and rated at the wrong altitude.'[33]

Combat experience over Dunkirk had shown that the original fabric-covered ailerons, despite their light weight, actually felt too heavy on the controls at high speeds, limiting the Spitfire in making high-speed turns and rolls, especially at speeds of 380 mph or over; above 430 mph, they were almost immovable. The fabric covering would 'balloon' off its framework. Fabric-covered ailerons required individual setting which had to be 'tuned' to match the aeroplane, requiring test flying and modifications that slowed deliveries.[34]

The first ailerons covered with aluminium alloy were tested in autumn 1940. They required only 9 lb of stick force to roll at 350 mph, while fabric-covered ailerons had required 43 lb. Jeffrey Quill, who carried out the required test flying, felt with the new ailerons the Spitfire was 'transformed'.[35] In the weeks that followed, the RAF retrofitted its Spitfires with the new ailerons, which were produced and installed as fast as possible. Douglas Bader used his formidable pull to ensure that the squadrons he led were among the first to receive the new ailerons, contractual formalities be damned.

Reconnaissance Spitfires had played an important role in the Battle of Britain. Spitfire Mk I PR Types A, B and C, operational from July 1940, watched the build-up and subsequent build-down of invasion barges in the Channel ports. The improved long-range Spitfire PR IV (modified Spitfire Vs different from the Griffon-powered Spitfire IV prototype), in 1941, gave Britain a vital strategic weapon that could fly over Europe and into Germany in daylight, unarmed, above the effective altitude of interceptors. Other reconnaissance Spitfires operated at low altitude, watching how German radar was being emplaced along the Channel coast. An armed version of the Spitfire PR IV, designated Type G and redesignated PR VII, carried oblique-mounted cameras for low-altitude photography.

The BF 109F

Willy Messerschmitt's reputation had suffered. The Bf 109E had been fought to a standstill by Spitfires. The unstable Me 210 had undergone a protracted and painful development, marked by many crashes, in 1939–41, and was still not ready for production. He needed another success.

In late 1940 and early 1941, German fighter units in northern France received the improved Bf 109F. The design team in Augsburg had made fundamental structural changes: a redesigned wing with rounded wing tips and a retractable tailwheel (though this proved unreliable and was removed on later versions), reducing drag. It was designed with self-sealing fuel tanks. During production, the Bf 109F was equipped with an artificial horizon and radio compass, allowing it to climb through overcast skies. The propeller spinner and radiator designs had also been streamlined. The redesigned tail, like the wing tips, was rounded (the Bf 109E's tail had been angular) and had no external bracing, again reducing drag. Its streamlined cowling demonstrated that Messerschmitt had fixed one of the Bf 109E's major drawbacks: the supercharger air intake was inefficient in forcing air into the engine, only two-thirds as good as that on the Spitfire IA's Merlin.[36] The radiator design was similarly improved.

The Bf 109F had a performance edge over the Spitfire II, especially in climbing and diving. Compared with the Bf 109E, it provided an additional 40 km/h (25 mph), a 10 per cent higher rate of climb (5 minutes 12 seconds to 5000 metres altitude), and more manoeuvrability (18 seconds rather than 25 seconds for a full turn at 1000 metres altitude). The initial F-1 version used the DB 601N engine, running on 96 octane; nitrous oxide injection was added on some F-2 versions, and the F-3 version used the 1300 hp DB 601E (running on 87 octane).

There was no armament in the Bf 109F's redesigned wings, but rather one engine-mounted cannon firing through the propeller hub and two synchronised 7.92mm machine guns, allowing a concentrated armament aligned with the pilot's gunsight. The Bf 109F-1 used the same 20mm FF engine-mounted version unsuccessfully tried on the Bf 109E-3. This was replaced by a 15mm cannon in the Bf 109F-2 model. Though an accurate weapon, most pilots thought its shells lacked explosive power, and the F-4 version went back to 20mm. Designing the wings without internal guns kept them simpler and lighter, while nose-mounted guns were more accurate. The Spitfire was designed from the outset to have all its armament in the wing; the compact Merlin design would have been hard to fit with an engine-mounted weapon.

Many veteran Bf 109 pilots remember the early Bf 109Fs as providing the best flying of any version. Franz Stigler, who was to score twenty-eight victories (while surviving being shot down seventeen times), recalled that 'I preferred the 109F because it flew well at any altitude, was as fast as most . . . had a superior rate of climb and could dive very well. Most of all, it instilled confidence in its pilot.'[37] Günther Rall, who went on to score 275 victories, said, 'The Bf 109F was my ideal fighter.'[38]

Others were not so sure. Hauptmann Walter 'Gulle' Oesau, a leading ace, refused to give up his Bf 109E and its firepower. Galland at first thought the same way. He later had a Bf 109F modified with 20mm cannon in the wings. Assurances that Messerschmitt's previous problems with using an engine-mounted weapon had been cured were only slowly accepted.

In early 1941, Bf 109Fs in action in northern France experienced a series of structural failures. Tail sections came off the aircraft in flight. Pilots watched in horror as Bf 109Fs pulling up from diving attacks would 'clap hands', their wings folding up in mid-air. Major Wilhelm Balthasar, the forty-seven-victory ace commanding JG 2, who had started his career over Spain, was killed when a wing of his Bf 109F came off in a dogfight with Spitfires on 3 July 1941. He was buried in a German Great War cemetery in France, next to his father. Oesau, still flying his Bf 109E, took over in his place.

Faced with the widespread failures in the development – Udet's responsibility – and production of aircraft by the spring of 1941, Göring granted Milch extensive authority over the aircraft industry.[39] He could terminate programmes, build or close factories, and transfer or fire designers and technicians. In May, he formed the RLM's industrial council (*Industrierat*) to provide peer review of designs and procurement plans. Milch resolved to implement mass production, expand the labour force, and end the politicised competition for contracts, which discouraged cooperation and defeated attempts to prioritise resource allocation.

Messerschmitt's troubles with Berlin increased. Hitler still thought him a genius, but his credibility had suffered from over-optimistic promises on aircraft development and production and now the Bf 109F crashes. When Udet had wanted him to concentrate on a few fighter designs, Messerschmitt instead worked on jets, rockets, bombers and huge powered gliders, competing with other companies for resources. Messerschmitt asked Berlin for investment in new aircraft designs, but, with victory imminent, the RLM provided no prioritisation, minimal direction, and few resources for development of these aircraft.[40] His team, starting in mid-1940, was working on a second piston-engine successor to the Bf 109, designated the Me 309, designed by Waldemar Voight, in parallel to the Me 209 II.

In Berlin, the leadership – especially Milch – was outraged at yet more structural failures of Messerschmitt designs. The problems of the Bf 109F brought back everything Milch had said about Willy Messerschmitt since 1931: that he was an aerodynamicist, not a structural engineer, that in his desire to create advanced designs he made aircraft structures too light, and that his designs failed, especially in the tail.

Milch started unravelling the mismanagement of aircraft programmes and production that had expanded unchecked under Udet. Germany had increased aircraft output only by 30 per cent from 1939 to 1941, but this had required doubling the amount of resources allocated. In 1941, Germany produced only a little over half as many aircraft as Britain (11,776 versus 20,094) but consumed a greater amount of aluminium and labour. Messerschmitt had a large amount of freedom from RLM strictures. Germany was short of aluminium. But the RLM allocated each factory the same amount of aluminium for each aircraft to be built, regardless of size, and with no procedures for reallocating material.[41] Factories building the twin-engine Ju 88 bomber found themselves chronically short of aluminium; the plane was redesigned to use less material. Messerschmitt's factories, building smaller Bf 109s, were awash in the scarce metal with no way to return it. Messerschmitt was soon producing portable buildings, ladders, and frameworks for grape-growing, all from surplus aircraft aluminium. Milch, furious, put an end to these product lines.[42]

Milch wanted to meet the need for skilled labour in the German aircraft industry with foreigners, including prisoners of war. Albert Speer complained that 'Internal politics prevented a general use of women in industry.'[43] But, in reality, German women already made up a higher percentage of the overall labour force than in Britain, especially in agriculture. German women were less available for rapid recruitment into the aircraft industry.[44] Some German firms, such as Messerschmitt and its engine-maker, Daimler-Benz, were so short of workers they recruited women. This was vital to them because Messerchmitt's Regensburg plant was among the first to use unskilled labor and Daimler was the first German engine manufacturer to build engines on an automotive-style assembly line.[45] The Germans were reluctant to turn to automotive firms for aircraft and engines, as the British and Americans had done (although the Opel plant at Russelheim became the largest source of Bf 109 undercarriages).

Göring and the Luftwaffe leadership still saw bombers as the highest priority. Anyway, the war would be won in a year, leaving Britain isolated and doomed.

Messerschmitt's old friend, deputy leader Rudolf Hess, flew to Scotland on 10 May 1941 in a Bf 110 taken from the Augsburg factory. Hess thought he was going to bail out and negotiate peace. Instead, he became a prisoner. Still a frequent factory visitor, Hess had convinced Willy Messerschmitt to let him fly the Bf 110 and suggested fuel tank and radio modifications that Messerschmitt had ordered to be implemented. At Augsburg, as had happened with the grounded Bf 108A back in 1934, no one questioned Hess's orders when he wanted to fly a Messerschmitt plane.

In the aftermath of Hess's flight, Messerschmitt was summoned to Munich by Göring. By arguing that he was obliged to carry out unquestioningly the orders of any high official, Messerschmitt avoided possible charges of conspiracy.[46] Messerschmitt's personal relationship with Hitler remained strong. Germany needed him.

Messerschmitt's access to Hitler was important. Rather than rely on the technophobe Göring, who had let him down at Dunkirk and in the Battle of Britain, Hitler informed himself about aircraft and the war in the air by talking directly to men such as Messerschmitt and Galland, both of whom thought he had a greater understanding of technical matters and the situation they faced than did the Luftwaffe leadership. Hitler often made decisions based on these conversations, rather than through a transparent staff process.

The Bf 109F crashes did not stop. Udet took the pilots' concerns to Willy Messerschmitt personally. On 4 April, he sent Messerschmitt a letter summarising twenty-five urgent design flaws in the Bf 109F that had been reported to him. On 27 June, he wrote a personal letter: 'Dear Messerschmitt: The difficulties which have arisen in recent years with your designs ... which have resulted in severe loss of life and time, force me to be completely frank with you for once ... might I remind you of the wing reinforcements on the 109.' The same day, he wrote to Theo Croneiss, holding him responsible for relations with the RLM.[47]

Udet wrote again on 29 July, addressing the long-standing undercarriage problems. 'Let us get one thing completely clear, dear Messerschmitt, it must not occur again that aircraft are destroyed when flying from normal airfields because of an insufficiently strong undercarriage.'[48] Udet's concerns reflected a looming crisis in the Luftwaffe. Even the best pilots, such as Galland, had landing accidents. Indeed, over the course of 1941, the Luftwaffe lost over 650 single-engine fighters to enemy action, but even more – over 750 – to accidents.[49]

Eventually, the Messerschmitt design team worked up a solution to the structural failure problem. The new, rounded tail section had proven too sensitive to certain vibrations. As an interim solution, four external strips were added to the rear fuselage, replaced later on by four additional connecting bolts holding the tail section to the fuselage. Undercarriage problems lacked a comparable solution.

Willy Messerschmitt had his design team working on a new version of the aircraft, the Bf 109G, intended to retain the Bf 109F's superior performance while avoiding its structural flaws. But these would not be available until mid-1942. The Bf 109G would be the first chance for Messerschmitt to incorporate the combat lessons of the Battle of Britain in the design. But he remained committed to retaining his basic design and his original 'light fighter' concept. Minimising changes from the Bf 109F would reduce disruption to production when the new model was introduced.

Fighter Command takes the offensive
In the spring of 1941, the Blitz ended. London had been bombed for seventy-six consecutive nights, and cities throughout the United

Kingdom had been attacked. Over a million houses in London had been destroyed or damaged, and 40,000 civilians had been killed, half of them in London. The Luftwaffe's bombers, unable to operate effectively by day in 1940, had delivered powerful blows by night that much of the RAF, including its Spitfires, could not prevent.

The end of the Blitz, on 10 May 1941, was the result less of improving British night defences than of the fact that Hitler needed the bombers for his next conquests. Fighter Command was still uncertain of Germany's next move; a resurgence of the daylight air offensive was expected. The radar coverage of Britain was extended, and the Chain Home Low system of tower-mounted radar stations for low-altitude coverage, started in 1939 with first deliveries in 1940, was operational in 1941.

Politically, Britain needed to take the offensive against Germany somewhere. The only way this could be done was in the air. The RAF's night bombing of Germany had, so far, inflicted only a fraction of the damage caused by the Blitz. The burden of taking the offensive fell on the RAF's fighters.

Despite Trenchard's Great War doctrine to 'use scouts offensively', the RAF had considered that the main mission of its fighters was to defend the United Kingdom. Using fighters integrated with offensive air power – as the Germans had done since Spain – was secondary. Sholto Douglas had been stating accepted RAF wisdom when he said in March 1940, 'The conclusion had been reached that the escort fighter was really a myth.'[50] Bomber Command, committed to attacking Germany at night, was not interested in escort fighters. The RAF had no one to champion a long-range single-engine escort fighter as Freeman or Dowding had helped pull the Spitfire into service as an interceptor.[51] Long range meant two engines or two seats. Even RAF Beaufighters were at the same disadvantage against Bf 109s in daylight as Bf 110s had been against Spitfires.

A further factor reducing the Spitfires' range was that, over France, they had to cruise at high speed, otherwise they would be vulnerable to Bf 109s diving from higher altitude. Because the Bf 109 accelerated faster in a dive than the Spitfire, diving away from an attack to accelerate was not practical. Spitfires taking the offensive had to keep their speed up or be vulnerable.

The RAF's offensive fighter tactics were improvised, largely by the fighter leaders who had survived the Battle of Britain. Fighter Command started to take the offensive over France in December 1940. The initial offensive missions, codenamed 'Rhubarbs', were penetrations of the Continent, generally at low altitude, by small groups of fighters looking for targets of opportunity, which were usually attacked by strafing. For Johnnie Johnson, who had survived the brevity of his OTU training and an operation for a separated shoulder that had kept him out of most of the Battle of Britain, Rhubarbs were a waste of planes and pilots. 'I loathed these Rhubarbs with a deep, dark hatred. Apart from the flak, the hazards of making a let-down over unknown territory and with no accurate knowledge of the cloud base seemed far too great a risk for the damage we inflicted.'[52] Fighter sweeps, the RAF equivalent of the German *freie Jagd*, were codenamed 'Rodeos'. Three Spitfire squadrons flew the first one on 9 January 1941.[53]

Fighter Command's defensive mission was still a priority. The bombers might return in daylight. Luftwaffe fighter-bomber attacks, especially against airfields and aircraft factories, and high-altitude fighter sweeps were launched as the weather permitted. Fighter Command's air defence system remained much as before, with squadrons held at readiness and waiting the order to scramble.

They were called on to scramble much less often than they had been the year before. The Luftwaffe was not going to make a major effort to defeat the British in daylight in 1941. Instead, the Luftwaffe was moving away. Headquarters, bombers and fighters alike all left the airfields where they had been operating since the summer of 1940, when it seemed that England was going to be overcome much as France had been. By June 1941, the Luftwaffe's defensive fighter force in northern France was effectively reduced to two *Geschwadern*, JG 2 'Richthofen' (the unit had been renumbered before the war) and JG 26 'Schlageter'.[54] Other units went back to Germany to refit and re-equip with the Bf 109F, then returned to fight the RAF, but it was clear that this was an economy-of-force effort by the Luftwaffe. The Bf 109s were needed elsewhere.

Commanding JG 26, Galland now turned his view from the cockpit and his goals from improving his victory score. The Germans still lacked an integrated air defence system that would allow them to intercept

RAF offensive missions effectively. Galland was among those who started to improvise a solution to fighting a defensive air war – something the Luftwaffe had not considered a priority since the long-ago staff studies of 1933 – while the higher leadership was preparing offensives larger and more extensive than anything carried out the year before.

The Bf 109F, first introduced to combat in October 1940, offered improved performance compared to the Spitfire V, which entered operational service in February 1941. Douglas was told, 'When it comes to fighter vs. fighter and the struggle for the altitude gauge, we must expect for the time being to be at a disadvantage as compared with the improved Me 109 we are now meeting.'[55] Leigh-Mallory, commanding 11 Group and responsible for most daylight offensive operations, considered that 'the Me 109F has a slightly superior performance to the Spitfire V'. Johnnie Johnson, flying Spitfires with Douglas Bader, agreed. 'I also thought the Bf 109F was slightly superior to the Spitfire V.'[56]

By mid-1941, the German fighter units in northern France were receiving upgraded Bf 109F-3 and F-4 versions, powered by the new 1350 hp DB 601E engine that could run on the Luftwaffe's standard 87-octane fuel. With two speeds to its single-stage supercharger, making it more capable of maximising engine power, it could outrun a Spitfire V by 30 km/h (20 mph). Its critical altitude was 1000 feet higher than that of the Bf 109E-3. In the Bf 109F-4 model the 15mm engine-mounted cannon was replaced by the improved 20mm MG151 cannon. Survivability was enhanced by a 'cutoff' switch to the cooling system, allowing the Bf 109 to limp home on one of its two radiators, highly appreciated by pilots who thought, like the ace Oberstleutnant Eduard Neumann, 'The coolant was the Achilles' heel of our Messerschmitts.'

The Germans retained their 1940 advantage due to superior tactics, though the gap was closing. German fighter pilots were still predominantly those who had been superbly trained before the war, although some hastily introduced replacements had undergone curtailed training. The reduced operational tempo now gave them time to increase their skills.

As the weather improved in the spring and summer of 1941, in addition to the Rhubarbs and Rodeos, the RAF launched 'Roadsteads',

attacking shipping, and escorted bomber missions codenamed 'Circus'.
Formations of British bombers, usually with heavy escort, operated
over northern France, Belgium and the Netherlands. Sometimes the
bombers would hit targets out of Spitfire range, especially dockyards
and German capital ships sheltering in the harbour of Brest. But the
number of bombers was too small, their bomb load too limited and
their bombing too inaccurate. They were hitting few things important
to the Germans.

The Circus tactics, like those of the Luftwaffe in the Battle of Britain,
relied too heavily on escorting bombers and not enough on supporting
fighter sweeps or taking the offensive against enemy fighters as far as
possible with the Spitfire's limited range. The large RAF escort fighter
formations, known as 'Beehives', were often so unwieldy that the escorting squadrons got in each other's way. Individual German pilots found
they could slip through to make the vertical slashing attacks, climbing up,
attacking, then diving away, to which the Bf 109F was particularly well
suited, without having to fight Spitfires on their own terms. Spitfires
escorting bombers, at low speed and altitude, were particularly vulnerable. If they saw German attackers, they could rely on their superior
turning performance to evade while the Germans climbed away and
looked for less attentive Spitfires. Otherwise, they were at a disadvantage.
In the Battle of Britain, the Bf 109s had been forced to fight Spitfires to
defend their bombers; now they could choose when to intercept.

The aim of all these operations was to force the Germans into decisive air battles where Fighter Command would now have the advantage
of numbers. The RAF, like the Germans when they attacked the coastal
convoys in July 1940, thought that by threatening peripheral targets with
bombers, the enemy would rise to the bait.

These tactics did not lead to success. The Bf 109 units remaining in
the west had been tasked with avoiding losses. In July, they suspended
fighter-bomber raids and fighter sweeps over England. With a break
from December to February 1941, these had been carried out in diminishing numbers and frequency since the Battle of Britain. The Luftwaffe
was willing to fight for few targets within Spitfire range. After the
Luftwaffe had withdrawn many fighters, those that remained waited for
RAF mistakes or for when they could fight at an advantage. The

Bf 109F was suited for these tactics. It was able to climb quickly, attack, usually in a dive, and disengage, then climb back to attack again.

Douglas Bader, promoted to wing commander, led in combat the wing based at Tangmere in Sussex. This by itself was a tactical improvement. Previous RAF multi-squadron fighter formations committed to battle had no single, permanent commanding officer but rather had one of the squadron commanders in charge. From now on, Spitfire and Hurricane operations from English bases would be predominantly offensive rather than defensive. The wing, with about thirty-six Spitfires in the air, would be the basic fighting formation, rather than the twelve-Spitfire squadron formations employed during the Battle of Britain.

Bader smoked his pipe on combat missions, leading the Tangmere Wing over France, sometimes flying over the Great War cemetery where his father was buried. Backed by Leigh-Mallory (who had authorised the legless pilot to fly before the war), Bader had a great impact on the RAF. A man once called a legless invalid was now one of Fighter Command's highest-scoring aces. Along with Flight Lieutenant Cocky Dundas, who became one of his close associates, Bader took it on himself to work out new tactics that used pairs of Spitfires and flights of four, based on the German example.[57] Bader, with Dundas as a wingman, led four Spitfires on 8 May 1941 to try out 'the finger four' formation in combat. It was judged a success. All survived, Dundas barely. He glided his shot-up Spitfire back to RAF Hawkinge, having encountered a Bf 109 flown by Oberstleutnant Werner Mölders who had written up these tactics in Spain. Mölders claimed Cocky as his sixty-eighth victory, the second time he had shot him down. Fighter Command still had a way to go before they could equal German tactical expertise.

Moreover, Bader's iron will and flying skill did not directly lead to an understanding of the realities of air combat at the operational level. Bader, described by an admiring Cocky Dundas as 'mercurial, impatient, unconventional', was a man who evoked strong, polarising opinions. Leigh-Mallory admired his fighting spirit. Dowding and Park resented what they saw as his role in having them sacked. Flying Officer 'Nobby' Clarke – the 145 Squadron Spitfire pilot who thought German planes smelled of death – considered the 'Bader regime' at Tangmere unappealing and put in for a transfer. Dundas learned combat leadership lessons from Bader, applying them when he was given his own Hawker Typhoon squadron to command. Flying Officer Johnnie Johnson, arriving at Tangmere with 616 Squadron, started flying as one of Bader's and Dundas' wingmen and understudies. He found Bader an inspiration and a brilliant combat leader.

Although neither Bader nor Galland was in charge of overall fighter operations or tactical development, both did exert influence on how their air arms would fight and what tactics they would use. Both were first and foremost fighter pilots, leading from the cockpit. Both had come away from the Battle of Britain with a fighter-centric view of air warfare. For several months, their planes – Spitfire Vs and Bf 109Fs – units and tactics shaped air combat over northern France.

On the offensive, the Spitfire's limited range was still a handicap, much as the Bf 109E-3's had been over England the year before. The RAF needed its Spitfires and Hurricanes to be able to fly longer distances. The Norwegian campaign of 1940 and the need to ferry fighters in the Middle East had brought this lesson home. As a result, Supermarine modified some Spitfire IIs with a single fixed external fuel tank holding 40 gallons. Three squadrons were equipped with this modification. Combat performance was reduced and handling atrocious, especially if trying to land with the external tank full. 10 Group reported 'strong protests by the pilots' assigned to fly it.[58]

The next step was for Supermarine to design 30- and 45-gallon drop tanks that could be carried under the fuselage centreline, which required adding hardpoints to attach the tank and plumbing to feed the engine.[59] These would not be tested and operational until early 1942.

An internal 29-gallon rear fuselage tank was designed and fitted to some Spitfires, also capable of using the drop tanks, but this would not be tested and approved until July 1942. The Spitfire's design was finely balanced. Additional fuselage tanking would move the centre of gravity to the rear, affecting stability and performance; those Spitfire Vs and later with additional rear fuselage tanks were not supposed to use them unless they would be empty in combat. The Spitfire's thin wing section had little room for fuel along with the armament. (Unarmed reconnaissance Spitfires with wing tanks were capable of longer range.)

When on the offensive, the RAF's Spitfire squadrons had all the disadvantages that the Germans experienced over Britain. Their pilots were captured or lost in the Channel if shot down or victims of engine failure. While, in 1940, the Germans had the first effective air–sea rescue organisation to pick pilots out of the Channel with seaplanes, the RAF only slowly put together a similar capability.

Some RAF units still flew in the three-plane 'vic' that had been common in 1940. But few other wings had adopted Bader's more flexible tactics outright. Others had switched to four-plane sections but often flew in line astern or relied on the 'weavers' who had proved vulnerable so often in the Battle of Britain.[60]

The bitter lessons of 1940 often had to be relearned by new squadrons. Before the end of 1941, the BCATS (formerly EATS) graduates arrived in Spitfire squadrons. But even after they had been through the expanded Fighter Command OTUs, those trained in the blue skies of Canada often lacked sufficient experience with British weather.

The RAF remained short of veteran fighter pilots.[61] In 1941, forty-six new squadrons were created in Fighter Command. Each of these required a veteran cadre of leaders, further diluting the number of skilled pilots available. Even before the heavy attrition of 1941's spring and summer battles, RAF fighter squadrons averaged only five experienced pilots.[62] This raised accident rates; pilots overstressed Spitfire Vs, causing structural failures. The experienced fighter leaders of 1940 had rotated out of squadron command or been shot down. As the number of pre-war pilots was reduced by losses or promotions, the average age of Spitfire pilots decreased to twenty-one or less. Yet morale remained high, despite the heavy losses to both the Germans and the risks of wartime flying. The new British pilots were drawn from throughout society, an improvised meritocracy. Churchill said of them in 1941, 'They have saved this country; they have the right to rule it.'[63]

British Spitfire pilots were also joined by increasing numbers of pilots from the Commonwealth and occupied Europe, who formed their own Spitfire squadrons. By 1941, even in RAF squadrons, Spitfire pilots were multinational. Most wore the RAF blue uniform, neckties and all. Some wore the dark blue of the Royal Australian Air Force or the khaki of the South African Air Force. Poles wore elements of their national uniform and affected soft brown leather riding boots. The most important uniform element, next to the wings and any decoration ribbons, were the shoulder tabs bearing the name of their home country.

Fighter pilots wore the top button of their tunics unbuttoned. They joked in a slang-laced banter reserved for themselves alone and intended to be opaque to outsiders, and in the two separate worlds of the officers' and sergeants' messes, called each other by their nicknames, with only the most senior officer being 'sir'. While parties in the officers' mess were limited by operational requirements and shortages of drink, they sometimes became joyful alcohol-fuelled bedlam that shocked USAAF fighter pilots.[64] The sergeants' mess, where youthful pilots were often presided over by the formidable figure of the older (non-flying) station warrant officer and other senior ground personnel, tended to be a more sedate establishment. This contributed to the appeal of the local pub. Most fighter stations had different 'locals' for flying and ground personnel. There, they drank and talked alongside the local civilians, whose concerns did not include the unspoken presence of violent death in the air on a daily basis; even when not in combat, fighter pilots still had to deal with flying in British weather conditions, potentially more lethal than the Luftwaffe. While many of the most successful pilots were serious-minded and abstemious (like Bader), youth and high spirits, coupled with an acute but always unspoken awareness of impending mortality, made alcohol important to most fighter pilots on both sides of the conflict.

The squadrons that fought and partied together had changed from the more static pre-war models into fighting organisations created from countless reciprocal interactions and expectations between superiors and subordinates, some defined by the King's Regulations, more by custom, personality (such as the 'Bader regime') and the unspoken but powerful expectations made of an RAF fighter pilot. Spitfires may have been constructed of interchangeable parts, but their pilots were as individual as possible in a mass military organisation of the industrial age. The web of human behaviour established on a daily basis on the ground had impact in combat in the air.

RAF Fighter Command recruited pilots and technicians among escapees from every occupied country in Europe. Because of their shortage of replacement aircrew, the exiles' air arms concentrated on fighter units. Reports of the Battle of Britain had inspired volunteers for the RAF worldwide: from neutral Eire, Mexico, Argentina, Brazil and Thailand. The first few US volunteers had flown in the Battle of Britain. Their numbers soon expanded. By the time of Pearl Harbor, the RAF had three Spitfire-equipped Eagle squadrons of US pilots. These were not the only US volunteers. About 15 per cent of the RCAF's aircrew in 1941 were Americans.

Some Spitfire squadrons took on a multiracial character, as the first few pilots from Africa and the West Indies – authorised in June 1940 – completed training. Their example inspired other young men from their homelands to enlist: over 5000 West Indians served as RAF ground personnel, over 300 as aircrew, plus 50 from west Africa. The perceived differences between the RAF and the other British services, more than neckties for all, included the presence of fewer racial barriers.[65]

Those who could not volunteer to fly could volunteer their money. Lord Beaverbrook set up a 'Spitfire Fund'. In return for a donation to the war effort, you named 'your' Spitfire. Money came in from all over the world, £13 million by April 1941. The red-haired women of Australia contributed for 'Gingerbread', a Spitfire flown by a red-haired Australian pilot. The value was not so much the money, but the emotional commitment to the RAF and Britain's victory that came with it.

Fighters over France – 21 June, 2 July, 9 August 1941
When Circus 17 crossed the French coast at about 1220 hours on the bright sunlit afternoon of 21 June 1941, the German radar system and fighter ground control provided about forty-five minutes' warning. The Circus consisted of some fifty RAF fighters escorting six Blenheim bombers of 21 Squadron, flying at 11,000 feet, heading for the German airfield at St Omer. Hurricanes and Spitfires, stacked up in the cloudless sky above the bombers, flew at 25,000 feet and beyond. The Polish Northolt Wing was providing the escort, with 303 Squadron flying above the Blenheims, while twelve Hurricane IIs of Bader's old 242 Squadron, now commanded by the New York-born multi-millionaire (and pre-war Auxiliary Air Force pilot) Squadron Leader Whitney

Straight MC, flew close escort. He reported that the Hurricanes 'were flying in pairs, in line astern, three on each side of the bombers'. But one of the Blenheims was straggling, out of formation. Straight thought it had turned for home, but it was instead pressing on, by itself, behind the formation.[66]

Adolf Galland had been alerted while doing paperwork in his office. After a quick briefing, he and his wingman, Oberfeldwebel Bruno Hegenauer, were in the first Bf 109F-2s off the ground at the headquarters strip at Audembert at 12.24 p.m. They climbed quickly, while a further thirty Bf 109s of JG 26 formed up to intercept. Some six minutes after scrambling, Galland and Hegenauer were above and up-sun from the incoming formation. They had not attracted the escort's attention. Galland quickly assessed the situation.

'The best approach to a battle is surprise,' Galland said. Rather than wait and form up for a mass attack, potentially losing the element of surprise and letting the bombers hit their target, Galland and Hegenauer hurtled down in a diving attack, from out of the sun, aiming at the straggling Blenheim, alone and vulnerable. Galland's cannon hit one of the Blenheim's engines. It exploded. Galland had time to see at least two of the Blenheim's crew parachute out.

Neither the Canadian Hurricanes nor the Polish Spitfires had been able to halt Galland's attack until he had hit the Blenheim. Galland went diving past, then climbed back for another attack. By this time, the five remaining Blenheims had bombed St Omer airfield and were heading for home. Galland could not see any of JG 26's Bf 109s attacking them. Before diving to attack again, he gave the order over the radio: '*Angriff!* [Attack!]'

In his second assault, Galland was alone. Hegenauer had not been able to follow him through the attack. Galland could not see him. Galland's personal tactics, using long vertical dives and tight pull-outs, made it difficult for wingmen to stay with him, often leaving them vulnerable.

Four minutes after his first attack on the bombers (and eight minutes after scrambling), Galland attacked another of the Blenheims, again diving from behind. This time Straight, alerted, saw him. 'One yellow nosed Bf 109F dived down through the escort and made an above and astern attack on the leading bombers.'

This time, to make sure he had the chance to land a lethal blow before he overshot his (slower) target, Galland throttled back his Bf 109F–2.

He pulled the twin triggers on the control stick with a three-second burst.

The Blenheim's rear gunner returned fire, but Galland had the greater firepower. The Blenheim was hit. Galland claimed the victory though the Blenheim managed to limp back to England.

Straight came to the aid of the stricken Blenheim. 'I turned and opened fire. When the enemy aircraft was about 500 yards from the Blenheim, it broke away, upwards.' But even with his Hurricane IIB's two-speed supercharged Merlin XX engine, Straight, who had been throttled back to keep pace with the Blenheims, could not catch Galland, who used the momentum from his diving attack to pull up into a zoom climb. Straight, the fleeting target in his gunsights, pushed the trigger button on his control stick. 'I fired continuously for about seven seconds.' But Straight scored no hits with his four 20mm cannon. He 'did not pursue but rejoined the formation'.

Galland quickly accelerated to maximum speed (causing smoke to billow from his exhausts, which led Straight to think he had hit him) and climbed away from the stricken Blenheim, leaving Straight behind.

'Make your attack and disappear and start a new attack. Don't get engaged and make it a dogfight' was Galland's maxim but not, at that instant, what he did. Instead, he flew directly into the Spitfires of 303 Squadron. Rather than disengage, he turned to attack from below and behind the Spitfire flown by Pilot Officer Marian Belc. Galland 'pulled up and cut power to make my enemies overshoot, and I extended flaps to further slow me down, and then I kicked the rudder hard to yaw right. One Spitfire flew past and I snapped a quick shot and scored some good hits.' Galland hit the Spitfire before it could react.

Pilot Officer Boleslaw 'Gandhi'[67] Drobinski, Belc's friend and a veteran of the Battle of Britain, swiftly turned into firing position behind Galland's climbing Bf 109 from below, now at low speed and highly vulnerable. He framed the wings in the inner illuminated circle of his reflector sight, before pressing the trigger button on the top of the

Spitfire's control stick with one gloved finger. 'I opened fire, hitting the Messerschmitt beneath the fuselage,' he recalled.

Galland, focused on Belc's Spitfire, was surprised when the Bf 109F was hit in its right wing and immediately broke off his attack. Galland started going down, trailing white smoke from his damaged radiator. Drobinski, following orders, did not follow Galland down to finish him off. He watched Galland dive 'away in the direction of Calais with a thick trail of smoke coming from his engine'. Straight also saw Galland going down. Belc made it back to England (Galland claimed him as a victory, but this was not officially confirmed).

Galland was able to keep control of the damaged Bf 109, diving down into clouds. 'The engine oil light went on. Some smoke began entering the cockpit; I lost power and threw the throttle full open to get more power to get out of there. I radioed my plight and headed for the deck.' His engine stopped. But Galland used his glider-pilot skills to belly-land safely on a German airfield. A quick flight in a Bf 108 brought him back to home base.

Hegenauer was less fortunate. Separated from Galland after the first attack, he found himself the target of a Spitfire flown by Wing Commander 'Johnny' Kent, the Canadian ace leading the Northolt Wing of Polish Spitfire squadrons. 'I couldn't have fired many rounds when there was a brilliant flash on the starboard wing root of the 109 and the whole wing came off.' Hegenauer was able to parachute out.

Then Kent was separated from his own wingman. 'I had not gone far before I was attacked by five Messerschmitts.' Kent's superb flying and the over-aggression of the Bf 109 pilots – two almost collided, each trying to finish off the seemingly doomed lone Spitfire – kept him alive. Then he saw an opportunity to escape. 'Like a flash I whipped into a left-hand turn, rolled onto my back to accelerate more quickly, and then as I gained speed rolled right way up again, diving for the sea at full throttle.' Kent made it home.[68]

Galland was scrambled a second time that day at 1630 hours against another RAF Circus formation on its way home. This time, his Bf 109F-2 destroyed, he was flying a Bf 109E.

Once again, he was one of the first Bf 109 pilots off the ground and, as before, rather than forming up with the other Bf 109s for a mass attack, he climbed to intercept the British. With Hegenauer injured, he was alone. Douglas Bader's Tangmere Wing, their Spitfires flying in the loose finger-four formations adapted from the Germans, was the vanguard, ahead of the bombers to 'de-louse' the airspace.

Climbing to 20,000 feet, even though he could see the rest of I/JG 26 forming up, Galland attacked the Tangmere Wing by himself. He had used cloud cover to enable lone attacks before. He would make a single pass and then dive away.

Galland spotted six Spitfires of 616 Squadron heading for home over the Channel. He attacked the 'tail end Charlie', the most vulnerable Spitfire in the formation, flown by Pilot Officer Edward Brown. Opening fire from 100 metres range, Galland reported it shot down in flames. Brown did not survive.

Galland then 'did something stupid. I was following the burning Spitfire down when I was bounced and shot up badly.'[69] Galland had not seen the Spitfires of 145 Squadron coming up behind him. Sergeant Reginald 'Reg' Grant, a New Zealander flying a cannon-armed Spitfire IIB, reported that 'a 109E suddenly loomed out of the haze in front of me at 20,000 feet'. Grant turned towards the tail of Galland's Bf 109E. 'I throttled back and gave him a three-second burst with my cannon at 100 yards closing to 50 yards. Black smoke burst from the cockpit and he rolled over slowly to the left and dived into the sea. I was rather excited and circled around, watching him go in. Luckily he was alone and I was not attacked.'[70]

Galland heard and felt the Bf 109 hit by 20mm cannon fire. 'This RAF fighter pilot shot exceedingly well,' he recalled.[71] Grant had riddled the Bf 109 with cannon shells. Fragments wounded Galland: 'My plane was on fire, and I was wounded. I saw blood splatter in the cockpit against the inside of the canopy.'

Galland was losing blood. The Bf 109 was losing fuel and coolant. The engine was shaking and making loud grinding noises. Still at 17,000 feet, he flicked off the damaged engine's ignition switch to reduce the risk of fire. But, rather than going into the Channel, as Grant thought, Galland broke away into the low clouds and headed back to the airfield. En route, the leaking fuel exploded. 'Smoke filled the cockpit, and flames were visible just under the inside of firewall, under the control panel. I had lost rudder and aileron control. All the glass had been shattered, the canopy cracked, and the throttle had been shot away. The joystick where my hand had been had lost about two inches of height from a round that struck it. I could hear the wind whistling through the broken canopy Plexiglas.'

Galland's Bf 109E was blazing. He unstrapped himself from his seat and released the cockpit canopy, ready to bail out. The canopy had been damaged by Grant's gunfire. It jammed.

Galland heaved on the canopy jettison lever. Nothing happened. Then, standing up on his seat, using one leg to hold the control stick forward to prevent the plane from going into a spin, he threw his weight against the jammed canopy with his body. It gave way.

Galland followed it – halfway out. He was stuck. Parts of the damaged canopy frame had stayed in place on the Bf 109E. 'The fighter rolled over, inverted, and I could see the ground quite clearly.'

In desperation, with the burning plane now starting to spin, he wrapped his arms round the radio antenna behind the cockpit and heaved. He pulled himself from between the jagged edges of the remaining pieces of the canopy. He popped out.

His parachute was undamaged. Galland was able to open it just before impact. On landing, he injured his ankle. Unable to move, he was rescued by French farmers. Rushed to a German military hospital, Galland recovered sufficiently to insist on smoking cigars on the operating table.[72] He was notified that he had become the first recipient of Germany's new top decoration for heroism, the Knight's Cross with Oak Leaves and Swords.

On the morning of 2 July, despite being medically grounded from his previous wounds and having been officially taken off operations, Galland watched his ground crew chief, Unteroffizer Gerhard Meyer, who had kept his personal Bf 109s flying since the Battle of Britain, install a section of armour plate in his new Bf 109F-2, delivered to replace that lost on 21 June.

But then the order came just after noon: '*Alarmstart!* [Scramble!]'

For his first combat mission since being shot down twice on 21 June, Galland hastily strapped himself into the cockpit. He leaned back to slide his feet into the rudder pedal stirrups. Then Galland 'felt as if I had been hit in the head with a club. I could not really focus for a minute, the pain was so intense.' He had banged his head against the armour plate that Meyer – standing on the wing in his black overalls, helping Galland to strap in – had just installed.

'*Dummkopf!*' Galland cursed Meyer, then slammed the canopy and taxied out for take-off. Galland formed up a formation of JG 26 against the incoming Circus, heading for a power station at Lille. He 'reached a favourable position for attacking. I gave the order for the attack and I was the first to dive down through the English fighter escort on to the bombers.' Again, he opened with a diving attack on the Blenheims despite the large fighter escort.

'Flying in a shallow right bank, I fired from a distance of about 200 yards right down to ramming distance at one of the Blenheims in the first row of the formation.'

Galland's skill as a marksman told. 'Pieces of metal and other parts broke away from the fuselage and from the right engine. Then she went up in flames and smoke.'[73]

The escorts recovered from their surprise. Galland and his wingmen fought a swirling dogfight with the Spitfires. Galland turned behind a Spitfire V, flying at about 15,000 feet. Its pilot seemed not to see him. Galland closed into firing position, concentrating on the target, setting up a shot, ready to open fire when he was too close to miss.

Galland's Bf 109F shuddered as if hit by a huge stick. He felt the force of impact and pain in his back. He had been hit from behind by a 20mm cannon shell. 'Everything rattled inside my crate. My cockpit was shattered. But what is more, my head got it again. Warm blood was running down my face. I was afraid of a blackout. I must not lose consciousness!'[74]

Galland had not seen Squadron Leader Marian Pisarek's Spitfire VB turning into firing position behind him. Pisarek was the wrong man for Galland to have there. A five-victory Polish ace who had recently taken command of 308 Squadron, Pisarek 'saw an Me 109 attempting to make a surprise attack. I flew towards him and fired a short burst at 100 yards range. The enemy aircraft immediately burst into flames and black smoke.'[75]

'With a great effort I succeeded in shaking off my pursuer,' Galland later recalled.

Pisarek had no time to watch Galland go down or try to finish him off. He was attacked by other Bf 109s from JG 26. 'I noticed cannon shells burst on my tail unit and machine gun bullets struck my wings, tail and engine.' Pisarek half-rolled his Spitfire inverted into a dive and disengaged, chased by two Bf 109s, one following him 'half-way across the Channel' before it gave up.

Smoke was streaming from Galland's Bf 109F. Pisarek's cannon shell had hit just behind the cockpit. Once again injured, Galland crash-landed back at his field. He was taken back to the same surgeon who tolerated cigar smoking.

Without the armour plate installed that morning, Galland would have been killed instantly. On recovery, he gave Meyer a three-day pass, champagne from his private stock and 100 Reichsmarks in cash, saying, 'That's how much my head is worth.'

'An excellent weapon and luck had been on my side, to be successful the best fighter pilot needs both.' Galland's experience – shot down three times on three consecutive combat missions – shows the mounting odds against even the Luftwaffe's most talented fighter pilots and the irreplaceable value of pure luck.[76] With a total of seventy victories, Galland was now one of Germany's national heroes. His smiling face was put on postcards for use back in Germany. In addition to ensuring a constant supply of drink, cigars and female admirers, he used his hero status to set up a model railway layout in his headquarters. He was able to get his two younger brothers, Wilhelm-Friedrich 'Wutz' and Paul, who had completed fighter pilot training, transferred to JG 26. He even got elder brother Fritz into fighter training, forgiving him for childhood rivalries. Galland was summoned to Germany to receive his Knight's Cross with Oak Leaves, Swords and Diamonds from Hitler himself. The ornate medal, worn around the neck, proved too heavy for its issue ribbon. One of his girlfriends volunteered a garter. Galland tucked it under his collar and suspended the medal from it.

The RAF continued the daylight offensive. Churchill had demanded longer-ranged fighters for escorts. Air Chief Marshal Sir Charles Portal, the Chief of Air Staff, had told him this was not possible. Churchill was unconvinced. 'We have got to adapt machines to the distances that have to be traversed.'[77] The RAF had not, before the war, envisioned the need for long-range offensive fighters. They had not thought such aircraft were necessary or even feasible. Now, they started to feel their lack of such a capability.

On 12 August, fifty-four Blenheims made a daylight low-level raid on targets in western Germany. Spitfire IIs with non-jettisonable long-range tanks flew as part of the escort. RAF losses – ten Blenheims and four Spitfires – meant that even escorted operations could not be sustained. The RAF wanted to use Spitfire Vs with 30-gallon external drop tanks for longer-range operations. These would be ready in 1942. The RAF built up its night bomber forces. But it would be 1942 before they could inflict substantial damage.

Wing Commander Douglas Bader, with twenty-two and a half victories, was shot down during the Circus operation on 9 August 1941, probably a 'friendly fire' victim of another Spitfire.[78] With his Spitfire going down, the tail section shot off and the side of the cockpit smashed, Bader jettisoned the cockpit canopy, raised his arms, grabbed the windscreen and heaved himself out of the cockpit with all his might. He made it halfway out of the cockpit, into the slipstream. That was as far as he got. Bader was trapped.

He yanked at his right leg where the mangled aluminium was holding him fast. The straps holding his artificial leg parted. Bader was able to escape the tumbling tailless Spitfire by parachute, a Bf 109 circling close by and watching the seemingly one-legged pilot.

When Bader dropped in, Galland welcomed him to dinner with JG 26, showed him his model railway, introduced him to a one-legged Luftwaffe pilot and allowed him to sit in the cockpit of a Bf 109F. Bader's request for a test flight was refused. Galland asked his higher headquarters to radio a message to England so that Bader could receive his spare legs from Tangmere.[79] The RAF insisted on having them dropped by parachute from a Blenheim bomber over the German airfield at St Omer. Bader entered captivity with his usual in-your-face response to adversity. He was finally hauled off to a prisoner-of-war camp in Germany, planning escape.

Bf 109s' Blitzkrieg

In spring 1941 many of the Bf 109s redeployed from northern France were committed to the German campaign in the Balkans. The Luftwaffe had already been playing a major role in consolidating Germany's position, helping to secure alliances with Romania and Bulgaria with promises of supplying aircraft and training pilots.[80]

Yugoslavia's accession to a pro-German Balkan pact on 25 March 1941 proved so unpopular that within two days a coup by General Dušan Simović, the *Vazduhplovstvo Vojske Kraljevine Jugoslavije* (VVKJ, Royal Yugoslav Air Force) chief of staff, established a new government in the name of King Peter. Hitler flew into a rage and ordered the army to overrun Yugoslavia and the Luftwaffe to level its capital.[81]

The German invasion of Yugoslavia again brought Bf 109Es into action *against* the Luftwaffe. Germany and Britain had both used the supply of combat aircraft as a way to try to influence Yugoslavia. Germany supplied eighty-three Bf 109E-3s in 1939–41. The British matched them by supplying Hurricanes (and a manufacturing licence). By the time Germany invaded, only forty-six Bf 109Es were operational in Yugoslavia.

German air attacks on Belgrade on 6 April inflicted devastating damage. Despite matching Bf 109Es against each other, the air battles over Belgrade were hardly an even fight. The Luftwaffe had the advantage of surprise, combat experience, numbers and superior tactics. Yugoslavia had been forced to cut back on flight hours due to economic constraints in previous years. The German Bf 109Es all had armour, self-sealing fuel tanks and the improved Revi gunsights that their opponents lacked.

One of the Bf 109E pilots defending Belgrade on 6 April was Narednik-vodnik I klase (Sergeant) Karlo Strebenk.[82] He damaged a German Bf 109 before being shot down twice. The first time he glided back to his airfield and took off in another Bf 109E; the second time he was killed. Near Pazova, Adjudant Zvonimir Halambek was flying one of four Bf 109Es surprised by a large formation of Bf 110s of I/ZG 26.

In front of us, the pair of Lieutenant Kolarov and Sergeant Milošević were hit and flamed by the enemy. They bailed out. I moved in front of my leader, Capitain Ercigoj, as he apparently did not see this. I turned left and positioned myself behind the enemy formation . . . From the distance of some 400 meters the gunners opened fire at me. At the same moment, I also opened cannon and machinegun fire into the middle of the formation: the third plane on the right went into an abrupt dive, smoking and then in flames. I continued to fire. Suddenly, I felt my aircraft jolt. An aircraft made a chandelle next to me. I thought it was Captain Ercigoj. I looked closer and saw it was a Me 110. I immediately rolled inverted from horizontal flight and dived from an altitude of 4200 meters until I found myself at 600 meters.

Halambek, despite damage from the Bf 110's attack, managed to make a successful belly landing.[83] But fifteen Yugoslavian Bf 109Es were shot down or damaged beyond repair on the first day of the war. On 7 April, the second day of the war, fifteen Yugoslavian Bf 109Es were sent against twenty-six Ju 87 Stukas attacking rail targets. Some twenty Luftwaffe Bf 109Es came to the aid of the Stukas, shooting down seven without loss in a swirling low-altitude dogfight. Yugoslavia lost a total of nine more Bf 109Es on the second day. The survivors fought on until resistance collapsed.

Luftwaffe Bf 109 units participated throughout the campaign that saw Yugoslavia and Greece quickly overrun. With air superiority achieved, this included numerous fighter-bomber and ground strafing missions. Bomb-carrying Bf 109Es were used against ships during the battles off Greece and Crete; on 22 May, they inflicted damage on the battleship HMS *Warspite* and the cruiser HMS *Fiji*. The latter was finished off by dive-bombing Ju 88s.

But soon, the participating units moved into forward airfields in German-occupied Poland, ready for Operation Barbarossa, the invasion of the Soviet Union. Luftwaffe fighter units had not recovered from the Balkan campaign or even from the Battle of Britain. Germany was producing less than a quarter of the number of fighters built by Britain and the US, now available to the British under Lend-Lease. Eight hundred and thirty Bf 109s led the invasion, fewer than had been involved in the invasion of France the year before. Most of the single-engine fighters were Bf 109Es, now increasingly worn out. Spare part shortages were unabated. Milch, aware of the Luftwaffe's limitations, urged Göring to go to Hitler and oppose the invasion; Hitler was not interested in reasons not to invade.[84] Jeschonnek, the Luftwaffe chief of staff, remained convinced Hitler was infallible.

Operation Barbarossa opened on 22 June 1941 with attacks on airfields. The Soviet Air Force had not been dispersed and large numbers were destroyed on the ground, over 1200 on the first day alone. Those Soviet planes that took off were defeated by the attackers. Some 322 Soviet aircraft were shot down on the first day, five by Hauptmann 'Fürst' Wilcke alone.[85] Stalin, having never trusted anyone else in his life, had so relied on Hitler that he considered warnings of the impending invasion from Churchill and his own intelligence sources alike mere attempts at provocation. The initial blow had hit unprepared defences.

Bf 109s fought differently in the east than they had over Britain. It was a low-altitude air war, with air combat seldom taking place at over 15,000 feet. Formations tended to be smaller, not the hundreds of bombers that had attacked London. While radar was vital in the west and aircraft were integrated into an air defence system, in the east the use of radar was more limited. The Soviets were behind both the British and Germans in developing radar technology. Soviet radar was kept primarily in defence of cities. Few German radars operated in the east.

In 1941, although many Soviet fighter units still flew the same I-16 *Rata* that the Bf 109B had outperformed in 1937, the Germans were surprised also to encounter numbers of modern fighters powered by in-line engines, including the Yak-1 and MiG-3. But these were unable to hold off the Luftwaffe. The Soviets, emphasising numbers of aircraft produced, had made insufficient spare parts to sustain the new fighters in combat. Most Soviet fighter aircraft had been delivered without radios. In the months before the invasion, the Soviets had inadequate training time and flying hours for their pilots to become proficient and work out tactics that would take advantage of their new fighters' performance. The combat lessons of Spain had made little impression on Soviet fighter tactics. The Soviet Air Force had suffered from defeats in the 1939–40 Russo-Finnish War as well as the effects of Stalin's purges (and were in the throes of a renewed round when the Germans attacked).[86]

The heavy Soviet losses of 1941 wiped out many of their cadre of experienced pre-war leaders and pilots. The Soviets sent inexperienced pilots into combat against Bf 109 aces. Oberleutnant Herbert Kaiser flew Bf 109s in III/JG 77. 'Against the early Russian aircraft, the Me 109E was untouchable. The Soviet planes were slower and could not climb with us. They were, however, highly maneuverable, especially the I-15 and I-16 and one could not allow an encounter to deteriorate into a contest of turns. This was easily avoided because we always had the element of surprise, due to our high speed and advanced communications systems.'[87] Many victories were scored by skilful German pilots in a target-rich environment. Gerhard Barkhorn, who had flown over 100 combat missions in 1940 without scoring a victory, shot down many hastily trained Soviet pilots. 'Many of them never looked around to clear their tails. They never looked around in the cockpit and it was relatively easy to approach a flight of them and score several kills before they knew what was happening.'[88]

The size of the eastern front and the failure of the German logistics system led to air operations being restricted by lack of fuel, parts and ordnance as early as July 1941. The motorised forward support units that followed the German Army's advance, as in Poland and France, allowed the Luftwaffe's own units to provide continuous support to its planes. But by the beginning of October, only some 58 per cent of the Bf 109s on the eastern front were serviceable.[89] While the 1941 campaign against the Soviets was, for Bf 109 units, a victory rather than the defeat they had suffered against Britain, the number of losses they suffered was comparable. Neither was sustainable. Up until November, the Luftwaffe was losing an average of 240 Bf 109s and 73 pilots monthly on the eastern front.[90]

Then 'General Winter' took charge of air operations. Bf 109-equipped units on the eastern front found themselves unable to deal with the Russian climate. Some Bf 109 units had spent the previous winter operating in Norway or central Poland, but any lessons learned had been pushed aside by the assumption of a quick and easy victory. The Luftwaffe had winter clothes that the ground troops lacked. Much else was inadequate. Metal tools became brittle. Engines froze unless started regularly, or unless the planes were enclosed in heated sheds. In the absence of direction from the RLM, adaptation came from local improvisation or from desperation. Former Soviet Air

Force personnel −10–15 per cent of the ground staff in many units – showed the Germans how to warm up an in-line engine by building a petrol fire under it before it could be started.

The arrival of winter coincided with the return of the Soviet Air Force, rebuilt after the summer's losses with units from the Far East, including veterans of combat against the Japanese. During the crucial battles in November–December, Soviet fighters had the advantage of operating from pre-war airfields near Moscow, with depots and repair facilities, while the Germans were at the end of an unsustainable supply line.

Soviet counter-attacks to save Moscow began on 5 December, supported by 1376 aircraft (859 serviceable) which flew an average 400 sorties a day. The Bf 109s – only 200 were serviceable – were unable to deal with winter weather and an opposition that, if not yet improving in tactical effectiveness, was always resolute and already increasing in numbers.[91] 'We could not fly many times due to heavy snow and bad weather, and when we could fly it was hard to know how to get back unless you flew totally on instruments, and landings were often more hazardous than combat,' recalled Oberleutnant Walter Krupinski, flying as Barkhorn's wingman in JG 52. The Luftwaffe logistics system collapsed and air operations ground to a halt.[92] Serviceability dropped to 30 per cent.[93]

As the Soviets advanced, serviceability declined further, to near zero. Trained technicians had to hold the front lines as infantry. Göring embraced this practice, forming Luftwaffe field units that constituted his own private army. The Luftwaffe already controlled all the paratroopers and once Göring had added tank units (named for himself), they effectively competed with the army and SS, absorbing personnel and resources from the air war.

The Luftwaffe's victory in the east had proven as costly as its defeat over Britain. By 5 December, it had lost 2093 aircraft, including 568 Bf 109s, from all causes in the east.[94] In return, the Bf 109 units had claimed 7300 air-to-air victories; Soviet figures show their total losses up to December as over 21,200 aircraft, 10,600 of them in air combat.[95] But with Soviet factories and training fields now re-established out of reach of the Germans, their air power could be reconstituted, unhindered by air attacks.

New threats to Fighter Command

No one knew what it was. On 17 August, Belgian Flight Lieutenant Victor 'Vicky' Ortmans of 609 Squadron reported fighting a 'radial engine Messerschmitt'. On 27 September 1941, RAF Spitfires encountered a new German fighter in combat over northern France. Tremendously fast, with a rapid rate of roll and powered by what appeared to be an air-cooled radial engine, it was not a new version of the Bf 109.

At first, RAF intelligence officers told the Spitfire pilots that this was a sign of Luftwaffe desperation, using Hawk 75s captured from the French. They were laughed at. The Hawk 75 had been outclassed by the Spitfire I in 1940. This new fighter was outfighting even the latest production Spitfire Vs.

The Fw 190 appeared in combat after a difficult two-year development. Back in 1937, Kurt Tank had set out to design a fighter that was everything the Bf 109 was not. It had a radial engine, a broad-track undercarriage, and a heavier structure than the Bf 109. Its basic design was four years more recent than the Bf 109's. The Fw 190's weakness was that it lacked high-altitude performance.

Richard 'Batchy' Atcherley, who had flown the S.6B racer and was now a group captain, commanding the sector station at Kenley, became one of many Spitfire pilots shot down by Fw 190s:

I caught sight of an Fw 190 right behind me,[96] and two others a bit further back and above. I was too late. I started an immediate turn in the opposite direction, but was cold meat. I heard his cannon strikes and saw my dashboard splinter . . . I seemed to be receiving the full blast of four cannons. I saw everything and heard everything, but in the excitement of the moment felt nothing – although in fact I was hit down my throttle arm by an explosive shell. The armour plate behind my seat made a noise like a drum, but gave me full protection.[97]

Luckier than many, he was picked up by the Royal Navy after he bailed out over the Channel.

Reports came in to the RAF from hard-fought air battles over France

that demonstrated the Fw 190's superiority over the Spitfire V. The
Fw 190 was some 20–35 mph faster at low and medium altitude, with a
superior rate of climb, faster dive and greater rate of roll. The RAF's
Circus operations, which sent Spitfires into battle as escort to bombers,
meant they would meet the Fw 190 at below 20,000 feet, rather than at
higher altitudes where the Spitfire would have the advantage. Only the
Spitfire V's superior turning performance, combined with the limited
numbers of Fw 190s and their continued technical problems – its engine
was considered so unreliable that Fw 190s were not to fight out of gliding range of land – kept the Spitfires from defeat over the Continent.

Douglas characterised the Fw 190 as 'the best all-around fighter in the
world today'.[98] He stated, 'there was no doubt in my mind, nor in the
minds of my pilots, of the Fw 190's superiority'. Johnnie Johnson agreed
about its impact: 'As the number of 190s increased so the depth of our
penetrations over France decreased, they drove us back to the coast.'[99]

This imposed a painful cost on the RAF in terms of Spitfires shot
down. In August 1941, the RAF cut back its offensive daylight operations; there was concern that a Soviet collapse might lead to a renewed
invasion threat in the spring. On 13 November 1941 the Air Staff issued
a directive curtailing RAF offensive operations over Europe. But this primarily reflected the winter weather. Some senior RAF leaders, such as
Air Marshal Sir Wilfrid Freeman, then vice chief of Air Staff, considered
the Spitfire offensive over France as too costly for its limited results and
that once it was apparent that the Luftwaffe was concentrated in the east,
Spitfire units should be sent to the Middle East or even the eastern front
(where an RAF Hurricane wing was to be sent). But the political necessity of maintaining offensive operations from Britain meant that, weather
permitting, these operations would continue into the next year despite
the threat posed by the Fw 190.

Adapting the Spitfire II to the Merlin 45 engine had created the
Spitfire V in 1940. Joe Smith, Alan Clifton and the Supermarine team
now worked on adapting the Spitfire V to use Rolls-Royce's new
1560 hp Merlin 61 engine with a two-speed, two-stage supercharger.[100]
This improved its performance at both high and low altitudes. The new
engine was fitted in the prototype Spitfire III – which had been put
aside by the decision to push the Spitfire V into production – and first

flew on 27 September 1941. The first Griffon-engine prototype Spitfire IV (not to be confused with the Merlin-powered Spitfire PR IV) flew on 27 November 1941, but with the new threat posed by the Fw 190, this promising development received less of the design team's scarce resources. Even though 750 Spitfire IVs had been ordered in June, it would be months before any were produced. Because the change-over would disrupt Spitfire V production, the Spitfire IV was put aside, its prototype converted to that of the more advanced Spitfire XX, and the orders and Supermarine's ongoing development of an advanced Griffon-powered Spitfire shifted to that type.

While the new engines were being flight tested, Smith's team was adapting them to the Spitfire and further developing the basic design.[101] Using the Merlin 61, they designed the Spitfire VII (with a pressurised cockpit for high-altitude operations) and Spitfire VIII (with an unpressurised cockpit), major redesigns incorporating improvements created for the Spitfire III that could not be used on the Mark V. These new Spitfires had a strengthened fuselage, elegant extended pointed wings (for improved climb and ceiling) and rudder (for more surface area, reflecting the more powerful engine forces), stronger structure (the main spar had the lengths of its overlapping sections extended and made from a higher-grade light alloy), a reinforced undercarriage (to carry more weight) and a retractable tailwheel. The longer cowling necessary for the Merlin 61 further reduced ground visibility. For longer range, a 14-gallon self-sealing tank was squeezed into each wing between the weapons and the fuselage tanks increased to 98 gallons. But the Spitfire VII and VIII were still in development in 1941 when the Fw 190 outmatched the Spitfire V.

The RAF needed a Spitfire capable of countering the Fw 190. The Supermarine design team continued working on the Spitfire VIII (as well as the Griffon-engine developments) but made its priority paralled development of an interim design using the new Merlin 61 engine. Work started immediately on the Spitfire IX. Its airframe was to be as close as possible to that of the current Spitfire V, forgoing many of the Spitfire VII and VIII improvements.

To meet the Fw 190 threat, Spitfire Vs their wing tips cut back and squared off. By increasing wing loading, this led to a larger turning circle, higher landing speed but improved rate of roll, in which the Spitfire V had been outperformed by the Fw 190. The impeller of the Merlin 45's single-stage supercharger – the fan-like blades which forced air into the engine's intake manifold – was cropped in size to permit greater power at low altitude at the expense of high-altitude performance, making it a small, quick-turning intake fan rather than a larger, slower-turning one. These modified fighters were redesignated Spitfire LF (low-altitude fighter) Mks VB and VC. To their pilots, they were called 'clipped, cropped and clapped'. 'Clipped' referred to the wing tips, giving an advantage over the Fw 190 at low altitudes and speeds.[102] 'Cropped', the Spitfire LF V had one of the highest low-level climb rates of any wartime fighter, although it reached its critical altitude at only 5900 feet, conceding the enemy an advantage at high altitude. 'Clapped' referred to the planes' physical condition, which too often included repaired battle damage and engines worn out from having to fly at high speeds. Flight Lieutenant David Glaser flew them with 234 Squadron. 'I really loved it because it had a super rate of roll and you could really put it in. We did mainly escort work and it was ideal for that height (10,000–12,000 feet). I found it was very good against the Fw 190 and I never had any trouble dealing with them.'[103]

The Luftwaffe responds

Göring had given Milch 'full power' over aircraft production on 29 June 1941. Production had been near-static for a year and Milch demanded expansion, in the 'Elch' and 'Hermann Göring' production programmes. Encouraged by combat reports of Fw 190 victories, Milch was enraged that Willy Messerschmitt seemed to be more interested in developing his jet and rocket fighters than mass-producing Bf 109s. He ordered work halted on a jet fighter prototype, the Me 262, that Messerschmitt had been working on since 1939. On 21 October 1941, Milch announced that Fw 190 production would be increased to comprise over 75 per cent of single-engine fighters.[104] Messerschmitt would be back to building others' designs under licence.

Messerschmitt protested that the dip in production from the change-over to building Fw 190s at his factories would leave the Luftwaffe with too few fighters. He received support from Luftwaffe operational commanders. The Fw 190, formidable at low and medium

altitudes but less effective above 20,000 feet, could not replace the
Bf 109 for high-altitude combat.

German fighter pilots could see the different design philosophies
behind the two fighters. A well-known joke among them was: 'When an
Fw 190 crashes, they take the wreckage to Kurt Tank and he strength-
ens the parts that failed. When a Bf 109 crashes, they take the wreckage
to Willy Messerschmitt and he lightens the parts that stayed together.'[105]
The Fw 190's broad-track undercarriage was also appreciated. But the Fw
190 suffered from reliability and manufacturing problems. Few were available, even though the Arado and AGO aircraft factories, which had been
producing Bf 109s under licence, were now switching to building Fw
190s. The Fw 190's BMW 801 radial engine was in short supply and its
development problems would not be cured until 1942. Messerschmitt
had fitted one on a Bf 109F; it proved incompatible with the airframe
design.

Though his power over the German aircraft industry continued to
increase, Milch was forced to backtrack. He made the decision to keep
the Bf 109 in mass production regardless of the Fw 190's performance.
Ernst Udet had been unable even to start to answer how long it would
take to convert Bf 109 production lines to make Fw 190s, or whether
the Fw 190 lacked high-altitude combat performance. Friedrich Seiler,
the banker and director who had acted as an intermediary between
Milch and Messerschmitt for years, had to provide the answers. On 12
November 1941, Milch decided to keep Bf 109 production intact. Seiler
received the thanks of all concerned and a bonus of 420,000
Reichsmarks from Messerschmitt AG.[106] Five members of the board of
directors shared a 1-million-Reichsmarks bonus for Messerschmitt's performance in 1940–1. Other directors received different benefits. The
Baroness's youngest son, Eberhard von Stromeyer, worked at Augsburg
as a test pilot and on the Bf 109 design team, keeping him out of
combat.

Udet was made neither the resurgent Milch's superior nor his subordinate, but rather a competitor. Milch fired Udet's staff. Udet's
credibility had been undercut by the failures in the Battle of Britain and
the invasion of the Soviet Union. His friends Willy Messerschmitt and
Ernst Heinkel had failed to deliver the Me 210 fighters and He 177

bombers he had counted on as 'standard types' to re-equip the Luftwaffe. He saw mounting Luftwaffe casualty figures of aircrew as a 'Verdun of the air', a massive losing battle of attrition rather than the quick victory he had planned to enable.[107] Depressed, Udet drank heavily and swallowed amphetamines. On 15 November his former chief of staff, back in Berlin after being exiled to the eastern front by Milch, told Udet about widespread German atrocities. Two days later, Udet committed suicide.

Propaganda had it that Udet died in a plane crash, but the truth was widely known in the Luftwaffe. 'We knew already when the funeral took place,' Galland later recalled. Milch took over Udet's responsibilities as Director General of Equipment in addition to his own. Mölders was killed in a plane crash flying in from Russia for Udet's funeral. Galland was stunned: 'I think perhaps the greatest leader was still Mölders.' He was appointed to Mölders' position as *General der Jagdflieger*. This was not a command position, but rather that of a *Waffengeneral*, responsible for the training and tactics of Germany's fighter forces. With regret, Galland left JG 26, his comrades and brothers to fly a desk in a Berlin office building confiscated from a Socialist newspaper.[108]

JG 26 would miss Galland's leadership, although no doubt some pilots noticed that his single-plane attacks often alerted RAF formations before others could engage and he had lost multiple wingmen while increasing his own score.[109] One of these was Leutnant Peter Göring, Hermann's nephew, killed by the gunner of a Blenheim bomber on 13 October.[110] JG 26 had, on any given day, some 120 to 140 Bf 109 pilots. Yet Galland had been personally responsible for some 14 per cent of the unit's total air-to-air victories.[111] This showed not only Galland's tremendous skill and luck, but that a few highly skilled aces scored a large percentage of the victories, while, increasingly, new pilots were shot down by a now numerically superior enemy before they could have much of an impact themselves.

From 14 June 1941 to the end of the year, 411 British and 103 German fighters were lost in action.[112] Despite this, buoyed by overclaiming by RAF pilots (Galland himself was claimed four times on 21 June alone), the RAF remained committed to the fighter offensive over France, the Circuses and even the Rhubarbs.[113] Yet, even though 1941 had been a year of successes for Galland and the Bf 109 units opposing the RAF in northern Europe, the latter's relentless if costly offensive and numerical superiority were inflicting increasing attritional damage. While the RAF rotated pilots out of combat to training, staff, and research and development assignments before combat fatigue burned them out, the Luftwaffe kept their fighter pilots in combat until killed, injured too badly to fly, or, like Galland, promoted out of the cockpit. Being a Luftwaffe fighter pilot started to look less like a ticket to sharing Galland's matinee-idol fame and more like a death sentence.[114] But volunteers for pilot training were never scarce.

A change in the Spitfire versus 109 struggle

From the Spitfire's inception until late 1941, no fighter in the skies of Europe could outmatch it. The only fighter that could match it was the Bf 109. The contests between the Spitfire I and the Bf 109E, or between the Spitfire V and the Bf 109F, had both proven to be near-even, with each plane having its own advantages and disadvantages. Pilot skill, tactics and the overall operational situation most often determined success or failure. At the end of 1941, the Spitfire V, outperformed by the Fw 190 and hard-pressed to stay competitive with improved Bf 109Fs, was no longer the gold standard in fighter combat.

The competition between the Spitfire and the Bf 109 entered a new phase. The capabilities of these two fighters had previously tipped the course of the war successively in their country's favour – the Bf 109 in the Battle of France and the Spitfire in the Battle of Britain. Now, the conflict had become truly global with the US entry into the war after the Japanese attack on Pearl Harbor on 7 December.

The people involved had changed. At the highest levels, Churchill, Hitler and Göring still held power. But other figures who had shaped the course of the war in the air were gone, such as Beaverbrook (moved to the Ministry of Supply in 1941 and appointed Lord Privy Seal in 1942) and Udet. Dowding and Park had lost their commands. Galland was flying a desk. Bader was on his way to a punishment camp after repeated escape attempts. Those who replaced them would never achieve the same heroic stature, in part because the size of the conflict had so expanded that it overshadowed them.

The daylight air battles between Spitfires and Bf 109s over France were a secondary front compared to the vast war raging in the east. Different types of aircraft would join the fight, as the Fw 190 already had, and the air war over Europe would become more intense. The Bf 109 continued to lose the battle of production. Some 2628 were delivered to the Luftwaffe in 1941, only 40 per cent more than the previous year.

Fighter Command had expanded in 1941 – it had fifty-eight Spitfire (and thirteen Hurricane) squadrons by December – yet had lost more pilots and inflicted far fewer casualties than the year before, when they had been outnumbered and had won the Battle of Britain. In 1941, the RAF had lost two and a half fighters for every one they shot down. In return, Fighter Command had achieved no strategic advantage for Britain. The duel of Spitfire and Bf 109 that had held centre stage from their design now became only one element of a global air war. Udet's 'Verdun of the Air' would be dominated by larger numbers of many different types of aircraft.

9

A Widening Air War

February 1941–November 1942

RAF Flight Lieutenant James MacLachlan's head was constantly swiv-elling. He looked into the winter morning's sun, as close as he could, reflecting the message of the old RAF tactics posters: 'Beware of the Hun in the Sun'. He looked at the five other Hurricane I fighters he was leading at 20,000 feet in that day's cold blue skies over the RAF airfield at Luqa, making sure no one was straggling or out of position, an easy mark. 'I could see Malta spread out below me like a map,' it seemed to him. But he was in no position to contemplate the island's geography or its vital geostrategic location in the Mediterranean. On the morning of 15 February 1941, MacLachlan was hunting for Bf 109s. He had not found them. Yet.

The Bf 109 had entered combat over Malta in the preceding days. While RAF Hurricanes had been able to defeat the Italian Air Force's attacks on Malta, which had started soon after Italy's entry into the war in June 1940, the Bf 109 was now showing its capability. The RAF's Hurricanes, slower than the Bf 109, had demonstrated over France and England in 1940 that, either by attacking first or, failing that, manoeu-vring the Bf 109 into a turning dogfight, they could even the odds. That is what MacLachlan was aiming to do high over Malta that morning.

MacLachlan and his flight did not find the Bf 109s. *They* found *him*. Six Bf 109E-4s dived in from behind the Hurricanes, in a slashing attack.

The Hurricanes, their chance of seizing the initiative gone, pulled into hard right turns. Keeping all six together, so the attackers could not concentrate on part of the flight at a time, MacLachlan led them into a tight defensive ring, where the Hurricane's smaller turning circle could prove decisive, especially at lower speed. At that altitude, at 240 mph, a Hurricane could pull 6 g forces without stalling, a Bf 109 only a little more than 5 g.

The Hurricanes turned hard away from their attack. The Bf 109 pilots showed their hard-earned battle experience. Instead of turning after the Hurricanes, they used the momentum from their initial dive and their superior rate of climb to regain the altitude advantage. As the Hurricane pilots squinted to follow their flight, the Bf 109s turned, high in the sunlight. Leaving two Bf 109s at higher altitude as top cover to watch for RAF reinforcements, four German planes dived on MacLachlan and his flight.

'I could see four more Messerschmitts coming down out of the sun. I turned back under them, and they all overshot me.' This gave MacLachlan the chance he was looking for, a turning fight with the Messerschmitts. 'I looked round very carefully but could see nothing, so I turned back on the tail of the nearest Hun, who was chasing some Hurricanes in front of him. We were all turning gently to port so I cut the corner and was slowly closing in on the Hun.'

But MacLachlan lost track of at least one of the Messerschmitts. 'I was determined to get him, and must have been concentrating so intently on his movements that, like a fool, I forgot to look in the mirror until it was too late.'[1] Had he looked in the mirror, MacLachlan would have seen muzzle flashes from the two machine guns and two cannon of the Bf 109E-4 of Oberleutnant Joachim Müncheberg, Adolf Galland's former wingman. Their concentrated fire shredded the Hurricane in two seconds.

Badly wounded, MacLachlan managed to parachute from his Hurricane, observing the map-like abstraction of Malta below him as it all too soon resolved itself into stony ground.[2] He had just become Müncheberg's twenty-sixth victory. The Bf 109 was challenging the RAF for control of the sky above Britain's beleaguered fortress island, the site of the most intense air combat in the Mediterranean theatre of war that also covered air operations over the Balkans and north Africa.

Bf 109s head south

Despite Malta's potential importance as an air and naval base against the lines of communication from Italy to north Africa, the RAF had not spent much time or effort before the war in considering how it might be defended against air attack. Italian air attacks in 1940 and early 1941 had been unable to defeat the British defences. With the island undefended by fighters except for a trio of Sea Gladiator carrier biplanes, the RAF brought in Hurricanes and radar.[3] The Italian Air Force lacked many things, including a fighter comparable to the Bf 109 in performance.

All this changed with the arrival in the Mediterranean theatre of the Luftwaffe and its Bf 109s. Italian defeats in Libya, Greece and in the air had led Hitler to order a major commitment of German forces to that theatre. But all that they could afford to commit to operations over Malta was a single *Staffel*, detached from Galland's JG 26 in northern France. Its strength never exceeded nine Bf 109s able to fly on any day.

The Bf 109E was able to dominate the Hurricane I when no Spitfires were present to provide top cover. While the Hurricane shared the Spitfire's Merlin engine, superb manoeuvrability and eight-gun armament, the greater drag of its older-technology design limited speed, acceleration and rate of climb. The Germans had an advantage in tactics, pilot skill and experience, and, being on the offensive, could determine when they would fly over Malta and at what altitude. As during the Battle of Britain, the Hurricanes' primary mission was intercepting bombers, and their pilots would concentrate on this task even when it increased their vulnerability to Bf 109s.

The Bf 109E entered the long-running air campaign over Malta on 12 February 1941, when Müncheberg led his *Staffel* over Malta, shooting down three Hurricane Is. Three days later, he repeated his success with MacLachlan in his gunsights. Out of Galland's shadow, Müncheberg demonstrated his skill as a fighter leader.

In the large-scale air battles over Britain or northern Europe, a single *Staffel* was a small part of the overall action. In 1941 in the Mediterranean theatre, it could shape the course of the air war. In its four months operating against Malta, with breaks to participate in the

German invasions of Yugoslavia and Greece, Müncheberg's *Staffel* claimed forty-two victories (half by its leader) without a Bf 109 shot down. Like many of the successes of German fighter units, it was made possible by a single ace, backed up by enough highly skilled comrades to cover his tail.

The German air raids on Malta in March–April 1941 gave notice that the dynamics of the air, land and sea campaign in the Mediterranean and its littoral had fundamentally changed. From then on, while Italian aircraft continued to play a major role in the attacks on Malta, the Luftwaffe was the most significant air force in the Mediterranean. At the same time, German air superiority helped enable German land forces to overrun Greece, forcing a British evacuation of the forces they had committed to defend that country against the Italians. A German airborne assault drove the British from Crete.

Bf 109s in north Africa

One of the first Bf 109 pilots to arrive in Africa was Leutnant Hans-Joachim Marseille. The son of a general, he had claimed eight victories in the Battle of Britain. His comrades did not originally consider him an outstanding Bf 109 pilot, but rather thought him what his 3 Squadron Royal Australian Air Force (RAAF) opponents would have called 'a bullshit artist'. He tended to wander away from formations. Several of his victory claims, while officially approved, were thought spurious. He had been shot down at least three times and crashed at least once. His flying in northern France came to an official halt through his interest in drink and women. On more than one occasion, he was found to be in no condition to fly a scheduled mission. Oberleutnant Johannes Steinhoff, his commanding officer (who had attacked the Wellingtons over Heligoland in 1939), sent in Marseille's name for a transfer to a unit under orders to deploy to north Africa.

When Marseille arrived in north Africa with his new unit, JG 27, he found a different type of air war from that they had left behind over Britain. Over north Africa, the air battles primarily took place at low altitude. Both sides flew in small formations. Marseille would often fly by himself. He was shot down or forced to crash land several times and, as ever, it was luck rather than skill that enabled him to get back in another Bf 109 each time. One Hurricane pilot, Capitaine James Denis of the Free French Alsace Squadron, shot Marseille down twice in thirty days.

North Africa became important to the Luftwaffe after the initial German attacks on Malta ebbed in spring 1941. The aircraft involved were diverted to the east or to support the operations of General Erwin Rommel's Afrika Korps. This was the German mechanised force that had been sent to redeem Italy's initial defeats in Egypt and Libya. The first Bf 109Es went into action in north Africa on 19 April 1941, after being equipped with hastily improvised air filters to deal with the omnipresent sand and dust. The Afrika Korps' initial advance, covered by the Bf 109s, brought it to the Egyptian frontier, besieging the Libyan port of Tobruk.

Bf 109s, while never present in large numbers, had an immediate impact on the situation in north Africa. They were able to dominate any Allied fighters they encountered in the absence of Spitfires. In 1941, the RAF squadrons in north Africa, including those from the Free French, Royal Australian and South African air forces, flew no Spitfires. When the first Bf 109Fs arrived in north Africa in September 1941, the advantage became even more pronounced.

Marseille had learned from hard experience. To his commanding officer, Oberstleutnant Eduard Neumann, 'It was as if once he was in the aircraft his personality changed, completely opposite from what he was on the ground.' Marseille discovered an amazing talent for deflection shooting. He could, by eye, precisely estimate where he needed to point his Bf 109 so that when he pulled the two triggers on the control stick, he would hit even a violently manoeuvring enemy aircraft. He started running up a high victory score, primarily of British fighters.

The Bf 109Fs outperformed their opponents, mainly Hurricane Is and US-built Curtiss Tomahawks, which could carry out their missions in the face of Bf 109F opposition only by accepting heavy losses. Tactics also gave the Bf 109F the advantage. Since most of the fighting was at low altitude, the advantage of the Merlin-powered Hurricane's higher critical altitude was negated. The Tomahawk could take on superior fighters if it attacked from higher altitude and at high speed.[4] The RAF, lacking both effective aircraft and tactics, sent them into battle at low altitude and, escorting bombers or carrying bombs, defending at slow speed.

'The Middle East was crying out for Hurricanes and Spitfires for the Western Desert,' according to Harold Balfour, Parliamentary Under-Secretary for Air, but the Chief of the Air Staff kept the Spitfires in Britain.[5] The absence of the Spitfire, the only fighter that could then meet the Bf 109 at even odds, shaped the course of the first year of the desert air war. Radar coverage was limited to areas near the Suez Canal. But despite the lack of Spitfires and radar, the RAF had increasing numbers and determination.

Just as the air war was becoming too large and too global for any single airman or type of aircraft to shape its course, Marseille and his Bf 109 did precisely that in Africa. He had the advantage of flying along with combat-experienced pilots, who, even if they did not achieve victory scores comparable to his own, still maintained a qualitative edge over their opponents. Soon Marseille was noticed by the propaganda machine that had previously turned men like Mölders and Galland into heroes.

Other German pilots followed Marseille's lone-wolf example. Oberleutnant Herbert Kaiser, transferred from the east, flew with Marseille in JG 27: 'We were forced to this lone sortie tactic of surprise due to the overwhelming supply of Allied aircraft and, in this way, were able to spread ourselves over more area ... The speed and durability of the Me 109 lent itself very well to this type of tactic. If we were over-matched, we could always break off.'[6]

Both sides' air forces were at the end of lengthy supply lines. Undercutting the combat power of Britain's fighters in north Africa were the failings of the most humble item of military hardware, the four-gallon petrol can. Called a 'flimsy', it would break and leak with ease. It was too fragile to be airlifted in the RAF's few transport aircraft. It ensured that much of the aviation fuel brought to forward airfields through this tortuous supply line would be wasted; still worse, it increased the possibility of terrible accidents when trying to refuel under combat conditions.

The few airfields in the Western Desert of Libya and Egypt became important objectives. They were supplemented by even more Spartan desert landing grounds. Support facilities were, if lucky, tents and the backs of lorries, more likely just sand. It was a far cry from the Luftwaffe fields in northern France, farther still from RAF Fighter Command's pre-war sector stations.

In the desert, the sun discoloured and cracked canopies. It made metal too hot to touch. Sand was everywhere. As Flight Lieutenant Bill Olmstead recalled, it 'got into our hair, our eyes, and our mouths, and more disastrously, into our aircraft. We stuck our Mae West life jackets into the air scoops to keep out the sand.'[7] Sand in carburettors destroyed engines. It required the fitting of large, performance-reducing filters in engine air intakes. Sand permeated everything in each plane, instruments and equipment alike. Parts that should have lasted for many weeks were often sandblasted into junk in a single flight, with the nearest replacements on other continents. Ground crewmen improvised, conducting repairs and reusing parts that would have been scrapped anywhere else.

Both Luftwaffe and RAF pilots and ground crew shared the same experience of flying and maintaining aircraft in a hostile environment at the end of a logistics shoestring. They ate the same monotonous stomach-churning food that mixed poorly indeed with heat, accompanied by the omnipresent flies that were part of every mouthful, while enduring the smell of aviation fuel and the effects of high-g air combat manoeuvres. The RAF ate tinned 'bully beef'. The Luftwaffe ate Italian-provided mystery meat in tins marked 'AM', said to stand for *asino morte* (dead donkey). The conditions served to break down barriers. While RAF units in Britain maintained the pre-war separation of different messes for officers and sergeants, in the Desert Air Force all aircrew lived and messed together. Bill Olmstead recalled it 'encouraging a great deal of cooperation and mutual assistance as we struggled to make the best of our primitive living conditions and the monotonous diet of canned foods'.[8] Both the Luftwaffe and the RAF also shared the same way of ending each day, in the mess tent, tuning the radio to Radio Belgrade to hear Lale Andersen sing 'Lili Marlene'.

When Operation Crusader, the British counter-offensive to relieve Tobruk, opened in November 1941, the Bf 109F was still the dominant fighter over north Africa, even though torrential rains had flooded airfields and drowned JG 27 personnel. In September–December 1941, the RAF's 112 Squadron lost twenty-four of its Curtiss Tomahawks, with their signature shark's mouth markings, to Bf 109s, while claiming ten in return (but, in reality, getting five). The British had the advantage of numbers. But even the improved Curtiss Kittyhawk, used for air-to-air combat, was still unequal to the Bf 109F. The British increasingly used Hurricanes and Tomahawks as fighter-bombers, supplementing twin-engine bomber units for attacks on Axis forces and logistics. The RAF's fighters had to escort their bombers, fly ground attack and tactical reconnaissance missions, and defend their own ground forces against Axis bombers. They suffered two losses for every one they inflicted on German fighters, but they ensured that British bombers and fighter-bombers hit their targets while limiting Axis air attacks. The success of Operation Crusader was achieved at the cost of heavy losses of fighters, especially at the hands of Bf 109Fs. Air Marshal Arthur Tedder, commander-in-chief of the RAF's Middle East Command, said with regret: 'One squadron of Spitfire Vs would have been worth a lot.'[9] But the Spitfires had remained in Britain.

Malta – 1942

After the initial German air attacks in 1941 ended when the bombers withdrew to the eastern front, British bombers and submarines based on Malta were able to threaten Axis supply lines. This action was instrumental in weakening the Axis armies in north Africa and contributed to their defeat in Operation Crusader.

The Axis response was an increased bombing offensive against Malta, starting in December 1941, with units Germany had pulled off the eastern front. Both sides now had better fighters than had met in combat earlier in 1941. But Bf 109Fs, based in Sicily, were still able to outperform the Hurricane IIs defending Malta.

The renewed bombing of Malta, starting in January 1942, enabled Axis resupply convoys to reach north Africa, reinforcing Rommel, who launched his own spring counter-offensive. Axis bombers were able to prevent British convoys getting through to Malta. Resupply could be carried out only by fast warship, submarine or night-time flying boats.

On one of these flying boats, Squadron Leader Percival Stanley 'Stan'

Turner, DFC arrived on Malta in February 1942 and soon took command of the hard-pressed 249 Squadron, flying Hurricane IIs. A Canadian, and one of Douglas Bader's flight commanders in the Battle of Britain, he had been Bader's protégé in the Tangmere Wing in the summer of 1941. Hard-drinking and frank before authority (his response to Bader's first speech as a squadron commander had been 'That's horseshit, sir'), Turner was a skilful pilot and a powerful fighter leader in his own right.

Turner soon applied the tactics he had learned over England, getting his Hurricanes to fight in Bader's version of Luftwaffe-style 'finger-four' formations. But he realised that changes in tactics alone could not counter the Bf 109F's superiority, especially as the Italians were now able to make a strong contribution to the air battle, having deployed the Macchi MC 202 fighter, with performance comparable to that of the Bf 109. Powered by the same German-designed DB 601 engine as the Bf 109E, imported or built under licence in Italy, the MC 202, more manoeuvrable than its German counterpart, was a formidable design, only prevented from changing the balance of air combat by its light armament (two synchronised 12.7mm machine guns), poor oxygen and radio systems, and ineffective Italian fighter tactics.

To lose the air battle over Malta could mean invasion. The Axis plan for 1942 included supporting Rommel's spring counter-offensive in north Africa with a renewed bomber offensive against Malta, to be followed by an invasion in August–September. The Axis prepared for such an invasion.[10]

Malta needed Spitfires or it would fall. Reports had been sent from Malta for months about the need for Spitfires. Turner told Air Vice Marshal Hugh Pughe Lloyd, commanding the RAF on Malta, 'Either, sir, we get the Spitfires here within days, not weeks, or we're done. That's it.'[11] Lloyd echoed these words in his signals to London. Air Marshal Sir Arthur Tedder sent London an urgent request for Spitfires to Malta on 24 March.

RAF Hurricanes and US-built fighters were suffering heavy losses wherever they had been committed without Spitfires for top cover in Malta, north Africa and, now, against the Japanese in the Far East. They could no longer have Spitfires fight only from Britain.

Ensuring that Spitfires made it to Malta before the Axis invaders would be a challenge. Spitfires could not fly the 1100 miles from Gibraltar. Nor could they be crated and sent by ship, as only submarines or fast warships could make it through to Malta.

There was no solution but to launch Malta-bound Spitfires off a Gibraltar-based Royal Navy aircraft carrier, which would not have to come close to the Axis bombers based in Sicily and southern Italy. The nearest a carrier could get to Malta was 660 miles. Spitfire Vs were modified for a long-range mission. They received a 90-gallon 'slipper' fuel tank (it could slip off in flight) under the fuselage, extending practical range to 1060 miles at 20,000 feet. A large and drag-inducing tropical air filter – required for a Merlin to survive on Malta's dusty airfields – was fitted under the nose. Cocky Dundas was to have led the mission, but he had broken his leg playing indoor rugby in the mess.

The technique for taking off from the carrier was for the pilot to bring the engine to maximum power while standing on the Spitfire's brakes on the carrier deck. Then, when given the signal to take off, he would go to full maximum boost, release the brakes, and point the nose of the Spitfire at the front of the flight deck as it rolled. To make this possible, wooden wedges were positioned to keep the Spitfire's flaps open at the right angle, determined by its weight and take-off position on the flight deck, to maximise lift and minimise drag. Once in flight, the flaps were quickly extended to drop the wedges, then retracted.

The Spitfires were on their way. On Malta, Turner told 249 Squadron what was at stake. 'The chips are down on the table. This goddamn operation has just got to succeed. If it doesn't, God help us, no kidding.'[12]

The first attempt to launch Spitfires from a carrier to reinforce Malta, on 28 February 1942, was called off due to problems with the unloved slipper tanks. On 7 March, HMS *Eagle* sent fifteen Spitfires to Malta. Two more missions by the *Eagle* delivered thirty-one Spitfires by the end of the month. On arrival, the Spitfires were sent into an intense battle, starting on 10 March. Losses were high.

Unlike the Battle of Britain, the Germans (and Italians) kept the pressure on the Maltese airfields. In one twenty-four-hour period, on 20/21 March, RAF Takali, where Spitfires were based, was hit by 295 tons of bombs, the most intense airfield attack in the entire war. Only the extensive use of stone revetments enabled some defending fighters to survive the onslaught.

Over the next month, the Axis forces launched an average of over 300 sorties a day against Malta. The RAF had to withdraw from the island bombers that had been operating against Axis shipping in the Mediterranean. Malta's air defences were reduced to a few fighters, backed up by anti-aircraft guns. Again, carrier-launched Spitfire re-inforcement was the only option to prevent collapse.

While Hitler, recalling the heavy losses his forces had suffered invad-ing Crete in 1941, was reluctant to order an invasion of Malta, Churchill was committed to its defence. He told the House of Commons that Malta's 'effective action against the enemy communications with Libya and Egypt is essential to the whole strategic position in the Middle East'[13]. Malta had to be held. Following a request by Churchill directly to President Roosevelt, the US Navy had committed one of its aircraft carriers to the mission, bringing two squadrons of Spitfires from Britain to Malta. The carrier USS *Wasp* had left its US Navy air group ashore except for one squadron of F4F-3 Wildcats to provide self-defence. Spitfires were stowed everywhere they could fit on board. Spitfires lacked the folding wings of carrier aircraft. Some were suspended from the hangar roof, with others parked beneath them.

None of the embarked RAF fighter pilots had ever flown from a carrier before, except for Squadron Leader Edward 'Jumbo' Gracie, DFC, who had flown in the first reinforcements from the *Eagle* and was now a Malta combat veteran. He would lead the mission. He was soon called 'the Confectioner', from his repeated assurance to the nervous Spitfire pilots on board the carrier that the whole operation was a 'piece of cake'. As the *Wasp*'s flight deck was longer than that of a British carrier, they could dispense with the wooden wedges for take-off.

On 20 April 1942, the *Wasp* launched forty-seven Spitfires, with Gracie flying the first one off the deck. Following him was Pilot Officer Michael Le Bas, who, like many of the reinforcement pilots, had never fired a shot in anger. On the flight deck of the *Wasp* 'the deck officer began rotating his checkered flag'. This was the 'wind-up', the signal to get ready:

I pushed forward my throttle until I had maximum rpm. His flag then fell and I released the brakes and pushed the throttle to emergency override to get the last ounce of power out of my Merlin. The Spitfire picked up speed rapidly in its headlong charge down the deck, but not rapidly enough. The ship's bows got closer and closer and I still had insufficient airspeed and suddenly – I was off the end. With only 60 feet to play with before I hit the water, I immediately retracted the undercarriage and eased forward on the stick to build up my speed. Down and down went the Spitfire, until, about 15 feet above the waves, it reached flying speed and I was able to level out.[14]

All except one of the Spitfires reached its destination. At the same time as these Spitfires, low on fuel, arrived over Malta, so did some 140 Bf 109Fs and 90 Italian Macchi MC 202s, with hundreds of German and Italian bombers. The Germans, watching the operation, had timed a large-scale attack on Malta's airfields to coincide with the Spitfires' arrival.

Most of the *Wasp*'s Spitfires were destroyed in combat, either in the initial onslaught or within a few days. Despite the intensity of air combat over Malta, for some of the pilots committed to the mission the flight off the carrier to the beleaguered island was their first operational Spitfire flight; in one squadron seven of twenty-three pilots had no operational experience and four had less than twenty-five Spitfire flight hours, while in another squadron twelve out of twenty-three pilots had seen no combat.[15]

Malta was the first time significant numbers of Spitfires had been committed to battle outside the UK. Spitfires had operated close to where they were built, mainly from well-established bases and serviced by well-trained technicians. On Malta, everything was in short supply, the bases were under constant air attack, and while fighter pilots could fly in, the too-few ground crews had to be supplemented by soldiers and Maltese. Flight Lieutenant Percy 'Laddie' Lucas, DFC, a journalist who was one of Turner's flight commanders in 249 Squadron, saw that 'the do-it-yourself, make-do-and-mend, cobble-the-parts of three damaged aircraft together to make one fly concept ruled everywhere'.[16]

Once they arrived, the Spitfires were modified to meet Maltese conditions. The Spitfire VCs that were defending the island had been flown off the carriers with four 20mm cannon in the wings. The defenders removed two of the cannons to improve rate of climb and to conserve ammunition.

The British were able to maintain radar coverage that extended to Axis bases in Sicily, providing warning so Spitfires could climb to altitude before each incoming raid. Fighter controllers, veterans of the Battle of Britain, directed planes or, if there were too many attackers, provided a running commentary on the enemy's number and location and left it to the airborne fighter leaders to intercept as they felt appropriate.

Once they had scrambled, Spitfires headed south, away from the incoming raids, until they had the advantages of altitude and sun direction. The raiders had usually dropped their bombs and were heading for home by the time the Spitfires were in a position to intercept. Air raids were often met by no more than six fighters, four to intercept the bombers and two to cover the other four, when, low on fuel and ammunition, they would have to fight their way through superior numbers of Axis fighters to land. For Malta to survive, Britain would have to send more Spitfires.

Churchill personally asked Roosevelt to delay the *Wasp*'s urgent transfer to the Pacific to enable it to re-enter the Mediterranean with more Spitfires. Roosevelt agreed. 'Jumbo' Gracie and other Malta veterans flew off Malta in a night flying boat to Gibraltar to lead another 'piece of cake'. On 9 May, the *Wasp* and the *Eagle* together flew off sixty-four Spitfires to Malta; sixty arrived on the island.

This time, the RAF had planned the arrival of the Spitfire reinforcements. As soon as each Spitfire landed on Malta, its exhausted pilot was hauled out of the cockpit and replaced by one with Malta combat experience; the second the ground crews had refilled the fuel tanks and armed the guns, he took off in turn to cover the arrival of the rest of the reinforcements. When the Luftwaffe arrived to destroy the Spitfires, they found them already in the air, having climbed to altitude, waiting for them up 'in the sun'.

The new fighters were able to blunt the Axis air offensive. When the Axis launched four massive air attacks on the British resupply ship HMS *Welshman* in Malta's Grand Harbour on 9 May, the RAF was able to keep it from being hit, putting up thirty-seven Spitfires and thirteen Hurricanes. More large-scale attacks on 10 May were also defeated. Churchill wired Roosevelt, 'Who says a Wasp cannot sting twice?'

The May reinforcement Spitfires forced the Axis powers to switch more of their bombing effort to night. German bomber units blamed the failure of the Bf 109 units to provide escort. Galland, visiting the fighter fields on Sicily, found the pilots exhausted and embittered. Looking at their air reconnaissance photographs, the Germans decided that they had destroyed everything worth destroying on Malta without a costly invasion. The Axis had dropped more bombs on Malta in two months than they had dropped on London throughout the Blitz. The Germans transferred aircraft to support offensives in north Africa and on the eastern front, bringing the spring air offensive to a halt.

The Spitfire arrives in north Africa

This was the high point in Marseille's career. His status as a celebrity ace had permitted him the nearest thing to a bohemian lifestyle possible in north Africa, where his portable gramophone was a luxury item. In defiance of regulations, he flaunted untrimmed hair, a personal command car (captured from the British) and Matthias, his batman, a black South African prisoner of war. When Galland inspected Marseille's unit, Marseille 'played his banned American jazz records so loudly that I was sure the British could hear it in Egypt' and ordered a commemorative marker to be painted and set up in front of the latrine Galland had used, a reminder to his comrades that the great man was now a desk general visiting the war.[17]

Marseille had learned from all the times he had been shot down, yet kept his natural gunnery skill. On 3 June, escorting Stukas attacking Free French troops at Bir Hakeim, Marseille and his wingmen took on nine Tomahawk IIBs of 5 Squadron, South African Air Force, three of them flown by aces. Six of the Tomahawks formed a defensive circle. Marseille climbed above them and, diving down, hit one with a short burst of fire in a high-deflection shot before the one covering its tail could engage him, then made a zoom climb back to altitude for another attack. He did this six times in succession. In an epic dogfight, Marseille shot down four planes and damaged two.

Axis reinforcements allowed Rommel to resume his offensive on 26 May 1942. The Luftwaffe had 120 Bf 109Fs. Opposing them, the RAF had been reinforced by about six Spitfire Vs (Tedder had asked London for Spitfires in March), by fewer still photo reconnaissance Spitfire PR IVs – which had first arrived in Egypt in March – and by the first mobile radar station for day fighter control.

Like those on Malta, Spitfires in north Africa had to be equipped with an air filter. The model initially fitted was the Vokes air filter, which reduced maximum speed by at least 11 mph and critical altitude by over 1000 feet. These were later replaced on some aircraft by the improved Aboukir air filter, designed and produced in Egypt, which still reduced performance (by at least 8 mph). The Bf 109F's air filter, in comparison, created less of a reduction in performance.

Axis success on the battlefield forced the RAF to withdraw from their airfields, including El Adem near Tobruk, and then from their forward landing grounds. This, for the first time, forced the RAF to allow Axis bombers to operate freely. When Rommel took Tobruk on 20 21 June, he was able to bomb his way through the defences and suppress counter-attacks. German and Italian Ju 87 Stukas, their 1940 sirens reattached, flew multiple sorties. It was the high point of Axis air power in north Africa.

In the six weeks from the opening of Rommel's offensive, the RAF lost 202 fighters. Bf 109s had been able to inflict heavy losses on these fighters, but had never been able to drive them from the skies, except for a few vital days, such as the taking of Tobruk. Otherwise, despite the Bf 109F's qualitative superiority, RAF fighters enabled the bombers of the Desert Air Force to continue their attacks on Axis supply routes. RAF Kittyhawks as well as Hurricanes and Tomahawks were modified to carry bombs in the increasingly important fighter-bomber role. The RAF was able to use its numerical resources and superior support infrastructure (despite the supply lines stretching back to Britain) to absorb the losses imposed by the Bf 109Fs. Generalleutnant Otto Hoffman von Waldau, the *Fliegerführer Afrika*, said that, despite this, RAF 'combat effectiveness has been maintained, and indeed increased, by the assignment of new and excellent trained Spitfire squadrons from England. The employment of the Spitfires has given the enemy the confidence he needs to hold his own against our Me 109s.'[18]

Following the taking of Tobruk, Rommel advanced into Egypt as far as the British defensive position at El Alamein. The Luftwaffe operated at the end of an ever-lengthening supply line. The RAF retreated closer to its Egyptian bases. They received increased numbers of Spitfires, Hurricane IIs and Kittyhawks. The USAAF arrived in Egypt, operating fighters and bombers as well as C-47 transports that were able to fly 55-gallon drums of aviation fuel and spare engines into forward desert landing grounds.[19]

Air Vice Marshal Keith Park, who had commanded 11 Group in the Battle of Britain, arrived in July as Air Officer Commanding Egypt, subordinate to Tedder. After having served in Training Command since 1940, he was pleased to have received the opportunity for another high-level operational command that had been denied his patron Dowding. In Egypt, Park helped turn the RAF around from the shock of the British defeat.

The Spitfire defends Malta

Sergeant George 'Screwball' Beurling, a Canadian serving in the RAF (he had been rejected by the RCAF), had seen combat over northern Europe. While he had demonstrated great flying and gunnery skills at OTU, he had disdained teamwork in air combat, which was seen as making him a liability for any squadron. 'Laddie' Lucas took the new arrival into his flight: 'Untidy, with a shock of fair tousled hair above penetrating blue eyes. He smiled a lot and the smile came straight out of those striking eyes ... he was highly strung, brash and outspoken, something of a rebel.'[20]

Beurling, for his part, was delighted to see that Malta constituted a different air war from that over the Channel. Soon after his arrival, he saw three Bf 109s 'whipping out of nowhere and go frisking across the field at Takali no more than ten feet off the ground, doing rolls and helling around generally. Then twisting back and shooting the joint up, like a bunch of horse-opera cowboys going to town.'[21]

Beurling promptly established himself as the new sheriff. He shot down twenty-seven aircraft in fourteen (non-consecutive) days of intense combat, earning promotion to flight lieutenant and a chestful of decorations. Beurling improvised his own tactics. He possessed a tremendous visual acuity, which he credited with much of his success, stating that 'the flyers who see first usually shoot first, for they have already won half the battle'. He often reverted to Great War-style individual interceptions rather than fighting as part of a team. This was made possible by his natural skill at deflection shooting and his situational awareness. He could concentrate on accurate shooting. Having once seen an enemy aircraft, he could keep its likely location in his mind's eye, rather than relying on a wingman.[22] For most fighter pilots, his tactics would have been suicidal. Beurling was able to make them work. Over Malta, Beurling seized the last opportunity for a lone-wolf pilot with a miraculous ability to aim through a reflector sight to make a difference to a major battle. Elsewhere, the size, scope and intensity of the air war was now such that even air marshals could not steer its course as it consumed vast numbers of aircraft and aircrew.

More carrier-launched reinforcement Spitfires flew off to Malta. But each carrier load was worn down by relentless attrition. The Spitfires delivered by each carrier-launched reinforcement mission were all eventually destroyed, either in air combat or by air attack. How long they would last and how many of their pilots would survive would determine victory or defeat. In June, two convoys were launched to resupply Malta, one from Alexandria and one from Gibraltar. But neither of the two merchant ships to make it through to Malta was a tanker.

A shortage of aviation fuel limited RAF flying on Malta. Spitfires were soon being kept on the ground for lack of fuel. In the Battle of Britain, the critical shortage had been trained fighter pilots. Malta had more pilots than fighters. In May, 150 Spitfire pilots on the island had barely 60 Spitfires. But Malta-based Spitfire pilots suffered from exhaustion due to the intense combat. Poor rations and dysentery put many out of action. At the end of June, the situation in north Africa had deteriorated so much that a Spitfire squadron was sent from Malta to Egypt.

The 1942 defence of Malta was the Spitfire's most intense and desperate battle. In addition to the Bf 109s that would, along with Italian fighters, escort the attacking bombers, the Germans sent over Bf 109s on *freie Jagd* missions, timed to catch British fighters heading back to their airfields after they had intercepted the bombers and were almost out of fuel and ammunition. As in north Africa, many of the most intense battles were fought at low altitude, a few British fighters keeping the Bf 109s at bay from others, vulnerable at take-off or landing.

The RAF improvised new tactics. By 1942, all the British fighters defending Malta were trained to fight in finger-four formations, copied from the Germans. But due to the shortage of fighters, the British often sent up formations of two or three planes. With the nearest enemy airfields in Sicily, only sixty-five miles away, fighters needed to attain altitude quickly. Many times a pair or even a single Spitfire had to break up an incoming raid or fighter sweep. With only enough fuel to launch a handful of fighters, the skill of every pilot mattered.

Flying in from Egypt, Keith Park took over command of Malta's air defences on 21 July 1942. In his familiar pre-war white flying overalls, he soon impressed the squadron commanders by his willingness to listen to them and their pilots and by his lack of patience with paperwork, but he made it clear that he would be the one making the decisions on tactics. Park sent home many exhausted leaders, including Turner and Lucas, and changed the defensive air tactics. But by August, fuel shortages were so acute that air operations from Malta were severely curtailed. If, this time, a tanker could not get through, by September there would be no aircraft flying from Malta at all. In mid-August, Operation Pedestal, one of the most intense air–sea battles of the war, fought a convoy through to the island. Losses were heavy: nine of fourteen merchant ships and many warships (including the *Eagle*). But the desperately needed tanker *Ohio* made it to Malta on 15 August.

The *Ohio's* fuel made reinforcement possible. For the first time, Malta had over 100 Spitfires. RAF bomber squadrons returned to the island. Park wanted to take the offensive against Sicily. Spitfires were modified as fighter-bombers. Equipped with bomb racks made from material cannibalised from destroyed aircraft, these could carry two 250 lb bombs. As fighter-bomber missions were usually flown at low altitude and

Spitfires were vulnerable when weighed down with bombs, these tactics had not been used in England-based operations. Now, Spitfires took the offensive, including attacks on ground targets.

Malta also received additional reconnaissance Spitfires. The first such Spitfires had operated from Malta back in January 1941, but the intense bombing had limited the numbers surviving to fly over Italian ports. Squadron Leader Adrian 'Warby' Warburton, whose reconnaissance missions from Malta over Italian harbours to spot convoys getting ready to sail for Africa had already made him a legend, took command of 69 Squadron. Its Spitfires would provide vital information to guide the Allied offensive action that would break the Axis hold on the Mediterranean.[23]

The decisive battles over Malta

In October, the Axis renewed the air offensive against Malta, aiming to neutralise its airbases. The October offensive proved to be the most massive use of Axis air power in the Mediterranean theatre, including 125 Bf 109s in four *Gruppen* and a similar number of Italian fighters. Major Heinz 'Pritzl' Bär, now commanding II/JG 77, brought his *Gruppe* west from intense combat on the eastern front. Some 150 Ju 88 bombers, about 75 Italian bombers, and new Bf 109Gs gave the Germans hope of achieving air superiority.

This time, the RAF had five squadrons with 130 Spitfire VCs (with two-cannon armament) on Malta and fuel to meet the Axis on even terms. As he had in the Battle of Britain, Park emphasised intercepting the enemy before they dropped their bombs, coordinating multiple squadrons. The first Spitfire squadron off the ground would climb high, to take on any top cover Bf 109s. The second squadron would attack the close escort. The third, and any additional squadrons to get into the battle, were to go straight for the bombers. It was a far cry from the spring when such 'wings' consisted of ten RAF fighters.

The Axis October air offensive against Malta started out with large formations of bombers. These proved vulnerable to intercepting Spitfires despite large numbers of escorts, like those in the climactic Luftwaffe attacks on London in the Battle of Britain. At the height of the offensive, some 2400 sorties were launched against Malta over the course of

nine days. But Malta's airfields remained operational. Formations as large
as eighty Ju 88 bombers, escorted by nearly double that number of
fighters, were defeated. 'Screwball' Beurling destroyed a Bf 109 on
14 October but went down to the German's wingman. He survived,
wounded, his score at twenty-eight.

By 15 October, the Axis powers had scaled back their attacks, with
as few as 14 bombers escorted by 100 fighters. On 18 October, the Axis
gave up using bombers over Malta in daylight. Bf 109 fighter-bombers
took over the air attacks. Fighter sweeps and high-altitude fighter-
bomber attacks were increasingly used against Malta instead of bombers.
A Luftwaffe analysis realised: 'This was the turning point in the German
air campaign in the Mediterranean area; the strength of the British
defences was superior to the offensive powers of the Luftwaffe.'[24]

The Spitfire was the capstone element in another defensive air victory. If smaller than the Battle of Britain, the battle over Malta was no
less intense. Malta became the second great climactic duel of the Spitfire
and the Bf 109. The defeat of the October 1942 offensive demonstrated,
like the defeat of the Luftwaffe over London on 15 September 1940, that
even with a Bf 109 escort, German bombers could not sustain daylight
attacks against such opposition; although, as over Britain, Bf 109s shot
down more Spitfires, who were aiming for the bombers, than the
reverse. In the 1942 battles, 204 Spitfires were lost in air combat (148
shot down and 66 force-landed). Of these, thirty-four were lost to Italian
fighters, fifteen to German bombers and two to Italian bombers; the rest
all to Bf 109s. In addition, fifty-nine Spitfires were lost in accidents,
thirty-three to bombing and strafing, six to friendly and two to enemy
anti-aircraft fire. In return, Spitfires shot down eighty-two Bf 109s, fifty-
one Italian fighters, ninety-seven Ju 88s and thirty-six other Axis
aircraft.[25] When losses to other RAF aircraft, and to anti-aircraft fire,
were added (over twenty-five Bf 109s), it was apparent that the Axis had
suffered a major defeat.

Axis defeat in north Africa
In August–September 1942, three squadrons of Spitfires were in Egypt,
providing air defence for British forces defending against Rommel's last
attempt to break through to Cairo, which was stopped at the Battle of

Alam Halfa. Unlike Tobruk, the Luftwaffe could not help the Germans break through. The Germans were at the end of an unsustainable supply line. German road convoys, fuel dumps and ports were all targets of integrated day and night interdiction attacks of RAF and USAAF bombers. Their bombing of Rommel's supplies contributed to bringing the German offensive to a halt.[26]

The Spitfires prevented German reconnaissance and air attacks on Allied forces as they built up for the major counter-attack that was to push the Axis out of north Africa. On 24 August, a stripped-down Spitfire V managed to intercept a Ju 86P-2 high-altitude reconnaissance aircraft at 37,000 feet and damage it. After subsequent encounters, the Germans were forced to stop their missions over Egypt.

By late 1942, the RAF in north Africa had become proficient in cooperating with the ground forces which had been overshadowed by the strategic bombing and air defence missions prewar.[27] The Desert Air Force was able to set the pattern for air–land cooperation that would be maintained and refined for the remainder of the war, plus demonstrating close integration with the USAAF and the continued reliance on Commonwealth squadrons and aircrew.

As the Luftwaffe and their allies tried to enable Rommel to break through to El Alamein, they were reinforced by the arrival of the first Bf 109G-2s. Spitfire squadrons newly arrived from Britain had a hard time matching Luftwaffe veterans. Marseille claimed a total of sixteen Spitfires.

But Marseille was exhausted. On 26 September, after two dogfights with Spitfire Vs flown by Malta combat veterans, he had to be helped from the cockpit of his Bf 109. Oberstleutnant Eduard Neumann, his commanding officer, 'saw Marseille break down'. But he did not take him off operations; JG 27 relied on Marseille in the air too much for that. Marseille had beeen promoted to *Hauptmann* and had gone home on leave several times, rare boons for a German fighter pilot in north Africa. After one such trip, it was rumoured that, after learning of Nazi atrocities at home, he had declined to receive a decoration from Hitler and had intended to refuse to return to combat until the secret police had a word with him and explained that he would still be useful to the Reich as a dead hero. Whether the story was true or not, it eventually became part of his legend.[28]

Soon after his last battle with the Spitfires, Marseille's engine caught fire, a common problem with early production Bf 109Gs. Their DB 605A engine was prone to overheating. An oil line had broken. He baled out but his parachute failed to open. The death of Marseille proved a painful blow for German airpower in north Africa. Neumann recalled, 'His loss was a very serious morale issue for the unit.' Marseille's final score of 158 victories on 388 combat missions would prove to be the highest any German ace would achieve against the western Allies. Significantly, only four of those victories were against bombers. Marseille and the other German fighter pilots in north Africa were unable to prevent the defeat in the air that preceded the Axis defeat on the ground at El Alamein.

The RAF's fighter units, even those with Spitfire Vs, were not equal to JG 27's Bf 109Gs and Fs on a one-to-one basis. But this did not stop the Desert Air Force from successfully carrying out its missions. Reports of the Afrika Korps being pounded by bombers reached Hitler in Berlin. 'Do you hear that, Goering? Saturation bombing in the desert now!'[29]

When the Allied counter-offensive started at the Battle of El Alamein on 23 October, fighter units, except for Spitfire squadrons, flew mainly air-to-ground missions, attacking enemy troops with bombs and machine-gun fire. Spitfires ensured that the Germans would not be able to concentrate their bombers against Allied ground units and that Allied bombers would be able to get through to their targets. The air–land battle contributed to Rommel's defeat.

The Luftwaffe reinforced north Africa with some fifty Bf 109s that had been based in Sicily, operating against Malta, but these had little effect. The Luftwaffe's bombers were forced to fly in fuel to enable Rommel's retreat to Tunisia to start on 5 November.[30]

Operation Torch: the Seafire goes into action

Operation Torch, the Allied amphibious invasion of French north Africa starting on 8 November 1942, saw US and British troops coming ashore in Morocco and Algeria then advancing to try to beat the Germans to occupy Tunisia. The invasion took place outside the range of most shore-based air cover. To defend against Vichy French aircraft, the Allies relied on fighters operating from aircraft carriers until bases could be established ashore.

Royal Navy aircraft carriers now carried the Supermarine Seafire, the navalised version of the Spitfire. Six squadrons of Seafires flew from five carriers in Operation Torch, assuring superiority over Vichy D.520 and Hawk 75 fighters that came up to challenge the invasion fleet.

The Seafires that flew over the invasion fleet during Operation Torch were the results of a lengthy development and deployment process. The Royal Navy had maintained its interest in operating Spitfires from its aircraft carriers even after the RAF rebuffed their attempt to procure them in 1940. It was only in autumn 1941 that they received authorisation to convert 400 Spitfire Vs for carrier operations.

The Spitfire had not been designed for carrier operations. Most previous carrier aircraft, British as well as US or Japanese, had been designed as such from the outset, with folding wings for hangar deck parking, a reinforced structure and undercarriage and treatment against sea water corrosion, as well as receiving the arrester hook that, then as now, was essential to land successfully on an aircraft carrier. With no viable alternatives to the 'Sea Spitfire' – soon contracted to Seafire – available, it entered production in 1941.

Seafire IAs and IBs – Spitfire VAs and VBs fitted with hooks for arrested deck landings, lift points for being lifted by crane onto carriers at dockside, and navy-compatible radios – were hastily pressed into Fleet Air Arm (FAA) service. In December 1941, deck handling tests led to a modification of the Spitfire VB as the Seafire IIB and the Spitfire VC as the Seafire IIC, retaining its Merlin 45 engine. In 1942, Seafire IIs started to come off the production lines at Supermarine and Westland, fitted to allow them to make use of catapults when being launched off carrier decks. They also had structural reinforcement against the shock of carrier landings. Without folding wings, Seafires could not fit on the elevators of several Royal Navy carriers; they stayed on the flight deck when not flying. The Seafire IB went into service with the FAA in mid-1942. Its fighter squadrons were delighted to receive a plane that would give them a chance of catching modern bombers such as the Ju 88 and could hold its own against the Bf 109. Lieutenant Eric 'Winkle' Brown, Distinguished Service Cross (DSC), was an experienced FAA carrier pilot who had been given the job of testing Seafires before Operation Torch. 'Never designed for shipboard use, the Seafire was difficult to take off, deck-land and it acted like a submarine when ditched. In spite of this, it was the fastest shipboard fighter in the world at the time of Operation Torch.'[31]

The Seafire pilots involved in Operation Torch found that the most dangerous part of their mission would not be dealing with the Vichy French or German bomber attacks, but landing on the carriers afterwards – a challenge for any aircraft of the period, even those designed from the outset for carrier operations. A returning Seafire pilot would join the pattern for landing, flying down the port side of the ship in the direction opposite to its course. First, he lowered the flaps. They went to full down, the only position on a Seafire – which shared the Spitfire's limited flap settings – providing additional lift but lots more drag. This required a quick retrimming of the Seafire, the pilot's hand going down to the elevator trim wheel, keeping the controls in balance. Then he lowered the undercarriage and the arrester hook. The Seafire slowed further as these hit the airflow, creating more drag.

The pilot would next switch the propeller pitch to full fine, which provided a low blade angle that again increased drag. He would hear the rising hum of the Merlin engine as the pitch changed. Then, he would select the engine's mixture to full rich – more fuel, less air – and complete the rest of his pre-landing checklist.

The pilot would then turn the Seafire towards the carrier, flying the crosswind leg of the pattern. The final approach took less than a minute, but it felt like an age of pure adrenaline. Lining up with the carrier's wake was the obvious thing to do, but it was dangerous. The pilot's view of the carrier deck would be blocked by the Seafire's nose. Doing an S-turn on final approach to keep in sight the spot at which he needed to land to hook one of the carrier's arrester wires would not work. There would not be enough time and distance to be properly lined up for touchdown, it was an invitation to land sideways. The result would likely be a damaged undercarriage or, worse, going off the flight deck on landing and displaying the Seafire's ditching qualities. 'Not many pilots survived an "over-the-side" in a Seafire,' Jeffrey Quill observed. The underwing radiator, on contact with the sea, would pitch the nose underwater.[32]

Rather, the pilot would throttle back and trim for a constant rate of descent – a manoeuvre made possible because the Seafire retained the Spitfire's excellent lateral stability. He would glance at the instrument panel, check the airspeed for the last time. Then he would approach the carrier in a curving left-hand turn, cockpit canopy opened, goggles on, head thrust from the left side of the cockpit into the punishing slipstream that tore his cheek. No more looking at instruments. The pilot's eyes would now be fixed on 'Paddles', the batsman. This was the deck landing control officer. He was an experienced pilot, standing on an elevated platform at the edge of the flight deck. Holding the signalling paddles from which he received his universal nickname, he would be dressed in a high-visibility suit, holding his arms straight out at the shoulder, mimicking the desired alignment of the Seafire's wings. A screen behind him provided a contrasting background for his performance and some cover from the wind. A safety net below gave him an escape route other than the ocean in case of a landing accident.

The Seafire pilot had a few seconds to see Paddles and then follow directions expressed by the body gestures as he directed the Seafire to touchdown. If the descent was steady, Paddles would have his arms outstretched, raising or lowering them depending on whether the pilot was high or low on final approach. He would tilt his body to one side to signal corrections to keep the wings level as the Seafire went through the slipstream caused by the carrier's superstructure and funnel gases.

If the Seafire's approach was not right, Paddles would 'wave off' with a flurry of his signalling paddles, the signal to go around again and try another landing. The signal the Seafire pilot wanted to see, as the end of the flight deck appeared to be rushing up at him, was the cut, a slashing two-handed signal by Paddles. Pull back the throttle. Gently. Keep the stick centred. Too sudden a loss of power would lead the Seafire to drop on the deck, bouncing or damaging the undercarriage.

If all went to plan, the Seafire would make a three-point landing, its two main wheels and tailwheel touching down together. The arrester hook would grab one of the wires stretched across the carrier deck. The pilot would feel the sudden wrench, flight helmet thrust back against the headrest. If he had not tightened his shoulder straps, he would then whiplash forward again.

Once hooked, powerful hydraulic cylinders attached to the wire would decelerate the Seafire from landing speed to a dead stop in a few dozen yards. Sailors would quickly unhook the Seafire and direct it to taxi to the forward end of the flight deck, to the deck park. If everything worked right, a carrier could land a flight of four Seafires every two minutes.

But too often, everything did not work right. Seafires incurred a high rate of deck accidents. If the pilot hooked a wire too fast or the Seafire had been damaged, the violent deceleration could pull its tail structure off. It had only local reinforcement against the shock of an arrested landing.

More commonly, the source of the problem was what Lieutenant Hugh Popham, a Seafire pilot, deplored as 'its silly little undercarriage, which was quite inadequate against the rough-and-tumble of deck landing ... Minor damage was frequent, for apparently faultless landings often buckled an oleo-leg or bent a propeller tip.'[33] The Spitfire's narrow-track undercarriage had not been designed for a carrier's deck, likely to be rolling and pitching. Winkle Brown recalled that a pair of tyres would only last for six take-offs.[34] Unless a landing was perfectly made, the force of the plane being arrested by the wires and violently decelerated could cause the Seafire's nose to lever down. Its propeller blades would strike the carrier deck. Called 'pecking', a mild strike could be cured by shaving off the damaged tips of the propeller blades. A severe impact could damage the carrier deck and the Seafire's engine mount.

Other problems were potentially even more serious. If the arrester hook failed to engage any of the deck wires, the Seafire would 'take the barrier'. The barrier was a reinforced wire net raised across the flight deck to stop a crashing plane before it ran into aircraft and sailors in the forward deck park. The barrier could do severe damage to a Seafire. A two-point landing on the main undercarriage, acceptable on an airfield, could became a disaster if a Seafire bounced. It could easily leap the crash barrier and smash into planes parked on deck.

Jeffrey Quill, the Supermarine test pilot who had flown Spitfires with the RAF during the Battle of Britain, had become an experienced carrier pilot and knew all about the problems Seafires encountered. 'Failure to engage an arrester wire with the aircraft's hook meant an immediate crash into the cable barrier which separated the landing area from the forward deck park [usually full of aircraft]. Misjudging the approach speed, or getting a few feet off line, could result in a broken undercarriage and a damaged hook and a fair chance of going over the ship's side ... The Seafire was undoubtedly accident prone.'[35]

The Seafires protected the Torch invasion from air action until Allied fighters – mainly Spitfires – flew in from carrier decks or from Gibraltar to start operations from former French airfields. One FAA Seafire pilot, seeing a US Army tank column advancing inland, simply looked for a suitable open field, landed near the lead tank, walked over, introduced himself to the unit commander, and asked if they needed any reconnaissance missions flown.

The invasion of French north Africa in November 1942 was soon followed by six RAF Spitfire squadrons and two USAAF Spitfire-equipped fighter groups, equivalent to RAF wings, deploying to Algeria: 90 British and 130 American Spitfires. But the Germans were able to seize the airfields in Tunisia. With Malta undefeated and Allied forces advancing on Tunisia from both Libya and Algeria, the Luftwaffe fighter force faced renewed air combat. Once again, it would be the Spitfire that represented its main threat.

10

Fighters in a Changing Air War

1942

Generalmajor Adolf Galland never liked fighting the war from a desk in Berlin. He took every opportunity in his post as *General der Jagdflieger* to visit German fighter units. He would borrow a fighter and fly some combat missions. So, when the high command needed him to return to the Channel coast for one more operation, he was happy to go back and see his two brothers and the other pilots of JG 26. Unlike the RAF (and, later, the USAAF), which rotated fighter pilots out of combat assignments to be instructors or serve on staffs after a set tour, the Luftwaffe, increasingly pressed on all fronts, tended to keep them in action until lost or, like Galland, promoted.

Galland's mission was going to be a demanding one. Three of the German Navy's major warships were in the French port of Brest, within striking range of British bombers. They wanted to run them through the English Channel back to Germany without the British sinking them. Galland planned the interlocking relays of fighter cover the ships would rely on to protect them from air attack.[1]

As a young fighter pilot, Galland had considered the radio in his Bf 109 so much dead weight, but now he set up a command post in a Ju 52 transport with multiple radios so he could communicate with German radar and radio-monitoring stations, control the air battle over the Channel and commit reinforcements as required. Galland made sure that a set of fighter aircraft radios and one of the Luftwaffe's most effective fighter controllers would be aboard the ships to coordinate their air defence. He had to brief his plan to Hitler himself. Galland later recalled, 'When I had finished, he took me aside and asked, "Do you believe this operation will be successful?" I replied, "*Mein Führer*, this will depend completely on surprise."'[2]

On 11 February 1942, Galland executed his plan. Making use of bad weather, the element of surprise, and the qualitative edge of the Fw 190A and Bf 109F over the RAF Spitfire V, the 'Channel Dash' was a tactical success. While two of the ships were damaged by mines dropped by RAF bombers along their route, Galland had demonstrated that he could win battles as a commander as well as a fighter pilot, with some forty-one British aircraft being shot down (most by flak) in exchange for seventeen German fighters lost.[3] The Fw 190's engine problems had eased. Operating over the Channel was no longer more hazardous to its pilots than Spitfires were.

Fighter Command realised that 'This year we are worse off for formation leaders and experienced pilots than we were in 1941.'[4] In March 1942, Fighter Command resumed large-scale offensive operations over the Continent. In April alone, over 100 Spitfires were lost carrying out offensive operations; the RAF was losing more aircraft than the Luftwaffe by a ratio of four to one. Sholto Douglas' response was to intensify efforts, aiming to increase German fighter losses (which intelligence reports drastically overestimated). On 24 April 1942, he gave the order to start 'Super Circus' operations. RAF losses mounted as the Fw 190 continued to demonstrate superior performance to the Spitfire V. German radar cover and fighter control had also improved since 1941.

On 13 June, by which time Fighter Command had lost 259 fighters since March, the Air Staff realised that 'the balance of casualties [was] turning against us' and instructed Douglas to 'restrain' offensive operations. In response, on 17 June, Douglas instead told Leigh-Mallory, commanding 11 Group, and his other subordinates, 'our pressure on the enemy should not be weakened ... We shall inflict casualties in the fighting whilst the additional flying that is forced upon the enemy will increase his normal wastage.'[5] Fighter Command would continue its war of attrition. Douglas projected that it would cost Fighter Command 330 Spitfires and 112 pilots per month.[6] They had shot down fifty-eight German aircraft (though claimed over three times that number). But, in July, the RAF flew only half the offensive sorties of the previous month. It was going to need a new fighter before it could effectively take on the numerically inferior Luftwaffe on even terms.[7]

A new fighter

The Fighter Command Development Centre at RAF Duxford asked Ronnie Harker, Rolls-Royce's senior test pilot and a combat veteran of the Battle of Britain, to test the new North American Mustang I tactical reconnaissance fighter. Powered by an Allison engine, its performance at high altitude appeared inadequate compared to the latest German fighters. Working with Supermarine's Jeffrey Quill, Harker had been heavily involved in developing the Spitfire IX, integrating the new Merlin 61 engine into a reinforced Spitfire V airframe to provide the RAF's Spitfire squadrons with a desperately needed capability against the Fw 190 threat.

Harker flew the Mustang I three times at Duxford on 23 April 1942. Recognising a remarkable design, he recommended that the Mustang be re-engined with the Spitfire IX's Merlin 61 engine. Air Marshal Sir Wilfrid Freeman, who had pulled the Spitfire into production and who listened to test pilots, contacted senior USAAF generals in support of producing a Merlin-engine Mustang. Freeman also persuaded Churchill to get in touch with President Roosevelt about the new fighter's potential.

As the Spitfire had been in the 1930s, the Mustang was pushed from below at the same time it was pulled from above by high-level supporters. Without RAF Spitfires, there would have been no USAAF P-51s. The bottom-up push for the Merlin-engine Mustang came, in part, from USAAF fighter pilots in the England-based Eighth Air Force. Having started flying Spitfires in the RAF's Eagle squadrons of American pilots, they loved the Spitfire and its superb manoeuvrability. They learned to trust the Merlin. They wanted to fight behind a Merlin, but over Berlin. With the Merlin in a Mustang instead of a Spitfire, that would be possible. Among the advocates for the

Merlin-engine Mustang was Squadron Leader Donald 'Don' Blakeslee, an American in the RCAF, who was commanding officer of 133 (Eagle) Squadron, RAF. In September 1942 he became, with a change of uniforms, Colonel Blakeslee, USAAF, commanding officer of the 4th Fighter Group.

USAAF chief of staff General Henry 'Hap' Arnold and many senior officers were suspicious of this Anglo-American hybrid with British advocates. Eventually, they were won over. Mustangs, powered by Merlins built in the US by Packard, were ordered for the USAAF as the P-51B/C. The RAF would receive some under Lend–Lease; a senior Ministry of Aircraft Production official later identified the failure to produce P-51s in Britain as one of the major planning setbacks of the war. But it would be over a year before significant numbers would be available in England to enter the air war over Europe.[8]

The openness of the British and, eventually, the US aircraft development and procurement systems paid dividends throughout the war, but never more so than in the creation of the P-51. Outsiders could, if they received high-level 'pull', change aircraft and equipment. Sometimes this could happen swiftly, as with the provision of constant-speed propellers on Spitfire Is. More usually, it was months or years before a change could go through the whole process of identifying a need, generating a requirement, designing, testing, evaluation and, finally, incorporation in production or service aircraft.

Spitfire IX

It was now the turn of Fw 190 pilots to demand explanations from clueless intelligence officers. They had encountered Spitfires that outperformed them. Rushed through development and into production, the Spitfire IX first flew on 20 September 1941 and first went into action with 64 Squadron, based at RAF Hornchurch, on 28 July 1942. Two days later, Flight Lieutenant 'Don' Kingaby claimed the first Fw 190 in a dogfight with twelve of them over Boulogne. 'I broke down and right and caught another Fw as he commenced to dive away. At 14,000 feet approx, I have a burst of cannons and machine guns, hitting the enemy aircraft along fuselage. Pieces fell off and enemy aircraft continued in a straight dive nearly vertical.'[9]

As it looked just like a Spitfire V, the new high-performance Spitfire IX was a surprise to the German fighter pilots who encountered it. Johnnie Johnson recalled, 'The Spitfire IX was the best Spitfire. When we got the IX, we had the upper hand, which did for the 190s.'[10] The Spitfire IX was able to achieve superiority over both the Fw 190A and the new Bf 109G.

With the RAF in desperate need of a Spitfire with better performance than the Mark V, the Spitfire IX was gladly received. Jeffrey Quill, instrumental throughout in Spitfire upgrades, described the introduction of the Spitfire IX and its Merlin 61 engine as one of two quantum jumps in Spitfire performance achieved during the war.[11] British advantages in supercharger technology and engineers such as Stanley Hooker, Geoffrey Wilde and Cyril Lovesey were able to push the Merlin design.[12]

Originally designed for high-altitude bombers, the Merlin 61 engine was the reason for the success of the Spitfire IX. Its two-stage supercharger essentially consisted of two supercharger blowers in series, one feeding the other, separated by an intercooler that reduced the temperature of the air and increased its density. It was a highly effective way of grabbing as much thin air as possible, cooling it to prevent detonation, and cramming it, concentrated, into a Merlin's hungry intake manifold. The Merlin 61 required a four-bladed propeller to absorb the extra power and a second enlarged underwing radiator to cool the intercooler. Ideally, a larger diameter three-bladed propeller would have been more efficient, but the limited ground clearance provided by the Spitfire's undercarriage prevented this.

At sea level, the Merlin 61 produced 1560 hp, compared to 1470 hp for the Merlin 45 powering the Spitfire V. But the real advantage was apparent at 30,000 feet, when the Merlin 61 was capable of 1020 hp as opposed to 720 hp for the Merlin 45. Automatic controls cut in the blowers for optimal power, depending on altitude. More power at high altitude delivered superior performance to that of the Bf 109G and the Fw 190A.

Rolls-Royce were able to incorporate the Merlin 61's additional blower in a slightly enlarged cowling. It could be installed in a Spitfire with minimum redesign. The Spitfire IX's structure was reinforced, weighing 600 lb more than that of the Spitfire V. Most Spitfire IXs were armed with two

20mm cannon and four .303 machine guns. Some, especially in fighter-bomber roles, carried a battery of four 20mm cannon, but this firepower imposed a weight penalty many Spitfire pilots wished to avoid. US-made .50-calibre (12.7mm) Brownings were also used in place of pairs of .303 machine guns on some Spitfire IXs and later marks.[13]

Modified versions of the basic Merlin 61 powerplant led to a range of Spitfire IX sub-types. The Spitfire LF IX was not really a low-altitude aircraft. Rather, its Merlin 66 engine's two-stage supercharger was designed to turn on automatically at low and medium altitudes, to provide optimal performance against the Fw 190s that preferred to fight there. Because of its two-stage supercharger, it had two critical altitudes: 10,800 and 22,000 feet (rather than 16,000 and 28,000 feet with a Merlin 61).

The Merlin 66 introduced the Bendix Stromberg floatless carburettor, some two years after the need for it became apparent in the combat. This replaced the Rolls-Royce zero g carburettor that had succeeded 'Miss Shilling's Orifice' in Spitfires' Merlins. These new carburettors were, like 100-octane aviation fuel and VHF radios, technology of US origin that contributed to the Spitfire's evolution. But the Bf 109 still could accelerate faster in a dive and maintain a steeper angle. Diving away from Spitfires remained the Bf 109's 'escape corridor', but its stiff controls and the need to apply physical force to pull out of a high-speed dive meant that many less thoroughly trained pilots were unwilling to use it.

Wing Commander Al Deere, the Battle of Britain ace now leading the Biggin Hill Wing, went into combat in Spitfire IXs:

The Biggin Hill squadrons were using the Spitfire LF IXB (Merlin 66) [an unofficial designation], a mark of Spitfire markedly superior in performance to the Fw 190 below 27,000 feet. Unlike the Spitfire IXA [unofficial designation], with which all other Spitfire IX wings in the [11] Group were equipped, the Spitfire IXB's supercharger came in at a lower altitude and the aircraft attained its best performance at 21,000 feet or at roughly the same altitude as the Fw 190. At this height it was approximately 30 mph faster, was better in the climb and vastly more manoeuvrable. As an all-around fighter the Spitfire IXB was supreme and undoubtedly the best mark of Spitfire produced.[14]

Throughout 1942, Spitfire Vs equipped most of Fighter Command. Not enough Spitfire IXs were coming off the production lines. Shortages, especially of skilled labour, limited production. At Castle Bromwich, now finally reaching its potential production levels, only about an eighth of the workforce was considered skilled, half the industry average. This led to quality control issues with their Spitfires; it also meant that Castle Bromwich could effectively only build a single mark of Spitfire at any one time. To keep up production numbers, large numbers of hydraulic power press tools had been put into service, starting in 1941. These proved efficient in fabricating the Spitfire's compound curves, but changing tooling required a major effort. New spar-milling equipment proved effective, but to get their full benefit the Spitfire's main spar would have to be redesigned. This task was assigned to the Supermarine design team, but it would be years before the new spar was available. Disruptions to airframe production, increasingly reliant on machine tools and unskilled labour rather than adaptable manual jigs used by craftsmen, resulted from the changeover to new marks; as a result, the economist Sir Alec Cairncross, working for the Ministry of Aircraft Production, found that 'A clarion call for more fighters was almost an annual event.'[15] Air Marshal Sir Wilfrid Freeman, now the ministry's chief executive, had to enable the production of the aircraft types that he had supported developing earlier in his career.

A shortage of Merlin 61s and subsequent versions with two-stage superchargers was a production bottleneck. The Ford-operated shadow factory at Crewe, designed from the outset for mass production, had previously produced Merlins faster and more cheaply than Rolls-Royce, but now production dipped as it required complete retooling in order to build the new engines.[16] Spitfire HF (high-altitude fighter) IXs were eventually produced with Merlin 70 engines, providing two critical altitudes (one for each supercharger stage) of 15,900 and 27,800 feet. As Cairncross pointed out, 'Nothing was more disruptive of production than interruption of the line to introduce some modification.'[17] These were major modifications considering the Spitfire IX was an interim design.

The British economy was now approaching full mobilisation and was creaking under the strain. RAF technicians were taken away from their units and temporarily deployed to troubled factories. Part of the answer was to bring more women into the factories. By 1941, the aircraft industry's workforce had become 30 per cent female. Peggy Carpenter was one of these women. Bombed out of her home in London, she became secretary to the chief of the personnel department at the Vickers factory in Blackpool.[18]

Other, specialised, Spitfire versions also entered RAF service. The Spitfire PR IX was an interim measure, produced in 1942; fifteen Spitfire IXs configured for high-altitude photo reconnaissance, with long-range wing fuel tanks in place of armament. These increased daylight high-altitude coverage of Germany, enraging Göring, who told Milch, Messerschmitt and other German aircraft industry leaders on 13 September 1942, 'It is amazing how the Spitfire flies so high, with its cameras, beyond Köln and Frankfurt. They have become a great hindrance. How they do so is unknown.'[19]

The Spitfire PR XI was produced from December 1942, and started photo reconnaissance operations in 1943. Powered by the Spitfire IX's Merlin 61 engine, it could cruise at 42,000 feet – at which altitude it was above the reach of almost all Luftwaffe fighters – and fly to Berlin and beyond, and it provided both the RAF and USAAF with vital photographs. A pressurised version with the 1655 hp Merlin 77, the Spitfire PR X, did not fly until 4 April 1944. Only sixteen were produced. Other Spitfire IXs were modified for fighter reconnaissance, with cameras in the fuselage, retaining armament. The Spitfire PR XIII was a 1645 hp Merlin 32-powered armed low-altitude photo reconnaissance version; twenty-six were converted from earlier production versions and were first operational in March 1943.

The Spitfire VI was designed for high-altitude combat in answer to the RAF's concern, following the German high-altitude fighter-bomber offensive of autumn 1940, that the Luftwaffe would eventually resume daylight bombing over England by flying higher than the defending Spitfires and Hurricanes could operate. The first Spitfire VI had flown on 26 June 1941, using a high-altitude Merlin 47, greater wing area, and cockpit pressurisation. But its internal fuel of 84 gallons was used up in climbing to its 39,000-foot ceiling, after which it had to turn around and come down. Cockpit heating and window fogging were also problems.

When the high-altitude bomber threat to England failed to materialise, Spitfire VI production was cut back to ninety-seven. They flew top cover for multi-squadron offensive operations. Pilots disliked them, not least because the canopy had to be bolted in place before take-off (though it was jettisonable in an emergency), a step which became known as 'nailing the coffin'. Spitfire VIs were used, without much success, to intercept German reconnaissance aircraft such as the Ju 86P, which had diesel engines and a pressurised cabin that enabled it to fly at 40,000 feet.

Even as Joe Smith and his design team were rushing to make incremental changes that would put upgraded Spitfires in production and in the hands of the squadrons, both they and the Air Ministry realised that the Spitfire needed to remain a viable design for years to come. There was no other more advanced fighter that could supplant it in production.

Sydney Camm's team at Hawker was getting ready to fly the Tempest, an improved version of the Typhoon with thinner wings for higher speed and using the troubled Napier Sabre engine. Britain's first jet fighter, the Gloster Meteor, was also getting ready to fly. But its engines were still an unproven technology and, being fuel-thirsty, provided the fighter with limited range.

Many more promising designs were on drawing boards throughout England, including those at Supermarine, but the RAF lacked an obvious replacement for the Spitfire. Ever since the Battle of Britain, Smith and the Supermarine team had wanted to incorporate all the upgrades to the Spitfire design that the emphasis on interim designs and minimising production disruption had led them to put aside. Work continued on a thorough redesign, which built on that done for the never-built Spitfires IV and XX, using a new elliptical wing, which would eventually become the Spitfire 21. The wing, designed by Alan Clifton, was intended to be stronger and stiffer, able to accommodate both fuel and armament, with ailerons that were more effective at high speed (and required less brute force to move) than those of current Spitfires. In addition, the RAF, impressed by the potential performance increase unrealised in the Mustang's laminar flow wing, issued Specification F.1/43, calling for this technology to be used on a new fighter using the Spitfire VIII fuselage. Laminar flow technology was also to be adapted to Spitfire production, and was intended to go on a version of the Spitfire 21, designated the Spitfire 23.

The designers at Supermarine responded to requirements from the Air Ministry to improve performance and fix problems that had been identified in testing, by research and development institutions (such as the RAE) or by operational users. At the same time, all the multiple factories producing Spitfires and Seafires had to meet the output set by the Ministry of Aircraft Production. To do so, Smith managed multiple Spitfire upgrades and design changes at the same time. He followed Mitchell's example: listening to test pilots, impatient with bureaucracy. 'Joe was never satisfied with the rate of progress,' said Alan Clifton. 'James Bird [Supermarine general manager] . . . and Joe hatched many a plot to surmount any difficulties in the way of getting the new [Spitfire] marks to the production stage.'[20] One test pilot recalled how, in meetings with Smith, if a problem was identified, Smith would immediately pick up the phone, call the Air Ministry, and get authorisation for design changes on the spot.[21] Paperwork would follow.

Tip and run

Luftwaffe Bf 109s based in France, on the defensive throughout most of the year, had resumed making strafing attacks on targets in England on Christmas Day 1941.[22] Intended as 'nuisance raids' (*Störangriff*), these were followed by fighter-bombers carrying out extreme low-level attacks, flying in strict radio silence and coming in under the radar – the Chain Home Low system was still incomplete – mainly against coastal shipping and towns on the English south and east coasts. The Germans expanded their fighter-bomber force based in France. Unlike the *JaBos* of 1940, this time the pilots were trained in bombing.

As the weather improved, in late March and April 1942, two or three raids by small formations were taking place each week. Initially, Bf 109Fs were the main attackers. Starting in May, Fw 190s with their superior range, bomb load and low-altitude speed did more of the bomb-carrying, and by August they had taken over the fighter-bomber role, flying sixty-eight sorties compared to nineteen by Bf 109Fs. Both were faster than Spitfire Vs at low altitude once they had dropped their bombs; on 6 July two Spitfires chased a Bf 109F for over twenty miles and were left behind. From June to August, the RAF flew some 12,000 patrols against the raiders without destroying a single one. Too few

British low-altitude anti-aircraft guns and fire control radars defended targets vulnerable to the attackers.

Unteroffizer Oswald Fischer of the specialist *JaBostaffel* of JG 26 was flying on a two-plane mission across the Channel in a bomb-laden Bf 109F on 20 May 1942. 'Low flight over the Channel and hedge-hopping over the British countryside and right into the harbour at Brighton. I saw a large ship and told my wingman, "Let's hit it hard". In we went. The flak sprayed like a firehose, but we made it and struck the ship with both bombs. As we exited, I got hit. I could hear the impact.'[23] He belly-landed his Bf 109 and became a prisoner of war.

Strafing and 'nuisance raids' also continued along with the often-escorted operations of the specialised *JaBos*. Many German fighter pilots disliked flying them, seeing them as the counterparts to the RAF's costly low-level two-plane Rhubarb missions over France. All German low-level attackers suffered a higher loss rate than the fighter units running up victory scores against the RAF over France, where a belly landing did not mean capture.

These 'tip and run' raids reached their height in May 1942, with 105 attacks, and the *JaBo* force, reinforced to 118 aircraft in June, presented the RAF with an operational problem. The raiders, striking also at London and across the North Sea, were usually detected too late for RAF fighters to be scrambled and intercept them. Fighter Command kept Spitfire standing patrols airborne. But even these were often outrun by the attackers once they had dropped their bombs. The minutes of the 7 September meeting of the War Cabinet in Whitehall summed up the inability to defeat these raids: 'RAF wanting: patrols and coast [anti-aircraft] guns v. expensive'.[24] A relatively small number of German Bf 109 and Fw 190 fighters and fighter-bombers had tied up large numbers of fighters and anti-aircraft guns without suffering prohibitive losses in return.

In response to the 'tip and run' threat, the Air Ministry expanded radar coverage with the Chain Home Extra Low system and had the Supermarine design team develop a Spitfire designed for high-speed, low-altitude interception, to be powered by the Griffon engine. Although a high-priority effort, it would be months before the new design was tested and ready.

The Eighth Air Force

On 17 July 1942, twelve Boeing B-17 bombers of the US Eighth Air Force, based in England, flew their first combat mission against the rail yards at Rouen. Escorted by six squadrons of Spitfires, the B-17s suffered no losses and encountered few German fighters; Spitfires kept them at a distance at a cost of two Spitfire IXs shot down. The mission demonstrated to both sides what was to follow. As the number of US bombers based in England increased, their missions over France started to draw Luftwaffe interceptors. Churchill and the RAF's high command thought daylight attacks on Germany were doomed to defeat. USAAF heavy bombers, however, fundamentally changed the daylight air war over Europe.

The RAF's Spitfire squadrons soon discovered that escorting the B-17 required different tactics. The B-17s bristled with .50-calibre machine guns. USAAF gunners would shoot down any fighter that appeared to point its nose at a bomber. The Spitfires provided more effective escort when staying outside gun range of the bomber formations.

As well as providing escort for bomber operations, the Spitfire was instrumental in the creation of effective US fighter forces in Europe. In September 1942, the three RAF American-manned Eagle squadrons and their Spitfires were transferred from the RAF to the USAAF, where they became the 4th Fighter Group. They were joined by other Americans who had been flying with the RAF and RCAF. Many of the pilots were sorry to leave the multinational Fighter Command. A few declined to transfer. For most, pay increases of up to 400 per cent provided consolation.

The USAAF was at first not happy to receive the Eagle squadrons. Many of their leaders had no use for pilots trained in RAF rather than USAAF tactics, techniques and procedures. They did not want the Spitfire. They were planning to ship their own fighters to Britain: the same P-39s and P-40s the RAF had earlier considered outperformed by the Bf 109, plus the twin-engine P-38.

In the summer of 1942, as the first USAAF fighter units arrived in Britain, their leadership realised that the RAF was right. To survive, the USAAF adopted a version of the RAF fighter tactics that had been developed through a painful process of trial and error since 1940. They had already trained in the US using interception tactics based on those seen by US observers during the Battle of Britain. Instrument flying skills improved as a matter of survival. The 4th Fighter Group, based in England, while unhappy at having to relinquish their familiar Spitfires for the new US P-47C Thunderbolt, would provide the cornerstone of the Eighth Air Force's VIII Fighter Command.

Dieppe

The diplomatic and political pressure that had forced RAF Spitfires into offensive action over Europe also led to the disastrous Allied amphibious raid on the French port of Dieppe on 19 August 1942. With massive battles raging in Russia, Churchill demanded action.

The RAF saw the raid as an opportunity to bring the Luftwaffe to battle on its terms. The RAF would commit no less than forty-eight squadrons of Spitfires over Dieppe, almost seven times the number that 11 Group had used on the climactic day of the Battle of Britain: forty-two with Mark Vs, two with high-altitude Mark VIs, four with the new Mark IXs. Most of the Spitfire IXs were flying top cover for a diversionary Eighth Air Force B-17 attack on the German fighter field at Abbeville, making use of their superior high-altitude performance. They were joined by three USAAF Spitfire VB-equipped squadrons. Trafford Leigh-Mallory, commander of 11 Group and in charge of the air portion of the operation, had a total force of seventy squadrons, many flying fighter-bomber missions. The RAF was able to achieve a numerical superiority of some three to one against Luftwaffe fighters.

The air battle over Dieppe did not work out as the RAF had planned it. The air fighting was mainly between Spitfire Vs and Fw 190As, at low altitude over the ships and troops on the ground. RAF Fighter Command and their USAAF allies put up a maximum effort that day, with 171 squadron-sized patrols. Spitfires flew 2050 sorties in one day (out of a total of 2600 Allied sorties). German fighters put up some 600 sorties. The air operations covering the Dieppe raid were the single most intensive day of combat in the Spitfire's history.

Overshadowed by the bloody repulse of the Canadian troops raiding Dieppe, the air battles saw the highest losses ever for Fighter Command: 59 out of a total of 106 Allied aircraft lost were Spitfires. In return, the

Luftwaffe lost forty-eight aircraft, twenty of them Fw 190s, and only three Bf 109s. Dieppe, far from showing an Allied capability to strike at the Channel coast by land, sea and air, instead demonstrated the effectiveness of outnumbered Luftwaffe fighters.[25]

Fighter Command's offensive was cut back, reflecting losses over Dieppe and the need to make Spitfire units ready to deploy for overseas theatres. Sholto Douglas protested at his Spitfires being sent away. By the end of October only eight of forty-nine Spitfire squadrons were equipped with the Spitfire IX. As the autumn weather set in, escort missions for USAAF bombers, fighter sweeps, and Rhubarbs replaced the Super Circus campaign.

Despite the setback over Dieppe, Leigh-Mallory realised his ambition to replace Douglas as commander-in-chief of Fighter Command in November 1942. Unlike Douglas he did not object to the deployment of Spitfires overseas, although he shared his predecessor's commitment to keep up offensive operations against the Luftwaffe. But the increasing importance of the England-based US Eighth Air Force was changing the air war. Fighter Command's offensive operations would have to support them.

German fighter units in France were now increasingly engaging USAAF four-engine bombers. The Germans found out that the USAAF was a different type of opponent from the RAF. The USAAF's numbers, the armament of the bombers, and the realisation that they were soon going to commence massive daylight raids on Germany provided an impetus for the Luftwaffe to invest more resources in building up an integrated air defence system. Losses of Bf 109s and Fw 190s were mounting. In the last quarter of 1942, some 797 were lost, mainly in western Europe.

The Bf 109G

In the near term, to meet this new threat, the Luftwaffe relied on the Bf 109G. US bombers flew at 25,000 feet, above the altitude where the Fw 190 was most effective. The Bf 109G, nicknamed 'Gustav' (from the German phonetic alphabet), was, like the Spitfire IX, intended as an interim measure. The Bf 109G adapted the DB 605A engine to the Bf 109F airframe with minimal changes. It was the first

Bf 109 version to reflect 1940 combat lessons, having been designed by Messerschmitt's Augsburg design staff after the Battle of Britain. Willy Messerschmitt had provided high-level direction, splitting his time between many programmes, including his jet and rocket designs. Messerschmitt himself worked with the designers for a V-tail Bf 109 project that was intended to avoid the tail structure problems of the Bf 109F.

The DB 605A engine was an enlarged and faster-turning version of the DB 601 series that had powered earlier Bf 109s. It produced more power (1450 hp) and also had a larger capacity (35.7 litres as opposed to 33.9), and was heavier (756 kg rather than 700). It was designed to operate for 200 hours between overhauls, running on 87-octane fuel. While the DB 605A retained the single-stage supercharger of the DB 601, its barometrically controlled hydraulic clutch constantly adjusted the supercharger's compressor speed to different altitudes (rather than just having gears for two speeds); this made it more efficient. Galland found that 'This engine in the beginning had very great difficulties. The placing of the engine and the exhaust was not functioning properly, and a delay in the mass production took place so it was not [started] until 1943.'[26]

The DB 605A had provision for nitrous oxide injection, allowing for boost to higher speed. It also added water–methanol (MW) injection. A DB 605A-powered Bf 109G using water–methanol injection could increase its power by the equivalent of 120–150 hp at sea level for ten minutes. Unlike nitrous oxide, this provided more power below the supercharged engine's critical altitude, rather than above it. The water was injected into the supercharger inlet to cool the fuel–air mixture, acting as an anti-detonant and enabling higher compression ratios than would otherwise have been possible. However, it required scarce 96-octane fuel to work effectively.

The plumbing and weight for the engine additives, along with armament, armour plate and radio equipment, were difficult to integrate into the small package of the basic Bf 109 airframe design. The Bf 109G's handling qualities suffered. 'With the steady increase of the wing loading, the demands on the pilot also increased. Attempts to improve the roll rate of approximately five seconds per full aileron roll, compared to the four seconds of the Fw 190, never ceased,' said Messerschmitt test pilot Heinrich

Beauvais.[27] Winkle Brown, flying a captured Bf 109G, found that 'in a dive at 400 mph (644 km/h) the controls felt as though they had seized!'[28]

Göring said, 'The Me 109 ... has now reached the peak of its performance, no further improvement is possible.'[29] The limitations of Willy Messerschmitt's original 1934 design and those of the wartime Luftwaffe and the German aircraft industry were combining to reduce its effectiveness. The original concept of a light fighter limited armament options, which were more important now that the heavily armed and armoured USAAF bombers were in action. The radio equipment required by the Luftwaffe's increasingly effective but improvised air defence system imposed weight penalties. The narrow-track undercarriage had been acceptable when it was being flown by skilled pre-war pilots. Now, Bf 109s weighed down with cannon, radios, armour plate and larger engines were exacting a heavy toll on hastily trained wartime pilots. Galland told Göring, 'On damp fields, in wheel landings [on the two main wheels], it wants to groundloop or overturn. I know. I did that once myself.' Göring replied, 'The problem is the 109. I'm no engineer, but it is clear to me.'[30]

The Fw 190, with a broader-track undercarriage but weighed down even more, proved almost as hazardous in landing to its pilots. Lack of instrument training for the Luftwaffe's new pilots led to a still higher accident rate.[31]

The first Bf 109G-1s came off the production lines in March 1942, armed with a 20mm MG 151 cannon firing through the propeller hub and two synchronised 7.92mm machine guns. Two small air scoops aft of the propeller aided cooling, but – as Marseille found – the DB 605A engine (with its integral GM-1 injection system), inserted in a cowling designed for the smaller DB 601 engine of the Bf 109F, proved prone to overheating and catching fire. The Bf 109G-1 had a pressurised cockpit for high-altitude operations (which proved difficult to maintain), thick double-glazing for the canopy (reducing visibility) and a water-methanol tank that led to centre-of-gravity problems. The cockpit and canopy drawbacks were omitted from the otherwise similar, more widely produced, unpressurised Bf 109G-2. The Bf 109G-3 was a modified G-1 version, only fifty were produced. The Bf 109G-3 was similar to the G-2 version with an improved undercarriage and radios.

Despite incorporating improvements introduced during Bf 109F production, the Bf 109G suffered from a rash of structural failures. Wings came off Bf 109Gs in flight. While some of the failures were the result of putting a larger engine in an airframe that had received only minimal reinforcement – the Spitfire IX had suffered failures from the same cause – others resulted from encountering transonic phenomena as, in dives from high altitude, Bf 109Gs approached the sound barrier.

The Fw 190, with its thicker wing, had already encountered this problem. At high speeds (approaching 500 mph at 20,000 feet, about seven-tenths the speed of sound), shock waves on the wings could so disrupt airflow that the pilot would have no control.

The first Bf 109Gs to go into action in June 1942 deployed to Fw 190-equipped units in France. With a critical altitude of 18,700 feet, their superior high-altitude performance allowed them to function as top cover for the Fw 190 against Spitfires. By August 1942, however, only about thirty Bf 109Gs were operational.

The battles between the Spitfire IX and the Bf 109G represented the third stage of evolution of the duel between the two fighter designs The Spitfire IX was slightly faster and could out-turn, out-roll and out-climb the Bf 109G, which still retained its diminished 'escape corridor' of superior acceleration in a dive. While the introduction of the Bf 109F had given the Luftwaffe the edge, even against the Spitfire V, the 'quantum leap' of the Spitfire IX gave the RAF a clear-cut performance advantage that the Bf 109G could not reverse. Göring browbeat the German aircraft industry with his claim, 'The Spitfire . . . is now absolutely and unquestionably superior to the Me 109.'[32]

At the end of September 1942, with the storm about to break over Stalingrad, in Egypt, and in the daylight skies over Germany, the Luftwaffe had only 981 Bf 109s (683 serviceable) and 517 Fw 190s (381 serviceable), fewer fighters than in 1940. Now, the Germans were starting to lose the qualitative battle in the air as they had lost the quantitative one.

Luftwaffe reaction

While the RLM was still in charge of aircraft procurement, the new minister of armaments, Dr Albert Speer, who had assumed the post on 8 February 1942, was soon making major decisions. Even the Luftwaffe's high command began to realise the importance of fighters; Milch had persuaded Göring to support a series of RLM programmes designed to increase production. In 1942 single- and twin-engine fighters only made up a third (34.7 per cent) of overall German production, a figure it was decided in July to increase to 60 per cent. More Bf 109s would have to be produced.

The German fighter pilots were finding out that air combat, against both the USAAF and the RAF, was becoming more deadly. With more Spitfire IXs coming into service daily, there were no more easy victories. Of the 107 German aces who scored more than 100 victories, only 8 started their careers after mid-1942.[33]

Losses increased. They included Generalmajor Galland's youngest brother, Leutnant Paul Galland, who had claimed 17 victories in 107 combat missions, despite his brother Adolf recalling 'he had difficulties in the beginning'. On a cold and blustery 31 October 1942, he lost a deadly game of hide-and-seek among the low grey autumn clouds of late afternoon between Canterbury and France, killed while flying escort for the last major 'tip and run' raid of the year. He and his wingman had turned back to look for a Fw 190 that had called that it was under attack when two Spitfire VBs dropped out of the cloud deck at 3000 feet altitude.

Flying Officer Jean Maridor and his wingman, Flying Officer Jean-Pierre Lux, were French pilots flying with 91 Squadron. What followed was a classic dogfight. For ten minutes, the two pairs of fighters turned and manoeuvred, with neither side getting in position for a kill.

Maridor, facing the superior performance of the Fw 190s, repeatedly called for help over the VHF radio. None came. He was able to get some bursts off at the Fw 190s, but nothing told.

Finally, he was able to put his reflector sight on an Fw 190 at 'almost full deflection', meaning he was trying to hit a manoeuvring fighter he was basically broadside to, the most difficult shot a fighter pilot could take. Maridor pressed the trigger button on the top of the Spitfire's control column.

The plane 'burst into flames and went into the sea'.[34] Maridor claimed an Fw 190, his second victory. Paul Galland was flying the only Fw 190 lost to Spitfires that day.[35] His brother later recalled that his inadequate instrument flying skills had contributed to his loss. The low-level attack on Canterbury had otherwise been a success and was followed up by an attack by twin-engine night bombers.[36]

The long-feared high-altitude bomber offensive against Britain started on 24 August 1942. It consisted, at first, of only two planes, modified Ju 86Rs used in a bomber role, which could fly higher than even the high-altitude Spitfire VIs. These were nuisance raids to show the German population that the Luftwaffe was striking back at British cities. But their potential political impact required a response. On 12 September, the War Cabinet, chaired by Churchill, reviewed the situation. 'Spitfire VI won't make the height. Blower being fitted. Spitfire IX will do the height, but no pressure cabin. Spitfire VII has both – but not ready until Dec[ember]. Pilots specially trained.'[37]

Even as the War Cabinet was considering the threat, the RAF hastily modified Spitfire IXs for high altitude, stripping out armour and equipment. The Merlin 61's two-stage supercharger was the key to its capability. On 12 September, a Spitfire IX flown by Pilot Officer Prince Emanuel Galitzine, a RAF officer of Russian background, caught a Ju 86P flown by Feldwebel Horst Götz and Leutnant Erich Sommer at 40,000 feet. Despite the bomber climbing to 43,500 feet, the prince stuck with the Ju 86P, damaging it – a single hit on the wing – before it could escape into cloud.[38] The highest air battle of the war ended the high-altitude bombing of Britain.

In addition to flying 'Ramrod' missions as bomber escorts, in place of the earlier Circus operations, and continuing to fly Rhubarbs and Rodeos, Fighter Command had to intercept the 'tip and run' raids. Improvements in tactics remained uneven. Some squadrons still flew three-Spitfire elements and line-astern formations. Losses remained high. Squadron Leader Brian Lane, who had flown with Bader's 'big wing' over London, was shot down and killed by an Fw 190 over the North Sea on 13 December 1942.

Over France, the Germans would only come up and fight USAAF bombers being escorted by Spitfires if they appeared vulnerable. The first 1100 bomber sorties within Spitfire range, by November 1942, had a loss rate of only 1.6 per cent. But those that had gone outside of Spitfire range suffered 6.4 per cent losses.[39] This did not shake the confidence of the USAAF leadership that larger attacks would penetrate to distant strategic targets without fighter escort when raids against Germany itself started.

The eastern front

The Bf 109 continued as the mainstay of the German fighter force in the east. Bf 109s were frequently used for fighter-bomber missions throughout the German offensives in 1942 that led them to the Crimea, the Volga and the Caucasus.[40] Cluster-bomb units, canisters containing a total of ninety-six 2 kg SD-2 fragmentation bomblets, were added to the BF 109's air-to-ground armament. Bf 109s flew fewer *freie Jagd* missions, which had inflicted heavy losses on the Soviet Air Force.[41]

In summer 1942, the Luftwaffe was concentrated to allow the German Army to seize the city of Stalingrad on the Volga, which Hitler had insisted be taken regardless of cost. The Soviet Air Force, rebuilt since the previous year, was able to match them with numbers but not yet in quality. Major Johannes Steinhoff observed: 'Never before had we found the hunting as good as it was then, for the Russians were throwing in every fighter they possessed so as to protect their troops from the dreaded Stukas. We marked up victory after victory.'[42]

The Luftwaffe, especially its Bf 109 units, were already exhausted when the November 1942 Soviet counter-attack encircled the German forces in Stalingrad. Hitler ordered them to stand fast while supplies were sent in by air. The Soviets were able to concentrate much of their rebuilt air power and anti-aircraft defences. This, combined with the Russian winter, defeated the airlift, despite the arrival of German fighter reinforcements. Galland recalled, 'When the Russians started their offensives, fighter schools, reserves, were all closed down' and rushed to the east. Steinhoff led escort missions in his Bf 109. 'The worrying aspect was the ever-increasing distance between the front itself and the Stalingrad pocket. More and more of our time was spent escorting the old Ju transports, a job we found deeply depressing.'[43] 'Fürst' Wilcke – still a *Hauptmann* – was put in charge of all fighter operations over Stalingrad. Milch flew from Berlin to organise the airlift personally, but it was beyond even his capabilities.[44]

The Soviet advance forced Bf 109 units from forward airstrips. Others were transferred to Tunisia. As the Germans retreated, Bf 109s lacked the range for escort missions. The airlift had to switch to night operations. It was unable to resupply the Germans encircled in Stalingrad.

The Bf 109's superiority in air combat could do nothing to prevent the most disastrous failure of German air power since 1940. Bf 109Gs were operating inside the Stalingrad pocket until a few days before the final collapse. Feldwebel Kurt Ebeners flew one. 'Most of the Me 109s had bullet damage ... With the longer approach routes the supply aircraft used up their fuel themselves and were no longer able to provide us with any. The bitter cold and the dwindling rations scale which we, pilots and ground crews, shared with the ground troops made it equally difficult for us.'[45]

Those fighters operating outside the pocket lacked the endurance to escort the airlift. The capability of the Bf 109 and the skill of its pilots were unable to prevent the Soviets, weather and German logistical problems creating a decisive defeat at Stalingrad. By the time resistance collapsed and the Germans surrendered, 226 German bombers and 269 transports had been destroyed during the failed attempt to sustain Stalingrad by air. Over 1000 trained aircrew, including many irreplaceable instructors, were lost. Future Bf 109 pilots would not learn to fly on instruments because their instructors had died at Stalingrad.

Göring had spent the final weeks of the Stalingrad battle in a prolonged gala celebration of his fiftieth birthday. He had sneered at Milch's desperate messages from the collapsing airlift: 'anyone who goes to the front immediately loses his clear view of the front'. Even after the surrender, he blamed the defenders: 'If the men had fought harder, particularly in Stalingrad itself, we would still have the city today.'[46]

Galland found a different attitude from Jeschonnek, the chief of staff, whom he considered 'a follower of Hitler'. Galland recalled years later, 'I talked to Jeschonnek: "This is the end. What do we do?" His reply: "When we lost the offensive in the spring, the war was lost." He had no answer for Galland. No one in Germany did.[47]

Turmoil at Messerschmitt

By 1942 politics had turned ugly for Willy Messerschmitt. He remained a stubborn individualist, always focused on advancing his projects on the basis of the most important and interesting challenge in aircraft design, rather than what was needed for the Luftwaffe.[48] His friendships with Rudolf Hess and Ernst Udet had turned into political liabilities, now that the pair were gone. Messerschmitt now depended on the esteem of Göring and especially Hitler. But he was unwilling to confront them with the unpalatable truth about trends in the air war or explain how the ideas on his drawing boards could be translated into operational capabilities. Messerschmitt's credibility with Göring had never recovered from the Me 210 programme. While Me 210 deliveries had finally started in spring 1942, poor performance led to production being cancelled on 14 April 1942 after only 184 of 1000 ordered had been built. Parts of 800 Me 210s were hauled away for scrap.

Following Udet's death, Milch's status in Berlin and power in the RLM increased. He received a personal birthday card from Hitler, with a cheque for 250,000 Reichsmarks, tax free, tucked inside.[49] On 17 April 1942, Milch used the Me 210 failure and his increased leverage to secure Göring's agreement with his demands that Messerschmitt be removed as chairman of the board and managing director of his company. He would be restricted to acting as a designer and barred from management duties. His personal Bf 108, D-IMTT, was taken away and impressed into the Luftwaffe. Roluf Wilhelm Lucht, a senior RLM engineer who had worked closely with Udet, sent down from Berlin to inspect the Messerschmitt factory at Augsburg on 19 April, reported that Willy Messerschmitt seemed a broken man.[50] Göring joined in the pressure on Messerschmitt. In August 1942 he threatened with court-martial any industry leaders reporting inaccurate figures. In September, he threatened to nationalise the aircraft industry and sack its management.[51]

The demotion was a powerful personal blow to Messerschmitt. But he retained his extensive (and profitable) stock holdings and investments and soon was effectively running things behind the scenes. Messerschmitt's friend Theo Croneiss, chair of the stockholders' committee, was promoted to Messerschmitt's positions as well as becoming manager of the expanding Regensburg factory. Milch hated Croneiss but left him in his position. Croneiss was Göring's friend. All Milch could do was threaten to sack him too if he failed to clean up the mess Messerschmitt had left. The board of directors continued to support Messerschmitt; its members included Croneiss, the Baroness (Messerschmitt's long-time girlfriend and still a major stockholder), Friedrich Seiler (the banker who had signed his performance bond for Milch) and Michel Konrad (the lawyer who had extracted the settlement from Milch in 1931). Rakan Kokothaki, another friend and colleague, remained in high-level management. Profits reached a height of over 256 million Reichsmarks in 1943.

Milch reorganised all Messerschmitt Bf 109 production facilities as an integrated multi-firm 'circle', *Sonderausschuss* (special production centre) F2, although this remained under the control of Fritz Hentzen, one of the Messerschmitt directors who had shared huge bonuses in 1940–1. Linking together all the licensed production facilities, it initially concentrated final assembly at the Messerschmitt plants at Regensburg and Wiener Neustadt and the Erla plant in Leipzig. This increased vulnerability to bombing; almost all machine tools involved in Bf 109 production were concentrated in only six factories.[52]

Milch went beyond Udet's limited policies to extract more capability from occupied countries. In 1942, Bf 108 production was moved from Regensburg to Les Mureaux in France.[53] France's Caudron was told to develop the Bf 109S, intended to have improved landing characteristics. The French did only enough work to keep themselves from being deported for forced labour in Germany, not enough to complete the programme.

In response to the increased wing loading of the Bf 109G, Messerschmitt's design team had started work in 1941 on the Bf 109H, a version with an extended wing, hence a larger wing area and a lower wing loading. It was originally intended as a high-altitude fighter, but it became apparent that improved engines on standard Bf 109s or new designs could do the job equally well. A few Bf 109H-1s were however produced and used operationally for high-altitude photo reconnaissance.

The Me 155 was another large-wing Bf 109 development, turned over for development to the French aircraft industry, who did little to advance the programme. Essentially a Bf 109G fuselage with extended Me 209 II wings, Galland recalled it as 'a "109" with enlarged wings for higher altitudes'.[54] The Me 155 was cancelled by Milch in 1942, but revived to be developed by Blohm and Voss as the Bv 155. It was heavily redesigned; their design team found the basic lightweight Bf 109 structure inadequate. It did not fly until 1945.

In 1942, the RLM confronted Messerschmitt with reports that twenty Bf 109Gs had suffered accidents in two months following dives from high altitude. At the Augsburg factory, the flight testing department received a terse order, initialled with the familiar bold 'MTT', that the diving characteristics of the Bf 109G needed investigation.[55] The results led the Germans to begin conducting research into transonic flight, to allow fighters to operate close to the sound barrier. While a Bf 109G could only do so in a dive, the upcoming jet fighters had the potential to operate at these speeds in level flight.

The first jet-powered Me 262 fighter prototype flew on 18 July 1942. It had survived cancellation and the reallocation of resources, but its primitive turbojets meant it was still far from a developed design. Hitler's order of 11 September 1941 had reiterated Göring's of the previous year: stop all aircraft development that would take over one year. Messerschmitt's bombers and jet and rocket fighters were among the obvious targets, but work had continued on them at Augsburg. As Messerschmitt himself wrote: 'They were designed for speeds around 1,000 kmph (600 mph) and constructed with special consideration to the aerodynamic forces involved ... This excellent plane, which seemed predestined for the role of a successful fighter, failed to capture the attention of the Air Ministry [RLM] and the German Air Force Command. At this time they were interested solely in long-ranged fighters and bombers.'[56]

With limited support forthcoming for his jet fighter projects, Messerschmitt also developed piston-engine fighters. The Me 309 first flew on 18 July 1942. Intended to replace the Bf 109G in production, the Me 309V1, the first prototype, was demonstrated for Galland and flown to Rechlin for evaluation in November 1942. The second prototype crashed on its first flight the same month. Following a negative evaluation, the RLM ordered development suspended.

Work on the Me 209 II piston-engine fighter design continued under Richard Bauer, who had been part of the original Bf 109 team. It was to have 65 per cent commonality with the Bf 109G to keep up production numbers. The design team lacked the resources or time to start from scratch. Powered by the DB 603 engine or the similarly troubled Junkers Jumo 213E,[57] it was effectively competing with the improved Fw 190D and the Ta 152H, Kurt Tank's ultimate re-engined development of his Fw 190 design, optimised for high-altitude combat. Milch said, 'We are very much afraid the enemy bombers will appear at great altitude above the effective ceiling of the 109 and 190.'[58] B-17 bomber formations at 25,000 feet were hard to counter. The Luftwaffe needed high-altitude fighters, and until these new fighters could be developed, the Bf 109 was the nearest thing.

Theo Croneiss died after a short illness on 7 November 1942 and was replaced by Friedrich Seiler as chairman of the board of Messerschmitt AG, Kokothaki as operations manager, and Roluf Lucht of the RLM as titular manager of the Regensburg factories. Messerschmitt gave the eulogy at Croneiss' memorial service at the factory. He did not emphasise Croneiss' achievements as a fighter pilot and record-setting aviator, which might have been expected from an aircraft designer, nor his role as a Brownshirt, which would have been politic in Nazi Germany. Instead, Messerschmitt talked about the efforts Croneiss had made on behalf of those who had worked for him.[59]

That year, 1942, had been a frustrating one for Messerschmitt. Germany had counted on winning a short war; even though this obviously was not going to happen, production for a sustained conflict still lagged despite increasing mobilisation. Many in the Luftwaffe, including Jeschonnek, the chief of staff, saw little need to increase fighter production while Germany was on the offensive. Total production of 2664 Bf 109s was only thirty more than had been built in 1941. This was despite improvements in fabrication that allowed a Bf 109 to be built in 6000 man-hours.[60] Messerschmitt and the German aircraft industry had put in place improvements in production over the preceding five years, though they remained limited by shortages of capital and labour. The Bf 109 factories now made extensive use of machine tools, using large presses to create fuselage skin sections and stamp out structural components, a complex Messerschmitt-developed process requiring multiple operations and precise alignment. Welding replaced riveting wherever possible. The total number of employees fell from 15,000 to 12,800, as more were conscripted into the military than could be replaced by women or foreign workers.[61] Messerschmitt AG had been a leader in recruiting women; by 1942 they constituted 24.6 per cent of the workforce. But this source was now increasingly tapped out as German industrial mobilisation increased and women's absenteeism rose as they had to queue for hours for their families' rationed food. While industry had originated and put in place most of the improvements in fabrication, Milch continued to demand a shift to a programme that stressed the building of more fighters by methods of mass production, making maximum use of unskilled labour; he was backed up by a decree issued by Hitler in 3 December 1941 that had demanded a shift to mass production. To obtain labour, the Messerschmitt AG board of directors asked for concentration camp inmates to be provided in October 1942.

So, when the SS, Heinrich Himmler's powerful security service, now seeking to expand its control of the German war economy, called to offer 3000 prisoners from the Dachau concentration camp as workers, it was an attractive proposition. The German aircraft industry desperately needed workers and it was never safe to refuse SS offers in Nazi Germany, but it was no longer up to Willy Messerschmitt to accept.

The Bf 109, designed from the outset to be lightweight and easy to produce, proved suitable to being built by a workforce dominated by unskilled and forced labour. Messerschmitt's design made possible a form of mass production never previously envisaged. Slave labour was to become an integral part of the German war effort. With German women already largely committed to war work, it provided a source of workers that allowed German males to be conscripted into the military, replacing the mounting losses in the east. The aircraft industry would, in practice, lead the way, with Messerschmitt AG living up to its entrepreneurial traditions (and keeping up its competition with Heinkel) by changing its manufacturing methods to make maximum use of concentration camp inmates.[62] One of these innovations was to make increasing use of Jewish prisoners. In both Germany and the occupied countries, the SS, which supplied concentration camp labour in return for payment from industry, would provide accommodation and security.[63] Satellite concentration camps soon appeared alongside German industrial plants of all types.[64]

Both paid and enslaved foreign workers built aircraft in Germany and in the occupied countries, as at the former Polish LWS aircraft factory at Lublin. There, however, output was limited by lack of food for workers and SS demands to send Polish workers to Germany and Jewish workers to concentration camps; so much so that Ernst Heinkel told Milch that he thought it was impossible to build his aircraft there.[65] Max Auerbach, a Jewish Pole, started work at Lublin in April 1943. 'Our duty was to build skeletons for Messerschmitt, which would be part of the planes. It was just a body, not the engine itself. Our instructors would show us how it goes and I was always playing dumb, and a lot of times got my head very, very beaten for it, because they thought I could do better, which I didn't want to, and I was risking my life, because they could shoot me too.'[66]

A new battle – for survival inside Germany's aircraft industry – was beginning. From now on, the story of the German aircraft industry would be linked not only to the Luftwaffe, but also to the system of deportations, forced labour and concentration camps on which they – and especially Messerschmitt AG – became dependent.

11

A Global Air War

The Mediterranean Theatre

Major Joachim Müncheberg, now a high-scoring ace and *Kommodore* of JG 77 on the eastern front, had become, like Galland, a star of the German propaganda effort. Unlike Galland, he was still flying a Bf 109, not a desk, with 111 total victories. He received orders to move his *Geschwader* to north Africa and to take command of the fragmented fighter units. Flying off in his Bf 109G in advance of his unit, he and his wingman headed via refuelling stops in Sicily and Tunisia to the forward landing ground in Libya nearest the enemy. Müncheberg wanted to see the situation for himself. Making his final approach to the desert airstrip that was his ultimate destination, he noticed that all the parked vehicles and aircraft had British markings. The RAF was closer than any German in Tunisia had known. Müncheberg quickly opened his throttle, retracted his landing gear, and managed to make it back to Tunisia, now the focus of air operations throughout the Mediteranean theatre, including the Aegean, Sicily, Italy and the Balkans.[1]

Tunisia
The Luftwaffe deployed more aircraft to Tunisia than it had done in the desert campaign. About 200 Bf 109Gs (including fighter-bombers) arrived, while experienced Fw 190 units were pulled from the Channel coast. Flight Lieutenant Douglas Benham was then leading a flight of

Desert Air Force Spitfires: 'The 109s could just be held on equal terms by the Spitfire VBs. When the 190s came, unless we were able to pounce on them from above, we really had a fight on our hands. The more 190s arrived, the more problems we had.'[2]

Major Heinz Bär, commanding I/JG 77, brought the unit to north Africa after the October offensive over Malta. He had improved his personal score to 114 victories. Galland left his desk in Berlin and visited his old friend Müncheberg, who introduced him to Bär.

But if Galland found good friends in Tunisia, he also found an unwinnable tactical situation and Allied numerical superiority. Luftwaffe fighter pilots were able to achieve high individual scores as they encountered USAAF units, inexperienced and without veteran fighter leaders, especially against twin-engine P-38 Lightnings. RAF Spitfire units committed to Tunisia from Britain had few experienced pilots and inadequate tactics. Their Spitfire Vs were fitted with the drag-inducing Vokes air filters or no filters at all, which left them choking on dusty forward airstrips. The tactics of even the three experienced Desert Air Force Spitfire squadrons still lagged behind the Malta Spitfires.[3] Despite this, though, Allied bombers pounded Axis troops, ports and airfields.

The Luftwaffe, operating from pre-war permanent airfields in Tunisia, had an advantage when heavy rains in December turned the Allied forward airfields to seas of mud.[4] But this was only a temporary respite for the Luftwaffe.

The USAAF quickly learned. They were willing to borrow RAF tactics, which they had studied in north Africa since before Pearl Harbor, as well as RAF Spitfires.[5] USAAF fighter units' performance steadily improved throughout 1943. The USAAF became good at air combat because it first became good at learning and adapting.

In Tunisia, Stukas, sirens screaming, returned to the battlefield, hitting US forces during the Battle of Kasserine Pass. This threatened the entire Tunisian campaign. Control of the air would be impossible if German fighters held the upper hand. In January 1943 US Army generals, their green troops shaken by Stuka attacks, had demanded that the Allied fighters be diverted to maintaining combat air patrols over them. The Allied commander-in-chief, General Dwight Eisenhower of the US

Army, turned to his airmen. They told him that such patrols would be vulnerable to concentrated German attacks. The answer was to achieve air superiority over all of Tunisia rather than protecting a few locations. On 12 January 1943, Eisenhower told the RAF back in the UK of his need for Spitfire IXs.

In March, the RAF made an emergency deployment of Spitfire IXs, pulled out of Britain-based squadrons. Among the first units to fly the Spitfire IX in Tunisia was the Polish Fighter Team, a composite squadron of pilots with extensive combat experience. The USAAF's 31st and 52nd Fighter Groups (FGs) also received Spitfire IXs in addition to their Spitfire Vs. RAF radar and the 'Y' service deployed to support the air war over Tunisia, increasing the situational awareness of all Allied fighters. The IFF Mark III transponder was introduced for both US and British aircraft. Forward fighter control tactics were developed; radar would help fighters on the offensive as well as defending.

Before the Spitfire IX could challenge the Fw 190 over Tunisia, the Luftwaffe pulled most of the survivors back to France. The Bf 109G would have to fight alone against the growing weight and skill of Allied air power. Franz Stigler was a Bf 109G pilot who encountered the Spitfire IX. 'We had a very bad time with them since their speed had jumped nearly 50 mph and they were now carrying 20mm cannon.'[6]

Oberfeldwebel Herbert Boldt was one of many pilots who found that the appearance of the Spitfire IX encouraged a 'Spitfire complex' in Luftwaffe fighter units. Faced with any Spitfires, they would 'dive away and make off at high speed'.[7]

On his 500th combat mission, on 23 March 1943, Müncheberg and his wingman, Leutnant Gerhard Strasen, were flying their Bf 109Gs near Sened on a *freie Jagd*. They spotted, beneath them, two Spitfire Vs of the 52nd Fighter Group.

Müncheberg manoeuvred behind the Spitfires and launched a diving attack. He took the lead Spitfire, flown by Captain Theodore 'Sweetie' Sweetland. Strasen took the other, flown by Captain Hugh Williamson.

The two Americans never saw the two Bf 109s diving down out of the sun. Müncheberg dived under Sweetland, then pulled up. His Bf 109 was in the American's blind spot, below and directly behind the tail. Müncheberg waited until he was so close he could not miss.

He squeezed the two triggers on the top of the Bf 109's control column as he had done so many times before. The first burst of gunfire smashed into Sweetland's Spitfire, setting it on fire. It was Müncheberg's 135th victory.

For Williamson, the first warning that they were under attack was seeing Sweetland on fire. Müncheberg's Bf 109 climbed past the stricken Spitfire. It seemed to Williamson that Sweetland, rather than bailing out, then rolled the Spitfire into the climbing Bf 109, striking it in a fiery mid-air collision. Müncheberg jumped, but his parachute failed to open.[8] Whether this had happened or whether Müncheberg, misjudging his attack, had flown too close to his target, Williamson did not have long to consider.

Strasen, behind him, opened fire. His Spitfire in flames, Williamson managed to bail out.

The USAAF's bombers were a threat that the Luftwaffe was unable to counter. The Luftwaffe did airlift in radar and set up an improvised air defence system to intercept air attacks on Tunisia's ports. Luftwaffe fighter pilots, however, flying whenever their fuel supplies permitted, were exhausted, facing a numerically superior and qualitatively improving enemy. It was a harbinger of the future. Victory, seemingly inevitable a year before, was fading. So were the chances of survival.

Bf 109Gs could not defend against devastating Allied interceptions of German and Italian transport aircraft, bringing in supplies. Nine Bf 109Gs were lost defending transports on 18 April 1943 in a battle soon named 'The Palm Sunday Massacre'. Allied fighters inflicted heavy losses on the transport aircraft the Axis relied on to resupply Tunisia.

By April 1943, Spitfire IXs, flying fighter sweeps, aimed to bring the remaining Bf 109Gs to battle. Douglas Benham appreciated the performance of the Spitfire IX. 'In the climate of North Africa the improvement in performance over the [Spitfire] VB was particularly noticeable.'[9] Flight Lieutenant Neville Duke, a Desert Air Force ace leading a flight in 92 Squadron, found, 'While we were reasonably effective with the Mark V, the advent of the Mark IX was a revelation and a source of great joy. For the first time one felt on equal terms with anything the enemy had to offer and the improvement in speed, climb and altitude performance was a wonderful thing to experience.'[10] But most of the Allied fighter operations were fighter-bomber missions against ground targets. These played an important role in the ultimate defeat of the Axis armies in Tunisia.

Heinz Bär, sick and exhausted, was medically evacuated just before the Axis surrender in Tunisia in May 1943. He had scored some 60 victories, bringing his total to 174. But he had also been shot down several more times. On his return to Germany, he used the opportunity of a meeting with Göring to tell him what had happened in Tunisia: too few fighters and fighter pilots, more and more Allied aircraft, getting better all the time. Göring responded with an accusation of cowardice. Bär, outraged, directed a particularly pointed and bitter retort to Göring. Only his combat record limited his punishment to demotion to *Hauptmann* and transfer to a training unit. Losing him in this way hurt morale. One of his pilots said, 'the spirit of Bär has entirely vanished from the *Gruppe*'.[11] By 1943, German fighter units were becoming reliant on just a few leaders.

There would be no Axis evacuation from Tunisia. The Allies controlled the air and sea. In early May, the Axis flew out their remaining fighters to Sicily. Bf 109 pilots were able to pack three ground crew in the rear fuselage or sitting in the pilot's lap, leaving behind radios and armament as required.

While the battles over Malta and the desert had been shaped by the duels of a relatively few Bf 109s and Spitfires that represented the highest-performance fighters in combat, the air war over Tunisia subsumed the rivalry between the Spitfire and the Bf 109 in a more massive and destructive conflict in which these were only two of many types of combat aircraft involved and in which the RAF was, in daylight combat, increasingly secondary to the USAAF and its emphasis on heavy bombers. Tunisia turned out to be a major defeat for the German fighter force. In the first six months of 1943, 902 Bf 109s and Fw 190s were lost in the Mediterranean theatre, almost as many as on the entire eastern front (908). But both numbers were overshadowed by 1677 lost over Germany and the west. The defence of the *Reich* was becoming the decisive battle for the Luftwaffe's fighter force as Stalingrad had been for the German Army.

Malta on the offensive

With the defeat of the last German bomber onslaught in October 1942, the role of Malta's Spitfires shifted to being the spearhead of an air offensive. While Axis fighters were fed into the Tunisian debacle from which few returned, Park's offensive operations would be built around the Spitfire in the fighter-bomber role. From August 1942, RAF units in Malta modified their Spitfires as fighter-bombers, carrying two 250 lb bombs. While the first Spitfire fighter-bombers on Malta used equipment scavenged from destroyed aircraft, Supermarine quickly developed a conversion kit based on that developed in the field.

Throughout the first half of 1943, forces in Malta were built up, ready to execute the decision, made at the Casablanca conference earlier that year, to invade Sicily (its 30 airfields now held only 130 Bf 109s) by July. By mid-1943, Malta-based Spitfire squadrons started receiving Spitfire IXs. They soon demonstrated the same qualitative superiority to Bf 109Gs and Fw 190As that England-based squadrons had done the year before. No less than twenty-five squadrons of RAF and USAAF Spitfires flew from Malta and nearby Gozo (where Americans had quickly built a fighter strip on ground previously thought suitable only for goats). Drop tanks holding 30 and 45 gallons provided Spitfires with the range to strike Sicily. Cocky Dundas, now a wing commander, was sent down from Britain to lead a wing of five Spitfire squadrons: 'at least once a day and sometimes twice, I led the wing across sixty miles of sea to patrol over Sicily'.[12]

Malta's Spitfires were the spearhead of the aerial offensive that achieved air superiority over Sicily. The Germans had brought in specialist anti-shipping bombers and, short on fighters, massed flak guns. Neither these nor the German and Italian fighters could prevent air attacks on Sicily and southern Italy, or stop US and British heavy bombers striking throughout Italy. Galland came down from Germany to take personal charge, but proved unable to recreate his operational success of the Channel Dash the year before.

Göring, seeking to counter Allied material and numerical superiority with a racial and national spiritual power, announced that cowardice was the only reason his fighter units were being defeated. He ordered one pilot from each unit to be court-martialled.[13] When all the *Geschwaderkommodoren* in the Mediterranean theatre put down their own names as the defendants, the idea was dropped. This expanded the searing contempt separating Göring, in his flash uniforms that said more about the narcissism of power than the banality of evil, from Germany's fighter leaders: skilled, increasingly fatalistic men with high victory scores and decreasing life expectancy.

On 10 July, when the invasion of Sicily opened, Axis bombers could not stop the powerful naval forces. They sank only twelve ships out of an armada of 3000, defended by Malta-based Spitfires, joined by Seafires from Royal Navy aircraft carriers. Nor was flak able to prevent Allied bombers striking throughout Sicily and southern Italy.

With twin-engine bombers and Stukas too vulnerable to fight by daylight, the Luftwaffe used fighter-bombers at low altitude, as they had over England. This included Bf 109G-6/R2 versions armed with time-fused 210mm rockets, originally intended for use against US bomber formations, now fired at the invasion fleet.

Bill Olmstead was flying one of the Malta-based Spitfires protecting the invasion:

> The Germans would watch us patrol and just before we got to a turning point at one end of our run, a bomber would be sent in at the other end to attack a ship or ground target. The bombers appeared to have perfect coordination and we would sometimes be surprised after completing a turn to find a tanker or a landing craft going up in smoke at the other end of our run. We then split our squadron into smaller sections to cover the beach more effectively. The Germans took advantage of this by sending out enough fighters to give the small sections a very desperate, often one-sided, fight.[14]

Within three days, Spitfire units had arrived on forward airstrips in Sicily. These were able to intercept German attempts to use transport aircraft, with Bf 109 escorts, to resupply their forces. Attempts to interdict German supplies flowing across the Strait of Messina from Italy, mainly at night, were blocked by the intensive flak and an equally intensive effort by the last eighty Bf 109Gs. Olmstead's 'final impression was the vast amount of intense accurate flak which the enemy was able to put up around the Messina Straits . . . so heavy the bursts would virtually create a cloud cover over the defended area'.[15] Flak, not Fw 190s or Bf 109s, would be the Spitfire's main enemy from now on.

The Germans evacuated Sicily in August, most of their forces escaping through Messina. Again, the fighter units flew out, cramming ground crew into their Bf 109Gs. They took off from their airfields on Sicily after pouring their little remaining fuel over any cannibalised fighters that could not fly – Allied bombing had cut off the supply of spare parts – and flew away as the last German fighters on the island went up in smoke.

Like the Bf 109G pilots flying away from Sicily for the last time, watching the island where they had not long before set out to subdue Malta gradually disappear into the haze, fighter pilots throughout the Luftwaffe saw their past of victory and optimism recede. The old spirit of comradeship and loyalty still held, and the personal oaths to Hitler went unquestioned, but as more and more of the veteran pilots went down and their enemies became stronger, it all tasted increasingly of bitter resolve and desperation.

The Aegean

Churchill believed that his latest initiative, the Aegean campaign of 1943, had the potential to roll back the occupation of the Balkans. It opened with high-altitude reconnaissance Spitfires, based in Cyprus, detecting what appeared to be German weakness in the eastern Aegean islands. The British occupied Kos, Leros and Samos. Spitfires flew into the only airfield, on Kos. But the US, committed to the Italian campaign, refused to deploy forces, including the long-range P-38 fighters, to the Aegean.

Within a few days, the Germans were able to muster a strong force of Bf 109s against the islands occupied by the British and pro-Allied Italians. Ju 88 bombers, unable to operate over Sicily by day, attacked the liberated islands with Bf 109 escort. The Germans massed aircraft from throughout the Mediterranean, including sixty Bf 109s. They opened their air offensive on 18 September. As on Malta, German strafing attacks led to low-altitude dogfights over the airfields as the outnumbered Spitfires took off and landed. By 27 September, only four Spitfires were operational on the airfield. Spitfire reinforcements flew in from Cyprus.

On 3 October, German fighters provided air cover for transport aircraft and an invasion fleet. Even Stukas, massacred many times by Spitfires, were back in action in daylight. The last four Spitfires, without fuel, were captured on the airfield by paratroopers. Kos fell.

On 12 November, the Germans invaded Leros. Again, Bf 109s seized air superiority. The Stukas dive-bombed as in their days of glory. Germans had nearby airfields on Rhodes, while the nearest Spitfire base was 390 miles away on Cyprus.

Three floatplane Spitfire Vs were rushed to Egypt and made ready to deploy to Leros, but the island fell before they could go into action. Originally intended for service in the Pacific, the floatplane Spitfire was only 30 mph slower than the standard Spitfire V and retained excellent handling qualities. Jeffrey Quill did the test flying. 'The aircraft turned out to be a most beautiful floatplane.'[16] The floats were designed by Arthur Shirvall, a member of R.J. Mitchell's original team, who had been responsible for the floats for the Schneider Cup racers, and was now head of Supermarine's project office. With the moment they were needed in the past, no more were converted. The Great Bitter Lake soon corroded away those that had deployed. The Spitfire's limited range had shaped the outcome of Churchill's campaign in the Aegean. It was the last time the Bf 109 was able to win air superiority that allowed the Germans to defeat numerically superior Allied forces.

Italy

Following the liberation of Sicily, massive air attacks on targets in Italy helped collapse Mussolini's regime and disrupted the Luftwaffe's ability to interfere with the coming invasion. Instead, a few Italian units re-equipped with Bf 109G-6s. Many Italian fighter units stayed fighting alongside the Germans. Others, joining the new Allied Italian government, eventually flew Spitfire Vs.

The Allied invasion of Italy at Salerno on 9 September 1943 was covered by fighters, including Spitfires now based on Sicily's airfields. Spitfire IXs, flying two 150-minute sorties a day, carried 90-gallon slipper tanks that enabled them to spend thirty minutes on station over the beachhead, up to 200 miles from their bases, backing up longer-range USAAF P-38s. This represented an effective doubling of the Spitfire's radius of action. Allied bombers attacked German airfields. The German fighter force, not recovered from their defeat over Sicily, lost heavily to long-range strafing attacks by P-38s.

Introduced during the carrier reinforcement missions to Malta, the slipper tank had a tendency to hit the Spitfire when jettisoned. Slipper tanks were not pressurised to assure fuel flow, and since they did not have a fuel gauge, problems with fuel starvation ensued. The British-designed slipper tanks proved a poorly designed solution, but the Spitfire IX had enough power that its handling qualities were little affected by their addition. Some Spitfire IXs, like the Spitfire Vs that preceded them, had an extra rear fuselage tank (26 gallons), but this affected stability and was not intended for use on combat missions. Corporal Ray Honeybone was an RAF technician in Gibraltar attaching slipper tanks. 'In the end a man from Supermarine was flown to Gibraltar to help us get them to work ... I said the man who designed the system ought to jump off Beachy Head. He said "Don't say that corporal, I designed it."'[17]

Off Salerno, Royal Navy Seafires repeated their role of providing carrier-based air cover until fighter fields could be established ashore. These were mainly improved Seafire L IICs, with a low-altitude Merlin 32 engine and clipped-back wing tips. They were built mainly by Westland and Cunliffe-Owen; Castle Bromwich and Supermarine were at capacity with Spitfires. Seafires were directed by radar on ships off-shore and broke up several German bombing attacks, flying 713 sorties from carriers and 56 from shore bases. While no Seafires were lost in combat, some 30 were destroyed and 53 damaged in accidents. An average of 11 per cent of all deck landings resulted in a serious accident, seven pilots being killed and three injured. The Seafires were operating mainly from small escort carriers. Inexperienced pilots, reduced deck length, light winds, and tactical restrictions on the speed the carriers could achieve all ratcheted up the accident rate. The Royal Navy admiral in command was unfamiliar with the Seafire's limitations and did not manoeuvre the carriers to mitigate them. The lessons of Salerno led to a high-priority development effort to reduce Seafire deck landing attrition.

Over Salerno, Spitfires and Seafires defended the Allied fleet against a new threat. In the week following the invasion, German bombers, escorted by between fourteen and twenty Bf 109s to overwhelm combat air patrols, were able to use anti-ship guided missiles and bombs to damage several capital ships severely, but were unable to halt the invasion. The first RAF Spitfires flew into forward airstrips in the Salerno beachhead on 12 September.

Spitfires from British, Commonwealth and US air arms, eventually joined by those flown by French, Italian Co-Belligerent and Yugoslav units, were a vital part of the air war in Italy. Most of the Spitfire's combat flying in Italy was air-to-ground, as most of the Luftwaffe fighters were held back in the north to defend against bomber attacks. By November 1943, the Germans had only 150 fighters in all of Italy.

On 5 December, Lieutenant Albert 'Bertie' Sachs, SAAF, of 92 Squadron, encountered a *Staffel* of Fw 190 fighter-bombers with Bf 109G escorts near Pescara. Sachs was originally from Germany; his brother was flying Bf 109Gs with the Luftwaffe in Italy.[18] The squadron's operational record book contemporaneously recorded:[19]

He positioned himself behind the twelve-plus fighter-bombers while two others attacked the fighter cover. After destroying an Fw 190 with a one-second burst, Lt. Sachs saw another on the tail of a Spitfire, so he turned into it, firing a 30-degree deflection shot, then fired again from point-blank range astern.

The aircraft blew up, and portions hit Sachs' windscreen, smashing it, while another large piece struck his starboard wing.

Fw 190s were then diving on him from both sides and one shell exploded on his tail plane, blowing off his starboard elevator. He turned toward another FW 190 which was attacking him at point-blank range on his port side, and felt a jar as he collided with it. The enemy aircraft dived away out of control minus its fin and rudder.

The attack continued and finally, after his elevator and aileron control were useless, Lt. Sachs was forced to bail out. He landed safely in his own lines within 60 yards of the wreckage of his Spitfire.[20]

Fighter units of the French Air Force in north Africa had started re-equipping with Spitfires in early 1943, first with Spitfire Vs, and by mid-year with new Spitfire IXs. French Spitfires, along with RAF squadrons, saw their first combat as part of the north Africa–based Allied Coastal Air Force. Commanded by Air Vice Marshal Hugh Pughe Lloyd, who had defended Malta, this now protected shipping in the Mediterranean with RAF and USAAF fighters guided by a network of radar and ground control stations. In September 1943, the French units started to deploy to liberated Corsica, along with RAF Spitfire units.

In January 1944, the Allied invasion on the Italian coast at Anzio, near Rome, strained the capabilities of their fighter units. The invasion relied for air cover on aircraft based in Italy. Spitfires were used for naval gun-fire spotting. It was six hours after the invasion before a single Bf 109 on a reconnaissance mission was able to penetrate the airspace over the beaches and bring confirmation to the German command.

Anzio brought more German aircraft in from throughout the theatre. German fighters were needed to defend against bomber attacks on rear areas, which targeted airfields and maintenance facilities. German bombers increasingly shifted to night operations. Spitfire units provided dawn and dusk patrols over Anzio. Additional training for the pilots was required, as these patrols demanded that the Spitfires either take off or land at their forward airstrips in darkness. Again, the Germans failed to disrupt the invasion. At Anzio, as throughout the Italian campaign, Spitfires were primarily used as fighter-bombers. In April the RAF stated, 'The present intention is to convert all Spitfire VIIIs and IXs into fighter bombers.'[21] Their improved air-to-ground tactics were based on those developed in north Africa. Massive Allied air power helped defeat German counter-attacks on Anzio; 1,700 sorties were flown on 17 February alone.

With the Germans pushed back out of Spitfire range, Malta was now effectively a rear area. Park was sent home. The entire RAF Middle East force came under the command of Sholto Douglas, promoted 'upstairs' from Fighter Command, as many senior airmen, British and American, returned to Britain to plan and lead the upcoming invasion of France.

The last Luftwaffe fighter units were withdrawn from Italy to the defence of the Reich in June 1944. The Germans continued to deliver

Bf 109Gs and 96-octane fuel to Mussolini's puppet air force, which went on fighting to the end. Messerschmitt AG set up support facilities for them in Italian aircraft factories. With no more German fighters within range, the USAAF's two Italy-based Spitfire groups re-equipped with P-51 Mustangs and joined the strategic air offensive over the Balkans and Germany. The German and Romanian Bf 109s defending the vital Ploesti oil fields were soon in losing battles with increased numbers of P-38s and P-51s escorting Fifteenth Air Force bombers.

Hauptmann Helmut Lipfert was a top-scoring ace in II/JG 52, pulled off the eastern front to the defence of Ploesti. 'It was quite different from flying against the Russians. The number of aircraft was amazing. Behind the large formations were long, thick condensation trails; one simply couldn't miss them. Above the bombers, probably up to 10,000 metres, the sky swarmed with fighters. There were so many I didn't dare look up.' But Lipfert was aware that what he encountered over Ploesti was dwarfed by the air battles over the Reich. 'We knew all too well that it was a virtual death sentence for anyone who had to move to the Reich ... Everyone who flew in the Reich was "burned" sooner or later.'[22]

Lipfert returned to the air war in the east after Ploesti was destroyed by US bombers and finally denied to the Germans when Romania joined the Allies. However, almost all the German fighter pilots who had fought in the Mediterranean, knowing what it would mean for them as well as Lipfert did, were committed to the defence of the Reich.

12

A Global Air War

The Eastern Front

Spitfires. Eight of them. That is what the enemy appeared to be to Leutnant Alfred Grislawski, an experienced Bf 109 pilot with 100 air-to-air victories, all on the eastern front. His wingman, Leutnant Erich 'Bubi' Hartmann, had been flying within him since late 1942 and was starting to show promise, but had only seen Spitfires in the recognition books.

On their third mission of 29 April 1943, over the Kuban bridgehead on the shores of the Black Sea, Grislawski and his flight from III/JG 52 encountered the Spitfires, apparently a combat air patrol protecting the Soviet troops at Krymskaya.

The Spitfires also saw the Bf 109Gs. They too were led by an experienced pilot, Kapitan Viktor Chernetsov, though neither knew the other's identity. Chernetsov had survived the 1941 and 1942 campaigns flying I-16s. Now, his unit re-equipped with Spitfire VBs, he was able to fight Bf 109s on an even basis. And this time, he had the advantage of numbers.

A swirling dogfight ensued, the altitude too low for the Bf 109s to be able to dive away. But neither side was able to ambush the other without the element of surprise. No aircraft were lost. Even the experienced Grislawski was unable to get into firing position.

Grislawski's commanding officer did not believe his report of fighting

Spitfires over the Kuban, although Hauptmann Günther Rall, in the same *Gruppe*, had shot one down the preceding day. But on the next day, Oberleutnant Gerhard Barkhorn – who had encountered Spitfires over Britain before becoming an ace on the eastern front – and his wingman, flying Bf 109Gs, each claimed a Spitfire. The Germans realised that the Spitfire had joined the air war in the east.

Chernetsov was back in action the next afternoon, leading an eight-Spitfire mission that fought four Bf 109Gs without loss, while claiming one shot down. Other Spitfires were attacked by a nearby Soviet fighter unit, unfamiliar with its silhouette.

Grislawski's flight was providing top cover for Ju 88 bombers when he met the Spitfires – and Chernetsov – again on 7 May. Chernetsov, leading six Spitfires, went for the bombers, apparently unaware of the Bf 109Gs with their height advantage. Grislawski led his flight down in a diving attack, aiming for the lead Spitfire.

Grislawski hit Chernetsov with his first burst of fire. But before he could close in and finish the Spitfire off, he had to break off to defend himself against Chernetsov's wingman, Serzhant Limonov. As had happened the last time Grislawski met Spitfires, a savage turning dogfight resulted. Another Spitfire, attacked by two Bf 109s, was shot down. Two more Spitfires, damaged, made it back to their airfield. Chernetsov managed a belly landing and was soon back in combat.

Grislawski, seeing Chernetsov heading for home, realised he had not managed to score a victory over the Spitfires. But these Soviet pilots and their Spitfire VBs were different from the opponents that had made it possible for German pilots to amass such high victory totals in previous years. One JG 52 pilot recalled, 'These pilots were not your average Russian. These fellows knew their business.'[1]

Soviet Spitfires in eastern front combat

These were not the first Spitfires on the eastern front. A Soviet test pilot had flown a captured Spitfire I in Germany in March 1941, while the Hitler–Stalin pact held. A few Spitfire PR IVs, flown by RAF pilots, operated from Vaenga near Murmansk in September–November 1942. They watched German warships, based in Norway, that threatened the northern convoy routes to the Soviet Union. These planes were later handed over to the Soviet naval air arm, which operated a few Spitfires, primarily in the reconnaissance role, in support of the Red Banner Northern and Black Sea fleets.[2] (RAF reconnaissance Spitfire detachments subsequently deployed to northern Russia in April 1943 and February 1944.)

The Spitfires that Grislawski had encountered over the Kuban bridgehead were part of the ongoing British resupply efforts to the Soviet Union. The British had agreed to supply the Soviets with 200 fighters a month on 1 October 1941. In October 1942, Stalin had personally asked Churchill for Spitfires. Originally to be sent along with RAF air and ground crew to fight on the eastern front – Churchill had proposed deploying the RAF to the southern end of the eastern front in March 1942 – the Soviet Air Force instead received 143 overhauled ex-RAF Spitfire Mk VBs, many being veterans of air combat over France. All were equipped with the obsolescent TR-9D HF radio, as the Soviet Air Force did not then use VHF radio (it was only in 1943 that all Soviet fighters were delivered with radios and reflector gunsights). The Spitfires were shipped to Iran and assembled before being ferried to the Soviet Union and initially used to re-equip the 57th GIAP (Guards Fighter Air Regiment). The unit had a cadre of combat veterans, but some of its pilots were sent to fly Spitfires straight from training. Without British instructors or even manuals, the Soviets had to teach themselves to fly and maintain the Spitfire. They re-equipped near Baku from December 1942 to March 1943. Committed to the air battles over the Kuban bridgehead in April–May 1943, by 1 June, after over a month of intense air combat, the 57th GIAP, which had gone into battle with twenty-nine Spitfires, had only four serviceable. It had lost thirteen Spitfires in air combat, claiming forty-eight victories (including twenty-five Bf 109s). Chernetsov flew a few more Spitfire missions. On 20 May and 7 June he shot down Great War-style observation balloons the Germans had been using over the Kuban.

The 57th was pulled out of the line to re-equip with US-built P-39s. It turned its surviving Spitfires over to the 821st IAP (Fighter Regiment), which had been training with other Spitfire VBs. While this unit lacked experienced pilots, in six weeks it claimed thirty-two victories while losing sixteen Spitfires in combat and four in accidents. One of these victories was achieved through deliberate ramming of a Fw 189 reconnaissance aircraft. With few spare parts and encountering widespread failures with the Merlin engines, the 821st gave up its Spitfires for P–39s in August 1943. The crucial battles on the eastern front that saw the defeat of the German Army would take place without Spitfires.

The Kuban air fighting demonstrated that the Soviet Air Force was coming back from its defeats of the previous two years. The Spitfires and all Soviet fighters over the Kuban suffered from the defensive orientation of their tactics, cover of ground troops being seen as the primary objective and most missions being flown by keeping up small standing patrols that could be overwhelmed by concentrated German attacks. Tactics worked out over the Kuban became the basis for those refined over the following two years. New Soviet fighter tactics were devised by pilots who had fought alongside the Spitfires. They stressed the importance of the *para* (pair) of fighters, operating like a German *Rotte*. *Okhotniki* (free hunter) missions, introduced to catch Ju 52s heading for Stalingrad, were expanded to use larger forces. Even though the Spitfires represented only a small percentage of overall Soviet air power, their role in the crucible of Soviet fighter tactics in the Kuban and their status as one of the most complex fighters operated in the field by the Soviet Air Force up to that time meant that Spitfire VBs had an impact on the Soviet air war out of proportion to their limited numbers.

Improved fighter tactics and the increasing number of more effective fighter aircraft – mainly Soviet-built planes such as the Yak-9 and radial-engine La-5, but with significant numbers of Lend–Lease fighters as well – contributed to the Soviet Air Force's ability to prevent the Luftwaffe from achieving and using air superiority as they had repeatedly done throughout 1941–2. Soviet fighters were designed for mass production. They had an average combat life of just eighty hours, so many of the refinements made on aircraft such as the Spitfire were simply not cost-effective.

The shipment of Spitfire VBs to the Soviets was not repeated. After the intense Kuban bridgehead fighting, the Soviet Air Force found that sustaining the limited number of Spitfire VBs remaining was difficult for their logistics system. To keep them flying, the Soviets carried out field modifications, including the replacement of armament and tyres with

Soviet models. The Soviets appreciated the Spitfire's excellent rate of climb and oxygen system. But the Spitfire proved to be less adaptable to the conditions of air combat on the eastern front than aircraft such as the US-built P-39 and B-25, supplied under Lend–Lease, new production aircraft where the Spitfires had been hard used, if overhauled before delivery. The British considered the weather, the primitive conditions on Soviet forward airstrips, and the limitations of Soviet maintenance, with technicians used to simpler aircraft, as the underlying causes.[3]

Spitfires defend Soviet airspace
After the Kuban battles, the remaining Spitfire VBs were pulled out of the 57th GIAP. The Luftwaffe, encountering no more Soviet Spitfires, assumed they had destroyed them. They were reassigned to air defence units around Moscow and other high-value targets. They intercepted Ju 86P high-altitude German reconnaissance aircraft, shooting one down on 15 October 1943 (after another had escaped a Spitfire over Moscow on 22 August). The 7th Naval Fighter Air Regiment of the Black Sea Fleet used twenty Spitfire VBs for the air defence of Novorissok. The planes saw little combat.[4]

The Soviets used their Spitfires to counter a new threat. In 1943, German He 177 four-engine strategic bombers appeared in the East, after years of difficulty-plagued development. The Soviets reinforced their air defence system around Moscow, Leningrad, Murmansk and other strategic targets.

Starting in 1944, 1148 Spitfire IXs were delivered, mainly by sea through Iran. Most were used for interceptor missions. The Air Defence Force (PVO) 802nd IAP deployed with Spitfire IXs to the Ukraine in 1944 to help cover US shuttle bombing bases. Operational in daylight only, they were unable to defend against a devastating Luftwaffe night bomber attack on the airfield at Poltava that destroyed dozens of B-17s and curtailed these missions (providing at the same time a reminder of the importance of Fighter Command in preventing such attacks against bases in England).

Late-war Soviet fighter Spitfires saw little combat. On 1 May 1945, the Soviets had 847 Spitfires, 683 operating with the PVO.[5] The Spitfire played an important role in the transition of Soviet air defences around key cities to regional integrated systems, using radar and a command and control network; twenty-two PVO regiments were equipped with Spitfires in 1946 and served until at least 1949–50.

The Bf 109 in the east

Bf 109s rarely encountered Spitfires again on the eastern front, but they found themselves fighting other Soviet opponents that increased in both numbers and quality. With Fw 190s mainly used for fighter-bomber missions, the Bf 109 remained the mainstay of German fighter units in the east. There were insufficient numbers of both planes to deal with resurgent Soviet air power. At the time of the German offensive at Kursk in July 1943, the Luftwaffe could mass only 700 Bf 109s and Fw 190s; Soviet fighters outnumbered them by over three to one. In the two months of fighting around Kursk, the Germans lost 1272 aircraft. Lacking the long reach to control the air over German airfields, the Soviet Air Force's fighter units were never so grimly efficient at destroying Luftwaffe fighters as their USAAF counterparts. That was not the job of the Soviet fighters. Rather, they were supposed to prevent German air power being used against the Soviet Army while enabling Soviet bombers to strike targets on the battlefield and in rear areas.

Germany's allies on the eastern front received Bf 109s. Slovakia, Croatia and Spain all had *Staffel*-sized units in 1941. Romania and Hungary used Bf 109Es in 1942. In 1943, the Luftwaffe made Bf 109Gs available to their allies.[6] Finland, Slovakia, Croatia, Hungary and the puppet government in northern Italy received Bf 109Gs. But all these countries maintained separate units; Luftwaffe fighter units were never multinational. The Swiss received twelve Bf 109G-2s (in exchange for destroying an interned lost German night fighter full of radar equipment) and were shocked by the poor workmanship compared with their pre-war Bf 109E-1s.

The Finnish Air Force, with a cadre of pilots with combat experience going back to the Winter War of 1939–40, received their first Bf 109G 2s in February 1943.[7] Faced by increasing numbers of Soviet aircraft, they claimed 270 shot down for the loss of 22 Bf 109Gs and 11 pilots, a higher ratio than the Germans achieved even in 1941. The highest scoring non-German ace, Eino Juutilainen, claimed ninety-four victories, many while flying Bf 109s. He was never shot down. This contrasts with major German aces, almost all of whom were shot down in air combat numerous times.[8]

The Bf 109 pilots flying on the eastern front included aces who achieved the largest scores ever. Erich Hartmann, who started as Grislawski's wingman, ultimately claimed 352 victories scored in 825 combat missions, almost all Soviet (except seven USAAF P-51s) and all while flying the Bf 109. Gerhard Barkhorn was awarded 301 victories in some 1100 combat missions. A total of 15 fighter pilots had scores of over 200 victories, and 107 over 100.

While Luftwaffe fighter pilots were subject to the same inclination to over-claim as other combatants, evidence suggests that, overall, they were no more so inclined. Nor were German rules about confirmation of victories particularly lax (they varied unit by unit in practice). The large scores gained in the Bf 109 by German aces are as believable as most fighter pilots' claims. In the east, from 1943 on, they reflected the target-rich environment and the relentless operational tempo that sent German fighter pilots into the air on multiple short missions – their airfields were close to the front line – every day until they went down. They all went down. Hartmann was shot down seventeen times. Because the Germans were on the defensive after 1943, most came down behind friendly lines.

The repeated shooting down of even the best German fighter pilots showed that there were no easy days in the east. While the Luftwaffe, unlike the German Army, suffered the majority of its casualties outside the eastern front, that theatre still represented, from 1943 on, a series of desperate missions punctuated by retreats. Every success against Soviet aircraft was tempered by the knowledge that they would be back again, if not tomorrow then the next day, and there would be more of them and they would be better than before. The young pilots, fresh from training – for often the Germans tried to send them to the east to gain experience before committing them to the lethal battles over Germany – would see this and ask their more experienced *Gruppenkommandeure* if there would be better fighters. They would carry on with Bf 109s. They asked if there would be reinforcements. Any reinforcements would be needed in Germany. Then, sir, they asked, what shall we do? Came the answer: we will do as much as we can for as long as we can.

Major Günther Rall was one of those answering the young pilots' questions, aware that the Luftwaffe depended heavily on a few leaders and aces to keep their fighter units operating. 'Hundreds are putting their trust in the "old man" to lead them out of this catastrophe alive. The "old man", that's what we are even to those under our command that are twice our age.'[9] But Rall would not be on the eastern front to offer leadership. He was one of many called back to defend the Reich against the escalating bomber offensive. He packed his kit, shook hands with all those who would remain, and caught a transport plane back to a now badly bombed Berlin to receive his next command assignment.

13

A Global Air War

The War against Japan

Smoke rose from Darwin, the dark skyward pillars visible far away. Closer, the intense heat from the fires added to that from the tropical southern-hemisphere midsummer. Darwin harbour was where the smoke rose thickest and the fires burned most fiercely. Of the forty-five ships in the harbour, twenty-three had been sunk. Burning aircraft added to the pall of smoke and the fear of defeat. The only air defences had been eleven USAAF P-40E Kittyhawks. The Japanese shot down ten. The Japanese had bombed Darwin in Australia's North West Territory on 19 February 1942. The newspapers had called it Australia's Pearl Harbor. Many thought invasion was imminent.

It was now 2 March 1943: the Japanese were back over Darwin in force on this clear morning. Clive Caldwell saw them, ahead and slightly to port, from the cockpit of his Spitfire VB. He was leading six Spitfires, in the air behind him. The Japanese had just attacked an Australian airfield. Intended to deliver a powerful blow, they had destroyed only a lone Beaufighter. Caldwell had been looking for the attackers, now on their way home, heading back over the sea to Timor, and had been in the air for ninety minutes. He calculated that he would have time for just one pass at the Japanese, a formation of three twin-engine G4M2 'Betty' bombers escorted by fifteen A6M2 'Zero' and A6M3 'Hap' fighters, stacked up above the bombers with an altitude advantage over the Spitfires.

Caldwell led his Spitfires at the bombers and their close escort of three Zeros, diving down in a straggling line-astern formation to set up a high-deflection shot from the side of the three Zeros. The Japanese pilots, looking behind them, did not see the Spitfires' diving attack.

Caldwell was superb at deflection shooting. Over the desert, he had even surprised Marseille, the German master, shooting down one of his wingmen with an 'impossible' shot. Caldwell aimed carefully at the Japanese aircraft, waited until he was at close range and then pressed the firing button on the top of the Spitfire's control column. He saw his fire hit the target.

In an instant, he had flashed past the Zero, using the momentum the Spitfire had built up in the diving attack to make a zoom climb, to position himself for another attack.

He did not get the chance.

All fifteen Japanese fighters, now alerted, turned on the attacking Spitfires. The remaining Spitfire pilots, lacking Caldwell's deflection shooting skills, missed the Zeros. They found themselves fighting for their lives in individual dogfights, losing mutual support.

Caldwell took on several of the Japanese fighters one at a time. A glance at the Spitfire's airspeed indicator showed Caldwell he was doing 280 mph. With one Zero, he started a tight-turning dogfight, the two fighters each trying to turn inside the other's turning circle and get behind on the enemy's tail. Caldwell had the control stick pulled back almost in his lap. He stood the Spitfire on its pointed wing tip and hauled it into its tightest possible turn, with the familiar juddering on the brink of a stall that had scared off less experienced pilots. Maintaining situational awareness, he looked up at the fighter and found to his surprise that he could clearly see the pilot in its cockpit, looking at him; two fighter pilots who had both come a long way to try to kill each other, turning in circles with their canopies opposite each other.

Caldwell had talked before to the USAAF P-40E Kittyhawk pilots who had met the Japanese over Darwin. They told him: whatever you do, never dogfight with a Zero, especially at low speed. Caldwell had not believed them. An experienced fighter pilot, like Adolf Galland he had increased his victory score by being able to use his flying skill to out-turn fighter planes that were more manoeuvrable on paper but whose pilots lacked the skill to wring out every last bit of performance.

Caldwell thought, 'Now here's a golden opportunity to see how we turn with the Zero.' He – and the RAF – had never encountered a fighter able to out-turn a Spitfire flown to the limits of its performance.

Until now.

The two fighters were turning as tight as they could, inducing drag, slowing down. As they turned more tightly and flew more slowly, the Japanese fighter's superiority – it had indeed been designed for unmatched low-speed manoeuvrability – became terribly apparent to Caldwell. By the end of their second complete 360-degree circle, Caldwell could see the Zero was turning inside him, using his smaller turning circle to close on the Spitfire's vulnerable tail. A glance at the airspeed indicator showed that the turns had brought the Spitfire's speed down to 180 mph.

Caldwell had not lived to be an experienced fighter pilot without having a back-up plan at all times. He 'parked everything in the left hand corner', violently throwing his control column forward and hard to the left, while at the same time kicking his left foot, in its RAF-issue wool-lined flying boot, pushing the rudder pedal to its extreme forward limit as his right hand eased the throttle as far forward as it would go, 'through the gate' of the aluminium wire stop, to get maximum power from his Merlin engine.

The Spitfire's nose was violently yanked down. Caldwell's vision was suddenly turned to blood red, leaving him seeing nothing else.

He had 'redded out', the blood rushing to his head under the violent negative-gravity manoeuvre. But the Merlin, fitted with an upgraded carburettor, did not cut out, as it had when Spitfire pilots first used this manoeuvre in the Battle of Britain.

Caldwell, literally flying blind, now rolled his Spitfire inverted by feel and pulled back the control stick hard again into his lap. His vision returned for an instant before it was slammed shut again by blackness. Now, all his blood had rushed to his feet under the powerful positive-g inverted manoeuvre.

Again flying blind, Caldwell sustained the inverted dive for a moment. Then he pulled the Spitfire's nose up and immediately threw it into a tight turn. Caldwell looked behind him to see if the Japanese fighter had followed his manoeuvre. It had not.

As he looked around, Caldwell saw another Spitfire diving away, followed by a Zero. Coming to the Spitfire's aid, Caldwell dived after the attacking Zero and, turning in towards the six o'clock position of the diving Japanese plane, directly behind, opened fire. The Zero went down. Caldwell thought he saw it crash into the sea.

The six Allied pilots were lucky to have survived the Spitfire's first combat against Japanese fighters. While the Spitfires claimed three shot down (which higher headquarters promptly doubled to six before calling the news media), two by Caldwell, in reality all the Japanese made it home to their base in Timor, unimpressed with their Spitfire opponents. They misidentified them as P-39s and Brewster Buffalo fighters, which they had outperformed many times in the past year.

Spitfires to Australia

By the end of 1942, Australia had been bombed fifty-one times from Japanese bases in Timor. The USAAF and RAAF both lacked suitable fighters and radar to defend the North West Territory.[1] This provided an opportunity for Britain to come to the defence of Australia.

Since Pearl Harbor, Australia had depended on the US rather than Britain to defend against invasion. The Australian government insisted that its army divisions return to defend their homeland before joining the fight in New Guinea. But Australian airmen were still an integral part of the British air arms in all theatres. With the USAAF having been unable to defend the country, the foreign minister, Dr Herbert V. 'Doc' Evatt, stated that 'three Spitfire squadrons would have a tremendous effect on Australia'.[2]

Australian Wing Commander Clive R. Caldwell, DFC and Bar, a twenty-two-victory Tomahawk ace (ten of them Bf 109s) nicknamed by the press 'Killer' (which he hated), was coming home a hero. He had joined up in 1940 as a 29-year-old clerk, thought too old for pilot training, but had thrived in the multinational world of RAF fighter squadrons and in eight months' fighting in north Africa had gone from 'sprog' newcomer to squadron commander. Australian newspapers published photographs of his Tomahawk with its shark's mouth squadron insignia (copied by the American 'Flying Tigers' in China) and the many swastikas and fasces painted under the cockpit that marked his victories. Surely this man would save Australia from the Japanese bombers.

Caldwell was not coming to Australia alone. Known as the 'Churchill Wing', because of the prime minister's personal promise that it would demonstrate Britain's continued commitment to defend Australia, the RAF's 1 Fighter Wing, equipped with tropicalised Spitfire VCs, deployed from airfields in England, via a long sea voyage around the Cape of Good Hope with their planes in crates. They arrived at a number of airfields in the Darwin area, accompanied by British and Australian radar and ground controllers.

Caldwell was confident to the point of arrogance in his ability to defeat the Japanese. After all, he had beaten Germans while flying aircraft inferior to the Spitfire. Before heading off to Australia, Caldwell had been sent to England to learn how to lead a Spitfire wing in battle. But there was no time to train him up, just a few operations over France and some instruction about the importance of operating *en masse*, in big 'wings', and at high altitude, very different tactics from what Caldwell was used to over the desert.

But of the ninety-five pilots in the wing's one RAF (54) and two RAAF (452 and 457) squadrons, only thirty-seven had seen combat. About six were experienced in Spitfires; others, including some of the squadron commanders, had never flown fighters before. 54 Squadron's Battle of Britain veteran pilots had all long since rotated out of the unit.

From the outset, the Spitfires relied on a long supply line from Britain for parts and supplies; even bottles of Australian beer were 'unusual'.[3] Darwin itself was so remote that when one of the wing's pilots was forced down in the outback, it took fifteen days to find him (he was alive).

Spitfires were designed to operate in temperate climates, not in conditions where the temperature varied rapidly between the extremely dusty (in the dry season) or tropical airfields and the extremely humid cold of high altitude that caused repeated failures of the radio, the 20mm cannon and the propeller constant speed unit (CSU). Spitfires crashed in flight. Others were grounded until replacements could be fitted. The Spitfire's short range and lack of drop tanks were major drawbacks. They had to operate over huge distances. The pilots, coming from Britain, were only briefly trained in the tactics US and Australian fighter pilots had already found effective against the Japanese.

The Spitfires, marked with their new blue-and-white Australian roundels (removing the RAF's red centre that could be confused with a Japanese *hinomaru*), were operational in February 1943.

Spitfires versus the Japanese

Japanese Army Ki 46 'Dinah'[4] reconnaissance aircraft, whose high-altitude photographs had identified British weakness before the invasion of Malaya in 1941, started to fly over Darwin. Even the USAAF's stripped-down P-40Es could not catch the fast unarmed Dinah, one reason the Australians wanted Spitfires to defend Darwin. Dinah over-flights preceded major Japanese air attacks.

Radar tracked a Dinah on 7 March and vectored two Spitfires to intercept:

> The tally ho was given by Flight Lieutenant MacLean who gave chase with Flight Sergeant McDowell. Both pilots delivered the attacks at close range upon the enemy reconnaissance aircraft 'Dinah' when it was heading for home over the sea about 15 miles from Darwin. There was no return fire from the aircraft, which plunged, burning fiercely, into the sea. The 'destroyed' claim was shared between the two pilots. In the evening, the 'first blooding' of the squadron was celebrated in the traditional manner, despite a shortage of liquor.[5]

But Caldwell knew that this was just a preliminary combat. The serious air battles were to follow and he made sure that he would then be in the air leading the wing. The Imperial Japanese Navy started attacks on northern Australia with A6M2 Zeros and A6M3 Haps escorting G4M2 Betty bombers. The initial interception, on 2 March, had actually resulted in no losses on either side.[6] The Spitfire wing was not ready for the attack. Caldwell was off for a doctor's appointment.

On 15 March, the Japanese hit the harbour facilities at Darwin. 54 Squadron recorded in its operational record book: '22 bombers and an unknown number of Zeros as escort. The formation coming over in bright sunlight was very reminiscent of the Battle of Britain and most of us had not seen such a sight since that time.' The interception was, in the words of Flight Lieutenant 'Bob' Foster of 54 Squadron, 'a complete shambles'.[7]

Squadron Leader T. Smith, DFC, who led the wing sections, gave 'Tally ho' and turned in front of the bombers, placing the Zeroes between the wing aircraft and the bombers. The wing aircraft were separated and were jumped out of the sun by Zeroes. 54 Squadron aircraft were already by this time engaged with the bombers and the fighters. A general dogfight ensued with the Zeroes over Darwin harbour, while the bombers made slight damage in Darwin. As the bombers turned and made away from the coast our aircraft kept out a running attack until the enemy were 90 miles away.[8]

Four Spitfires were lost to combat or mechanical failure. One Zero was shot down. The loss of three pilots killed in action on 15 March convinced Caldwell that something had gone badly wrong. The Spitfires had tried to form up into a wing-sized formation and engage the attacking Japanese, but had failed. Caldwell remained convinced that 'big wings' were needed to defeat the Japanese, and that the fault lay with the inexperience of his pilots and the failure at altitude of Spitfire cannon.

A larger attack – twenty-five Betty bombers escorted by twenty-seven Zeros – on 2 May again penetrated Australian defences. The Spitfire pilots found that the highly manoeuvrable Zero was dangerous even if a Spitfire was on its tail. 'Squadron Leader James closed for an astern attack, but the enemy aircraft half-looped for a head-on attack and closed, head-on, upside down. James commenced firing at 200 yards and continued until the enemy filled up and overfilled his sights. Bits of the enemy fuselage were seen to break off.'[9]

'Wing Commander Caldwell led the squadron up to attack.'[10] Some thirty-three Spitfires had taken off, but five had to abort with mechanical problems. The Spitfires failed to repulse the bombers. Five Spitfires were shot down in air combat, with no Japanese losses (although they suffered fourteen aircraft damaged). A running battle brought the Spitfires off-shore and out of range of their airfields. More Spitfires were lost from fuel starvation and mechanical failures. A total of fourteen Spitfires were lost that day and, Foster recalled, 'several pilots had to make forced landings all over the place'. The loss of Spitfires that simply ran out of fuel was particularly painful. Drop tanks were introduced after this setback.

The 2 May battle marked the failure of the 'big wing' tactics that Caldwell had relied on. Yet, even though the Americans did not try to use such tactics, he remained convinced they were the way to beat the Japanese. He pointed to the wing's tactical advantage when engaging Japanese planes, with the advantage of higher altitude and being up-sun; the setback was not the fault of his tactics. Some sixteen Spitfires had suffered armament failures.

On 10 May, a Japanese fighter sweep, following Beaufighters returning from a mission to Timor, surprised the defenders. Pilot Officer Bruce Little's Spitfire had been damaged in the initial combat and had to return to the airfield at Millingimbi, north-east of Darwin. Just as the main wheels of his Spitfire touched down, three Zeros roared over the field, strafing the returned Beaufighters. Little immediately pushed his throttle full forward and took off again. One of the Zeros turned around from the strafing attack and, for ten minutes, it and Little's Spitfire put on a highly lethal low-level air display over the airstrip, 'a series of climbing turns from 100 feet to 300 feet'.

Until the Zero flew Little into the ground. 'Little took his eyes off the enemy aircraft and found himself approaching the ground, which he struck.' The Zero turned back and strafed the wreckage. Little survived with cuts and bruises, walking back to the airfield.[11]

After the hard-fought battles, the wing developed improved tactics, despite the shortage of combat-experienced Spitfire pilots in Australia.[12] 457 Squadron recorded that pilots 'discuss little else but tactics'.[13] In a horizontal turning fight, the Spitfire V could dogfight with the A6M2 at high speed and win.[14] Unless the Spitfires were able to fight at high speed or dive on A6M2 Zero fighters, they would be at a disadvantage. Spitfire tests against a captured improved A6M3 Hap fighter determined that 'the Spit is outclassed by "Hap" at all altitudes over 20,000 feet'.[15] Caldwell remained committed to Spitfires operating together as a 'big wing', as he had seen in England, rather than relying, as the US did, on smaller, more flexible formations or his own experience from north Africa.

When large-scale Japanese attacks resumed on 28 May, Spitfires managed to shoot down Japanese bombers for the first time, but two Spitfires were shot down and one crash-landed. Between then and September, Spitfires intercepted multiple escorted bomber raids. Both sides, with finite numbers of aircraft and at the end of long supply chains, found that their air efforts were running down due to their inability to sustain their surviving aircraft.

The number of Spitfires available to intercept each raid declined as they came up against additional raids on 20, 28 and 30 June that saw a dozen Spitfires lost. On 20 June, 452 Squadron 'made an excellent interception'.[16] But the Japanese Army had taken over the air offensive with Nakajima Ki 43 'Oscar' fighters escorting Ki 48 'Lily' and Ki 49 'Helen' bombers. 'Bob' Foster tried turning with an Oscar during the 20 June battle. 'The pilot was soon turning inside me, almost straight away. They were so quick those fighters and it was impossible to turn with him, so I broke off as quickly as I could.'[17] The Japanese Army had been expecting a 'milk run' to Darwin but instead encountered heavy opposition, losing at least two fighters and five to eight bombers. Caldwell claimed an Oscar shot down with his machine guns after his cannon froze. The Japanese Army never returned to bomb Darwin. Their units were transferred to New Guinea, where the USAAF destroyed them in the air and on the ground by relentless attacks.

The Spitfire's mechanical problems continued throughout these battles. The CSU on the propellers was still vulnerable to overspeed: 'Flying Officer J. Halse, after his combat, dived away and experienced the now-common 4000 rpm and was forced to crash land by a road'; 'Cannon and machinegun stoppages again subscribed to the lack of success of this squadron and steps are being taken to remove the faults, i.e. freezing of mechanisms and faulty ammo.'[18]

On 30 June, with Caldwell leading them, four Spitfires were lost to Zeros, but this reflected the wing's focus on attacking the bombers. Only the poor deflection shooting of the Spitfire pilots and widespread armament failures saved the Japanese from heavy losses. Caldwell demanded remedial gunnery training.

The 6 July air battle brought the Japanese Navy back to hit the USAAF bomber base at Fenton near Darwin with twenty-six Zeros and twenty-two bombers; the fighting cost seven Spitfires. Despite mechanical and supply problems – a ship carrying replacement Spitfires had been sunk en route – the Spitfires were still able to intercept Japanese raids through August but fought fewer pitched battles. In return, RAAF and USAAF bombers hit Japanese airfields on Timor; Spitfires lacked the range to take the offensive against these Japanese bases.

The Japanese daylight raids ended after a final offensive operation (a fighter sweep) on 7 September. The Japanese switched to unescorted night attacks, against which Spitfires were used as night fighters. These ended in November, not due to losses, but rather because the Japanese crews and aircraft were needed elsewhere. Instead of duelling with Spitfires, they were destroyed by the USAAF and the US Navy.

The 1943 air campaigns over Darwin and Timor were overshadowed by the more intense fighting in New Guinea and the Solomon Islands, and none of the bombing on either side did significant damage. Air combat losses, a small fraction of the total, were twenty-eight Spitfires against four Zeros, one Oscar, four Dinahs and fourteen bombers. Caldwell had turned the wing and its Spitfires into an effective fighting force, which neither had been when they first arrived in Australia. The wing itself lost 109 Spitfires from all causes over the course of 1943, most due to operational accidents at forward airfields.

The Spitfire wing held its own in air combat only on those occasions when it could put sufficient numbers into the air – a rare occurrence, due to the mechanical and logistics problems – and had warning enough to climb to gain the altitude advantage over the attackers. The Spitfires, located at dispersed bases and often lacking sufficient warning from radar to climb, were often unable to do this. The wing's mechanical problems reflected the fact that in Australia, unlike north Africa and Burma, the

Spitfires did not fight alongside combat-tested Hurricane squadrons (which were able to make Merlins turn in the worst conditions) and lacked combat support infrastructure or experienced leadership above wing level.

In the end, Caldwell and the wing had won. But, despite the exaggerated victory totals published by the press, the Spitfire did not save Australia in 1943, as it had appeared to save Britain in 1940. The RAAF command resented that they had not been able to show their American counterparts that they could succeed without them. Caldwell, after a spell as an instructor, put in to go back to flying with the RAF but was turned down.

With the end of the Japanese air offensive, the wing was reinforced and re-equipped with fast-climbing Spitfire VIIIs, modified to overcome the problems encountered over Darwin. They waited for any return of the Japanese air offensive. In late 1943, a fourth Spitfire squadron deployed to north-east Australia. By late 1944, six squadrons were equipped with Spitfire VIIIs, one wing in Australia to defend Darwin and another deployed for offensive operations over New Guinea and the Solomons. By the time these were committed to combat, few Japanese aircraft within their range were capable of flying.

Spitfires over India and Burma

The first Spitfires to arrive in India were two reconnaissance Spitfire IVs, which had carried out high-altitude reconnaissance missions over Burma from October 1942. 607 and 615 squadrons, based at Alipore in India, started to convert from Hurricanes to Spitfire VCs in September 1943. These were followed by reconnaissance Spitfire PR XIs, arriving the following month.

The Indian weather proved the biggest threat to Allied aircraft. Monsoons shut down air operations for several months a year. Warrant Officer Francis 'Chota' Brown, RNZAF, was flying a Spitfire PR IV on 8 June 1943, returning from a reconnaissance mission over Japanese-occupied Mandalay, when he had to penetrate a frontal system at 23,000 feet – the Spitfire lacked fuel to fly around or above:

For 20 minutes I was on instruments with flying conditions becoming rougher with the engine continually icing up and losing power, which could only be overcome by vigorous pumping on the throttle. The aircraft then struck a series of terrific bumps which sent the instruments haywire. I could see my artificial horizon up in the top corner of the dial while the turn and bank indicator appeared, as far as I could see, to be showing conditions of a spin. Deciding that I must be in a spin, I applied correction for it, but this was my last conscious thought.[19]

Brown came to falling through space at 3000 feet, his Spitfire ripped into small pieces. After plummeting through the storm, he opened his parachute and survived (though suffering a back injury that ended his flying). His Spitfire was scattered over twenty square miles around Fulbachiga, India.

The first Spitfires to arrive in India, along with increased numbers of air defence radar installations, had a tremendous impact on air combat throughout the theatre. As in Australia, the fighter Spitfires' initial task, which they started in November, was to close Allied airspace to the high-altitude Dinah reconnaissance aircraft. Four Dinahs were claimed in a month.

RAF Spitfire strength increased, including the arrival of combat-experienced squadrons, equipped with the Spitfire VIII, deployed from the Mediterranean theatre. These were able to defeat Japanese daylight air attacks following the end of the 1943 monsoon. The Japanese air offensive started in December; on the 5th an attack on Calcutta did considerable damage to the dock area. The Japanese flight path had been planned to avoid the Spitfires' airfields. By the end of the month, Spitfires were intercepting the raiders and, with improved radar warning, dived on them with the advantage of being high and up-sun. The combination of radar, ground controllers and Spitfires, with their superior climbing performance, meant that they were able to gain the altitude advantage against the Japanese. The introduction of Spitfires allowed Hurricanes to be replaced as interceptors and used as fighter-bombers. The Japanese switched to night bombing of Calcutta (until halted by Beaufighters rushed from Egypt).

After defeating the Japanese air attacks against targets in India, the Spitfire's introduction to combat in Burma enabled Allied forces to fight using the integrated air and ground operations that would ultimately defeat the Japanese. On the battlefield, the Allies relied on air transport. Spitfires ensured that the Japanese were unable to interfere. Spitfire VIIIs forward deployed to support the 'Chindits' behind Japanese lines, operating from hastily cleared forward strips such as those codenamed Broadway and Aberdeen, although the lack of radar coverage made them vulnerable to strafing Japanese fighters. Spitfires fought desperate low-altitude battles against these highly manoeuvrable attackers to protect these airstrips. One Spitfire VIII squadron detached their extended wing tips, designed to enhance high-altitude performance, to increase low-altitude rate of roll.

Throughout 1942–3, the Japanese had been able to defeat numerically superior Allied ground forces by infiltrating behind them, cutting their supply lines. The Allies then had to fight their way to the rear, through Japanese ambushes, to avoid being cut off. In what became known as 'The Battle of the Admin Box', in February 1944, an Indian Army division dug into defensive positions instead of retreating and relied on transport aircraft to airdrop food and ammunition. Faced with an unmoving defensive position rather than retreating troops, the Japanese Army was forced to launch frontal attacks on the defenders, which were repulsed with the aid of fighter-bomber attacks. Flight Lieutenant David Dick was flying fighters over Burma. 'It was the Spitfires that enabled the supply-dropping Dakotas to do their work, because if they had not been able to deliver the supplies the battle would have been lost.'[20]

The Japanese responded to the Allied airdrops by committing their fighters to intercept the transport aircraft. The Imperial Japanese Army's Ki 43 Oscar was a lightweight, manoeuvrable fighter, able to out-turn even the Zero. Previously, the Oscars had an advantage over Hurricanes. Now, Flying Officer Alan Peart, DFC, RNZAF, appreciated that 'the Spitfire VIII had a considerable advantage over the Oscars, being armoured, more highly powered, faster, and because of its two-stage supercharger, had the advantage of altitude ... Our tactics were to position ourselves above the Oscars, attack at speed using the sun, surprise if possible, and power to climb away out of range. Thus we could mount continuous attacks with relative impunity.'[21]

With Spitfires committed to air combat over the Burmese jungles, based at forward airstrips, the Japanese were unable to stop the transports. In the air battles over the 'Admin Box', sixty-five Japanese aircraft were destroyed or damaged for the loss of three Spitfires. These battles allowed the Allies to integrate transports, bombers, fighter–bombers and ground forces together and be ready when the Japanese launched their invasion of India in 1944. Seven Spitfire VIII squadrons were operational by March 1944.

Throughout the campaign, RAF Spitfire squadrons found themselves at the end of a tenuous supply line. Consumable items, especially tyres, were scarce. The Spitfire's narrow-track undercarriage led to many accidents on rough jungle airstrips, choked with mud during the monsoon season. Three-quarters of the ground crews suffered from malaria or dysentery. Spitfires needed to be based as far forward as possible because of their short range.

During the Japanese offensive against Imphal in India in 1944, Spitfire squadrons dug in on their airfields so that they could operate even under enemy ground attack, forming their own versions of the 'Admin Box'. 'One Spitfire box looked like a honeycomb. Each section, of pilots, armourers, fitters, riggers, electricians, wireless technicians and maintenance crews was responsible for its own dugout and all were arranged to guard the perimeter. Pilots, armed, stayed with their aircraft.'[22] The defence of Imphal and Kohima defeated the Japanese offensive. Spitfires made possible daytime fighter-bomber attacks and air resupply.[23]

Spitfires provided air cover for the subsequent Allied offensive into Burma. Once again, the Spitfire's limited range proved a drawback, but USAAF fighters and Lend–Lease RAF P-47 Thunderbolts led the assault on Japanese bases and escorted bombers. Allied fighters achieved a five-to-one numerical superiority over Japanese fighters in the theatre. Even as Japanese fighters became scarce, however, the hastily constructed forward airstrips, the lack of spare parts and, above all, the weather exacted a heavy toll. On 10 August 1944, sixteen Spitfires of 615 Squadron tried to penetrate a front. Half were destroyed. The surviving pilots struggled so hard to control their Spitfires that they landed with hands bleeding.

14

The Allied Bomber Offensives

January–October 1943

17 January 1943. They were coming: USAAF B-17 four-engine bombers, flying close together for mutual defence provided by the thirteen machine guns that armed each one, in tight formations refined over the previous months. The bomber formation was so close that it amounted to a single entity, intensely disciplined yet committed to inflicting destruction, lethal and magnificent, making ominous and stately progress towards Germany. The target was the U-boat shipyards in Wilhelmshaven. At 25,000 feet that day, each B-17 marked its track by white contrails, vivid in the freezing cold of winter which at high altitude could instantly turn the water molecules in engine exhaust to ice crystals.[1] But it was not just from the contrails, or from the radar that had tracked the approach of the formations across the North Sea, that the Germans knew they were coming.

The Bf 109 and the USAAF bomber offensive
B-17s attacking Wilhelmshaven on 17 January 1943 – the start of day-light strategic bombing of Germany – were no surprise to Generalmajor Adolf Galland. For the past six months, German fighter pilots had been intercepting US B-17 and B-24 heavy bombers over occupied Europe and the Mediterranean theatre. The initial German single-seat fighter attacks, from astern, had been ineffective. In

November 1942, German fighter units had improvised new tactics, aiming to attack the bomber formations head-on.[2] Galland heard of these tactics, studied them, and pushed for their use throughout the Luftwaffe. The head-on attacks offered less of a chance for the fighter to be hit and gave more of a chance to hit the bombers' vulnerable cockpit and engines.

Galland's authority did not allow him to redeploy fighter units, but he did have frequent interaction with those who decided which units should move and which aircraft should be produced, including Hitler, Göring and Milch. Galland had repeatedly told Göring that a single integrated air defence system, and more fighters and trained pilots, was required for the Luftwaffe to defend Germany. Göring resisted the message. Galland told Hitler that Germany would need three to four fighters for each attacking unescorted bomber. Göring resisted this even more; he wanted bombers to take the offensive to the enemy, not expend resources on radar, command centres, and technologies he made a point of ignoring. The Luftwaffe's senior uniformed leaders, still fighting an offensive war, wanted resources for that. Germany had trained 1662 single-seat fighter pilots in 1942, with an average of 200 flight hours before going into combat. That had not been enough to make good losses, let alone build up forces for a prolonged defence of Germany.

Milch had known the bombers would be coming: Germany needed to build more day fighters.[3] He had read the intelligence reports of the US strategic bomber build-up in England. In 16 December 1942 RLM Study 1013 had called for a tripling of fighter production in 1943.

Hitler had been fully aware since mid-1942 of the potential of US air power.[4] But he saw both the war in the air in general and the potential US impact on it through ideological filters.[5] On 17 January 1943, German armies were facing defeat, at Stalingrad and in Tunisia. The British night bombing campaign against Germany had intensified. The German people wanted retaliation. Hitler demanded continued investment in bombers, and in weapons projects, secret even from other Nazi leaders, that offered the potential to change the course of the war in Germany's favour, rather than defences against the bombers.[6]

The Luftwaffe's leadership had known they were coming. They had seen shot-down and captured US-designed aircraft: good workmanship, but lacking in combat performance. But their priorities were not the defence of Germany, but trying to restart the offensive to redeem the losing battles at Stalingrad and in Tunisia. That day, as the B-17s approached Wilhelmshaven, few German fighters defended Germany against daylight bombing: four *Gruppen* of JG 1, two each based in northern Germany and the Netherlands, and one from JG 54, based in central Germany, all flying Bf 109s and Fw 190s. US bombers operated at high altitude, while the Fw 190 was best at low and medium altitudes. The Luftwaffe day fighter force would have to rely on the Bf 109.

On 17 January 1943, over Wilhelmshaven, the Luftwaffe destroyed only three of the fifty-five attacking bombers that made it over the target. It would have to inflict more losses than that if it was to defeat a daylight bomber offensive as the RAF had done over Britain and Malta. Even a month after this first USAAF daylight attack, only 145 Bf 109s and Fw 190s were deployed for air defence.

Bf 109G-6 'Kanonboot'

Willy Messerschmitt had known they would be coming. He had realised since 1939 that the US would eventually fight Germany.[7] Over a year ago, he had examined the wreckage of a shot-down B-17, an early model flown by the RAF. He saw a design intended for high-altitude daylight bombing. He knew that above 20,000 feet, any aircraft engine with a single-stage supercharger, even a two-speed type as on current production Bf 109s, would be at a disadvantage against such an opponent. He and others in German industry had called for increasing aircraft production soon after the US entered the war. The RLM had issued taskings; a design team led by Ludwig Bölkow started work on a response in the form of the Bf 109K, a version of the Bf 109G optimised for high-altitude combat.

Messerschmitt worked on jet fighters but realised the limits of the Me 262's turbojet technology. He first wanted to develop improved piston-engine fighters, even as he devoted much personal attention to dealing with Berlin. But the Me 309, following its poor RLM evaluation and the crash of the second prototype in November 1942, had lost support. Galland thought it offered little performance improvement over the Bf 109.[8]

It became increasingly apparent that the first Me 209 II fighter proto-type was unlikely to fly until late 1943. At a meeting at Karinhall in March 1943, Göring and Milch blamed Messerschmitt for the Me 209 II's problems. The meeting concluded with Milch promising to rip out Messerschmitt's few remaining hairs by the roots.[9] Milch, supported by Galland, halted the Me 309 and made development of the Me 209 II Messerschmitt's priority, a switch to jet aircraft being planned for an unspecified future date.[10] A plan for eventually starting Me 209 II pro-duction was submitted to the RLM in April 1943, while in the same month Messerschmitt also proposed to the RLM the high-altitude Me 209H with a DB 628 engine. He was told to concentrate instead on the high-altitude Bf 109H, likely to be ready more quickly.

Messerschmitt factories – no longer 'his' – began producing upgraded Bf 109G models. The increased weight of the Bf 109G's DB 605 engine required undercarriage legs with larger wheels. To accommodate these, the Bf 109G-4 and subsequent versions incor-porated streamlined fairings on top of the wing (along with the improved FuG 16ZY VHF radio, allowing new ground control tech-niques). The Bf 109G-5 and G-6 were essentially the same aircraft, identifiable by a raised vertical fin and rudder and powered by versions of the DB 605A engine, with the former having a pressurised cock-pit and the latter being much more widely produced. High-altitude performance was increased through the new engine, a more powerful supercharger, an improved water–methanol injection system and, for those fitted with the DB 605AM engine, reliance on 96-octane syn-thetic aviation fuel in place of the standard 87-octane, plus water–methanol injection, to achieve 2000 hp at sea level and 1800 hp at 16,400 feet.

In their first encounters with B-17 formations in 1942, the Luftwaffe realised their fighters' inadequacy. Analysis after the air battles showed that they shot down only 2.3 bombers per hundred attacks. German experience was that only about 2 per cent of the rounds fired by attack-ing fighters actually hit their targets. It took an average of twenty 20mm hits to bring down a bomber, which required twenty-three seconds of sustained firing, which was not feasible, especially in head-on attacks. Attacking fighters would have only two seconds from the moment they came in range of the bombers to when they flashed past them, diving away. Skilled fighter pilots might be able to shoot down bombers with fewer hits, aiming for the cockpit. Most Luftwaffe fighter pilots simply had to rely on luck to knock a bomber out of formation, where it would be vulnerable to subsequent attacks.[11]

Bf 109s needed heavier armament to damage a bomber like the B-17. In the Bf 109G-6, as in the G-5, the two nose-mounted synchronised 7.92mm machine guns were replaced by larger 13mm machine guns. To insert these larger (and heavier) weapons in the tight Bf 109 cowling required the addition of two large, drag-inducing external fairings for their breech mechanisms forward of the cockpit. This gave the new Bf 109Gs their nickname of '*Beule*' (bump). Starting in February 1943, over 12,000 Bf 109G-6s would be produced, over a third of total Bf 109 production.

These were divided into a vast number of sub-types, reflecting differences in engine capabilities and armament. Some Bf 109G-6s had a retractable tailwheel, reducing drag, while others had a tall non-retractable tailwheel for better ground handling. An improved radio navigation direction finder was introduced on the production lines from August 1943. At around the same time, the armour plate behind the pilot's head was replaced by bulletproof glass, increasing visibility. From the spring of 1944, DB 605D engines – which could use either nitrous oxide or water–methanol injection – were fitted on some production lines. Even with 87-octane fuel, this engine could produce 1850hp for take-off. Its cowling design eliminated the Bf 109G-6's signature 'bumps'.

Even the better-armed Bf 109G-6 lacked adequate firepower. In the head-on diving attacks used by the Luftwaffe in 1942 against US bomber formations, single-engine fighters had a closing speed of some 600 mph. An attacking Bf 109G-6 fighter could not put out a lethal volume of firepower with its two 13mm machine guns and one engine-mounted 20mm cannon.

Armament was increased: 20mm or 30mm cannon were added in external mountings under each wing, unlike the cannon in the Bf 109E, which had been mounted internally in the wing. Uparmed

Bf 109G-6s (designated Bf 109G-6/R-4 with 30mm cannon and Bf 109G-6/R-6 with 20mm cannon) were nicknamed '*Kanonboot*' (gunboat), a double-edged comment on the additional firepower and the wallowing boat-like manoeuvrability the external guns' weight and drag created. This modification increased the Bf 109G-6's firepower at the expense of performance. With the two underwing cannon mounted, it was slower and less manoeuvrable, and hence was vulnerable to enemy fighters.[12] Its handling, especially on landing, also suffered. The stiffness of the Bf 109's aileron control had increased with the shift to a rounded wing-tip design on the Bf 109F and now became more acute on the heavier Bf 109G-6.

The Bf 109G-6/R-1 was a fighter-bomber version, dispensing with the underwing cannon but able to carry a 500 kg (1100 lb) bombload. Starting in mid-1943, many Bf 109G-6s, especially those assembled at the now-dispersed Wiener Neustadt plant, had their engine-mounted 20mm cannon replaced by a 30mm MK 108 lightweight low muzzle-velocity cannon with sixty rounds of ammunition. Its development had been delayed by Ernst Udet, who had scorned 'heavy artillery'. Each of its shells packed equivalent power to four 20mm rounds, making the MK 108 a highly effective weapon. This modification had been a result of the perceived inadequacy of the Bf 109G's armament to inflict lethal damage on heavy bombers. The average of twenty 20mm hits to destroy a heavy bomber could be reduced to three from a 30mm (though these numbers could be reduced to a quarter or a third when attacking from head-on, where cockpit or engines were likely to be hit). A single 30mm hit would often destroy a fighter or medium bomber.[13]

The '*Kanonboot*' was limited by the small wing and the narrow-track undercarriage of the basic Bf 109 design. Its overloaded airframe and 1600 hp engine driving a broad-bladed three-blade propeller led to potentially lethal handling problems, especially if loaded down with external armament and the full fuel tanks and drop tanks often required for interception battles over Germany. Well-trained pilots were able to handle this. They even found the underwing 20mm cannon mounts well designed, with only a 20 km/h (12 mph) penalty off their top speed. But many of the hastily trained pilots committed to action in the Bf 109G-6 never even got them off the ground. Opening the throttle too rapidly during an *Alarmstart* take-off or trying to lift off too early would result in the plane rolling over on its back and crashing. While the Luftwaffe started using Fw 190s with even more armament and armour as bomber destroyers, the Bf 109's design limited how much could be added to it. Messerschmitt's basic wing design of 1934, lightweight and low drag, easy to produce, could not easily be adapted to carry the heavier armament now required in the air war.

The daylight bomber offensive opens
More B-17 and B-24 US bomber groups arrived in England and went into action. The Britain-based US Eighth Air Force had, from the start, been intended as a mix of bomber and fighter groups, unlike RAF Fighter and Bomber Command. But no Allied escort fighter capable of joining combat on even terms with a Bf 109 could fly to any German targets, let alone Berlin. Spitfires escorting US heavy bombers could not even reach the French Biscay coast. In April, Fighter Command made bomber escort missions – Ramrod missions – their top priority, supporting the Eighth Air Force, twin-engine day bombers from the RAF and the USAAF's Ninth Air Force and RAF fighter-bombers. Yet the Spitfire's range, even with 30- or 45-gallon drop tanks – eleven of Fighter Command's forty-eight Spitfire squadrons were equipped to use drop tanks and rear fuselage tanks by early 1943 – was increasingly relegating it to a peripheral role in the air offensive.

In May 1943, Eighth Air Force Fighter Command (VIII FC) P-47C fighters flew their first escort mission. But without drop tanks, the P-47Cs could not fly much further than Spitfires. The twin-engine P-38, despite its long range and powerful firepower, was limited by engine problems and inadequate high-altitude performance. These were being sent to the Pacific and Mediterranean theatres. Few were available for the Eighth Air Force.

Though German twin-engine bombers had proven unable to survive in daylight without fighter escorts over Britain in 1940, the USAAF believed that unescorted B-17 and B-24 bomber formations would now be able to strike at German industrial targets; the bombers' massed defensive gunfire would destroy so many fighters they would soon effectively decimate the Luftwaffe. As the intensity of the US air attacks increased, they came under the directive for the combined Anglo-American bomber offensive, codenamed Pointblank, issued on 10 June 1943, after Roosevelt and Churchill had reached agreement at the Casablanca conference. Pointblank's goal was the destruction of German air power with the intention of enabling the invasion of France in 1944. Until then, the bomber offensive would have to be the major western contribution to the war effort at a time when massive battles were raging on the eastern front.

The Germans modified their fighters and tactics.[14] A defence in depth was improvised, able to attack US bombers on their way to any target. The Germans increasingly relied on twin-engine fighters to shoot down bombers in daylight. Bf 110s, fighter versions of the Ju 88 and Me 410s (an improved version of the failed Me 210) carried the heavy armament needed to take out bombers from long range. The role of Bf 109 and Fw 190 attacks, head-on or from astern, was to knock bombers out of formation. Bf 109s, fitted with drop tanks and additional internal fuel tanks, could be concentrated from airfields throughout Germany against an incoming bomber attack.

With these aircraft, the Luftwaffe fighter force was able to inflict losses of over 5 per cent of the bombers taking off, unsustainable for the USAAF. But for Luftwaffe fighter pilots, attacking the formations of USAAF bombers was like no air fighting they had experienced before. Flying through the fire of bomber machine guns required a tremendous act of will, one RAF and USAAF fighter pilots were never called on to carry out on a sustained basis. Galland demanded that fighter pilots focus 'entirely on the destruction of the enemy and not their own success'. US bomber firepower had a powerful impact even on the most motivated and skilful fighter pilots; only massed attacks were observed to be effective.[15] Oberstleutnant Hans 'Fips' Phillips, then the Luftwaffe's highest-scoring ace, as *Kommodore* of JG 1, led many of the initial battles against B-17s over Germany. 'It is one thing to fight against 20 Russians out to kill you or to dogfight with a Spitfire. That kind of fighting is a joy. But to curve into 70 Fortresses is like seeing your whole life pass in front of you.'[16]

The most intense battle so far of the daylight bomber offensive was on 22 June, an attack on the Hüls chemical plant by 183 B-17s. When the smoke cleared from the target, the Germans saw the power of the US daylight bombing. Hüls, responsible for a third of Germany's synthetic rubber, was knocked out of production for a month. It took six months before its production was back at pre-attack levels. But the air battle had been a victory for the Luftwaffe's fighter force. Sixteen B-17s were shot down and over 100 damaged. Faced with these losses, the Eighth Air Force called off daylight attacks on Germany for a month. The chemical plant itself was not attacked again until repairs had been completed.

On 28 July, fierce air battles raged over northern Germany as the Eighth Air Force attacked aircraft factories at Kassel and Oschlersleben; 37 of 120 bombers attacking were shot down. German fighters were fitted with 210mm unguided air-to-air rockets mounted under the wing, enabling them to stay out of range of the bombers' defensive machine guns. A rocket's massive 40 kg high-explosive warhead had a time fuse, set to bombard bomber formations. Initially installed on twin-engine fighters, these rockets soon armed Bf 109Gs. But the rocket launcher's weight and drag reduced performance against enemy fighters.

As the bombers withdrew, the Germans encountered P-47C fighters, using US-produced 75-US-gallon drop tanks, that could just reach targets in northern Germany. This was the first time (except for a few occasions before May 1940) that Bf 109s had fought single-engine fighters over Germany.[17] The heavy P-47, designed around a turbo-supercharger,[18] had excellent performance at high altitude, including a rate of roll superior to the nimble Spitfire and even to the Fw 190. At 30,000 feet it was faster than both. However, in dogfights over England, ace P-47 pilots like Captain Francis 'Gabby' Gabreski had found out that 'as a defensive airplane over England, you couldn't beat the Spitfire IX'.[19] The P-47's armament of eight .50-calibre machine guns was massive firepower. British-built 108-US-gallon drop tanks, first used in August, allowed P-47s to achieve a 400-mile radius of action. Since the opening of the war, Bf 109 pilots, if they needed to disengage, had been able to dive away. The Bf 109, in a dive, had accelerated faster than any opponent, including the Spitfire. The P-47 out-accelerated the Bf 109 in a dive, closing that escape path. Colonel Hubert 'Hub' Zemke became a leading ace and fighter leader. 'Too many German pilots attempted to evade our attacks by trying to dive away, usually a fatal move as the P-47 could soon overhaul them.'[20]

Attacks from England were not the only threat to the German war effort. The southern front in the daylight strategic bombing campaign opened with a dramatic attack on 1 August 1943. One hundred and eighty USAAF B-24 bombers from bases in Libya hit the Ploesti oil refineries in Romania. While inflicting substantial damage, the B-24s suffered heavy losses, especially from German and Romanian Bf 109s (the latter had recently replaced British-built Hurricane Is). Fifty-four B-24s were shot down. Oberstleutnant Douglas Pitcairn, the former Bf 109 pilot, a ground-based fighter controller since a take-off accident in 1940, successfully coordinated the defensive air battle.

The surviving B-24s based in Libya attacked on 13 August another high-value target: the Bf 109 factory at Wiener Neustadt in Austria. In mid-1943, Wiener Neustadt was producing about half of all Bf 109s, compared with a fifth at the Messerschmitt Regensburg plant and a third at the Erla Leipzig plant. The Luftwaffe was not expecting a strike from the south. Only two of 101 attacking B-24s were lost. Heavy damage was done to the factory. Production dropped from 270 Bf 109s in July to 184 in August.[21] Its tools and workers were dispersed throughout Austria and the former Czechoslovakia, with final assembly carried out in the repaired factory.

The Eighth Air Force aimed to continue the offensive against the German aircraft industry by the deepest penetration attacks so far, striking simultaneously the Messerschmitt factory at Regensburg and the ball-bearing plant at Schweinfurt (each Bf 109 required 10,000 ball bearings). The attack would have P-47 escort to and from the German–Belgian border. The B-17s hitting Regensburg would then fly on to bases in north Africa, while those attacking Schweinfurt would return to England.

On 17 August, 376 B-17s attacked the two targets. The Luftwaffe committed over 300 fighters to intercept them. Many flew multiple sorties, attacking the bombers on both legs of the flight.

The Regensburg plant suffered 60 per cent damage, with some 400 of its 10,000 workers killed. Monthly production dipped to 77 the following month from an average of 200.[22] The Me 309V4 prototype, being developed as a bomber destroyer, was among the aircraft destroyed, bringing that programme to a halt. Two production lines were extracted from the rubble and moved to Overtraubling airfield.

P-47s were supposed to meet the returning Schweinfurt bombers at the point where they had dropped them off on the outward leg. But, as the P-47s had climbed to altitude and were cruising towards the rendezvous point, their pilots set their radios to the bombers' radio frequency.

They heard the bomber formations staggering under the weight of repeated German fighter attacks. Bombers were reporting they were out of ammunition and the barrels of their machine guns burned smooth. They heard orders to close up the formations tighter as bombers went down, calls to watch for parachutes, warnings of new attacks. Captain Robert S. Johnson heard 'the cries for help, the radio messages of the black-crossed fighters plunging in'.[23]

Without an order being given, the P-47 pilots opened their throttles, increasing their speed from the economical cruise settings, burning more fuel. They would have no reserve fuel to make it back to England. Even though it would make them more vulnerable to any German fighters that intercepted them, the P-47 pilots held on to their drop tanks until the last drops of fuel were drained. They needed to get to the bombers faster. The P-47s of the 56th Fighter Group reached the beleaguered B-17s before they left German airspace.

Captain Walker 'Bud' Mahurin saw from the cockpit of his P-47 'German fighter after German fighter flying through the bombers with cannons blazing. I could see hits on the bombers and several in trouble going down. The scene served to make me mad as hell. My only thought was: By God! They're hurting our boys.'[24]

Leading II/JG 26, Adolf Galland's younger brother Major 'Wutz' Galland was forming up his *Gruppe* for a massed attack, intended finally to shatter the bomber formation and allow the stragglers to be picked off individually. It was too far from England for him to have to watch for enemy fighters.

Until the 56th Fighter Group's P-47s dived down, out of the sun. Mahurin picked one Fw 190. 'Obviously the Jerry did not see me, because I came to within 500 yards dead astern before opening fire. When the ammunition from my eight machineguns hit the German, he sparkled like fireflies from the impact of explosive shells.[25] His aircraft immediately flipped over on its back and bobbed erratically upside down.'

'Wutz' Galland went down from the surprise attack, probably falling to Mahurin.

'*Herr Gott sakrament!*'

The cry over the radio of a horrified German pilot when Galland was hit was picked up by the British 'Y' service. 'Wutz' Galland had flown 186 combat sorties. He had claimed fifty-five victories, thirty-seven of them Spitfires. His brother Adolf, years after the war, recalled him as 'an excellent fighter pilot and excellent *Gruppenkommandeur*'. But he was among the first of the small cadre of veteran fighter leaders on whom the Luftwaffe depended to fall to the lethal type of air combat the USAAF was waging.

Those who replaced him reflected the shortage of resources that had led training for Luftwaffe fighter pilots to deteriorate in 1943. Only 40 per cent of the fuel required for fighter pilot training was available. The number of flight hours decreased from 260 hours in 1942 to about 175 (including 30 on Bf 109s) before joining a unit. Germany managed to train 3276 single-engine fighter pilots over the course of 1943 (to replace 2870 lost), but only by reducing their quality.[26]

It was not just fighter pilots that the Germans lacked. The production of more Bf 109s had not been matched by a comparable expansion of ground crews to support them. Experienced technicians were sent off to the infantry and replaced by untrained conscripts. Bf 109 pilots found it difficult to fly more than one sortie a day against bomber formations. It was a far cry from the six or seven sorties a day that had won battles for the Luftwaffe in earlier years.

Despite these signs of weakness, the Luftwaffe fighter force still managed a stunning victory. They had increased their rate of kills per hundred engagements from 2.0 in 1943 to 3.6. On 17 August, sixty US bombers had been shot down, 19 per cent of the force, an unsustainable loss rate. Many more bombers were damaged. While the bomber gunners claimed hundreds of German fighters shot down, actual German fighter losses were twenty-seven. Damage to the factories, without follow-on raids by day or night, proved temporary. Monthly Bf 109 output at Regensburg rose from about 50 in 1942 to over 250 by the end of 1943 despite the bombing, reflecting the rationalisation of production by Messerschmitt AG's technical director Karl Lindner.[27]

The Bf 109G and the RAF night bomber offensive

The RAF's first thousand-bomber attack, against Köln on the night of 30/31 May 1942, had concluded the night bomber offensive's long, frustrating and costly opening phase. Escalation continued in 1943. In addition to ever more powerful heavy bombers, the RAF was now sending over Germany the high-speed De Havilland Mosquito, a bomber made of plywood with no defensive armament, relying solely on speed and altitude for protection. Mosquitoes operated over Germany as night bombers and by day for reconnaissance, supplementing the photo-reconnaissance Spitfires.

Göring was particularly enraged by the Mosquito. In July 1943, the Luftwaffe formed two *Geschwadern* for anti-Mosquito operations, partially equipped with Bf 109Gs with GM-1 nitrous oxide-boosted engines. But only a few of these modified Bf 109Gs were available. The new units were not a success. Few Mosquitoes or Spitfires were intercepted by Bf 109s unless they were lucky enough to be in the path of the reconnaissance aircraft or, more often, the reconnaissance aircraft came down from cruising altitude because of engine or oxygen problems or to dive under high clouds to get the photographs they needed. The two *Geschwadern*, neither of which exceeded the strength of a single *Gruppe*, were committed to other roles. They were eventually disbanded before the end of 1943.[28]

The Bf 109 would be needed to carry out night operations, despite its limitations and the lack of night training its pilots received, as the Luftwaffe turned to using single-engine fighters at night. German radar-equipped night fighters using ground controlled interception (GCI) tactics, whereby fighter controllers watching radar screens directed them to the enemy bombers, were being overwhelmed by the concentrated RAF night bomber stream. Major Hans-Joachim 'Hajo' Hermann proposed using night fighters that did not depend on ground controllers.

His ideas excited the Luftwaffe high command, short on radars for night fighters, desperate for a way to counter the bomber attacks and willing to embrace a junior officer's idea (he could always be blamed if things went wrong). Galland, realising that the tactics would consume fighters he needed for the day battle, pointed out to Göring and Milch: 'The OKL [*Oberkommando der Luftwaffe*, the high command] in 1939 formed the first such *Gruppe*,' referring to the searchlight-guided Bf 109Ds that had proved ineffective.[29]

Fw 190s, with their heavier armament and broader-track under-carriage, were the first choice. After testing the concept using surviving Bf 109Ts, Bf 109Gs carrying 300-litre drop tanks (allowing two hours in the air) were also committed to the night battle.

First used in action on the night of 3/4 July 1943, Hermann's tactics, codenamed *Wilde Sau* (Wild Boar), relied on single-engine night fighters. Wild Boar fighters used the pilot's eyes, illumination from searchlights, and the fires of the German cities under attack to detect bombers over the targets, while their under-fuselage drop tanks allowed them to reach attacking bombers throughout Germany. The Luftwaffe embraced single-engine night fighting and eventually formed three *Geschwadern* for this mission. 'Hajo' Hermann was appointed *Kommodore* of JG 300. Hermann found 'the pilots with the 109s fly this type at night in preference to the 190, as it is rather more manoeuvrable, especially at high altitude'.[30] Most of their pilots, like 'Hajo' himself, were volunteers from bomber or transport units. They already knew instrument flying.

Wild Boars provided the most effective German air defence during the massive RAF attacks on Hamburg in July 1943. Extensive use of Window (chaff) by the attackers jammed German ground radar. Hamburg was devastated. But widespread fires gave many opportunities for the single-engine night fighters to detect and attack bombers.

In the short summer nights, 'Hajo' Herrmann led JG 300 into combat over a burning Berlin, flying a Bf 109G:

> I did not need the glare from the target; it was searchlight fighting that night. It was clear, no moon, and the searchlights were doing a good job. I tried for one bomber, but it was too fast and I went past him without firing ... I came up to the next one

more slowly, level from the rear, but before I could open fire
another chap coming down from above me attacked the bomber
and set it on fire ... I circled back over the target and had no difficulty finding a third bomber. Normally, if a fighter wanted to
attack a bomber in the searchlights, we should have fired a flare,
so that the flak would cease fire, but we Wild Boar men rarely
bothered to do this. We usually waited until the bomber weaved
or dived out of the searchlights and then attacked it. I shot that
bomber down.[31]

The accident rate, even of Bf 109s, was acceptable. The Wild Boar
units modified their Bf 109s with night-suitable lighting arrangements.
Others were polished for higher speed and their engines modified for
counter-Mosquito night operations.

Zahme Sau (Tame Boar) tactics sent up both single- and twin-engine
fighters but provided them with a running radio broadcast of the
location of enemy bombers rather than GCI's detailed directions, leaving each pilot to fly from one radio beacon to another until a controller
could direct them to the point where they were most likely to infiltrate
the bomber stream. The night-fighter pilot was then left to work out
how to get within radar or visual range of the enemy himself. Tame
Boar became a widespread German night-fighter direction system. It
was first used on the night of 27/28 August, but took longer to become
effective. Together, Wild Boar and Tame Boar fighters shot down 200
bombers in August 1943 alone, a record success.

Tame Boar was used with increasing regularity in the autumn of
1943. Wild Boar tactics declined in effectiveness as the nights became
longer, the weather became worse and the original instrument-trained
volunteer pilots were lost. Using the same fighters to fly night and day
missions proved impractical. 'Hajo' Hermann himself, the most successful Wild Boar, with nine bombers shot down in fifty missions, had
to parachute twice in bad weather. Those who replaced the more experienced pilots usually lasted just long enough to score some victories,
often stalking and attacking their own twin-engine Bf 110 night fighters. Then, one by one, their luck ran out and the German weather,
friendly fire or, more rarely, bomber gunners claimed them.

Some Tame Boar Bf 109s used the *Y-Gerät* (apparatus) guidance system which allowed fighter pilots to determine their location by reference to ground-based radio beacons. It also automatically reported the fighter's location to ground stations, similar to the 1940-vintage British Pipsqueak system.

This new equipment was also used by day fighters, although often only one fighter in each *Staffel* could be equipped with it. The German industrial base could not produce enough radio equipment. It contributed to the strength and resilience of the German night-fighter defences in the face of air attacks of unprecedented size and sophistication. But there were too few night fighters to prevent the start of the relentless destruction of German targets: Hamburg, the industrial Ruhr and Berlin, and Peenemünde, where the 'wonder weapons' Hitler put much stock in were being developed. On 18 August, Jeschonnek, the Luftwaffe's chief of staff, at odds with Göring and Milch and now recognising he had lost Hitler's confidence, shot himself. He was replaced by General Gunther Korten.

Messerschmitt under pressure

In May 1943, Adolf Galland flew a Me 262 jet fighter prototype at Augsburg. He said after his flight, 'I felt as if the angels were pushing.' It was once again as it had been when he was a glider pilot or when he first flew the Bf 109: he could ride the air, it was all his. He felt instinctively what Willy Messerschmitt had concluded years before: the future of the fighter was jet propulsion.

What Galland had not grasped was how many problems remained with jet engines, especially in making them suitable for mass production and extending their life beyond around fifteen hours. Galland wanted the Me 262 rushed into production, if necessary at the expense of Messerschmitt's piston-engine fighters, ending development of the Me 209 II and increasing Fw 190 production to keep numbers up.[32] Galland thought the Me 209 II was a diversion of resources from creating the all-important jets. It was not a game-changer, but only 'a drastically changed Me 109 ... a broader undercarriage, stronger elements and longer range ... The fuselage had to be extended.'[33] This meshed with Milch's proposed '224' programme, put forward now that his rival Jeschonnek was dead, to mass-produce new fighters, cutting back on Bf 109s. Milch, with Göring's approval, cancelled the Me 209 II programme on 25 May. The first production orders for the Me 262 were placed in May–June 1943. Hitler and Göring wanted bombers for retaliation; Milch now wanted the Me 262 as the only way of defeating the US bomber offensive.[34]

Willy Messerschmitt and other designers were summoned by Hitler to Obersalzburg on 27 June 1943. Messerschmitt was still working on the Me 209 II piston-engine fighter despite Milch's order to cancel the programme. Messerschmitt pushed for (and received) continued funding for it. He spoke of the importance of building high-altitude fighters to engage the US bomber threat and for continued production of the Bf 109.[35]

In the aftermath of this conference, the Me 262 became the Messerschmitt design team's top priority. While lack of resources and high-level mismanagement were indeed undercutting the Me 262, the most important obstacles remained, as he had said, those of its unreliable jet engine technology.[36] Messerschmitt resolved to continue the Me 209 II and, together with Speer, he worked to keep his Bf 109 production lines going.[37] Willy Messerschmitt met with Hitler, who ordered the Me 209 II reinstated by Milch on 13 August. Messerschmitt continued to press for a production order, leading to a dispute with his colleague Rakan Kokothaki, who was trying to push the Me 262 forward. Messerschmitt even tried to license the Me 209 II design to Japan.

After the Wiener Neustadt and Regensburg factories were bombed in August 1943, Messerschmitt AG faced increasing difficulties, with labour and material shortages, disrupted transport lines, and further air raids. Willy Messerschmitt wrote on 23 August to his old colleague from the Bf 109 design programme, Robert Lusser, saying that they 'could count on their fingers the remaining months that the German armament industry could survive'.[38]

On 7 September 1943, Messerschmitt again took his concerns directly to Hitler: Milch was incompetent, one-shift labour in the aircraft industry should be ended and the number of types in production reduced, more fighters should be built and investment made in massive production of the new V-1 land attack cruise missile, pulse-jet powered, and the first of the 'vengeance weapons'. Messerschmitt demanded more workers and told Hitler that he would produce, first, the Me 209 II – although its prototype had not yet flown – and then the Me 262, which could certainly also serve as a fighter-bomber. Hitler heard the last part. He insisted that future Me 262 development be as a bomber.[39] Göring, furious that Messerschmitt had gone over his head, threatened him with a court-martial and insisted that future meetings with him would have to be on the record, with a stenographer.[40]

Spitfires in new roles

Photo-reconnaissance Spitfires, along with Mosquitoes, flown by both the RAF and the USAAF, and the USAAF's F-5s (modified P-38s), were the 'eyes' of the bomber offensive and the Allied high command as a whole. The Spitfire PR XI went into action in mid-1943. Based on the Spitfire IX, but with extra fuselage and wing tanks, it carried multiple cameras, the number and type tailored to each mission's requirements. PR XIs could operate by day with virtual immunity from Luftwaffe interceptors. They provided the before-and-after-attack photographs that were often the best evidence as to whether bombers had hit their target and the effects they had caused. It remained dangerous work, and problems with an engine or oxygen flow in the cold dark blue world of high-altitude flight could easily become lethal.

RAF fighter Spitfires based in Britain took part in Ramrod bomber escorts, low-level tactical reconnaissance, and continued Ranger and Rodeo fighter sweeps. The costly Rhubarb strafing raids were discontinued. As more German fighters were concentrated to defend the homeland, the RAF encountered less airborne opposition and increasing anti-aircraft fire.

The RAF had improved its training over previous years, expanding OTU training and setting up advanced units to assist pilots trained in blue skies overseas in making the transition to surviving the potentially lethal mysteries of British weather. But operational losses remained high. Simply flying fighters in wartime was dangerous. Diana Barnato, ferrying a Spitfire IX when weather closed in, would have left it were it not for the fact that it would have meant parachuting while wearing a skirt. 'We were very modest in those days.'[41] She managed to avoid the high ground that claimed so many aircraft and groped her way to a landing on an RAF airfield.

Low-altitude German fighter-bomber 'tip and run' raids on England were opposed by the Spitfire XII, the first operational Spitfire to be powered by the Griffon engine. The Spitfire XII was an interim measure, developed from the Spitfire IV prototype that had first started development in 1940 and flown in 1941. But to get the Spitfire XII in production faster, it used the clipped-wing Spitfire V airframe with the Spitfire VIII's retractable tailwheel. The first Spitfire XII first flew on 10 April 1942. It went into service with two squadrons, with deliveries starting in February 1943.

Only 100 Spitfire XIIs were built. Its single-stage supercharger limited its effectiveness at high altitude. The powerful Griffon made it directionally unstable. Pilots found it a different Spitfire. Jeffrey Quill was concerned that the sudden changes in power could throw the Spitfire XII dangerously out of trim, but there was no time to fix this problem, only warn pilots about it. Test pilot H.A. Taylor recalled, 'Merlin Spitfires tried, fairly gently, to swing to port [on take-off], but the Griffon versions tried (very much less gently) to swing to starboard and full port trim as well as hard rudder pressure had to be applied to keep them straight.'[42] A new, enlarged rudder was designed to counter this swing at low speed (and was soon adopted for many subsequent Merlin-powered Spitfires). For Diana Barnato 'the Mark XII, with its clipped wing tips, had a plainer and more solid feeling. I didn't like the sound of the Griffon engine – not at all as comforting or glorious as the Merlin.'[43]

At low altitude, the Spitfire XII was able to catch Fw 190s, as was the faster Typhoon. But the RAF was never able to defeat these raiders fully. Even before the Spitfire XII went into action, the *JaBos* were switching tactics. The second large-scale low-level raid on London, on 20 January 1943, with ninety Bf 109s and Fw 190s, suffered substantial losses from Typhoons and Spitfire IXs once the defences were alerted. The raids were then shifted to targets on the south and east coasts.

In April, the remaining *JaBostaffeln* were concentrated for a renewed night offensive, to operate at higher altitudes along with twin-engine bombers (and the troubled four-engine He 177s). Fw 190 fighter-bomber operations against England increasingly, and, after July, exclusively, took place at night.[44] The Germans needed fighter-bombers in the Mediterranean, and in June they were transferred away from attacks on England. As a result, Spitfire XIIs switched from low-altitude interceptor to bomber escort and tactical reconnaissance missions, even though the thirsty Griffon and 84 gallons of internal fuel limited range to 425 miles.

The RAF redesignated Fighter Command as Air Defence of Great Britain (ADGB), its pre-1936 designation (the unpopular name change was reversed the next year), now commanded by Air Marshal Roderic Hill as Leigh-Mallory was promoted 'upstairs' to a new command. A large number of Spitfire squadrons were split off and placed under the 2nd Tactical Air Force (2 TAF). Created from the RAF's former Army Cooperation Command, this was intended to provide air power for the coming invasion of Europe. Fighter Command and Bomber Command both made major contributions of squadrons (more than half of Fighter Command's first-line strength was transferred) and personnel. Intended from the outset to fight in close cooperation with ground forces, using tactics developed in north Africa and Italy, 2 TAF brought together RAF fighters and bombers. It was not usually committed to the air defence of Britain or the air offensive over Germany. Like its US counterpart, the Ninth Air Force, now based in Britain, 2 TAF's twin-engine bomber squadrons hit targets in occupied Europe while its fighters flew escort missions.

2 TAF's Spitfire squadrons would have to control the air over the battlefield when the Allies invaded northern Europe, at a location within Spitfire range of British bases. 2 TAF had priority for Spitfire IXs, using them as dual-mission fighter-bombers, the role that would represent the Spitfire's largest mission for the rest of the war.[45] Spitfire pilots had been trained primarily for air-to-air combat. Air-to-ground tactics and equipment were largely improvised. Spitfires and Typhoons – the latter now transformed into a capable fighter-bomber rather than an unreliable fighter – would carry out an increasing burden of RAF fighter-bomber missions.

Not having been designed as a fighter-bomber, the Spitfire lacked the bombsight, dive brakes, extensive armour plate and bomb release crutch (swinging bombs clear of the propeller) of specialised dive bombers. The

Supermarine-developed fighter-bomber kit gave the Spitfire IX a capability of carrying a 250 lb bomb under each wing and a 500 lb bomb or a drop tank under the fuselage, later modified to two under-fuselage 500 lb bombs. The Spitfire was never as effective a fighter-bomber as the Typhoon or the US P-47. The liquid-cooled Merlin was about twice as likely to be knocked out by ground fire as the P-47's air-cooled radial engine,[46] the coolant pipes running to the underwing radiator being the Spitfire's Achilles' heel when subject to such fire. Captain John A.C. Andrews, a USAAF fighter pilot, 'saw many Spit pilots in prison camp with horribly burned faces, because the main fuel tank was behind the instrument panel (right in front of the pilot's face)'.[47] These injuries came from the Spitfire's upper fuselage fuel tank, protected but not self-sealing, that had concerned Dowding in 1940. In ground-attack missions, it was between the pilot and enemy firepower. But the Spitfire retained its performance and manoeuvrability, fully capable of fighting any enemy fighters it encountered once it had dropped its bombs.

While the RAF turned Spitfires into fighter-bombers, Joe Smith, Alan Clifton and the team at Hursley Park continued work on upgraded Spitfires and Seafires, powered by both Merlin and, increasingly, Griffon engines. A cut-down rear fuselage and a teardrop canopy for all-round visibility were first tested on a modified Spitfire VIII in August 1943 and incorporated in later Spitfire and Seafire versions.

The Merlin 61-powered high-altitude Spitfire VII with a pressurised cockpit first flew in April 1942 and entered service in early 1943. Its extended pointed wing tips improved ceiling and rate of climb, but at the cost of a 40 per cent reduction in rate of roll. Only 140 Spitfire VIIs were produced, serving alongside the Spitfire VI. Its pressurised cockpit was an advance over that on the Spitfire VI. Flying Officer Don Nicholson was in 131 Squadron when it re-equipped with Spitfire VIIs in early 1944. 'I liked the Mk VII. It was a good aeroplane. The highest I ever took one was to 39,000 feet; it could have continued climbing ... Our job was to prevent German reconnaissance planes taking photographs of the ports.'[48]

The Spitfire VIII had been intended to be the standard Merlin 61 series-powered Spitfire fighter. Incorporating structural upgrades, its production required the most extensive retooling effort of any Merlin-engine

Spitfire version, which enabled it to be used as the basis for future development with more powerful engines. Jeffrey Quill, the Supermarine test pilot, found it 'very pleasant to handle with a performance as good as the Mark IX, with many other advantages added on'.[49]

With the success of the interim Spitfire IX, there was little need for units based in Britain to adopt the Spitfire VIII; instead it was produced as a tropicalised version with an improved air filter and sent to the Mediterranean, Burma–India and Pacific theatres, where its increased fuel tankage was valuable. Many had their pointed wing tips cropped back to increase rate of roll at low altitude.

Luftwaffe victorious

As US bombing operations increased in number and intensity through the summer of 1943, they encountered additional German fighters, withdrawn from the east and Italy. Milch had advocated that 'Germany itself is the real front line, and that the mass of fighters must go to home defence.'[50] The operational commanders had agreed, pulling units out of Italy and the eastern front although they were desperately needed there. The Luftwaffe fighter force was now defending with increased numbers. In an attack on Stuttgart on 6 September, forty-five bombers were shot down. On 27 September, 300 escorted bombers attacked Emden, the operation marking the first large-scale use of radar to bomb through overcast conditions. This meant that, in future, to intercept bombers, German fighters might have to penetrate the overcast skies that dominated German weather. While the Bf 109G had at least minimal blind-flying instruments – an artificial horizon and a radio compass – that previous versions had lacked, German fighter pilots had inadequate training for flying by instruments alone.[51]

On 8 October, in an attack on Bremen and Vegeseck, Hans Phillips was shot down and killed while attacking B-17s escorted by P-47s.[52] He had flown over 500 combat missions and had 208 confirmed victories, 178 of them on the eastern front. Phillips' intuition – that the USAAF had the potential to wage a type of air war much more lethal than the one he had encountered from the RAF or the Soviet Air Force – was brought home to the Luftwaffe by his own death. Spitfires duelled; P-47s destroyed.

Some US bomber attacks were successful, such as that targeting the factories building Fw 190s at Ankelm and Marienburg on 9 October. Others were more costly: thirty bombers each were lost during attacks against aircraft factories in Bremen on 8 October and the city centre in Münster on 10 October. For a maximum effort against Schweinfurt on 14 October, no escort was possible beyond the German border. More German fighters joined the defence, pulled from the eastern front and the Mediterranean. The factory was hard hit – even Milch called it 'a brilliant attacking operation'[53] – but at a cost of sixty B-17s for thirty-three German fighters shot down. The Luftwaffe achieved five bomber kills per hundred fighter attacks.

Wing Commander Johnnie Johnson, leading the RCAF Spitfire squadrons of the Kenley Wing, escorted the B-17 formations on their withdrawal. 'We swept well behind the stragglers and drove off a few 109s and 110s ... How we longed for more drop tanks so that some of the many hundreds of Spitfires based in Britain could play their parts in the great battles over Germany instead of being confined to unprofitable sweeps.'[54]

US bombers pulled back from the daylight skies over Germany's industrial heartland. It seemed to many in the RAF that, like the German bombers in September 1940, they would never return except under cover of darkness. To the Germans, continued USAAF attacks on targets within fighter escort range meant that their victory had gained them no respite. With a continued shortage of fighters – monthly production of Bf 109s had dropped from 704 in July 1943 to 350 in December due to the bombing of aircraft and component plants – and fighter pilots, the Luftwaffe could not rebuild their defences. The USAAF, holding firm to its strategy emphasising daylight strategic bombing, would have to rely on new tactics, technology and aircraft.

15

The Defeat of the
Luftwaffe Fighter Force

October 1943–June 1944

USAAF chief of staff General 'Hap' Arnold, in Washington, was furious. His bombers had suffered unsustainable losses over Schweinfurt. The timetable for the invasion of Europe the following spring was in jeopardy. He was pushing the USAAF to expand the use of long-range fighter escort over Europe and wanted the RAF's fighters to do more to revive the stalled Pointblank strategic bombing plan: 'We are doing things the RAF cannot or will not attempt.'[1] When the USAAF was being defeated over central Germany, the RAF had a force of 1461 fighters based in Britain, defending the bases of the bomber offensive along with British cities. That this force had been unable to contribute to the decisive battles infuriated leaders and aircrew of the Eighth Air Force in England and RAF fighter pilots alike.

Air Chief Marshal Sir Charles Portal, chief of staff, saw no prospect of using the RAF's fighter strength over Germany. The Spitfire's short range had proven a significant drawback since 1941. But nor did Portal ever accept that any long-range fighter could prevail against Bf 109s or other high-performance interceptors.[2] The RAF, committed to night bombing against Germany, had no requirement for a daylight escort fighter.

The only short-term solution was to increase Spitfires' ability to operate over Europe by providing them with additional external fuel tanks, like the slipper tanks that had been used over Salerno. Supermarine and the RAF knew how to extend the range of the Spitfire. They had done it for the reconnaissance versions. It required removing the armament from the wing and using the strong box-like structure of the leading edge as a fuel tank.

The USAAF remained unsatisfied that more could not be done to extend the Spitfire's range.[3] Arnold called Portal. Five Spitfire IXs were quickly shipped to the US for range extension development (the RAF, apparently resentful of US pressure, 'neglected' to provide manuals and performance information to accompany them).

The Spitfire IX was built with an increased fuel capacity, but much of that capacity was required to feed the more powerful Merlin 61 and subsequent engines. While jettisonable flush-fitting slipper tanks under the fuselage were widely used the most common solution to extending the Spitfire's range became a single 50-gallon under-fuselage drop tank. Operational in 1943, it was soon widely produced, but it did not offer the Spitfire the radius of action of drop tank-equipped P-47s. A streamlined, bomb-shaped 200-gallon tank was tried, as were two of the underwing 108-US-gallon drop tanks being built in Britain for the USAAF. Neither arrangement was used operationally, mainly due to RAF concerns about weight and balance considerations affecting stability. A wide range of solutions were used. A total of over 300,000 external fuel tanks of different types were eventually produced for the Spitfire.[4]

The Luftwaffe adapts

Despite the bomber offensive, the German aircraft industry improved its production figures in 1943, with a 75 per cent increase following the 50 per cent increase in 1942. In May 1943, monthly production exceeded 1000 fighters for the first time. Hitler permitted resources to go to building more, smaller fighters rather than fewer, larger bombers, boosting the numbers.

Messerschmitt reassured a high-level meeting with Göring, Milch and other officials that he could build more fighters and, if given the resources, 'we have capacity for the Me 209 in addition to the 109'.[5] But the Me 209 II V5 did not fly until November 1943. Its handling problems proved to be prohibitive. Messerschmitt's design staff had not succeeded in putting a powerful engine in its small airframe. Willy Messerschmitt blamed the shortage of labour for the delay in production and demanded an additional 1000 workers. On 30 November 1943, Milch said, 'We cannot bring out the Me 209 before the end of 1945 or the beginning of 1946. According to my opinion, things like this should be brought before a court martial.'[6] Göring again ordered the Me 209 II programme cancelled in December 1943.

Messerschmitt had once more failed to produce a piston-engine fighter that surpassed the Bf 109. The Me 209 and 309 programmes had absorbed large amounts of resources without producing a single combat aircraft. Messerschmitt kept trying to adapt the DB 603 engine to the Bf 109 airframe for high-altitude operations, including a series of company-funded P.1091 design studies. None of these ever flew. Removed from overall management responsibility yet powerful behind the scenes, he continued to use company resources (and the cachet from his personal relationship with Hitler) in pursuit of advanced programmes that reflected his personal vision, even when this did not follow RLM priorities.

The German aircraft industry had been standardising and simplifying the aircraft being produced, with Messerschmitt plants reducing the construction time required for each Bf 109 by 53 per cent from prewar levels by 1942 and a further 15 per cent in 1943. As late as 1943, most of the German aircraft industry was working a single shift totalling forty-eight hours a week, whereas the Allied industries had been working round the clock for years. Women, always vital to the German war effort despite Hitler's and Göring's reluctance to mobilise them, played an ever greater role in the aircraft industry as German males were conscripted away from the factories and sent to the army, but there were too few not already employed available to solve the labour shortage.[7] Women were brought in to carry out Luftwaffe ground duties, many replacing ground crew sent to the front. To make up numbers, the Luftwaffe used foreigners in support roles. Units in the east used local and former Soviet personnel. Prisoners of war and local labour, both hired and forced, filled bomb craters in German runways.

The use of foreign labour became vital to German industry. Workers from occupied countries, like Belgium and France, had originally been hired (in the absence of jobs at home). Their numbers now included ever greater numbers of forced labourers and prisoners of war. Other workers were prisoners from Dachau, the concentration camp located near Munich. Willy Messerschmitt so appreciated the provision of inmate labour that on 20 July 1943 he sent a personal thank-you letter to Dachau's SS commandant, asking for more inmates. Messerschmitt AG outsourced sub-assembly manufacturing to be carried out behind barbed wire at Dachau. A satellite concentration camp was established at Haunstetten, near the Augsburg factory, housing both workers and workshops.[8]

At one aircraft plant with 12,500 workers, 2375 were German men, 4000 German women, 875 concentration camp inmates or prisoners of war, and 5250 'volunteer' or enslaved foreigners. The latter were concentrated in certain areas of production within plants; at Regensburg in 1943, 80 per cent of Messerschmitt AG metalworkers were labourers from the east. Milch suggested that if French workers shirked, the first step should be to shoot half of them as a warning to the survivors.[9]

The Luftwaffe victorious again

Udet's nightmare of 'a Verdun of the air' was terribly real. RAF Bomber Command's multi-month 'Battle of Berlin' ran through the winter into March 1944. Its goal was nothing less than the defeat of Germany by levelling its capital and other major cities. But the Luftwaffe defenders, especially the night-fighter force, were able to inflict a rate of loss on the attacking bombers too high for the offensive to be sustained, while the damage inflicted failed to match that seen in Hamburg or the Ruhr in 1943.

This series of attacks ended with the loss of ninety-six bombers, mainly to fighters, during a single massed attack on Nuremberg, on 30/31 March 1944, which failed to inflict significant damage to the target. The RAF lost more aircrew killed in one night (545) than it had defending against the Luftwaffe in the entire Battle of Britain (505), evidence of how the scale of the air war had increased. While, in the Battle of Britain, aircraft and aircrew had been the capstone of competing systems, of their organisations and institutions, now they were also an expendable raw material to be used in bringing about the defeat of Germany through strategic bombing. In thirty-five major attacks since 18 November, the RAF had lost 1047 aircraft. The night bombers shifted their attacks away from Berlin and cities to transport targets, including those in France. Once again, the Luftwaffe had prevented Allied strategy from being carried out. Churchill had been an advocate for the bomber offensive since it opened on 15 May 1940. Offensive air operations were vital to his vision of strategy, hoping to enable the defeat of Germany through minimising reliance on a decisive land campaign in western Europe that Britain could not afford, even as a junior partner in the wartime coalition with the US. But the British commitment to strategic bombing remained, even if what Churchill said about the bomber crews spoke more of grim determination than the soaring inspiration of his words about the fighter pilots in 1940. 'What we received was child's play compared to what we are now giving Germany,' he told the Commonwealth prime ministers, whose countries provided many of the aircrew who had fallen in the bomber offensive.

The Bf 109 had played a major role in the defeat of the day bombers months earlier. It had a more marginal but still significant role in the defeat of the night bombers, although most of the attacking bombers lost were shot down by multi-engine night fighters. By early 1944, the Bf 109G-6/N, a specialised night-fighter version, went into action in small numbers. In addition to heavier *Kanonboot* underwing gun armament, it was equipped with *Y-Gerät* and, in yet another 'bump' behind the cockpit, a *Naxos-Z* radar detector, which showed the pilot the bearing to radar used by British bombers. Some ten to twelve were equipped with *Neptun-J* radar, but the weight and drag it added, as well as the difficulty experienced by pilots flying a Bf 109 at night while using a radar set, made it unsuccessful.

Only a limited number of Bf 109G-6/Ns were built. Single-engine night fighters became less significant when the Wild Boar units were retrained for day fighting and fed into the climactic air battles over Germany. But even after that, the Luftwaffe continued to use single-engine night fighters. In May 1944, 183 such fighters, including Bf 109s, supplemented 466 twin-engine night fighters. Bf 109s continued, in diminishing numbers, to fight at night, seventy-one remaining operational on 31 December 1944.

The USAAF resurgent

On 27 December 1943, a cheerless 'Hap' Arnold sent his Christmas message to senior commanders in Europe. It set out the harsh reality that, unless the Luftwaffe was defeated in the coming months, invasion of France in 1944 would be impossible. German industry continued to increase aircraft production. The RAF's heavy losses in the 'Battle of Berlin' demonstrated the bomber offensive was succeeding neither by day nor by night. The Pointblank objectives were far from being met. Arnold's message concluded, 'This is a MUST – Destroy the Enemy Air Force wherever you find them, in the air, on the ground, in the factories.'[10]

Since attacking Schweinfurt on 14 October, the Eighth Air Force had concentrated on targets along the German periphery or within escort fighter range. US bombers used radar bombing to attack area targets through overcast skies. German single-engine fighters were forced to operate in bad weather. The lack of instrument training in the Luftwaffe's fighter units contributed to a high accident rate.

The means to defeat the Luftwaffe were already arriving on US airfields in Britain. With US production fully mobilised, more and more combat groups arrived in England and in Italy, where the Fifteenth Air Force was now part of the daylight air offensive. Uparmed B–17G and B–24J bombers arrived in larger quantities. New US fighter units deploying to Europe were equipped with twin-engine P–38 fighters, improved P–47D fighters and Merlin-powered P–51 Mustangs, and their pilots had received the sort of training that the Luftwaffe could no longer manage. The leaders were veterans who had seen combat in the Pacific, north Africa, or with the RAF.

Thanks to the immense productive capacities of the US industrial base and the organisational capacities of the USAAF, the P–51, an outsider's idea in 1942, was in a position to fight decisive air battles over Germany in early 1944. It was fitted with drop tanks giving a radius of action of over 600 miles, more than three times that of RAF Spitfires.

When P-51s arrived in England, the RAF Spitfire IX pilots who encountered them in the air were amazed: a fighter with the same Merlin engine as their own planes, weighing some 25 per cent more, but still 30 mph faster, while its range left the RAF envious. P-51s were going to take the fighter air war to Germany, Spitfires were not. The P-51 was a more advanced design, with air intakes and radiators designed to create less drag than those of the Spitfire, while its engine exhaust was channelled to provide additional thrust at high speed, making use of the 'Meredith Effect', discovered at the RAE in the 1930s, that Mitchell had used to align the exhausts on the original Spitfire design.

The first P-51 escort missions over Germany – to Emden on 11 December and Kiel on 13 December 1943 – changed the nature of the air war. Bf 109Gs had an advantage in rate of climb over the P-51s and were about even in rate of roll. In everything else – range, armament, speed, turning and diving – the P-51 had the edge even before pilot quality and tactics, both now USAAF advantages, were taken into account. The P-51's advantage was most pronounced at high altitude, where most of the air combats took place. Veteran Bf 109 pilot Franz Stigler found that 'The P-51 was something else. It was an awful antagonist, in the truest sense of the word, and we hated it. It could do everything we could do and do it much better.'[11]

German twin-engine day fighters – Bf 110s, Me 410s and Ju 88s – armed with externally mounted cannon and rockets, had been the biggest killers of bombers in 1943. The twin-engine fighters, manoeuvrability further reduced by their heavy armament, rapidly fell to attacking US fighters. Galland was ordered by Korten to provide single-engine fighter escorts for them, only to find that, tied to the twin-engine fighters, they suffered heavy casualties too. Bf 109s with external armament were equally vulnerable. Stigler recalled, 'It was worth your life to be caught flying a 109 with [under]wing cannon against a Mustang and most of the pilots in my squadron elected to stick with the 109G-6 with its two 13mm cowl guns and a single MG 151 20mm cannon firing through the propeller hub.'[12]

In January 1944, the US Eighth Air Force received a new commanding general. Lieutenant General 'Jimmy' Doolittle had commanded the Twelfth Air Force in north Africa and then the Fifteenth Air Force in Italy. He had become a national hero in 1942 when he led the first US air attack on Japan (Spencer Tracy played him in the movie version). In command positions, starting with Operation Torch, he had demonstrated the use of effective integrated airpower, bombers and fighters, strategic and tactical, RAF and USAAF, in the Mediterranean.

With the approval of his superiors, Doolittle decided that rather than waiting for German fighters to come to the bombers, US fighters would seek them out. He wanted to use the new long-range capabilities of US fighters, especially the P-51, to have them take the offensive ahead of the bombers and attack German fighters gathering into the large formations that had been used successfully to defeat unescorted bombers in 1943. Where before US fighters had not been supposed to operate at less than 18,000 feet, new orders were to pursue German fighters 'down to the deck'.

If they could not find them, US fighters would go directly to the source through strafing attacks on airfields. Organisations tend to value most what they can count. The decision that a German aircraft destroyed by strafing on the ground would count as a kill as much as one shot down in air combat was instrumental in denying the Luftwaffe sanctuary on its airfields, despite the rings of anti-aircraft guns defending them.

Doolittle made his point. On 21 January, he gave the new orders at a commanders' conference: 'Meet the enemy and destroy him rather than be content to keep him away.'[13] Visiting VIII FC headquarters, he ordered the replacement of a mission-statement sign that the command had inherited, 'The first duty of the Eighth Air Force fighters is bring the bombers back alive,' with one reading, 'The first duty of the Eighth Air Force fighters is to destroy German fighters.'[14]

What made this action possible was that the USAAF now had enough fighters both to escort the bombers and to take the offensive, something it had previously lacked. With US heavy bombers now able to strike German targets even when the skies were overcast, thanks to the use of radar, the Germans were allowed no respite. This marked the start of large-scale, industrial, mass destruction of Luftwaffe fighters and fighter pilots. The USAAF finally had the combination of strength and quality – aircraft, senior commanders, pilots, tactics – to carry out this objective. Combat experience had led the USAAF to abandon a doctrine that emphasised the use of unescorted bombers and precision visual bombing in favour of one stressing integration of bombers and fighters and radar bombing of targets. Years of US industrial and military preparation, building on British experience, and the hard-earned lessons of Eighth Air Force operations had made Doolittle's orders feasible.

USAAF fighter pilots started carrying out the new tactics, seeking out and destroying German fighters.[15] Captain Clarence 'Bud' Anderson caught a Bf 109. 'The tracers race upwards and find him. The bullets chew at the wingroot, the cockpit, the engine, making bright little flashes. I hose the Messerschmitt down the way you'd hose down a campfire, methodically ... My momentum carries me to him. I throttle back to ease my plane alongside, just off his right wing. Have I killed him? I do not particularly want to fight this man again ... and then he falls away suddenly.'[16]

Up to now, German fighters had been able to disengage by diving faster than their opponents, but no longer. Galland found German 'fighters were decimated by American fighters, all of which dived faster'.[17] When Galland started getting reports of the new US fighter tactics, he understood what Doolittle was aiming to accomplish. It was what Galland himself had wanted to do over England in 1940, this time unconstrained by the limited range of the Bf 109. Galland told Göring that the Luftwaffe must defeat the escort fighters or be defeated itself. He urged building up the interceptor forces to gain a numerical advantage and that the Luftwaffe make the defeat of the US fighters their priority.

Göring received the news with unflinching incomprehension. Initially, he did not believe any US single-engine fighter could ever fly over Germany, even when confronted with evidence in the form of shot-down P-47s. Göring insisted that the bombers – and the threat to Germany's industries and cities they represented – remained the primary target of German fighters. The political impact of not intercepting them was unacceptable, such was the pressure from officials whose cities and industries were bombed.[18] As late as December 1943, he had obliged Milch to cut back fighter production goals to make resources available to build bombers to carry out a renewed night bombing campaign against Britain (which failed to inflict any militarily significant damage, but pleased Hitler). Fighter units were able, in practice, to make early spoiling interceptions of US fighters, hoping to get them to jettison their drop tanks prematurely. But the defence stayed focused on the bombers.

The decisive air battles over Germany – Operation Argument

On 11 January 1944, the Luftwaffe fighter force managed to score another victory against US B-17 and B-24 bombers attacking the Fw 190 plant at Oschlersleben. Some sixty bombers were shot down. But the increased German losses – fifty-three fighters – compared with their 1943 successes reflected the power of US fighters. First Lieutenant Lester F. Rentmeester was flying a B-17 that day:

> All eyes followed the swarm of thirty or forty Focke Wulf and Messerschmitt fighters. They were at our altitude and about a mile ahead of us. Suddenly, a single P-51 Mustang fighter plane flashed through their formation from behind, sending two German fighters down in flames. Several times our little friends streaked through the swarm of German fighters. It was a complete surprise; for the first time, the German Me 109s and Fw 190s were confronted over their homeland by an equal, or superior opponent.[19]

For major missions, the Eighth Air Force would send up to 1300 B-17 and B-24 heavy bombers over Germany, with 800 P-38s, P-47s and P-51s flying one or two escort missions each. The Germans would commit many hundreds of Bf 109s, Fw 190s and twin-engine fighters to intercept them. Once the bombers fought their way through to their targets, they faced massive flak defences.

The attacks on the aircraft industry in Operation Argument were initiated in England's 'midwinter spring', a forecast week of clear weather, 'Big Week', in February 1944. From the opening of Operation Argument on 20 February, both the England-based Eighth Air Force and the Italy-based Fifteenth Air Force made repeated attacks on the German aircraft industry. The bombers hit twenty-three aircraft factories and three engine factories. February's aircraft deliveries were 20 per cent lower than those of January.

Bf 109 production was targeted. The Erla plant in Leipzig was badly damaged, with 180 aircraft destroyed. The Regensburg Messerschmitt plant was crippled; that at Augsburg was out of commission for two weeks, a third of its structures gutted and production machines damaged. Willy Messerschmitt described the 26 February attack on Augsburg as 'completely destroying' the factory; he lost his house to the bombing. He moved to the Baroness's country house, near Oberammergau, where 1400 design staff members (including 600 engineers and scientists) were evacuated from Augsburg.[20] There, he recalled 'some of the happiest days of my life'. He worked on advanced jet fighter designs, with swept-back wings, able to approach the sound barrier in level flight. He would play the piano in the evenings in a village church; his *Missa Solemnis* was thought excellent.[21]

By 26 February, the Luftwaffe had lost 355 fighters and 150 pilots defending the Reich. During the six days of 'Big Week', the USAAF had put 3800 bomber sorties over Germany and lost 226 bombers, a high but sustainable loss rate. P-47Ds, using new 165-US-gallon drop tanks, joined the increasing numbers of P-51s in taking the offensive against the German fighters. Only twenty-eight US fighters were lost.

German fighter units had been forced into battle in instrument flying conditions for which they were not equipped or trained. In February alone, over 1300 German aircraft were destroyed or damaged in flying accidents with 408 aircrew killed and 207 injured. Over 40 per cent of the accidents took place during landing or taxiing, long-standing areas of Bf 109 weakness.[22] Eventually, up to half of all accidents were considered due to inadequate training.[23]

More German fighter units were pulled out of the eastern front or the Mediterranean and fed into the massive battles over Germany. They did not last. Their cadre of fighter leaders, many of whom had been in combat throughout the war, went down, one after another, before the intense offensive fighter combat waged by the USAAF. The Luftwaffe fighter force could not recover from their loss.

At the end of February, four P-51 groups were flying from England. US industrial strength and mass-production capabilities, nurtured by contracts agreed with the British before Pearl Harbor, now provided a rapid build-up of P-51s, in contrast to the slower pace of Spitfire IX re-equipment in previous years.

In March 1944, new drop tanks extended the P-51's range still further, allowing it to fly to Berlin and on past, to Prague, Munich and Stettin. The P-38 and P-47D could range over most of Germany. Colonel Don Blakeslee, who had pushed hard for the USAAF to adopt the Merlin-engine P-51, succeeded in getting his 4th Fighter Group re-equipped with them. With no time to lose to training, he ordered: 'We can learn to fly them on the way to the target': Berlin.[24]

The first US attack on Berlin, on 4 March, was disrupted by bad weather. Bf 109s used the conditions to deal the P-51s one of their few defeats in air combat. One USAAF group, surprised, lost eight P-51s to a single attack. On 6 March, Don Blakeslee flew the lead P-51 over Berlin, escorting the next US daylight bombing attack on 'The Big City'. Sixty-nine bombers were lost, the highest single-day toll of the war, but sixty-six German fighters went down, sixty of them lost to US fighters.

A single dark blue US Spitfire PR XI followed the bombers over Berlin. Climbing up to 41,000 feet to avoid three Bf 109Gs with GM-1 boost that pursued it, the Spitfire made its pass in a high-speed shallow dive to 38,000 feet. The photographs were used to plan repeated US strikes on Berlin in the following days.

On 8 March, the Eighth Air Force attacked Berlin again. One more time, the Luftwaffe fought. The attackers lost forty bombers. But on the following day another attack on Berlin found German fighters too exhausted and limited by bad weather to respond. On 16 March, the USAAF again hit German aircraft targets, forcing the Luftwaffe to come up and fight; P-51s caught a formation of forty-three Bf 110s and shot down twenty-six. On 22 March, Eighth Air Force bombers came back to Berlin, bombing through the overcast. German fighters were again unable to respond. The USAAF had established daylight air superiority over Berlin.

By the end of March, under a relentless drumbeat of attacks, the

German fighter force was collapsing. It had lost 3091 fighters in the preceding three months, some 70.5 per cent of them in the defence of Germany and in the west. For the fighter units, this was like losing the Battle of Britain every month, repeated without ceasing. Over 300 German fighter pilots were casualties in March alone, when the Luftwaffe lost 56.4 per cent of its single-engine fighters and nearly 22 per cent of the pilots who had been available at the start of the month.[25] Among them was Major 'Fürst' Wilcke, of the painted-over swastikas, one of many who, despite achieving high scores in the east, could not survive the harsh Darwinism of the more lethal air battles over Germany. He had amassed 162 victories on 732 combat missions when, on 23 March, P-51s shot down his Bf 109 over Brunswick. While over 400 USAAF bombers and fighters had been lost in March, these had all been replaced.

At the end of March, the USAAF dispensed with RAF Spitfire escorts for its heavy bombers. So few German fighters would fly within Spitfire range that they were not needed. The bomber crews missed their 'little friends', flying close escort where they could see them, and orbiting over ditched bombers, calling in air–sea rescue.

The German industrial response

No sanctuaries were left for German fighter units. Twin-engine fighters could not survive without escort and by the end of March many had been withdrawn from daylight combat. Flight training and developmental flying within range of US fighters were severely curtailed. Galland said he 'confirmed his suspicion that formation leaders were obsessed with a fear of engaging American fighters, and when four Mustangs chased him from the Rhine to Brandenburg, he realized why'.[26] Galland believed the Bf 109 was now largely inadequate to deal with deep-ranging US fighter attacks and more powerful bomber formations. He stated at a high-level armament conference in April 1944 that he 'would rather have one Me 262 jet than five Bf 109s'.[27] But that was not an option. Trials of the Me 262 were only just beginning. Only eight were produced in May 1944. The rocket-powered Me 163 flew its first combat missions in mid-1944; but, with its limited range and high accident rate, it had little impact on the overall situation. It proved, in the words of Eric 'Winkle' Brown, 'probably more lethal to its pilots than its enemies', while Waldemar Voight, chief designer on Messerschmitt's team, said only of its pilots, 'they got used to it'.[28]

Under the direction of Albert Speer, the Reich armament minister, working together with his friend Milch, German industry increasingly dispersed in order to decrease its vulnerability to bombing. While some industries such as oil refineries could not be dispersed, Messerschmitt, along with the rest of the aviation industry, moved as much manufacturing as they could out of their factories, and put machine tools and assembly processes into storefronts, barns (dirt floors could support heavy machine tools) and caves. Underground salt mines were less successful. Roman Katzbach, a Jewish Pole, was forced to work in one. 'They discovered the salt was corroding the metals. So, it was a bad experiment.'[29]

Messerschmitt factories soon became dependent on carts pulled by donkeys to bring components from dispersed machine shops to the factories for final assembly. The Bf 109's lightweight design helped: the wings had been designed to be easily detached from the fuselage and three workers could lift a wing into a cart. Many workshops were hidden in forests near rail lines that could be used to deliver raw materials. Machine tools remaining in the factories had bunkers of sandbags and concrete built around them, making them invulnerable to anything except a direct hit from a bomb; losses were replaced with machine tools looted throughout Europe.

This led to dips in production until the new facilities were established. Quality control also suffered, as on-site supervision was divided between several facilities. Once the dispersed facilities were able to resume production, this increased. All workers were now on a seventy-two-hour week. Milch implemented this schedule by making arrangements, with Himmler, for summary execution of German absentees, giving orders for the use of physical violence against forced labourers, and demanding that prisoners of war be compelled to work or die: 'They are not handled strictly enough ... International law cannot be observed here.'[30] While the compulsion of foreign workers was successful, German absenteeism remained high despite threats of punishment; at the BMW motor works in Munich, it averaged 10 per cent in 1943, climbing to 19 per cent in August 1944.

Even before the damage caused by Big Week, the effects of British bombing of factories in the Ruhr in 1943 had led to the 'sub-components crisis' (*Zulieferungskrise*) that had halted Speer's 1943 production increases. Now, Milch told the leadership March production was anticipated to be 30–40 per cent of that in previous months and said, 'we can no longer continue by normal means'.[31]

On 3 March 1944, the Germans created the *Jägerstab* (Fighter Staff) under Speer's Armaments Ministry (rather than the RLM) and headed by Speer's assistant, Karl-Otto Saur. Milch and Willy Messerschmitt had, separately, both implored Hitler to create the *Jägerstab*. Messerschmitt had not however expected that Milch would run it, alongside Saur and with Ernst Kaltenbrunner of the SS, who proved invaluable in his ability to secure cooperation by threatening the managers of any industrial bottlenecks with a quick trip to Dachau.[32] Milch had strong ideas who this should include. He and Saur had made a personal tour of the aircraft industry in a special train, empowered to dispense summary courts-martial judgements. When the train reached Messerschmitt's Regensburg plant, they were horrified to see that Bf 109G output was only five aircraft a day. A local Nazi official was hauled back to Berlin and turned over to Kaltenbrunner. A *Hauptmann* of the construction battalion repairing bomb damage was court-martialled on the spot.[33]

Milch wanted more. At a conferece held in Obersalzburg on 23–5 May he got the *Jägerstab* to agree to his plan to close down all Bf 109 production. He wrote on 26 May 1944, 'If you want to clear this up, you will have to throw the whole Messerschmitt company into a concentration camp.' Friedrich Seiler, chairman of the board, was arrested during summer 1944 for links to anti-Hitler plotters.[34] While Seiler was released and resumed his duties, the example was noted. He was the target of subsequent investigations. Karl Wahl, *Gauleiter* of Swabia, recommended to Berlin that Willy Messerschmitt be brought back to replace Seiler. The *Jägerstab* brought a level of coercive violence to aviation industry management previously reserved for the victims of Nazi Germany; the fear of the concentration camps had arrived in the board rooms. Saur's staff called his management style 'the whip'.

Saur's representatives, armed, went into every aircraft factory with the authority to order arrests. A Nazi party official, *Gauamstleiter* Professor

Hans Overlach, had authority over the Messerschmitt organisation; he launched an investigation of the management. Rakan Kokothaki found that 'Mr Saur's staff consisted of a great number of people who had not the slightest idea of aircraft manufacturing.' He wrote, 'From this time on the factory's management was practically out of action because direct orders were issued by this new office.'[35]

Willy Messerschmitt's behind-the-scenes influence over management was curtailed. He was reduced to sending complaining letters to the same directors he had enriched a few years before.[36] He relied on the Baroness. She would drive him, alone, from Oberammergau to important meetings in the firm's Volkswagen. Messerschmitt's chauffeur recalled her as 'a vivacious divorcee of something over 55 years of age who used more than the usual ration of cosmetics'.[37]

Saur was concerned by the effects of bomb damage on the production numbers: 'Regensburg is the only remaining pillar of Me 109 production following the serious setbacks at Leipzig-Erla and Wiener Neustadt.'[38] Yet, despite the damage to Bf 109 factories, spring 1944 saw ever-rising factory output of Bf 109s: 660 in March, 719 in April, 1017 in May and 1206 in June. Only 4500 man-hours were required per Bf 109G built by Messerschmitt.[39] The quality of workmanship continued to decline. On Saur's order, engines received only half an hour running-in to conserve fuel.[40] Lacking ammunition, new fighters could not have their guns test-fired.

The Me 262 jet fighter was finally operational, but was not available in the numbers required. Milch now pushed the plane's production as Germany's last chance in the air. 'We need this before everything else. This is the only way you can sort out Germany's problem,' he told Speer's Armaments Ministry.[41] Hitler, despite his previous insistence that the Me 262 be used as a bomber, agreed, giving the programme special priority status on 22 June.[42]

Milch, though retaining his Luftwaffe posts, became Speer's nominal deputy. Saur then moved to cut Milch out of authority. By 20 June, Milch was fired, his plan of ending Bf 109 production forgotten, and the RLM was effectively dissolved. From now on, the decisions as to what modifications would be made to the Bf 109s, and how many would be produced, came from the *Jägerstab*, whose leaders were from neither the

Luftwaffe nor the aircraft industry. All Messerschmitt AG labour allocations were handled through the *Jägerstab*. Roluf Lucht left Messerschmitt AG's Regensburg plant to work for the *Jägerstab*, setting up dispersed factories in forests. The destruction of oil targets allowed Speer to increase his power by controlling allocation of the remaining resources; he told Hitler the Luftwaffe might well have to cease operations soon, while at the same time supporting Saur's demands for more fighter production, which meant keeping the Bf 109 in production, against Galland's recommendations to Speer to close it down and throw everything into building still-unready jets.[43]

The *Jägerstab* demanded that the aircraft industry immediately make changes in aircraft production to enable maximum use to be made of unskilled labour. This meant an increase in the use of enslaved labour. Göring had already asked Himmler for as many concentration camp inmates as possible for the aircraft industry.[44] Himmler, a believer in both industrial mass production and racial extermination, agreed, pointing out that he already had 36,000 inmates working on aircraft, that Bf 109G wooden tail sections were being built at the Butschowitz camp (Brno in Czechoslovakia) and that cowlings and radiator covers for Regensburg-assembled Bf 109s came from the camp at Flossenbürg. The tail sections were being built with the new all-synthetic P600 glue that had been developed by SS scientists. The SS took on a larger role in the German war economy, especially the aircraft industry, with their ability to allocate forced labour.[45] Flossenbürg's deliveries, and others controlled by the SS, increased so that by summer 1944 it was providing about one-third of the Regensburg factory's Bf 109 components; while many of the 20,000 dead at Flossenbürg had been working for the aircraft industry, the prisoners considered it much more survivable than quarrying or construction.

Despite these extreme efforts to boost production, the Luftwaffe experienced no increase in the number of operational fighters. Saur focused on boosting production numbers, producing few spare parts; the Bf 109G of 1944 had 9000 different parts. In 1941, spare parts had constituted only 30 per cent, by weight, of German aircraft production; yet this had been halved by 1944, a desperate short-term surge option. Spare parts were obtained by cannibalisation of otherwise repairable aircraft.[46]

Through the *Jägerstab*, Speer arranged for damaged aircraft to be returned to factories for repairs, rather than going through Luftwaffe depots and repair facilities. Many Bf 109s requiring relatively minor repairs were returned for rebuild at the factory, further boosting production figures. Every aircraft that was over 51 per cent damaged when turned over to the aircraft industry for repair essentially counted the same as a new production aircraft. German production totals probably reflected some 30 per cent overclaiming compared to comparable Allied figures.[47] In 1944, for the first time since 1939, Germany produced more aeroplanes than Britain (39,600 versus 26,500), but, with Britain building more bombers and Germany largely fighters, the total weight of British aircraft production was greater (208 million lb versus 174 million lb). Production overclaiming increased under the *Jägerstab*. Even Göring no longer believed Saur's statistics. 'Saur lived only for his numbers, numbers, and numbers.'[48]

The struggle inside the factories

Messerschmitt had started large-scale dispersal after the 1943 bombings of Regensburg and Wiener Neustadt. To manufacture components, workshops were set up in the quarries of Gusen in upper Austria as well as at Flossenbürg and its many sub-camps. Run by the SS *Deutsches Erd und Steinwerke* (DESt) organisation, Gusen, like Flossenbürg, used concentration camp labour. Gusen had started delivering components by late 1943; by mid-1944, seventy-seven full goods trains a month brought Gusen-built components to Messerschmitt plants.

After Big Week, the SS – Himmler had gained control of the creation of underground factories with Speer's approval – ordered 10,000 prisoners from Mauthausen concentration camp to excavate tunnels and underground workshops at Gusen, working many of them to death.[49] Shlamek Orzech, a Jewish Pole, helped to build the underground aircraft assembly facilities at Sankt Valentin, near Gusen. 'That underground working was so hard, the *Kapos* were beating so bad the people – and I think it was purposely – beating those people and the people couldn't hold it, and they unfortunately died at work.'[50] The death rate was highest during the building of the facilities, as construction workers received smaller rations than assembly workers.[51] The underground workshops were seen as an important way of bringing together processes that would otherwise have to be dispersed to multiple locations.[52] By creating underground mass-production factories, Himmler aimed to demonstrate that the SS could, through systematic brutal exploitation of labour, do what the Luftwaffe was unable to do with Bf 109s: protect the German aircraft industry from Allied bombers, while still achieving the Third Reich's genocidal goals; modernisation linked to extermination.

The workshops and factories producing Bf 109s received large numbers of inmates from concentration camps. As a result of a request from the *Jägerstab*, the SS selected some 100,000 inmates, many women and girls, for transfer to the aircraft industry. This was feasible because of the changes that had been made by the industry itself to move away from the craftsman-based model of pre-war years and set up mass-production assembly lines where unskilled labour could be effectively used.[53] Yet, although Messerschmitt AG had been using deported foreigners and prisoners from Dachau since 1942, neither prisoners nor industry were prepared for the new intakes.

Elli Friedmann, a teenager from Hungary, had survived Auschwitz, where she was selected for a 'transport' that eventually arrived at a railway siding serving the Messerschmitt factory at Augsburg.[54] '"Where is your luggage?" And everybody started laughing. "Luggage? We have no luggage." He says "But you have no personal belongings?" And we said, "No, we have nothing." And so it is obvious that now we are dealing with a totally new leadership here. They don't know anything about concentration camp inmates and how to treat them. They were very nice to us.'[55]

A network of satellite concentration camps appeared throughout Germany, providing inmates for dispersed industries. But, as Elli Friedmann found out to her relief, 'Augsburg is not a concentration camp in the conventional sense. It is a camp for inmates who labor 12 hours a day and live on rations below minimum, who are escorted to and from the toilet by SS guards and are not permitted any contact with the outside world or with other workers at the factory. But we are not subject to the standard abuses of Auschwitz – beating, maiming, exposure to the elements – and the selection.'[56]

The German aircraft industry became increasingly multinational. Messerschmitt AG at its height would have over 22,000 workers: half Germans, a fifth 'paid' foreigners, the remainder forced labour. In the final analysis, some of the foreign workers were almost as effective as their German counterparts; in the case of female Russians and skilled Czech workers, some 90–100 per cent, enslaved Jews only 30 per cent.[57] Workers, forced and salaried, civilian and military prisoners, Germans (the few remaining skilled craftsmen and the unskilled conscripted into the factories), Jews, Poles and prisoners from throughout Europe all worked together. But it was a workforce divided by National Socialist ideology even on the shop floor; a 1943 SS decree made fraternisation punishable by dispatch to a concentration camp or summary execution. The Nazi racial hierarchy permeated aircraft construction.

Once assembly work began, the aircraft industry had an economic incentive to keep workers alive. The death rate among the prisoners, high during construction, was kept down in non-SS factories through the provision of better rations and the use of less brutality among those doing aircraft assembly; if they died, others would have to be trained in their jobs. Elli Friedmann arrived at Augsburg with a group of 500 women; after some six months 498 were still there. In concentration camps, selection to work in the aircraft industry was considered a 'good transport', offering chances for survival.

Yet industry's interest in keeping prisoners alive was often undercut by the violent system. As Messerschmitt engineer Friedrich Messler stated, 'the *Messerschmitt-Werke* themselves gave the prisoners additional food'.[58] But Aron Tenenbaum, a Jewish prisoner from Poland, remembered: 'Messerschmitt would send milk for us, so we would have more strength to work. The *Kapo* was supposed to give us the milk together with our bread and soup, but instead he would take the milk for himself and his friends back at the camp.'[59]

Gusen was the most lethal aircraft plant. By late 1944, three concentration camps had been set up there for workers. The death rate continued to climb, reaching 3271 in March 1945 alone as the aircraft industry and food supplies collapsed from bombing attacks on the transportation system. Summary execution of suspected saboteurs and slackers was common, their bodies left hanging above the production lines.[60] 'Even after Mauthausen it was real hell,' recalled Vasiliy Kononenko, a Russian prisoner. 'Two months in Gusen was a long life,' said Felice Malgaroli from Milan. 'Seven was a record.'[61] Ironically, the fighter pilots who flew the aircraft they built had comparable life expectancies. Labourers, pilots and aircraft alike had all become raw material to be expended in the integrated military–industrial process to protect the Reich from Allied bombers.

German tunnelling and camouflage were again successful. The Allies, though aware of them, never bombed the Gusen facilities. Berl Tieger, a Jewish Pole who had been in camps since 1940, worked as a mechanic in Gusen. 'We worked from sunrise to sundown, no food, very little food. Beatings. We have to survive somehow. Not many of us survived there . . . Building planes was in the tunnel. Big tunnel. Everything was underground, because they were bombing.'[62]

Open rebellion was rare, but on 1 May 1944 some 200 Polish and Soviet slave labourers revolted and seized control of the Erla workshop in the Mülsen–St Micheln concentration camp, burning Bf 109 wings before they were massacred by German reinforcements. Twenty escaped. Two Soviet prisoners of war tried to escape from the Regensburg factory in February 1944 by stealing a Bf 109. It crashed on take-off; they were subsequently executed. More common was passive resistance, with workers setting machines incorrectly or mis-assembling parts. Some workers were willing to risk summary execution to sabotage production. One rocket-propelled Me 163 was found to have a piece of sharp scrap metal jammed between the pilot's seat and the fuel tank. Deceleration on landing would punch it through the fuel tank, creating a potentially spectacular fire. This work was accompanied by French-language graffiti on the aircraft structure: 'my heart is not in my work'.[63]

Most of the sabotage to aircraft was detected before it caused accidents, but it likely contributed to heavy losses, especially during ferrying. Saur complained of an incident where 'of 20 aircraft picked up by the ferrying service, eight were destroyed on take-off'.[64] However, the knowledge that some of those building their planes wanted them dead was unlikely to help pilot morale. Compounding the problem was that the standards of workmanship of much of the hastily trained workforce and the demand to keep up production numbers often resulted in a level of manufacturing quality indistinguishable from sabotage.[65] Elli Friedmann, making bomb-release mechanisms at Augsburg, found 'Mistakes were chalked up as deliberate negligence. Or worse. Sabotage. We were forewarned.'[66] The dispersal of the industry meant that many sites lacked inspectors who knew anything about aircraft.

New Spitfires

The RAF's Britain-based fighter Spitfires continued to fly Ramrod escorts, especially of twin-engine bombers based in England, and Ranger fighter sweeps. The potential of the Griffon-engine Spitfires in air combat was demonstrated on 20 October 1943. Spitfire XIIs, escorting medium bombers over northern France, were attacked by twenty-five Bf 109s and Fw 190s. Fighting at their critical altitude of 12,000 feet and below, the Spitfire XIIs claimed nine destroyed without loss. But they encountered fewer German fighters, since most had been pulled back for home defence.

In late 1943, the Mark II gyroscopic gunsight started to arrive in some Spitfire squadrons. Replacing the reflector gunsight, it used an analogue computer that calculated the lead if the pilot tracked a manoeuvring target for one second. The RAF estimated that the average pilot became up to twice as effective when using it. Johnnie Johnson was one of many aces who eschewed it; he could work deflection out instinctively and did not want to focus on a gunsight, but rather on the enemy. Another innovation was the 'g' suit, which helped counteract blacking- and redding-out during air combat. The original 'g' suit, Canadian designed, used bladders of water to exert pressure on a pilot's body. These were uncomfortable and an improved US-designed version, using air pressure, was used in combat from 1944. As with the gyroscopic gunsight, many experienced pilots preferred to go without, but it provided the average pilot with a considerable advantage.

The first flight, in 7 September 1943, of the Spitfire XIV, a modified Spitfire VIII airframe powered by a Griffon 61 (and subsequently a Griffon 65) engine was, in the view of Jeffrey Quill, the second 'quantum jump' in Spitfire performance.[67] The Spitfire XIV combined an improved engine with an existing airframe to minimise production disruption. There had been extensive investment in tools and jigs to facilitate Spitfire production, with the particular intention of solving the problems in fabricating the elliptical wing, its fairing with the fuselage, all of which had held back production in previous years. But changing the Spitfire design now meant changing all this machinery as well.

Rolls-Royce had rushed the Griffon 61 into production. To Winkle Brown, now flying as a test pilot, 'The performance of the Spitfire XIV was electrifying. It had lost none of the harmony of control that makes the classic Mk IX such a pleasant aircraft to fly and to fight. The Spitfire XIV was the greatest British fighter of World War II, incorporating as it did so many improvements over earlier models without losing anything in looks or handling.'[68] Johnnie Johnson disagreed. 'It's not a Spitfire any more.' He disliked the high torque forces, which required strong use of rudder controls to keep the plane's alignment on take-off and while cruising. He continued flying the Spitfire IX.

The Spitfire XIV's Griffon 61 had a two-stage supercharger, similar to that on the Merlin 61 that powered the Spitfire VIII and IX. Able to develop over 2035 hp at 7000 feet, the Griffon 61 had a cubic capacity a third greater than the Merlin. To translate this power to thrust, the Spitfire XIV was fitted with a five-blade propeller. A larger fin and rudder helped counteract the engine's torque forces. Two 25-gallon fuel tanks were fitted, around the guns, in the wing leading edge. These barely compensated for the Griffon's higher fuel consumption. Overall, a Spitfire XIV had almost twice the engine power and weighed over a ton more than a Spitfire I. Packing this power into the Spitfire design and still keeping it flyable was one of Joe Smith's and the Supermarine design team's greatest wartime achievements. For all this, the Spitfire XIV – like the Spitfire V, IX and XII – was considered an interim type, pending the introduction of what was to become the Spitfire 21, which would represent a thorough upgrade of the Griffon-powered design.

The Spitfire XIV flew its first combat operations in January 1944. But its first dogfights had been over England in both tests and unofficial air battles against the newly arrived USAAF P-51s. The two fighters were found to be closely matched. The Spitfire XIV had a tighter turning circle, higher rate of climb, and slightly higher speed at high altitude. The P-51 had faster acceleration in a dive (even though the Spitfire could dive faster) and a faster rate of roll. The two fighters were closely matched. What mattered most was that the P-51 could fight over Berlin. The Spitfire XIV could not.

As the Spitfire XIV was being made ready for production, the design team worked on the Spitfire 18, an improved 'interim' Mark XIV, incorporating advances that the hastily developed Spitfire XIV did not have. As with the Spitfire IX in 1942–3, the production rate of Spitfire XIVs was slow to increase. The Castle Bromwich production line remained committed to building Spitfire IXs. Shortages of Griffon engines and the problems of retooling Supermarine's dispersed production facilities meant that only a handful of squadrons were operational with Spitfire XIVs by spring 1944.

In 1943, Joe Smith and Alan Clifton had been working on the Spitfire XX, the improved version of the Mark IV that had been put aside in favour of the Mark XII and more Mark Vs in 1941–2. In turn, the Spitfire XX, an advanced Griffon-engine version, was put aside in favour of the Mark XIV and more Mark IXs in 1942–3. Work continued through 1943–4 on the 'super' comprehensive redesign that would become the Spitfire 21, which Joe Smith called 'a direct descendent of the Spitfire IV and XX'.

Also put aside thanks to the design team's emphasis on the Spitfire XIV was the Spitfire 23 (originally planned to be produced as the Supermarine Valiant), a redesigned Griffon-engine high-altitude interceptor with a laminar flow wing leading edge. Work on it had started in early 1943. Instead, the design team would add an entire new 'laminar flow' wing (like that on the P-51) to the Spitfire 21's fuselage and create a new fighter, the Spiteful, which had its origins back in Air Ministry Specification F.1/43.

With the intensifying Allied bomber offensive against targets in France, starting in May 1944, Spitfire squadrons flew more escort missions. Low-level reconnaissance missions over France and northern Europe were stepped up to provide information for planning the upcoming invasion. Photo-reconnaissance Spitfires helped make maps.

The USAAF's insistence that combat-capable Spitfires could have their range extended resulted in a high-priority development programme at Wright Field, Ohio, starting in March 1944.[69] Two Spitfire IXs had their internal fuel capacity increased with a large fuselage tank

Spitfire I and a Do 17Z. Still from a German 1940 propaganda film made with a captured Spitfire. (National Archives RG 306)

4 Squadron, newly re-equipped with Spitfire Is, demonstrates a scramble for the camera, 20 April 1940. In the Battle of Britain, when every second saved getting off the ground meant more altitude when the enemy was encountered, such action was considerably more kinetic. (Getty Images)

1941 109: Bf 109F–4. A more streamlined redesign. (National Archives RG-18-WP)

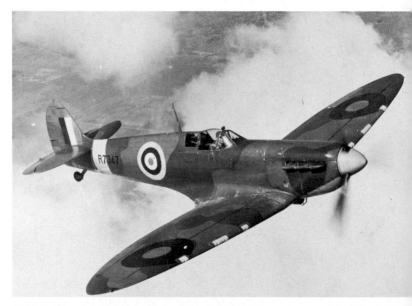

1941 Spitfire: Spitfire VA in flight, 6 April 1943. This version carried eight .303 guns; most Spitfire Vs had cannon. (National Archives RG-18-WP)

109 factories become targets: Regensburg burns on the afternoon of 17 August 1943. (National Archives RG-342-FH)

1942: the Spitfire VII, designed for high-altitude operations, with extended wingtips, a four-bladed propeller and a pressurised cockpit. (National Archives RG-18-WP)

From 1942 to 1945, the Bf 109G-6 was in constant combat. This version (bump and DF loop) was found at the Messerschmitt factory at Augsburg by the US Army in April 1945. (National Archives RG-342-FH)

From 1942 to 1945, the Spitfire IX was in constant combat. MH869 of 302 (Polish) Squadron escorts a USAAF bomber. (National Archives RG-342-FH)

Spitfire IX of the USAAF in North Africa. (National Archives RG-342-FH)

The tide recedes: wrecked Bf 109G abandoned on Trapani airfield, Sicily,1943.
(National Archives RG342-FH)

Spitfire FR XIV NH 373 in India after V-J Day. The porthole near the two-tone fuselage roundel is for a low-altitude reconnaissance camera (point wingtip at subject). (National Archives RG 342-FH)

Bf 109G-14 with Erla hood. (National Archives RG-18-WP)

Seafire III of 809 Squadron FAA takes the barrier on HMS *Stalker* and knocks off a propeller blade in the Pacific, 1945. (National Archives RG 80)

Defeat in air combat: Bf 109 with underwing 20mm gun pods caught in the gun camera of a USAAF fighter. (National Archives RG 342-FH)

Spitfire as symbol of a shared national past: Griffon-powered Spitfire PR 19 with a Lancaster and a Hurricane of the Battle of Britain Memorial Flight in the 1970s. Such flyovers have become part of British public occasions. (David Isby)

Bf 109G as artefact of a receding time: the Duxford flight line.
(David Isby)

and two 75-US-gallon drop tanks, retaining all armament. By May 1944, the Spitfires were able to fly 1200 miles. US engineers claimed they could achieve a 600-mile radius of action: Berlin! These two Spitfires concluded their testing programme by hopping across the Atlantic back to Britain in July 1944. Wright Field's engineers were proud of their achievement, but subsequent air tests in England showed the RAF considered it 'a lash-up' that lacked stability with the rear tank full.[70] Tests were made on Spitfire IX with a 170-gallon belly tank that provided a range of 1370 miles, but while officially adopted for ferry missions, this was never used on operations.[71] In a modification programme codenamed 'Fusank', additional fuselage tanks holding 72 gallons – reduced to 64 in aircraft with the teardrop canopy – were fitted to the Spitfire IX (and, in 1945, to the Spitfire XVI). But Fighter Command, who had never asked for these tanks, citing the stability issue, would not use them in combat and received Air Ministry approval for their removal from Spitfires being delivered to them.[72]

Bf 109: development under attack

By the spring of 1944, Messerschmitt's factories had to follow the goal of increasing production numbers while the resources of his design team were applied to jet programmes. Messerschmitt kept working on the Me 209 II project. He put the Me 209H V1 prototype, with the extended Bf 109H-type wing, into the air in June. It was not ordered into production; the Luftwaffe would receive instead the Ta 152.

For the past year, an array of modifications to the basic Bf 109G design had been produced. Messerschmitt's remaining design staff in Augsburg created upgrades that were incorporated on some production lines, contributing to a lack of standardisation. To improve rear vision, Adolf Galland ordered the armour plate behind the pilot's head (which had saved his own life back in 1941) to be replaced by bulletproof glass. A new wooden tail section design featured a taller fin with an adjustable rudder trim tab, something that the Bf 109 had lacked since its initial design. This had first appeared on some Bf 109G-5s in 1943. The shortage of aluminium required a redesign of the Bf 109 tail for wood construction. Woodworking shops joined the dispersed production 'circles'.[73]

Joining wood assemblies to a metal airframe proved difficult. The wooden tails started failing in flight, especially at high speeds. The Messerschmitt design team came to the conclusion that most of these failures were the result of poor materials (the SS-developed P600 glue came unstuck in bad weather) and workmanship at the dispersed workshops, problems that could not be effectively addressed.[74] The SS, which had seized control of the woodworking industry, could not provide quality assurance. Attempts to use more wood and plastic in the Bf 109 structure proved unfeasible.

Speer was demanding increased production numbers and was impatient with any changes that would disrupt production lines. At the same time, the Luftwaffe was insisting on improved high-altitude combat performance for combat in the west. A Bf 109G-6 engine managed, in Messerschmitt plant testing, to achieve a maximum critical altitude of 6600 metres (21,654 feet). But the standardisation and quality control of engines and airframe alike had become problematic, in part reflecting the proliferation of Bf 109 sub-types. To improve high-altitude performance, the Bf 109G-6/AS was powered by the DB 605AS instead of the standard DB 605A. It used the larger supercharger from the less reliable DB 603 engine.[75] This version introduced an improved cowling design (removing the hated 'bumps') and a new broad-blade propeller. Some 686 were produced, most converted from existing Bf 109Gs (including some G-5 models). The DB 605AM and 605ASM engines added MW injection (weighing some 300 lb) and were installed in multiple Bf 109G versions. These myriad engine sub-types show how the DB 605 design was pushed for incremental improvement. Because of the limits of weight and volume on the Bf 109 airframe, not every subtype could accommodate every upgrade.

The Bf 109G-10, with the more powerful DB 605D series engine with MW injection, was built as both a new production model and as re-engined early-production Bf 109Gs. When fitted with the DB 605DC engine, it was the fastest Bf 109 fighter yet – 428 mph at 24,607 feet – and was able to climb to 20,000 feet in less than six minutes. It was armed with an engine-mounted 30mm MK 108 cannon and two synchronised 13mm machine guns (with accompanying 'bumps'), but could carry additional weapons externally under the wings or fuselage.

It had a longer tailwheel (improving ground visibility if not perform-ance) that had been introduced on late-production Bf 109G-6s. During its production, the Bf 109G-10 received an enlarged wooden tail section. A new canopy, intended to provide increased visibility, replaced the heavy-framed side-opening design that had been used since the proto-type. First introduced at the Erla factory, it was known as the Erla hood or, more often but incorrectly, the Galland hood (even he did not claim to have invented it). The FuG25, a radio with an improved IFF transponder, capable of ground-based direction using the 'Egon' *Gerät* (apparatus), was also fitted.[76]

The Bf 109G-12 was a hastily converted Bf 109G-6 used as a two-seat trainer. The instructor in the rear cockpit could see so little at landing that even the experienced test pilot Winkle Brown took 'three frightening attempts' to land it.[77]

The Bf 109G-14 was powered by the DB 605A engine; a few had the more powerful DB 605AS or AM (with water–methanol injection). Saur said, 'The installation of high performance engines and the stan-dardisation of water–methanol injection is pressing forward.'[78] It was a modified Bf 109G-6 intended to make up numbers, along with the fewer Bf 109G-10s and their higher-rated DB 605D engine. An enlarged tail section compensated for the more powerful engine. The cowling lacked 'bumps' for the 13mm machine guns. Galland was enthusiastic about the Bf 109G-14 with the high-altitude DB 605AS. But only 120 had reached Luftwaffe fighter units at the time of the deci-sive battles over Germany in spring 1944 and not all were operational. Repeated incremental improvements to the DB 605 had reduced its use of scarce raw materials – from 27 to 19 kg of chrome per engine, for example – but pushed performance as far as it could go. Engine fires became more frequent under the strains of high-boost operation as qual-ity control decreased. The Bf 109G-16 was similar to the G-14; only a few were produced, used for night fighting or as fighter-bombers.

The defeat of the German fighter force

The daylight bomber offensive continued. In April 1944's air battles over Germany, the USAAF lost 409 four-engine bombers. The Luftwaffe, however, lost 43 per cent of its front-line fighters and over 20 per cent

of its pilots in that one month. At the end of April, Galland told the
RLM that over 1800 fighter pilots, 'including many of the best unit
leaders', had been lost over the past four months, 350 of them in April
alone.[79] Continuing the pressure on German fighter fields, the first
'Jackpot' mass strafing attack by 615 USAAF fighters took place on 15
April.

If they failed to encounter the Luftwaffe in the air, US fighters over
Germany would be encouraged to seek it out on the ground. Escort
missions completed, fighter leaders would leave their 'big friends' and
give the order over the VHF radio, 'I do not want to see any ammunition coming home.' Fighters would disperse and go 'down on the deck',
ranging throughout Germany, attacking targets of opportunity.

In 1942, before the threat from long-range US fighters emerged,
Oberst.i.G. Dr Georg Pasewaldt,[80] a highly decorated bomber pilot and
then chief of the Development Department of the *C-Amt*, had told
Willy Messerschmitt, 'The one-hundred-nine is still quite a good aircraft, but our need is for one with the same speed plus greater range and
a better rate of climb.' Messerschmitt had snapped back, 'What do you
want, a fast fighter or a barn door?'[81] Willy Messerschmitt now had
cause to remember. He was accompanying Pasewaldt to the airfield at
the Augsburg factory, where prototype aircraft flew. The air-raid sirens
blared. They both just had time to run and dive into a nearby slit trench.
A flight of USAAF P-47 fighters flashed over the airfield at treetop altitude, strafing any planes they could see, in a single pass, accelerating away
before the flak defences could react. Pasewaldt turned to Messerschmitt:
'*There* are your barn doors!'[82]

The Luftwaffe reeled from the impact of combat losses and the effects
of the bombing of German industry. It further suffered from the Anglo-
American bomber offensives' joint attacks on the synthetic oil and
transport industries, starting on 12 May. Albert Speer wrote, 'On that
day the technological war was decided . . . It meant the end of German
armaments production.'[83]

By May, USAAF fighters controlled the skies over Germany, flying
36,120 sorties, experiencing about a 1 per cent loss rate. German fighters flew 3600 sorties, experiencing a 10.7 per cent loss rate; including
non-combat causes, over 400 German fighter pilots were lost in May.

While the number of fighters shot down on each side was comparable, the impact was highly disparate. The Germans, flying only a tenth as many fighter sorties over their country as the enemy, were shot down ten times as often. At the same time, the new *Sturmgruppe* tactics and improved armament meant those German attacks that penetrated to the bombers were much more lethal. Luftwaffe fighters achieved 17.7 kills per 100 attacks made on the bombers.[84] But far fewer attacks were being made.

Most of the Bf 109s that came off the production lines were flown into combat by similarly mass-produced pilots of increasingly marginal skills. Both were simply ground up in the relentless process of attrition. The production of more Bf 109s had not been matched by a comparable expansion of ground crews to support them. By 1944, over Germany, Bf 109s found it difficult to fly more than one sortie a day.

The USAAF had the weight of numbers, but the Luftwaffe could still reverse this advantage when they succeeded in massing fighters that could break through to the bombers, overwhelming any escorts in the area. Even if the escorts overall outnumbered the interceptors, the escort force was divided to cover the whole of the larger bomber formations throughout the time they were over German territory.

Galland wanted his fighters to concentrate their efforts, as Park had done over Dunkirk in 1940. In 1943, a mass attack was one by a single *Gruppe*. In 1944, to break through to the bombers past fighter escorts required massing multiple *Gruppen* together in a *Gefechtsverband* (combat unit). Each *Geschwader* would have at least one Bf 109 *Gruppe* as a *Höhengruppe* (high group) to provide top cover against fighters. As the Germans formed *Sturmgruppen* (storm groups) of fighters weighed down with additional armament and armour to fight the bombers, the performance differences between types increased.

Any Bf 109 carrying the external armament required to destroy bombers would be so weighed down that it would be unable to manoeuvre against US fighters. As a result, heavily armed Bf 109s and Fw 190s required fighter escorts of their own. Galland realised that a *Gefechtsverband* of one *Gruppe* of single-engine fighters with external weapons had to be escorted by two *Gruppen* of fighters without them. Often, the Germans lacked enough fighters or time to gather into large

formations. Such massed formations proved successful on several occasions. More often, however, US fighters, ranging ahead of the bombers,
would take the offensive and attack first. Galland, despite his advocacy
of massed attacks, saw the vulnerability of these *Sturmgruppe* tactics. 'The
big formations flew purely defensively, with the fighter escort above and
to the side of the heavy Fw 190s. The escort fighters did not leave to
attack American fighters and the Fw 190s had strict orders to hold formation and fly to the bombers.'[85] The Bf 109Gs of the *Höhengruppen*
ended up fighting US fighters at high speeds and altitudes. At high
speeds, the control forces of a loaded Bf 109G were heavy indeed,
reducing directional stability as well as manoeuvrability and making it a
less effective gun platform. Despite engineering that extracted improved
high-altitude performance from upgraded versions of the Bf 109G's
DB 605 engine, it was still not equal to USAAF fighters with turbo-
superchargers at high altitude.

To pull together and use these formations effectively required both
capable leaders and pilots competent enough to be able to carry out
these tactics rather than simply trying to fly their Bf 109s. Both were
going down, more and more rapidly. Oberstleutnant Walter 'Gulle'
Oesau, *Kommodore* of JG1, who three years before had refused to replace
his Bf 109E, was now a 127-victory ace (at least thirty-eight of them
against Spitfires), but was exhausted from five years of air combat and
suffering from pneumonia. With his *Geschwader* having to send hastily
trained pilots against the USAAF every day, by leading them in the air
he might show some of them what to do and maybe keep some alive
through their first five or so combats, so that they might have a chance
of becoming useful fighter pilots. Göring incessantly goaded that fighter
pilots lacked courage while German cities were burning and that inadequate aircraft could easily be compensated for by the right spirit. For
whatever reason, on 11 May 1944, Oesau rose from his sickbed and into
the cockpit of his Bf 109G-6/AS. It was his last combat mission. He was
shot down and killed by P-38s. Next, it was the turn of Major Günther
Rall, with 275 victories, all but three in the east. His luck held one more
time: a .50-calibre bullet from a P-47 amputated his thumb, leaving him
four fingers with which to pull his parachute's ripcord.

In one month, May 1944, the Luftwaffe lost over 50 per cent of the fighter aircraft defending the Reich and over 25 per cent of the Bf 109 and Fw 190 pilots. By now, Bf 109 and Fw 190 units had lost over 100 per cent of the pilots they had at the start of the year. Luftwaffe fighters were unable ever again to inflict such losses on the US bombers as they had in April.

But May was only a prelude to two months of devastating raids on oil and transport targets. As part of the oil campaign, the Italy-based Fifteenth Air Force had begun its sustained attacks on Romania's Ploesti refineries. The synthetic aviation fuel on which the Luftwaffe relied was systematically targeted. Production fell from 180,000 tonnes in April to 53,000 tonnes in June. As average monthly consumption was 150,000 tonnes, both operations and flight training were further cut back. With fuel for delivery flights lacking, Bf 109s were often delivered from the factories to fighter units by rail, their wings unbolted. Allied strikes on transport links ensured many never arrived.

In April 1944, USAAF bombers had struck Hungary's Bf 109G licensed production line at Györ, which had supplied some planes to the Luftwaffe. German pilots, examining these aircraft, were astounded by the quality of the workmanship, reminiscent of pre-war German production. Romania's Bf 109G licensed production facilities at Brasov were gutted by a USAAF attack in May 1944.

16

Fighters over France and England

May–September 1944

On 13 May 1944, the sky was grey but spring weather was clear as Johnnie Johnson led some dozen Spitfire IXs of 442 Squadron of the RCAF's 144 Wing over the Channel to France, their finger-four formations arranged so that those closest to the morning sun flew higher. The Merlin engine of Johnson's Spitfire gave it enough power that it remained manoeuvrable and superbly responsive even with a 500 lb bomb under the belly (where the drop tank was normally carried) and, for shorter-range missions, another two 250 lb bombs under the wing.

Now a wing commander leading three Canadian Spitfire squadrons, Johnson had been flying Spitfires over France since he was one of Douglas Bader's wingmen back in 1941. In the previous months, Johnson's Spitfires had continued flying Ramrod escort missions for Allied bombers. But these missions, though bitterly opposed by massed flak, encountered few Luftwaffe fighters, most of which had been withdrawn to the defence of Germany. In 1944, throughout Europe, the Spitfire's primary opponent was flak, not German fighters. Johnson was aware that flak was more lethal to Spitfire pilots than fighters.

Since early 1944, fighter-bombers (including Spitfires) had joined USAAF and RAF bombers in escalating attacks against what were called

'Noball' sites in northern France's Pas de Calais region. Intelligence had linked these to German missile development. Most sinister were the 'ski sites', curved concrete structures that looked like ski jumps. It did not require access to highly classified intelligence to realise that something unpleasant would be using the ski sites for a quick trip to England.

Most Allied attacks, however, were launched against decoy sites. The actual sites remained camouflaged. But for Johnson's Canadian Spitfire wing and all of 2 TAF's Spitfire squadrons, attacks on Noball sites were a primary mission, alternating with Armament Practice Camps and joint training with ground forces in Britain, all making ready for the upcoming invasion. Today, the target was rail junctions near Cleves.

Spitfires would attack a target on their first pass, rather than overflying to identify it, alerting the defenders. Whenever possible, a clearly identifiable initial point (IP) on the ground would be selected. Over the IP, Spitfires would then turn on a pre-briefed heading for the time needed to bring them over the target. This required good photo reconnaissance in advance of the mission and thorough planning.

Johnson's Spitfire fighter-bombers approached the target from out of the sun, at about 8000–10,000 feet, above the worst flak. But still, he recalled, 'we were bracketed by many bursts of heavy flak'. Despite this, he 'had to make a steady approach to the target at a constant height'. He had to fly over the IP precisely. The Spitfires could not take their usual evasive action when fired at by flak. For a few moments, the Spitfire pilots felt terribly vulnerable and exposed, sitting targets. 'Near the target the flak increased and so did my respect for the bomber boys who had to put up with this sort of thing on all their missions,' Johnson said.

Following Johnson's Spitfire as he turned over the IP, 442 Squadron shifted to a loose echelon formation and throttled up to about 300 mph. When the target was opposite Johnson's Spitfire's wing tip, he pulled up in a climb, the control stick pulled back to kill airspeed, quickly looking around to make sure his flight was following him. Keeping his eyes on the target, he gave the radio call to attack. Peeling off from the formation, the control stick and rudder pushed hard over together, Johnson half-rolled and dived for a few moments, until he saw the target in the Spitfire's upside-down canopy.

Aligning the diving Spitfire with stick and rudder in seconds, he centred the target in his gunsight. Then he rolled, canopy up. The Spitfire,
accelerating, dived at an angle of sixty degrees. Johnson's hand flew to
the trim wheel in the cockpit. The Spitfire had to have its trim control
eased forward, giving it a nose-down trim, otherwise it would pull itself
out of the dive as it accelerated. Lacking dive brakes, the Spitfire was
soon diving at about 450 mph. The guns on the ground fired as fast as
they could.

Johnson held the aiming point of the reflector sight on the target as
it grew larger and larger.[1] It spilled past the illuminated rings on the flat
panel inside the windscreen thrown up by the reflector gunsight.

As the Spitfires, one after another, made their dives on the target,
Johnson wrote, 'the light flak came into its own'. These were not the
black bursts of heavy flak, time fused to spray shrapnel at a predetermined altitude. This light flak was largely the same type of 20mm
cannon and machine guns that armed German fighters. They were
aimed through an 'iron' (non-reflector) gunsight. Some would use tracer
rounds to allow the gunners to correct their aim, stitching bright lights
across the sky with each burst of fire, visible even on a grey spring
morning.

Johnson was one of the many Spitfire pilots who discovered by experience that 'the bombs did not possess the same line of flight as our
Spitfires and if you aimed directly at the target, then the bombs fell
short'.

Dive-bombing had to be judged by eye. The Spitfire's barometric
altimeter lagged in a high-speed dive. Aiming through the gunsight was
found to lead to 'target fascination' – in which the pilot pulled up too
late or, sometimes, not at all – concentrating on hitting the target. Many
Spitfires, in practice as well as on operations, flew into the ground while
dive-bombing. Johnson judged by the way the target rushed to expand
past the outer illuminated ring of the reflector gunsight. Gently, he
started a gradual pull-out, easing back on the stick. He counted to three.
Then he hit the bomb release.

The delay was needed for the Spitfire to survive. If a bomb, especially
a 500-pounder carried under the Spitfire's belly, was released in a dive,
it was likely to hit the propeller. Because the pilot was not looking at the

target at the moment when the bombs released, dive-bombing was inaccurate.

Johnson released his bomb at 5000-foot altitude, which meant the bombs would come off at about 4000 feet. The minimum safe altitude for bomb release was 3000 feet. If bombs were dropped from 1000 feet or less, they had to be fused with an eleven-second delay to prevent their fragments from damaging the Spitfire when they exploded. Bombs with a delay fuse would either dig themselves a hole before exploding, minimising blast and fragmentation effects, or would bounce on impact, further reducing accuracy. But that day Johnson and 442 Squadron claimed three hits plus near misses.

The Spitfire was now freed of the weight of the bomb. Johnson's first move was to get as far away as possible from the target (and everyone shooting at him) as fast as he could. A too-violent pull-up, hauling back on the stick, could overstress the Spitfire. While catastrophic failures were rare, strained structures were common on dive-bombing Spitfires. Wrinkled skin would appear on the wing above the undercarriage and cannon bays from high-g pull-outs to avoid bomb blasts, requiring first external structural reinforcement and then the use of thicker and stiffer metal skin. It was not just the flak that made these manoeuvres dangerous.

Throttling up, getting away from the flak at low altitude, Johnson rejoined his flight at a pre-briefed assembly point, climbing back to altitude where the squadron would reform, in case the Luftwaffe had put in an appearance and they would have to fight their way home.

That would not be happening today. Instead, one of Johnson's wingmen had been hit by flak – a trail of flame whipped by the slipstream poured from the engine of his Spitfire. Rather than take his chances with the Germans he had just bombed, he was able to keep the Spitfire in the air until it was over the Channel. He was almost back to the English coast before he had to use his parachute. After Johnson and the rest of his flight orbited over him, reporting his position by radio, he was picked up by an RAF amphibious air–sea rescue aircraft.

Different squadrons had to improvise these tactics for themselves.[2] Bill Olmstead, rotated back from Italy and now leading dive-bombing missions in his Spitfire IX, found, 'We were forced to use a trial and error method, for we had no special apparatus to aid us in aiming our bombs.'[3]

Ready for the invasion

Both at high and low altitude, reconnaissance Spitfires contributed to photographing 'the whole invasion area'.[4] Some Spitfire squadrons even trained in glider towing, to enable them to resupply themselves from England with cargo gliders once based across the Channel. Fortunately, this capability was never used in earnest.

ADGB used the still-rare Griffon-engine Spitfires and larger numbers of Spitfire IXs (or Spitfire Vs in less vital locations) to control the airspace over Britain. They could stop bombers, but a few piston-engine German reconnaissance aircraft were able to fly over in daylight in the weeks preceding the invasion and survive. Although between six and forty Spitfires were kept on standing patrols over them in daylight, some twenty-eight invasion ports were photographed in May alone by 'hit and run methods at high altitude in Me 109s, with each aircraft frequently having only enough time to make a few hurried exposures over a port before turning for home'. Leutnant Walther Warthol raced his Bf 109G-8 over British ports at 12,000 metres altitude, GM-1 fuel injection providing a boost to maximum speed that kept him alive.[5] But the German high command found such successes too infrequent to give them a coherent picture. Generaloberst Walter Warlimont, deputy chief of operations of OKW (*Oberkommando der Wehrmacht*, the armed forces high command), said: 'Air reconnaissance was made perhaps every fortnight, and even then was confined to photographs of possible points of embarkation.'[6]

Getting ready for the invasion were Spitfire air–sea rescue squadrons, which had operated since 1941 with unarmed Spitfire IIs and Vs carrying a life raft extra and fuel tanks. If he spotted survivors, the pilot dropped the life raft, then would stay in the area as long as fuel permitted to direct ships or amphibious aircraft for a rescue.

Trafford Leigh-Mallory, promoted from Fighter Command, was now serving as commander of the Allied Expeditionary Air Force, where he would coordinate 2 TAF and the US Ninth Air Force in the coming invasion. In May 1944, he launched Typhoon and Spitfire fighter-bombers in a systematic dive-bombing campaign attacking German radar stations; Johnnie Johnson led his wing on several of these attacks.

On 21 May, the strafing of passenger trains in France in daylight was authorised. In the first two weeks of the combined air offensive against transport targets in northern France, Spitfires were able to claim many of the 500-plus locomotives damaged or destroyed. The Germans attached flak guns mounted on goods wagons to the trains. These fought pitched battles with the fighters, shooting down sixteen Spitfires on 21 May alone and more on successive days: nine on 22 May, eight on 23 May. But daylight rail traffic was effectively halted, limiting the German ability to reinforce and supply the coming ground combat.

The final preparation for the invasion was on 4 June. Overnight, in response to secret, immediate orders coming over the teletypes, all Allied aircraft were painted with black and white stripes on their wings and fuselage: 'invasion stripes', intended as a recognition marking during the great events that were even then in progress.

Spitfires' D-Day
Ships and landing craft filled the English Channel off the Normandy beaches, before the grey and cloudy dawn on 6 June 1944. Nine RAF, RAAF and RCAF Spitfire squadrons arrived to provide the initial air cover at dawn, with more relieving them throughout the day.

Some Spitfire pilots were in the thick of the action, spotting the fall of shells from the naval gunfire of the invasion fleet and radioing back corrections. They included two RAF and four FAA squadrons, flying Spitfires and shore-based Seafires. Some Spitfire Vs were flown by the US Navy, using pilots from battleship and cruiser floatplanes, trained to observe and adjust naval gunfire, as Spitfires were more likely to survive the intense flak that would probably be encountered over Normandy. The spotters operated in pairs, one observing fire, the other looking for threats.

Only a handful of the many Spitfire pilots flying that day had also flown over Dunkirk, four years previously. They looked down on a different picture. The vast naval forces, with British and US battleships leading hundreds of warships and landing craft, were a far cry from the improvised flotillas of Dunkirk. Instead of the heroic little boats, ranks of landing craft, drilled and proficient, brought more and more troops into the battle ashore. Beyond the flames and smoke on the beaches, a powerful air and naval bombardment was striking German positions.

The sky over the invasion was filled with multinational Spitfire pilots, flying a plane designed and built in Britain but using resources from all over the world. The RAF had trained them all, put them in Spitfires and sent them into battle: so many different squadrons, many more nationalities. They were not simply diverse, they were very good, a long way from the force that had suffered heavy losses to numerically inferior German fighters two years before. The Spitfires flying over the invasion beaches were superior in performance, pilot skill, tactics and the all-important numbers.

Spitfire pilots flying over the D-Day invasion saw large numbers of other aircraft, especially other Spitfires. They did not see much of the Luftwaffe; Spitfires claimed only four Ju 88s in air combat on D-Day, while two Spitfires were lost in air combat, one likely in a friendly fire incident. Many German aircraft took off on D-Day, but almost all were shot down or unable to penetrate the barrier of fighters between their airfields and the beaches.[7] Two reconnaissance Bf 109G-8s survived a high-speed, high-altitude dash over the invasion fleet, bringing the German leadership its first photographs. But these were limited in their coverage and, above all, in their impact. General der Infanterie Günther Blumentritt, the chief of staff to *Oberbefelshaber West* (commander-in-chief west), thought that even with all the evidence of the invasion 'OKW did not know on 6 June 1944 whether the events in Normandy were the expected invasion and were to be taken seriously, or whether they were only a diversion.'[8]

The Allies had planned for a great air battle, like those over Dunkirk or Dieppe, potentially lasting for days. But it did not materialise. A total of twenty-seven Spitfire squadrons from 2 TAF and nine from ADGB were in the air over the invasion. 421 Squadron RCAF's Operational Record Book stated: 'The squadron carried out four patrols between dawn and dusk and not a thing was sighted in the air except apparent thousands of Allied aircraft all making their way towards Hitler's European Fortress. Returning pilots report that the Channel seems to be full of sea-going craft of all shapes and sizes.'[9]

Spitfire squadrons were assigned the difficult low cover missions, under the clouds that disrupted air operations throughout D-Day. Naval guns repeatedly fired at any fighters they could see. On D-Day, the Allies flew 12,015 sorties in support of the invasion; against it the Luftwaffe could manage only 319.[10]

Bf 109s over Normandy

The opening days of the battle in Normandy brought intense air combat between Spitfires and Bf 109s. While its military effect on the Allies was limited, the German fighter force's efforts over Normandy constituted a maximum effort. In the days after the invasion, some 1000 of the Bf 109s and Fw 190s defending Germany were deployed to France, as the Luftwaffe had been planning.[11] German fighter strength increased as Bf 109s and Fw 190s flew in to forward airfields in France from Germany, many configured as fighter-bombers. They were fed into the fighting.

Few survived against Allied fighters. On 11 June, five fighter *Gruppen* in France had to be withdrawn due to losses. By 12 June, the Germans ordered a halt to fighter-bomber sorties in Normandy.[12] Fighters weighed down by bombs could not survive long enough to reach a target. Subsequent Luftwaffe fighter air-to-ground missions in Normandy would be limited to strafing and rockets. The primary mission of Bf 109s and Fw 190s alike would be 'to fight the fighter-bombers . . . as these endanger the reinforcements and communications of the Army'.[13]

Galland flew from his office in Berlin to inspect the forward airfields. 'My impressions were shattering. In addition to the appalling conditions there was a far-reaching spiritual decline. This feeling of irrevocable in-feriority, the heavy losses, the hopelessness of the fighting, which had never before been so clearly demonstrated to us.'[14] He reported back to Berlin that 'the pilots were not good at the type of tree-top war fought over the Normandy beachheads . . . Supplies came very slowly over the bombed out railways.'[15] In return, fighter pilots on the forward airfields resented Galland flying back to Berlin while they were left to carry on against Allied air power with little hope of survival, let alone victory.

Reconnaissance sorties were even more dangerous. Leutnant Warthol's unit had one (rare) Bf 109H and because of that the high command 'demanded a mosaic of the whole coast, from Cherbourg to the mouth of the Seine'. This mission, likely to prove suicidal, was never carried out. 'Thank God, it was shot down by our own flak. Our commanding officer got out, he made a belly landing. The whole kite was burnt. We were glad.'[16]

Over Normandy, a few Bf 109Gs flew night sorties as control aircraft for the *Mistel*, a huge guided missile converted from unmanned radio-controlled Ju 88 bombers.[17] The Bf 109G was attached on struts to the explosive-filled bomber until it was time to launch it at its target. The Bf 109G pilot used radio-controlled guidance and miniature thumb-button controls to keep a large flare in the *Mistel*'s tail aligned with the target in his sights. Starting on the night of 24 June, Bf 109Gs launched *Mistel*s against ships offshore on four occasions, damaging a British headquarters ship. Despite its limited success, the *Mistel* appealed to a desperate Luftwaffe command. More were produced, though Bf 109Gs were increasingly replaced as control aircraft by more survivable Fw 190s.

The Luftwaffe fighter force had been defeated over Germany before D-Day, but it was the losses over Normandy, many of them inflicted by Spitfires, that ensured that it would not be able to recover as it had done from setbacks over Britain, Stalingrad and Tunisia. By 30 June, the Luftwaffe had lost 931 aircraft in combat over France, plus 67 from non-combat causes, mostly Bf 109s and Fw 190s.[18] Unteroffizer Gerhard Dolleisch of JG 2, whose Bf 109G-6 was shot down on his seventeenth combat mission on 24 July, told interrogators that the average life of a Bf 109 in his unit was twelve hours of flight time. Although replacement Bf 109G-14s were flown in straight from the production lines, Allied air superiority remained unchallenged. Yet the Luftwaffe fighter force diverted Allied fighters, especially Spitfires, that could otherwise have been used to support the ground battle. Half of the 2 TAF fighter sorties flown throughout June and July were in air-to-air missions, compared with about 40 per cent air-to-ground, with most of the remainder being tactical reconnaissance.

Spitfires against the German Army

Spitfires arrived on forward airstrips in Normandy and were operational by 10 June. Spitfire fighter-bombers needed to be based as close to their targets as possible; carrying an under-fuselage drop tank effectively halved the Spitfire's maximum bomb load. Free French Spitfire squadrons were overjoyed to be home. Other squadrons, used to England, had 'Mark XXX' Spitfires ferry in 18-gallon beer barrels under each wing, attached to the bomb racks. By 27 June, thirty Spitfire squadrons were based in France, many within range of German artillery, if not sniper fire, using fuel and ordnance brought across the beaches or flown in on transport aircraft. The dust raised on the hastily built forward strips, using prefabricated pierced steel planking (PSP) runways, clogged Merlins' air intakes. Hoses were used to wet down runways. Pilots switched to flying in army-issue battledress uniforms, in case they were forced down in the forward area. England-based Spitfires continued operating over Normandy, including the Spitfires and Seafires responsible for directing Anglo-American naval gunfire; fifty of these aircraft were put up to support the bombardment of Cherbourg on 25 June that preceded the German surrender.

Wing Commander Johnnie Johnson, despite the skill in air-to-air combat that made him the British Commonwealth's highest-scoring living ace with thirty-three victories, led his wing flying dive-bombing Spitfires in the climactic battles of the Normandy campaign. RAF fighter-bomber squadrons were part of a highly responsive system and could hit a target within an hour of being called for, within minutes if they were flying 'cab rank' combat air patrols. The troops could see these fighter-bombers circling just out of flak range during attacks, waiting to be called in.

On 29 June, two German SS Panzer divisions concentrated for a massed counter-attack. It was, in the words of their commander, General Paul 'Papa' Hausser, 'scheduled to begin at seven o'clock in the morning but hardly had the tanks assembled when they were attacked by fighter-bombers. This disrupted the troops so much that the attack did not start again until two-thirty in the afternoon.'[19] Such effects were more important than the number of tanks destroyed.

On 17 July, Spitfire fighter-bombers strafed and wounded

Generalfeldmarschall Erwin Rommel, the 'Desert Fox', now commanding German forces in Normandy. His staff car was one of the many German vehicles that found they could not move in daylight and survive on French roads. A month before, Rommel had sent a message to his superiors on the fighter-bombers. 'Our own operations are rendered extraordinarily difficult and in part impossible to carry out [owing to] the exceptionally strong and, in some respects, overwhelming superiority of the enemy air force. The enemy had complete control of the air over the battle zone and up to 100 kilometres behind the front and cuts off by day almost all traffic on roads.'[20]

A German armoured counter-attack against the US Army at Mortain, seeking to cut off the breakout from Normandy, was defeated on 7 August with the help of RAF rocket-firing Typhoons, supported by Spitfires with bombs and cannon.[21] The surviving German units tried to retreat north-west, through the Normandy town of Falaise, in the gap between the two advancing Allied armies.

Johnnie Johnson's Canadian squadrons were among those operating over the Falaise Gap, averaging six sorties per Spitfire per day. 'Immediately the Typhoons withdrew from the killing ground, the Spitfires raced into the attack. The tactics of the day were low-level strafing attacks with cannon shells and machine guns against soft-skinned transports, including all types of trucks, staff cars and lightly armoured vehicles.'[22] Frank Wooton, a RAF war artist, was carrying out research at the scene:

> The assault lasted for ten days and turned defeat into an utter rout. The aircraft took off in pairs, averaging over one thousand sorties a day. I went down to the battlefield together with the pilots. The ground was littered with burnt-out vehicles and armour, some caught nose-to-tail in deeply cut roads. The grey-clad bodies of German soldiers were everywhere, some still in their vehicles sprawled in the seats, others on the running boards staring up into the sky, while in the neighbouring fields lay those tried to seek safety off the roads.[23]

While many of the German Army's personnel escaped through the Falaise Gap, little of their equipment did.

There are no easy days in air combat. The 2 TAF Spitfire squadrons often needed to fight for air superiority and scored the vast majority of RAF victories over France (Typhoons did little dogfighting). This, and the reliance on strafing attacks, often limited Spitfires' dive-bombing. In August, 83 Group RAF's twelve squadrons of Spitfires were responsible for only 747 of its 6071 bombs dropped. Radar and 'Y' service detachments, arriving in Normandy, provided a vital edge in situational awareness. 83 Group's 'Y' service alone was credited with enabling ninety-five air-to-air kills in the eight weeks after D-Day.

Over Normandy, the Spitfire again played a major role in the air war. Together with USAAF P-47s and RAF and USAAF P-51s, they defeated a maximum effort by the Luftwaffe so completely that, years after, many were unaware that Normandy was where Germany lost any chance of reconstituting its fighter force.

Seafires over southern France
Air cover for Operation Dragoon, the amphibious invasion of southern France on 15 August, was provided by Royal and US Navy aircraft carriers. Offshore were ninety-seven improved Seafire IIIs, which had gone into production by Westland and Cunliffe-Owen in April 1943, powered by a Merlin 55 engine with the automatic supercharger boost control and four-blade propeller used by Spitfire IXs. Many (designated Mark LIII) had a supercharger using the fast-climbing Spitfire LF V's cropped impeller blades. Unlike its predecessors, the Seafire III had double-folding wings, the wing roots hinged to fold up manually and the wing tips hinged to fold down. They could be accommodated on a carrier's hangar deck elevator. A great improvement from the navy's standpoint, folding reduced the strength of the wings by 10 per cent and, as Joe Smith pointed out, 'resulted in increased weight'.[24]

Seafires flew air defence missions over the invasion, directed by controllers on radar-equipped cruisers. As the limited German air opposition faded, the Seafires shifted to more dangerous fighter-bomber, dive-bombing and armed reconnaissance missions. The Seafire accident rate was less than that experienced the year before during the Salerno invasion, reflecting improved procedures developed by experienced test pilots, including Winkle Brown and Jeffrey Quill.[25]

Seafires flew 1073 carrier-based sorties covering the invasion and 'wrote off' fourteen aircraft.

Within days, an RAF Spitfire wing and several French Air Force Spitfire squadrons flew in to southern France from Corsica, allowing the carriers and Seafires to withdraw. The RAF wing flew fighter-bomber attacks until deploying to Italy. The French Spitfire squadrons, back home, joined in the fight to complete *La Libération*.

Spitfire developments

Intelligence reports of the development of Messerschmitt's jet- and rocket-powered fighters had led to the development of the Griffon-engined Spitfire PR 19. It entered service in May 1944, using the Spitfire XIV's two-stage supercharger on a 2035 hp Griffon 65 engine powering the Spitfire XI's long-range airframe and cameras. Its improved pressurised cockpit made high-altitude flight more endurable, though its large wing tanks made it nose-heavy, especially on the ground. Capable of operating at 45,000–49,000 feet, it was the ultimate reconnaissance Spitfire.

An Anglo-American hybrid, the Spitfire XVI, started production alongside Mark IXs at Castle Bromwich in 1944 and went into service in December; its Spitfire IX airframe was powered by a US-built 1705 hp Packard Merlin 266. This helped ensure that Spitfire production would not be further disrupted by Merlin production bottlenecks (which had included a major strike in the Glasgow factory in November 1943); in February 1944 120 completed Spitfire airframes were awaiting engines. Many of the Packard engines suffered from quality control problems. Sustained high boost using 150-octane fuel led to engine failures and fires. Rolls-Royce were better at detecting minute cracks. Like Spitfire IXs, many Spitfire XVIs flying fighter-bomber missions had three feet of wing tip clipped back to reduce the aerodynamic stresses on the wing root after several fatal in-flight failures; this made the wing an estimated 10 per cent stronger.[26] The Spitfire LF XVI had the same supercharger performance as the LF IX.

Some Spitfires came off the production lines with a cut-down rear fuselage and a teardrop canopy for improved all-around visibility (but some loss of directional stability). The oxygen supply was relocated to the wings. In development since 1943, these modifications appeared on many late-production Spitfire IXs, XVIs and later marks, reaching operational units by early 1945. Taking her first flight in one of these Spitfires, Diana Barnato, the ATA ferry pilot, put it into a roll, spinning it along its axis, seeing the earth and sky quickly change places, enjoying the superb all-around vision provided by the new canopy. When she inverted the Spitfire, her compact slipped from her flight suit pocket and fell, hitting the canopy frame. The compact burst open. Everything in the Spitfire's cockpit was coated with powder, including the pilot. She arrived at her destination airfield with a stark white face.[27]

From 1941, most Spitfires had gone into combat armed either with two 20mm cannon and four .303 Browning machine guns or four cannon. In 1944, the two .303 machine guns in each wing were replaced by one US-built M2 .50-calibre machine gun, starting with the Spitfire IXE.

The Spitfire 21, powered by the 2035 hp Griffon 61 engine, had Alan Clifton's redesigned wing with a stronger internal structure that accommodated both armament and fuel tanks. Improved ailerons allowed effective control even at high speeds. The design incorporated many of the 'Super Spitfire' changes developed for the Spitfire IV and XX before they were cancelled, including flush riveting and undercarriage doors that completely enclosed the main wheels. Four-20mm-cannon armament was standard. Despite development problems after the first Spitfire 21 proper flew the following month, it was pushed into production in March 1944.

Initial service tests of the Spitfire 21 showed it was unstable. The best the RAF could say was that, while not a danger to its pilots, it was not likely to be a successful fighter. The Air Fighting Development Unit (AFDU) added a telling recommendation: the Spitfire design, pushed beyond its limits, should not be developed further.

Even though 3000 Spitfire 21s had been ordered, production was halted until the design could be modified. Supermarine again turned to Jeffrey Quill for the test flying. 'From the time I first flew the Spitfire 21, it was clear that we had a hot potato. There was too much power for the aeroplane and what was needed were much larger tail surfaces, both horizontal and vertical. The work to design these was already in hand, but would take several months to complete.'[28]

The redesigned larger tail made the Spitfire 21 more flyable. Incorporating changes meant that none would be in the hands of operational units in 1944. With the Royal Navy looking ahead to intense fighting off Japan, however, a Spitfire 21 was successfully deck-landed on a carrier in November 1944, leading to an urgent programme to build a Seafire version. The comprehensive changes and extensive fixes of the Spitfire 21 absorbed 165,000 design man-hours, more than any other mark since the original Spitfire I. It remained a success; despite their initial problems, Smith and the Supermarine design team had been able to once again design a better Spitfire. But with the end of the war approaching, and the threat of increased numbers of jet aircraft entering service with the Luftwaffe, even the best possible Spitfire might not be good enough to meet RAF needs.

Spitfires against the V-1

RAF Spitfires were once more defending England from a daylight air threat. Though German bombers could no longer get through to London, either by day or night, on a sustained basis, the V-1 offensive against England opened on 13 June. Over 2000 were launched from ground sites in northern France during the first nine days alone.

The V-1, first of Hitler's promised 'vengeance weapons', was a cruise missile. It flew like a high-speed aeroplane, powered by a pulse jet engine based on the ones Willy Messerschmitt had considered back in 1935. Its airframe was designed by Dr Robert Lusser, who had helped design the Bf 109. Messerschmitt had kept his interest in the V-1: in 1942 he had written to Theo Croneiss of its potential to bombard London; and later, he had personally urged Hitler to use them *en masse* or not at all.[29]

Initially, ADGB did not have effective tactics against the V-1. Spitfire IXs and XIIs proved not fast enough for V-1 interception missions. V-1s flew at 350–400 mph at 2500–3000 feet. Spitfire squadrons tried to gain speed: wings were waxed to smooth the airflow (gaining up to 9 mph), rear-view mirrors detached (another 1 mph), and armour and camouflage paint removed. But the V-1s were too fast for 11 Group controllers to scramble fighters against them. Fighters had to be kept aloft in standing patrols. Ground control was decentralised, broadcasting just the flight path of incoming V-1s. Fighters crowded to get the 'easy' V-1s, while others slipped through unintercepted.

Three squadrons of Griffon-engined Spitfire XIVs were committed to the defence of London, flying standing patrols. The RAF turned to Rolls-Royce and the RAE at Farnborough, whose engineers included 'Tilly' Shilling (of orifice fame).[30] In a quick-reaction development and testing programme, the top speed of the Spitfire and other fighters was increased by allowing a surge of increased supercharger boost, hence higher manifold pressure and greater speed. This was made possible by the use of 100/150-octane aviation fuel, which Eighth Air Force fighters had started using in June. The Spitfire XIV's top speed was increased by about 30 mph to some 400 mph at 2000 feet, although, Winkle Brown wrote, 'the engines would crack up unusually quickly'.[31]

Reinforcements included RAF Mustangs and the first Gloster Meteor jet fighters. But the RAF's Hawker Tempest V, faster than the Spitfire at the V-1's altitude, became the most effective interceptor. Bombing of the Noball launch sites increased. Anti-aircraft guns, redeployed, used US-provided fire control radar and proximity fuses.[32]

A small, receding target, the V-1 was almost impossible to hit at a range of over 300 yards. Yet, if a fighter closed in on a V-1, it was likely to be destroyed in the explosion of the missile's one-tonne Amatol high-explosive warhead, lethal at a radius of up to 150 yards and capable of damaging a fighter at up to 200 yards. One alternative, first demonstrated on 23 June, was for a Spitfire to fly alongside, slip its wing tip under the V-1's wing and then roll sharply. This tipped the V-1's stabilising gyro: it immediately plummeted and exploded on impact with the ground. A fighter overtaking a V-1 in a dive and catching it in its slipstream could also make it crash.

The RAF's veteran 91 Squadron flew Spitfire XIVs defending London from the V-1s. Losses were heavy. On 26 July, Flying Officer Eugene 'Gin' Seghers, an experienced Belgian Spitfire pilot, pressed his attack on a V-1 so close that he collided with it. He died when the warhead exploded. On 31 July, another 91 Squadron Spitfire XIV was lost and its pilot, Malta veteran Pilot Officer Patrick Schade, DFM, was killed in a collision with a Tempest. Both were attacking the same V-1.

On 3 August at 12.45 p.m., over Rolvenden in Kent, Flight Lieutenant Jean Maridor, DFC, intercepted a V-1.

Maridor had flown Spitfires since 1942 – scoring four victories (including Paul Galland) and ten V-1s – and had turned down promotion to command a French Air Force squadron to stay with 91 Squadron. No RAF fighter squadron was so multinational as this unit, which brought together fighter pilots from throughout the world, always including a number of Frenchmen. Maridor constantly reminded his squadron mates of the need to avoid collateral damage when operating over France.[33] He planned to get married to a WRAF officer on 11 August.

Diving, Maridor opened fire. He hit the V-1 at long range. It did not explode but went into a dive. Maridor could see it was seemingly heading directly towards Benenden School, which housed a hospital, marked by a large red cross.

Maridor dived his Spitfire after the V-1 as it plummeted closer to the hospital. He closed in so that he would be sure to hit. Then he fired again, apparently aiming at the warhead. It exploded. At that range, the blast took off the Spitfire's wing. According to those who witnessed the incident on the ground, Maridor had closed in to ensure he would destroy the V-1, even though this put him too close to its warhead to survive.

V-1 attacks on Britain were reduced after the launch sites in the Pas de Calais region were overrun in August–September. V-1 attacks on Britain continued at a reduced rate. Modified He 111 bombers provided nocturnal airborne launch platforms. With the reduced V-1 threat, the RAF retired the Spitfire XIIs, their engines burned out and airframes strained, and moved most Spitfire XIVs to airfields on the continent. Spitfires claimed over 630 V-1s shot down.

17

The Luftwaffe's Fighters at Bay

June 1944–January 1945

The Allied bomber offensive was entering its final phase; some 72 per cent of the total bomb tonnage to fall on Germany did so after 1 July 1944.[1] The Eighth Air Force had ten groups of P-51 fighters, eventually increased to fourteen. These were often joined by P-51s from the Ninth and Fifteenth air forces and the RAF and drop-tank-equipped P-47s and P-38s.[2] Luftwaffe fighters were damaging less than 1 per cent of the USAAF bombers attaching Germany; a year previously, that figure had been 18.2 per cent.[3]

Relentless attrition
On 28 June, Göring ordered an end to bomber production and crew training. While this instruction was never fully implemented, it meant the *Jägerstab* now controlled the whole aviation industry. Bomber pilots were sent to fighter units. German pilots received a maximum of eighty hours – usually half that – on an operational aircraft once they had completed initial flight training, Their RAF and USAAF opponents received 225 hours or more.

The destruction of poorly trained replacement fighter pilots and the inexorable hunting down of the surviving *Experten* accelerated. Only *Gruppe* and *Staffel* leaders had as much as six months' experience; a small percentage had three months'; most pilots had eight to thirty days' experience.[4] Everyone else was gone: killed, crippled or a prisoner of war.

Losses to accidents and USAAF fighters started even before combat. Pilots straight out of training were given a thirty-hour course in Bf 109Gs before being sent to combat units. Despite the use of modified two-seat trainer Bf 109G-12s, of just under a hundred pilots who started one such course in spring 1944, thirty-two were killed before they could complete their thirty hours.[5] Even those who survived training had limited instrument flying capabilities. Only two *Jagdgeschwadern* were capable of bad-weather operations; other pilots required a 500-metre ceiling and 2000 metres visibility to land and could not penetrate clouds denser than 700 metres.[6] Göring demanded greater capability, but there was insufficient fuel or instructors to carry out instrument training.[7]

Lieutenant Colonel Francis 'Gabby' Gabreski, a P-47 ace, found, 'The quality of the Luftwaffe pilots we were facing now had deteriorated markedly from the tough guys we had faced in the same skies in the previous summer.'[8] Johnnie Johnson said of German fighter pilots that 'except for a leader here and there, they seemed a poor lot who bore little resemblance to those fierce and highly trained pilots who had fought so well over Britain'.[9] Hauptmann Anton Hackl, a leading German ace, agreed: 'Our older pilots were very good, but the new ones coming from the training schools could do little more than take off and land the aircraft; they could not fly well enough to do much in action. I had my younger pilots fly with more experienced ones and told them to stay close to their leaders. Of course, if the leader was shot down, the inexperienced pilot was almost helpless.'[10]

On 22 June, Dr Josef Goebbels, minister of propaganda and an astute observer of Nazi Germany, noted in his diary that the Luftwaffe was in the midst of crises of both material and morale.[11] To Oberstleutnant Johannes Kogler, *Kommodore* of JG 6, 'It was terrible to be in command of a unit with young, idealistic pilots coming in from the training schools and knowing that two or three battles later most would be dead or maimed. And it was terrible for them as well, for they soon learned how slim were their chances of survival.'[12] Oberstleutnant Johannes Steinhoff saw that 'A man with virtually no chance of survival grows disillusioned and bitter and is not inclined to mince his words. But our sarcasm had assumed forms incomprehensible to anyone who was not so vulnerable.'[13]

It was apparent to Luftwaffe fighter pilots that they were all being shot down. They did not have to receive the accountings sent to Galland and the high command. They could see the turnover in their own units, every day. Yet they still went up and fought until they too went down. If they survived, they walked away from the wreckage or gathered up their parachute and went up again, until their luck ran out.

Then, they died or were crippled. They died sitting in the cockpits of their fighters, burning out in the air, burying themselves deep in German soil, or making a mistake on a final approach, leaving a wreck that had to be quickly taken away before it discouraged the replacement pilots. They died whenever the USAAF was in the air over Germany, or even when it was not, especially when the German weather closed in on them and the red 'fuel low' lights were burning in the cockpits. The poorly trained pilots died alongside the skilled veterans, who had lived to fight in the air and had decorations around their necks and dozens of victory scores, mainly from the east, painted on the rudders of their Bf 109s. They all died with an inevitability and a rapidity that neither RAF nor USAAF pilots had ever experienced. Yet they continued to go up, to demand more fuel and another chance at the bombers.

Coercion was part of their motivation, for industry and Luftwaffe alike. Over 5000 workers were executed in 1944.[14] At the Erla Bf 109 factory in Leipzig, 'troublemakers' were hanged as an example.[15] Many more workers were sent to concentration camps. Göring signed a succession of death sentences for cowardice and failure to fight to the end. These increased as Hitler blamed Luftwaffe cowardice for defeat over Germany. Ultra intercepted an order: 'The *Reichsmarschall* ... has empowered *Luftflotte* Reich to set up instant courts-martial to try offenders on the spot, and where cowardice is proved to shoot them in front of the assembled personnel.'

While the Luftwaffe never matched the army's widespread use of the firing squad, the vast apparatus of repression focused on fighter pilots as things fell apart. Galland, as the most visible fighter pilot, became a prime suspect. 'The Gestapo made many visits to front commands, even rear commands. I had more than one visit from these fellows, who were hoping to ferret out dissent.' The attempted assassination of Hitler on 20 July 1944 increased the regime's internal savagery. Korten, the Luftwaffe chief of staff, died in the blast. General Werner Kreipe, who had battled Spitfires over Dunkirk, was his appointed acting successor.[16]

In fighter units, commanders were able to enforce discipline by sending in for transfer to the infantry the names of pilots who seemed unwilling to fight. With fuel running out, over 200,000 Luftwaffe personnel, including fighter pilots, were sent to fight on the ground. A few more added in because they flinched in air combat went unnoticed. But Galland still saw disciplinary problems in the fighter force as 'almost non-existent'.[17] To ensure it remained so, German fighter pilots were sent on guided tours of bombed-out cities. Years after the war, Galland remembered how 'the population was suffering in such terrible ways'. The new jet fighters were publicised; these would turn the course of the air war. Wives were banished from within fifty kilometres of operational fighter fields, to ensure that the pilots were focusing on fighting rather than their families.[18]

Renewed air combat over Germany

Allied targeting of synthetic oil plants, begun in May, was sustained through the following months. Luftwaffe fighters could still inflict painful losses. On 20 June 1944, forty-nine US bombers and twelve fighters were shot down. The next day, forty-four US bombers were shot down, twenty by fighters. But at the end of June, the Luftwaffe had lost 4080 Bf 109s and Fw 190s in the preceding three months, 74.9 per cent of them in the west and defending Germany.

July 1944 marked the high point of German aircraft production, with fighters comprising three-quarters of the aircraft produced. Monthly production of Bf 109s and Fw 190s increased from 1016 in February to 2615 in July.[19] Bf 109 production rose from 6418 in 1943 to 14,213 in 1944. This was made possible by efficient use of labour, a few skilled technicians and masses of the unskilled and enslaved.

But it no longer really mattered how many Bf 109s came off German production lines. Due to the heavy losses, shortage of fuel and lack of trained pilots, this tremendous increase in production did not mean more fighters were available to defend Germany. At the end of June, the Luftwaffe had 1180 Bf 109s in the hands of its *Jagdgruppen* but only 1375 fighters in total were operational: 370 defending the Reich, 425 in western Europe, 475 in the east, 65 in the Balkans and 40 in Norway.[20] The Luftwaffe could still strike back by day only when it accumulated enough fuel, although the fewer night fighters remained highly lethal. At the same time, the Bf 109's enemies were increasing in numbers and capabilities. More P-51s were flying from bases in England and Italy.

The offensive against synthetic oil, like the attacks earlier in the year against the aircraft industry, forced the German fighter force to do battle. Sometimes, they could still inflict heavy losses; usually these were inflicted by heavily armed and armoured Fw 190 *Sturmjägers*, escorted by large numbers of Bf 109Gs. On 7 July, one successful *Gefechtsverband* attack accounted for most of the twenty-three B-24 bombers lost that day over Germany.

Attacks continued on the aircraft industry. The heavily bombed Erla Bf 109 factory at Leipzig dispersed to over twenty locations, with its remaining buildings used only for final assembly. A factory at Genshagen, near Berlin, producing the Bf 109G's DB 605 engine had its output cut by 40 per cent by air attacks in June–September. Its machinery was moved into a gypsum mine at Neckar-Els near Heidelberg, codenamed *Goldfisch*, where high humidity made working conditions unbearable and led to widespread corrosion. The Henschel plant at Kassel, also producing DB 605s, was bombed but able to resume production after dispersal. But it took until September 1944 for even half the engine industry's machine tools to be dispersed.

The Luftwaffe's massive losses continued, only being checked when, by the end of July, Allied bombing had knocked out the bulk of aviation fuel production, grounding most German fighters and curtailing training. New pilots received four or five hours' training on Bf 109G-12 two-seat trainers, then were sent to units. Their first combat mission was also their first solo Bf 109 flight and, for many, their last. Johannes Kogler described his experience: 'With 15 planes I attacked a formation of 60. Of these 15 planes not one returned. Next day, I took off with eight planes we had raked together and I was the only one to return.'[21]

With the oil attacks in full swing and the Luftwaffe fighter force reeling, the Spitfire joined the strategic air offensive over Germany. RAF bombers could now operate over Germany more safely by day than night. On 27 August, the RAF sent 200 heavy bombers over Meerbeck refinery in daylight. Escort to the target was nine squadrons, 117 ADGB Spitfires, with 90-gallon slipper tanks, operating at extreme range from bases in England. A further seven squadrons with over eighty Spitfires took over the escort for the return trip. The attack was a success. Encountering no fighter opposition, not a single bomber was lost. Meerbeck refined no more oil until the end of October. Ten days later, Spitfires joined with USAAF P-51s to escort 139 RAF bombers to the submarine yards at Emden. Following that, as Air Vice Marshal 'Boy' Bouchier recalled, 'We regularly escorted Bomber Command, in day-light, to their targets in Germany, with negligible and often no losses.'[22] RAF Lend–Lease Mustangs took over escort missions once the V-1 campaign ended.

On 6 September, 200 England-based Spitfires flew escort missions for large-scale Bomber Command daylight missions against German airfields in the Netherlands, encountering no air opposition. This was preparation for Operation Market Garden, the Allied airborne offen-sive in the Netherlands that ended with the unsuccessful attempt to secure a Rhine crossing at Arnhem. Even though the Luftwaffe com-mitted most of its remaining day fighters and fuel from Germany to try to defeat Allied air transport operations, Spitfires and other fighters pre-vented any sustained attacks on the unarmed transport aircraft, except on a single day, 21 September, when Luftwaffe fighters shot down twenty-six transports.

In September 1944, the Spitfire squadrons of 2 TAF moved from their forward airstrips in Normandy to Belgium and the Netherlands. The RAF managed to set up a logistics pipeline that kept them supplied with the 100/150-grade fuel. The fighters were soon fol-lowed by navigational beacons and radars from the Allied Microwave Early Warning (MEW) radar system.[23] Allied radar coverage over much of Germany provided enhanced situational awareness, supple-menting communications interception reported to fighter leaders in flight by the British 'Y' service and its USAAF counterparts (VHF radio transmissions were easier to pick up than from England).[24] Fighter-bomber formations were used to attack area targets through overcast conditions, directed by ground controllers using US-built SCR-584 microwave fire-control radars to track their flight path to a pre-computed bomb release point.

The ultimate developments

Both the USAAF and RAF had substantial numbers of fighters powered by engines in the 2000 hp class. It was 1944 before the Germans were able to produce such engines. The DB 605 series showed the limitations of German engineering that designed larger, slower-turning engines; the Bf 109's light fighter design limited the use of larger engines to achieve more power as had been done with the Spitfire. German engine design was hindered by lack of alloys. More powerful German engines had to use thicker steel, hence were larger, weighed more and were hard to fit on the Bf 109.[25] German engines could not achieve the levels of boost that the Merlin and the Griffon attained. Daimler-Benz, for all their skill, were never as good as Rolls-Royce with supercharger design and fabrication. A DB 605A engine had to be removed for inspection if it exceeded its maximum permissible revolutions per minute (rpm) by as little as 2 per cent; a Merlin had a comparable safety margin of 20 per cent. The lack of high-octane aviation fuel – many Bf 109s with engines designed for 96-octane were flying on 87-octane – meant the Germans had to achieve improved engine performance by use of nitrous oxide and water–methanol injections.

The Bf 109K was an attempt to integrate, in a Bf 109G airframe, the largest engine (the 2000 hp DB 605DCM with both nitrous oxide and water–methanol injections) and the largest cannon (an engine-mounted 30mm MK 108) that would fit. Cowlings without 'bumps', Erla hoods and improved-visibility cockpit designs, introduced on late-production Bf 109Gs, were standard. Reflecting Speer's influence, the attempt was made with the Bf 109K to impose one Bf 109 design that would be produced by all of the dispersed German aircraft industry.

The Bf 109K-1 and K-2 (with, respectively, pressurised and unpressurised cockpits) were little different from late-production Bf 109Gs and were not manufactured. The first production version, the

Bf 109K–4 – with a pressurised cockpit and DB 605DB or DC engine (more powerful DB 605D versions) – went into service in October 1944. The Bf 109K–6 was the most heavily armed version, with three 30mm cannon (two under the wing) and two synchronised 13mm machine guns and a DB 605DCM engine (with water–methanol injection). The tailwheel was both tall and retractable. This was the last Bf 109 version to go into production in Germany. The Bf 109K–14 was to have had a DB 605L engine with a two-stage supercharger, armed with one 30mm MK 108 cannon and two 13mm machine guns. It never saw combat. Still in prototype form was the Bf 109L, to be powered by a 1750 hp Jumo 213E engine.

The Bf 109K was never able to replace the Bf 109G. The powerful engine and the lack of a redesigned tail section to handle the torque led the Bf 109K, even when flown without external armament, to retain the potentially lethal handling characteristics of many of the Bf 109G series. The few Bf 109K–6s that made it to combat units usually had their underwing guns removed to improve handling and performance against the omnipresent Allied fighters.

Production problems increased. Many airframes never received engines. Dr Karl Frydag was managing aircraft production for Saur in 1944–5. 'At Regensburg they made the 109 and they went over to a new type of 109 that was called the K-4 or K-6. It was badly made and we took a machine to Tempelhof and showed the workers they had made bad work. This was the influence of the bombing.'[26]

By the time the Bf 109K was in service, the USAAF's main opponent over Germany – as elsewhere – was flak, not fighters. While almost every major Luftwaffe fighter ace was shot down, most several times, in air combat, they were unable, in return, to shoot down any major USAAF ace, but many of these were lost to flak, especially when strafing airfields.[27]

Defeat in the east

Fighter units on the eastern front had been spared the repeated cycles of destruction, rebuilding and more destruction seen in the west. There was no sustained Soviet effort to locate and destroy German fighters on their forward airstrips. But when the Soviet summer offensive opened on

22 June 1944, the increasing strength and capability of Soviet fighter units meant the Luftwaffe could prevent collapse only by massing their remaining fighters. Elsewhere, the Soviets controlled the air.

Finns, Romanians and Bulgarians all switched sides (and Slovakia tried) as the Soviets advanced. Romanian and Bulgarian Bf 109s saw combat as Allied aircraft. Romanian Bf 109s fought German Bf 109s.[28] One Romanian Bf 109G, hastily repainted in pre-war US markings, flew to Italy carrying a US prisoner-of-war colonel in the radio compartment. He arranged the airlift of the remaining prisoners. Hungarian Bf 109 units fought on alongside the Luftwaffe even as their homeland was overrun by the Soviets.

'A new breed of Russian pilots emerged, flying excellent native fighters,' found veteran Bf 109 pilot Oberstleutnant Dieter Hrabak.[29] These included La-7s and Yak-3s, with higher performance than the standard Yak-9 fighter. The Yak-3's low-altitude manoeuvrability led Luftwaffe fighter pilots to call it 'The Spitfire of the east'.[30] The Soviet Air Force in 1943, in the words of German Army Generalmajor Erich Dethleffsen, 'was a negligible factor, in 1944 an unpleasant one, and in 1945 a decisive one'.[31]

Air battles over Germany

When the Germans were able to repair enough of their synthetic oil plants to produce fuel and enough of their transport system to move it to fighter units, the costly battles continued. The Eighth Air Force recognised that the Luftwaffe had 'resumed aerial warfare'. Revised tactics included 'mass attacks against the rear of bomber formations ... As many as 20 fighters of single-engine types have been reported in one of the "fronts". Each "front" represented a wave and behind the first wave one or more waves have followed.'[32] With each new crisis, *Staffeln* or *Gruppen* of Bf 109s and a few tonnes of the now-precious aviation fuel were moved around, but the Germans had no way to stop the bombers.

On 11 September, over 1000 US and 379 RAF bombers hit oil targets in daylight. The RAF repeated their escort tactics, sending twenty squadrons of Spitfires, plus Mustangs and Tempests, over Germany. The Luftwaffe avoided the RAF, but some 500 German fighters intercepted the US bombers; US escort fighters claimed 115 shot down and 42 strafed, for the loss of 17 of their own. The next day the US fighters claimed 54 shot down and 26 strafed for the loss of 12. The attacks on oil targets on 11–13 September cost 91 US and 17 RAF heavy bombers, mainly to flak. Synthetic aviation fuel production fell to 7000 tonnes in September, less than 5 per cent of what it had been five months before. The heavy losses of Bf 109s even included two from the Swiss Air Force. Escorting a damaged B-24 bomber to a Swiss airfield, they were shot down by P-51s that obviously mistook them for attacking Germans.

Yet the Luftwaffe fighters could still strike back. Captain Leonard 'Kit' Carson, a P-51 pilot, would encounter formations of 'a hundred Me 109s flying top cover at 32,000 feet for a main attack group of 75 Fw 190s at about 28,000 feet'. On 27 September a combat wing of B-24s, off course and without escort, lost 26 bombers in three minutes to 100 single-engine fighters. The next day, another formation of some 100 single-engine fighters over Magdeburg overwhelmed the escort and destroyed 17 B-17s. 'The Reich defence forces during this period were quick to take advantage of any lapses,' according to a USAAF assessment.[33] But such successes were rare. By the end of September, the Luftwaffe had lost, in the preceding three months, 4936 Bf 109s and Fw 190s, 81.9 per cent of them in defence of Germany and in the west, and over 1000 fighter pilots killed or seriously wounded. Such losses came on top of two years of sustained attrition. In the two years since the US daylight bomber offensive had started, 21,139 Bf 109s and Fw 190s had been lost, 65 per cent of them over Germany and the west.

Spitfires against the jet fighters

On 5 October 1944, a bright and partially overcast autumn day, when it was increasingly obvious that the war was not going to be over by Christmas, the Spitfire had its first encounter with an Me 262. The jet was bombing, as Hitler had wanted. But, from over 13,000 feet, its two bombs fell inaccurately.

Near Nijmegen in the Netherlands, Squadron Leader 'Rod' Smith was leading a patrol of twelve Spitfire IXs from 401 Squadron RCAF at 13,000 feet, higher than 2 TAF Spitfires normally flew. Alerted by radar warnings relayed through a ground controller, he turned the patrol up-sun. He 'sighted an Me 262 coming head-on 500 feet below. He went into a port climbing turn and I turned starboard after him, with several other Spitfires chasing him.' The Canadians armed their guns and turned on their gyroscopic gunsights, all except Smith: a twelve-victory ace, he had been one of 'Stan' Turner's boys on Malta in 1942 and did his deflection shooting with his reflector sight.

Hauptmann Hans-Christof Büttmann, the KG 51 bomber pilot flying the Me 262, apparently did not like twelve-to-one odds. He decided to use the jet's superior speed to outrun his attackers. Smith reported, 'He then dived down towards the [Nijmegen] bridge twisting and turning and half rolling at very high speeds. He flew across Nijmegen turning from side to side.'

The chase was on. The Spitfires half-rolled after the Me 262, their engines at full boost.

Flight Lieutenant Hedley 'Snooks' Everard was part of the patrol. He trimmed his Spitfire, putting in forward trim because it became tail heavy in a dive, then joined the pursuit. 'My Spit was screaming for the deck about 800 yards behind the unrecognizable aircraft. A glance at the airspeed indicator confirmed that I had exceeded the maximum safe flying speed for Spitfires. Although the flight controls stiffened up alarmingly, I pursued my prey.'

Everard was facing not only the need to apply intense physical force just to move the control surfaces but also compressibility, as the Spitfire approached the speed of sound. The little white needle on his airspeed indicator had gone past the red line, which meant he was following the fleeing jet at a speed at which no Spitfire was designed or built to fly. The rational rules of aircraft control that a fighter pilot – any pilot – lived by did not apply at such speeds, in what the men who worked at drawing boards called the transonic flight regime. The Spitfire was buffeted as the airflow broke away from the elliptical wings rather than providing lift. Had Everard taken his eyes off the Me 262, he would have seen an opaque mist forming above each of the Spitfire's wings as this shock wave hit the moister air during his dive to low altitude. If the wings stayed on, control force reversal or unpredictable changes in trim could easily send him out of control, smashing down, the Spitfire's Merlin digging him so deep into the waterlogged Dutch soil that they would never find the bottom of the crater.

Büttmann spiralled down to low altitude, hoping to shake his attackers or that their wings would come off in the screaming dives.

Flying Officer John MacKay, Everard's wingman, followed him as the jet dived for the Rhine below them. MacKay, closing in on the fleeing jet, got in 'Rod' Smith's line of fire. Smith called out on the radio, 'For God's sake shoot – that Spitfire!'

That is what MacKay did. 'Following it down to the ground, firing whenever I could get my sight on the aircraft. Saw strikes on the after part of the fuselage and the port or starboard wing root.'

Everard fired too. 'I first opened fire from 900 yards and followed it chasing all the time.' Everard was already fighting the Spitfire's control forces as it encountered transonic flight diving after the jet. 'I "blacked out" as the excessive gravity forces buffeted my aircraft.'

Smith pulled up from his dive at 7000 feet to avoid another Spitfire. Now Büttmann had to pull up as well. Everard kept his eye on the Me 262. 'At 5,000 feet he began to level out, heading south.' He used the momentum from his dive to open his lead over the pursuers. Smith saw the Me 262 'was no longer trailing smoke and increasing its lead over several Spitfires, which were still chasing it but were then out of range'.

With his Spitfire now in thicker air and the speed limit for transonic flight rising, Everard was able to keep control, winding back the forward trim. Despite the blackout from the high-g pull-out from his dive in pursuit of the jet, he used the momentum from his transonic dive to close the range. The Me 262's wingspan now overfilled the six diamond points projected by the Mark II gunsight on the panel inside Everard's windscreen as the analogue computer worked out where he should aim.

Everard attacked. 'Throttling back, not to overshoot, I opened fire with machine guns only from 150 yards. A streamer of white smoke came from it and it accelerated rapidly, drawing away.'

After pulling up, Smith was back chasing the Me 262 in the pack of Spitfires. He had seen Everard's attack. 'I saw a Spitfire get some strikes on him and he streamed white smoke from the starboard wing root. He flew on at very high speed.'

Gaining every last bit of speed from his Spitfire, his throttle all the way forward, Smith went in for another attack. 'I managed to get behind him and fire two three-second bursts at 200 to 300 yards approximately.' Everard, through his peripheral vision, saw Smith come into range: 'glimpsed another Spitfire 200 yards astern pouring cannon fire into the crippled Hun'.

Büttmann was down on the deck, with no way to pick up speed through diving. Smith and Everard were sticking to him, desperately hanging on behind, wanting him dead. Büttmann now pulled back on his control stick and threw the Me 262 into a climb. Smith, above him, saw that 'it zoomed up in the most sustained vertical climb I had ever seen ... As it soared up to us, still climbing almost vertically ... its speed, though still very considerable, was beginning to fall off.'

Büttmann had traded airspeed for altitude, betting his life that the Spitfires would be unable to follow the jet in its spectacular climb. Smith was not going to let Büttmann shake him. As the jet started to climb away, Smith was 'able to pull up in an almost vertical position, to within 350 yards behind. I aimed at one of the engine nacelles and was able to fire a burst lasting about eight seconds.'

Everard also hung on to Büttmann's tail as he climbed. His Spitfire was able to follow the jet, firing all the way. 'Saw strikes on him in the port and starboard nacelles.'

Büttmann was now caught by the remainder of the Canadians, who had been above him, diving at high speed after him. As Everard saw, 'In rapid succession three other Spits made high-speed passes, all register-ing strikes on the now flame-streaked fighter.'

Badly hit, Büttmann's climb was slowing. Flight Lieutenant Gus Sinclair was able to close in. 'I turned in behind and fired four or five second bursts, saw strikes,' before he was crowded out by Smith and, closing in again, MacKay.

Each attacking Spitfire, at high speed from their dives in pursuit of Büttmann, overshot the climbing crippled jet and reversed, the Spitfire pilots kicking their rudder pedals and throwing their control sticks hard over to reverse direction as quickly as they could, to get another shot at the climbing jet, to stop him from getting away.

Büttmann, his damaged jet slowing even further in its climb, was out of airspeed but not yet out of ideas. As he approached a stall, his engines still throttled all the way up, he pressed his right rudder pedal full forward, stood the jet on its wing tip and pushed it into a stall turn, aiming to cartwheel around and go back into a dive. Smith, who had been behind him, hanging on, losing airspeed as he climbed, was also on the edge of a stall. He too reversed in a right stall turn, refusing to let Büttmann escape. 'Halfway through our stall turns, when our noses had come down level with the horizon but our wings were almost vertical, I felt as if I were in slow motion line abreast formation with the 262, directly below it.'

Smith 'broke to starboard under him and he turned down to starboard behind me'. Büttmann and Smith were now carrying out the same manoeuvre at the same time. But while, an instant before, they had been climbing with Smith behind, now they were diving with Büttmann behind the Spitfire.

Smith had become the hunted rather than the hunter. Flight Lieutenant Robert M. 'Tex' Davenport, an American in the RCAF, saw the instant flash of gunfire from the Me 262's nose. Büttmann's shot missed Smith. But Smith was vulnerable, his nose down. The Me 262, having turned, was pointing its nose with its four lethal cannon at Smith, in his blind spot, above and behind him.

John MacKay, following behind Smith, could only look on Büttmann's flying with admiration. 'The aircraft was extremely manoeuvrable. The pilot was hot and put the aircraft through everything in the book.'

But, before Büttmann could pick up airspeed again in the dive, 'Tex' Davenport's Spitfire 'closed to 300 yards astern and emptied the remainder of my guns' [ammunition] into the kite, observing strikes all over the engines and fuselage. The aircraft was burning all this time. The pilot seemed to be unhurt and put up a good fight all during this.'

Büttmann, his jet riddled and burning, its nose pointing down, had one last desperate move to make. 'I thought at that time he was trying to attack me, even though in flames,' Smith reported. MacKay saw it too. 'The aircraft pulled up to the right then dove down (burning) on a Spit (S/L Smith), seeming to want to ram the Spitfire.' 'Tex' Davenport saw the end: 'At the last realizing the fight was up he attempted to ram

Red 1 [Smith] on his way to the ground where he crashed and burned.'
Büttmann's plane was the first Me 262 to be shot down by Spitfires.

As 401 Squadron turned back to their airfield, their pilots saw, in a
field near the Rhine, the smoking crater, like an access manhole to
Erebus, where the jet that had shared their minutes of intense air combat
had finished its final flight. Johnnie Johnson recalled 'a great party to cel-
ebrate the event'. They did not know the name of the pilot, nor did they
find out for some days that Büttmann's parachute did not open. Galland
sadly recalled, 'These bomber pilots had no fighter experience, such as
combat flying or shooting, which is why so many of them were shot
down. They could only escape by outrunning the fighters in pursuit.'
But the twilight of the piston-engine fighter had started. Everard's
Spitfire barely survived its high-g pull-out following its encounter with
the sound barrier. 'Both wings of my Spit were wrinkled and I knew it
would never fly again.'[34]

Reconnaissance Spitfires were among the first targets for the new jet
fighters. From the summer of 1944, their pilots had to search so intently
that the condition known as 'PR neck' became widespread.[35] More than
ever, the reconnaissance aircraft had to fly either above or below the altitude where they would leave contrails. The Spitfire PR 19 was capable
of avoiding even the Me 262 and, if intercepted, could outmanoeuvre
it. But this required that the reconnaissance pilot spot the Me 262 first
and demanded of him a great deal of nerve, to wait until the jet was
almost in cannon range and then make a tight turn. The Me 262 could
not turn like a Spitfire. It would overshoot and come back for another
attack. Then the reconnaissance pilot had to do it again, until the
Me 262 ran out of fuel or got lucky. One German jet pilot, in frustration, rammed a Spitfire (the jet pilot survived). In the absence of
enough Me 262s, reconnaissance Spitfires increased their lone missions
over Germany, taking over from slower Mosquitoes.

18

Last Battles

1944–1945

The four Spitfires peeled off into a dive from 6000 feet, throttled back to 200 mph, then followed their leader as he rolled in on the target. A quick touch of the trim wheel and each of the four Spitfires was accelerating towards the target in a seventy-degree dive at some 360 mph. Looking through gyroscopic Mark II gunsights, each pilot positioned the aiming cross, illuminated on the flat Plexiglas panel between himself and his windscreen, just below the target. Then, as the target grew in the sight picture, surrounded by the six diamonds, each pulled back on the stick and released his bombs as he passed 3000 feet – never lower than 1500 – and turned away from the target at low altitude.

Flight Sergeant Thomas 'Cupid' Love, a short, wiry Scot, pulled his Spitfire XVI out of its dive-bombing attack, throttling up its US-built Packard Merlin to climb away from the flak defending the target in the woods north of The Hague in the Netherlands.

His 602 Squadron flight leader, Flight Lieutenant Raymond Baxter, DFC, was an experienced Spitfire pilot who could bomb accurately to within 25–30 metres of a target. As he sped away from the target, he swivelled his head around to observe the results of his flight's attack and called on the radio for the four Spitfire XVIs to double back for a strafing attack on that most dangerous of targets, a German flak emplacement. 'I must have been in a very aggressive mood,' Baxter recalled.

Love turned hard, so as not to come from the same direction over the target where he had pulled away, then, control stick forward, into a diving attack, centring the flak gun in his gunsight. With a quick touch of the trim control to set up the Spitfire in a twenty-degree dive, Love was ready to open fire.

'Kee-rist! Will you look at that?'

Love responded to the radio call. What he saw, straight in front of his Spitfire's nose, was an all-too-real vision of the future: a drab-green camouflaged ballistic missile blasting off in a massive, violently boiling grey-white cloud as its liquid-fuelled rocket engines ignited. It seemed to hang on its launcher, poised for its one-way trip through outer space to London. Baxter saw it too. 'I saw to my surprise, at a distance of 600 metres, a V-2 – out of the forest that we just had bombed – rising into the air, very slowly. Right in front of us. It was an incredible sight and it was so unexpected that I couldn't do anything about it.'

But 'Cupid' Love could. Instantly, he aimed his Spitfire at the missile and pushed the firing button of his four 20mm cannon. But it was all over in seconds. The V-2 accelerated and flashed upwards. 'He'd have blown us all up.' Baxter was glad that Love had missed the boosting missile with its liquid fuel and one-tonne high-explosive warhead. But the incident showed the difficulty Spitfires would have in countering Hitler's new threat to Britain.[1]

Spitfires against the V-2

The V-2 ballistic missile was Wernher von Braun's development of German rocket technology. Travelling through space and re-entering the atmosphere at several times the speed of sound, it could not be intercepted by aircraft or anti-aircraft fire like a V-1. Giving no warning from engine noise and undetectable by British radar, a V-2 announced itself by the explosion of its warhead that could destroy a city block. First hitting London on 8 September 1944, the V-2 had a greater impact on British life and morale than the V-1.[2] Years of rationed food and overtime work had already brought much of the population close to exhaustion.

'Cupid' Love's attempted boost-phase interception of a V-2 showed how difficult it was to detect the missiles on the ground. His flight of Spitfires had flown directly over the launch site moments before but he, Baxter and the other two pilots had all failed to spot the missile in its full upright launch position. The Germans had obviously carried on with their countdown despite the Spitfires flashing overhead.

Spitfires could not shoot down ballistic missiles but they were vital to the defence of Britain against the V-2s. The British soon realised that counterforce offensive operations were the only viable defence. Allied bombers attacked V-2 factories. The destruction of the German transport system limited production. Interdiction attacks on rail lines reduced the number of missiles fired. With 2 TAF and the US Ninth Air Force both fully engaged in supporting Allied ground forces, Fighter Command – the name had been restored in October 1944 – was given the primary responsibility of defeating the V-2 launch sites near The Hague.[3]

Unlike the V-1, which used a large fixed launcher, V-2s were kept hidden until, towed on mobile launch wagons by heavy trucks, they were taken to small pre-surveyed launch sites. Every day, the Germans launched all the V-2s they received from the factories. V-2 support operations were kept in densely inhabited areas to limit Allied ability to use bombers against them. The repeated attacks by large formations of bombers that had pounded the V-1 launch sites could not be used against the mobile V-2 launchers. On the one occasion twin-engine bombers attacked V-2 launchers, they inflicted many Dutch civilian casualties and no militarily significant damage.[4] For fear of collateral damage, Spitfires' 20mm cannon were the primary weapon used against the V-2 launchers and their support units. Despite frequent air reconnaissance patrols and the heroic actions of the Dutch resistance in locating V-2 launchers and radioing their location to Britain, Allied air power was unable to catch them. Heavy concentrations of flak made low-altitude Spitfire operations hazardous.

Even when air reconnaissance or the resistance was able to locate specific buildings being used to support the V-2 operations, fighter-bombers lacked the accuracy to destroy them without collateral damage. On Christmas Eve 1944, thirty-three Spitfires dive-bombed a building where the resistance, alerted by looting of food, had found out that V-2 launch crews were having a lavish holiday dinner. The intelligence was accurate, but the casualties were limited to three Germans. Spitfires were more successful against other infrastructure targets. Germans were producing liquid oxygen for the V-2s' engines at a plant in nearby Loosduinen. It was destroyed by Spitfires, making five separate attacks to minimise collateral damage, even though this increased exposure to the intense flak.

Armed reconnaissance sorties were frustrating. Squadron Leader Bill Olmstead, leading 422 Squadron RCAF, saw 'a V-2 rocket flash by a mile or two in front of us. As the monster spiralled skywards, we were close enough to fly through the trail of smoke and crystalline particles created by its engine. Search as we might, however, we were never able to locate the launch vehicle, even though we would be over the launch area within two minutes of the rocket being fired. Time and again the Germans proved themselves to be masters in the art of camouflage.'[5]

Spitfire attacks reduced the rate of V-2 fire and forced the Germans to fire them mainly at night, when fewer people massed together in their target cities of London and Antwerp. In one two-day period, the RAF kept relays of Spitfires over a wooded park that concealed a V-2 support facility, preventing more than a single launch over the two days. On those days when low cloud prevented Spitfire operations, their crews rapidly fired those V-2s they had amassed.

Evolving fighter combat 1944–5
In October–November, the Allies encountered a desperate German fighter force over Germany. Galland said that they 'used the *Sturmgruppe* tactics and succeeded in shooting down a goodly number of heavy bombers'.[6] The Luftwaffe fighter force had 3000 single-engine fighters, mainly fresh off the production lines, and had saved up fuel Galland planned to use in the 'Big Blow', a concentrated attack on a single day-light raid that he aimed to annihilate, thereby turning the course of the offensive.[7] But his pilots, many now with only three to five flight hours on two-seat Bf 109s before being sent into combat, were proving unable to carry out their missions.

On 2 November, the Luftwaffe made a maximum effort against US bombers attacking synthetic oil targets. Some 490 fighters were com-mitted to battle; 305 engaged the enemy, 133 were shot down, with 73 pilots killed and 42 wounded. Total US losses were forty-two bombers and sixteen fighters. The German single-engine fighter forces were pounded as the US bombers returned again and again to oil targets, suffering heavy losses from intense flak. On 21 November, the US shot down 119 fighters for the loss of 42 bombers and 11 fighters. On 26 November, US fighters claimed 114 German aircraft shot down as against 9 losses. On 27 November, the Luftwaffe did not shoot down a single bomber, but lost 81 fighters, shooting down 16 US fighters in return. On 5 December, the Luftwaffe again put up a maximum effort, this time to defend Berlin. The escort fighters claimed 91 German aircraft shot down for the loss of 17 of their own. The tally of one-sided air battles did not stop with the onset of autumn weather.

As a result of the December 1944 German offensive in the Ardennes, fighters and fuel being saved for Galland's proposed 'Big Blow' were instead expended in combat over the front lines. In a repeat of the defeat of the German fighter force over Normandy, they were lost with little effect on the outcome. One pilot, shot down by US ground fire, had written to his father: 'When one sees the front for the first time, you hear nothing, but below you see clouds of smoke and guns flash. The flak fires like mad. In this madhouse, you force yourself to be calm, seek your target, and shoot. I have four operational flights now, two against enemy bombers.'[8]

On 1 January 1945, Operation Bodenplatte, the Luftwaffe fighter force's last offensive operation, launched 800 fighters, including 17 *Gruppen* of Bf 109G/Ks, in strafing attacks on 27 Allied airfields throughout France, Belgium and the Netherlands. They destroyed 127 Allied aircraft, all but 6 on the ground. But few Allied aircrew were lost, while Luftwaffe losses included 270 fighters and over 150 pilots, including many of the surviving leaders.

The Luftwaffe intercepted a USAAF bomber attack on oil targets on 14 January. Escort fighters shot down 155 Germans for 11 of their own, the highest single-day victory score of the war in the west. One P-51 group encountered a massed formation of Bf 109s whose pilots could obviously barely fly, let alone manoeuvre, and shot down fifty-five. By February 1945, German synthetic aviation fuel production was down to a trickle. The Allied bomber offensive shifted to trans-port targets, effectively crippling dispersed German industries and preventing fuel from reaching fighter units. By 2 March, enough fuel had been saved up for German fighters once again to fight in defence of oil targets. The USAAF fighters claimed sixty-six shot down for the loss of thirteen. The lack of instrument flying training kept German fighters on the ground even when fuel was available; the USAAF flew above the overcast. As far back as September 1944, it had been commonplace for USAAF fighter pilots to rotate home, their tour of duty expired, never having seen a German aeroplane in the air; one fighter group commander estimated over 70 per cent of his pilots never had the chance to fire their guns in air-to-air combat.[9]

Cocky Dundas, at twenty-four the RAF's youngest group captain, was in Italy in 1945. He found few hostile fighters but intense flak and bad weather made Spitfire missions against targets in Italy and the Balkans, he thought, more lethal than fighting outnumbered during the Battle of Britain. Spitfires and pilots in Italy both reportedly had a life expectancy of some three months.[10] Spitfire fighter-bombers used napalm (jellied petrol) incendiary weapons, with an area effect compensating for lack of accuracy.[11]

Last gasps of the Luftwaffe

The *Jägerstab* organisation had on 1 August 1944 become the Armament Staff (*Rüstungstab*), responsible for *all* production. At Messerschmitt AG, Rakan Kokothaki found this made things worse. 'When the *Jägerstab* was extended to the whole German armament industry, it very soon lost its efficiency and activity.'[12] Following a 12 October Hitler decree, along with the remainder of the aircraft industry, Messerschmitt AG was effectively nationalised. Gerhard Degenkolb, previously Speer's V-2 production manager, was appointed general trustee and demanded immediate changes.

At the main assembly plants, where Bf 109s were put together from sub-assemblies produced by dispersed workshops, many complete aircraft were ready to fly except for one vital component that, due to the destruction of factories or disruption of transport, was missing. It took up to two weeks for goods trains of components to reach Bavaria from Germany's industrial heartland. They often never arrived at all. Messerschmitt production relied heavily on couriers with rucksacks, hitchhiking with needed parts.

From as far back as March 1944, some 10 per cent of the single-engine fighters that came off the production line had not actually reached the Luftwaffe. They were destroyed by bombs, during test flying, or during ferry missions by inexperienced pilots (Germany had no equivalent of the ATA).[13] Göring attributed the losses to 'the inexperienced pilots, especially in fighters'. In a twelve-month period, 2787 fighters were lost after they were produced but before they could be delivered.[14]

Milch was fired by Göring as Inspector-General of the Luftwaffe and effectively marginalised. After two years of acrimony, Adolf Galland had finally been relieved of his post of *General der Jagdflieger* by Göring in January 1945. Following this, many of the surviving fighter leaders had organised together and demanded changes in how the Luftwaffe's war was being fought. In what became known as 'the fighter pilots' mutiny', their distrust of Göring and the Luftwaffe command, growing since 1943, finally came out in the open when it was too late to do anything about it.

The participants in the 'mutiny' were sent back to their units, where they were desperately needed. Galland, though he had not directly participated, was put under house arrest and threatened with 'trial' before one of the summary courts-martial handing down death sentences on a daily basis.[15]

He started to think that Ernst Udet had had the right idea about the only way to stop dealing with the Nazis. But, instead of suicide, Galland slipped out to a pay phone. He called Speer on his private number. Speer called Hitler. Hitler, long fed up with Göring, assigned Galland an SS bodyguard and assured him all charges were dropped. With Hitler backing Galland, Göring, his influence waning, could not squash him.

Galland went back to leading fighters in combat. Though little aviation fuel was available, he was able to find some jet fuel. Enough Me 262s had been produced by February 1945 for Galland to organise *Jagdverband* (fighter unit) 44. He brought together many surviving German aces. Without fuel to fly Bf 109s or Fw 190s, *Experten* jumped at an opportunity to fight one last time. Many of the participants in the 'mutiny' joined him. 'Pritzl' Bär, now again leading a *Gruppe* as a *Major*, was one of Galland's volunteers. 'Bubi' Hartmann declined, sticking with his Bf 109G and his unit on the eastern front.

The Me 262 depended on Bf 109s and Fw 190s to defend it while taking off and recovering at its few operational airbases, as it required long concrete runways (or sections of the now-defunct *Autobahn*). It was also especially vulnerable when coming in to land, often low on fuel. The numerical superiority of Allied fighters allowed them to carry out 'capping' of the few airfields where the jets were operating, keeping combat air patrols in the air just out of range of the flak. 'We'd get them when they had to throttle back for landing,' said 'Gabby' Gabreski.[16]

Spitfire XIVs versus Bf 109Ks

Since their defeat of the Luftwaffe's fighters over Normandy, the majority of the Spitfires' missions had been air-to-ground or reconnaissance while fighting jets, cruise missiles, ballistic missiles and ever-present flak. To this was added another round in the decade-long duel between the Spitfire and the Bf 109. Against the Bf 109K, the Spitfire XIV was able to increase the Spitfire IX's margin of superiority over the Bf 109G. Numbers and pilot quality decided many of the Spitfire's victories. The Spitfire XIV and Bf 109K, deployed within range of each other, had both been designed as high-altitude fighters but fought usually at low altitude. Bf 109Ks constituted a quarter of Bf 109 strength at the end of 1944. Spitfire XIVs, deployed to 2 TAF bases in northern Europe, flew high-speed tactical reconnaissance missions. Spitfire FR (fighter reconnaissance) XIV versions had an oblique camera in the rear fuselage but retained four 20mm cannon. After finding that high-g manoeuvres led to the wrinkling of skin on the wings, Supermarine strengthened the Spitfire XIV's structure.

III/JG 27 had been running on desperation and high-octane fuel for months by 2 March 1945; too much of one and too little of the other. The unit's mixture of green replacements and former bomber pilots had been committed to the defence of Me 262s as they took off and landed from airstrips. They had been receiving new Bf 109K-4s since October, but were still flying some Bf 109G-10/14s. Because they were tasked with engaging enemy fighters, the unit did not carry underwing-mounted cannon. Another *Gruppe* nearby was flying the new Fw 190D-9, 'long nose' versions with DB 603 engines.

To catch Me 262s just outside the flak range of their airfields and before they could get to the bombers that morning, the RAF's 125 Wing of Spitfire XIVs, based at Eindhoven, launched a fighter sweep over their airfield. The Bf 109Ks and Fw 190Ds were scrambled to block them, at about 7.30 on a cloudy morning with a high overcast. The day started badly: one experienced pilot lost control of his Bf 109K-4 on take-off and fatally collided with a Bf 109G-14.

Allied radar spotted the climbing German fighters and ground controllers used radio to direct the Spitfires against them. The RAF saw the Fw 190D-9s first, climbing up from their field at Hesepe. 130 Squadron dived down to attack them at low altitude, leaving as top cover the seven Spitfire XIVs of 350 (Belgian) Squadron. The Belgians, alerted by fighter controllers, were vectored to intercept III/JG 27's Bf 109Ks, trying to join the fight. While the Luftwaffe had the advantage of numbers, some of the pilots were apparently barely able to keep formation among the overcast clouds.

This made 350 Squadron's day. Ron Ashman, who had flown with 350, described the Belgians as 'an absolute rabble of fliers, very tenacious and excitable. They acquitted themselves with glory, but discipline wasn't in their vocabulary . . . But what I liked about them was their devil may care attitude and no respect for rank.'[17] They were about to have an opportunity to extend this disrespect to the Luftwaffe.

Flight Sergeant Jacques 'Pichon' Greenensteen saw, between the towns of Tecklenburg and Saerbeck, 'a gaggle of enemy aircraft at about seven or eight thousand feet'. The Belgians attacked.

Greenensteen 'picked out a Me 109 which was flying at an angle of about 90 degrees to me. I turned and got on to his tail and the enemy aircraft began to turn.'

A turning fight with a Spitfire was never a good idea. 'I kept on his tail and I opened fire from 400 yards closing to about 100 yards.' The German did not have a chance.

'I was dead astern and I fired with cannon and machine guns. I had closed to what I estimate was about 50 yards when the pilot jettisoned his [canopy] hood, turned the aircraft on its back and baled out.' His parachute did not open.

Leading the Belgians that day was Flight Lieutenant Roger Hoornaert. He waded into the middle of III/JG 27's beleaguered Bf 109Ks, which were being chased in and out of the overcast by the aggressive Belgians.

'I joined in the dogfight and there were aircraft turning everywhere. I started to turn in the middle of them. I found that there was a Me 109 trying to get on my tail and there began a game of hide and seek in and out of the clouds. Finally I stayed underneath the clouds and I saw the enemy aircraft quite a long way away. So I opened up to full throttle and went after him. I caught him up and closed in to between 50 and 100 yards. I gave him everything I had. There was a big explosion. My windscreen became covered with oil and muck from the explosion. The enemy aircraft pulled up and I went underneath him. The enemy aircraft, after pulling up, dived down out of control. I saw it crash into a wood.'

Flight Sergeant Emile Pauwels was flying as Blue 4, wingman to Blue 3, Pilot Officer Louis 'Boum' Lambrechts. They dived together into the swirling dogfight. Lambrechts' Spitfire XIV demonstrated its excellent turning ability. 'I picked out a Me 109 that was turning very steeply. After two or three turns I got in behind the enemy aircraft. It then dived for the deck. I followed him. At about 2,000 feet I managed to get about 150 yards behind the enemy aircraft. I opened fire with all guns at a 10 degree angle-off. I saw strikes all over the engine and cockpit. The enemy aircraft immediately dived away, out of control. I followed as it crashed to the ground.'

Pauwels reported, 'My number 3 was chasing one Me 109 and I was following him when another Me 109 opened fire on me.'

Pauwels 'had to break away and I lost sight of my number 3. I climbed up and I found another 109 just in front of me. I opened fire with all my guns from about 200 yards dead astern and pieces flew off the enemy aircraft, including one very large piece. I was firing again when another 109 attacked me and I had to break off.'

All seven Belgians later enjoyed breakfast at Eindhoven. 350 Squadron claimed three Bf 109s shot down and a fourth (that hit by Pauwels) damaged. III/JG 27 had three Bf 109K-4 pilots shot down and killed: *Fähnreich* Unteroffizer Karl-Heinz Eidam, Feldwebel Karl Schaffhauser and Unteroffizer Erich Schulz. 130 Squadron's Spitfires, fighting Bf 109K-4s of III/JG 27 and seventeen Fw 190D-9s of III/JG 26, claimed four in return for two Spitfires shot down. Even though 350 Squadron's Spitfires were not fitted with the gyroscopic gunsight, the superior performance of the Spitfire XIV and the skills of RAF-trained pilots meant that, even on occasions, such as this one, when the Luftwaffe had numerical superiority in the air, they were nowhere near the force they had been even the previous year.[18]

Surviving Bf 109 pilots faced one more challenge: landing. This had always been difficult, even for experienced pilots. Major Willi Batz was a leading ace with JG 52 on the eastern front. 'In Austria, near the end of the war, we were operating from a base that had a bitumen runway. Such luxury! For years we had been operating from grass strips near the front. The unaccustomed experience of using the bitumen strip played havoc with our group. Out of 42 aircraft, 39 cracked up on landing due to the sensitivity of the Bf 109 to its brakes and the strange feel and response of a solid runway.'[19]

That day, the Bf 109s' pilots were lucky, even the pilot who had been shot up by Pauwels' 20mm cannon and whose plane was probably held together only by its control cables and shards of aluminium. The Spitfires, ammunition expended, were on their way home, rather than waiting for them outside flak range. There were no fresh bomb craters on the grass runway. The surviving Bf 109s, approaching their airfield at Hesepe, throttled down to some 290 km/h (180 mph).

As each Bf 109K's airspeed came down, its pilot lowered the undercarriage, checking that it was down and locked and the fixed tailwheel unlocked for landing, then, with his left hand, adjusted the trim wheel for final approach. Each Bf 109 slowed to 250 km/h (155 mph), and turned on to final approach, extended full flaps (40 degrees), lined up with the grass runway at about 225 km/h (140 mph). Inexperienced pilots 'chased' the airspeed indicator, trying to fly the right speed they had memorised, eyes on the instrument panel rather than the grass that loomed closer every instant.

The Bf 109K came over the trees at the edge of the grass runway at 180 km/h (112 mph). As the speed dropped through 160 km/h (100 mph), the left wing started to feel heavy and approaching a stall. Experienced pilots knew to keep the nose down, making a steep approach and giving a good view of the field; but, at this point, pilots with too little Bf 109 experience, watching the ground rushing towards them and fearing a stall, gunned the engine to full power and tried to go around again. A sudden burst of power would cause the left wing to drop even further. Even with the strength of desperation on the control stick and rudder pedals, the Bf 109 would fall into a left roll. Next, for many pilots, was a horrifyingly brief inverted dive, culminating with fighter and pilot alike burying themselves, in an instant, deep in a smoking crater in the green earth at the runway threshold.

But none of that would happen to III/JG 27 today. Perhaps the still-burning wrecks of the two 109s destroyed on take-off focused the minds of the pilots who had survived that morning's battle with the Spitfire XIVs. The blurred grass appeared to slow as the pilot cut the throttle, then gently pulled back on the control stick. Most pilots were able to put their Bf 109Ks on the runway at about 135 km/h (85 mph), all three wheels touching together with a creak as the undercarriage's long legs compressed under the weight of the plane. Rolling from the touch-down, each pilot in turn felt the rapid jar and bouncing from the grass field. Then the pilot applied the foot brakes. These could bring the landing roll to a quick halt.

Even then, the pilot's problems were not over. With poor forward vision from the huge engine and the upraised nose, he had to taxi to where he could be directed to a camouflaged dispersal parking spot. The flaps were raised again, to keep them from damage from stones thrown up by the propeller.

Turning into a dispersal site, the pilot carried out the shut-down checklist – radiators closed, mixture and throttle leaned back until the engine stopped, then cut the ignition switch, turn off the electrical power, and unstrap the shoulder and lap belts. The propeller slowly rotated to a stop. Quickly, tree branches and camouflage netting were thrown over the Bf 109K. A ground crewman jumped up on the left wing root and opened the 'Erla hood' canopy, much less confining than that on earlier versions. The ground crew drained any remaining fuel from the tanks, making it available to other aircraft and decreasing vulnerability to strafing attacks.

When all the surviving Bf 109s had landed, ground crew manually pushed Bf 109 hulks, stripped of spare parts, out of the woods where they had been camouflaged and left them in plain sight. These were decoys, each covered by concealed flak guns. With little fuel, teams of horses or spans of oxen moved Bf 109s into position for the next mission.

The Bf 109Ks had little chance in the air. Spitfire XIVs were estimated to have made some fourteen claims in air combat for every plane they lost. Galland said: 'The improved Spitfire was definitely superior. When we had the greater quantity and better training of your pilots to contend with, the feeling of technical inferiority on the part of our fighters was much greater than was warranted by the difference in performance.'[20]

The end of the Luftwaffe

The Luftwaffe fighter force still had many Bf 109s, but so little aviation fuel that their use was limited. Oberstleutnant 'Hajo' Herrmann, who had pushed the Wild Boar night-fighter tactics in 1943, now advocated another tactical innovation: air-to-air ramming by fighter planes. Seized upon by desperate men in the leadership – high-ranking Nazis had long been attracted to the idea of suicidal missions – Herrmann was able to secure support for his idea.

Planning started for Operation Werewolf. Stripped-down Bf 109s would deliberately ram USAAF bombers. This would not be a true *kamikaze* mission. The pilots were encouraged to bail out after collision (if possible). Most were committed but poorly trained, straight from their abbreviated flight training. Some were experienced pilots, who simply wanted one last chance to die fighting. *Sonderkommando* (special detachment) Elbe was formed for these attacks.

Hitler gave his personal approval for the ramming attacks in March. On 7 April, Elbe made its first attack. Its pilots managed to collide with eight bombers. Over sixty fighters were lost. Ramming would not save the Reich.

Other Bf 109 pilots volunteered for full *kamikaze* status, ten flying suicidal missions against the Soviet bridges over the Oder River on 16 April, followed by others on subsequent days.[21] The remaining *Mistel* combinations were also used against these bridges.

Hitler had held one last meeting with Willy Messerschmitt in Berlin on 26 March, as the Soviet Army was closing in on Berlin. Messerschmitt later said that the Führer talked of his faith in wonder-weapons to come and that his valediction was: 'it can all be traced to that damned Jew Milch'.[22] As Germany's remaining cities, including Berlin, were surrounded and Hitler was in his final bunker, Bf 109s were used to drop supply canisters to the cut-off defenders.

The USAAF launched massive strafing attacks on every German airfield between 9 and 16 April, claiming 1697 aircraft destroyed. Few German fighters had the fuel to take off in their own defence.

'Pritzl' Bär was nevertheless able to become the most successful Me 262 pilot of the war, claiming 16 victories, bringing his total to 221 (28 of them Spitfires). But the weapon that would have made the Me 262 truly lethal against heavy bombers, the R4M 55mm air-to-air rocket, only became available in quantity in the last weeks of the war. Another armament advance, the German copy of the gyroscopic gunsight, never entered service. Its factory had burned in the bombing of Dresden in February.

Galland's career as a fighter pilot came to an end on 26 April. He was shot down and wounded, for the last time, flying an Me 262, by a P-47D. Galland had scored 104 victories in over 400 combat missions. Bär took over the unit until the US Army took them all prisoner (and 'liberated' Galland's prized shotguns and last twenty boxes of cigars). All of Germany's jets and rocket aircraft destroyed a total of about 150 Allied aircraft while losing over 100 in air combat.[23]

Johnnie Johnson, with his Spitfires now based on former Luftwaffe airfields, finally did what he had wanted to do for years: lead a Spitfire wing over Berlin. The only fighters he encountered were large Soviet formations. Berlin was in ruins and the Luftwaffe defeated. The RLM's huge office building somehow survived both years of bombing and the Battle of Berlin. With swastikas removed and Göring's office subdivided, it housed Soviet Army headquarters and, later, most of East Germany's communist government. It seemed to fit them both well.[24]

German defences collapsed. The Regensburg factories were evacuated. Willy Messerschmitt tried to use his influence to have his home town of Bamberg declared an open city and ignored orders to arm his design staff as part of the *Volkssturm* militia. The regime turned its terror inwards, its targets including Luftwaffe personnel, but the bodies seen hanging from lamp-posts throughout Germany were often German soldiers, 'defeatist' civilians or foreign workers, sometimes Allied airmen, seldom Luftwaffe pilots.

In the final weeks, Bf 109 production ended; 2969 were produced in 1945, bringing total German Bf 109 production to over 33,984 (30,573 during the war), the highest total for any fighter ever designed. The last Luftwaffe fighter lost in the west was a Bf 109, caught at low altitude by a USAAF P-51 before the guns went silent on 8 May.

Of Germany's fighting men, no one except U-boat crews had less chance of seeing the end of the war than fighter pilots. Some 99,875 Luftwaffe aircrew were casualties up to February 1945; it is estimated that over 90 per cent of Luftwaffe fighter pilots were killed, seriously wounded or became prisoners of war before the end of hostilities.[25] Many of those who survived only did so by being sent into combat on the ground when the aviation fuel ran out.

Oberst Johannes Steinhoff, who had flown Bf 109s in combat on every front, scoring 158 victories, finished the war in hospital. One of Galland's Me 262 pilots, he had ended his last combat mission, unconscious, thrown clear of the crash, lying on his side in a pool of burning jet fuel which left half of his face and body terribly scarred. From all his years of air combat, he summed up, 'The war in the air is a technological war which cannot be won by a technologically inferior fighting force, however high its morale or dauntless its resolution.'[26]

Victory in the Far East
Air Marshal Keith Park took over the British air forces in south Asia in February 1945, replacing his old rival Leigh-Mallory, killed in an air crash. Supply lines and flying conditions still made Spitfire operations

difficult. Spitfire units leapfrogged to forward airstrips behind advancing troops. Japanese air reconnaissance was effectively closed down.

When the Japanese withdrew from the island of Akyab on 2 January 1945, Spitfires arrived to operate from its airfield six days later. The next day, the Imperial Japanese Army attacked with seven Ki-84 Frank fighters and twenty-eight Oscars (they relied on fighter-bombers when their twin-engine bombers were no longer survivable). Five Spitfires scrambled in time to shoot down four attacking Oscars without loss.[27] As of March 1945, four Spitfire squadrons flew air cover for the Fourteenth Army in Burma; others provided air defence in India.

With the collapse of Japanese air power in Burma, the majority of the missions became, as in Europe, air-to-ground. High-altitude reconnaissance Spitfires provided mapping. The Spitfire's relatively short range and limited bombload as a fighter-bomber were drawbacks as it took part in the 1945 advance in Burma. As in Europe, Spitfire tactics included elements that would become familiar in later conflicts.[28]

Spitfire squadrons started preparations for the invasion of Malaya. Plans called for Spitfires to fly from carriers into forward airstrips as soon as a beachhead was established. Griffon-engine Spitfire XIVs and PR 19s arrived in India to prepare for the operation.

Seafire operations against Japan started in earnest in 1945, with Royal Navy carrier attacks on oil refineries in Sumatra in January. In March–April, the Royal Navy launched carrier operations in the central Pacific, with Seafires in action over the Sakishima Islands and, in June, over Truk in the Carolines. Seafires were also used to direct naval gunfire (though with less success than in Normandy). Seafires flying from escort carriers provided air cover for amphibious operations in Burma in May 1945.

In 1944–5, the RAAF's Spitfire VIII-equipped 80 Wing moved to Morotai off Dutch New Guinea. Clive Caldwell was in command. Its pilots were trained in air-to-air combat, reflecting the lessons of the 1943 campaign over Darwin. But Japanese air opposition was absent. The last Dinah to fly over Australia was shot down by Spitfires in July 1944. RAAF Spitfires had encountered Japanese aircraft on only three occasions since the attacks on Darwin.[29] The Spitfires flew fighter-bomber missions.

To RAAF Spitfire pilots, braving anti-aircraft fire to attack targets of limited value when they wanted to take on Japan's remaining fighters seemed a bad idea. When Caldwell and other pilots made their commanders aware of this, the result was the 'Morotai Mutiny' of March 1945. The RAAF Spitfires advanced to airfields on Borneo after Australian troops landed, but did not get another chance at air combat against the Japanese. Caldwell was court-martialled for illicitly trading whisky for equipment with the Americans and left the RAAF as a flight lieutenant.

The Seafires flying from the Royal Navy carriers operating against Japan introduced themselves to the US Navy by holding a mass fly-past over Task Force 58's aircraft carriers, hoping to reduce friendly fire incidents. The Seafire had rarely been required to carry out the specific mission it was designed for: radar-directed interception at low or medium altitude. It finally got the chance off Japan and proved effective in the final months of the war. Its deck landing risks were reduced by the availability of experienced pilots, but the hazards of wartime carrier flying still claimed many more pilots than did the Japanese. Against Japanese *kamikaze* attacks, the Royal Navy used radar-directed 'stacked' combat air patrols (CAPs) of longer-range fighters at high altitudes and Seafires with external tanks at low altitude, backed up with fast-climbing Seafire LIIIs kept ready for take-off on the carrier deck.

Seafires flew offensive sorties against Japan. One Royal Navy carrier in the Pacific in 1945 was able to phase out 90-gallon slipper tanks for its Seafires by using 90-US-gallon drop tanks obtained by trading a US fighter group two crates of whisky. In the last British air-to-air combats of the Second World War, on 13 August 1945, eight Seafires flying a bomber escort mission over Japan were intercepted by twelve or fourteen A6M5 Zero fighters. The Seafires succeeded in protecting the bombers and claimed eight Zeros shot down for the loss of a single Seafire (its pilot was subsequently murdered on the news of Japan's surrender). On the afternoon of 15 August, the last desperate solo Japanese air attack on the British carriers ended, shot down by two Seafires.

The Seafire had introduced itself into the Pacific war with a mass fly-over. It now exited with the same, showing the power of Allied carrier air power, first over the battleship USS *Missouri* as the Japanese surrender was signed in Tokyo Bay and then, as British carriers fanned out to reclaim lost possessions, at Hong Kong, Singapore (where they joined up with Spitfires that had flown down from Burma) and the muchbombed former Japanese citadel of Rabaul. There, the sound of Merlin engines was among those signalling the end of the global conflict and the start of a post-war age in which both the aircraft and the country that had produced it were facing an uncertain future, one in which past glories would prove fleeting.

19

Fighters in a Cold War World

After 1945

On 15 September 1945, the fifth anniversary of the Battle of Britain was marked by a victory fly-past above London, led by a Spitfire flown by Group Captain Douglas Bader, liberated from captivity in Germany that had included three years in Colditz Castle as punishment for his repeated escape attempts. The fly-over tradition established, the RAF retained a handful of Spitfires and Hurricanes to carry them out, the precursors of the current Battle of Britain Memorial Flight.[1]

While Spitfire squadrons were part of British occupation forces in Germany, Austria and Japan, the RAF was demobilising.[2] Churchill, having lost the 1945 General Election, was now leader of the opposition. Most senior RAF leaders retired. Even Douglas Bader was getting out. He realised that the peacetime career prospects for a senior officer with artificial legs and a willingness to confront air marshals were limited.

The multinational world of the Spitfire squadrons dissolved for ever. The ATA disbanded. Some pilots stayed in the RAF: Johnnie Johnson eventually retired as an air vice marshal. Most went home. Spitfire pilots became leaders in their nations' air arms (including the US Air Force). Others went into business. Cocky Dundas' success earned him a knighthood. Some went into politics: Malta veteran 'Laddie' Lucas was one of many who served in the House of Commons. 'Sailor' Malan, back in South Africa, became one of the first anti-apartheid activists. Some Spitfire pilots became presidents or prime ministers: Ezer Weizman in Israel, Ian Smith in Rhodesia and Michael Manley in Jamaica. Dowding, who retired soon after he was relieved of his Fighter Command post, enjoyed skiing and spiritualism. At a Battle of Britain memorial service at Westminster Abbey, he said he could see the spirits of the fallen of Fighter Command.

Poles and Czechoslovaks who had flown for the RAF and now returned home were mainly sent to prisons or labour camps by Communist governments. Some of those who survived were rehabilitated after the death of Stalin. Wojciech Klozinski, who had flown his last combat mission on 15 August 1940, was a ground instructor at RAF Squire's Gate (where 'Jack' Carpenter had instructed since 1940). Like most Polish Spitfire pilots, he did not try to go home. He anglicised his name and emigrated to Canada. West Indians who had served in the RAF were among the first waves of emigrants to post-war Britain.

Production of the Merlin-engine Spitfire IXs (5665 built) and XVIs (1054) ended in June 1945. The Spitfire's structure was always difficult to adapt to mass production – in 1941–2 a Mark V had required about 13,000 man-hours for Supermarine to build at its dispersed facilities, 10,400 man-hours on Castle Bromwich's production line – but for an aircraft industry that lacked both the vast access to resources of the US and the compulsion available to the Germans, such figures constituted a tremendous achievement.[3]

Even though the RAF had only operated a single squadron of Gloster Meteor jet fighters in combat during the war, and its air-to-air victories had been limited to the destruction of V-1s, the future of military aviation now belonged to the jet. The RAF soon scrapped large numbers of Spitfires. Others were sold. After the war, Spitfires equipped air arms throughout Europe. Commonwealth air arms continued to fly Spitfires and Seafires (though Australia and New Zealand used US-designed fighters). Post-imperial air arms in Egypt, India, Pakistan, Syria and Burma (plus Thailand) flew Spitfires from former RAF airfields.

Post-war Spitfire development

Many wartime Spitfire and Seafire design improvements, which would have been introduced on a massive scale had the war continued, appeared on a much more limited scale in the post-war years. The Spitfire 18 was an improved 'interim' Spitfire XIV designed in parallel to more advanced Spitfire IV-XX-21 development.[4] Its airframe was strengthened, new high-strength alloys being used for a redesigned unitary main spar that proved difficult to machine properly and so delayed production. It could handle more powerful versions of the Griffon, which required a reinforced undercarriage, a larger rudder and a new propeller unit. Initial trials showed marked longitudinal instability, delaying the start of production until July 1945. Had the war continued, it would have replaced earlier Spitfire versions; instead, it went into production as the Spitfire FR (fighter reconnaissance) 18, re-equipping six RAF squadrons. It retained the Spitfire's superb manoeuvrability, and often outperformed the RAF's first-generation jet fighters.[5]

The troubled development of the Spitfire 21, the long-awaited redesigned 'Super Spitfire', now powered by the 2375 hp Griffon 64, resulted in only a few being operational in Europe before VE Day, flying 154 operational sorties for the loss of two to flak. It saw no air-to-air combat, flying armed reconnaissance missions against V-2 launchers and anti-shipping patrols, which included sinking a midget submarine (Spitfires had been flying patrols against this threat for several months). Its handling characteristics were no longer alarming, although Diana Barnato thought it 'wallowed a bit on final approach at slow speed'.[6] While 3000 Spitfire 21s had been ordered from Castle Bromwich, which had kept building Merlin-powered Spitfire II-V-IXs since 1940, production was halted at the end of the war; just 120 were built.

The Spitfire 22 – a Spitfire 21 with a cut-back rear fuselage, teardrop canopy and a new tail design to counter increased engine torque – had first flown in November 1944. The long and painful development paid off, even though too late to see combat in 1945, in an aircraft that retained the handling qualities that had been thought lost in the troubled original Mark 21 design. Jeffrey Quill said of the Spitfire 22: 'The thought occurred to me, as it had so many years before, after my first flight in the prototype – this aeroplane was a real lady. By then a much more powerful, noisy, tough and aggressive lady, certainly, but a lady just the same.'[7] Only one RAF fighter squadron flew the Spitfire 22 operationally, many of the 278 produced being exported.

The Spitfire 24, the final production Spitfire, was first flown in February 1945 and the first production aircraft were delivered in 1948; sixty were built. Similar to the Spitfire 22, it was powered by a Griffon 61 engine and delivered with two additional fuselage fuel tanks and a capability to use air-to-ground rockets. It equipped only one RAF fighter unit, 80 Squadron, in Germany and Hong Kong. To Jeffrey Quill, it was 'a little overpowered, perhaps – but a magnificent aeroplane'.[8] Group Captain 'EJ' Edwards Jones, who had first evaluated the Spitfire in 1936, found the Spitfire 24 'A disappointment to fly. To balance the extra weight of the enormous engine, various adjustments had been made and these gave the aircraft a heavy and unbalanced feel, although, of course, it was perfectly controllable. I thought back to the original prototype with its ideal handling qualities and regretted what "progress" had achieved!'[9]

Joe Smith had been working since early 1943 on adapting laminar flow wing technology – as used on the Mustang – to the Spitfire. After an interim design, the Spitfire 23, applied laminar flow elements to the Spitfire 21 wing (but did not provide enough of a performance improvement to merit production), the ultimate results of Smith's work were the RAF's Spiteful and the FAA's Seafang, powered by a 2375 hp Griffon 85. The fastest single-engine piston fighters ever put into production, they were capable of 476 mph in level flight, faster than the world record held by the Me 209 since 1939. Smith had aimed to achieve the laminar flow effects that had largely eluded the P-51, but it required smaller manufacturing tolerances than were practical.

The Spiteful and Seafang had shared the troubled development of the Spitfire 21. Integrating the immense power of the larger Griffon and dealing with its torque forces required a redesigned tail section, based on the Spitfire 21. It retained the Spitfire's elliptical horizontal stabiliser, but little else remained of Mitchell's original design. Only about two dozen Spitefuls and Seafangs were built.

In 1944 Smith had proposed to use the Spiteful design as the basis for a jet fighter. The Air Ministry responded by issuing Specification E.10/44, for an experimental jet Spiteful. Smith, handing over Spitfire design management to his long-time deputy Alan Clifton, designed a prototype which was first flown by Jeffrey Quill in July 1946. By that time, access to wartime German research, especially Messerschmitt's work on swept-wing transonic jet fighters, had made it apparent to Smith that 'swept back wings now appeared to be essential'.[10] Still, Smith's straight-wing jet design, renamed the Supermarine Attacker, was eventually produced in limited numbers for the Royal Navy and exported to Pakistan.

The Seafire XV, a navalised version of the Spitfire XII intended to chase down low-level attackers, first flew in November 1943 and went into production in 1944. First deliveries were planned for July 1944, but engine torque issues, adapting the 1850 hp Griffon VI engine to carrier operations, led to development problems. It went into service on carriers in the Pacific, but the war ended before it could see combat. Armed with the older-style mix of two 20mm cannon and four .303 machine guns, it was fitted during its production run with a more effective tail-mounted 'stinger' arrester hook, located aft of the tailwheel, rather than the amidships A-frame hook that all previous Seafires had used. The similar Seafire 17 had an improved undercarriage and plumbing to carry drop tanks under the wings. Cut-down rear fuselages and teardrop canopies were introduced to some of both types.

The Seafire 45, a navalised version of the Spitfire 21, was suitable only for carrier training (no folding wings). An interim type, the Seafire 46, first flew on 8 September 1944, but only twenty-five were produced. The Supermarine design team then created the Seafire 47. Drop tanks gave the Seafire 47 a maximum range of over 1000 nautical miles. A reinforced undercarriage could absorb over three times the landing impact of the original Spitfire's design. Powered by Griffon 87 and 88 engines, it used a six-blade contra-rotating propeller that was actually two propellers geared one behind another, going in opposite directions, thus negating the torque forces that made later Griffon-engine Spitfires and Seafires difficult to fly. Unreliable when first introduced on the Seafire 46, the new propeller was retrofitted to some

RAF Spitfire 21s after improvements were introduced on the Seafire 47. In addition, the Griffon 88 finally introduced a fuel injector to the Spitfire. The Seafire 47 went into production in 1946; only ninety were built, up to 1949, the last iteration of the classic Spitfire design.

The development of the Spitfire proved to be one of the great successes of the British aircraft industry. A total of 20,334 Spitfires and 2558 Seafires were built. Mitchell's basic design was capable of repeated upgrading. The total number of man-hours devoted to the multiple parallel projects all upgrading the Spitfire design in all the years after it went into production, an estimated 620,000, was about twice the 330,000 required for the original Spitfire I design.[11] Considering what the investment of these man-hours – a scarce resource – produced, the Spitfire design was efficient as well as effective. More adaptable than the Bf 109, the Spitfire design reflected Joe Smith's personal attitude that 'the good big 'un will eventually beat the good little 'un'. Slightly larger, the Spitfire was less limited in its evolution. The P-51, slightly larger again than the Spitfire, used the latter's engine and a half-generation more advanced design to be more adaptable than either.

The Bf 109 and its pilots after the war

There was no post-war need for Bf 109s or their pilots. Surviving Luftwaffe Bf 109s were scrapped and their pilots went to prisoner-of-war camps. Some on the eastern front, including 'Bubi' Hartmann, whose 352 air-to-air victories (all but seven of them Soviets) made him the highest-scoring fighter ace of all time, spent ten years in Soviet labour camps, as did 'Hajo' Hermann and Alfred Grislawski.

Those in British or American hands fared better. Milch had handed over his field marshal's ceremonial baton to a British commando brigadier, as an Age of Reason general would have done. Milch was stunned when the commando smashed him across the face with it and ordered him handcuffed; he had just come from the site of an atrocity. A few fighter pilots, including Galland and Bär, were taken aside for interrogation. Galland, as usual, took charge of the process, charming and impressing everyone, and made friends with his interrogators. He again encountered Douglas Bader, who gave Galland his first post-war box of cigars. Galland could no longer shape the outcome of the war, but he made sure he was going to shape the writing of its history.[12]

The foreign workers who had been building Bf 109s went into displaced persons camps. Some went home to tensions between those paid to work in Germany ('collaborators') and those who were deported ('victims'). Others went to new countries: the US, Britain, Israel. It was many years before agreement was reached on compensation for their labour.[13]

Willy Messerschmitt cooperated with the Allies. The designs on Messerschmitt's drawing boards were far in advance of the jet fighters now starting to equip the RAF and USAAF (to become, in 1947, the US Air Force). Future jet fighters would use design innovations of German origin. The US and the Soviet Union were able to have jet fighters with German-developed swept wings operational within five years. Britain was unable to serially produce comparable aircraft until the Supermarine Swift – designed by Joe Smith – of 1954. Smith himself, like Mitchell and test pilot 'Mutt' Summers, died prematurely, of cancer. Jeffrey Quill ended up in aerospace corporate management.

Many German leaders were put on trial. Göring, sentenced to death, cheated the hangman by committing suicide. Speer was given twenty years. Saur turned prosecution witness and walked. Hess, too insane to have been tried in an American court, and Milch, restating his loyalty to Hitler and explaining that the camps were nothing to do with him, both received life sentences. Milch felt that Messerschmitt was among those personally responsible for forced labour.[14] Speer and Hess served hard time; Milch got out after ten years (and had a skilled, sympathetic biographer tell his story). Willy Messerschmitt was held by the US for two years but never convicted. His personal fortune, which he had estimated at $50 million, largely in Messerschmitt AG stock, was wiped out.

With no German military or aircraft industry, Galland worked in Argentina, along with Kurt Tank. Other surviving German fighter pilots found employment during the Berlin Airlift of 1948–9, loading and unloading Anglo-American transport aircraft. Captain Gail 'Hal' Halverson, who flew during the airlift, did not then speak German. He became used to these men, often black with coal dust, coming up to him at Berlin's Tempelhof Airport, talking in emphatic German, shaking his hand, showing him their Luftwaffe pilots' wings, pinned inside their wallets, and pointing to the sky. What they were saying, he learned, was: 'In 1944, I was up there trying to shoot you down. Now, you are trying to feed and warm us. Thank you.'[15] When civil aviation restarted in Germany, some Bf 109 pilots went back in the cockpit. Heinz Bär, who had survived over 1000 combat missions, crashed and was killed doing low-altitude aerobatics.

A German court in Augsburg cleared Willy Messerschmitt of complicity in the use of forced labour; it had been neither his decision nor, at that time, his company.[16] When he was released from US military custody, Messerschmitt started a new company building sewing machines, before moving on to prefabricated buildings. A writer in 1950 found him 'a wildly impatient, chain-smoking bundle of struts and stresses, about as easy to interview as a man building a time bomb'. But Messerschmitt served notice that he was coming back in the aircraft business. 'I'm a self-made man, and just in case there were ever any doubts about it, I'm going to repeat the performance.'[17] He worked on aircraft projects in Spain, where Bf 109s were still being built, and Egypt. Then he moved on into motor vehicles, designing a three-wheel miniature car that competed with one designed by his old rival, Ernst Heinkel. In 1952, the Baroness and Willy married. He eventually became leader of Messerschmitt-Bölkow-Blohm (MBB), a major aircraft company. His last job, in retirement in the 1970s, was as a consultant for the design of Airbus airliners. He stressed the importance of being able to remove and reattach the wings easily.

With the rebirth of the Luftwaffe as an integral part of the North Atlantic Treaty Organisation (NATO) in the mid-1950s, many of the leading surviving Bf 109 combat pilots rejoined. These included Erich Hartmann, Gerhard Barkhorn, Günther Rall and Johannes Steinhoff, who, despite scarring from burns over half his body, retired as a four-star general after a twenty-five-year career, having been *Inspektur* of the Luftwaffe and chair of the NATO Military Committee.

German societal attitudes towards the surviving fighter pilots were more complex. While they had avoided the taint of widespread atrocities, they had been the 'glamour boys' of the Nazi regime and, most tellingly, they had failed to prevent Germany's cities from being levelled by the Anglo-American bomber offensive. Even if only a minority of fighter pilots had been committed to Nazi ideology, their strong nationalism, elitism, and the measure of devotion the vast majority had given the regime up to the end tended to make post-war Germany uneasy. After the war, German national opinion sought to distance itself from the Third Reich and its horrors. Average Germans perceived themselves as bystanders or victims of the conflict.[18] These were two categories into which Germany's surviving fighter pilots fitted poorly. Relatively few fighter pilots survived to put forward their story. Because many of their fellow Germans did not understand what they, and their more numerous fallen comrades, had gone through, Germany's fighter pilots often associated with each other or, in many cases, with those who had flown in the Allied air arms, whether NATO military or retired, that had shared the experience of war in the air.[19]

Such association was enabled by the perception that fighter pilots were examples of those Germans who had fought untainted by Nazism. Mölders was commemorated in the name of a warship and a fighter wing in the new German armed forces (both were scrapped in more politically correct recent years). Marseille was the subject of a romanticised biographical movie. Galland and Steinhoff both talked up the fighter pilots' antipathy with Göring (easily blamed for years of Luftwaffe failures and for decisions made and implemented by the allegedly 'non-political' uniformed leaders), and their roles in the 'fighter pilots' mutiny'.

The re-formed Luftwaffe did not offer Adolf Galland the four stars that he claimed were the only things that would make him put on a uniform again. He became personal friends with many of his former opponents, including Douglas Bader, whom he invited to be his guest at a reunion of German fighter pilots. On entering, Bader looked at the attendees with dismay. 'I didn't think we left this many of you bastards alive!' Galland, smooth as ever, replied, 'Oh, you didn't. Most of these bastards were on the eastern front. Come, I'll introduce you.'

Post-1945 combat

The years after 1945 saw Spitfires and Seafires in combat around the world. A squadron of RAF Spitfire VIIIs and XIVs was in action in 1945 against Indonesian nationalists in the Netherlands East Indies, until Dutch Spitfire IXs could be shipped out to take over the fight. Spitfires flown from aircraft carriers were the first RAF aircraft to be based in Malaya after the war. RAF Spitfire IXs supported ground forces in counter-insurgency in Palestine until, in 1946–7, they were replaced by Spitfire FR 18s.

A squadron of RAF Spitfire VIIIs were the first Allied fighters in French Indochina in 1945, flying a few combat missions in support of French garrisons against Vietnamese insurgents. French Air Force Spitfire IXs went into action in 1946 (their pilots had flown borrowed RAF Spitfire VIIIs and captured Japanese Oscars until their own Spitfires arrived from France). French Seafires, operating from carriers and shore bases, also saw extensive combat in Indochina.

RAF Spitfire VIIIs and IXs had already seen combat against Greek Communist insurgents in 1944–5. In street fighting in Athens, 'the Spitfires with their 20mm cannon proved invaluable in close support of the troops', reported Air Marshal John Slessor, commanding RAF oper-ations.[20] Greek Spitfire Vs and IXs were used against ground targets during the 1948–9 campaign of the civil war. Royal Indian Air Force Spitfire VIIIs, flying from Srinagar during the first conflict over Kashmir in 1947, started the strafing attacks that held back tribal militias, later reinforced by Spitfire XIVs and FR 18s.

Neutral Turkey and Portugal received Spitfire Vs during the war. Turkey lost two to Bulgarian flak in 1948, early Cold War casualties. Both countries continued to fly Spitfires after they joined NATO, with Turkey receiving Spitfire IXs after the war.

Bf 109s remained in service in Switzerland, Yugoslavia and Finland. Yugoslavia, its Spitfires and Hurricanes non-operational without spare parts and 100-octane fuel, obtained extra Bf 109Gs from Bulgaria and used them in its internal conflicts and in the confrontation with Italy over Trieste. They came up against, but did not fire on, USAAF and RAF aircraft and Italian Spitfire Vs, reinforced by post-war Spitfire IX deliveries.

Bf 109 production continued in Spain (where it had been licensed since 1944) and Czechoslovakia, where in 1944, as part of the disper-sal of the Wiener Neustadt Messerschmitt factory, twenty-four dispersed

Bf 109 production facilities had been set up. After the German surrender, Bf 109G-14s were completed for use by the restored armed forces
of Czechoslovakia. Designated the Avia S.199, they were adapted by
Czechoslovak aircraft designers to use the only engine available, the
Junkers Jumo 211F, never intended for the Bf 109 airframe. The resulting improvised design had poor performance and atrocious flying
characteristics, and was nicknamed the 'Mezec' (mule). Czechoslovakia
began casting around for a customer to take these planes off its hands.[21]

The 1948–9 Arab–Israeli War

That customer appeared in the form of the about-to-be-created country of Israel, desperate for combat aircraft. Czechoslovakia had first tried
to sell the S.199s to Arab countries, but the lure of Israel's US dollars
closed the deal. Subject to an arms embargo and facing an imminent
conflict with an Arab coalition, Israel would accept any fighters it could
get, even S.199s, designated *Messer* (knife) in Israeli service.

Boris Senior, a wartime SAAF fighter pilot, was one of the first Israeli
pilots to fly the S.199. 'It was rightly called the Mule, for taking off and
landing in one piece was an achievement. It has an unpleasant built-in
swing during these phases.'[22]

After their pilots were trained in Czechoslovakia and at a clandestine
field in Italy, the S.199s were flown to Israel, disassembled inside transport aircraft. They were made ready for action by 101 Squadron, the first
Israeli Air Force fighter squadron, which also operated a few Spitfires,
some salvaged from RAF scrapyards. The former RAF field at Ein
Shemer north-east of Natanya had a dump rich in Spitfire parts.

Israel had enough money to hire combat veteran pilots with RAF,
USAAF, US Navy, SAAF and RCAF experience – plus Jewish
Palestinians who had flown in the RAF, though most of the latter
lacked combat experience. The pilots were a diverse group. Some were
devoted Zionists and had ambitions for the new country, others wanted
to take the money and go home. 'Screwball' Beurling, at a loose end
since Malta, volunteered to join them, but was killed en route in a
transport crash in Italy. Ground crew were largely refugees, some survivors of slave labour in the German aircraft industry; a cadre was
RAF-trained.

What brought them all together was the evil little S.199. All of those who flew it had fighter experience; but none in Messerschmitts. Some, like Ezer Weizman, an RAF Spitfire pilot, had never seen air-to-air combat. Now, they would have to fight against Spitfires while flying S.199s.

The most significant opposition 101 Squadron's S.199s faced was the Royal Egyptian Air Force (REAF) with over thirty Spitfire Vs and IXs (although only some ten to twelve Spitfire LF IXs were initially operational, more joined them). It had operated Spitfires in the Second World War and had purchased additional planes from the British.[23] While some Egyptian pilots had flown under RAF command in the Second World War, none had seen combat. 'The combat effectiveness of the REAF is practically nil and it cannot be considered a striking force or even a defensive force ... The average Egyptian pilot cannot be considered at all proficient by standards used for rating an American or British pilot,' a US intelligence report concluded.[24] Egypt would also have to improvise an air force while fighting a war.

The first Egyptian Spitfire attack on 14 May 1948 targeted Israeli airfields; two unassembled S.199s were destroyed. This was followed by an attack on Tel Aviv on 18 May, losing one Spitfire to ground fire. On 19 May, four Israeli S.199s went into action for the first time; two were lost, one to ground fire and another to a landing accident.

On 22 May, Egyptian Spitfires attacked the RAF base at Ramat David in Palestine, which was to be occupied by Israel the next day. The RAF had been doing a good job of destroying Ramat David themselves; the night before, after a particularly jolly party, they had burned down the mess. Egyptian Spitfires, their pilots thinking the Israelis were already in occupation, destroyed two RAF Spitfire FR 18s on the ground. Subsequent Egyptian Spitfire attacks were met by RAF anti-aircraft fire; two were shot down. RAF Spitfire FR 18s scrambled and shot down two more Egyptian Spitfires. 'Caught them up from behind and opened up at point blank range at sitting targets,' Flying Officer Gregory Middlebrook saw from the ground.[25] These Egyptian Spitfires became the last air-to-air victories by RAF fighters.

By 29 May, supported by Spitfire attacks, the Egyptian Army had advanced as far as Ashdod, twenty-five miles south of Tel Aviv. To halt the advance, the Israelis now relied on attacks by S.199s, fitted with improvised bomb racks. Ezer Weizman flew on the first mission. 'I let go my two bombs, speeding them on their way with a prayer that they would delay the column that was moving northwards. Anti-aircraft fire harried us from all sides. I dove once more, blasting away with my 20mm cannon, which soon jammed.'[26] Ground fire on that first day cost two S.199s and one pilot, but Israeli fighter attacks, along with logistics difficulties, helped halt the Arab advance.

101 Squadron used the S.199 to score Israel's first air-to-air victories: one Egyptian C-47 transport, serving as an improvised bomber, shot down and another damaged on 3 June. On 7 June, two S.199s intercepted four bomb-carrying REAF Spitfires, shooting one down. After two S.199s were lost attacking observation aircraft, probably after their synchronisation gear had failed and they had shot off their own propellers, another three S.199s surprised two Egyptian Spitfire VCs and shot one down on the evening of 18 July. Boris Senior attributed the Israeli success in air combat to the wartime experience of its fighter pilots, who enlivened life on the ground with drinking, partying and recreational car theft.[27]

At the start of a truce on 18 July, only three S.199s were operational, reflecting ground fire and landing accidents. Czechoslovakia, having already sold twenty-three S.199s, now sold Israel fifty-six Spitfire LF IXEs. Getting these to Israel proved an epic journey; some were flown inside transport aircraft, most covertly ferried and refuelled in Yugoslavia.

Starting with a strafing attack on El Arish airfield on 15 October, breaking a UN ceasefire, the Spitfire IX took over the burden of Israeli fighter operations. Their main opponents were Egyptian Spitfire LF IXs, with over forty in service. Deliveries had continued until mid-1947. Egypt used a cadre of USAAF-trained technicians, adept in improvisation and cannibalisation, to put unserviceable Spitfires back in the air. RAF dumps and crash sites in the desert were scoured for essential parts. Spitfire VCs were withdrawn for coastal patrol duties. The REAF lacked trained pilots.[28]

Faced with strong opposition, Israel also kept its S.199s in action through cannibalisation. One bellied in following a dogfight with REAF Spitfires on 16 October, but by 21 October, eight S.199s and five Spitfires were operational, with more coming. That day, the Israelis scored their first Spitfire versus Spitfire air combat victory. Israel acquired three B–17s, using S.199s and Spitfires as escorts for them, and converted transports, against REAF Spitfires. A few Spitfires were modified with cameras for reconnaissance. Ezer Weizman led two of these, with S.199 escort, on the first mission over Damascus on 19 November 1948.

The air war expanded as Egypt put Italian-built MC 205s and Fiat G.55s into action and Israel acquired its first P–51s. But the number of fighters continued to decrease, the Israelis flying Malta-style lone interceptions until more Spitfires could arrive from Czechoslovakia. By the time the war ended on 7 January 1949, only five Israeli S.199s were still flyable, but increased numbers of Spitfires and foreign volunteer pilots gave the Israeli Air Force the decisive edge that it has never relinquished. Israeli aircraft shot down some twenty-one Arab aircraft, losing two to four in air combat and some forty to ground fire or accidents.

The S.199, along with the Spitfires and ground forces equipment that also came from Czechoslovakia, had proven decisive. David Ben Gurion, Israel's first prime minister, said, 'They saved the State. There is no doubt of this. Without these weapons, it is doubtful whether we would have won. The arms deal with the Czechs was the greatest assistance we received.'[29]

RAF high-altitude reconnaissance flights over the Arab–Israeli War had halted on 20 November 1948 after an Israeli P–51 shot down an RAF Mosquito (S.199s had previously failed to intercept them). On 7 January 1949, four RAF Spitfire FR 18s, on a tactical reconnaissance mission over the ceasefire lines, flew over an Israeli column that had just been attacked by REAF Spitfire IXs. Expecting another attack by Spitfires, the Israeli ground forces opened fire. One Spitfire FR 18 was shot down.

The remaining RAF Spitfires orbited around the shot-down pilot. Their pilots had their eyes fixed on the ground when they were attacked by two Israeli Spitfire IXs. These were flown by Chalmers 'Slick' Goldin, a former US test pilot who had flown Spitfires in the RAF; and John McElroy, a nine-victory RCAF ace who had been one of 'Stan' Turner's boys on Malta in 1942. They had thought they were attacking the same Spitfires that had been reported attacking the ground column. Two of the RAF Spitfires were quickly shot down by McElroy. 'It wasn't one of ours, so I just dropped my sights on him – it was about 400 yards – and I let fly. I got strikes all over him. Right down the fuselage and the engine. And I didn't wait around,' he recalled of his second attack.[30] Goldin shot down the remaining RAF Spitfire after it turned on him and opened fire.

There followed an intermission, as Israeli Spitfires and P-51s fought REAF MC 205s, shooting one down. In the afternoon, the RAF sent up a further four Spitfire FR 18s and fifteen Tempest IIs. Only the Spitfires and some of the Tempests carried ammunition; seven Tempests, though armed, had their guns uncocked. The mission was considered a show of force to look for the missing Spitfires. Israelis sent up four Spitfire IXs, led by Ezer Weizman, now 101 Squadron operations officer, still looking for his first victory.

Weizman later said he thought he was intercepting Egyptian reinforcements. The RAF formation was looking for its lost Spitfires when the Israelis attacked them. One Tempest was shot down and two others damaged. Weizman fought with two Tempests. 'I caught one, sat on his tail and let him have it. I observed hits but I did not see him catch fire or crash. In a fight lasting about two minutes we scattered them in all directions.'[31] Weizman's Spitfire IX was slightly damaged. Unarmed Tempests ran for home; others turned on the escorting RAF Spitfires, thinking them attackers. The Israelis disengaged before the RAF Spitfires could join the fight in what Group Captain Alan Anderson, flying one of the Tempests – no one was leading – called a 'fantastically misplanned operation'. The Spitfire's last air combat victories had been against the RAF.[32]

Cold War Spitfires
Defending the UK, Germany and Austria in the opening years of the Cold War, RAF Spitfire fighters remained in service until replaced by jets by 1951, reconnaissance versions until 1957. During the Communist insurgency in Malaya, starting in 1948, RAF Spitfire XIVs, FR 18s and PR 19s and FAA Seafires were used in air-to-ground and reconnaissance roles. The last ground attack mission by an RAF Spitfire was on

1 January 1951 over Malaya. Photo-reconnaissance Spitfire PR 19s took part until 1954; high-level photographs detected insurgent base camps (and the crops grown to sustain them).

During the 1950–3 Korean War, Spitfire FR 24s defended Hong Kong. They never saw combat. Hong Kong-based Spitfire FR 18s and PR 19s flew more than sixty reconnaissance sorties over China, including low-level missions to Hainan after its occupation by the People's Liberation Army. They did not encounter opposition. The South African Air Force trained a fighter squadron for Korea using Spitfire HF IXs. It re-equipped with F-51 Mustangs before going into action.

Royal Navy Seafire 47s, operating from the carrier HMS *Triumph* off the Korean coast, had been in combat over Malaya before they fought the North Koreans through the summer of 1950. The Seafires provided defensive air protection and were kept on deck alert against low-altitude attackers, flew armed photo-reconnaissance missions and took part in air-to-ground and anti-shipping missions. 'We rocketed and strafed trains and ammunition dumps,' said Lieutenant John Treacher.[33] Only one Seafire was lost in air combat, when the pilot inadvertently pointed his nose at a US Air Force B-29 bomber. A gunner, keeping up wartime traditions, shot the Seafire down. The pilot survived.[34]

The improved performance of the Seafire 47 had resulted in increased weight. Structural damage from arrested landings was common. By the time the *Triumph* sailed for home, just four of its Seafires were flyable and only one fit for combat. With the Seafire 47 out of production since 1949 and no replacement aircraft available, they were withdrawn from combat.

From 1948 to 1961, Burma's Spitfires and Seafires (reinforced with ex-Israeli aircraft) carried out fighter-bomber missions and tried to intercept (without shooting any down) resupply flights to Chinese Nationalist forces operating in the north of the country.[35]

The Egyptian Air Force used Spitfires in the 1956 war after their jet aircraft had either been destroyed in Anglo–French air attacks or evacuated out of range. Spitfire 22s were all the Egyptians had left for combat missions over the Sinai. They did not encounter Israeli fighters.[36] Israel had retired its Spitfires just before the war. They last saw combat in 1951 border fighting with Syria.

In 1963, a Spitfire PR 19 from the Battle of Britain Memorial Flight flew battle trials against an English Electric Lightning Mach 2 jet interceptor. The RAF needed to know how Singapore-based Lightnings could take on Indonesia's P-51s if the confrontation over Borneo escalated.

Spain

Spain was where the Bf 109 had first gone into combat. The Spanish Air Force, flying Bf 109s since 1938, sent a volunteer *Staffel* to fly Bf 109Es with the Luftwaffe on the eastern front in 1941–2. A Bf 109G-2 production line had been set up in Spain in 1944. After the war, the lack of a suitable engine limited operations. They were built as HA 1109 fighters with indigenous engines, starting in 1945, with the 1300 hp Hispano-Suiza 12.7Z fitted in sixty-seven HA 1112-K1L versions, starting in 1951. In the 1950s, the aircraft were redesigned in Spain to accommodate the Merlin, available in quantity from Britain, as the Hispano HA 1112-MIL *Buchon*, eventually serving in the Spanish Air Force alongside Lockheed F-104C Starfighters capable of Mach 2. HA 1112 production continued until 1958. They saw action against insurgents in the Spanish Sahara from 1957 to 1964, flying from airfields at Al Aoun and in the Canary Islands, the plane's final combat operations. In 1967, as the HA 1112 was finally leaving Spanish Air Force service, twenty-three were purchased.

They were going to be used in making a movie: *The Battle of Britain*, a wide-screen, full-colour account of the events of 1940 with a huge budget. Previously, Bf 108s, which had been produced in France after the war, had been flown for the cameras for the highly profitable *The Longest Day*; as had Spitfires which had been towing targets for gunnery practice in Belgium until the early 1960s. Now it was to be the turn of the Bf 109.

The Spitfire and Bf 109 on screen: The Battle of Britain

Neil Williams rolled his Spitfire into a near-vertical bank and went into a tight turn to get behind the Messerschmitt Bf 109. Concentrating, he was able to keep his eyes focused on the Bf 109 as his peripheral vision faded, blackness edging it against the brilliant blue sky. With his Spitfire turning tight, he felt increasing g forces compressing him into his seat, until, pushing his control stick forward, smoothly coordinating with his rudder pedals, he rolled the Spitfire back into level flight. He was where he needed to be, directly behind and below the Messerschmitt, in its pilot's blind spot. The Bf 109 stayed at cruise speed in level flight. Williams instinctively swivelled his head around and checked the Spitfire's rear-view mirror, 'clearing his tail'.

What he saw was the brightly painted twin-engine B-25 camera aircraft, nicknamed 'The Psychedelic Monster', keeping a safe distance, filming his simulated attack on the Messerschmitt. This dogfight was not taking place over England in the summer of 1940, but over Spain in 1968, as part of the filming of the classic movie *The Battle of Britain*. Neil Williams' brilliant flying had been captured on film.

Despite high-profile efforts to ensure accuracy – Adolf Galland was one of the technical advisors and, filming in Spain, made his last flight at the controls of 'his' fighter – the film had many anachronisms and dramatic compromises. The actual characters were mixed with thinly disguised fictional versions of their historical counterparts. The heroine (Susannah York) wore 1960s lingerie for her bedroom scene. But Hugh Dowding, aged eighty-six, wheelchair-bound from arthritis, wept, overcome with emotion, watching Laurence Olivier, himself a wartime FAA pilot, sit at his old desk and play him. Keith Park was less happy with his portrayal. Galland walked off the set.

The real stars were the aeroplanes. The HA 1112s, modified and painted like Bf 109E-3s, still revealed, by shape and sound, their Merlin engines. Spitfires were played by a wide range of mainly late-production versions, Merlin and Griffon powered.

The movie itself gathered much publicity but limited critical esteem and did not earn back its production costs. Yet, though a box-office disappointment, it had a long-lasting impact. The aircraft assembled for the movie were dispersed to collections and museums worldwide. Individuals and organisations have paid the substantial costs to keep them airworthy and put more into the air, some being recovered wartime wrecks. More Spitfires and Bf 109s were flyable in 2011 than when the movie was made. [37]

20

From Fighters to Legends

Duxford

If you like your history with insights, you cannot do better than to watch the flying at Duxford on a fine English autumn day. Legends are not what the Imperial War Museum's facility at Duxford, just south of Cambridge, is about. The Imperial War Museum is about serious history. But the legends are there all the same. Legends still thrive, invited in through the front gate of popular culture and imagination, and are maintained by myths, much as fighters must be maintained by ground crew. The legends and myths are often what end up being valued, a past people can invest with their emotions and significance for their own lives. It is no easy matter to distinguish legends and myths from facts; all alike come camouflaged. The legends started at the same time as the planes were designed (by heroic designers) and only grew as they went into action (with heroic pilots). The widespread desires for an understandable narrative and admirable heroes remain difficult to reconcile with the complex events of the Second World War and the complex technologies of the late industrial age.

The wartime airfield – Douglas Bader twice led its 'big wing' of fighters to defend London in the climactic battle of 15 September 1940 – is home base to a large collection of painstakingly restored historical aircraft. Many of them still fly. At air displays, held several days a year, Duxford hosts large crowds who see and hear the actions and sounds that, seventy years ago, could be seen and heard at airfields worldwide.

Today's Duxford-based Spitfire is treated with all the care that a complex, well-preserved and valued artefact merits. The man in the cockpit is a professional, with extensive experience flying for an airline or an air force, and has on his own acquired experience with once-common technologies, such as piston engines and tailwheels. He is not only older and more professional, he is as distant from the young men – often quickly trained, and considered, like their plane, expendable – who long ago took the Spitfire to war as today's museum at Duxford is from its past as a front-line airfield.

No Spitfire was built to be flyable seventy years after it came off the assembly line. To transform an expendable aeroplane into something that will endure has been a remarkable achievement. It also means transforming the experience. In wartime flying, fear and risk were as much a part of flying a Spitfire as the sound of the engine. People died in Spitfire cockpits every day. Today, while preserved aircraft have been known to crash and kill even the most skilful pilots,[1] care and professionalism can allow a 70-year-old aircraft to fly on a regular basis.

The ground crew preparing a restored Spitfire for flight does not look like its wartime counterparts. Even in the absence of haste, the technicians are distinguished by their age, their clean civilian overalls and the digital equipment keeping the Spitfire flying, but they show equal professional competence and concern as they accompany the pilot, doing the walk-around inspection. Like their wartime counterparts, they mount the wing root to assist the pilot in easing down into the seat in the cockpit, then help him to strap in.

It is now up to the pilot to perform the cockpit check, until, finally, he gives one last look around. The warning shout 'Clear prop' precedes the starting of the Merlin. The propeller blades turn over, slowly at first, then the engine appears to burst into noisy and immediate life, with puffs of smoke from the exhaust.

The pilot throttles back the Merlin. More checks are carried out in the cockpit until the pilot signals: chocks away. The chocks holding the main undercarriage wheels in place are pulled away by the ground crew using long ropes. The pilot releases the brakes. Slowly and carefully – a Fabergé egg held in the hand – the Spitfire taxis out from the flight line to the taxiway, then turns and taxies along it to the end of the active runway – although, at Duxford, tailwheel aircraft will operate from the grass field when wind conditions permit.

The engine is revved up with a roar, both magnetos checked, then throttled back. Finally, the Spitfire turns onto the runway and lines up with the centre line. The pilot gently opens the throttle. The Spitfire picks up speed down the runway. The tailwheel rises, followed by the whole tail and the main wheels. As the Spitfire starts to climb above the runway, the two main undercarriage legs retract into the underside of the wing. This one Spitfire is, for the moment at least, back in its element.

O! I have slipped the surly bonds of earth . . .

The words of the poem are brought, unbidden, to mind as the Spitfire, its main wheels retracting, climbs away into the afternoon sky from the Duxford runway. Few opening lines in twentieth-century poetry are better known than that of 'High Flight', written by a Spitfire pilot, John Gillespie Magee. He, like many of the technologies and people in the Spitfire's story, had roots on both sides of the Atlantic. An American with a British mother and an English public school education, he had turned down attending Yale to volunteer to fly with the RCAF in England. He was killed in 1941 when his Spitfire crashed after a mid-air collision. His best-known poem is about flying, writing and, appearing only at the end, the hand of God.

I've chased the shouting wind along, and flung
My eager craft through footless halls of air

Magee's 'eager craft' was both flying Spitfires and writing poems. It was the poem Ronald Reagan eloquently used to memorialise the lost astronauts of the Space Shuttle *Challenger*.

It is not just the earth that the Spitfire, now climbing over the motorway to Cambridge and London along the airfield's eastern perimeter, has left behind. It is today's world. Yet the past represented by the Spitfire, though real, remains for those watching from the ground as far out of reach as Magee's 'shouting wind'. Chase the past for a lifetime, you'll never catch it, even though you can study it and measure it. The past is not a museum (as RAF Duxford has become), which conserves. Nor is it a prison (as RAF Eastchurch became), which confines. But, like museums and prisons, and, indeed, the wind itself, the past is real. It is a presence that can warm you or, sometimes, even on an English autumn day, chill you to the bone.

The Spitfire and Bf 109 today

The past of violent struggles between European powers has receded. Few of those living today anticipate that their lives and futures will be violently altered by war, as previous generations experienced in 1914 and 1939. But if the struggles – and the vast majority of those who participated in them – have passed, their impact has not. Hitler remains the personification of barbarous tyranny, Churchill of democratic leadership in a crisis. Such lasting impact is not limited to people. The Spitfire and the Bf 109 both remain more than interesting examples of outdated technologies. Vintage automobiles and preserved steam locomotives are both those things. But no one used to die in them. These aircraft present the past not as a construct, perceptions and prejudices agreed upon, but as evidence of actual world-shaping events, however open to changing interpretation.

The Spitfire was a legend and a symbol even while the war was in progress. That is why Britain collected money for the Spitfire Fund during the war. A film based on R.J. Mitchell's life and his development of the Spitfire was a major 1942 cinematic release. No other aeroplane of the Second World War carries the same associations, a part of history contributing to today's sense of identity. The Spitfire will always invoke the Battle of Britain, part of the Second World War when Britain was alone and forced to defend itself, without moral dilemmas to trouble the post-modern observer. It required not Spitfires but the vastly more destructive and morally ambiguous forces of the Soviet Army and the Anglo-American bomber offensive to secure victory in 1945. That is part of the past that chills.

The Spitfire remains a British icon. In an age when Britain cannot build an aeroplane by itself and its international role has become that of a junior partner in coalitions, the Spitfire is a symbol of British innovation, unique greatness and, above all, skill and courage in self-defence.

Anything powerful – symbols, memory, the past itself – makes people perceive it as part of what they are. They try to control or use it. In 2009, the fringe British National Party made the news when it used a photograph of a Spitfire as a nationalist image on a poster opposing immigration from eastern Europe. This turned into self-parody when they selected a photograph of a Spitfire belonging to one of the RAF's Polish squadrons.[2]

History is important, even if its political expression often tends to be in the form of over-generalisation and inaccurate clichés. The Spitfire still projects an image, one the BNP clumsily attempted to appropriate. The Spitfire is recognisable even to those who are only experiencing it as received history or through stories told by their relatives – an object of worldwide and national emotional investment.

Duxford is one of the few places where, on occasion, a Bf 109 can be seen, still flying, alongside a Spitfire. Sometimes, those who played a part in their intertwined stories can been seen watching the planes together. Spectators appreciate the rarity of a flying Bf 109. But the legend of the Bf 109 *is* different. Germany remains proud of its history of technological innovation. The Deutsches Museum in Munich, close to the university where Willy Messerschmitt earned his degree, has among its exhibits a Bf 109E and a Me 262, the two aircraft designs of which, in his long career, he was most proud. They are remembered as masterpieces of aircraft engineering.

The preserved Bf 109 in Luftwaffe markings at Duxford presents an artefact of Hitler's Germany, evoking high-performance fighter planes and brave pilots, contesting the skies, not the distant enemy in Berlin committed to murder and conquest. The multinational world of the Spitfire, with its story of bravery and hard-won success, is present at Duxford; the opposing multinational effort, that which built the Bf 109, is absent. However different the two sides were, their aircraft were similar, as were their fighter pilots and the squadrons they flew in. Both fighters' stories had similar characters: the brilliant designer, the brave fighter pilots, all volunteers; ground crews and factory workers, often conscripts during the war. But the Bf 109's story includes many characters who had no counterpart: the totalitarian and criminal national leadership, the failed Luftwaffe leaders, the enslaved workers, the heroic, yet nameless, saboteurs. As capstone systems, the fighters are only the most visible parts of the two complex and inter-twined stories.

The future of the legends

The world that created the Spitfire and the Bf 109, like the war that was the reason for their existence, is increasingly distant. On the seventieth anniversary of the Battle of Britain, in 2010, it was estimated that some eighty of The Few, the RAF fighter pilots who had defended Britain in 1940, were still alive. Their German equivalents, inevitably, are even fewer. Those who made up the story of the Spitfire and the Bf 109 are almost gone, but their aeroplanes remain.

Even when the few remaining people who were part of these events appear at the Duxford flightline to watch the planes, they are emissaries from the vanished world, the actions of their younger selves seemingly as heroic and as incredible as anything in the *Iliad* or the *Odyssey*, and seemingly as distant. For many, if not most, their wartime flying was the central fact of their life's story. When they die, their obituaries – rattling good reading – tend to summarise their post-1945 lives in a conclud-ing paragraph. When they talk among themselves, they speak of a fellowship outsiders cannot share. They remain untouched by the post-modern insistence on ironising their experience. It was all important to them, all real, and they remember the all too many members of that fel-lowship who, unlike them, never had the chance to grow old. The differences between the causes for which the Spitfire and Bf 109 fought were enormous, but little distinguishes the few remaining survivors watching the aeroplanes that defined and shaped their lives decades ago. The rare elderly Germans at Duxford differ from their British coun-terparts only in that they have travelled farther and tend to be better dressed.

Looking at a preserved and restored, airworthy Spitfire flying over Duxford, it requires a feat of imagination to recall that, in the Battle of Britain, a few hundred of those planes appeared to be the last defence against what Churchill called, in his 'finest hour' speech of 18 June 1940, 'the abyss of a new dark age made more sinister, and perhaps more pro-tracted, by the lights of perverted science'. Historic artefacts, no matter how well preserved and how perceptively curated, present but shadows of the world in which they once played a vital, even decisive, role. Yet they are important as a link to the past, without which the present is chaos and the future unreadable.

The context of the Spitfire and the Bf 109 was one of struggle. This means the struggle of the Allies against Nazi Germany, that of RAF Fighter Command against the Luftwaffe in the Battle of Britain, but also the countless individual struggles that, only in the light of history, can be linked together through these two aeroplanes. It was the struggle of the dying R.J. Mitchell, working to finish the Spitfire, listening to flight tests in the back seat of his car when he could no longer go to his office. It was the struggle of the Bf 109 pilots of 1944–5, both in the wartime skies over Germany and in their own minds as they faced near-inevitable death fighting for a defeated country. It was the struggle of forced labourers, compelled to build Bf 109s, deciding to risk their lives to slow or sabotage production, even though no medals were awarded for their actions and no historians recorded their deeds. The technology of the Spitfire and Bf 109 may today be of only historical interest. The human dimension revealed by their stories remains as applicable as ever.

High flight

Turning gently and gracefully as it reaches pattern altitude, the Spitfire's elliptical wings flash in the sunlight. Those wings were Mitchell's design decision, made back in 1935, when he was trying to do his best in the brief time permitted him to provide Britain with the fighter it would need for the coming conflict. The wings literally shaped the Spitfire and its story. Mitchell's elliptical wings were what made it possible for Spitfires to out-turn Bf 109s over London and impossible for fighter Spitfires to fly to Berlin until the last days of the war, when it no longer mattered.

Coming overhead above the field, the song of the Spitfire's Merlin becomes stronger, but never discordant. Like a song, or a poem, the Merlin means different things to each listener, depending on what he or she brings to it. The Merlin does sound a musical note. Those who heard the Merlin in their youth know it for the rest of their lives.

To those living or serving in Britain during the Second World War, whether in uniform, in industry, or just trying to grow up, hearing the Merlin was a shared experience. *I heard that, I remember that, I was there.* Some few in France, Belgium or the Netherlands remember it, often heard during the years of Rhubarbs, Circuses and Ramrods. Johnnie Johnson remembered how they 'would look up at the sound of our engines and wave frantically when they saw our RAF roundels'.[3] It provided substance to the words broadcast over the BBC: that Britain was fighting, and that Frenchmen, Belgians, Dutchmen and men from around the world were also flying Spitfires.

The dying R.J. Mitchell, sitting in his vehicle in 1936, listened to the engine of the prototype. It told him about the slow flight characteristics of the aeroplane that was to be, as 'High Flight' was for Magee, his final yet best-known creation. It is not noise to those who know it and understand it.

Knowing and understanding the Spitfire and the Bf 109 requires more than appreciating artefacts and acquiring antiquarian knowledge. It is an open door to the world that really was just the day before yesterday, for all that the heroism of those in the story – and the numbers who died during it – evokes a distant Homeric past.

Never more so than on those occasions when one of the few flyable Bf 109s – much rarer than Spitfires – joins its former opponent in the skies over Duxford. Most of the surviving Bf 109s are Spanish-built HA 1112 versions, ironically re-engined with Merlins. You cannot tell them apart from the sound, just as you cannot tell, by looking at the few elderly gentlemen and ladies among the crowds watching them, which side they flew for or built aircraft for, seventy years ago.

At Duxford, the Spitfire and the Bf 109 fly. Not in the wartime sky, touched with fire, but in the cold sunlight of history.

Comparative Ranks

RAF	USAAF	Luftwaffe
		Reichsmarschall
Marshal of the Royal Air Force	General of the Army	*Generalfeldmarschall*
Air Chief Marshal	General	*Generaloberst*
Air Marshal	Lieutenant General	*General der Flieger*
Air Vice Marshal	Major General	*Generalleutnant*
Air Commodore	Brigadier General	*Generalmajor*
Group Captain	Colonel	*Oberst*
Wing Commander	Lieutenant Colonel	*Oberstleutnant*
Squadron Leader	Major	*Major*
Flight Lieutenant	Captain	*Hauptmann*
Flying Officer	First Lieutenant	*Oberleutnant*
Pilot Officer	Second Lieutenant	*Leutnant*
Officer Cadet	Aviation Cadet	*Oberfähnreich/Fähnreich*
Warrant Officer	Flight Officer	*Oberfeldwebel*
Flight Sergeant	Master Sergeant	*Stabsfeldwebel*
Sergeant	Staff/Technical Sergeant	*Feldwebel*
Corporal	Sergeant	*Unterfeldwebel/Unteroffizer*
Leading Aircraftsman	Corporal	*Obergefreiter*
Aircraftsman First Class	Private First Class	*Gefreiter*
Aircraftsman Second Class	Private	*Flieger*

Major Production Version Chronology

Numbers show production of versions (for German 109s, in thousands for entire sub-type). Brackets indicate non-Spitfire/109 type. Years indicate when entered service or first flown (for prototype or experimental aircraft)

Bf 109	Spitfire
1934 – [Bf 108A] prototype	1934 – [Type 224]
1935 – [Bf 108B]	
1935 – Bf 109V1 prototype (Kestrel engine)	1935 [Hurricane prototype]
1936 – Bf 109V2 (Jumo engine)	1936 – Type 300 (Spitfire prototype)
1937 – Bf 109B/C (Jumo 210D/G engine, 3/4 MGs) 0.4	1937 – [Hurricane I]
1938 – Bf 109D (Jumo 210D engine, 4 MGs) 0.65	1938 – Spitfire I (first production Spitfire, Merlin III engine) 1583
1938 – Bf 109E-1 (DB 601A engine), 4×MG 3.6	
1939 – [Fw 190V1 prototype]	
1940 – Bf 109T (carrier version with increased span, as E-3) 0.07	1940 – Spitfire II (developed from Mk I, Merlin XII engine) 920
1940 – Bf 109E-3 (DB 601A engine), 2×20mm wing cannon	1940 – Spitfire III experimental (developed from Mk I, Merlin XX engine)
1940 – Bf 109E-4 (DB 601A engine), wing cannon. E-4/BN version with DB 601N engine and bomb racks.	1940 – Spitfire PR IA-C (converted from Mk I, Merlin III engine) 29 (redesignated Spitfire PRIII)

Bf 109	Spitfire
1940 – Bf 109E-7 (DB 601A engine), wing cannon, bombs or drop tanks	
1940 – Bf 109E-8 (DB 601N engine), wing cannon, E-9 was camera-equipped recon version	
1940 – Bf 109F-1 (DB 601N engine), single engine cannon (20mm), 2xMG, aerodynamically redesigned 2.7	1940 – [Hurricane II] (Merlin XX)
	1941 – Spitfire V (interim version, developed from Mk II with improved Merlin 45 thru 55 engines) 6479
1941 – Bf 109F-2 (DB 601N engine), engine cannon (15mm) 2xMG	1941 – Spitfire IV experimental (first Griffon II engine version)
1941 – Bf 109 F-3/4 (DB 601E engine) engine cannon (15mm) 2xMG	1941 – Spitfire PR ID (developed from Mk I, redesignated PR IV) 2
1941 – [Fw 190A]	1941 – Spitfire PR IV (developed from Mk V, Merlin 45 thru 55 engines) 229
	1941 – Spitfire PR VII (developed from Mk PR IV and Mk V, Merlin 46 engine) 43
	1941 – [Typhoon I]
	1941 – [Hurricane IV]
1942 – Bf 109G-1/G-2 (developed from Bf 109F with DB 605A engine) engine cannon (20mm), 2xMG 23	1942 – Spitfire VI (high-altitude version with Merlin 47) 100 1942 – Seafire IB (developed from Mk V, Merlin 45–46) 166
	1942 – Seafire II (developed from Seafire IB, Merlin 32 or 55) 302
	1942 – Seafire III (developed from Seafire II, Merlin 32 or 55) 1220
	1942 – P-51A Mustang (Allison engine)]
	1942 – Spitfire PR XIII (developed from Mk PR VII, Merlin 32) 18
1943 – Bf 109G-5/G-6 (DB 605 with increased armament 'bump') engine cannon (20mm). MG replaced by HMG. Many armament options.	1943 – Spitfire VII (redesigned upgraded Merlin 71 high-altitude version) 140

Bf 109	Spitfire
1943 – Bf 109G-8 (recon version of G-6)	1943 – Spitfire VIII (redesigned upgraded Merlin 61 thru 70 version) 1658
1943 – Bf 109G-10 (DB 605D engine) engine cannon (30mm)	1943 – Spitfire IX (interim version, Mark V modified with two-stage supercharger Merlin 61 thru 70 engine) 5665
1943 – Bf 109G-12 (2-seat trainer)	1943 – Spitfire XII (interim version, modified Mark V with Griffon III/IV engine) 100
1943 – [Fw 190D]	1943 – Spitfire PR XI (developed from Mk PR IV and Mk IX, Merlin 61/70 engine) 471
1943 – Bf 109G-14 (DB 605AS engine) engine cannon (20mm)	1943 – Spitfire XX experimental (developed from Spitfire IV and XII with Griffon II B engine)
1943 – Bf 109H (high-altitude fighter/recon with extended 11.9 m wingspan) 0.1	1943 – [P-51B Mustang (Packard Merlin engine)]
	1944 – [Hawker Tempest]
1944 – Bf 109K-1/K-2 prototype (DB 605ASCM engine) 3.6	1944 – Spitfire XVI (Mark IX with US-built Packard Merlin 266 engine) 1045
1944 – Bf 109K-4/6 (DB 605 DCM engine) 1×cannon, 2×HMG, underwing armament options	1944 – Spitfire PR X (developed from Mk PR XI and MK VII) 16
1944 – [Ta 152]	1944 – Spitfire XIV (interim version, developed from Mk VIII with Griffon 61 thru 67) 957
1944 – [Me-262 jet fighter]	1944 – Spitfire PR XIX (Griffon 65–66 version, developed from Mk XIV and PR XI) 225
	1944 – [Gloster Meteor jet fighter]
	1944 – Spitfire 21 (Griffon 61–64 engine, developed from Mk XX, most extensive redesign) 120
	1944 – Seafire XV (Griffon VI engine, developed from Mk XII and Seafire III) 390
	1944 – Seafire 17 (Griffon VI engine, developed from Seafire XV) 232
	1944 – Spitfire 23 experimental (Mk 21 with Griffon 61, laminar flow technology, never built)

Bf 109	Spitfire
1945 – Bf 109K-14 prototype (DB 605L engine)	1945 – Spitfire 18 (Griffon 65–67 engine, developed from Mk XIV and XX) 300
	1945 – Spitfire 22 (Griffon 61–64 engine, developed from Mk 21) 260
1945 – HA 1109 (Spanish HS 127Z-89 engine Bf 109G-2 version, 2x20mm) 24	1945 – Seafire 45 (Griffon 61 engine, developed from Mk 21) 50
1945 – Avia S.199 (Jumo 211F engine Czechoslovak Bf 109G-14 version, 2xHMG, 2xMG) 44	1945 – Seafire 46 (Griffon 61–87 engine, developed from Mk 22 and Seafire 45) 24
	1945 [Spiteful and Seafang]
	1946 – Spitfire 24 (Griffon 61 engine, developed from Mk 22 and Mk 18) 81
	1946 – Seafire 47 (Griffon 87–88 engine, developed from Mk 24 and Seafire 46) 90
1951 – HA-112-K1L (Spanish HS 127Z-17 engine Bf 109G-2 version) 65	
1954 – HA 1112-MIL (Merlin engine, Spanish Bf 109G-2 version) 143	

Notes

1 Introduction: Over London, 15 September 1940

1 Peggy Carpenter Isby described the incident while sitting outside this pub (The Royal Oak), on the same bench, in the summer of 1972. By that time, the former RAF Eastchurch had become a prison and the former RAF Duxford was becoming a museum. Britain had more prisons, more museums and few armourers, fewer still those whose lives were centred around flying, operating or building actual military aircraft.

2 A 'chiefy' is a senior NCO. http://www.perth.igs.net/~long/slang.htm

3 That German success in achieving air superiority over England would be followed by invasion no longer appears as inevitable as it did at the time. The Royal Navy remained undefeated. However, if Hitler was not serious about preparations for invasion, he did not tell his generals.

2 The Race to Design the Modern Fighter: to October 1936

1 James P. O'Donnell, 'The Secret Fight that Doomed the Luftwaffe', *Saturday Evening Post* (8 April 1950), pp. 22–3, 100–05, at p. 23.

2 On the rise of Bfw, see Lutz Budrass, *Flugzeugindustrie und Luftrüstung in Deutschland, 1918–1945* (Düsseldorf: Droste Verlag, 1998), pp. 20, 90–6; USSBS, *Subject: Prof. William Messerschmitt*, Interview 6, 11–12 May 1945, US Strategic Bombing Survey, pp. 1–4, National Archives (US), RG 243 Entry 32 Box 4; Rakan Kokothaki, 'A Contemporary Internal Messerschmitt History' in Walter J. Boyne, *Messerschmitt Me 262: Arrow to the Future* (Atglen, PA: Schiffer, 1994), pp. 165–81.

3 Wolfgang Wagner, *Kurt Tank: Focke Wulf's Designer and Chief Test Pilot*, The History of German Aviation, trans. Don Cox (Atglen, PA: Schiffer, 1998), p. 35. Tank's all-metal flying boats for Rohrbach were seminal in the US, convincing industry and military the future was all-metal. Peter W. Brooks, *The Modern Airliner* (London: Putnam, 1961), pp. 19, 39–44.

4 David Irving, *Goering: A Biography* (New York: Avon Books, 1990), pp. 94, 131, 136. Hitler's use of airliners to present himself as a national figure, a moderniser, and to descend from the clouds as a mystical deliverer was memorably portrayed in the opening of Leni Riefenstahl's documentary *Triumph of the Will*.

5   Kokothaki, 'Messerschmitt History', p. 173.

6   R.J. Mitchell, 'Racing Seaplanes and Their Influence on Design', *The Aeroplane, Aeronautical Engineering Supplement* (25 December 1929), pp. 1429–30, at p. 1429.

7   Ibid.; 'Schneider Winner', *Aeroplane Monthly* (September 2011), pp. 22–3 at p. 22.

8   'Batchy' is a contraction of Atcherley and 'barmy', one of many RAF terms for crazy (for the same reason the Inuit are said to have many terms for snow). Nicknames, common as a form of self-definition outside the mainstream of (ground-based, rules-based, feminised) society in the earlier years of the twentieth century, have endured in military aviation and, in conscious imitation, some aspects of civil aviation (which is why the author is known at some local airfields as 'Dismal' Isby). Nicknames were commonplace among those involved in aviation in that period (air-centric, achieve-ment-based, male-dominated) to an extent that seems strange in the twenty-first century, dominated as it is by a celebrity culture. The focus on achievement rather than rules helps show why repressive regimes have trouble with their fighter pilots (and jazz musicians) and why many fighter pilots obsessed over their victory scores (and, especially Germans, decorations) and transgressed regulations.

9   John Pudney, *A Pride of Unicorns: Richard and David Atcherley of the RAF* (London: Oldbourne, 1960), pp. 80–1.

10   Gordon Mitchell, *R.J. Mitchell: Schooldays to Spitfire* (Stroud: Tempus, 2006), p. 156.

11   J. Smith, 'R. J. Mitchell – Aircraft Designer', *The Journal of the Royal Aeronautical Society*, vol. 58 no. 521 (May 1954), pp. 311–28, at p. 314.

12   Jeffrey Quill, *Spitfire: A Test Pilot's Story* (Manchester: Crecy, 1998), chs 2 and 3.

13   Lee Kennett, *A History of Strategic Bombing* (New York: Scribner's, 1982), pp. 39–104; Williamson Murray, *Strategy for Defeat: The Luftwaffe 1933–45* (Maxwell AFB: Air University Press, 1983), pp. 1–26, 321–36; R.J. Overy, *The Air War* (New York: Stein and Day, 1980), pp. 5–25.

14   AIR 20/40, *Air Staff Memorandum No 11A*, March 1934, National Archives (UK); AIR 41/88, *Signals, Fighter Control and Interception*, vol. 5, Air Historical Branch, 1952, pp. 5–7, National Archives (UK); *RAF War Manual Part I, Operations* (May 1935), pp. 1, 57, National Archives (US), RG 18 Entry 223 Box 1; R.J. Overy, 'Air Power and the Origins of Deterrence Theory Before 1939', *The Journal of Strategic Studies*, vol. 15 no. 1 (March 1992), pp. 73–101; Barry D. Powers, *Strategy Without Slide-Rule: British Air Strategy 1914–1939* (London: Croom Helm, 1976), pp. 158–207; Scott Robertson, 'The Development of Royal Air Force Strategic Bombing Between the Wars', *Airpower Journal*, vol. 12 no. 1 (Spring 1998), pp. 37–52.

15   David Irving, *The Rise and Fall of the Luftwaffe: the Life of Field Marshal Erhard Milch* (Boston: Little Brown, 1974), p. 144.

16   Richard Blunk, *Hugo Junkers: Ein Leben für Technik und Luftfhart*, 2nd edn (Düsseldorf: Econ-Verlag, 1951), pp. 82–4, 166–70, 222–5; Budrass, *Flugzeugindustrie*, pp. 320–35; Olaf Gröhler and Helmut Erfurth, *Hugo Junkers: ein politisches Essay* ([East] Berlin: Militärverlag der Deutschen Demokratischen Republik, 1989), pp. 48–54; Irving, *Rise and Fall of the Luftwaffe*, pp. 37–8; Günter Schmitt, *Hugo Junkers Und Seine Flugzeug* (Stuttgart: Motor Verlag, 1986), pp. 214–18.

17 Edward L. Homze, *Arming the Luftwaffe: the Reich Air Ministry and the German Aircraft Industry, 1919–39* (Lincoln, NE: University of Nebraska, 1976), p. 197; Eugene M. Emme, 'The Renaissance of German Air Power 1919–1932', *Air Power Historian* (July 1958), pp. 139–51; Prof. Richard Suchenwirth, *Command and Leadership in the German Air Force*, USAF Historical Studies, no. 174 (Maxwell AFB: USAF Historical Division, 1969), pp. 75, 93; Karl-Heinz Völker, *Die Entwicklung der Militärischen Luftfahrt in Deutschland 1920–1933* (Stuttgart: Militar Geschichtlichen Forschungsamt, 1962), p. 125.

18 Donald Caldwell and Richard Muller, *The Luftwaffe Over Germany: Defence of the Reich* (London: Greenhill, 2007), ch. 1; Williamson Murray, *Luftwaffe* (Annapolis: Naval and Aviation, 1989), p. 16; James S. Corum, *Wolfram von Richthofen: Master of the German Air War* (Lawrence, KS: University Press of Kansas, 2008), pp. 105–8.

19 For details of the specification, see Rüdiger Kosin, *The German Fighter Since 1915* (London: Putnam, 1988), p. 14.

20 Mitchell, *Schooldays to Spitfire*, p. 44.

21 Mitchell, *Schooldays to Spitfire*, p. 232.

22 Letter to the Editor, Robert McLean, *The Sunday Times* (18 August 1957), p. 13; 'Spitfire's Origin in a "Crazy Experimental Thing"', *The Times* (19 August 1957), p. 9. The Air Ministry was actually more receptive to new technologies in fighter design than McLean recalled over twenty years later. Colin Sinnott, *The RAF and Aircraft Design, 1923–39, Air Staff Operational Requirements* (London and Portland, OR: Frank Cass, 2001), pp. 84–103; Eric B. Morgan and Edward Shacklady, *Spitfire, the History* (Stamford, Lincs: Key Books, 2000), p. 15.

23 Sinnott, *RAF and Aircraft Design*, pp. 97–8.

24 Smith, 'R.J. Mitchell', p. 314.

25 Mitchell, *Schooldays to Spitfire*, p. 140.

26 Mitchell, *Schooldays to Spitfire*, pp. 90–2.

27 Smith, 'R.J. Mitchell', p. 313.

28 Beverly Shenstone, 'Shaping the Spitfire', in Alfred Price, *Spitfire: A Documentary History* (London: Macdonald and Jane's, 1977), pp. 31–4, at p. 34.

29 Joseph Smith, 'Development of the Spitfire and Seafire', *Journal of the Royal Aeronautical Society*, vol. 51 no. 2 (February 1947), pp. 339–83; 'Spitfire and Seafire Development described by Supermarine Chief Designer', *Flight* (26 December 1946), pp. 707–10, at p. 707; Morgan and Shacklady, *Spitfire*, pp. 103–4, 404–5; Jeffrey Quill with Sebastian Cox, *Birth of a Legend: The Spitfire* (Washington: Smithsonian Institution Press, 1986), ch. 10.

30 Sinnott, *RAF and Aircraft Design*, p. 98. The 24-cylinder Napier Dagger never solved its cooling and noise problems, limiting the utility of those aircraft produced with it and leading to problems with its larger successor, the Sabre. Herschel Smith, *Aircraft Piston Engines* (New York: McGraw Hill, 1981), p. 171.

31 G.C. Peden, *British Rearmament and the Treasury* (Edinburgh: Edinburgh University Press, 1979); Robert P. Shay, *British Rearmament in the Thirties* (Princeton: Princeton University Press, 1971).

32 Air Marshal Sir Ralph Sorley, in Smith, 'R.J. Mitchell', p. 326.

33 Milch was at the meeting that identified Brownshirts to be murdered by their fellow Nazis. He recollected adding no names to the list, though it was read out in his presence. Irving, *Rise and Fall of the Luftwaffe*, pp. 40–2.

34 Irving, *Rise and Fall of the Luftwaffe*, pp. 51–2, 439 fn 4; Bryan Mark Rigg, *Hitler's Jewish Soldiers: The Untold Story of Nazi Racial Laws and Men of Jewish Descent in the German Military* (Lawrence, KS: University Press of Kansas, 2007), pp. 29–30, 177–9.

35 Heinz J, Nowarra, *The Messerschmitt Me 109: A Famous German Fighter* (Los Angeles: Aero Publishers, 1963), p. 13. Quoted in Martin Caidin, *Me 109: Willy Messerschmitt's Peerless Fighter* (New York: Ballantine, 1968), p. 17.

36 Irving, *Rise and Fall of the Luftwaffe*, pp. 43, 332–4.

37 Ernst Heinkel, *My Stormy Life* (Stuttgart: Aviatic Verlag, 1991) suggests, overall, that Milch's characterisation may have been an accurate one. Heinkel declined to join the Nazi party. This may also have been a factor.

38 Göring's 20 October 1933 letter to Croneiss is reproduced in Peter Schmoll, *Nest of Eagles: Messerschmitt Production and Flight Testing at Regensburg 1936–1945* (Hersham: Classic, Ian Allan, 2004), p. 169.

39 Kosin, *German Fighter*, p. 93.

40 Willy Messerschmitt interview by Manfred W. Hentschel and Dr Alexander von Hoffmann, 'Kein Platz für Deutsche Flugzeug?', *Der Spiegel* (Hamburg) (15 January 1964), pp. 34–7, at p. 36.

41 Willy Messerschmitt interview, *Der Spiegel*, pp. 35–6. However, the text of the specification and the treatment the Bf 109 design received suggests that the RLM's thinking was more advanced than Messerschmitt recalled over thirty years later.

42 Letter from Willy Messerschmitt to Prof. Dr-Ing Paul Brenner, Vereinigte Leichtmetallwerke GmbH, Bonn, 12 March 1955. Quoted in Hans J. Ebert, Johann B. Kaiser and Klaus Peters, *Willy Messerschmitt, Pioneer of Aviation Design* (Atglen, PA: Schiffer, 1999), p. 116.

43 Frank Vann, *Willy Messerschmitt: First Full Biography of an Aeronautical Genius* (Yeovil: Patrick Stephens, 1993), p. 201. Lachmann had developed slats for Rumpler aircraft in Germany during the Great War. Licensing payments from Germany helped keep Handley Page in business in the 1930s.

44 Statistiches Reichsamt, Abt. VII, *Industreielle Productionstatistik, A., Die Flugzeugindustries 1933–36*, National Archives (US), RG 242 T-177 Reel 32 Frames 3720917–20; *Flugzeug Beschaffungsprogramm*, LA/LC Nr. 1/35. g. Kdos., 1.1.35, National Archives (US), RG 242 T-177 Reel 48 Frame 37338956; Eugene M. Emme, 'The Genesis of Nazi Luftpolitik 1933–35', *Aerospace Historian* (January 1959), pp. 10–23; Eugene M. Emme, 'Emergence of Nazi Luftpolitik as a Weapon in International Affairs 1933–35', *Aerospace Historian* (April 1960), pp. 92–105.

45 Kosin, *German Fighter*, p. 106.

46 Hans-Detlef Herhudt von Rohden, ed., *Die Deutsches Luftrüstung 1935–1945*, Europäische Beiträge sur Geschichte des Weltkrieges II 1939–45, Bild 6, n.d. [*c.* 1946], National Archives (US), RG 242 T-971 Roll 26 Frames 969–70.

47 Willy Messerschmitt interview, *Der Spiegel*, p. 36.

48 A commercial or airline pilot.

49 Adolf Galland, 'Quarter Century of Greatness', in Caidin, *Me 109*, p. 6.

50 Galland, 'Quarter Century', p. 7.

51 Heinrich Beauvais, 'My Experiences during Trials of the Bf 109 (Me 109) and on Other Types', in Wolfgang Späte, ed., *Test Pilots* (Bromley, Kent: Independent Books, n.d.), pp. 68–81, at p. 69.

52 One 'g' force equals the force of gravity on an aircraft in level flight; multiple g forces refers to the amount of lifting airload imposed on an aircraft in relation to this. Commercial flight normally subjects passengers and crew to a maximum of 1.15 g force, corresponding to a 30-degree banked turn.

53 AIR 20/2371, Ralph Sorley, *Factors Involved in the Conception of the 8 Gun Fighter*, Memorandum, 6 May 1945, National Archives (UK); Quill, *Birth of a Legend*, pp. 62–5. Basil Collier, *Defence of the United Kingdom* (London: Naval and Military Press, 2004), p. 43. Despite this, aside from Brooke-Popham, the Air Ministry was generally in favour of heavier armament even before Sorley's advocacy. Morgan and Shacklady, *Spitfire*, p. 15; Sinnott, *RAF and Aircraft Design*, p. 114.

54 Shenstone, 'Shaping the Spitfire', p. 32; Morgan and Shacklady, *Spitfire*, pp. 18–25.

55 Shenstone, 'Shaping the Spitfire', p. 34.

56 On Spitfire stall performance, see J.R. Vensel and W.H. Phillips, *Stalling Characteristics of the Supermarine Spitfire VA Aircraft*, National Advisory Committee on Aeronautics, Langley Field, VA, September 1942: http://ntrs.nasa.gov/archive/nasa/casi.ntrs.nasa.gov/19930092581_1993092581.pdf

57 Shenstone, 'Shaping the Spitfire', p. 33.

58 The Spitfire design minimised both parasite drag (caused by profile area) and induced drag (caused by producing lift). Total drag profile area of the Spitfire IA was 5.182 sq ft, compared to 4.875 sq ft for the Bf 109E-3. Murray Rubenstein, *Messerschmitt Bf 109E-3 vs. Supermarine Spitfire IA*, Fighter Comparison No. 2 (Teaneck, NJ: Tacitus Publications, 1973), p. 9.

59 Keith Hayward, *The British Aircraft Industry* (Manchester: Manchester University Press, 1989), p. 20; Collier, *Defence of the United Kingdom*, pp. 41, 68. Resources for mobilising industry, including the shadow factories, were in practice limited until 1938–9.

60 Quill, *Birth of a Legend*, pp. 76–7.

61 Air Marshal Sir Ralph Sorley, in Smith, 'R.J. Mitchell', p. 326.

62 AIR 20/2371, p. 7; C.F. Andrews, *Supermarine Aircraft Since 1914* (London: Putnam, 1981), p. 223; K.J. Meekcoms and E.B. Morgan, *The British Aircraft Specifications File: British Military and Commercial Aircraft Specifications 1920–1949* (Tonbridge: Air Britain, 1994), pp. 217–18.

63 Air Marshal Sir Humphrey Edwards Jones, 'The Spitfire from Prototype to Mk 24', in Mitchell, *Schooldays to Spitfire*, pp. 298–300.

64 AIR 2/2824, *Memoranda: Handling Trial of the Spitfire K5054*, Aeroplane and Armament Experimental Establishment, Martlesham Heath, September 1936, p. 3, National Archives (UK).

65 Willy Radinger and Walter Schick, *Messerschmitt Bf 109: the World's Most Produced Fighter from Bf 109 A to E* (Atglen, PA: Schiffer, 1999), p. 18. That no one was

much interested in the Focke Wulf and Arado designs and that Bfw had a chance to repair the Bf 109V1 after its undercarriage failure (unlike Tank's design) suggest that Messerschmitt was not as much an 'outsider' as he recalled after the war.

66 Lukas Schmid, 'When the 109 Put its Ears Back', in Späte, *Test Pilots*, pp. 82–103, at p. 90.

67 Schmid, 'When the 109 Put its Ears Back', pp. 90, 93.

68 This description of the spinning tests of the Bf 109 is from Beauvais, 'My Experiences', p. 70.

69 Ibid.

70 This description of a Bf 109 in a spin is from Norbert Hanning, *Luftwaffe Fighter Ace: from the Eastern Front to the Defense of the Homeland* (Mechanicsburg, PA: Stackpole Books, 2009), p. 65.

71 Budrass, *Flugzeugindustrie*, pp. 295–6; Ebert, Kaiser and Peters, *Willy Messerschmitt*, p. 195; Kokothaki, 'Messerschmitt History', p. 177. On Bf 109 development, see Jochen Prien, Gerhard Stemmer, Peter Rodeike, Winfried Beck, *Der Jagdfliegerverbände der Deutschen Luftwaffe 1934 bis 1945, Vorkriegszeit und Einsatz über Polen – 1934 bis 1939*, Teil 1 (Eutin: Struve's Buchdruckerei under Verlag, 2000), pp. 30–50.

3 The Race to Deploy the Modern Fighter: June 1936–September 1938

1 Michael M. Postan, *British War Production* (London and Nendeln: HMSO and Kraus Reprint, 1975), pp. 96, 436. Folland, Cunliffe-Owen and General Aviation were other 'fringe' firms soon involved in Spitfire production.

2 C.R. Russell, *Spitfire Odyssey: My Life at Supermarine, 1936–57* (Southampton: Kingfisher, 1985), p. 156.

3 J.D. Scott, *Vickers: A History* (London: Weidenfeld and Nicolson, 1962), p. 269.

4 Knighted for his work in 1942 as Sir Robert Watson-Watt.

5 AIR 41/88, pp. 9–16; Sir Robert Watson-Watt, *Three Steps to Victory: A Personal Account by Radar's Greatest Pioneer* (London: Odhams, 1957), pp. 80–6; Collier, *Defence of the United Kingdom* pp. 37–40; Tony Devereux, *Messenger Gods of Battle* (London: Brassey's, 1990), pp. 78–84; T.C.G. James, *The Growth of Fighter Command 1936–1940*, ed. Sebastian Cox (London and Portland, OR: Whitehall History Publishing in Association with Frank Cass, 2002), p. 26.

6 Henry E. Guerlac, *RADAR In World War II*, vol. 1, *The History of Modern Physics 1800–1950,* vol. 8 (n.p.: Tomash, 1987), p. 131.

7 Francis K. Mason, *Battle Over Britain* (Garden City, NY: Doubleday, 1969), pp. 90–2.

8 On the Sabre, see Fredrick R. Banks, *I Kept No Diary* (Shrewsbury: Airlife, 1978), pp. 134–9; Sir Alec Cairncross, *Planning in Wartime: Aircraft Production in Britain, Germany and the USA* (New York: St Martin's, 1991), pp. 90–1; Bill Gunston, *The Development of Piston Aero Engines* (Yeovil: Patrick Stephens, 1993), pp. 170–1; Postan, *British War Production*, p. 329.

9 Vincent Orange, *Dowding of Fighter Command: Victor of the Battle of Britain* (London: Grub Street, 2009), p. 90.

10 AIR 16/51, *Fighter Command Attacks – 1938*, RAF, National Archives (UK). On
    their origins, see Air Vice Marshal Sir Cecil 'Boy' Bouchier, *Spitfires in Japan, From
    Farnborough to the Far East: a Memoir*, ed. Dorothy Britton (Lady Bouchier),
    (Folkestone: Global Oriental, 2005), p. 177.

11 CAB 24/273, Sir Thomas Inskip, *Defence Expenditure in Future Years*, 15 December
    1937, CP 316 (37), National Archives (UK); Malcolm Smith, *British Air Strategy
    Between the Wars* (Oxford: Oxford University Press, 1984), ch. 6; Quill, *Birth of a
    Legend*, pp. 83–5. James, *Growth of Fighter Command*, p. 29.

12 The Luftwaffe came to the same conclusion. On formation in 1935, its uniforms
    included neckties for everyone to be worn with the tunic, not only officers. The
    Luftwaffe issued multiple uniforms that owed much to Göring's love of flash
    clothes. *German Military Uniforms and Insignia 1933–45* (Old Greenwich, CT: WE
    Inc., 1967), pp. 128–9, 133.

13 On implementing policy through personnel decisions in the pre-1939 RAF, see
    John James, *The Paladins: A Social History of the RAF Up to the Outbreak of World War
    II* (London: Macdonald, 1990); Herford Montgomery Hyde, *British Air Policy
    Between the Wars* (London: Heinemann, 1976), pp. 214–23.

14 Quoted in Morgan and Shacklady, *Spitfire*, p. 47.

15 Known to the Spanish Loyalists as the *Mosca* (fly). On the I-16, see Corum,
    Richthofen, p. 138; Yefim Gordon, *Soviet Air Power in World War 2* (Hinckley:
    Midland, 2008), pp. 256–71; Gerald Howson, *Aircraft of the Spanish Civil War
    1936–1939* (Washington: Smithsonian Institution Press, 1990), pp. 197–201; Vaclav
    Nemecek, *The History of Soviet Aircraft from 1918* (London: Willow Books, 1986),
    pp. 18–24.

16 Personal conversation with Adolf Galland, Washington DC, 16 November 1978.

17 Collier, *Defence of the United Kingdom*, p. 38.

18 CAB 16/181, *Cabinet Meeting of 23 July 1937*, National Archives (UK). Watson-
    Watt, *Three Steps*, pp. 173–83.

19 Hans Herlin, *Udet: A Man's Life* (London: MacDonald, 1960), p. 202.

20 Homze, *Arming the Luftwaffe*, p. 234.

21 Wolfgang Falke, *The Happy Falcon: An Autobiography by the Father of the Night Fighters*
    (Hamilton, MT: Eagle Editions, 2003), pp. 39–40, 94–5. Had they had to take the
    original He 112 into combat, rather than the He 112Bs they actually flew, they may
    have thought otherwise.

22 James S. Corum, *The Luftwaffe: Creating the Operational Air War 1918–1940*
    (Lawrence, KS: University Press of Kansas, 1997), pp. 201–4; Jesus Salas Lazarrabal,
    Air War over Spain, trans. from Spanish by Margaret A. Kelley (Shepperton: Ian
    Allan, 1968), p. 68; Karl Ries and Hans Ring, *The Legion Condor: A History of the
    Luftwaffe in the Spanish Civil War, 1936–1939*, trans. David Johnston (West Chester,
    PA: Schiffer, 1992), p. 123. That Bf 109s flew escort missions over Guernica is not
    explicitly confirmed by post-war sources; most Spanish government sources assert
    or assume they did so.

23 'Vati' means 'daddy', a reference to Mölders' leadership (and his reluctance to party
    as hard as other German fighter pilots in Spain). Corum, *Operational*, p. 207; Ernst

Obermaier and Werner Held, with the help of Luise Petzolt-Mölders, *Jagdflieger Oberst Werner Mölders* (Stuttgart: Motorbuch Verlag, 1982), p. 14. Fritz von Forell, *Werner Mölders, Flug zur Sonne: Die Geschichte des Grossen Jagdfliegers* (Leoni am Stamberger See: Druffel Verlag, 1976), pp. 24–6.

24 Quill, *Birth of a Legend*, p. 91.

25 AIR 2/2964, *Employment of Two-Seater and Single-Seater Fighters in a Home Defence War*, Air Staff Note, 17 June 1938, National Archives (UK); Alec Brew, *Boulton Paul Aircraft Since 1915* (London: Putnam, 1993), pp. 235–69; Orange, *Dowding*, pp. 87–8, 103–4.

26 BA-MA ZA 3 3/357, Luftflottenkommando 2, Nr. 7093/39, *Mitschraft der Abschlüssbesprechung des Planspieles 1939*, 13.5.39, pp. 28–32 (minelaying), *Militärarchiv*; Murray, *Luftwaffe*, pp. 90–2. Klaus A. Maier, 'The Luftwaffe', in Paul Addison and Jeremy A. Crang, eds, *The Burning Blue: A New History of the Battle of Britain* (London: Pimlico, 2000), pp. 15–21, at pp. 16–17; Völker, *Militärischen Luftfahrt*, pp. 99–100.

27 Richard Suchenwirth, *The Development of the German Air Force, 1919–1939* (New York: Arno, 1970), p. 68.

28 Squadron Leader D.H. Clarke, DFC, AFC, *What Were They Like to Fly* (Shepperton, Middlesex: Ian Allan, 1964), p. 23.

29 AIR 41/88, pp. 28–9; Watson-Watt, *Three Steps*, pp. 20–1.

30 Norman M. Ripsman and Jack S. Levy, 'Wishful Thinking or Buying Time? The Logic of British Appeasement in the 1930s', *International Security*, vol. 33 no. 2 (Fall 2008), pp. 149–81, at p. 180.

4 The Race to Decisive Combat: October 1938–May 1940

1 Alfred Price, 'The World's First ELINT Platform', *Journal of Electronic Defense*, vol. 28 no. 3 (March 2005), pp. 50–4.

2 James, *Growth of Fighter Command*, pp. 18–19; Wesley K. Wark, 'British Intelligence on the German Air Force and Aircraft Industry, 1933–39', *The Historical Journal*, vol. 25 no. 3 (September 1982), pp. 627–48, at pp. 639–42.

3 Sir A.H. Roy Fedden, 'Aircraft Power Plant – Past and Future', *Journal of the Royal Aeronautical Society*, vol. 48 no. 405 (September 1944), pp. 337–89, at p. 375; Homze, *Arming the Luftwaffe*, p. 82; Herschel Smith, *Aircraft Piston Engines*, p. 84.

4 USSBS, *Minutes of Meeting with Reichsminister Albert Speer*, Flensburg, 18 May 1945, US Strategic Bombing Survey, p. 6, National Archives (US), RG 243 Entry 32 Box 1.

5 Kosin, *German Fighter*, p. 127.

6 Ulrich Steinhilper and Peter Osbourne, *Spitfire on my Tail: A View From the Other Side* (Bromley, Kent: Independent Books, 1990), p. 155.

7 Juan Araez Cerda, *Les Messerschmitt Espagnols: Des Premiers 109V aux Derniers Buchon*, Avions Hors Série 5 (Paris: Lela Presse, 1997); Corum, *Operational*, pp. 219–23; Howson, *Aircraft of Spanish Civil War*, pp. 231–5; Ries and Ring, *Legion Condor*, p. 235. On Bf 109 exports, see Budrass, *Flugzeugindustrie*, pp. 402–3.

8 USSBS, *Minutes of Meeting with Speer*, p. 9. On RLM standardisation policies (evolving for years), see Budrass, *Flugzeugindustrie*, pp. 562–3, 682–96.

9   Suchenwirth, *Command and Leadership*, p. 93.

10 Quoted in Antony Kay and L.R. Smith, *German Aircraft of the Second World War* (London: Putnam, 2002), p. 254.

11 Mark P. Friedlander Jr and Gene Gurney, *Higher, Faster and Farther* (New York: William Morrow, 1973), p. 50; Homze, *Arming the Luftwaffe*, p. 247.

12 Beauvais, 'My Experiences', pp. 69, 81.

13 Willy Messerschmitt, *The German Jet Fighter Me-262 (Development, Success and Prospects)*, n.d. [*c.* 1946], p. 3, US Navy Operational Archives, Washington DC, Essays by German Officers and Officials, Box T69; USSBS, Messerschmitt Interview, p. 11.

14 AIR 41/88, pp. 35–6; James, *Growth of Fighter Command*, pp. 41–2; R.J. Overy, 'The German Pre-War Aircraft Production Plans, November 1936–April 1939', *The English Historical Review*, vol. 90 no. 357 (October 1975), pp. 778–97, at p. 796.

15 Alan Deere, *Nine Lives* (Manchester: Crecy, 2009), p. 38.

16 Christopher Shores and Chris Ehrengardt, *Fledgling Eagles: The Complete Account of Air Operations During the 'Phoney War' and Norwegian Campaign, 1940* (London: Grub Street, 1991), p. 15. On Poland, see Corum, *Richthofen*, pp. 152–82; Prien et al. *Vorkriegszeit und Einsatz über Polen*, Teil I, pp. 110-43.

17 Steinhilper and Osbourne, *Spitfire on my Tail*, p. 180.

18 Corum, *Operational*, pp. 242–3; Shores, *Fledgling Eagles*, pp. 149–50; Jochen Prien and Peter Rodeike, *JG 1 und JG 11, Jagdgeschwader 1 und 11: Einsatz in der Reichsverteidigung von 1939 bis 1945, Teil 1, 1939–43* (Eutin: Struve-Druck, 1994), pp. 7–21; Watson-Watt *Three Steps*, pp. 107-9; Hans-Detlef Herhudt von Rohden, ed., *The Battle for Air Supremacy Over Germany (German Air Defenses)*, European Contributions to the History of World War II 1939–45, Air War, Book 4, n.d. [*c.* 1946], n.p. [p. 3], National Archives (US), RG 242 T-971 Roll 26 Frame 667 Document 4(b); Hans-Detlef Herhudt von Rohden, ed., *Reich Air Defense 1939–1945, A Strategic-Tactical Survey*, European Contributions to the History of World War II 1939–45, *Air War*, Book 3, August 1946, n.p., National Archives (US), RG 242 T-971 Roll 26 Frame 206 Document 3(b).

19 Horst Boog, *Die Deutsche Luftwaffenführung 1935–1945: Führungsprobleme, Spitzengliederung, Generalstabsausbildung* (Stuttgart: Deutsche Verlags-Anstalt, 1982) pp. 67–9; Homze, *Arming the Luftwaffe*, p. 229; FD 4355/45 no. 43, Letter from Messerschmitt to Tscherisch, RLM, 13 March 1940, Speer Collection, Imperial War Museum, quoted in Richard J. Overy, 'Air Power in the Second World War: Historical Themes and Theories' in Horst Boog, ed., *The Conduct of the Air War in the Second World War* (Providence, RI: Berg, 1992), pp. 7–28, at p. 28.

20 AIR 20/7706, Air Historical Branch, Translation VII/107, 'Luftwaffe Strength and Serviceability Tables, August 1938–April 1945' in *Translations from Captured Enemy Documents, Vol. VII, 1941–1952*, National Archives (UK). Pilot numbers from: BA/MZ, RL 2 III/707, General Quartier 6 Abteilung (1), *Übersicht über Soll, 1st-bestand, Einstatzbereitschaft, Verluste and Reserven der fliegenden Verbände*. Quoted in Murray, *Luftwaffe*, pp. 43–4.

21 Adolf Galland, *The First and the Last* (New York: Ballantine, 1965), p. 3; Adolf

Galland, 'General of the Fighters', in Colin D. Heaton and Anne-Marie Lewis, eds, *The German Aces Speak: World War II Through the Eyes of Four of the Luftwaffe's Most Important Commanders* (Minneapolis: Zenith, 2011), pp. 74–139 at p. 82.

22   Charles Christeinne and Pierre Lissarague, *History of French Military Aviation* (Washington: Smithsonian Institution Press, 1986), p. 335; Patrick Facon, *L'Armée de l'Air Dans La Tormente: La Bataille de France, 1939–1940* (Paris: Economica, 1997), p. 14.

23   Lee B. Kennett, 'German Air Superiority in the Westfeldzug, 1940' in F.X. Homer and Larry D. Wilcox, eds, *Germany and Europe in the Era of Two World Wars* (Charlottesville: University Press of Virginia, 1986), pp. 141–55, at p. 145; Stuart W. Peach, 'A Neglected Turning Point in Airpower History: Air Power and the Fall of France', in Sebastian Cox and Peter Gray, eds, *Air Power History: Turning Points from Kitty Hawk to Kosovo* (London and Portland, OR: Frank Cass, 2002), pp. 142–72, at p. 156.

24   Corum, *Richthofen*, pp. 196–8, 201; Murray, *Luftwaffe*, p. 41.

25   Alistair Horne, *To Lose a Battle: France, 1940* (London: Macmillan, 1969), p. 339.

26   An idea of Udet's, who had advocated dive-bomber development. Herlin, *Udet*, p. 206. Sirens were also attached to bombs.

27   Horne, *To Lose a Battle*, p. 339.

28   Brian Cull and Bruce Lander with Heinreich Weiss, *Twelve Days in May* (London: Grub Street, 1999), p. 135; Horne, *To Lose a Battle*, pp. 268–9.

29   Cull, Lander and Weiss, *Twelve Days in May*, p. 113.

30   AIR 16/352, *Operations Over France, May–June 1940*, 11 Group, p. 6, National Archives (UK); James, *Growth of Fighter Command*, pp. 86–8.

31   In a *Geschwader* the *Staffeln* were numbered consecutively in Arabic numerals, *Gruppen* in Roman. The 5th *Staffel* was part of II *Jagd Gruppe*; *Jagdgeschwader* 26, II/JG 26. Especially later in the war, *Staffeln* could be shuffled between *Gruppen*.

32   AIR 50/85, Combat Report, G.A. Brown, 66 Squadron, 13 May 1940, National Archives (UK).

33   The description of Spitfire high-speed stalling is from *Pilot's Notes*, Spitfire V, 12 (ii), *The Spitfire V Manual* (London: Arms and Armour, 1976); Peter Caygill, *Flying to the Limit: Testing World War II Single Engine Fighter Aircraft* (Barnsley: Pen and Sword, 2005), p. 19.

34   James, *Growth of Fighter Command*, p. 139; Robert Wright, *Dowding and the Battle of Britain* (London: MacDonald, 1969), p. 103.

35   CAB/65/13, *W.M. (40) 124th Conclusion, Confidential Annex*, 16 May 1940, Minute 1, National Archives (UK).

36   AIR 41/14, Letter, Sir Hugh Dowding to Under-Secretary of State, 16 May 1940 (Reference FC s.19043), National Archives (UK); James, *Growth of Fighter Command*, Appendix 11.

5 The Battle Opens: May–August 1940

1   General der Flieger Wilhelm Speidel, *The Campaign for Western Europe 1939–40* (1956), p. 156. USAF Historical Research Agency document K113.107–152 vol. 1.

2 Werner Kreipe, 'The Battle of Britain', in Seymour Freiden and William Richardson, eds, *The Fatal Decisions* (New York: Berkley, 1958), pp. 19–35, at p. 21.

3 Ibid. The Spitfires Kreipe is referring to may be misidentified Hurricanes of 17 Squadron, which shot down several of KG 2's Do 17s. This is an example of the Luftwaffe's 'Spitfire syndrome': any fighter that beat them appeared to be a Spitfire.

4 *Einstatz des II. Fliegerkorps bei Dünkirchen am 27.5.40: Schwere Tag des II. Fliegerkorps*, USAF Historical Research Agency document, K113.306-3, vol. 3. A *Fliegerkorps* is a Luftwaffe formation consisting of multiple types of aircraft, smaller than a *Luftflotte* (similar to a USAAF numbered air force) but larger than a *Geschwader*.

5 Norman Franks, *The Air Battle of Dunkirk* (London: William Kimber, 1983), p. 201.

6 William L. Shirer, *Berlin Diary* (New York: A.A. Knopf, 1941), entry for 24 May 1940, p. 378.

7 Quoted in Franks, *Air Battle of Dunkirk*, p. 142. Michael Robinson, *Best of the Few: 92 Squadron 1939-40* (Bletchley: privately published, 2001), pp. 130–1.

8 Franks, *Air Battle of Dunkirk*, p. 29. Cazenove did not identify the destroyers where he was invited to 'f— off'. His Spitfire, left on Calais beach, was covered in sand, rediscovered in 1980, and flew again in 2011.

9 James, *Growth of Fighter Command*, p. 94.

10 AIR 16/352, p. 16; James, *Growth of Fighter Command*, pp. 94–5. On the pre-war emphasis on intercepting attackers with small formations of RAF fighters, see Dilip Sarkar, *Bader's Duxford Fighters: The Big Wing Controversy* (Worcester: Victory Books, 2006), pp. 14–23.

11 Douglas Bader, *Fight for the Sky: The Story of the Spitfire and Hurricane* (Garden City, NY: Doubleday, 1973), p. 15.

12 Paul Brickhill, *Reach for the Sky* (New York: Ballantine, 1967), p. 144.

13 Michael G. Burns, *Bader: The Man and His Men* (London: Cassell, 1998), p. 42.

14 Ibid.

15 A wartime USAAF study showed that close-range firing at full (90 degrees) deflection, as Bader reported, was only about 10 per cent as effective against a bomber-size target as a burst fired from directly behind the target. *Relation of Closing Speed to Effectiveness of Frontal Attacks on Bombardment Aircraft*, Conference Report of the AAF Center, Orlando, 30 October 1945, AAF Board Project No. 4277A3731, National Archives (US), RG 80 Box 1972.

16 Brickhill, *Reach for the Sky*, p. 144.

17 Ibid.

18 AIR 50/85, Flight Lieutenant D.R.S. Bader, Combat Report, 1 June 1940, National Archives (UK).

19 Galland, *First and the Last*, pp. 6–7.

20 Vincent Orange, *Park: the Biography of Air Chief Marshal Sir Keith Park* (London: Grub Street, 2001), p. 87.

21 USSBS, *Interview, Field Marshal Albert Kesselring*, no. 61, 23 June 1945, US Strategic Bombing Survey, p. 5, National Archives (US), RG 243 Entry 31 Box 1.

22 AIR 20/7706, 'Luftwaffe Strength and Serviceability Tables'.

23 Sebastian Ritchie, *Industry and Air Power: The Expansion of British Aircraft Production 1935–41* (London and Portland, OR: Frank Cass, 1997), pp. 56, 233; Quill, *Birth of a Legend*, pp. 150–1.

24 Alec Harvey-Bailey, *The Merlin in Perspective: The Combat Years* (Derby: Rolls-Royce Heritage Trust, 1985), p. 32. Ian S. Lloyd, *Rolls-Royce: The Merlin at War* (London: The Macmillan Press, 1978), pp. 23, 72–4, 118–25.

25 Orange, *Dowding*, p. 134; Postan, *British War Production*, p. 116.

26 Ritchie, *Industry and Air Power*, p. 234.

27 Quill, *Spitfire*, p. 287.

28 In 1944, the ATA had 551 male and 108 female pilots (supplemented by RAF and FAA pilots, all male, awaiting transfer to operational units). Diana Barnato started flying Spitfires on 31 October 1942. Diana Barnato Walker, *Spreading My Wings* (London: Grub Street, 2008), pp. 43, 68–9.

29 Postan, *British War Production*, p. 316; Ritchie, *Industry and Air Power*, p. 233.

30 Gavin Bailey, 'The Narrow Margin of Criticality: The Question of the Supply of 100-Octane Fuel in the Battle of Britain', *English Historical Review*, vol. 123 (April 2008), pp. 394–411; Russell Warren Howe, 'Dr Sweeney's Secret Formula', *Air Force* (February 1978), pp. 64–7; A.C. Lovesey, 'Development of the Rolls Royce Merlin from 1939 to 1945', *Aircraft Engineering* (July 1946), pp. 218–26, at pp. 222–3; Morgan and Shacklady, *Spitfire*, pp. 54–5.

31 AIR 16/327, Commander-in-Chief Fighter Command Memoranda to Under-secretary of State for Air, 6 June 1940, National Archives (UK).

32 Clarke, *What Were They Like*, p. 26; AIR 41/88, pp. 16–17, 49.

33 AIR 41/88, pp. 43–5, 49–50; E.R. Hooton, *The Luftwaffe: A Study in Air Power 1933–1945* (Hersham: Classic Publications, Ian Allan, 2010), pp. 71–2, 78.

34 AIR 14/385, *Armament of Aircraft*, Air Fighting Development Unit Report No. 18, 1938, National Archives (UK). The RAF, at Sorley's urging, had given the go-ahead for a cannon-armed Spitfire in 1939. Sinnott, *RAF and Aircraft Design*, p. 118; Morgan and Shacklady, *Spitfire*, pp. 57–61.

35 Leo McKinstry, 'How Labour Unrest Nearly Lost Us the Battle of Britain', *The Spectator*, 17 November 2007, http://proquest.umi.com; Russell, pp. 87–8. Labour problems continued at Castle Bromwich through 1941–2.

36 Overy, *The Air War*, p. 77.

37 Johnson, *Full Circle*, p. 127.

38 Roger A. Freeman, *The Fight for the Skies* (London: Arms and Armour, 1998), p. 23.

39 On the Swiss–Luftwaffe battles of 1940, see *Bericht des Kommandanten der Flieger- und Fliegerabwehrtruppen über den Aktivdienst 1939–1945* (Bern: Buchdruckerei Rösch, Vogt and Co, 1946); Georg Hoch, *Messerschmitt Me 109 in Swiss Air Force Service*, trans. Christine Wisowaty (Atglen, PA: Schiffer Military History, 2008), pp. 95–114; Philippe Osché, *Les Messerschmitt Bf 109 Suisses*, Avions Hors Série 4 (Paris: Lela Press, 1996); Karl Ries, *Deutsche Luftwaffe über der Schweiz 1939–1945* (Mainz: Verlag Dieter Hoffmann, 1978); John Cilio, 'Defending Neutrality, the Swiss Air Force in World War II', *Warbirds* (February 2011), pp. 36–9.

40 R.J. Overy, 'Mobilization for Total War in Germany 1939–1941', *The English Historical Review*, vol. 103 no. 408 (July 1988), pp. 613–39.

41 This became a favourite Galland story, told by him several times in print and in interviews with researchers. As with many of Galland's stories, it is not verifiable from other sources. David Baker, *Adolf Galland, The Authorised Biography* (London: Windrow and Greene, 1996), p. 87; Johnson, *Full Circle*, p. 119; ADI(K) Report No. 373/1945, *The Birth, Life and Death of the German Day Fighter Arm (Related by Adolf Galland)*, 15 August 1945, National Archives (US), RG 165 Entry 79 Box 23, p. 12. The Luftwaffe officially eschewed the Anglo-American convention that five victories made an ace, recognising instead that ten victories made an *experte*.

42 Corum, *Richthofen*, p. 221 for the percentages. On Erla in Antwerp and Brussels, see Budrass, *Flugzeugindustrie*, p. 691. Subsequently, other overhaul facilities in occupied countries were also run by German industry.

43 Rubenstein, *Messerschmitt Bf 109E-3*, p. 11.

44 Prewar Bf109s required 10,000–12,000 man-hours. Ebert, Kaiser and Peters, *Willy Messerschmitt* p. 128; Postan, *British War Production* p. 171.

45 Overy, 'German Pre-War', p. 796.

46 Quotes from Adolf Galland interview at his home in Remagen, Germany, with Donald Lopez, curator of the National Air and Space Museum, 1991. Reproduced in DVD form in: *Adolf Galland, Ace of the Luftwaffe* (Santa Ana, CA: Virginia Bader Fine Arts, 2010).

6 The Battle of Britain: 15 August 1940, 'Black Thursday'

1 Times are Greenwich Mean Time. British Summer Time was one hour later; the Germans used local (French) time.

2 The term radar, now universal, was not widely used until 1942. What was informing Park's judgement he then knew as radio direction finding (RDF).

3 ADI(K) Report No. 373/1945, p. 14; Hooton, *Luftwaffe*, pp. 76–7.

4 Bouchier, *Spitfires in Japan*, p. 217.

5 Hugh Dundas, *Flying Start: A Fighter Pilot's War Years* (New York: St Martin's Press, 1989), p. 38; AIR 41/88, p. 51; Galland, 'General of the Fighters', p. 89.

6 Collier, *Defence of the United Kingdom* p. 198.

7 On the 1940 performance of what was to become the 'Y' service, see R.H. Hinsley, *British Intelligence in the Second World War: Its Influence on Strategy and Operations*, vol. 1 (London: HMSO, 1979), p. 180; Aileen Clayton, *The Enemy is Listening* (London: Hutchinson, 1980), p. 49. The latter remains a classic intelligence memoir.

8 Heinz Bär, 'Typical Orders for a Fighter Escort to a Geschwader (Battle of Britain)', in David C. Isby, ed., *The Luftwaffe Fighter Force: the View from the Cockpit* (London: Greenhill, 1998), p. 60.

9 Unlike a sustained turn (which, as the name implies, can be sustained as long as fuel permits), an instantaneous manoeuvre induces sufficient drag on the aircraft that it must lose airspeed or altitude, or usually both. When an aircraft's specific excess

power (SEP: the amount of power it needs above that required to keep it in steady-state level flight) equals zero, it must give up airspeed or altitude. Making (instantaneously) a high-g manoeuvre when climbing had slowed down his Spitfire (he had traded airspeed for altitude faster than his engine, even at emergency boost, could bring it up) was how George Brown stalled over Rotterdam while turning. One wing, generating less lift, stalled first, leading to a spin. Francis J. Hale, *Introduction to Aircraft Performance, Selection and Design* (New York: John Wiley and Sons, 1984), pp. 103–9. Details of sustained Spitfire and Bf 109E performance from AVIA 6/2394, *Messerschmitt Me. 109, Handling and Manoeuvrability Tests*, Royal Aircraft Establishment, Farnborough, September 1940, National Archives (UK).

10   Murray Rubinstein provided this information in 1979, working out the calculations from the in-depth analyses of the Bf 109E-3, Spitfire IA and Hurricane I he made in his studies of these aircraft's comparative air combat performance. Such a turn would exceed the Bf 109's 7 g limit (and would require great physical strength). The lowest speed at which an aeroplane can manoeuvre at its maximum g limit was called (post-war) its corner velocity. Such a manoeuvre induces drag and reduces airspeed.

11   Chris Goss, *Brothers in Arms* (Manchester: Crecy, 1994), p. 139.

12   Jochen Prien, *Jagdgeschwader 53, A History of the 'Pik As' Geschwader, March 1937–May 1942* (Atglen, PA: Schiffer, 1997), p. 143.

13   Baker, *Adolf Galland*, pp. 86–7.

14   Galland, *First and the Last*, p. 28.

15   ADI(K) Report No. 373/1945, p. 13; On JG 26's support for Galland, see the interrogation of Hauptmann Rolf Pingel: AIR 40/2406, A.I.1 (K) Report No. 396/194, 'Report of the Me 109F of Stab. I/JG 26 Brought Down on the South Coast on 10/7/41', *Interrogation of German and Italian Prisoners of War: Reports 301–400*, vol. 12, 1941, June–July, p. 4, National Archives (UK). Andy Saunders provided a copy of this document.

16   USSBS, *Interview, General Galland (Part I)*, no. 34, 4 June 1945, US Strategic Bombing Survey, p. 9, National Archives (US), RG 243 Entry 32 Box 2.

17   Hence the equivalent of a current RAF pilot being nicknamed 'Yorkie' Barr or a US pilot 'Hershey' Barr.

18   Bär was heavily engaged in the Battle of Britain. See Franz Kurowski, *Luftwaffe Aces: German Combat Pilots of World War Two* (Mechanicsville, PA: Stackpole, 2004), pp. 43–105; Franz Kurowski, *Oberstleutnant Heinz Bär, Als Jagdflieger an Allen Fronten* (Wurzburg: Flechsig, 2007); Ernst Obermaier, *Die Ritterkreuzträger der Luftwaffe*, vol. I, *Jagdflieger* (Mainz: Verlag Dieter Hoffmann, 1966), p. 39; *Heinrich 'Heinz' Bär, Ritterkreuz Träger Profile 6* (Saarbrucken: UNITEC, 2008). On his flying on 15 August, see Erich Zschocher, *Die Kämpfe des Hauptmanns Heinz Bär* (Berlin: Max Schwalbe Verlag, 1943), p. 139. Thierry Kleinprintz provided this.

19   Erik Mombeeck and Jean-Louis Roba with Chris Goss, *In the Skies of France: A Chronicle of JG 2 'Richthofen'*, vol. 1, *1934–40* (Linkebeek, Belgium: ASBL, 2008), p. 203.

20   Galland, *First and the Last*, p. 18; Obermaier, *Ritterkreuzträger*, vol. I, p. 41; Hans-Joachim Röll, *Major Joachim Müncheberg* (Würzburg: Fleschig, 2010), pp. 25–55.

21 Hans-Ekkehard Bob, 'Memories of a German Veteran', in Addison and Crang, *The Burning Blue*, pp. 123–8, at p. 127.

22 Arman van Ishoven, *Messerschmitt Bf 109 at War* (Shepperton: Ian Allan, 1974), p. 58.

23 Mombeeck, *In the Skies of France*, vol. 1, p. 207.

24 Galland's description of this battle is from: conversation with Galland, 16 November 1978; Baker, *Adolf Galland*, pp. 111–15. It does not mesh with the times and places for his victory claims in Prien et al., *Einsatz am Kanal und Über England, 26.6.40 bis 21.6.41*, Teil 4/I (Eutin: Struve's, n.d.), p. 336.

25 AIR 64/82, Central Fighter Establishment, *Visual Acuity of Fighter Pilots*, Report 76, 5.9.46, p. 31, National Archives (UK).

26 Quill, *Spitfire*, p. 175.

27 Franks, *Air Battle of Dunkirk*, p. 27.

28 J.A.D. Ackroyd and P.J. Lamont, 'A Comparison of Turning Radii for Four Battle of Britain Fighter Aircraft', *The Aeronautical Journal* (January 2000), pp. 53–8.

29 Personal conversation with Adolf Galland, Washington DC, 16 November 1978.

30 Chris Goss, *The Luftwaffe Fighters' Battle of Britain* (Manchester: Crecy, 2000), p. 23.

31 Deere, *Nine Lives*, p. 146.

7 'Battle of Britain Day':15 September 1940

1 Matthew Parker, *The Battle of Britain July–October 1940: An Oral History of Britain's Finest Hour* (London: Headline, 2000), p. 275.

2 Derek Wood and Derek Dempster, *The Narrow Margin* (London: Arrow Books, 1967), pp. 332–3.

3 AIR 2/7355, *Enemy Air Offensive Against Great Britain: Air Attacks on England, 8 August–10 September 1940*, report to Commander-in-Chief, Fighter Command from Air Officer Commanding, 11 Group, 22 September 1940, para. 28, National Archives (UK); Orange, *Park*, pp. 103–7.

4 Generaloberst Franz Halder, *Kriegstagebuch*, vol. 2 (Stuttgart: W. Kohlhammer, 1962), pp. 98–9. On German invasion planning, see Klaus A. Maier, ed, *Germany and the Second World War, vol. III Germany's Initial Conquests in Europe* (Oxford: Oxford University Press, 1991), pp. 374–81.

5 Orange, *Park*, p. 109.

6 Frank Usmar, Imperial War Museum oral history, 10588, Imperial War Museum, London.

7 Laddie Lucas, ed., *Out of the Blue* (London: Grafton, 1989), p. 98.

8 Clarke, *What Were They Like*, p. 66.

9 This took place on 4 June 1941 over Le Havre. The man who waved, Oberleutnant Klopf, survived, although wounded. The Stuka crash-landed. John Beaman provided information on this incident. Genst. 6.Abt. (III A), *Front Flugzeug Verluste, 1941, v. 5, 30.5.41–31.7.42*, Imperial War Museum (Duxford), GER-MISC-MCR-18 Reel 3; John Foreman, *Air War 1941: The Turning Point*, Part 2, *The Blitz*

to the Non-Stop Offensive (Walton on Thames: Air Research Publications, 1994), p. 283; Christopher Shores, *Those Other Eagles: A Companion Volume to Aces High* (London: Grub Street, 2004), p. 104; Clarke, *What Were They Like*, p. 111.

10 AIR 50/30, Flt Lt J.W. Villa, Combat Report, 15 September, 1940, National Archives (UK).

11 Alfred Price, *Battle of Britain Day: 15 September 1940* (London: Greenhill Books, 2000), p. 40.

12 AIR 50/30, Pilot Officer F.G. Whitaker, Intelligence Officer, 72 Squadron, Fighter Command Combat Report, 72 Squadron, 15 September 1940, National Archives (UK). Contemporary photos show that 'Pancho' Villa wore his moustache in (non-regulation) imitation of his namesake.

13 The reproduction of the plot table and tote board on display at the Battle of Britain Museum in Hendon shows what Park and Churchill saw at this moment.

14 This was the 11 Group controller, Wing Commander Lord John Willoughby de Broke.

15 Winston Churchill *The Second World War*, vol. 2, *Their Finest Hour*, (New York: Mariner Books, 1986), pp. 294–5.

16 AIR 50/30, Squadron Leader Brian Lane, Combat Report, 15 September 1940, National Archives (UK); Dilip Sarkar, *Spitfire Squadron at War* (Malden, Surrey: Air Research Publications, 1990), pp. 66–9, 152–4.

17 Unwin complained when he was left out of the first mission to Dunkirk. Bader, then Unwin's flight commander, retorted 'Shut up, grumpy.' Until his death in 2006 at the age of ninety-three, he remained 'Grumpy' Unwin. 'Wing Commander G A Unwin, DSO, DFM and Bar', *The Daily Telegraph* (22 June 2006), http://www.telegraph.co.uk/news/obituaries/1522658/Wing-Commander-Grumpy-Unwin.html

18 Baron Ismay, *The Memoirs of Lord Ismay* (London: Heinemann, 1960), pp. 179–80.

19 Scars still visible in the station façade opposite the bus shelters, above and around the pedestrian entry arch to the tube station, are from this crash.

20 Gottfried Leske, *I was a Nazi Flier*, ed. Curtis Reiss (New York: The Dial Press, 1941), p. 219.

8 The Continuing Battle: 18 September 1940–end of 1941

1 Steinhilper and Osbourne, *Spitfire on my Tail*, p. 286.

2 Prien, *Jagdgeschwader 53*, p. 164. Prien et al., *Einsatz am Kanal und Über England*, Teil 4/I, pp. 178–9, 186. Pilots were upset because JG 53's CO had been relieved and denied a decoration, reportedly for having a non-Aryan wife. They had been ordered to paint out their ace-of-spades unit insignia. There had been high-level unhappiness over the unit's combat performance. Wilcke suffered delayed promotion from then on, where before it had been rapid; why remains unknown. The relieved *Kommodore* and spouse both survived the war. On Wilcke, see Obermaier, *Ritterkreuzträger*, vol.I, p. 41.

3   [Air Historical Branch, RAF], *The Rise and Fall of the German Air Force, 1933 to 1945*, W.H. Tantum IV and E.J. Hoffschmidted. eds (Old Greenwich, CT: WE, 1969), p. 82.

4   On numbers and allocations of E-3 and E-4 versions, see Prien et al., *Einsatz am Kanal und Über England*, Teil 4/I, p. 67.

5   Baker, *Adolf Galland* p. 148.

6   ADI(K) Report No. 373/1945, pp. 18–19; Steinhilper and Osbourne, *Spitfire on my Tail*, pp. 9–19.

7   Paul Deichmann, *German Air Force Operations in Support of the Army* (Maxwell AFB: USAF Historical Division, 1962), USAF Historical Studies, no. 163, pp. 26–7; *The German Photographic Reconnaissance and Photographic Intelligence Service*, 25 April 1946, ACIU, A.I.12, USAFE, p. 170, National Archives (US), RG 341 Entry 268 Box 123 Report 49785; Galland, 'General of the Fighters', p. 84.

8   Chris Starr, 'Developing Power, Daimler-Benz and the Messerschmitt Bf 109', *The Aeroplane* (May 2005), pp. 42–7, at p. 42.

9   ADI(K) Report No. 373/1945, p. 17; Galland, *First and the Last*, pp. 28–9.

10 Minutes of *Generalluftzeugmeister* meeting, 19 July 1940, quoted in Heinz Mankau and Peter Petrick, *Messerschmitt Me 110, 210, 410* (Raumfahrt: Aviatic Verlag, 2001), p. 24. The *Gruppe* was II/JG 26. Prien et al., *Einsatz am Kanal und Über England*, Teil 4/II, pp. 431–3.

11 Caidin, *Me 109*, p. 9.

12 Detonation occurs when the fuel–air mixture in an engine cannot be forced into the cylinders and will not burn smoothly after ignition by the spark plug but literally detonates. It can result in the crown of the piston burning through. It is also known as knocking or pinking. Bill Gunston, *The Development of Piston Aero Engines* (Yeovil: Patrick Stephens, 1993), pp. 30–5.

13 This was the constant speed unit (CSU), which included a small hydraulic pump, fed by oil from the engine, that adjusted the pitch of the propeller blades.

14 AIR 16/327, Memorandum by Commander-in-Chief Fighter Command to Under-Secretary of State, Air Ministry, 22 June 1940, National Archives (UK).

15 AIR 41/88, p. 54; Hooton, *Luftwaffe*, p. 78.

16 Alan Clifton, 'Joe Smith – A Colleague's Memoir', *Flight*, 6 April 1956, p. 378.

17 AVIA 10/311, *UK New Aircraft Deliveries by Firms*, Ministry of Aircraft Production, n.d., National Archives (UK), based on figures for last quarter of 1940 and first quarter of 1941.

18 Ritchie, *Industry and Air Power*, p. 233.

19 C.R. Russell, *Spitfire Odyssey: My Life at Supermarine, 1936–57* (Southampton: Kingfisher, 1985), p. 85.

20 Derek N. James, *Westland Aircraft Since 1915* (Annapolis: Naval Institute Press, 1991), p. 40.

21 Wood and Dempster, *The Narrow Margin*, pp. 461, 470.

22 Ted Hooton, *Spitfire Special* (Shepperton: Ian Allan, 1974), pp. 12–13. The total figures were provided by Christer Bergström from his book. *Luftstrid Över Kanalen* (Stockholm: Leanden and Elcholm, 2007), p. 207.

23 Murray, *Luftwaffe*, p. 45.

24 Quoted in Martin Gilbert, ed., *The Churchill War Papers*, vol. II, *Never Surrender, May–December 1940* (New York: Norton, 1995), p. 1012.

25 Letter of Marshal of the Royal Air Force Sir John Salmond, Director of Armament Production, Ministry of Aircraft Production to Winston S. Churchill, 5 October 1940, quoted in Martin Gilbert, ed., *Churchill War Papers*, vol. II, p. 903; Harold Macmillan, *The Blast of War 1939–1945* (London: Macmillan, 1967), p. 85. Sarkar, *Bader's Duxford*, pp. 147–84, emphasises the 'big wing' controversy as leading to Dowding's sacking.

26 Letter, Winston S. Churchill to Sir Archibald Sinclair, 10 July 1940, Churchill Papers, 20/2, reproduced in Gilbert, ed., *Churchill War Papers*, vol. II, p. 498; Orange, *Dowding*, pp. 210–23. General A.P. Wavell, Britain's other 1940 victor, was similarly sacked after he was proved right over Greece. Admiral Charles Forbes, commanding the Home Fleet, was also right (over Trondheim) and also sacked. Wavell went on to command against the Japanese and become Viceroy; Churchill's 1941 suggestion that Dowding become Air Officer Commander-in-Chief, Middle East, was turned down by the Air Ministry.

27 Bouchier, *Spitfires in Japan*, p. 217.

28 AIR 41/18, *The Air Defence of Great Britain: The Beginning of the Fighter Offensive, 1940–1941,* vol. 4, Air Historical Branch, n.d. [*c.* 1949], paras 33–48, National Archives (UK).

29 James, *Westland Aircraft*, p. 270.

30 Martin Freudenberg, *Negative Gravity: A Life of Beatrice Shilling* (Taunton: Charlton, 2003), pp. 41–8. On the pioneer female leadership figures at the RAE, see James, *The Paladins*, p. 190.

31 AIR 19/286, Douglas, AOC-in-C Fighter Command, to Under-Secretary of State, 17 July 1942, National Archives (UK).

32 Barnato Walker, *Spreading My Wings*, p. 69.

33 Quoted in Peter Caygill, *Spitfire Mark V in Action: RAF Operations in Northern Europe* (Shrewsbury: Airlife, 2001), p. 227. 'Rated' refers to the critical altitude/full throttle height.

34 Morgan and Shacklady, *Spitfire*, pp. 157–65; Quill, *Spitfire*, p. 198; Smith, 'Development', p. 341; 'Spitfire and Seafire', p. 708. Peggy Carpenter's older sister, Lily, spent much time 'tuning' control surfaces at Vickers and met her future spouse, Charles Lane, working on the same tasks.

35 Quill, *Spitfire*, p. 199.

36 Rubinstein, p. 11. The Bf 109E intake and radiator designs set up a boundary layer that pushed air away from them at high speeds when they needed to suck in as much air as they could. M.B. Morgan and R. Smelt, 'Aerodynamic Features of German Aircraft', *Journal of the Royal Aeronautical Society*, vol. 48 no. 404 (August 1944), pp. 271–331, at pp. 312–15.

37 Quoted in Joseph V. Mizrahi, *Knights of the Black Cross* (Granada Hills, CA: Sentry Books, 1972), p. 25.

38 Talk given at NASM, Dulles, VA.

39 Murray, *Luftwaffe*, pp. 102–4.

40 Letter, Messerschmitt AG to RLM, 20.5.41, National Archives (US), RG 242 T-177 RLM File 228 Roll 19 Frame 3704483; Murray, *Luftwaffe*, pp. 88–107.

41 *The Light Metal Industry of Germany*, USSBS Report 20, 1947, p. 13; Irving, *Rise and Fall of the Luftwaffe*, p. 126; R.J. Overy, *Goering: The Iron Man* (London: Routlege and Kegan Paul, 1984), p. 148.

42 Minutes of Conference chaired by Milch, 25 March 1944, translation of Document NOKW-017, *USA v. Erhard Milch*, Prosecution Exhibit 54, p. 18 (original document); Budrass, *Flugzeugindustrie*, p. 394; Overy, *Air War*, pp. 192, 219, 226.

43 USSBS, *Excerpts: Interview with R/M Albert Speer 15 to 22 May 1945*, US Strategic Bombing Survey, Physical Damage Division, National Archives (US), RG 243 Entry 32 Box 1.

44 R.J. Overy, 'Mobilization for Total War', pp. 627–8.

45 The conversion to production lines at both Daimler and Messerschmitt-Regensburg was not completed until autumn 1943 (following bomb damage at Regensburg), enabling subsequent increases in Bf 109 production. Neil Gregor, *Daimler-Benz in the Third Reich* (New Haven: Yale University Press, 1998), pp. 70, 123.

46 USSBS, Messerschmitt Interview, p. 12.

47 Armand van Ishoven, *Bf 109 at War* (London: Ian Allan, 1977), p. 107.

48 Budrass, *Flugzeugindustrie*, p. 715; Kosin, *German Fighter*, p. 130.

49 Genst. 6.Abt. (III A), *Front Flugzeug Verluste, 1941* BA/MA, RL 2 II/1025. Quoted in Murray, *Luftwaffe*, pp. 80–1; Walter Krupinski, 'The Count', in Heaton and Lewis, *The German Aces Speak*, pp. 21–74 at p. 25.

50 AIR 16/1024, *Minutes of the 20th Meeting of the Air Fighting Committee, held at the Air Ministry, Whitehall*, 12 March 1940, National Archives (UK).

51 John Terraine, *A Time For Courage: The Royal Air Force in the European War, 1939–45* (New York: Macmillan, 1985); Appendix G deals with this issue. Sinnott, *RAF and Aircraft Design*, p, 226. Morgan and Shacklady, *Spitfire*, p.159, details proposed Spitfire modifications.

52 AIR 41/18, paras 8–26; J.E. Johnson, *Wing Leader* (New York: Ballantine, 1965), p. 66.

53 John Foreman, *Air War 1941: The Turning Point*, Part 1 (Walton on Thames: Air Research Publications, 1993), p. 43.

54 Named for a 1920s German nationalist martyr.

55 AIR 16/903, Memorandum to Air Marshal Sholto Douglas, Air Officer Commanding-in-Chief Fighter Command, from the Senior Air Staff Officer, 27 April 1941, National Archives (UK). Douglas, like Leigh-Mallory, had an interest in pointing to the Spitfire V's limitations rather than strategic failure to explain RAF losses.

56 AIR 16/745, Air Vice Marshal Sir Trafford Leigh-Mallory, *Memorandum by AOC 11 Group on the Results of 'Circus' Operations*, 5 September 1941, p. 2, National Archives (UK). For Johnson quote, see Dilip Sarkar, *Bader's Tangmere Spitfires* (Yeovil: Patrick Stephens, 1996), p. 170. Eduard Neumann, 'Mentor to Many', in Heaton and Lewis, *The German Aces Speak,* pp. 141–70 at p. 146.

57 AIR 41/18, paras 105–15; Dundas, *Flying Start*, p. 63.

58   AIR 16/327, *Spitfire Aircraft Fitted with Long Range Tanks*, Memorandum from Headquarters, 10 Group to Headquarters, Fighter Command, 29 July 1941, National Archives (UK).

59   AIR 16/327, *Spitfire Aircraft, Long Range Tanks*, Under-Secretary of State for Air to Air Chief Marshal H.C.T. Dowding, 2 June 1940.

60   AIR 16/334, *Tactical Memorandum No. 8, Fighters vs. Escorted Bombers*, Fighter Command, 29 May 1940; *Tactical Memorandum No. 9, Operations of Fighter Forces by Day*, Fighter Command, n.d. [*c.* December 1940], National Archives (UK).

61   AIR 41/18, paras 49–58.

62   AIR 41/18, paras 66–89; AIR 16/373, Memorandum to A.M. Douglas, Air Officer Commanding-in-Chief Fighter Command, from Wing Commander (Tactics), 7 March 1941, National Archives (UK).

63   John Colville, *Fringes of Power: Downing Street Diaries 1939*–45 (London: Hodder and Stoughton, 1985), entry for 30.8.41, p. 433.

64   See, for example, Roger Freeman, *The Hub: The Story of Hub Zemke* (Shrewsbury: Airlife, 1988), p. 26.

65   Santiago A. Flores, 'Mexican Spitfire Pilots in the RCAF: Unheralded Participants in the Allied Air War', *C.A.H.S.: The Journal of the Canadian Aviation Historical Society*, vol. 33 no. 4 (October 1995), pp. 126–35; Claudio Meunier, Carlos A. Garcia and Oscar Rimondi, *Alas de Trueno (Wings of Thunder): The Histories of Argentine Volunteer Aircrews in the RAF and RCAF during the Second World War* (Buenos Aires: Claudio Meunier, 2004); Roger Lambo, 'Achtung! The Black Prince: West Africans in the Royal Air Force, 1939–46', *Immigration and Minorities*, vol. 12 no. 3 (November 1993), pp. 145–63; Michael S. Healy, 'Colour, Climate and Combat: The Caribbean Regiment in the Second World War', *The International History Review*, vol. 22 no. 1 (March 2000), pp. 65–85, at p. 77.

66   All Straight quotes from AIR 50/92, Combat Report, S/L Straight, 242 Squadron, 21 June 1941, National Archives (UK). 'MC' meant he had been awarded the Military Cross, for heroism in ground combat (in Norway, in his case). More common were the DFC (Distinguished Flying Cross) or AFC (Air Force Cross, for actions not in the face of the enemy). NCOs received medals (DFM and AFM) instead of crosses. Command personnel were eligible for the Distinguished Service Order (DSO).

67   A common nickname in the Polish Air Force, applied to any pilot who partied less than the (considerable) norm and so was considered an ascetic. He had been with 65 Squadron in the Battle of Britain and had been reluctant to transfer to a Polish squadron. On the action, see Foreman, *Air War 1941*, Part 2, pp. 342–51.

68   Group Captain J.A. Kent, *One of the Few* (London: William Kimber, 1971), pp. 160–1.

69   Quoted in Colin D. Heaton, 'Interview with World War II Luftwaffe General and Ace Pilot Adolf Galland', *World War II* (January 1997), http://www.historynet.com/interview-with-world-war-ii-luftwaffe-general-and-ace-pilot-adolf-galland.htm. Galland's recollection that he was flying a Bf 109E is contradicted by sources showing he was flying a Bf 109F-2. Prien et al., *Einsatz am Kanal und Über England*, Teil 4/I, p. 275.

70   AIR 50/62, Combat Report, Sgt Grant, 145 Squadron, 21 June 1941, National Archives (UK).

71   Caidin, *Me 109*, p. 9.

72   Galland's version is from Baker, *Adolf Galland*, pp. 165–8; Galland, 'General of the Fighters', pp. 86–8. See also Donald Caldwell, *The JG 26 War Diary, Volume One 1939–42* (London: Grub Street, 1996), pp. 137–9; Galland, *First and the Last*, pp. 59–60; Robert Michulec and Donald Caldwell, *Galland* (Redbourn: Stratus for Mushroom Model Publications, 2003), pp. 37–42; Edward H. Sims, *The Greatest Aces* (New York: Ballantine, 1967), pp. 200–23; ADI(K) Report No. 373/1945, pp. 21–2.

73   Galland, *First and the Last*, p. 60.

74   Galland, *First and the Last*, p. 65; Galland, 'General of the Fighters', p. 85.

75   AIR 50/120, Personal Combat Report, S/L Pisarek, 308 Squadron, National Archives (UK). It is uncertain whether it was Pisarek who shot Galland down that day, but his report seems to fit Galland's description of the action most closely. Pilot Officer Joseph 'Larry' Robillard, RCAF, of 145 Squadron, claimed Galland as a victory on 2 July before he was himself shot down that day and subsequently evaded capture.

76   On Galland's version of the events of 2 July, see Caldwell, *JG 26 War Diary*, pp. 143–4; Michulec and Caldwell, *Galland*, p. 42; Christer Bergström, 'Adolf Galland and the Dramatic Air Combat, July 1941', http://www.elknet.pl/aces-tory/galland/christer.bergstrom@blackcross-redstar.com

77   Winston S. Churchill to ACM Sir Charles Portal, *Lengthening the Range of Fighter Aircraft*, 2 June 1941, Churchill Papers 20/30, reproduced in Martin Gilbert, ed., *The Churchill War Papers*, vol. III, *The Ever-Widening War 1941* (New York: Norton, 2001), p. 748. On the evolution of the RAF offensive, see AIR 41/16, paras 39–52.

78   On this incident, see Bader, *Fight for the Sky*, pp. 31–3; Brickhill, *Reach for the Sky*, pp. 238–43; Burns, *Bader*, pp. 185–92; Andy Saunders, *Bader's Last Fight* (London: Grub Street, 2007), pp. 37–43, 114–18. Saunders' research points to friendly fire.

79   Galland, *First and the Last*, p. 70.

80   *Rise and Fall of the German Air Force*, p. 120.

81   Murray, *Luftwaffe*, p. 78.

82   Christer Bergström, *Max-Hellmuth Ostermann* (Crowborough, East Sussex: Chevron, 2007), pp. 19–21; Sime Ostric, *Les Messerschmitt Yugoslaves, Les Me-109E-3, les Me-108 Taifun et l'Unique Me-110 de l' Aviation Royale Yougoslave*, Avions Hors Série no. 26 (Paris: Lela Presse, 2009), pp. 46–75; Prien et al., *Einsatz in Mittelmeerraum Oktober 1940 bis November 1941*, Teil 5 (Eutin: Struve's, 2003), pp. 238–326; Christopher Shores and Brian Cull with Nicola Malizia, *Air War for Yugoslavia, Greece and Crete, 1940–41* (Carrollton, TX: Squadron Signal, 1987), pp. 194–219. Boris Ciglic provided information on these operations.

83   Quoted in Boris Ciglic, *Twelve Days in April: The Royal Yugoslav Air Force at War*, (unpublished manuscript), p. 4. A chandelle is a vertical climbing 180-degree turn. The Bf 110 had dived while the Bf 109E was attacking the formation, then climbed up in firing position.

84   Irving, *Rise and Fall of the Luftwaffe*, pp. 118–25; *Rise and Fall of the German Air Force*,

p. 161; Prof. Richard Suchenwirth, *Command and Leadership in the German Air Force*, USAF Historical Studies, no. 174 (Maxwell AFB: USAF Historical Division, 1969) p. 169. On Göring's views on the invasion, see Generalleutnant Herman Plocher, *The German Air Force Versus Russia, 1942*, USAF Historical Studies, no. 154 (Maxwell AFB: USAF Historical Division, 1966), pp. 2–7.

85   8 Abt., OKL, *Der Luftkrieg in Osten*, 1942, National Archives (US), RG 242 T-971 Reel 18 Frame 793; Murray, *Luftwaffe*, pp. 84–5.

86   Hooton, *Luftwaffe*, p. 154.

87   Quoted in Mizrahi, *Knights of the Black Cross*, p. 71. On Kaiser, see Obermaier, *Ritterkreuzträger*, vol.I, p. 147.

88   Quoted in Mizrahi, *Knights of the Black Cross*, p. 84.

89   AIR 20/7706, 'Luftwaffe Strength and Serviceability Tables'.

90   BA/MA, RI 2III/715, Gen. Qu. 6 Abt (I) *Ubersicht Über Soli, Istbestand, Verluste and Reversen der fliegenden Verbände*, 1.11.41. Quoted in Murray, *Luftwaffe*, p. 93.

91   Christer Bergström, *Barbarossa – The Air Battle: July–December, 1941* (Hersham, Surrey: Midland, 2007), p. 111; Krupinski, 'The Count' p. 27.

92   Richard Muller, *The German Air War in Russia* (Baltimore: Naval and Aviation, 1993), p. 61; Prien et al., *Winterkampf im Osten, 6.12.41 bis 30.4.42*, Teil 9/I, (Eutin: Struve's, n.d.), pp. 1–19; Dr Generalmajor i.G. Klaud Rheinhardt, *Die Wende vor Moskau, Das Scheiten der Strategies Hitlers in Winter 1941/42* (Stuttgart: Deutsche Verlags-Anstalt, 1972), pp. 68–79.

93   *Rise and Fall of the German Air Force*, p. 172; Corum, *Richthofen*, p. 278.

94   Bergström, *Barbarossa*, p. 117.

95   Bergström, *Barbarossa*, p. 116.

96   Flown by Unteroffizer Konrad von Jutrezenka of I/JG 26, who claimed a Spitfire over the Channel on 26 May 1942. Dennis Burke provided this information. Atcherley had never done air-to-air gunnery training before encountering Fw 190s.

97   Quoted in Pudney, *A Pride of Unicorns*, p. 174.

98   Letter, 17 July 1942, to Lord Sherwell, Under-Secretary of State for Air. Quoted in Alfred Price, *Focke Wulf 190 at War* (New York: Charles Scribner's Sons, 1977), pp. 41–2.

99   Dilip Sarkar, *Spitfire Ace of Aces: the Wartime Story of Johnnie Johnson* (Stroud: Amberley, 2011), p. 90.

100 On development of the Merlin 61, see Sir Stanley Hooker, *Not Much of an Engineer: An Autobiography* (Shrewsbury: Airlife, 1984), pp. 52–6; Lovesey, 'Development of the Rolls Royce Merlin', pp. 219–22.

101 Smith, 'Development', p. 341; 'Spitfire and Seafire', p. 708.

102 AVIA 18/1302, F/Lt. D.R.H. Dickinson, *The Effect of 'Clipping' Spitfire Wings*, Aircraft and Armament Experimental Establishment, Boscombe Down, 27 March 1943, National Archives (UK). The clipped Spitfire outrolled the Fw 190A at 10,000 feet at 220 mph or less. Langley Research Staff, *Summary of Lateral Control Research*, National Advisory Committee on Aeronautics, Langley Field, VA, Report 868, 14 February 1946, p. 166, http://naca.central.cranfield.ac.uk/reports/1947/naca-report-868.pdf

103 Quoted in Caygill, *Spitfire Mark V*, p. 226.

104 Irving, *Rise and Fall of the Luftwaffe*, pp. 133–4.

105 Erich Schwarz, a long-serving JG 26 pilot, to Don Caldwell, US author and researcher, who provided this information.

106 Budrass, *Flugzeugindustrie*, pp. 695–6. Seiler's bonus alone was about the cost of nine Bf 109s, reckoned at their cheapest cost; equating it to nine current fighters priced the same way, it would amount to about $400 milllion. Considering that non-management members of the design staff had received 4800–9600 Reichsmarks a year in 1939, the directors became very wealthy in 1940–1, especially Seiler.

107 Galland, *First and the Last*, p. 74. Verdun was a massive Great War battle of attrition.

108 Richard Brett-Smith, *Hitler's Generals* (Novato, CA: Presidio, 1977), p. 133; Galland, interview with Donald Lopez; Galland, 'General of the Fighters', p. 133; Herlin, *Udet*, pp. 227–38; Suchenwirth, *Command and Leadership*, p. 104.

109 Ulrich Steinhilper had noticed the year before that the fighter leaders most concerned with improving their own victory scores seemed to lose more wingmen that way. He did not mention Galland's name. Steinhilper and Osbourne, *Spitfire on my Tail*, p. 302.

110 Galland, *First and the Last*, p. 77.

111 James S. Corum, *Richthofen*, p. 224.

112 AIR 41/49, *The Air Defence of Great Britain: The Struggle for Air Supremacy, January 1943–May 1944*, vol. 5, Air Historical Branch, n.d. [*c.* 1949], p. 88, National Archives (UK); Caldwell, *JG 26 War Diary*, pp. 93, 103–4.

113 AIR 16/846, *Report, Air Office Commanding Fighter Command, November 1940–December 1941*, report by Marshal of the RAF Sir Sholto Douglas; supplement to *The London Gazette*, 14 September 1948, no. 38404, http://www.ibiblio.org/hyperwar/UN/UK/LondonGazette/38404.pdf; AIR 37/483, *Fighter Command Offensive Operations*, April–June 1942, Operational Research Section Fighter Command Report No. 359, 18 October 1942, National Archives (UK).

114 Even to Galland. Galland, *First and the Last,* pp. 24–5.

9 A Widening Air War: February 1941–November 1942

1 Quoted in Christopher Shores and Brian Cull with Nicola Malizia, *Malta: The Hurricane Years 1940–41* (London: Grub Street, 1987), p. 155.

2 MacLachlan lost his arm at the elbow from his injuries but returned to fighter combat, shooting down six German aircraft before being shot down and killed in 1943. Röll, *Müncheberg*, pp. 63–74.

3 *The Middle East Campaigns, Malta, June 1940–May 1943*, vol. 11, Air Historical Branch, n.d. [*c.* 1950], chs 1–2; AIR 41/88, p. 59; Prien et al., *Einsatz in Mittelmeerraum*, Teil 5(, pp. 328–40. On numbers available, see Shores, Cull and Malizia, *Malta: The Hurricane Years*, pp. 5–7 and Appendix III, pp. 369–73.

4 On Marseille, see Neumann 'Mentor to Many', p. 153. The Flying Tigers'

Tomahawks, over China, were able to take off and climb to higher altitude with the benefit of warning from ground observers. Without having to loiter, they could fly at high speed. Murray Rubinstein, *The Curtiss P-40C vs. the Mitsubishi A6M2 Model 21 Zero-Sen* (Biloxi: Gamescience, 1976).

5   Harold Balfour, *Wings Over Westminster*, entry for 19 September 1941, reproduced in Gilbert, *The Churchill War Papers*, vol. III, *The Ever-Widening War 1941*, (New York: Norton, 2001) p. 1238.

6   Mizrahi, *Knights of the Black Cross*, p. 72.

7   Bill Olmstead, *Blue Skies: The Autobiography of a Canadian Spitfire Pilot in World War II* (Toronto: Stoddart, 1987), p. 73.

8   Olmstead, *Blue Skies*, p. 82.

9   Arthur Tedder, *With Prejudice: The War Memoirs of Marshal of the Royal Air Force, Lord Tedder* (Boston: Little, Brown, 1967), p. 202. Tedder had previously been director of development at the Ministry for Aircraft Development, under Beaverbrook.

10 *Rise and Fall of the German Air Force*, p. 134.

11 Laddie Lucas, *Malta, The Thorn in Rommel's Side, Six Months That Turned the War* (London: Penguin, 1993), p. 47.

12 Lucas, *Malta*, pp. 51–2.

13 Hansard, 8 September 1942, http://www.ibiblio.org/pha/policy/1942/420908b.html

14 Price, *Documentary History*, p. 87.

15 AIR 16/626, Message to Air Ministry received from AVM Lloyd, 25 April 1942, on the quality of fighter pilots on Malta, National Archives (UK); AIR 41/49, p. 156.

16 Lucas, *Malta*, pp. 162–3.

17 Galland, 'General of the Fighters', pp. 100–1.

18 Quoted in J.R.O. Playfair, *The Mediterranean and Middle East: British Fortunes Reach their Lowest Ebb*, vol. III (London: HMSO, 1960), p. 337. Hoffman von Waldau had been chief of the Luftwaffe operations staff and a strong supporter of Jeschonnek until he was sent to Africa in April 1942.

19 The Germans had found out in Spain and pre-war exercises, and demonstrated in Poland and France, how important it was for fighters coordinating with ground forces in mobile combat to have air transport. The C-47 similarly enabled the RAF and USAAF. David C. Isby, *C-47/R4D Units of the ETO and MTO* (Oxford: Osprey, 2005), pp. 13–14.

20 Anthony Rogers, *Battle over Malta: Aircraft Losses and Crash Sites 1940–42* (Stroud: Sutton Publishing, 2000), p. 178.

21 Quoted in Brian Cull and Frederick Galea, *Screwball Beurling, Malta's Top Scoring Ace* (Rabat, Malta: Wise Owl, 2010), p. 33.

22 This facility of Beurling was similar to that of another Canadian, Wayne Gretzky, playing ice hockey, who had the locations of all the players and the puck at any instant in his mind's eye. I would like to thank the anonymous Canadian who provided me with this insight (and a bottle of Molson).

23 William K. Carr, 'Getting the Picture: Memories of a Photo-Reconnaissance Unit Spitfire Pilot', *C.A.H.S.: The Journal of the Canadian Aviation Historical Society*, vol. 39 no. 4 (October 2001), pp. 124–33.

24 AIR 20/7700, 8 Abt., OKL, 'German Air Force Activities in the Mediterranean Tactics and Lessons Learned, 1941–43', 30 October 1944. Translated by RAF Air Historical Branch, Translation No. ADI (K) VII/11, p. 5 in *Translations from Captured Enemy Documents*, Vol. I, *1940–45*, National Archives (UK). On 1942 Bf 109s over Malta, see Prien et al., *Einsatz in Mittelmeeraum, November 1941 bis Dezember 1942*, Teil 8/I (Eutin: Struve's, 2004), pp. 1–27.

25 Christopher Shores, Brian Cull and Nicola Malizia, *Malta: The Spitfire Year, 1942* (London: Grub Street, 1992), p. 646 and estimated from numbers in the text.

26 *Rise and Fall of the German Air Force*, p. 142.

27 Brad Gladman, 'The Development of Tactical Air Doctrine in North Africa', in Sebastian Cox and Peter Gray, eds, *Air Power History: Turning Points from Kitty Hawk to Kosovo* (London and Portland, OR: Frank Cass, 2002), pp. 188–205, p. 191.

28 This incident was included in the 1950s German-made biographical film, *Star of Africa*. His commanding officer recalled that Marseille 'heard rumours' about the Holocaust. Neumann, 'Mentor to Many', pp. 161–3.

29 Irving, *Goering*, p. 361.

30 *Rise and Fall of the German Air Force*, p. 144; E.R. Hooton, *Eagle in Flames: the Fall of the Luftwaffe,* (London: Brockhamption, 1999), pp. 218–20.

31 Captain Eric M. Brown, RN, *Duels in the Sky: World War II Naval Aircraft in Combat* (Annapolis: Naval Institute Press, 1988), p. 117.

32 Postan, *British War Production*, p. 342 (airframes), p. 411 (engines); Quill, *Spitfire*, p. 275.

33 Hugh Popham, *Sea Flight* (London: William Kimber, 1954), pp. 144, 168.

34 Personal conversation, Captain Eric 'Winkle' Brown, National Air and Space Museum, Washington, 8 January 1982; Kev Darling, *Supermarine Seafire,* (Marlborough: Crowood Press, 2008), pp. 28–33, 88–9.

35 Quill, *Spitfire*, pp. 275–6.

10 Fighters in a Changing Air War: 1942

1 Galland's planning is set out in Adolf Galland, 'Protection of Naval Forces and Convoys by Fighter Forces' in Isby, *The Luftwaffe Fighter Force*, 1997), pp. 93–9.

2 Galland interview with Donald Lopez.

3 AIR 16/738, *11 Group Report on Operation Fuller*, n.d., National Archives (UK); AIR 41/49, pp. 92–102. On Galland and the Channel Dash, see Galland, *First and the Last*, chs 12–13; Hooton, *Eagle in Flames*, pp. 114–16; ADI(K) Report No. 373/1945, pp. 30–1.

4 AIR 16/548, *GAF Wastage*, Fighter Command, 18 April 1942, National Archives (UK).

5   AIR 15/546, Air Marshal W. Sholto Douglas, *Appreciation on Methods of Causing by Air Action the Greatest Possible Wastage of the German Air Force in the West*, Headquarters Fighter Command, 14 April 1942, National Archives (UK).

6   Ibid., p. 4.

7   AIR 16/538, Assistant Chief of Air Staff (Operations) to AM Douglas, Air Officer Commanding-in-Chief Fighter Command, 13 June 1942, National Archives (UK); AIR 16/538, AM Douglas, Air Officer Commanding-in-Chief Fighter Command to Numbers 10, 11, 12 Groups, 17 June 1942, National Archives (UK). AIR 41/49, pp. 112–15, appendix 10, National Archives (UK).

8   Cairncross, *Planning in Wartime*, p. 69. The P-51 wing achieved only limited laminar flow, but this appellation, somewhat inaccurately, has come to reflect the technology used in its design. On the rise of the Merlin-powered Mustang, see J.L. Atwood, 'We Can Build You a Better Airplane than the P-40', *Aeroplane Monthly* (May 1999), pp. 30–7; Bernard L. Boylan, 'Search for a Long Range Escort Plane, 1919–1945', *Military Affairs*, vol. 30 no. 2 (Summer 1966), pp. 57–67; Paul Kennedy, 'History from the Middle: The Case From the Second World War', *The Journal of Military History* (January 2010), pp. 45–51, at pp. 46–8; Paul A. Ludwig, *P-51 Mustang: Development of the Long-Range Escort Fighter* (Hersham: Classic Publications, Ian Allan, 2003); Stephen L. McFarland, 'The Evolution of the American Strategic Fighter in Europe 1942–1944', *Journal of Strategic Studies*, vol. 10 no. 2 (June 1987), pp. 189–208; Postan, *British War Production*, p. 330; Ray Wagner, *Mustang Designer: Edgar Shmued and the P-51* (Washington: Smithsonian Institution Press, 2000).

9   AIR 50/120, Personal Combat Report, F/L D.E. Kingaby, 64 Squadron, National Archives (UK).

10 Quoted in Sarkar, *Spitfire Ace of Aces*, p. 116.

11 Quill, *Spitfire*, p. 119.

12 Lovesey, 'Development of the Rolls Royce Merlin', pp. 218–26; Quill, *Birth of a Legend*, pp. 57–9.

13 AIR 16/327, Memorandum from Air Ministry to Air Officer Commanding in Chief Fighter Command, 13 January 1945, National Archives (UK).

14 Deere, *Nine Lives*, p. 258.

15 AVIA 15/1852, Labour File, Memorandum by Deputy Director of Labour, 8 October 1942, Ministry of Aircraft Production, National Archives (UK); Cairncross, *Planning in Wartime*, p. 56; Morgan and Shacklady, *Spitfire*, p. 445. On Castle Bromwich quality issues see Ritchie, *Industry and Air Power*, pp. 238, 263. Sir Wilfrid Freeman worked effectively with the minister, Beaverbrook's replacement, Sir Stafford Cripps.

16 Lloyd, *Rolls-Royce*, pp. 120–3.

17 Cairncross, *Planning in Wartime*, p. 64.

18 This happened after her family's home in London was bombed during the Blitz and after she had worked retyping ships' actuarial tables for a maritime insurance syndicate in Liverpool at the height of the Battle of the Atlantic in 1942–3. On women workers, see Postan, *British War Production*, pp. 218–24. On the importance

of personnel and labour issues to the British aircraft industry: Ritchie, *Industry and Air Power*, pp. 260–1.

19 BA-MA ZA 3/263, *Stenographischer Bericht über die Besprechung Reichsmarshalls Görings mit Vertertern der Luftfhartindustrie über Entwicklungstragen am 13.9.42*, p. 6, *Militärarchiv*.

20 Alan Clifton, 'Joe Smith, A Colleague's Memoir', *Flight* (6 April 1956), p. 378.

21 Don Robertson, *Those Magnificent Flying Machines: An Autobiography* (Poole, Dorset: Blandford, 1984), p. 94.

22 AIR 41/49, pp. 16–24; *Rise and Fall of The German Air Force*, p. 196. Collier, *Defence of the United Kingdom*, pp. 304, 309–11, 321–2; Chris Goss with Peter Cornwell and Bernd Rauchbach, *Luftwaffe Fighter-Bombers over Britain: The Tip and Run Campaign 1942–43* (Mechanicsville, PA: Stackpole, 2003).

23 Quoted in Caldwell, *JG 26 War Diary*, p. 241.

24 CAB/195/1, *W.M. (42) 121st Meeting*, 7 September 1942, National Archives (UK).

25 Headquarters Staff, *Fliegerführer Atlantik*, 'Principles Governing the Conduct of Operations By Fliegerführer Atlantik and an Appreciation of the Types of Aircraft Available', 3 December 1943, in David C. Isby, ed., *The Luftwaffe and the War at Sea 1939–45* (London: Chatham, 2005), pp. 259–69. On Dieppe, see AIR 41/49, pp. 117–29; Lord Douglas of Kirtleside, *Years of Command* (London: Collins, 1966), pp. 174–5; Norman Franks, *Dieppe: The Greatest Air Battle, 19th August 1942* (London: Grub Street, 2010).

26 USSBS, Galland Interview 35, p. 2.

27 Beauvais, 'My Experiences', p. 69.

28 Brown, *Wings*, p. 151.

29 Hermann Göring, at a conference he chaired at Karinhall on 18 March 1943. AIR 20/7709 Air Historical Branch, Translation no. VII/136, 'Extracts from Conferences on Problems of Aircraft Production', in *Translations from Captured Enemy Documents: Vol. X, 1942–1944*, 18 March 1943, p. 2, National Archives (UK).

30 BA/MA RL 3/60, *Stenographische Niederscrift für die Besprechung beim Reichsmarschall am 7.10.43, 11.30hr, Atelierhaus Speer, Thema, Heimatsvertedigungsprogramm*, p. 13 [p. 11 original document], *Militärarchiv*.

31 USSBS, Galland Interview 34, pp. 7–11.

32 AIR 20/7709, 'Extracts from Conferences on Problems of Aircraft Production', 18 March 43, p. 2.

33 Obermaier, *Ritterkreuzträger*, vol. I, p. 21.

34 AIR 50/39, Intelligence Form 'F'. FO Maridor, 91 Squadron, National Archives (UK).

35 Maridor's claim reflects the time and place of Paul Galland's loss, at 1815 20 km west of Calais. Prien et al., *Einsatz im Westen, 1.1. bis 31.12.1942*, Teil 7, (Eutin: Struve's, n.d.), p. 401. Caldwell, *JG 26 War Diary*, pp. 299–300, states that Flying Officer Ronald Gibbs of 91 Squadron, flying a Spitfire V, shot down Galland and was in turn shot down and killed by Galland's wingman, Feldwebel Johann Erdmann. One II/JG Fw 190 was lost to anti-aircraft fire, another badly damaged in air combat.

36 *Rise and Fall of the German Air Force*, p. 198.

37 CAB 195/1, *W.M. (42) 121st Meeting*, 7 September 1942, National Archives (UK). On the Ju 86R campaign, see AIR 41/49, pp. 24–9; Winston G. Ramsey and Kenneth Wakefield, *The Blitz, Then and Now*, vol. 3 (Hemel Hempstead, Herts: Battle of Britain Prints, 1989), p. 158.

38 Alfred Price, *Blitz on Britain* (London: Ian Allan, 1977), pp. 138–40; Price, *Documentary History*, pp. 99–107.

39 Murray, *Luftwaffe*, p. 127.

40 8 Abt., OKL, *Der Luftkrieg in Rusland*, 1944, National Archives (US), RG 242 T-971 Reel 51 Frames 522–34. Prien et al., *Vom Summerfeldzug 1942 bis zur Niederlage von Stalingrad 1.5.1942 bis 3.2.1943*, Teil 9/II, (Eutin: Struve's, n.d.), pp. 1–13; Jochen Prien and Gerhard Stemmer, *Jagdgeschwader 3 'Udet' in World War II, Stab and I/JG 3 in Action with the Messerschmitt Bf 109* (Atglen, PA: Schiffer, 2002), pp. 185–97. A contemporaneous account of the effective use of the Bf 109 in direct support for the army is *Erfahrungsbericht über den Einsatz des Me. 109 in Erdkampf*, September 1942, National Archives (US), RG 242 T-314 Reel 997 Frame 115.

41 Christer Bergström, *Stalingrad – The Air Battle, 1942 through January 1943* (Hinckley: Midland, 2007), pp. 24–5; Corum, *Richthofen*, p. 270; Johannes Steinhoff, *Messerschmitts Over Sicily* (Harrisburg: Stackpole, 2004), p. 78.

42 Steinhoff, *Messerschmitts Over Sicily*, p. 220.

43 Hermann Plocher, *The German Air Force versus Russia, 1942*, USAF Historical Studies No. 154 (Maxwell AFB: USAF Historical Division, June 1966), pp. 260–329, 344–6; Steinhoff, *Messerschmitts Over Sicily*, p. 221. Considering their losses, the Ju 52 aircrew were probably even more depressed.

44 Bergström, *Stalingrad*, pp. 118–23; Joel S.A. Hayward, *Stopped at Stalingrad: The Luftwaffe and Hitler's Defeat in the East* (Lawrence, KS: University Press of Kansas, 1998), pp. 286–310; Hooton, *Eagle*, pp. 184–7; Irving, *Rise and Fall of the Luftwaffe*, pp. 185–99, Prien et al., *Vom Summerfeldzug 1942 bis zur Niederlage von Stalingrad*, Teil 9/II, pp. 14–17, 35–42.

45 Prien and Stemmer, *Stab and I/JG 3*, p. 237.

46 Irving, *Goering*, p. 379.

47 Galland interview with Donald Lopez.

48 Suchenwirth, *Command and Leadership*, p. 93.

49 *Trials of War Criminals before the Nuremberg Military Tribunals under Control Council Law No. 10, October 1946–April 1949*, vol. 2 (Washington: Government Printing Office, 1949), p. 678. This amounts to the cost of three to six complete Bf 109Es in 1941: 86,000 (58,000 without engine) Reichsmarks each according to Olaf Gröhler *Geschichte des Luftkriegs, 1910 bis 1970* ([East] Berlin: Militärverlag der Deutschen Demokratischen Republik, 1981), p. 171. Bf 109Fs cost 50,000–62,000 Reichsmarks, mass-produced 109Gs 43,000-45,000 Reichsmarks each according to Ebert, Kaiser and Peters, *Willy Messerschmitt*, p. 201. These latter figures appear to be without engine.

50 Armand van Ishoven, *Messerschmitt, Aircraft Designer* (London: Gentry Books, 1973), p. 164; Kokothaki, 'Messerschmitt History', p. 179; Schmoll, *Nest of Eagles*, p. 40.

51 BA-MA ZA 3/263, *Stenographischer Bericht üueber die Besprechung Reichsmarshalls Goerings mit Vertertern der Luftfhartindustrie üueber Entwicklungstragen am 13.9.42*, pp. 2–3, 12–14, Militärarchiv.

52 USSBS, *Interview Number 7, Mr.* [Friedrich] *Seiler*, US Strategic Bombing Survey, 16 May 1945, p. 3, National Archives (US), RG 343 Entry 31 Box 1; USSBS, Messerschmitt Interview, p. 6; Ebert, Kaiser and Peters, *Willy Messerschmitt*, p. 191; Gregor, *Daimler-Benz in the Third Reich*, pp. 94–5, 115–18. The use of such production 'circles' had pre-war roots, was initiated by Milch in 1940 and was expanded in 1944–5. Overy, 'Mobilization for Total War', p. 632. The building of Bf 109s under licence by multiple firms reflected the need for a central authority over all production of this type.

53 Letter, *Generalluftzeugmeister* an Messerschmitt AG, 30 October 1940, National Archives (US), RG 242 T-177 RLM file 228 Roll 19 Frame 3704666.

54 USSBS, Galland Interview 35, p. 3. Milch had previously cancelled the programme on 25 May 1943. Ebert, Kaiser and Peters, *Willy Messerschmitt*, p. 243.

55 Schmid, 'When the 109 Put its Ears Back', p. 84.

56 Willy Messerschmitt, *The German Jet Fighter Me-262 (Development, Success and Prospects)* n.d. ([*c.* 1946]), p. 3, US Navy Operational Archives, Washington DC, Essays by German Officers and Officials, Box T69.

57 Ebert, Kaiser and Peters, *Willy Messerschmitt*, p. 146; William Green, *Warplanes of the Third Reich* (Garden City, NY: Doubleday, 1970), p. 608; Ralf Schabel, *Die Illusion der Wunderwaffen: die Rolle der Düsenflugzeuge und Flugabwehrraketen in der Rüstungspolitik des Dritten Reiches* (Munich: R. Oldenburg, 1994), pp. 162–4.

58 AIR 20/7709, 'Extracts from Conferences on Problems of Aircraft Production', 25 August 1943, p. 10.

59 Vann, *Willy Messerschmitt*, pp. 217–19. Croneiss, in addition, held several Nazi party posts. He delegated his many responsibilities and only appeared, in one of his many uniforms, to welcome official visitors.

60 Budrass, *Flugzeugindustrie*, p. 27; Ebert, Kaiser and Peters, *Willy Messerschmitt*, p. 128. Hitler considered man-hours for Bf 109 construction greater than for comparable foreign-designed fighters; see *Hitler's Table Talk: His Private Conversations, 1941–44*, introduced and with a new preface by Hugh Trevor-Roper, trans. Norman Cameron and R.H. Stevens (New York: Enigma Books, 2000), p. 221.

61 On the labour issue, see Ulrich Herbert, *Hitler's Foreign Workers: Enforced Foreign Labour in Germany Under the Third Reich*, trans. William Templer (Cambridge: Cambridge University Press, 1997).

62 Budrass, *Flugzeugindustrie*, pp. 797–98; Adam Tooze, *The Wages of Destruction: The Making and Breaking of the Nazi Economy* (New York: Viking, 2006), pp. 611, 630; Daniel Uziel, *Arming the Luftwaffe: The German Aviation Industry in World War II* (Jefferson, NC, and London: McFarland, 2011), pp. 179–80.

63 John Cornwell, *Hitler's Scientists: Science, War, and the Devil's Pact* (New York: Penguin, 2003), p. 341.

64 Herbert, *Hitler's Foreign Workers*, p. 10.

65 Budrass, *Flugzeugindustrie*, p. 784.

66　Mark [Max] Auerbach, interview by Lauren Kempton, 5 January 1997, interview 24423, video recording, USC Shoah Foundation Institute for Visual History and Education, Los Angeles. On production in the former Poland and Czechoslovakia, see Budrass, *Flugzeugindustrie*, p. 657; Gregor, *Daimler-Benz in the Third Reich*, pp. 201–14

11 A Global Air War: The Mediterranean Theatre

1　Jack Parsonson, *A Time to Remember* (Usk, Washington: Aviation Usk, 1993), p. 57. One of the 111 victories was Marian Pisarek, who in 1941 had shot down Galland.

2　Christopher Shores, Hans Ring and William N. Hess, *Fighters over Tunisia* (London: Spearman, 1975), p. 393.

3　Shores et al. *Fighters over Tunisia*, p. 406; ADI(K) Report No. 373/1945, p. 38.

4　*Rise and Fall of the German Air Force*, p. 148.

5　1 Lt G.N. Robinson, *Tactical Doctrine RAF*, BES-263, Maxwell Field, AL, 15 October 1941, The Air Corps Tactical School, USAF Historical Research Agency document 248.211-65B. Captain James Roosevelt, the president's son, had been with the RAF in Greece and Crete in 1941. Shores et al. *Air War for Yugoslavia*, p. 320.

6　Mizrahi, *Knights of the Black Cross*, p. 26.

7　*Report of Interrogation of Pilot of Me 109G Shot Down Near the River Sangro, 30 November 1943*. CSDIC (UK), HQ A 295, 31 December 1943, p. 3, National Archives (US), RG 165 Entry 79 Box 640 Folder 4. The 'Spitfire complex' dated to 1940. Any Luftwaffe pilot damaged in air combat would attribute it to 'Spitfires'. Conversely, any victory was over a 'Spitfire', as seen over Rotterdam on 13 May 1940.

8　Shores et al., *Fighters over Tunisia*, pp. 260–1; Tom Ivie and Paul Ludwig, *Spitfires and Yellow Tail Mustangs: The 52nd Fighter Group in World War Two* (Crowborough, Sussex: Hikoki, 2005), pp. 37–8; Röll, *Müncheberg*, pp. 147–9.

9　Shores et al., *Fighters over Tunisia*, p. 392.

10　Shores et al., *Fighters over Tunisia*, p. 404.

11　*Report of Interrogation of Pilot of Me 109G*, p. 3.

12　Dundas, *Flying Start, p.* 119.

13　Norman Caldwell, 'Political Commissars in the Luftwaffe', *The Journal of Politics*, vol. 9 no. 1 (February 1947), pp. 59–79, at p. 71; Steinhoff, *Messerschmitts Over Sicily*, pp. 44, 53–7.

14　Olmstead, *Blue Skies*, p. 114.

15　Olmstead, *Blue Skies*, p. 120.

16　Quill, *Spitfire*, p. 287; Morgan and Shacklady, *Spitfire*, pp. 380–6; Price, *Documentary History*, pp. 116–19; Alfred Price, *Spitfire in Combat* (Stroud: Sutton, 2003), ch. 11; Phil Butler, 'The Spitfire Floatplanes', *Air Britain Aeromilitaria,* vol. 37 no. 146 (June 2011), pp. 89–91.

17　Quoted in Alfred Price, *Spitfire at War 3* (Shepperton: Ian Allan, 1990), p. 58. On the origins and problems of external tanks, see documents and minutes in AIR 16/327, *Long Range Fighters*, Air Ministry Memorandum, n.d. [*c.*1941], including

Sholto Douglas, Minute 120, 19 February 1942 and, in response, Air Ministry, Minute 137, 4 March 1942, National Archives (UK); Morgan and Shacklady, *Spitfire*, pp. 148–51, 167.

18 Burns, *Bader*, p. 288.

19 AIR 27/743, *92 Squadron Operational Record Book*, July–December 1943, National Archives (UK).

20 However, German records show the loss of no aircraft in that area that morning, let alone the three claimed by Sachs. Genst. 6.Abt. (III A), *Front Flugzeug Verluste, vol. 24. 02.12.43-02.01.44*, Imperial War Museum (Duxford), GER-MISC-MCR-18, Reel 12 has no reference to it, neither does AIR 20/7710, Air Historical Branch, Translation VII/150, *Luftwaffe Losses – Mediterranean, September–December 1943*, National Archives (UK). But Sachs was apparently not exaggerating; there were other Spitfires involved and, as the combat was over Allied lines, seemingly ground observers as well. Andrew Arthy provided information on this incident.

21 AIR 15/721, *Tactical Bulletin No. 36, Tactics of the Desert Air Force During the Spring of 1944*, 29 April 1944, p. 2, National Archives (UK).

22 Helmut Lipfert and Werner Girbig, *The War Diary of Hauptmann Helmut Lipfert, JG 52 on the Russian Front 1943–1945* (Atglen, PA: Schiffer, 1993), pp. 117–18, at pp. 113–14.

12 A Global Air War: The Eastern Front

1 Christer Bergström with Vlad Antipov and Claes Sundin, *Graf and Grislawski: A Pair of Aces* (Hamilton, MT: Eagle Editions, 2003), pp. 156–61; Krupinski, 'The Count', p. 31. On Soviet Spitfires, see Carl Frederick Geust and G.F. Petrov, *Lend-Lease Aircraft in Russia, Red Star*, vol. 4 (Tampere: Apali Oy, 2002), pp. 190–1. Mr Geust provided updated information. Igor Zlobin, *Spitfires Over the Kuban*, trans. James Gebhardt, http://lend-lease.airforce.ru/english/articles/spit/index.htm

2 Oberleutnant Walter Schuck shot one of these down with his Bf 109G over Finland on 17 June 1944, his 113th victory claim. Walter Schuck, *Abschuss! Von der Me 109 zur Me 262* (Aachen: Helios Verlag, 2007), p. 156; Michael Paterson, *Battle for the Skies* (Newton Abbot: David and Charles, 2004), pp. 159–60; Gordon, *Soviet Air Power*, pp. 495–501.

3 AIR 41/49, p. 160.

4 Walter Schwabedissen, *The Russian Air Force in the Eyes of German Commanders*, USAF Historical Studies no. 175 (New York: Arno Press, 1960), p. 197. *Losses V-VS* (excluding PVO, VDV), 1944, TsAMO, Podolsk, f.35, ip. 12258, g. 460, pp. 46–8. Christer Bergström provided a copy of this document. PVO strength of 16-13 Spitfires in 1943–4 from http://ipilot.narod.tsifra/gl_3/3.121.html. The shooting down of a Ju 86P remains uncertain. See Hooton, *Eagle*, p. 207, n. 54; Aleksandr Zablotskiy and Roman Larincev, *Ju 86 Losses on the Eastern Front 1941–43*, http://www.airwar.ru/history/av2ww/axis/ju86loss1/ju86loss1.html

5 On later Soviet Spitfires, see http:// ilpilot.narod.ru/vvs_tsifra/GL-3/3.121.html; Gordon, *Soviet Air Power*, pp. 498–502.

6   On Bf 109Gs to Romania, see Letter, Reichsmarschall and Oberbefehlshaber der
    Luftwaffe an Generalleutnant Spiedel, 13.5.42, National Archives (US), RG 242
    T-405 Reel 55 Frame 4895511.

7   In terms of books published per combat aircraft, the Finnish Air Force is proba-
    bly the best documented in history. Unfortunately, most of these works are
    untranslated. Eino Luukkanen, *Fighter Over Finland: The Memoirs of a Fighter Pilot*,
    trans. Mauno A. Salo, ed. William Green (London: Macdonald, 1963); Kari
    Stenman, *Aigles Finlandais Contre Etoile Rouge, La Guerre de Continuation*, Part 2,
    Avions Hors Série no. 54 (Paris: Lela Presse, 2011); Kari Stenman and Kalevi
    Keskinen, *Finnish Aces of World War 2* (Oxford: Osprey, 1998).

8   The one major German ace never shot down was Adolf 'Addi' Glunz, with 68 vic-
    tories (all in the west) in 574 combat sorties (and who once shook a P-47 off his
    tail by flying *through* a B-17 formation). Obermaier, *Ritterkreuzträger*, vol. I, p. 72.

9   Günther Rall, *My Logbook, Reminiscences 1938–2006*, ed. Kurt Braatz, trans. John
    Weal (Moosburg: 296 Verlag, 2006), p. 192.

13 A Global Air War: The War against Japan

1   Bernard Baeza, *Soleil Levant Sur L'Australie* (Paris: Lela Presse, 2008), pp. 245–323;
    Anthony Cooper, *Darwin Spitfires: The Real Battle for Australia* (Sydney: University
    of New South Wales Press, 2011); Wing Commander R.W. Foster, DFC, AE with
    Norman Franks, *Tally Ho! From the Battle of Britain to the Defence of Darwin* (London:
    Grub Street, 2008), pp. 94–169; Jim Grant, *Spitfires Over Darwin: No. 1 Fighter Wing*
    (Melbourne: Jim Moore, 1995); George Odgers, *Air War Against Japan, 1943–45*
    (Canberra: Australian War Memorial, 1957), chs 3 and 4; Jeffrey Watson, *Killer
    Caldwell: Australia's Greatest Fighter Pilot* (Sydney: Hodder Australia, 2006),
    pp. 101–68. These all cover the origins of the wing and Caldwell's first fight over
    Australia.

2   Cooper, *Darwin Spitfires*, pp. 9–10; Ian MacFarling, 'Australia and the War in the
    Pacific, 1942–45', in Cox and Gray, *Air Power History*, pp. 224–45, at p. 243;
    Odgers, *Air War*, pp. 38–67, 104–21.

3   *452 Squadron (RAAF) Operational Record Book*, National Archives of Australia, A
    9186, 137, 1119412, entry for 2.2.43, pp. 144–5; Cooper, *Darwin Spitfires*,
    pp. 124–73.

4   These are US-assigned code names, male for fighters and female for bombers and
    recon. Most Japanese military aircraft received one. 'Zero' comes from the plane's
    original Japanese designation, Type 00 Carrier Fighter, based on the Japanese cal-
    endar–660 years in advance of that used in the west. A 'Hap' is a Zero with clipped
    wing tips. When this became known, the name was dropped.

5   *457 Squadron (RAAF) Operational Record Book*, National Archives of Australia, A
    9186, 143, 1160749, entry for 7.3.43, p. 110; Grant, *Spitfires Over Darwin*, p. 50.

6   Sources for the 2 March air battle include Baeza, *Soleil Levant*, pp. 145–57; Cooper,
    Darwin Spitfires, pp. 47–68; Foster, *Tally Ho!*, pp. 132–3; Grant, *Spitfires Over
    Darwin*, pp. 45–7; Watson, *Killer Caldwell*, pp. 113–18.

7 Foster, *Tally Ho!* pp. 134–7.

8 *457 Squadron ORB*, entry for 31.3.43, p. 111.

9 *457 Squadron ORB*, entry for 2.5.43, p. 116; Cooper, *Darwin Spitfires*, pp. 141–2; Grant, *Spitfires Over Darwin*, pp. 78–86; Odgers, *Air War*, pp. 46–9.

10 *452 Squadron ORB*, entry for 2.5.43, p. 156.

11 *457 Squadron ORB*, entry for 10.5.43, p. 118; Cooper, *Darwin Spitfires*, pp. 196–202; Grant, *Spitfires Over Darwin*, pp. 88–92; Odgers, *Air War*, pp. 51–3. The Spitfire, recovered from the bush after the war, is in the Point Cook air museum.

12 Group Captain A.L. Walters, *Spitfire Versus Zeke – Tactics*, Headquarters, No. 1 Fighter Wing, 7/7/Air, 26 May 1943. National Archives of Australia, AWM 66, 7/7 Air, A 11231, 300087076; Cooper, *Darwin Spitfires*, pp. 100–17, 303–6, 401–2.

13 *457 Squadron ORB*, entry for 31.3.43, p. 113.

14 Cooper, *Darwin Spitfires*, pp. 110–11.

15 F/L C.R. Warm, *Report of Trials Conducted at Eagle Farm on 14th, 17th, and 18th August 1943 Between Spitfire 5C and Mark 2 Zero*, National Archives of Australia, AWM 66, 7/7 Air, A 11231, 300087076.

16 *452 Squadron ORB*, entry for 20.6.43, p. 171.

17 Foster, *Tally Ho!*, p. 154.

18 *457 Squadron ORB*, entry for 28.6.43 p. 123, entry for 30.6.43, p. 124; Grant, *Spitfires Over Darwin*, pp. 97–117; Odgers, *Air War*, pp. 59–65.

19 Hilary St. George Sanders and Denis Richards, *The Fight is Won: Royal Air Force, 1939–1945*, vol. 3 (London: HMSO, 1954), p. 364. Wing Commander H.L. Thompson, *New Zealanders with the Royal Air Force* (Wellington: Historical Publications Branch, 1959), p. 299.

20 A Dakota is what the RAF called a C-47 or DC-3. *The RAF and the Far East War*, Bracknell Paper No. 6, 24 March 1995, RAF Historical Society, pp. 86–8.

21 Christopher Shores, *Air War Over Burma* (London: Grub Street, 2005), p. 206. See also Alan McGregor Peart, DFC, *From North Africa to the Arakan* (London: Grub Street, 2008), chs 15–18.

22 Sanders and Richards, *The Fight Is Won*, p. 320.

23 Air Commodore Henry Probert, *The Forgotten Air Force: The Royal Air Force in the War Against Japan, 1941–1945* (London: Brassey's, 1995), pp. 168, 192. Dr Sebastian Ritchie, 'Rising from the Ashes', *RAF Air Power Review* vol. 7 no. 3 (Autumn 2004), pp. 17–29.

14 The Allied Bomber Offensives: January–October 1943

1 What it looked like was vividly portrayed in William Wyler's classic documentary film, *The Memphis Belle*, http://www.archive.org/details/MemphisBelle. Most of the combat footage was shot over Wilhelmshaven, but on a subsequent (26 February 1943) mission. The dialogue over the bomber's intercom was re-recorded by the crew of the *Memphis Belle* after they had returned to the US. For a description of a typical B-17 combat sortie, see David C. Isby, *Boeing B-17 Flying Fortress* (London: HarperCollins, 1999).

2 Caldwell and Muller, *Luftwaffe Over Germany*, pp. 63–4, 97–8; Adolf Galland, 'Experiences in Combat Against Boeing Fortress II and Consolidated Liberator', in Isby, *The Luftwaffe Fighter Force*, pp. 199–200; ADI(K) Report No. 373/1945 pp. 34–5.

3 Irving, *Rise and Fall of the Luftwaffe*, p. 126. AIR 20/7709, 'Extracts from Conferences on Problems of Aircraft Production', p. 20.

4 Boog, *Luftwaffenführung*, pp. 106–7, 118–22; Budrass, *Flugzeugindustrie*, pp. 707–8; R.J. Overy, 'Hitler and Air Strategy', *Journal of Contemporary History*, vol. 15 no. 3 (July 1980), pp. 405–21.

5 Werner Jochmann, ed., *Adolf Hitler, Monologe im Führerhauptquartier 1941–1944*, Die Aufzeichnungen Heinrich Heims (Hamburg: Albrecht Knaus, 1980), 10–11.8.41, p. 57; Henry Picker, ed., *Hitler Tischengespräche in Führerhauptquartier* (Stuttgart: Seewald, 1971), 3.7.42, pp. 174–8; Boog, *Luftwaffenführung*, pp. 119–21; von Rohden Book 4 [pp. 15–17].

6 Boog, *Luftwaffenführung*, p. 145.

7 USSBS, Messerschmitt Interview, p. 8.

8 ADI(K) Report No. 373/1945, p. 40.

9 Irving, *Rise and Fall of the Luftwaffe*, p. 212; Vann, *Willy Messerschmitt*, p. 147.

10 Ebert, Kaiser and Peters, *Willy Messerschmitt*, p. 128; Jeffrey Ethell and Alfred Price, *World War II Fighting Jets* (Annapolis: Naval Institute, 1994), p. 13; Irving, *Rise and Fall of the Luftwaffe*, p. 147.

11 *German Fighter Tactics Against American Fortresses and Liberator Bombers*, 11 Group Tactical Memorandum 18, n.d. [probably early 1943], Royal Air Force, USAF HRA document, 512.6403-18.

12 Initial testing with wooden mockups for a later gun pod showed that drag alone imposed a 4 mph penalty. Messerschmitt AG Flight Testing Report Nf.109 14 L 43 12.8.43, at http://www.ww2aircraftperformance.org/me109/me109g-15562-mk108.html

13 USSBS, *Armament in the Air War*, US Strategic Bombing Survey, 13 August 1945, pp. 9–10, National Archives (US), RG 243 Entry 6 Box 476. There is a photograph of a Spitfire fuselage ripped apart by a 30mm hit in Alfred Price, *World War II Fighter Combat* (London: Macdonald and Jane's, 1975), p. 84.

14 Adolf Galland, 'Tactical Regulations for SE and TE Fighter Formations in Air Defense', in Isby, *The Luftwaffe Fighter Force*, pp. 201–4; von Rohden Book 3; von Rohden Book 4 [pp. 18–21]; ADI(K) Report No. 373/1945, pp. 37–8; *German Fighter Tactics Against Flying Fortresses*, Headquarters, Eighth Air Force, 8 December 1943, USAF HRA document.

15 BA-MA RL 36/55, Report of Oberstleutnant Anton Mader, *Kommodore* JG 11 to Generalmajor Adolf Galland, *General der Jagdflieger*, Nr. 1018/43 g. Kdos., *Erfahrungsberichte über die Bekämplung viermotoriger Flugzeuge*, 2.7. 1943, pp. 3–5; Galland cover letter pp. 1–2, at p. 2, *Militärarchiv*.

16 BA-MA ZA 3/337, *Oberst a.d.* Hannes Trautloft, *Kurzbiographie Hans Phillips*, 14.2.1957; Mizrahi, *Knights of the Black Cross*, p. 88; Obermaier, *Ritterkreuzträger*, p. 40 vol. I, *Militärarchiv*.

17   Prien and Rodeike, *JG 1 und JG 11*, pp. 375–82, 396–7.

18   Unlike the superchargers in the Spitfire and the Bf 109, which were driven by engine power, a turbosupercharger was driven by engine exhaust gases through a turbine wheel.

19   National Air and Space Museum lecture, Washington, 10 April 1997.

20   Quoted in Roger Freeman, *The Hub: The Story of Hub Zemke* (Shrewsbury: Airlife, 1988), p. 146.

21   Caldwell and Muller, *Luftwaffe Over Germany*, p. 106; Manfred Rauchsteiner, *Der Luftangriff auf Wiener Neustadt, 13 August 1943* (Vienna: Styria Verlag, 1983), p. 43; Wernfried Haberfellner and Walter Schroeder, *Wiener Neustädter Flugzeugwerke* (Grasz: Weishaupt Verlag, 1993).

22   Ebert, Kaiser and Peters, *Willy Messerschmitt*, p. 197.

23   Robert S. Johnson with Martin Caidin, *Thunderbolt* (New York: Ballantine, 1966), p. 151. On German actions, see Prien et al., *Reichsverteidiging 1943, 1.1 bis 31.12.43*, Teil 10/III (Eutin: Struve's, n.d.), pp. 228–46.

24   Walker Mahurin, *Honest John* (New York: G.P. Putnam's Sons, 1962), pp. 124–5.

25   Unlike 20mm cannon shells, .50-calibre machine-gun bullets are not explosive. Mahurin saw the kinetic energy flash from the impact of the bullets.

26   ADI(K) Report 28/1944, *GAF Training: Training of a Fighter Pilot, 1943*, 21 January 1944, National Archives (US), RG 498 Entry UD231 Box 1260; Murray, *Luftwaffe*, p. 241. Alfred Price, *The Luftwaffe Data Book* (London: Greenhill, 1997), pp. 226–9. Comparative training hours from USSBS, *Overall Report (Europe)*, p. 21.

27   Ebert, Kaiser and Peters, *Willy Messerschmitt*, p. 189.

28   Prien et al., *Reichsverteidigung 1943*, Teil 10/III, pp. 204–17.

29   BA/MA RL 3/60, *Stenographische Niederschrift für die Besprechung beim Reichsmarschall am 7.10.43, 11.30hr, Atlierhaus Speer, Thema, Heimatsvertedigungsprogramm*, p. 74, *Militärarchiv*.

30   AIR 20/7709, 'Extracts from Conferences on Problems of Aircraft Production', 6 July 1943, p. 9.

31   Martin Middlebrook, *The Berlin Raids: R.A.F. Bomber Command Winter, 1943–44* (London, New York: Viking, 1988), pp. 47–8. On Wild Boar, see Gerhard Aders, *History of the German Night Fighter Force 1917–1945* (London: Arms and Armour, 1979), pp. 97–107, 141–7; Peter Hinchcliffe, *The Other Battle: Luftwaffe Night Aces Versus Bomber Command* (Shrewsbury: Airlife, 1996), pp. 131, 150–1, 179–92; ADI(K) Report No. 373/1945, p. 40; *Der erste grosse Einsatz der 'Wilden Sau'*, Auszug aus der G-L Besprechung am 20.8.43. USAF HRA document, K113.312-2, v.3; 1st Lt. William H. Pierce, *Tactics of Enemy Night Fighters*, Headquarters, 3rd Bombardment Division [Eighth Air Force], 27 September 1943, USAF HRA document.

32   Ebert, Kaiser and Peters, *Willy Messerschmitt*, p. 148; Ethell and Price, *Fighting Jets*, p. 219.

33   USSBS, Galland Interview 35, pp. 2–3; Schabel, *Illusion der Wunderwaffen*, pp. 162–70.

34 BA-MA ZA 3/194, *Mitschrift der Besprechung, Prof. Messerschmitt am 14.10.43*, pp. 1–13, *Militärarchiv*. This meeting with Milch, Göring and others saw much talk of long-range bombers, little of jet fighters. Irving, *Rise and Fall of the Luftwaffe*, p. 279.

35 Ebert, Kaiser and Peters, *Willy Messerschmitt*, p. 148; Irving, *Rise and Fall of the Luftwaffe*, p. 223; Ishoven, *Messerschmitt*, p. 312; Schabel, *Illusion der Wunderwaffen* pp. 168–72.

36 Ebert, Kaiser and Peters, *Willy Messerschmitt*, p. 150; Schabel, *Illusion der Wunderwaffen*, p. 168. Manfred Boehme, *JG 7, The World's First Jet Fighter Unit*, 1944–45 (Atglen, PA: Schiffer Military History, 1992) pp. 13–44. On the engine, see Schabel, *Illusion der Wunderwaffen*, p. 234.

37 Budrass, *Flugzeugindustrie*, pp. 858–67.

38 Imperial War Museum FD 4355/45, vol. 3. Quoted in Ferenc A. Vajda and Peter Dancey, *German Aircraft Industry and Production, 1933–1945* (Warrendale, PA: SAE International, 1998), p. 81.

39 On the 7 September conference, see excerpt from Report of Führer Conference, 11–12 September, 1943, 14 September 1943, *Trials of War Criminals before the Nuremberg Military Tribunals under Control Council Law No. 10, October 1946–April 1949*, vol. 2 (Washington: Government Printing Office, 1949), p. 442; Budrass, *Flugzeugindustrie*, pp. 862–3 quoting *Entwurf für Besprechung mit dem Führer*, Imperial War Museum FD 4355/45 vol. 1, folder 1; Nicolaus von Below, *Als Hitlers Adjutant 1937–45* (Mainz: Hase and Kohler, 1980), p. 350; Irving, *Rise and Fall of the Luftwaffe*, pp. 238–30; Schabel, *Illusion der Wunderwaffen*, pp. 165–8; USSBS, Messerschmitt Interview, pp. 9–11.

40 As demonstrated by BA-MA ZA 3/194, *Mitschrift der Besprechung, Prof. Messerschmitt am 14.10.43,* Militärarchiv.

41 Barnato Walker, *Spreading My Wings*, p. 75.

42 H.A. Taylor, *Test Pilot at War* (Shepperton: Ian Allan, 1970), p. 128. On the Spitfire XII, see Morgan and Shacklady, *Spitfire*, pp. 403–8.

43 Barnato Walker, *Spreading My Wings*, p. 69.

44 AIR 41/49, pp. 171–208, National Archives (UK). Chris Goss, *Luftwaffe Hit-and-Run Raiders: Nocturnal Fighter Bomber Operations over the Western Front 1943–45* (Hersham, Surrey: Classic, Ian Allan, 2009).

45 This had been proposed in 11 Group in 1940 and was recognised as early as 1942–3. AIR 16/776, Air Officer Commander-in-Chief Fighter Command to Groups, 24 January 1942; *The Use of the Spitfire-Bomber (Bombfire)*, HQ Fighter Command, Air Tactics Branch, 16 March 1943, p. 1, National Archives of Canada, A 5218, #598.

46 AVIA 6/11899, A.P. Goode, *Battle Damage to British Fighter Aircraft*, Farnborough, September 1945, Royal Aircraft Establishment, RAE Technical Note No. S.M.E. 330, p. 16, National Archives (UK).

47 John A.C. Andrews, 'The Forty, the Spit and the Jug', in Robin Higham and Carol Williams, eds, *Flying Combat Aircraft of the USAAF-USAF*, vol. III (Manhattan, KS: Sunflower UP, 1981), pp. 23–8, at p. 27.

48   Quoted in Price, *Spitfire at War 3*, p. 73.

49   Quill, *Test Pilot*, p. 221.

50   AIR 20/7709, 'Extracts from Conferences on Problems of Aircraft Production', 23 February 1944, p. 20.

51   Boog, *Luftwaffenführung*, pp. 28–30; von Rohden Book 3; von Rohden Book 4 [p. 27].

52   Prien and Rodeike, *JG 1 und JG 11*, Teil 1, pp. 495–9, 610. While this attributes his loss to a B-17, he may have been shot down by a P-47, possibly that flown by Captain Robert S. Johnson of the 56th Fighter Group, who scored his third victory that day on his forty-second combat mission. Caldwell and Muller, *Luftwaffe Over Germany*, p. 126.

53   Minutes, 25 March 1944 conference, p. 14 (original document). On Luftwaffe operations, see Prien et al., *Reichsverteidiging 1943,* Teil 10/III, pp. 341–57.

54   J.E. Johnson, *Full Circle* (New York: Ballantine, 1968), p. 226.

15 The Defeat of the Luftwaffe Fighter Force, October 1943–June 1944

1   Major General John W. Huston, ed., *American Airpower Comes of Age: General Henry H. 'Hap' Arnold's World War II Diaries*, vol. 2 (Maxwell AFB, AL: Air University Press, 2002), pp. 42, 48–51.

2   Charles Webster and Noble Frankland, *The Strategic Air Offensive Against Germany, Endeavour*, vol. 2 (London: HMSO, 1961), pp. 42–5.

3   AIR 41/49, p. 281; H.H. Arnold, *Global Mission* (New York: Harper, 1949), pp. 494–5.

4   Smith, 'Spitfire and Seafire', p. 356.

5   BA-MA ZA 3/194, *Mitschrift der Besprechung, Prof. Messerschmitt am 14.10.43*, p. 18.

6   G-L Conference 30 November 1943, stenographic record, p. 7930, at Prosecution Exhibit 145, Document NOKW-228, National Archives (US), RG 238 M-888 Roll 8 Frame 687. On the Me 209 development and cancellation, see Ebert, Kaiser and Peters, *Willy Messerschmitt*, p. 150; Schabel, *Die Illusion,* pp. 160–70.

7   Overy, 'Mobilization for Total War', pp. 637–9. On this issue in general and fears that women working would undercut Germany's eventual victory in what the Nazis saw as a war not between armed forces or even nations, but rather races, see Claudia Koonz, *Mothers in The Fatherland: Women, the Family and Nazi Politics* (New York: St. Martin's, 1987). Despite Britain's conscription of civilian labour, including women, such concerns were found there as well. John Costello, *Love, Sex and War: Changing Values 1939–45* (London: William Collins, 1985), pp. 204–6, 215–16.

8   Messerschmitt letter, 20.7.43, IWM FD 4355/45, folder 3; Schabel, *Die Illusion*, p. 145; Uziel, *Arming*, p. 180; Vann, *Willy Messerschmitt*, p. 151.

9   Gröhler, *Geschichte* p. 414; Schmoll, *Nest of Eagles*, p. 55.

10   Quoted in Wesley Frank Craven and James Lea Cate, eds, *The Army Air Forces in World War II, Europe: ARGUMENT to V-E Day*, vol.3 (Washington: Office of Air Force History, 1983), p. 8

11   Mizrahi, *Knights of the Black Cross*, p. 29.

12   Galland, 'General of the Fighters', p. 113; Mizrahi, *Knights of the Black Cross*, p. 59.

13   *Minutes of Commander's Meeting*, January 21 1944, USAF Historical Research Agency Document A520.141-1A, 'Commander's Meetings'.

14   James H. Doolittle, *I Could Never Be So Lucky Again* (New York: Bantam Books, 1991), pp. 380–1.

15   On the USAAF's evolution and implementation of fighter tactics over Germany, see *Tactics and Techniques Developed by VIII Fighter Command*, Army Air Forces Evaluation Board, Analysis Section, 27 October 1944, USAF Historical Research Agency 138.4-33A; *The Long Reach: Deep Fighter Escort Tactics*, VIII Fighter Command, 29 May 1944, USAF Historical Research Agency 524.502A; Lt. Col. Lynn Farnol, *To the Limit of their Endurance: A Family Story of the VIII Fighter Command*, n.d. [probably late 1944], USAF Historical Research Agency 534.107A; Lt. Col. Waldo A. Heinrichs, *A History of the VIII Fighter Command*, n.d. [probably late 1944]; Stephen L. MacFarland and Wesley P. Newton, *To Command the Sky: The Battle for Air Superiority Over Germany, 1942–44* (Washington: Smithsonian Institution Press, 1991).

16   Col. Clarence E. Anderson, *To Fly and to Fight* (New York: Bantam, 1991), p. 10.

17   ADI(K) Report No. 373/1945, p. 36.

18   BA/MA RL 3/60, *Stenographische Niederschrift für die Besprechung beim Reichsmarschall am 7.10.43, 11.30hr, Atlierhaus Speer, Thema, Heimatsvertedigungsprogramm*, p. 46.

19   Lester F. Rentmeester, 'Big Brothers and Little Friends: A Memoir of the Air War Against Germany', *The Wisconsin Magazine of History*, vol. 74 no. 1 (Autumn 1990), pp. 30–47, at p. 43. He was in the 401st Bomb Squadron, 91st Bomb Group at RAF Bassingbourn, serving with Joseph Shackleton.

20   AVIA 10/113, *Visit to the Messerschmitt Plant at Oberammergau Bavaria, June 19–25, 1945, by Mr. D.M. Clarkson, DeHavilland Aircraft Company*, Ministry of Aircraft Production, National Archives (UK), pp. 1–2; Helena Waddy, *Oberammergau in the Nazi Era: The Fate of a Catholic Village in Hitler's Germany* (New York: Oxford University Press, 2010), pp. 212–16.

21   O'Donnell, 'Secret Fight', p. 103. Messerschmitt, working on advanced aircraft projects, may not have been aware how quickly those building and flying his creation were dying; casualty reports went up the Luftwaffe command chain, while the SS and Saur were responsible for determining and reporting the Flossenbürg and Gusen death rate. But he had many connections in the Luftwaffe and industry, so what he knew, what he could have done and whether he cared are all unclear.

22   Von Rohden Book 4 [p. 48].

23   Dr Horst Boog, 'The Policy. Command and Direction of the Luftwaffe in World

War II', *Royal Air Force Historical Journal*, no. 41 (2008), pp. 66–85, at p. 75.

24 Johnson, *Full Circle*, p. 228.

25 Generalstab 6 Abteilung (IIIA), *Front Flugzeug Verluste*. RL 2 II/329, *Übersicht über Soll, Istbestand, Einstatzbereitschaft, Verluste und reserven der fliegender Verbände*, BA/MA, RL 2 III/1025, quoted in Murray, *Strategy for Defeat*, p. 136.

26 ADI(K) Report No. 373/1945, p. 46.

27 AIR 20/7709 Air Historical Branch, Translation no. VII/137, 'Fighter Staff Conferences' in *Translations from Captured Enemy Documents: Vol X, 1942–1944*, 25 April 1944, p. 9, National Archives (UK); Galland, *First and the Last*, pp. 260–1; Schabel, *Illusion der Wunderwaffen*, p. 290.

28 Captain Eric Brown, *Wings of the Luftwaffe* (Shrewsbury: Airlife, 1993), p. 17; AVIA 10/113, p. 22.

29 Kenneth Roman [Roman Katzbach], interview by Shirley Murgraff, London, 31 March 1995, interview 40310, video recording, USC Shoah Foundation Institute for Visual History and Education, Los Angeles.

30 *Law Reports of Trials of War Criminal Prepared by the United Nations War Crimes Commission* (New York: H. Fertig, 1994), pp. 31–2; Minutes, 25 March 1944 conference, p. 18 (original document). On the 72-hour week, see AIR 20/7709, 'Fighter Staff Conferences', 21 April 1944, p. 6, National Archives (UK). On absenteeism, see *Bayerische Motorwerke AG*, USSBS Report 18, Aero-Engine Plant Report 4 (Washington: US Strategic Bombing Survey, 22 October 1945), p. 5; Gregor, *Daimler-Benz in the Third Reich*, pp. 206–8. Germany had used conscription of (German) labour since 1938. Absenteeism was high among conscript German workers (waiting in line for rationed food often took all day).

31 AIR 20/7709, 'Extracts from Conferences on Problems of Aircraft Production', 23 February 1944, pp. 17–21; AIR 41/42, *The Full Offensive, February 1943 to February 1944: The RAF In the Bombing Offensive Against Germany*, vol. 5, Air Historical Branch, n.d. [*c.* 1949], p. 164, National Archives (UK); Tooze, *Wages of Destruction*, p. 598.

32 For Milch on *Jägerstab* organisation, see Minutes, 25 March 1944 conference, p. 5 (original document); Milch letter in BA/MA RL 3/1, quoted in Willi A. Bölcke, 'Stimulation and Attitude of the German Aircraft Industry in Rearmament and War', in Boog, *Conduct of the Air War*, pp. 55–84, at p. 76; Murray, *Luftwaffe*, p. 241.

33 Schmoll, *Nest of Eagles*, pp. 139–42.

34 Affidavit of Friedrich Wilhelm Seiler-Vierling, Nuremberg, August 1947, defence exhibit Mummenthy-65, NMT 04, *USA v. Oswald Pohl et al.*, English transcript, p. 7550 (16 September 1947). Seiler was holding high-level meetings with Saur's staff as late as April 1945. A *Gauleiter* was head of a regional branch of the Nazi party. On Saur's whip, see USSBS, *Subject: Dr. Karl Frydag*, Interview 44, 9 July 1945, US Strategic Bombing Survey, p. 12, National Archives (US), RG 243 Entry 32 Box 3.

35 Budrass, *Flugzeugindustrie*, p. 449–50; Kokothaki, 'Messerschmitt History', p. 181. On Wahl: Der Kommandant Rüstungkommando Augsburg:Führung frt Fa.

Messerschmitt AG, 22 February 1945, National Archives (US), RG 242 T-73 Reel 30 Frame 3159025.

36   Kokothaki, 'Messerschmitt History', p. 180; Vann, *Willy Messerschmitt*, pp. 219–23. On the Speer–Hitler conference, replacing the RLM, see Willi A. Bölcke, ed., *Deutschlands Rüstung im Zweiten Weltkrieg, Hitlers Konferenzen mit Albert Speer 1942–1945* (Frankfurt: Akademische Verlagsgesellschaft Athenaion, 1969), p. 376.

37   The chauffeur, conscripted when there was no more petrol for the company cars, ended up a PoW. ADI(K) Report No. 278/1945, p. 1, National Archives (US), RG 243 Entry 6 Box 238 File 11B.

38   AIR 20/7709, 'Fighter Staff Conferences', 27 April 1944, p. 7.

39   This does not include the man-hours from other furnished equipment, such as weapons and radios. Ebert, Kaiser and Peters, *Willy Messerschmitt*, p. 201. This is significant because Milch himself identified equipment as generating some 52 per cent of the total man-hours. *Stenographischer Bericht über die Besprechungmit den Flotteningenieuren und Oberquartiermeistern unter Vorsitz von Generalfeldmarschall Milch am Sonnabend 25 Maerz 1944*, National Archives (US), RG 238 M-888 Reel 6 Frame 328 (p. 14 original document).

40   He set the maximum at forty-five minutes to one hour. AIR 20/7709, 'Fighter Staff Conferences', 17 June 1944, p. 12.

41   Secretary of State/GLM/RuK meeting, 19 January 1944, BA-MA RL 3/32, 1153. Quoted in Williamson Murray, *Luftwaffe* (Annapolis: Naval and Aviation, 1989), p. 119.

42   Schabel, *Illusion der Wunderwaffen*, p. 234.

43   Memoranda from Speer to Hitler: 30 June 1944, 28 July 1944, 29 July 1944; National Archives (US), RG 242 T-971 Roll 28 Frame 231 (28 July); RG 243 Entry 6 Box 224 (30 June and 29 July); Galland, 'General of the Fighters' p. 113.

44   On 14 February 1944. See International Military Tribunal Sitting at Nuremberg, Germany, *The Trial of Major German War Criminals: Proceedings of the International Military Tribunal Sitting at Nuremberg, Germany*, 24 vols (London: HMSO, 1946), vol. 2, p. 338.

45   Michael Thad Allen, *The Business of Genocide: The SS Slave Labor, and the Concentration Camps* (Chapel Hill: University of North Carolina, 2002), pp. 1–2, 14, 58–63; Tooze, *Wages of Destruction*, p. 630. The SS developed wood glue because the RLM had concentrated on metal structures. As the RLM controlled aluminium supplies, the SS obtained wood from the labour organisation, *Organization Todt*.

46   USSBS, *German Air Force Supply and Maintenance*, US Strategic Bombing Survey, n.d. [*c.* 1946], p. 8, National Archives (US), RG 243 Entry 6 Box 476; US Strategic Bombing Survey, *Aircraft Division Industry Report* Report 4 (Washington: USGPO, 1947), Exhibit VIA. On Bf 109 parts, statement by Dr Frydag, Minutes, 25 March 1944 conference, p. 53 (original document).

47   Murray, *Luftwaffe*, p. 190 n. 196, p. 241; US Strategic Bombing Survey, *The Defeat of the German Air Force* (Washington: Military Analysis Division, January 1946), pp. 35–9; USSBS, *Overall Report (Europe)*, p. 7; Caidin, *Me 109*, p. 13. This was

known in Germany during the war. See, for example, *Report of Information Received from PW OS/1499, Oberst [Hans] Höffner, Pz Gren Regiment 29, Captured nr Düren*, CSDIC (UK), 25 March 1945, p. 5, National Archives (US), RG 165 Entry 79 Box 664 Folder 1. After the war, when Saur was asked where the thousands of airplanes he had reported building but could not be accounted for might be found, he answered simply, 'That, I do not know.' US Strategic Bombing Survey, *Minutes of Interview with Herr Saur*, 7 June 1945, p. 28, National Archives (US) RG 243 Entry 32 Box 5.

48   US Strategic Bombing Survey, *Subject: Reichsmarschall Hermann Goering*, Interview No. 46, 29 June 1945, p. 3, National Archives (US), RG 243 Entry 32 Box 2. Reproduced in Richard Overy, *Interrogations: The Nazi Elite in Allied Hands, 1945* (London: Penguin, 2001), p. 297. That this critique also applied to the economists who ran the US Strategic Bombing Survey went unnoticed by them.

49   Minutes, ibid., p. 6 (original document); Rudolf A. Haunschmied, Jan-Ruth Mills and Siegi Witzany-Durda, *St. Georgen Gusen Mauthausen: Concentration Camp Mauthausen Reconsidered* (Sankt Georgen an der Gusen: Books on Demand – http://www.gusen.org, 2008); Schmoll, *Nest of Eagles*, p. 162.

50   Stanley [Shlamek] Orzech, interview by Carol Stulberg, 8 March 1995, interview 2355, video recording, USC Shoah Foundation, Institute for Visual History and Education, Los Angeles. A *Kapo* was an inmate-overseer, known for sadistic brutality.

51   Allen, *Business of Genocide*, pp. 8–9, 77, 228.

52   USSBS, *Minutes of Meeting with Speer*, 18 May 1945.

53   *Stenographischer Bericht über die Jägerstab Besprechung am Freiburg, 17 Maerz 1944*, National Archives (US), RG 238 M-888 Roll 6 Frames 662–3 (pp. 35–6 original document).

54   Livia Bitton-Jackson [Elli Friedmann], *I Have Lived a Thousand Years: Growing Up in the Holocaust* (New York: Simon Pulse, 1999), p. 149.

55   Livia Bitton-Jackson [Elli Friedmann], interview by Martha Frezer, New York, 31 May, 1995 interview 2916, video recording, Survivors of the Shoah Visual History Foundation, Los Angeles.

56   Bitton-Jackson, *I Have Lived*, p. 144.

57   Budrass, *Flugzeugindustrie*, p. 799; Lutz Budrass, Jonas Scherner and Jochen Streb, *Demystifying the German 'Armament Miracle' During World War II: New Insights From Annual Audits of German Aircraft Producers* (New Haven: Economic Growth Center, Yale University, January 2005), Center Discussion Paper No. 905, p. 13; Lutz Budrass and Manfried Gieger, 'Die Moral der Effizenz. Die Beschäftigung von KZ-Häftlingen am Bespiel des Volkswagenwerks unter der Henschel Flugzeug-Wekre', *Jahrbuch für Wirtschaftgeschichte*, no. 2 (1993), pp. 89–136. That some workers were so close to the German baseline performance suggests either they were motivated (by self-preservation, bonuses (food or cigarettes), or identification with the task) and/or that the baseline reflects low productivity.

58   Affidavit, Friedrich Messler, Nuremberg, 13 August 1947, defence exhibit Mummenthey-53, NMT 04, *USA v. Oswald Pohl et al.*, English transcript, p. 7547 (16 September 1947).

59　Quoted in Anshell Pfeffer, 'Dark Skies', *The Jerusalem Post* (11 February 2007), http://www.jpost.com/Magazine/Features/Article.aspx?id=50824

60　Schmoll, *Nest of Eagles*, p. 164.

61　Quoted in Pfeffer, 'Dark Skies'.

62　Barry Tiger [Berl Tieger], interview by Adele Black, Morris Plains, New York, 7 October 1996, interview 20714, video recording, USC Shoah Foundation Institute for Visual History and Education, Los Angeles.

63　Uziel, *Arming*, p. 229 states that the revolt destroyed '100–200' Bf 109 wingsets (intended for the Leipzig factory). Me 163 information provided at the National Air and Space Museum's Garber facility, 1980. This Me 163 never flew. Sabotage was detected when it was being restored as an exhibit.

64　AIR 20/7709, 'Fighter Staff Conferences', 18 April 1944, p. 4. Saur blamed equipment failure (tyres bursting).

65　For example, Lipfert and Girbig *War Diary*, p. 174; Alfred Price, *The Last Year of the Luftwaffe: May 1944 to May 1945* (Osceola, WI: Motorbooks, 1991), p. 15.

66　Bitton-Jackson, *I Have Lived*, p. 147.

67　Quill, *Spitfire*, p. 119. On the Spitfire XIV, see Morgan and Shacklady, *Spitfire*, pp. 410–20.

68　Captain Eric M. Brown, RN, *Duels in the Sky: World War II Naval Aircraft in Combat* (Annapolis: Naval Institute Press, 1988), pp. 200–1.

69　*Case History of the Spitfire Airplane Range Extension*, Historical Division, Intelligence T-2, Air Technical Service Command, Wright Field [Ohio], 27 February 1946, pp. 1–3, National Archives (US), RG 18 Entry 22 Box 62.

70　AIR 16/327, *Spitfire LF IX MK 210, Long-Range Fuel Tank Installation by Wright Field Installation*, 4 September 1944, Aircraft and Experimental Establishment, Boscombe Down; *Spitfire IX MK 210, Functioning Tests with Long-Range Fuel Tank System (Wright Field Installation)*, 23 July 1944, Aircraft and Experimental Establishment, Boscombe Down, included as appendix to *Case History of the Spitfire*.

71　AIR 16/327, *Release of Aircraft for Service Use After Major Modification of the Spitfire 5C Fitted with Additional Fuel Tanks*, Air Ministry Memorandum, 31 October 1942; AIR 16/327, *Spitfire Mark IX 170 Gallon Auxiliary Drop Fuel Tank Installation*, Air Ministry Memorandum, 27 April 1945.

72　AIR 16/327, Memoranda by G/C W.R. Worstall, Senior Air Staff Officer, Fighter Command, 27 November 1944; Memoranda from Air Ministry to Air Officer Commanding in Chief Fighter Command, 13 January, 1945, National Archives (UK).

73　Before being sacked, Milch had been anxious to add them to his bureaucratic control. *Stenographischer Bericht über die Jägerstab Besprechung unter Vorsitz von Generalfeldmarschall Milch an Montag 20 Maerz 1944*, National Archives (US), RG 238 M-888 Reel 6 Frame 328 (p. 49 original document).

74　The tail failure issue led to a meeting at Messerschmitt's Regensburg plant on 21 July 1944 and a subsequent flight test programme. Schmoll, *Nest of Eagles*, p. 75.

75　The DB 603 encountered extensive design difficulties and absorbed much technical effort and factory space. US Strategic Bombing Survey, *Aircraft Division Industry*

Report 4 (Washington: USGPO, 1947), p. 96; Vajda and Dancey, *German,* pp. 78, 84.

76 AIR 20/1650, *German Control of Fighters by the Benito and Egon Methods,* Air Scientific Intelligence Report 33, Assistant Directorate of Intelligence (Science), 20 April 1945, National Archives (UK).

77 Brown, *Wings,* p. 157.

78 AIR 20/7709, 'Fighter Staff Conferences', 6 July 1944, p. 34.

79 AIR 20/7709, 'Fighter Staff Conferences', 27 April 1944, p. 8.

80 The suffix *i.G., in Generalstabdienst,* designates a General Staff officer.

81 Nowarra, *Famous Fighter,* p. 74; Heinz J. Nowarra, *Messerschmitt Me 109: Aircraft and Legend* (Yeovil: Haynes, 1989), p. 114. Pasewaldt was *Amstgruppenchef für Flugzeugentwicklung* from June 1942 to October 1943. Boog, *Luftwaffenführung,* p. 329.

82 Nowarra, *Famous Fighter,* p. 74. After the war, Messerschmitt still complained about the RLM's 1942-era desire for longer-range fighters. Messerschmitt, *The German Jet Fighter,* p. 3.

83 Albert Speer, *Inside the Third Reich* (New York: Macmillan, 1970), p. 346.

84 All figures on kills per 100 attacks from USSBS, *Defeat,* p. 16.

85 ADI(K) Report No. 373/1945, p. 58.

16 Fighters over France and England: May–September 1944

1 AIR 16/498, *An Analysis of Fighter Bomber Accuracy,* 9 August 1945, Operations Research Section, Fighter Command, National Archives (UK); AIR 20/6857, Air Historical Branch, *Tactics used by Spitfire Day Fighter/Bomber Squadrons of the 2nd Tactical Air Force During the Campaign in Western Europe,* Tactical Paper No. 4, September 1947, National Archives (UK); Hugh Godefroy, *Lucky 13* (Toronto: Stoddart Publishing, 1983), p. 237.

2 AIR 37/569, *Survey of Fighter OTU Training,* 6 April 1944, p. 1, National Archives (UK); AIR 27/1882, *442 Squadron (RCAF) Operational Record Book,* entry for 13.5.44, National Archives (UK); Johnson, *Wing Leader,* pp. 199–200.

3 Olmstead, *Blue Skies,* p. 179.

4 AIR 41/24, Air Historical Branch, *The Liberation of Northwest Europe, vol. III, The Landings in Normandy* (London: Royal Air Force, 1947), p. 14, National Archives (UK).

5 AIR 41/49, p. 188; ADI(K) Report 486/1944, *The German Photographic Reconnaissance and Photographic Intelligence Service,* 26 August 1944, National Archives (US), RG 498 Entry UD 231 Box 1258, p. 172.

6 Quoted in David C. Isby, ed., *The German Army at D-Day: Fighting the Invasion* (London: Greenhill Books, 2004), p. 92.

7 8 Abt., OKL, *Dokumente, Auszüge, Entwürfe u/w für das Thema Invasion in Frankreich, 1944,* National Archives (US), RG 242 T-971 Reel 8 Frames 4376–474.

8 Quoted in David C. Isby, ed., *Fighting in Normandy: the German Army from D-Day to Villers-Bocage* (London: Greenhill Books, 2001), p. 245. Blumentritt was memorably played by Curt Jürgens in the film *The Longest Day.*

9   *No. 421 Squadron Operational Record Book*, National Archives of Canada, Record Group 24, Microfilm C-12295.

10 Caldwell and Muller, *Luftwaffe Over Germany*, pp. 207–9; Jean-Bernard Frappé, *La Luftwaffe Face de Debarquement Allie* (Bayeux: Heimdal, 1999); Thomas A. Hughes, 'Normandy: A Modern Air Campaign?', *Air and Space Power Journal*, vol. 17 no. 4 (Winter 2003), pp. 16–29; Richard Overy, *Why the Allies Won* (New York: Norton, 1997), p. 124; John Keegan, *Six Armies in Normandy* (New York: Viking, 1982), p. 143.

11 BA-MA RL 211/5 *Reichsmarschall* and *Oberbefehlshaber der Luftwaffe*, *Drohende Gefahr West*, Nr. 9221/44 g. Kdos, 27.2.1944, Militärarchiv, Caldwell and Muller, *Luftwaffe Over Germany*, pp. 207–9.

12 DEFE 3/171, KV 7815 [Ultra Decrypt], 13.6.44 0715Z, National Archives (UK).

13 AIR 20/7701 Air Historical Branch, Translation no. VII/31, 'Normandy Invasion – June 44', 6 August 1944 in *Translations from Captured Enemy Documents: Vol II, 1939–1947*, 23 June 1947, p. 7, National Archives (UK); 8 Abt., OKL *Invasion in Frankreich, 1944*.

14 Galland, *First and the Last*, p. 218.

15 ADI(K) Report No. 373/1945, p. 51.

16 RAF transcript quoted at http://www.ghostbombers.com/recon/bf109h_3.html. Nick Beale provided this reference.

17 On the *Mistel*, see Robert Forsyth, *Mistel: German Composite Aircraft and Operations 1942–1945* (Hersham: Classic Publications, 2001).

18 AIR 20/7709 Air Historical Branch, Translation no. VII/136, 'Luftwaffe Losses on the Western Front (Luftflotte 3)', June 1944 in *Translations from Captured Enemy Documents: Vol. X, 1942–1944*, National Archives (UK); von Rohden Book 4 [p. 99]; Dolleisch quoted in ADI(K) Report No. 297/1944, 30 July 1944, National Archives (US), RG 498 UD 231 Box 1258.

19 L.F. Ellis with G.R.G. Allen, A.E. Warhurst Sir James Robb, *Victory in the West* (London: HMSO, 1962), p. 284.

20 Terraine, *A Time For Courage*, p. 637.

21 AIR 41/67, Air Historical Branch, *The Liberation of Northwest Europe, vol. III, The Break-Out and the Advance to the Lower Rhine*, Royal Air Force, 1947, pp. 81–93; AIR 2/7870, *Report on Attacks on Enemy Tanks and MT in the Mortain Area 7th August 1944*, Operational Research in North West Europe, Report No. 4, Operational Research Section, 1951, National Archives (UK).

22 J.E. Johnson and P.B. Lucas, *Winged Victory* (London: Stanley Paul, 1995), p. 166. Johnson, *Wing Leader*, pp. 235–6.

23 David Larkin, ed., *The Aviation Art of Frank Wooton* (New York: Bantam, 1976), n.p.

24 J. Smith, comments in Commander F.M.A. Torrens-Spence, DSO, DSC, AFC, RN, 'Operational Flying', *The Journal of the Royal Aeronautical Society*, vol. 51 no. 10 (October 1947), pp. 831–62, at p. 853; Smith, 'Spitfire and Seafire', pp. 362–3.

25 Quill, *Spitfire*, ch. 23.

26 AIR 16/327, Memoranda from Air Ministry to Air Officer Commander in Chief

Fighter Command, 13 January 1945. The Glasgow factory inherited the stormy labour relations of the 1930s Clyde shipyards. Ritchie, *Industry and Air Power*, p. 163.

27 Barnato Walker, *Spreading My Wings*, p. 85.

28 Quill, *Spitfire*, p. 290; Price, *Documentary History*, pp. 131–7. On design man-hours, see Postan, *British War Production*, p. 340.

29 Letter, 15 September 1942, Imperial War Museum, FD 4355/45 v. 4, quoted in Irving, *Rise and Fall of the Luftwaffe*, p. 417, fn 7.

30 Freudenberg, *Negative Gravity*, pp. 76–8.

31 Brown, *Wings on My Sleeve*, p. 60.

32 This allowed shells from the British 3.7-inch and US 90mm anti-aircraft guns to detonate when they received radar reflections from an enemy aircraft, rather than having a time fuse determine the altitude they would explode, as German 88mm and larger flak shells continued to do. Smaller flak shells exploded on contact.

33 On Maridor, see Marcel Julian, *Jean Maridor: Chasseur de V1* (Paris: Le Livre Contemporain, 1955), p. 132 and generally. AIR 41/55, *The Air Defence of Great Britain: The Flying Bomb and Rocket Campaign, 1944–1945*, vol. 6, Air Historical Branch, n.d. [*c.* 1949]; AIR 41/88, pp. 228–30; Collier, *Defence of the United Kingdom*, pp. 353–97; Brian Cull with Bruce Lander, *Diver! Diver! Diver! RAF and American Fighter Pilots Battle the V-1 Assault over South-East England* (London: Grub Street, 2008), p. 262; Frank W. Heilenday, *V-1 Cruise Missiles Against England: Lessons Learned and Lingering Myths from World War II*, RAND report P-7914 (Santa Monica: RAND, 1995).

17 The Luftwaffe's Fighters at Bay: June 1944–January 1945

1 Kenneth P. Werrell, 'The Strategic Bombing of Germany in World War II: Costs and Accomplishments', *The Journal of American History*, vol. 73 no. 3 (December 1986), pp. 702–13, at p. 711.

2 AIR 41/49, pp. 326–7. The RAF insisted that RAF Mustang IIIs and IVs have the aft-fuselage 85-US-gallon internal fuel tank removed despite the fact that the USAAF had used it to great effect on missions over Germany. When full, it made the aircraft unstable and was the first tank to be emptied on a mission. The USAAF found this acceptable, the RAF did not. David Lednicer, 'World War II Fighter Aerodynamics', *Sport Aviation* (January 1999), pp. 85–91, at p. 87.

3 USSBS, *Defeat*, p. 15.

4 USSBS, *Subject: Field Marshal Hugo Sperrle*, Interview 32, 30 May 1945, US Strategic Bombing Survey, p. 1, National Archives (US), RG 243 Entry 32 Box 5.

5 Alfred Price, *Battle Over the Reich* (New York: Scribner's, 1973), p. 133.

6 Von Rohden Book 4 [p. 27].

7 Göring letter, Nr 2460/44 g. Kdos, 16.3.44, National Archives (US), RG 242 T-321 Reel 10 Frame 474669.

8 Francis Gabreski and Carl Molesworth, *Gabby: A Fighter Pilot's Life* (New York: Orion, 1991), p. 164.

9 Johnson, *Full Circle*, p. 244.

10 Jeffrey L. Ethell and Alfred Price, *Target Berlin, Mission 250: 6 March 1944* (London: Arms and Armour, 1989), p. 25.

11 Hartmut Mehringer, ed., *Die Tagebücher von Joseph Goebbels, Teil II Diktate (Dictations) 1941–1945* (Munich: K.G. Saur Verlag, 1995), p. 520.

12 Ethell and Price, *Target*, p. 156.

13 Steinhoff, *Messerschmitts Over Sicily*, p. 249.

14 Gregor, *Daimler-Benz in the Third Reich*, p. 151.

15 These apparently included survivors of the 1 May 1944 Mülsen rising. *Stenographischer Bericht über die Jägerstab Besprechung am 2 Mai 1944*, National Archives (US), RG 238 M-888 Roll 6 Frames 931–2 (pp. 4–5 original document); Gröhler, *Geschichte*, p. 415.

16 The German military passed death sentences on an estimated 30,000 of its own personnel (compared to about 200 soldiers executed in the Great War). Fritz Wüllner, *Die NS-Militärjustiz im Dienste des Nationalsozialismus, Zersrtörung einer Legende* (Baden-Baden: Nomos, 1987), p. 203; Gerhard L. Weinberg, 'Unexplored Questions on the German Military During World War II', *The Journal of Military History*, vol. 62 no. 2 (April 1998), pp. 371–80, at p. 375. How many of these were fighter pilots is uncertain. Göring demanded authority over the execution of Luftwaffe personnel after an incident when three pilots were shot by the army in 1940. Caldwell, 'Political Commissars', pp. 76–7; Galland, 'General of the Fighters', p. 131; Suchenwirth, *Command and Leadership*, p. 157.

17 Adolf Galland, 'German Fighter Pilots: Equipment and Service', in David C. Isby, ed., *The Luftwaffe Fighter Force: the View from the Cockpit* (London: Greenhill, 1998), pp. 57–62, at p. 61. Galland made many exculpatory statements in his long post-war career. Despite Hitler's boasts about 'his' National Socialist Luftwaffe, the (admittedly self-serving) memoir literature suggests fighter pilots were no more committed to Nazi ideology than any other comparable technically proficient elite group and potentially considerably less.

18 USSBS, Galland interview 34, p. 13; Interview 35, pp. 13–15.

19 Lutz Budrass, *Flugzeugindustrie und Luftruestung in Deutschland, 1918–1945* (Dusseldorf: Schriften des Bundesarchivs, 1988), p. 868.

20 *Rise and Fall of the German Air Force*, p. 363; von Rohden Book 4, [p. 99]. Bf 109 numbers from BA/MA document RL2 III 880–2, quoted at http://www.ww2.dk.

21 WO 208/4169, CSIDC (UK) Report, SRGG 1140, 15 March 1945, pp. 8–9, National Archives (UK); 'GAF Office Reviews German Air Force Strategy and Tactics 1939 to 1945', *Headquarters AAF Intelligence Summary*, No. 45–8, 30 April 1945, pp. 10–12, at p. 11, National Archives (US), RG 243 Entry 6 Box 476; ADI(K) Report 159/1945, *The Memoirs of a Fighter Kommodore*, 10 February 1945, National Archives (US), RG 498 Entry UD 231 Box 231.

22 Bouchier, *Spitfires in Japan*, p. 252; AIR 41/49, pp. 325–8; ADI(K) Report No. 169/1945, *German Fighter Tactics: Attack on RAF Day Bombers, 12th December 1944*, 19 February 1945, National Archives (US), RG 165 Entry 79 Box 21. This latter (involving RAF Mustangs, not Spitfires) marked the Bf 109's first daylight battle with RAF heavy bombers since 1942.

23 HQ, 65th Fighter Wing, Eighth Air Force, *Colgate Calling: Offensive Fighter Control, ETO, 1943–45* (Saffron Walden, June 1945), USAF Historical Research Agency; AIR 41/88, pp. 231–48; Guerlac, *RADAR In World War II*, vol. 2, pp. 803–8; Squadron Leader C.A. Martin, *Front Line Radar* (London: Foster Groom, 1946); USSBS, *Defeat*, pp. 11–13.

24 *Relative Performance of British and American Fighters Against German Fighters 1940–45*, US Strategic Bombing Survey, 1945, p. 9, National Archives (US), RG 243 Entry 6 Box 476, USAF Historical Research Agency 137.306-5; *Eighth Air Force Tactical Development August 1942–May 1945*, Eighth Air Force and Army Air Forces Evaluation Board, 9 July 1945, USAF Historical Research Agency 520.04-11.

25 Martin W. Fleischmann, *General Summary, Report on Alloy Steel Development in Germany*, CIOS, Item 21, Metallurgy, G-2 SHAEF (rear), p. 3, National Archives (US), RG 243 Entry 36 Box 36.

26 USSBS, Frydag Interview, p. 17.

27 Having gained more than twenty victories, Captain Ralph 'Kid' Hofer's P-51 was shot down by flak over Yugoslavia after being damaged by a Bf 109 over Hungary. Claims have been made for 'Bubi' Hartmann (unlikely) and Major Aladar Heppes of the Hungarian Air Force, but neither would amount to a shoot-down. Mahurin's P-47 was shot down by a Do 217 bomber gunner.

28 Many Souffair, *Les Messerschmitt Bf 109 Romains*, AirMag Hors Série (Paris: AirMagazine, 2002), p. 61.

29 Colin D. Heaton, 'Interview: Messerschmitt Master on the Eastern Front', *World War II* (February 2004), pp. 42–8, at p. 46.

30 Leutnant Klaus Neumann, 'Allied Aircraft', in Isby, *The Luftwaffe Fighter Force*, p. 221.

31 USSBS, *Subject: Major General Dethleffsen*, Interview 19, 9 June 1945, US Strategic Bombing Survey, p. 1, National Archives (US), RG 243 Entry 32 Box 2. He had served on the eastern front and in Hitler's headquarters.

32 *Joint Conference of 8th Air Force Bomber-Fighter Personnel (29 September 1944 at HQ, VIII Fighter Command)*, p. 2, USAF HRA document; Oberstleutnant Walther Dahl, 'Conduct of a Company Front Attack', in Isby, *The Luftwaffe Fighter*, pp. 196–8.

33 Leonard 'Kit' Carson, *Pursue and Destroy* (Granada Hills, CA: Sentry Books, 1978), p. 94; *The Contribution of Air Power to the Defeat of Germany* [Spaatz Report], Assistant Chief of Staff A-2, HQ USAFE, 7 August 1945, Appendix A, p. 29, National Archives (US), RG 341 Entry 268 Boxes 120–1.

34 *No. 401 Squadron Operational Record Book*, National Archives of Canada, Record Group 24, Microfilm C-12264; AIR 50/134, 401 Squadron Combat Reports for 5 October 1944 for S/L Smith, F/Lt Davenport, F/Lt Everard. F/O MacKay, F/O Sinclair, National Archives (UK); David L. Bashow, *All the Fine Young Eagles* (Toronto: Stoddard, 1996), pp. 306–9; Ethell and Price, *Fighting Jets*, pp. 27–8; Hedley Everard, *Mouse in My Pocket* (Picton, ON: Valley Floatplane Services, 1988), pp. 375–6; John Foreman and S.E. Harvey, *The Messerschmitt Me 262 Combat*

Diary (Walton on Thames: Air Research, 1990), pp. 68–72; Galland, 'General of the Fighters', p. 119; ADI(K) Report No. 373/1945, p. 56.

35 Constance Babington Smith, *Evidence in Camera* (North Pomfret, VT: David and Charles, 1974), p. 242.

18 Last Battles, 1944–1945

1 The incident that gained 'Cupid' Love his place in the history books occurred on 14 February 1945. Craig Cabell and Graham A. Thomas, *Operation Big Ben: The Anti-V2 Spitfire Missions, 1944–45* (Staplehurst, Kent: Spellmount. 2004), pp. 109–10; Bill Simpson, *Spitfire Dive Bombers Versus the V2: Fighter Command's Battle with Hitler's Mobile Missiles* (Barnsley, Yorks: Pen and Sword, 2007), pp. 194–6; Collier, *Defence of the United Kingdom*, pp. 413–19. Baxter (after the war a well-known journalist and BBC television commentator) statement at: http://www.v2rocket.com/start/deployment/denhaag.html

2 Norman Longmate, *Hitler's Rockets: The Story of the V-2s* (London: Hutchinson, 1985), pp. 227, 347.

3 AIR 41/55, pp. 272–84, 289–96, 305–9; Collier, *Defence of the United Kingdom*, p. 412.

4 Simpson, *Spitfire Dive Bombers*, pp. 170–6. The two-day maximum effort followed the Loosduinen attack and made use of good weather on 21/22 February 1945. AIR 37/427, J. Wiseman, *84 Group versus V Weapons, October 1944 – March 1945*, 2 TAF Intelligence Report, April 1945, National Archives (UK). The bombers, on 3 March 1945, put most of sixty-nine tons of bombs on the nearby town of Bezuidenhout.

5 Olmstead, *Blue Skies*, p. 199.

6 ADI(K) Report No. 373/1945, p. 58.

7 USSBS, Galland Interview 34, p. 4. Adolf Galland et al., 'The Evolution of the Defense of the Reich', in Isby, *The Luftwaffe Fighter Force*, pp. 171–81, at p. 179; ADI(K) Report No. 373/1945, p. 59.

8 The letter, unmailed, was in his pocket when captured following a mission on 3 December. *JG 4's Appearance in Strength Over the Western Front*, APWIU (Ninth AF) 84/1944, 6 December 1944, National Archives (US), RG 398 UD 235 Box 1266.

9 *Joint Conference of 8th Air Force Bomber-Fighter Personnel (29 September 1944 at HQ, VIII Fighter Command)*, p. 2, USAF HRA document.

10 Dundas, *Flying Start*, pp. 140–62; Bader, *Fight for the Sky*, p. 168.

11 AIR 23/1458, *Notes on New Developments in Air-Ground Cooperation*, January 1945, National Archives (UK); AIR 37/956, *Use and Effectiveness of Napalm Fire Bombs*, 8 February 1945, National Archives (UK).

12 Kokothaki, 'Messerschmitt History', p. 181.

13 On the collapse of transportation, see Uziel, *Arming*, p. 200. On German ferry pilots, see *German Air Force List of 'Civilian' Ferry Pilots*, A.I. 12, US Air Forces Europe, 22 January 1946, National Archives (US), RG 243 Entry 36 Box 176;

Status and Duties of Civilian Pilots in the German Air Force, A.I. 12 Intelligence Report 114, US Air Forces Europe, 22 January 1946, National Archives (US), RG 165 Entry 79 Box 47.

14 USSBS, Goering Interview, p. 6; Kosin, *German Fighter*, p. 195; William W. Haines, *Ultra: History of the US Strategic Air Force Europe vs. German Air Force* (Frederick, MD: University Publications of America, 1980) p. 199.

15 *Reichsmarschall Befel*, Nr. 12, 23/1/45, National Archives (US), RG 242, T-971, Roll 10 4376/817; *Reichsmarschall Befel*, Nr. 14, 17/2/45, National Archives (US), RG 242, T-971, Roll 12 4376/3315; ADI(K) Report No. 373/1945, pp. 62–3.

16 Gabreski and Molesworth, *Gabby*, p. 332.

17 R.V. Ashman, *Spitfire Against the Odds* (Wellingborough: Patrick Stephens, 1989), p. 143.

18 AIR 50/134, 350 Squadron Combat Reports for 2 March 1945 for F/Sgt Groensteen, F/Lt Hoornaert, P/O Lambrechts, F/Sgt Pauwels, National Archives (UK); AIR 26/185 *125 Wing Operational Record Book January–March 1945*, entry for 2 March 1945, National Archives (UK); AIR 27/1746 *350 Squadron Operational Record Book*, entry for 2 March 1945, National Archives (UK); Peter Kassak, *An Ordinary Day in 1945* (Redbourn: Stratus for Mushroom Model Publications, 2005), pp. 7–12; Christopher Shores and Chris Thomas, *2nd Tactical Air Force, vol. 3: From the Rhine to Victory, January to May 1945* (Hersham: Classic, Ian Allan, 2006), pp. 440–1; ADI(K) Report No. 165/1945, 31 March 1945, National Archives (US), RG 398 UD 231 Box 1262.

19 Trevor J. Constable and Col. Raymond F. Toliver, *Horrido! Fighter Aces of the Luftwaffe* (New York: Ballantine, 1968), p. 264.

20 USSBS, Galland Interview 35, p. 6. On the Spitfire XIV victory ratio, see Christopher Shores and Chris Thomas, *2nd Tactical Air Force,* vol. 4 (Hersham: Midland, 2008), p. 586.

21 Christer Bergström, *Bagration to Berlin – The Final Air Battles in the East: 1944–45* (Hersham: Classic, Ian Allan, 2008), pp. 118–20; Alfred Price, *The Last Year*, p. 161. On ramming attacks, see ADI(K) Report 294/1945, *New German Ramming Units,* 26 April 1945, National Archives (US), RG 165 Entry 79 Box 22; Caldwell and Muller, *Luftwaffe Over Germany*, pp. 279–81; Manfred Griehl, *Last Days of the Luftwaffe* (Barnsley: Frontline, Pen and Sword, 2009), pp. 34–8, 171–88; Adrian Weir, *The Last Flight of the Luftwaffe* (London: Cassell, 1997).

22 O'Donnell, 'Secret Fight', p. 105.

23 Ethell and Price, *Fighting Jets*, p. 50.

24 As of 2011, it was occupied by the German Ministry of Finance.

25 A.I. 12, *OKL Intelligence Report* 7, June 1945, National Archives (US), Entry 79 Box 45. Unofficial estimates are that some 28,000 men in total flew fighters for the Luftwaffe in the Second World War, and 1400 remained at the end. It is estimated that those leaving the *Jagdwaffe* before the end of the war included 8500 killed, 2700 missing or prisoners and 9100 wounded. The figure of 90 per cent was provided by Günther Rall at the National Air and Space Museum, Washington, 1 March 1986.

26　Steinhoff, *Messerschmitts Over Sicily*, p. 200.

27　Shores, *The Air War for Burma*, p. 307.

28　AIR 64/29, *Visit to Southeast Asia by Tactics Branch, Central Fighter Establishment, 1 February–7 April 1945*, National Archives (UK).

29　Odgers, *Air War*, pp. 498–9.

19 Fighters in a Cold War World: After 1945

1　'Last Spitfires Are Retired, Ceremonial Flights Only in Future', *The Times* (12 July 1957), p. 6; Warren James Palmer, *Battle of Britain Memorial Flight* (Epsom: Ripping, 1996), p. 9.

2　AIR 41/93, *The RAF In the Post War Years: The RAF in Germany, 1945–1978*, Air Historical Branch, 1979, National Archives (UK); Bouchier, *Spitfires in Japan*, ch. 33; Wolfgang Etschmann, 'Spitfires Over Austria: Die Royal Air Force in Öster- reich 1946–47', *Österreichische Militärische Zeitschrift*, vol. 37 no. 2 (March 1999), pp. 183–90; Bill Taylor, *Royal Air Force Germany Since 1945* (Hinckley: Midland, 2007), chs 1 and 2.

3　AVIA 10/268, Production File, Table by Deputy Director General of Statistics and Programmes, 14 May 1942, National Archives (UK); AVIA 10/269, *Labour Statistics, 20 October 1942 to 16 August 1944*, Ministry of Aircraft Production National Archives (UK). In comparison, by 1945, a Lancaster required 20,000 man-hours.

4　Smith, 'Development', p. 346; 'Spitfire and Seafire', pp. 708–10. The change to Arabic from Roman numerals to distinguish different marks of Spitfire was made in an incremental and uneven way and not completed until 1949.

5　AIR 64/164, *Tactical Trials, Far East, Vampire III, Singapore, May, 1948*, Central Fighter Establishment, National Archives (UK).

6　Barnato Walker, *Spreading My Wings*, p. 69; Morgan and Shacklady, *Spitfire*, pp. 464–77.

7　Quill, *Spitfire*, p. 295.

8　Quill, *Spitfire*, p. 209.

9　Edwards Jones, 'Spitfire from Prototype to Mk 24', p. 300; Morgan and Shacklady, *Spitfire*, pp. 489–90.

10　J. Smith comments in Torren-Spence, 'Operational Flying'.

11　Postan, *British War Production*, p. 340. Compared to the German He 111 bomber's 4 million man-hours, it was highly efficient. Homze, *Arming the Luftwaffe*, p. 213.

12　Just as Galland had instinctively understood the concept of 'situational awareness', he also understood 'if you can't win the fight, get home first and win the debrief'.

13　Ulrich Volklein, 'German Business Reveals Its Sins', *World Press Review* (July 1995), pp. 17–18; 'The Final Reckoning: Businesses Agree to Compensation for Wartime Germany's Forced Labor Policies, but Where's the Money', *Time International* (31 July 2000), pp. 16–18.

14　Interrogation of Erhard Milch by Mr C. Koch on 14 October 1946, translation of Document NOKW-317, *USA v. Erhard Milch*, p. 3 (original document); Irving,

Rise and Fall of the Luftwaffe, p. 335. Milch's life sentence resulted in large part from his having approved lethal human experiments, related to aviation medicine research, on concentration camp inmates.

15   Halverson, National Air and Space Museum lecture. The famous 'candy bomber', he dropped sweets to Berlin children using miniature parachutes. On former Luftwaffe personnel in the airlift, see Roger G. Miller, 'Tunner and the Luftwaffe Connection with the Berlin Airlift', *Air Power History* vol. 56 no. 4 (Winter 2009), pp. 28–35.

16   'Obituary: Willy Messerschmitt, Fighters for the Luftwaffe', *The Times* (16 September, 1978) p. 14.

17   O'Donnell, 'Secret Fight', pp. 22–3.

18   Such attitudes have never been limited to post-war Germans. Peter Fritzsche, *Life and Death in the Third Reich* (Cambridge, MA: Harvard University Press, 2008), p. 18.

19   James Diehl, *Thanks of the Fatherland: German Veterans After the Second World War* (Chapel Hill: University of North Carolina Press, 1993); Robert Moeller, *War Stories, the Search for a Usable Past in the Federal Republic of Germany* (Berkeley: University of California Press, 2003); Helmut Schmitz, ed., *A Nation of Victims? Representation of German Wartime Suffering from 1945 to the Present* (New York: Rodopi, 2007). German fighter pilots formed a cohesive veterans' organisation (and published a well-edited newsletter) that had no direct counterpart among USAAF and RAF veterans.

20   Vincent Orange, *Slessor, Bomber Champion: The Life of Marshal of the RAF Sir John Slessor* (London: Grub Street, 2005), p. 168.

21   Shlomo Aloni, *101 – Israeli Air Force First Fighter Squadron* (Bat-Hefer, Israel: IsraeDecal Productions, 2007), pp. 6–45; Brian Cull and Shlomo Aloni with David Nicolle, *Spitfires Over Israel* (London: Grub Street, n.d. [c. 1992]), pp. 121, 217; Lon Nordeen, *Fighters over Israel* (New York: Orion, 1990), pp. 6–25; Bill Norton, *Air War on the Edge: A History of the Israeli Air Force and its Aircraft since 1947* (Hinckley: Midland, 2004), pp. 109–13; Murray Rubinstein and Richard Goldman, *Shield of David: An Illustrated History of the Israeli Air Force* (Englewood Cliffs, NJ: Prentice Hall, 1978), pp. 25–57; Alex Yofe and Lawrence Nyveen, *Avia S-199 in Israeli Air Force Service 1948–1950* (San Jose, CA: White Crow, 2007), pp. 2–31.

22   Boris Senior, *New Heavens: My Life as a Fighter Pilot and a Founder of the Israeli Air Force* (Dulles, VA: Potomac, 2005), p. 207.

23   Lon Nordeen and David Nicolle, *Phoenix Over the Nile: A History of Egyptian Air Power 1932–1994* (Washington: Smithsonian Institution Press, 1996), pp. 72–90.

24   *Air Study of Egypt*, 23 October 1946, Air Intelligence Division Study 96, p. 3, National Archives (US), RG 241 Entry 268 Box 129 Report KO63648.

25   Quoted in Alfred Price, *Spitfire: A Complete Fighting History* (n.p.: PRC, 1994), p. 144. RAF pilots have shot down aircraft since then, flying FAA, USAF or RAAF fighters.

26   Ezer Weizman, *On Eagles' Wings* (New York: Macmillan, 1976), pp. 67–8.

27 Senior, *New Heavens*; Yofe and Nyveen, *Avia S-199*, p. 64.

28 Nordeen and Nicolle, *Phoenix Over the Nile*, pp. 74–111.

29 Zeev Schiff, *A History of the Israeli Army, 1874 to the Present* (New York: Macmillan, 2008), p. 37. On Israeli Spitfires, see Norton, *Air War on the Edge*, pp. 114–21; Alex Yofe, *Spitfire, Star of Israel* (Wellington, NZ: Ventura Publications, 1996); Alex Yofe, *Spitfire Mk. IX in Israeli Air Force Service* (San Jose, CA: White Crow Publications, 2005).

30 Quoted in Rubinstein and Goldman, *Shield*, p. 56. The RCAF appeared to accept his explanation. Reinstated on his return from Israel, he flew with the RCAF into the 1960s.

31 Weizman, *On Eagles' Wings*, p. 81. Post-war Tempest IIs were powered by a Bristol Centaurus radial and differed considerably from wartime Tempest Vs.

32 AIR 28/1030, *324 Wing Operational Record Book*, National Archives (UK); AIR 27/2464, *208 Squadron Operational Record Book*, National Archives (UK); AIR 27/2769 *213 Squadron Operational Record Book*, National Archives (UK); Cull, *Spitfires Over Israel*, p. 197; Zeev Tzahor, 'The 1949 Air Clash Between the Israeli Air Force and the RAF', *Journal of Contemporary History*, vol. 26 no. 1 (January 1993), pp. 75–101; Squadron Leader Bruce Williamson, 'The RAF in Palestine 1948–49: The Wrong Place at the Wrong Time', *Royal Air Force Historical Society Journal*, no. 28 (2007), pp. 12–23.

33 Quoted in Graham Thomas, *Furies and Fireflies Over Korea* (London: Grub Street, 2004), p. 20.

34 Brian Cull and Dennis Newton, *With the Yanks in Korea*, vol. 1 (London: Grub Street, 2000), pp. 262–3; Darling, *Supermarine Seafire*, pp. 140–5; Thomas, *Furies and Fireflies*, pp. 17–24.

35 Peter R. Arnold and Ken Ellis, 'Burmese Lions, British Fighter Exports to Burma', *Air Enthusiast*, no. 71 (September–October 1997), pp. 48–52; Clarence Fu, 'Round Out: From Taiwan', *Air Enthusiast*, no. 72 (November–December 1997), p. 78; Daniel Ford, 'Double Fury, The Two Seat Hawker Sea Furies', *Air Enthusiast*, no. 58 (Summer 1995), pp. 28–36. Alex Smart provided these references.

36 Brian Cull with David Nicolle and Shlomo Aloni, *Wings Over Suez: The First Authoritative Account of Air Operations During the Sinai and Suez Wars of 1956* (London: Grub Street, 1996), pp. 139–40; Nordeen and Nicolle, *Phoenix Over the Nile*, p. 161.

37 Personal conversation with Neil Williams, Beaumont's Aviation Bookstore, Old Street, London, summer 1970. He later expanded on this description in a number of articles in *Aviation News* during the 1970s. On the movie, see Tony Aldgate, 'The Battle of Britain on Film', in Addison and Crang, *Burning Blue*, pp. 207–16; S.P. MacKenzie, *The Battle of Britain on Screen: 'The Few' in British Film and Television Drama* (Edinburgh: Edinburgh University Press, 2007), pp. 75–97, 143–51; Leonard Mosley, *'Battle of Britain', The Making of a Film* (New York: Ballantine, 1969).

20 From Fighters to Legends: Duxford

1 As were Neil Williams, veteran pilot of restored Bf 109s Mark Hannah, and the author's friend and co-author Jeff Ethell.

2 'BNP Uses Spitfire in Anti-immigration Poster', *The Daily Telegraph* (4 March 2009), http://www.telegraph.co.uk/news/newstopics/politics/4935429/ BNP-uses-Polish-Spitfire-in-anti-immigration-poster.html

3 Johnson, *Wing Leader*, p. 190.

Select Bibliography

Addison, Paul and Jeremy A. Crang, eds. *The Burning Blue: A New History of the Battle of Britain*. London: Pimlico, 2000.

Aders, Gerhard. *History of the German Night Fighter Force 1917–1945*. London: Arms and Armour, 1979.

Allen, Michael Thad. *The Business of Genocide: The SS Slave Labor, and the Concentration Camps*. Chapel Hill: University of North Carolina, 2002.

Aloni, Shlomo. *101 – Israeli Air Force First Fighter Squadron*. Bat-Hefer, Israel: IsraeDecal Productions, 2007.

Anderson, Col. Clarence E. *To Fly and to Fight*. New York: Bantam, 1991.

Andrews, C.F. *Supermarine Aircraft Since 1914*. London: Putnam, 1981.

Araez Cerda, Juan. *Les Messerschmitt Espagnols: Des Premiers 109V aux Derniers Buchon*. Avions Hors Série 5. Paris: Lela Presse, 1997.

Arnold, H.H. *Global Mission*. New York: Harper, 1949.

Ashman, R.V. *Spitfire Against the Odds*. Wellingborough: Patrick Stephens, 1989.

Bader, Douglas. *Fight for the Sky: The Story of the Spitfire and Hurricane*. Garden City, NY: Doubleday, 1973.

Baeza, Bernard. *Soleil Levant Sur L'Australie*. Paris: Lela Presse, 2008.

Baker, David. *Adolf Galland, The Authorised Biography*. London: Windrow and Greene, 1996.

Banks, Francis R. *I Kept No Diary*. Shrewsbury: Airlife, 1978.

Barnett, Correlli. *The Audit of War*. London: Macmillan, 1986.

Bashow, David L. *All the Fine Young Eagles*. Toronto: Stoddard, 1996.

von Below, Nicolaus. *Als Hitlers Adjutant 1937–45*. Mainz: Hase and Kohler, 1980.

Bergström, Christer. *Bagration to Berlin – The Final Air Battles in the East: 1944–45*. Hersham: Classic, Ian Allan, 2008.

—. *Barbarossa – The Air Battle: July–December, 1941*. Hersham: Midland, 2007.

—. *Luftstrid Över Kanalen*. Stockholm: Leanden and Elcholm, 2007.

—. *Max-Hellmuth Ostermann*. Crowborough, East Sussex: Chevron, 2007.

— with Vlad Antipov and Claes Sundin. *Graf and Grislawski: A Pair of Aces*. Hamilton, MT: Eagle Editions, 2003.

Bitton-Jackson, Livia [Elli Friedmann]. *I Have Lived a Thousand Years: Growing Up in the Holocaust*. New York: Simon Pulse, 1999.

Boehme, Manfred. *JG 7, The World's First Jet Fighter Unit, 1944–45*. Atglen, PA: Schiffer, 1992.

Boiten, Theo and Martin Bowman. *Battles with the Luftwaffe, The Bomber Campaign Against Germany 1942–45.* London: HarperCollins, 2001.

Bölcke, Willi A., ed. *Deutschlands Rüstung im Zweiten Weltkrieg, Hitlers Konferenzen mit Albert Speer 1942–1945.* Frankfurt: Akademische Verlagsgesellschaft Athenaion, 1969.

Boog, Horst. *Die Deutsche Luftwaffenführung 1935–1945: Führungsprobleme, Spitzengliederung, Generalstabsausbildung.* Stuttgart: Deutsche Verlags-Anstalt, 1982.

—, ed. *The Conduct of the Air War in the Second World War.* Providence, RI: Berg, 1992.

Bouchier, Air Vice Marshal Sir Cecil 'Boy'. *Spitfires in Japan, From Farnborough to the Far East: a Memoir* ed. Dorothy Britton Lady Bouchier. Folkestone: Global Oriental, 2005.

Boyne, Walter J. *Clash of Wings, World War II in the Air.* New York: Simon and Schuster, 1994.

—. *Messerschmitt Me 262: Arrow to the Future.* Atglen, PA: Schiffer, 1994.

Brew, Alec. *Boulton Paul Aircraft Since 1915.* London: Putnam, 1993.

Brickhill, Paul. *Reach for the Sky.* New York: Ballantine, 1967.

Brooks, Peter W. *The Modern Airliner.* London: Putnam, 1961.

Brown, Captain Eric M., R.N. *Duels in the Sky: World War II Naval Aircraft in Combat.* Annapolis: Naval Institute Press, 1988.

—. *Wings of the Luftwaffe.* Shrewsbury: Airlife, 1993.

Budrass, Lutz. *Flugzeugindustrie und Luftrüstung in Deutschland, 1918–1945.* Düsseldorf: Droste Verlag, 1998.

Burns, Michael G. *Bader: The Man and His Men.* London: Cassell, 1998.

Cabell, Craig and Graham A. Thomas. *Operation Big Ben: The Anti-V2 Spitfire Missions, 1944–45.* Staplehurst, Kent: Spellmount, 2004.

Caidin, Martin. *Me 109: Willy Messerschmitt's Peerless Fighter.* New York: Ballantine, 1968.

Cairncross, Sir Alec. *Planning in Wartime: Aircraft Production in Britain, Germany and the USA.* New York: St Martin's, 1991.

Caldwell, Donald. *The JG 26 War Diary,* 2 vols. London: Grub Street, 1996, 1998.

— and Richard Muller. *The Luftwaffe Over Germany: Defence of the Reich.* London: Greenhill, 2007.

Carson, Leonard 'Kit'. *Pursue and Destroy.* Granada Hills, CA: Sentry Books, 1978.

Caygill, Peter. *Flying to the Limit: Testing World War II Single Engine Fighter Aircraft.* Barnsley: Pen and Sword, 2005.

—. *Spitfire Mark V in Action: RAF Operations in Northern Europe.* Shrewsbury: Airlife, 2001.

Christienne, Charles and Pierre Lissarague. *History of French Military Aviation.* Washington: Smithsonian Institution Press, 1986.

Churchill, Winston. *The Second World War,* 6 vols. New York: Mariner, 1986.

Clarke, Squadron Leader D.H., DFC, AFC. *What Were They Like to Fly.* Shepperton, Middlesex: Ian Allan, 1964.

Clayton, Aileen. *The Enemy Is Listening.* London: Hutchinson, 1980.

Collier, Basil. *Defence of the United Kingdom.* London: Naval and Military Press, 2004.

Colville, John. *Fringes of Power: Downing Street Diaries 1939–45*. London: Hodder and Stoughton, 1985.

Constable, Trevor J. and Col. Raymond F. Toliver. *Horrido! Fighter Aces of the Luftwaffe*. New York: Ballantine, 1968.

Cooper, Anthony. *Darwin Spitfires: The Real Battle for Australia*. Sydney: University of New South Wales Press, 2011.

Cornwell, John. *Hitler's Scientists: Science, War, and the Devil's Pact*. New York: Penguin, 2003.

Cornwell, Peter. *The Battle of France, Then and Now*. Hemel Hempstead, Herts: After the Battle, 2008.

Corum, James S. *The Luftwaffe: Creating the Operational Air War 1918–1940*. Lawrence, KS: University Press of Kansas, 1997.

—. *Wolfram von Richthofen: Master of the German Air War*. Lawrence, KS: University Press of Kansas, 2008.

Costello, John. *Love, Sex and War: Changing Values 1939–45*. London: William Collins, 1985.

Cox, Sebastian and Peter Gray, eds. *Air Power History: Turning Points from Kitty Hawk to Kosovo*. London and Portland, OR: Frank Cass, 2002.

Craven, Wesley Frank and James Lea Cate, eds. *The Army Air Forces in World War II*, 6 vols. Washington: Office of Air Force History, 1983.

Crosley, Commander R.M. 'Mike', DSC and Bar. *They Gave Me a Seafire*. Shrewsbury: Airlife, 1986.

Cull, Brian and Shlomo Aloni with David Nicolle. *Spitfires Over Israel*. London: Grub Street, n.d. [c. 1992].

— and Frederick Galea. *Screwball Beurling, Malta's Top Scoring Ace*. Rabat, Malta: Wise Owl, 2010.

— with Bruce Lander. *Diver! Diver! Diver! RAF and American Fighter Pilots Battle the V-1 Assault Over South-East England*. London: Grub Street, 2008.

— and Bruce Lander with Heinreich Weiss. *Twelve Days in May*. London: Grub Street, 1999.

— with Nicola Malizia and Frederick Galaea, *Spitfires Over Sicily*. London: Grub Street, 2002

— and Dennis Newton. *With the Yanks in Korea*, vol. 1. London: Grub Street, 2000.

— with David Nicolle and Shlomo Aloni. *Wings Over Suez: The First Authoritative Account of Air Operations During the Sinai and Suez Wars of 1956*. London: Grub Street, 1996.

Darling, Kev. *Supermarine Seafire*. Marlborough: Crowood Press, 2008.

Deere, Alan. *Nine Lives*. Manchester: Crecy, 2009.

Devereux, Tony. *Messenger Gods of Battle*. London: Brassey's, 1990.

Doolittle, James H. *I Could Never Be So Lucky Again*. New York: Bantam Books, 1991.

Lord Douglas of Kirtleside [William Sholto Douglas]. *Years of Command*. London: Collins, 1966.

Dundas, Hugh. *Flying Start: A Fighter Pilot's War Years*. New York: St Martin's Press, 1989.

Ebert, Hans J., Johann B. Kaiser and Klaus Peters. *Willy Messerschmitt, Pioneer of Aviation Design*. Atglen, PA: Schiffer, 1999.

Ellis, L.F. *The War in France and Flanders 1939–40*. London: HMSO, 1953.

— et al. *Victory in the West*, 2 vols. London: HMSO, 1962, 1964.

Ethell, Jeffrey L. and Alfred Price. *Target Berlin, Mission 250: 6 March 1944*. London: Arms and Armour, 1989.

—. *World War II Fighting Jets*. Annapolis: Naval Institute, 1994.

Everard, Hedley. *Mouse in My Pocket*. Picton, ON: Valley Floatplane Services, 1988.

Facon, Patrick. *L'Armée de l'Air dans la Tormente: La Bataille de France, 1939–1940*. Paris: Economica, 1997.

Falke, Wolfgang. *The Happy Falcon: An Autobiography by the Father of the Night Fighters*. Hamilton, MT: Eagle Editions, 2003.

Fernandez-Sommerau, Marco. *Messerschmitt Bf 109 Recognition Manual*. Hersham: Classic, Ian Allan, 2004.

von Forell, Fritz. *Werner Mölders, Flug zur Sonne: Die Geschichte des Grossen Jagdfliegers*. Leoni am Stamberger See: Druffel Verlag, 1976.

Foreman, John. *Air War 1941: The Turning Point*, 2 vols. Walton on Thames: Air Research Publications, 1993, 1994.

— and S.E. Harvey. *The Messerschmitt Me 262 Combat Diary*. Walton on Thames: Air Research Publications, 1990.

Forsyth, Robert. *Mistel: German Composite Aircraft and Operations 1942–1945*. Hersham: Classic, Ian Allan, 2001.

Foster, Wing Commander R.W., DFC, AE, with Norman Franks. *Tally Ho! From the Battle of Britain to the Defence of Darwin*. London: Grub Street, 2008.

Franks, Norman. *The Air Battle of Dunkirk*. London: William Kimber, 1983.

—. *Dieppe: The Greatest Air Battle, 19th August 1942*. London: Grub Street, 2010.

Frappé, Jean-Bernard. *La Luftwaffe Face de Debarquement Allié*. Bayeux: Heimdal, 1999.

Freeman, Roger. *The Hub: The Story of Hub Zemke*. Shrewsbury: Airlife, 1988.

Freiden, Seymour and William Richardson, eds. *The Fatal Decisions*. New York: Berkley, 1958.

Freudenberg, Martin. *Negative Gravity: A Life of Beatrice Shilling*. Taunton: Charlton, 2003.

Gabreski, Francis and Carl Molesworth. *Gabby: A Fighter Pilot's Life*. New York: Orion, 1991.

Galland, Adolf. *The First and the Last*. New York: Ballantine, 1965.

Geust, Carl Frederick and G.F. Petrov. *Lend-Lease Aircraft in Russia, Red Star*, vol. 4. Tampere: Apali Oy, 2002.

Gilbert, Martin, ed. *The Churchill War Papers*, 3 vols. London: Heinemann, 1993–2000.

Godefroy, Hugh. *Lucky 13*. Toronto: Stoddart Publishing, 1983.

Gordon, Yefim. *Soviet Air Power in World War 2*. Hinckley: Midland, 2008.

Goss, Chris. *Brothers in Arms*. Manchester: Crecy, 1994.

—. *The Luftwaffe Fighters' Battle of Britain*. Manchester: Crecy, 2000.

—. *Luftwaffe Hit-and-Run Raiders: Nocturnal Fighter Bomber Operations Over the Western Front 1943–45*. Hersham: Classic, Ian Allan, 2009.

— with Peter Cornwell and Bernd Rauchbach, *Luftwaffe Fighter-Bombers Over Britain: The Tip and Run Campaign 1942–43*. Mechanicsville, PA: Stackpole, 2003.

Grant, Jim. *Spitfires Over Darwin: No. 1 Fighter Wing*. Melbourne: Jim Moore, 1995.

Green, William. *Warplanes of the Third Reich*. Garden City, NY: Doubleday, 1970.

Greenhous, Brereton et al. *The Crucible of War 1939–1945, The Official History of the Royal Canadian Air Force Volume III*. Toronto: University of Toronto Press 1994.

Gregor, Neil. *Daimler-Benz in the Third Reich*. New Haven: Yale University Press, 1998.

Griehl, Manfred. *Last Days of the Luftwaffe*. Barnsley: Frontline, Pen and Sword, 2009.

Gröhler, Olaf. *Geschichte des Luftkriegs, 1910 bis 1970*. [East] Berlin: Militärverlag der Deutschen Demokratischen Republik, 1981.

Guerlac, Henry E. *RADAR In World War II*, vol. 1. The History of Modern Physics 1800–1950, vol. 8. n.p.: Tomash, 1987.

Gunston, Bill. *The Development of Piston Aero Engines*. Yeovil: Patrick Stephens, 1993.

Haberfellner, Wernfried and Walter Schroeder, *Wiener Neustädter Flugzeugwerke*. Graz: Weishaupt Verlag, 1993.

Haines, William W. *Ultra: History of the US Strategic Air Force Europe vs. German Air Force*. Frederick, MD: University Publications of America, 1980.

Halder, Generaloberst Franz. *Kriegstagebuch*, vol. 2. Stuttgart: W. Kohlhammer, 1962.

Hale, Francis J. *Introduction to Aircraft Performance, Selection and Design*. New York: John Wiley and Sons, 1984.

Hanning, Norbert. *Luftwaffe Fighter Ace: from the Eastern Front to the Defense of the Homeland*. Mechanicsburg, PA: Stackpole Books, 2009.

Harvey-Bailey, Alec. *The Merlin in Perspective: The Combat Years*. Derby: Rolls-Royce Heritage Trust, 1985.

Haunschmied, Rudolf A., Jan-Ruth Mills and Siegi Witzany-Durda. *St. Georgen Gusen Mauthausen: Concentration Camp Mauthausen Reconsidered*. Sankt Georgen an der Gusen: Books on Demand – http://www.gusen.org, 2008.

Hayward, Joel S.A. *Stopped at Stalingrad: The Luftwaffe and Hitler's Defeat in the East*. Lawrence, KS: University Press of Kansas, 1998.

Hayward, Keith. *The British Aircraft Industry*. Manchester: Manchester University Press, 1989.

Heaton, Colin D. and Anne-Marie Lewis, eds. *The German Aces Speak: World War II Through the Eyes of Four of the Luftwaffe's Most Important Commanders*. Minneapolis: Zenith, 2011.

Heinkel, Ernst. *My Stormy Life*. Stuttgart: Aviatic Verlag, 1991.

Heinrich 'Heinz' Bär. Ritterkreuzträger Profile 6. Saarbrucken: UNITEC, 2008.

Herbert, Ulrich. *Hitler's Foreign Workers: Enforced Foreign Labour in Germany Under the Third Reich*, trans. William Templer. Cambridge: Cambridge University Press, 1997.

Herington, John. *Air Power Over Europe 1944–45*. Canberra: Australian War Memorial, 1963.

—. *Air War Against Germany and Italy 1939–43*. Canberra: Australian War Memorial, 1959.

Herlin, Hans. *Udet: A Man's Life*. London: Macdonald, 1960.

Higham, Robin and Carol Williams, eds. *Flying Combat Aircraft of the USAAF-USAF*, vol. 3. Manhattan, KS: Sunflower University Press, 1981.

Hinchcliffe, Peter. *The Other Battle: Luftwaffe Night Aces Versus Bomber Command*. Shrewsbury: Airlife, 1996.

Hinsley, F.H. et al. *British Intelligence in the Second World War*, 4 vols. London: HMSO, 1979–90.

Hitler's Table Talk: His Private Conversations, 1941–44, introduced and with a new preface by Hugh Trevor-Roper, trans. Norman Cameron and R.H. Stevens. New York: Enigma Books, 2000.

Hoch, Georg. *Messerschmitt Me 109 in Swiss Air Force Service*, trans. Christine Wisowaty. Atglen, PA: Schiffer, 2008.

Homer, F.X. and Larry D. Wilcox, eds. *Germany and Europe in the Era of Two World Wars*. Charlottesville: University Press of Virginia, 1986.

Homze, Edward L. *Arming the Luftwaffe: the Reich Air Ministry and the German Aircraft Industry, 1919–39*. Lincoln, NE: University of Nebraska, 1976.

Hooker, Sir Stanley. *Not Much of an Engineer: An Autobiography*. Shrewsbury: Airlife, 1984.

Hooton, E.R. *Eagle in Flames: the Fall of the Luftwaffe*. London: Brockhampton, 1999.

—. *The Luftwaffe: A Study in Air Power 1933–1945*. Hersham: Classic, Ian Allan, 2010.

Hooton, Ted. *Spitfire Special*. Shepperton: Ian Allan, 1974.

Horne, Alistair. *To Lose a Battle: France, 1940*. London: Macmillan, 1969.

Howson, Gerald. *Aircraft of the Spanish Civil War 1936–1939*. Washington: Smithsonian Institution Press, 1990.

Huston, Major General John W., ed. *American Airpower Comes of Age: General Henry H. 'Hap' Arnold's World War II Diaries*, vol. 2. Maxwell AFB, AL: Air University Press, 2002.

Hyde, Herford Montgomery. *British Air Policy Between the Wars*. London: Heinemann, 1976.

Irving, David. *Goering: A Biography*. New York: Avon Books, 1990.

—. *The Rise and Fall of the Luftwaffe: the Life of Field Marshal Erhard Milch*. Boston: Little, Brown, 1974.

Isby, David C. *Boeing B-17 Flying Fortress*. London: HarperCollins, 1999.

—. *C-47/R4D Units of the ETO and MTO*. Oxford: Osprey, 2005.

—, ed. *Fighting the Bombers: The Luftwaffe's Struggle Against the Allied Bomber Offensive*. London: Greenhill, 2003.

—, ed. *Fighting in Normandy: the German Army from D-Day to Villers-Bocage*. London: Greenhill, 2001.

—, ed. *The German Army at D-Day: Fighting the Invasion*. London: Greenhill, 2004.

—, ed. *The Luftwaffe and the War at Sea 1939–45*. London: Chatham, 2005.

—, ed. *The Luftwaffe Fighter Force: The View from the Cockpit*. London: Greenhill, 1998.

van Ishoven, Armand. *Bf 109 at War*. London: Ian Allan, 1977.

—. *Messerschmitt, Aircraft Designer*. London: Gentry Books, 1973.

Baron Ismay [Hastings Lionel Ismay]. *The Memoirs of Lord Ismay*. London: Heinemann, 1960.

Ivie, Tom and Paul Ludwig. *Spitfires and Yellow Tail Mustangs: The 52nd Fighter Group in World War Two*. Crowborough, Sussex: Hikoki, 2005.

James, Derek N. *Westland Aircraft Since 1915*. Annapolis: Naval Institute Press, 1991.

James, John. *The Paladins: A Social History of the RAF up to the Outbreak of World War II*. London: Macdonald, 1990.

James, T.C.G. *The Growth of Fighter Command 1936–1940*, ed. Sebastian Cox. London and Portland, OR: Whitehall History Publishing in Association with Frank Cass, 2002.

—. *The Battle of Britain*. Oxford: Taylor and Francis, 2000.

Jochmann, Werner, ed. *Adolf Hitler, Monologe im Führerhauptquartier 1941–1944*. Die Aufzeichnungen Heinrich Heims. Hamburg: Albrecht Knaus, 1980.

Johnson, J.E. *Full Circle*. New York: Ballantine, 1968.

—. *Wing Leader*. New York: Ballantine, 1965.

— and P.B. Lucas. *Winged Victory*. London: Stanley Paul, 1995.

Johnson, Robert S. with Martin Caidin. *Thunderbolt*. New York: Ballantine, 1966.

Jones, R.V. *Most Secret War: British Scientific Intelligence, 1939–45*. London: Hamish Hamilton, 1979.

Julian, Marcel. *Jean Maridor: Chasseur de V1*. Paris: Le Livre Contemporain, 1955.

Kassak, Peter. *An Ordinary Day in 1945*. Redbourn: Stratus for Mushroom Model Publications, 2005.

Kay, Antony and L.R. Smith. *German Aircraft of the Second World War*. London: Putnam, 2002.

Keegan, John. *Six Armies in Normandy*. New York: Viking, 1982.

Kennett, Lee. *A History of Strategic Bombing*. New York: Scribner's, 1982.

Kent, Group Captain J.A. *One of the Few*. London: William Kimber, 1971.

Klinkowitz, Jerome. *Their Finest Hours: The RAF and the Luftwaffe in World War II*. London and New York: Marion Boyars, 1990.

Koonz, Claudia. *Mothers in The Fatherland: Women, the Family and Nazi Politics*. New York: St Martin's, 1987.

Kosin, Rüdiger. *The German Fighter Since 1915*. London: Putnam, 1988.

Kurowski, Franz. *Luftwaffe Aces: German Combat Pilots of World War Two*. Mechanicsville, PA: Stackpole, 2004.

—. *Oberstleutnant Heinz Bär, Als Jagdflieger an Allen Fronten*. Wurzburg: Flechsig, 2007.

Larkin, David, ed. *The Aviation Art of Frank Wooton*. New York: Bantam, 1976.

Lazarrabal, Jesus Salas, *Air War Over Spain*, trans. Margaret A. Kelley. Shepperton: Ian Allan, 1968.

Leske, Gottfried. *I was a Nazi Flier*, ed. Curtis Reiss. New York: The Dial Press, 1941.

Lipfert, Helmut and Werner Girbig. *The War Diary of Hauptmann Helmut Lipfert, JG 52 on the Russian Front 1943–1945*. Atglen, PA: Schiffer, 1993.

Lloyd, Ian S. *Rolls-Royce: The Merlin at War*. London: The Macmillan Press, 1978.

Longmate, Norman. *Hitler's Rockets: The Story of the V-2s*. London: Hutchinson, 1985.

Lucas, Laddie. *Malta, The Thorn in Rommel's Side: Six Months That Turned the War*. London: Penguin, 1993.

—, ed. *Out of the Blue*. London: Grafton, 1989.

Ludwig, Paul A. *P-51 Mustang: Development of the Long-Range Escort Fighter*. Hersham: Classic, Ian Allan, 2003.

MacFarland, Stephen L. and Wesley P. Newton. *To Command the Sky: The Battle for Air Superiority Over Germany, 1942–44*. Washington: Smithsonian Institution Press, 1991.

Macmillan, Harold. *The Blast of War 1939–1945*. London: Macmillan, 1967.

Mahurin, Walker. *Honest John*. New York: G.P. Putnam's Sons, 1962.

Mankau, Heinz and Peter Petrick. *Messerschmitt Me 110, 210, 410*. Raumfahrt: Aviatic Verlag, 2001.

Martin, Squadron Leader C.A. *Front Line Radar*. London: Foster Groom, 1946.

Mason, Francis K. *Battle Over Britain*. Garden City, NY: Doubleday, 1969.

Meekcoms, K.J. and E.B. Morgan. *The British Aircraft Specifications File: British Military and Commercial Aircraft Specifications 1920–1949*. Tonbridge: Air Britain, 1994.

Mehringer, Hartmut, ed. *Die Tagebücher von Joseph Goebbels*, Teil II, *Diktate* [*Dictations*] *1941–1945*. Munich: K.G. Saur Verlag, 1995.

Michulec, Robert and Donald Caldwell. *Galland*. Redbourn: Stratus for Mushroom Model Publications, 2003.

Middlebrook, Martin. *The Berlin Raids: R.A.F. Bomber Command, Winter 1943–44*. London, New York: Viking, 1988.

Mitchell, Gordon. *R.J. Mitchell: Schooldays to Spitfire*. Stroud: Tempus, 2006.

Mizrahi, Joseph V. *Knights of the Black Cross*. Granada Hills, CA: Sentry Books, 1972.

Molony, C.J.C., et al. *The Mediterranean and Middle East*, 3 vols. London: HMSO, 1969–74.

Mombeeck, Erik, Jean-Louis Roba with Chris Goss. *In the Skies of France: A Chronicle of JG 2 'Richthofen'*, vol. 1, *1934–40*. Linkebeek, Belgium: ASBL, 2008.

Morgan, Eric B. and Edward Shacklady. *Spitfire, the History*. Stamford, Lincs: Key Books, 2000.

Muller, Richard. *The German Air War in Russia*. Baltimore: Naval and Aviation, 1993.

Murray, Williamson. *Luftwaffe*. Annapolis: Naval and Aviation, 1989.

—. *Strategy for Defeat: The Luftwaffe 1933–45*. Maxwell AFB: Air University Press, 1983.

Nordeen, Lon. *Fighters Over Israel*. New York: Orion, 1990.

— and David Nicolle. *Phoenix Over the Nile: A History of Egyptian Air Power 1932–1994*. Washington: Smithsonian Institution Press, 1996.

Norton, Bill. *Air War on the Edge: A History of the Israeli Air Force and its Aircraft since 1947*. Hinckley: Midland, 2004.

Nowarra, Heinz J. *Messerschmitt Me 109: Aircraft and Legend*. Yeovil: Haynes, 1989.

—. *The Messerschmitt Me 109: A Famous German Fighter*. Los Angeles: Aero Publishers, 1963.

Obermaier, Ernst. *Die Ritterkreuzträger der Luftwaffe*, Band I, *Jagdflieger*. Mainz: D. Hoffmann, 1966.

— and Werner Held, with the help of Luise Petzolt-Mölders. *Jagdflieger Oberst Werner Mölders*. Stuttgart: Motorbuch Verlag, 1982.

Odgers, George. *Air War Against Japan, 1943–45*. Canberra: Australian War Memorial, 1957.

Olmstead, Bill. *Blue Skies: The Autobiography of a Canadian Spitfire Pilot in World War II*. Toronto: Stoddart, 1987.

Orange, Vincent. *Dowding of Fighter Command: Victor of the Battle of Britain*. London: Grub Street, 2009.

—. *Park: the Biography of Air Chief Marshal Sir Keith Park*. London: Grub Street, 2001.

—. *Slessor, Bomber Champion: The Life of Marshal of the RAF Sir John Slessor*. London: Grub Street, 2005.

Osché, Philippe. *Les Messerschmitt Bf 109 Suisses*. Avions Hors Série 4. Paris: Lela Press, 1996.

Ostric, Sime. *Les Messerschmitt Yugoslaves, Les Me-109E-3, les Me-108 Taifun et l'Unique Me-110 de l'Aviation Royale Yougoslave*. Avions Hors Série 26. Paris: Lela Presse, 2009.

Overy, Richard J. *The Air War*. New York: Stein and Day, 1980.

—. *Goering The Iron Man*. London: Routledge and Kegan Paul, 1984.

—. *Interrogations: The Nazi Elite in Allied Hands, 1945*. London: Penguin, 2001.

—. *Why the Allies Won*. New York: Norton, 1997.

Parker, Matthew. *The Battle of Britain July–October 1940: An Oral History of Britain's Finest Hour*. London: Headline, 2000.

Parsonson, Jack. *A Time to Remember*. Usk, Washington: Aviation Usk, 1993.

Paterson, Michael. *Battle for the Skies*. Newton Abbot: David and Charles, 2004.

Peart, Alan McGregor, DFC. *From North Africa to the Arakan*. London: Grub Street, 2008.

Peden, G.C. *British Rearmament and the Treasury*. Edinburgh: Edinburgh University Press, 1979.

Picker, Henry, ed. *Hitler Tischengespräche in Führerhauptquartier*. Stuttgart: Seewald, 1971.

Playfair, J.R.O. et al. *The Mediterranean and Middle East*, 3 vols. London: HMSO, 1958–60.

Plocher, Generalleutnant Herman. *The German Air Force Versus Russia, 1942*. USAF Historical Studies no. 154. Maxwell AFB: USAF Historical Division, 1966.

Popham, Hugh. *Sea Flight*. London: William Kimber, 1954.

Postan, Michael M. *British War Production*. London and Nendeln: HMSO and Kraus Reprint, 1975.

Potsdam Institute for the Study of Military History. *Germany and the Second World War*, 9 vols. Oxford: Oxford University Press, 1990–2008.

Powers, Barry D. *Strategy Without Slide-Rule: British Air Strategy 1914–1939*. London: Croom Helm, 1976.

Price, Alfred. *Battle of Britain Day: 15 September 1940*. London: Greenhill, 2000.

—. *Battle Over the Reich*. New York: Scribner's, 1973.

—. *Blitz on Britain*. London: Ian Allan, 1977.

—. *Focke Wulf 190 at War*. New York: Charles Scribner's Sons, 1977.

—. *The Last Year of the Luftwaffe: May 1944 to May 1945*. Osceola, WI: Motorbooks, 1991.

—. *The Luftwaffe Data Book*. London: Greenhill, 1997.

—. *Spitfire: A Documentary History*. London: Macdonald and Jane's, 1977.

—. *Spitfire at War 3*. Shepperton: Ian Allan, 1990.

—. *Spitfire in Combat*. Stroud: Sutton, 2003.

—. *World War II Fighter Combat*. London: Macdonald and Jane's, 1975.

Prien, Jochen. *Jagdgeschwader 53, A History of the 'Pik As' Geschwader, March 1937–May*

1942. Atglen, PA: Schiffer, 1997.

— and Peter Rodeike. *JG 1 und JG 11, Jagdgeschwader 1 und 11: Einsatz in der Reichsverteidigung von 1939 bis 1945*, 2 vols. Eutin: Struve Druck, 1994, 1996.

— and Peter Rodeike. *Messerschmitt Bf 109F, G, and K Series*. Atglen, PA: Schiffer, 1995.

— and Gerhard Stemmer. *Jagdgeschwader 3 'Udet' in World War II, Stab and I/JG 3 in Action with the Messerschmitt Bf 109*. Atglen, PA: Schiffer, 2002.

— and Gerhard Stemmer. *Jagdgeschwader 3 'Udet' in World War II, II/JG 3 in Action with the Messerschmitt Bf 109*. Atglen, PA: Schiffer, 2003.

—, Gerhard Stemmer, Peter Rodeike and Winfried Beck. *Der Jagdfliegerverbände der Deutschen Luftwaffe 1934 bis 1945*, 12 vols. Eutin: Struve Druck, 2000–12.

Probert, Air Commodore Henry. *The Forgotten Air Force: The Royal Air Force in the War Against Japan, 1941–1945*. London, Brassey's, 1995.

Pudney, John. *A Pride of Unicorns: Richard and David Atcherley of the RAF*. London: Oldbourne, 1960.

Quill, Jeffrey. *Spitfire: A Test Pilot's Story* Manchester: Crecy, 1998.

— with Sebastian Cox. *Birth of a Legend: The Spitfire*. Washington: Smithsonian Institution Press, 1986.

Radinger, Willy and Walter Schick. *Messerschmitt Bf 109: the World's Most Produced Fighter from Bf 109 A to E*. Atglen, PA: Schiffer, 1999.

—. *Secret Messerschmitt Projects*. Atglen, PA: Schiffer, 1996.

Rall, Günther. *My Logbook, Reminiscences 1938–2006*, ed. Kurt Braatz, trans. John Weal. Moosburg: 296 Verlag, 2006.

Ramsey, Winston G., ed. *The Battle of Britain, Then and Now, Mk V edition*. Hemel Hempstead, Herts: After the Battle, 1990.

—, ed. *The Blitz, Then and Now*, 3 vols. Hemel Hempstead, Herts: After the Battle/Battle of Britain Prints, 1987–9.

Rauchsteiner, Manfred. *Der Luftangriff auf Wiener Neustadt, 13 August 1943*. Vienna: Styria Verlag, 1983.

Rheinhardt, Dr. Generalmajor i.G. Klaud. *Die Wende vor Moskau, Das Scheiten der Strategies Hitlers in Winter 1941/42*. Stuttgart: Deutsche Verlags-Anstalt, 1972.

Richards, Denis and Hilary St George Sanders. *Royal Air Force, 1939–1945*, 3 vols. London: HMSO, 1952–4.

Ries, Karl and Hans Ring. *The Legion Condor: A History of the Luftwaffe in the Spanish Civil War, 1936–1939*, trans. David Johnston. West Chester, PA: Schiffer, 1992.

Rigg, Bryan Mark. *Hitler's Jewish Soldiers: The Untold Story of Nazi Racial Laws and Men of Jewish Descent in the German Military*. Lawrence, KS: University Press of Kansas, 2007.

Ritchie, Sebastian. *Industry and Air Power: The Expansion of British Aircraft Production 1935–41*. London and Portland, OR: Frank Cass, 1997.

Robertson, Bruce. *Spitfire – The Story of a Famous Fighter*. Fallbrook, CA: Aero Publishers, 1961.

Robertson, Don. *Those Magnificent Flying Machines: An Autobiography*. Poole: Blandford, 1984.

Robinson, Michael. *Best of the Few: 92 Squadron 1939–40*. Bletchley: privately published, 2001.

Rogers, Anthony. *Battle Over Malta: Aircraft Losses and Crash Sites 1940–42*. Stroud: Sutton Publishing, 2000.

Röll, Hans-Joachim. *Major Joachim Müncheberg*. Würzburg: Fleschig, 2010.

Rubinstein, Murray. *The Curtiss P-40C vs. the Mitsubishi A6M2 Model 21 Zero-Sen*. Biloxi: Gamescience, 1976.

—. *Messerschmitt Bf 109E-3 vs. Supermarine Spitfire IA*. Fighter Comparison No. 2. Teaneck, NJ: Tacitus Publications, 1973.

— and Richard Goldman. *Shield of David: An Illustrated History of the Israeli Air Force*. Englewood Cliffs, NJ: Prentice Hall, 1978.

Russell, C.R. *Spitfire Odyssey: My Life at Supermarine, 1936–57*. Southampton: Kingfisher, 1985.

Sarkar, Dilip. *Bader's Duxford Fighters: The Big Wing Controversy*. Worcester: Victory Books, 2006.

—. *Bader's Tangmere Spitfires*. Yeovil: Patrick Stephens, 1996.

—. *Spitfire Ace of Aces: the Wartime Story of Johnnie Johnson*. Stroud: Amberley, 2011.

—. *Spitfire Squadron at War*. Malden, Surrey: Air Research Publications, 1990.

Saunders, Andy. *Bader's Last Fight*. London: Grub Street, 2007.

Schabel, Ralf. *Die Illusion der Wunderwaffen: die Rolle der Düsenflugzeuge und Flugabwehrraketen in der Rüstungspolitik des Dritten Reiche*. Munich: R. Oldenburg, 1994.

Schiff, Zeev. *A History of the Israeli Army, 1874 to the Present*. New York: Macmillan, 2008.

Schmoll, Peter. *Nest of Eagles: Messerschmitt Production and Flight Testing at Regensburg 1936–1945*. Hersham: Classic, Ian Allan, 2004.

Schuck, Walter. *Abschuss! Von der Me 109 zur Me 262*. Aachen: Helios Verlag, 2007.

Schwabedissen, Walter. *The Russian Air Force in the Eyes of German Commanders*. USAF Historical Studies no. 175. New York: Arno Press, 1960.

Scott, J.D. *Vickers: A History*. London: Weidenfeld and Nicolson, 1962.

Senior, Boris. *New Heavens: My Life as a Fighter Pilot and a Founder of the Israeli Air Force*. Dulles, VA: Potomac, 2005.

Shay, Robert P. *British Rearmament in the Thirties*. Princeton: Princeton University Press, 1971.

Shelton, John. *Schneider Trophy to Spitfire, The Design Career of R.J. Mitchell*. Yeovil: Haynes, 2008.

Shirer, William L. *Berlin Diary*. New York: A.A. Knopf, 1941.

Shores, Christopher, *Aces High*, 2 vols. London: Grub Street, 2002, 2004.

—. *Air War Over Burma*. London: Grub Street, 2005.

—. *Fighters Over the Desert*. New York: Arco, 1972.

—. *Those Other Eagles: A Companion Volume to Aces High*. London: Grub Street, 2004.

— and Brian Cull with Nicola Malizia. *Air War for Yugoslavia, Greece and Crete, 1940–41*. Carrollton, TX: Squadron Signal, 1987.

— and Brian Cull with Nicola Malizia. *Malta: The Hurricane Years 1940–41*. London: Grub Street, 1987.

— and Brian Cull with Nicola Malizia. *Malta: The Spitfire Year, 1942*. London: Grub Street, 1992.

— and Chris Ehrengardt. *Fledgling Eagles: The Complete Account of Air Operations During* the 'Phoney War' and Norwegian Campaign, 1940. London: Grub Street, 1991.

— , Hans Ring and William N. Hess. *Fighters Over Tunisia*. London: Spearman, 1975.

— and Chris Thomas. *2nd Tactical Air Force*, 4 vols. Hersham: Classic, Ian Allan, 2002–6.

Simpson, Bill. *Spitfire Dive Bombers Versus the V2: Fighter Command's Battle with Hitler's Mobile Missiles*. Barnsley: Pen and Sword, 2007.

Sims, Edward H. *The Greatest Aces*. New York: Ballantine, 1967.

Sinnott, Colin. *The RAF and Aircraft Design, 1923–39, Air Staff Operational Requirements*. London and Portland, OR: Frank Cass, 2001.

Smith, Constance Babington. *Evidence in Camera*. North Pomfret, VT: David and Charles, 1974.

Smith, Herschel. *Aircraft Piston Engines*. New York: McGraw Hill, 1981.

Smith, Malcolm. *British Air Strategy Between the Wars*. Oxford: Oxford University Press, 1984.

Souffair, Many. *Les Messerschmitt Bf 109 Romains*. AirMag Hors Série. Paris: AirMagazine, 2002.

Späte, Wolfgang, ed. *Test Pilots*. Bromley, Kent: Independent Books, n.d.

Speer, Albert. *Inside the Third Reich*. New York: Macmillan, 1970.

Steinhilper, Ulrich and Peter Osbourne. *Spitfire on my Tail: A View From the Other Side*. Bromley, Kent: Independent Books, 1990.

Suchenwirth, Richard. *Command and Leadership in the German Air Force*. USAF Historical Studies no. 174. Maxwell AFB: USAF Historical Division, 1969.

—. *The Development of the German Air Force, 1919–1939*. New York: Arno, 1970.

Tantum, W.H., IV and E.J. Hoffschmidt, eds. *The Rise and Fall of the German Air Force, 1933 to 1945*. Old Greenwich, CT: WE Inc., 1969.

Taylor, Bill. *Royal Air Force Germany Since 1945*. Hinckley: Midland, 2007.

Tedder, Arthur. *With Prejudice: The War Memoirs of Marshal of the Royal Air Force, Lord Tedder*. Boston: Little, Brown, 1967.

Terraine, John. *A Time For Courage: The Royal Air Force in the European War, 1939–45*. New York: Macmillan, 1985.

Thomas, Graham. *Furies and Fireflies Over Korea*. London: Grub Street, 2004.

Thompson, Wing Commander H.L. *New Zealanders with the Royal Air Force*. Wellington, NZ: Historical Publications Branch, 1959.

Tooze, Adam. *The Wages of Destruction: The Making and Breaking of the Nazi Economy*. New York: Viking, 2006.

Uziel, Daniel. *Arming the Luftwaffe: The German Aviation Industry in World War II*. Jefferson, NC and London: McFarland, 2011.

Vajda, Ferenc A. and Peter Dancey. *German Aircraft Industry and Production, 1933–1945*. Warrendale, PA: SAE International, 1998.

Vann, Frank. *Willy Messerschmitt: First Full Biography of an Aeronautical Genius*. Yeovil: Patrick Stephens, 1993.

Völker, Karl-Heinz. *Die Entwicklung der Militärischen Luftfahrt in Deutschland 1920–1933*. Stuttgart: Militärgeschichtlichen Forschungsamt, 1962.

Waddy, Helena. *Oberammergau in the Nazi Era: The Fate of a Catholic Village in Hitler's*

Germany. New York: Oxford University Press, 2010.

Wagner, Ray. *Mustang Designer: Edgar Shmued and the P-51.* Washington: Smithsonian Institution Press, 2000.

Wagner, Wolfgang. *Kurt Tank: Focke Wulf's Designer and Chief Test Pilot,* trans. Don Cox. The History of German Aviation. Atglen, PA: Schiffer, 1998.

Walker, Diana Barnato. *Spreading My Wings.* London: Grub Street, 2008.

Watson, Jeffrey. *Killer Caldwell: Australia's Greatest Fighter Pilot.* Sydney: Hodder Australia, 2006.

Watson-Watt, Sir Robert. *Three Steps to Victory: A Personal Account by Radar's Greatest Pioneer.* London: Odhams, 1957.

Webster, Charles and Noble Frankland. *The Strategic Air Offensive Against Germany,* 4 vols. London: HMSO, 1960–5.

Weir, Adrian. *The Last Flight of the Luftwaffe.* London: Cassell, 1997.

Weizman, Ezer. *On Eagles' Wings.* New York: Macmillan, 1976.

Wood, Derek and Derek Dempster. *The Narrow Margin.* London: Arrow Books, 1967.

Wright, Robert. *Dowding and the Battle of Britain.* London: Macdonald, 1969.

Wüllner, Fritz. *Die NS-Militärjustiz im Dienste des Nationalsozialismus, Zerstörung einer Legende.* Baden-Baden: Nomos, 1987.

Yofe, Alex. *Spitfire Mk. IX in Israeli Air Force Service.* San Jose, CA: White Crow Publications, 2005.

—. *Spitfire, Star of Israel.* Wellington, NZ: Ventura Publications, 1996.

— and Lawrence Nyveen. *Avia S-199 in Israeli Air Force Service 1948–1950.* San Jose, CA: White Crow, 2007.

Zschocher, Erich. *Die Kämpfe des Hauptmanns Heinz Bär.* Berlin: Max Schwalbe Verlag, 1943.

Index